THE
Common
Good
OF
Constitutional
Democracy

MARTIN RHONHEIMER

THE

Common Good

OF

Constitutional Democracy

Essays in Political Philosophy and
on Catholic Social Teaching

EDITED WITH AN INTRODUCTION BY
WILLIAM F. MURPHY JR.

The Catholic University of America Press
Washington, D.C.

Library of Congress Cataloging-in-Publication Data
Rhonheimer, Martin, 1950–
The common good of constitutional democracy : essays in political philosophy
and on Catholic social teaching / edited by William F. Murphy Jr.
p. cm.
Includes bibliographical references and index.
ISBN 978-0-8132-2009-3 (pbk. : alk. paper)
1. Political science—Philosophy. 2. Christian sociology—Catholic
Church. 3. Catholic Church—Doctrines. 4. Christianity and politics.
5. Christianity and politics—Catholic Church. 6. Democracy—
Religious aspects—Catholic Church. 7. Democracy—Religious
aspects—Christianity. 8. Economics—Religious aspects—Catholic
Church. 9. Economics—Religious aspects—Christianity.
I. Murphy, William F. II. Title.
JA71.R465 2013
261.7—dc23   2012030748

Contents

Acknowledgments

Chapter 1, "Why Is Political Philosophy Necessary? Historical Considerations and a Response," was originally published as "Perché una filosofia politica? Elementi storici per una risposta" in *Acta Philosophica* 1.1 (1992): 233–63. It was translated by Joseph T. Papa and is republished with permission.

Chapter 2, "The Liberal Image of Man and the Concept of Autonomy: Beyond the Debate between Liberals and Communitarians," was originally published as "L'immagine dell'uomo nel liberalismo e il concetto di autonomia: al di là del dibattito fra liberali e comunitaristi," in *Immagini dell'uomo. Percorsi antropologici nella filosofia moderna,* edited by I. Yarza (Rome: Armando, 1997). It was translated by Robert A. Gahl and is republished with permission.

Chapter 3, "The Democratic Constitutional State and the Common Good," was originally published as "Lo Stato costituzionale democratico e il bene comune" in *Con-tratto—Rivista di filosofia tomista e contemporanea* VI (1997) and in *Ripensare lo spazio politico: quale aristocrazia?* edited by E. Morandi and R. Panattoni (Padua: Il Poligrafo, 1998), 57–122. It was translated by Joseph T. Papa and is republished with permission.

Chapter 4, "*Auctoritas non veritas facit legem:* Thomas Hobbes, Carl Schmitt and the Idea of the Constitutional State," was originally published as "Autoritas non veritas facit legem: Thomas Hobbes, Carl Schmitt und die Idee des Verfassungsstaates" in *Archiv für Rechts- und Sozialphilosophie* 86 (2000): 484–98. It was translated by Gerald Malsbary and is republished with permission.

A shortened version of Chapter 5, "The Open Society and the New Laicism: Against the Soft Totalitarianism of Certain Secularist Thinking," was originally published as "Laici e cattolici: oltre le divisioni" in *Liberal* 17 (2003): 108–16. The original and longer text in this present volume was translated by Joseph T. Papa and is republished with permission.

Chapter 6, "The Political and Economic Realities of the Modern World and Their Ethical and Cultural Presuppositions: The Encyclical *Centesimus annus,*" was originally published as "La realtà politica ed economica del mondo moderno e i suoi presupposti etici e culturali. L'enciclica *Centesimus annus*" in *Giovanni Pa-*

olo Teologo—Nel segno delle encicliche, edited by Graziano Borgonovo and Arturo Cattaneo, with preface by His Eminence Camillo Cardinal Ruini (Rome: Edizioni Arnoldo Mondatori, 2003): 83–94. It was translated from the Italian by Joseph T. Papa and is republished with permission.

Chapter 7, "The Political Ethos of Constitutional Democracy and the Place of Natural Law in Public Reason: Rawls's *Political Liberalism* Revisited," was originally published in the *American Journal of Jurisprudence* 50 (2005): 1–70 and is republished with permission.

Chapter 8, "Rawlsian Public Reason, Natural Law and the Foundation of Justice: A Response to David Crawford (2009)," was originally published in *Communio: International Catholic Review* 36.1 (Spring 2009): 138–67 and is republished with permission.

Chapter 9, "Can Political Ethics Be Universalized? Human Rights as a Global Project," was not previously published in this form, although parts of it were included in Rhonheimer's "Christian Secularity, Political Ethics and the Culture of Human Rights," which was published in the *Josephinum Journal of Theology* 16:2 (August 2009): 250–72.

Chapter 10, "Christian Secularity and the Culture of Human Rights," was originally presented as a conference paper in 2006 and published in a more developed form as "Christian Secularity, Political Ethics and the Culture of Human Rights," in the *Josephinum Journal of Theology* 16:2 (August 2009): 250–72. It is republished with permission.

Chapter 11, "Multicultural Citizenship in Liberal Democracy: the Proposals of C. Taylor, J. Habermas and W. Kymlicka," was originally published as "Cittadinanza multiculturale nella democrazia liberale: le proposte di Ch. Taylor, J. Habermas e W. Kymlicka," *Acta Philosophica* 15:1 (2006), 29–52. It was translated by Joseph T. Papa and is republished with permission.

Chapter 12, "Christianity and Secularity: Past and Present of a Complex Relationship," was originally published as "Cristianesimo e laicità: storia ed attualità di un rapporto complesso" in *Laicità: la ricerca dell'universale nella differenza,* edited by Pierpaolo Donati (Bologna: il Mulino, 2008), 27–138. It was translated by Joseph T. Papa and is republished with permission.

As further detailed in the first note of the essay, parts of Chapter 13, "Benedict XVI's 'Hermeneutic of Reform' and Religious Freedom," were previously published in German, French, and Spanish. The complete text was then published in *Nova et Vetera,* English edition 9:4 (Fall 2011): 1029–54. It was translated by Joseph T. Papa and Matthew Sherry, with the assistance of William F. Murphy Jr. It is republished with permission.

Chapter 14, "Capitalism, Free Market Economy, and the Common Good: The Role of the State in the Economy," was originally published in *Free Markets and the Culture of Common Good,* edited by M. Schlag and J. A. Mercado (Springer: Dordrecht, Heidelberg, New York, London, 2012), 3–40. It is republished with permission.

Some of the translation and editing expenses for this volume were generously funded by the Cardinal Pio Laghi Chair of the Pontifical College Josephinum, and others were funded by grants from the Our Sunday Visitor Foundation. Other expenses were funded by a generous grant by Michael J. Barberi.

Special thanks are offered to the translators—especially Drs. Joseph T. Papa and Gerald Malsbary—and to Damian X. Lenshek for his assistance with several aspects of the project. Thanks are also offered to the staff of the Catholic University of America Press, including especially James Kruggel, Theresa Walker, and Beth Benevides, whose skills and labors have been indispensable in making these volumes available.

Carol A. Kennedy skillfully copyedited this large and complex text, and Anna M. Lenshek carefully reviewed the page proofs. Any remaining errors are, of course, the responsibility of the author and the volume editor. Finally, thanks are owed to Richard Lender for his outstanding work in preparing a detailed index.

Preface

The title of this book, *The Common Good of Constitutional Democracy*, contains a twofold message. First, there is a common good, including a set of socially shared values, which morally legitimates both the basic political structure of constitutional democracy and the outcome of the political process shaped by its legal and political institutions. Second, the basic legal and political institutions of constitutional democracy *are themselves* a common good, not only for individuals but also for social communities. These institutions are a common—shared—good of citizens living in a modern, pluralistic, and free society, a good therefore supported by those citizens in order to make possible social cooperation in peace, liberty, and justice.

The legal and political institutions of constitutional democracy—which, in the following pages, I will usually call the "democratic constitutional state"—are the product of a long history, rooted in the fertile soil of Christian civilization, yet further shaped by the tradition of modern liberal constitutionalism. To acknowledge one's debt to this tradition is nothing else than an acceptance of historical truth. Western modernity and what we call the Enlightenment would certainly not have been possible without the Judeo-Christian transformation of ancient Greek and Roman culture. But the ideas and creeds of Christianity alone were not sufficient to bring about the political culture of constitutional democracy and human rights as they are understood in the classical liberal-constitutionalist tradition. Neither could democracy *as such* survive without being firmly anchored in this tradition; it would necessarily degenerate into a despotism of the majority, which, eventually, is nothing other than state despotism. As I firmly believe and will argue in this book, however, Western modernity is essentially the fruit of a civilization shaped by Christianity and needs, in order to survive as an intrinsically human order, the oxygen of the values by which the Judeo-Christian heritage has enriched human history.

As a Catholic, I consciously and wholeheartedly espouse the political and legal ideals of the classical liberal-constitutionalist tradition. I do this not naively, because I am aware of the dangers of secularism and moral relativism often promoted by contemporary liberalism. Notice, however, that an American "liberal" is not necessarily a liberal in the European sense, and the author of this book is European. American liberals correspond instead to what those in the Old World call a social democrat: someone, that is, who believes in state intervention, bureaucratic control of the market economy and of private life, the welfare state, and egalitarian redistribution of income and property. Continental liberals, on the other hand, although they are not necessarily conservatives in the American sense, essentially uphold the ideas of limited government, personal responsibility (and corresponding solidarity, not to be delegated to the state), the protection of private property, and the conviction that only a market economy unfettered by state intervention can best guarantee what is commonly called social justice. Therefore, in some aspects they are closer to what in America is called a libertarian, without, however, sharing the anarchical traits of many libertarians. Moreover, continental European liberals commonly hold that solidarity is not to be implemented by the omnipresent welfare state, but, in accordance with the principle of subsidiarity, has rather to be an achievement of civil society and of both individual and group charity.

I am very happy to be now able to present this collection of essays in political philosophy and on Catholic social teaching to the English-speaking public; most of them have never been published in English before. They cover a range of time of twenty years and, therefore, also a certain development in my views. I am especially grateful to Dr. William F. Murphy, who not only promoted the idea of this book, but also did everything necessary to realize it, including bringing into English many texts originally published in German and Italian and so carefully editing it. I especially appreciate his thoughtful and detailed introduction—as I am convinced it is extremely helpful for those who set out reading this book—which happily relieves me from the challenging task of presenting and summarizing the different chapters myself. Once more, as in preceding cases, I offer warm thanks to Dr. Joseph T. Papa for translating into English most of the text, to my colleague Robert A. Gahl Jr. for generously translating a substantial chapter from the Italian original, and to Gerald Malsbary for translating a chapter from German. Finally my thanks go to the director and staff of the Catholic University of America Press who—after having published several other books of mine—have now published yet another with their usual high-standing professional competence. I consider this a special sign of confidence toward me as an author, for which I wish to sincerely express my gratitude.

Martin Rhonheimer, Easter 2012

Introduction

The present volume makes available, for English-language readers, a substantial collection of essays in political philosophy by the Swiss philosopher Martin Rhonheimer. In this preface, I will offer first some general introductory remarks to locate this work, which will be followed by a sketch of some basic themes and emphases of the fourteen included essays to give the reader an initial sense of the whole.

The Importance, Distinct Contribution, and Organizing Thesis of This Collection

This collection is quite different from anything in print, and—as I will explain below—there is good reason to expect that it will make a significant contribution to enriching the scholarly conversation, especially at the intersection of political philosophy and what is typically called Catholic social teaching or social doctrine. The distinctive contribution of this volume includes several interdependent dimensions. The first is the philosophical rigor with which it proceeds, which will both demand attentive perseverance from the reader and pay rich rewards. The second is the range of key questions it addresses, especially those that arise when a tradition such as Catholicism—with its deep roots in Scripture, magisterial teaching, and classical philosophy—enters into deep dialogue with the central features of the modern political culture of constitutionally established human rights. The third factor, inseparable from the second, is the range of interlocutors it engages, including a broad and deep encounter between Anglophone and Continental thought. Fourth, this volume engages these various questions and thinkers through the integrated work of a single scholar, one who is adept at not only the philosophical but also the historical aspects of the topics under discussion, and whose strength is to make detailed arguments based on a careful reading of the relevant texts.[1] Fifth, this collection is distinguished by fact that the essays in-

1. For a recent collection addressing some of the same subject matter, but in less depth, and through the work of several authors, see Kenneth L. Grasso and Robert P. Hunt, eds., *Catholicism and*

cluded can each be seen as contributing in its own way to support what can be understood as the organizing thesis of the book.

Although the essays were originally written and published separately, mostly in the European languages (primarily in Italian, but also in German, Spanish, and French), their joint publication in this volume offers a distinct advantage. In particular, it helps the reader to see how they form a multifaceted argument for the thesis suggested by the title, *The Common Good of Constitutional Democracy.* The idea is not so much that the democratic constitutional state is itself part of the common good,[2] but that its key institutions (not just the political institutions themselves, but the legal order, "rule of law," democratic procedures, etc.) form a fundamental part of the common good, and properly are a "common good" of citizens who strive to live together and cooperate in an ethos of peace, freedom, and justice. In the first place, therefore, the "common good" is not a goal or "pattern" that is predefined to be pursued and achieved, but the institutions themselves by which the democratic constitutional state, or constitutional democracy, is defined.[3] As an essential part of the common good, these key institutions of the

---

Religious Freedom: Contemporary Reflections on Vatican II's Declaration on Religious Liberty (Lanham, Md.: Rowman and Littlefield, 2006). For an earlier and worthwhile collection of essays from an American context, which seeks to foster a renewed and mutually enriching interaction—from philosophical, theological, and political perspectives—between liberalism and Catholicism, see R. Bruce Douglass and David Hollenbach, eds., *Catholicism and Liberalism: Contributions to American Public Policy,* Cambridge Studies in Religion and American Public Life (Cambridge: Cambridge University Press, 1994). Another recent contribution to the literature is Christopher Wolfe's *Natural Law Liberalism* (Cambridge: Cambridge University Press, 2006), which engages contemporary theorists of liberalism from the perspective of what he calls "classic natural law" (p. 1) to argue for what he calls "natural law liberalism." See also the collection edited by Wolfe, *Liberalism at the Crossroads: An Introduction to Contemporary Liberal Political Theory and Its Critics,* 2nd rev. ed. (Lanham, Md.: Rowman and Littlefield, 2003).

2. The technical term "democratic constitutional state" is the literal translation of the German *Demokratischer Verfassungsstaat,* most common in German for what in English is called "constitutional democracy." The German term happily expresses the historical three-stage composition of the "democratic constitutional state": the principles of the modern "state," of "constitutionalism," and of "democracy," as is further explained in the book. Based on considerations of length and aesthetics, the title of the book uses "constitutional democracy," which also in other places is used as a synonym for "democratic constitutional state." It may be helpful to also clarify that Rhonheimer is not at all a defender of "liberalism" in the sense of American politics, but rather a liberal in the sense of a "constitutionalist" in the continental liberal tradition. Second, his use of the word "constitutionalism" refers to what in German is *Verfassungsstaat:* that is, the modern secular constitutional state characterized by the rule of law, based on fundamental rights, a state that historically presupposes the modern sovereign territorial state and through successive democratization evolved to the democratic constitutional state.

3. For a similar emphasis on the institutional dimension of the common good, see no. 7 of Pope Benedict XVI's encyclical *Caritas in veritate.* It states, for example, "To take a stand for the common good is on the one hand to be solicitous for, and on the other hand to avail oneself of, that complex of institutions that give structure to the life of society, juridically, civilly, politically and culturally, making it the *pólis,* or 'city'"; and "This is the institutional path—we might also call it the political path—of charity." In chapter 14 of this collection, Rhonheimer will argue that whereas John Paul II's 1991 encyclical *Centesimus annus* established the doctrine that the first and principal task of the state regarding the common good was to establish and ensure the proper functioning of the basic institutions (political, economic, legal, and social) *Caritas in veritate* can be understood (by insisting that charity requires justice) as adding the requirement that the common good requires an ethics of institutions, that is, norms that establish and secure these institutions.

democratic constitutional state—in support of the foundational political ethos of peace, freedom, and justice—should be understood as a historical, philosophical, and political achievement. The brief introductory remarks on each essay that follow in the second part of this introduction will bring out some of the ways in which they contribute to this thesis.

Primary Audiences

The essays in this volume will be of interest to a multifaceted and influential audience among whom the promotion of sober and carefully reasoned dialogue is desirable, not simply to facilitate understanding of political philosophy and its relation to Catholic social teaching, but also for the broader benefits that can be expected therefrom. This audience includes at least the following four groups. It is comprised, first, of Catholic philosophers who are looking to engage the tradition of Catholic social teaching and put it into thoughtful dialogue with modern and contemporary political philosophy. Second, it includes moral theologians working in the field of Catholic social teaching, who recognize that their discipline requires not just ongoing reflection on the philosophical issues at stake, but the support of more adequate philosophical resources to relate the *philosophia perennis* to the significant developments in recent generations of political philosophy. Third, this audience includes contemporary political philosophers who are interested in considering the most sophisticated examples of how the resources of classical and modern political philosophy have been employed by Catholics to clarify and support the tradition of Catholic social teaching. Fourth, it includes other Christian and religious thinkers who are looking for philosophical resources to help them think through the relation of their traditions to the contemporary democratic constitutional state, taking into account the broad tradition of Western political philosophy. In different ways, these audiences will each recognize this book as taking up the unfinished agenda of the Second Vatican Council's Decree on Religious Liberty, *Dignitatis humanae,* by making many of the significant philosophical contributions needed to relate Catholic social teaching to contemporary political philosophy.

A Brief Personal and Intellectual Biography
of Martin Rhonheimer

Martin Rhonheimer was born in Zurich, Switzerland, in 1950 and grew up in an environment where his extended family included both Jews and Protestants, which developed in him an inclination toward intellectual exchange.[4] From the

---

4. This paragraph is adapted from the editor's introduction to Rhonheimer's *The Perspective of the Acting Person: Essays in the Renewal of Thomistic Moral Philosophy,* ed. with an introduction by William F. Murphy Jr. (Washington, D.C.: The Catholic University of America Press, 2008), xiv.

age of thirteen to twenty he studied at a boarding school run by the Benedictines, where he developed a love for philosophy through a full two-year program of Thomistic philosophy. His studies in history, philosophy, and political science culminated in a M.A. in general history and a Ph.D. in philosophy from the University of Zurich. From 1972 to 1978 Rhonheimer was an assistant to Professor Hermann Lübbe, who is one of the more prominent contemporary German philosophers; he was also a research assistant for Professor Otfried Höffe at the University of Fribourg from 1981 to 1982, and worked under a scholarship at the University of Bonn with Professor Wolfgang Kluxen. Rhonheimer was ordained a Catholic priest in 1983, and he is incardinated in the personal prelature of the Holy Cross and Opus Dei. He is currently professor of ethics and political philosophy at the School of Philosophy of the Pontifical University of the Holy Cross in Rome. In addition, he spends several months per year in Zurich, Switzerland, doing pastoral work. Rhonheimer is a member of the editorial board of the *American Journal of Jurisprudence,* a member of the scientific board of *Acta Philosophica,* and a corresponding academician to the *Pontifical Academy of St. Thomas Aquinas.*

Rhonheimer lists his three primary areas of philosophical interest as follows: first, political philosophy, including the history and theory of liberalism, questions regarding constitutional democracy and the common good, the secular state, religious freedom, and pluralism; second, fundamental and applied ethics; and third, the philosophical problems related to the theory of evolution.[5] Before focusing on his political philosophy, the next subsection provides a brief summary of his work in fundamental and applied ethics.

Rhonheimer's Work in Fundamental and Applied Virtue Ethics

Over the last decade, Rhonheimer has become well known to Anglophone moralists as several major works have been translated from the European languages. In fundamental ethics, these have included, first, his *Natural Law and Practical Reason: A Thomist View of Moral Autonomy,*[6] which was published in 2000.[7] This study documented his extensive exploration of primary and secondary literature to understand the sense in which one should understand "nature" as the basis of morality, a question that remains at the center of the postconciliar moral debate among Catholic scholars, a debate that led to the 1993 publication of John

5. A forthcoming work in German is entitled *Ziellose Evolution? Mensch und Schöpfung im Licht der heutigen Evolutionstheorie,* which might be rendered in English as Purposeless evolution? Man and creation in the light of contemporary evolution theory.

6. Trans. Gerald Malsbary (New York: Fordham University Press, 2000).

7. For a discussion on the development of Rhonheimer's work in fundamental ethics and a more detailed overview of the main works, the reader is again referred to the editor's introduction of *Perspective of the Acting Person.*

Paul II's moral encyclical *Veritatis Splendor. Natural Law and Practical Reason* was followed by a series of his works from the Catholic University of America Press. The first of these was Rhonheimer's *The Perspective of the Acting Person: Essays in the Renewal of Thomistic Moral Philosophy* (2008), which includes a number of essays through which Rhonheimer advanced his retrieval of Thomistic virtue ethics, in dialogue with a variety of interlocutors and in support of *Veritatis Splendor*. This collection was followed in 2011 with the publication of his *The Perspective of Morality: Philosophical Foundations of Thomistic Virtue Ethics,* in which he offers a systematic articulation of Thomistic virtue ethics for our day, including a carefully nuanced engagement with the key questions that have been raised by the leading moral philosophers after Aquinas.[8] Although it has been largely ignored by Catholic revisionists, for whom it provides a profound challenge (as it does for the main representatives of alternative ethical approaches), Rhonheimer's work in Thomistic moral theory has already been central to the last several years of debate, especially among what we might call more neo-Thomistic Catholics in the United States around the key question of the object of the moral act.[9] There are good reasons, moreover, to expect this debate in moral theory to broaden to include revisionists, both because it includes a systematic refutation of their basic approach (proportionalism, consequentialism) and because the discussion of applied cases includes extensive criticism of their analyses. The book also has the potential to broaden the discussion with consequentialists, Kantians, and advocates of the "discourse ethics" that traces to Jürgen Habermas and Karl-Otto Apel.

In applied ethics, Rhonheimer has recently published—also through the Catholic University of America Press—two volumes that build upon his work in Thomistic moral theory or fundamental ethics. Both of these applied works have already shown the promise of offering a further stimulus to contemporary ethical discussion in the wake of *Veritatis Splendor* and within the ongoing renewal of Thomistic ethics. The first of these is entitled *Vital Conflicts in Medical Ethics: A Virtue Ap-*

---

8. Among his major works in ethical theory, this leaves his yet-to-be-translated *Praktische Vernunft und Vernünftigkeit der Praxis: Handlungstheorie bei Thomas von Aquin in ihrer Entstehung aus dem Problemkontext der aristotelischen Ethik* (Berlin: Akademie Verlag, 1994), which might be rendered in English as *Practical Reason and the Rationality of Praxis: Thomistic Action Theory in the Context of Its Origin in Aristotelian Ethics.*

9. The initial interlocutors have primarily been critics publishing in journals that, contrary to the expected protocols for scholarly exchange, will not publish responses, and are especially "generous" in the criticisms they publish. Although this is not the place to make the case, it is a straightforward matter to show that—as a reflection of the atrophy of reason that has followed from the postconciliar balkanization of Catholic ethics—such critics have not yet come to recognize sufficiently either the problems that Rhonheimer tries to address or the solutions he proposes. The failure of the critics to raise themselves to the level of the real discussion is evident in the lack of works by them addressing the following: the debate regarding how to specify the moral relevance of "nature" and the related rise of revisionist ethics as treated in *Natural Law and Practical Reason;* the difficult questions of applied ethics as in *Ethics of Procreation* and *Vital Conflicts;* or a systematic articulation and defense of Thomistic virtue ethics as in *Perspective of Morality.*

proach to Craniotomy and Tubal Pregnancies (2009).[10] It attempts to resolve one of the most difficult classes of cases in Catholic moral theology, one that has been debated for well over a century. These involve those situations during pregnancy in which the life of the embryo or fetus (whose pathological situation immediately threatens the life of the mother) cannot be saved, while the mother can be, but only through a procedure that the traditional moral theories of the manuals would consider as a direct—and thus illicit—abortion, and in which, if this procedure is omitted, both mother and child will die.[11] The second applied work is entitled *Ethics of Procreation and the Defense of Human Life: Contraception, Artificial Fertilization, Abortion* (2010).[12] It similarly addresses some of the most difficult and contested questions in ethics upon the theoretical basis discussed above, and with a high degree of circumspection, precision of argument, and persuasive power. Because it deals not only with disputed questions such as contraception,[13] artificial fertilization, and abortion but also with those aspects of political philosophy concerning the defense of life in constitutional democracies, it acts as an apt transition to the present volume and a work to be kept in mind by the readers of the latter. Those familiar with the way Pope Benedict XVI's 2009 social encyclical *Caritas in Veritate* "forcefully maintains" the "*strong links between life ethics and social ethics*" (no. 15, emphasis in original) will recognize that Rhonheimer's broad body of work in practical philosophy—from fundamental ethics, to applied ethics, to political philosophy—is arguably the primary contemporary resource that pro-

10. Ed. William F. Murphy Jr. (Washington, D.C.: The Catholic University of America Press, 2009).

11. As Rhonheimer writes in the preface, although it should be read as reflecting his own views, it "was drafted for the Roman Congregation for the Doctrine of the Faith and ... submitted to the Congregation in 2000. After it was carefully studied in the Congregation and by its then prefect, Cardinal Joseph Ratzinger, the Congregation in turn asked that it be published, so that the theses it contains could be discussed by specialists." Despite the fact that the CDF obviously wanted the text to be carefully studied by specialists, because it departs from both some traditional analyses and the ensuing and more stringent conclusions, it has been subject to an unprecedented set of critical reviews in the last two years. As I try to show in my "Craniotomy and Treatments for Tubal Pregnancy: Progress toward Consensus on Extreme Vital Conflicts?" in *Angelicum* 87 (2010): 871–910, the first several of these criticisms have not been effective and have thus indirectly strengthened Rhonheimer's case. Unlike the debate on the moral object, the current one on vital conflicts has benefited from the fact that there have been venues in the scholarly journals for both sides to make their case. For Rhonheimer's latest major response, see his "Vital Conflicts, Direct Killing, and Justice: A Response to Rev. Benedict Guevin and Other Critics" in the *National Catholic Bioethics Quarterly* 11, no. 3 (Summer 2011): 519–40.

12. Ed. William F. Murphy Jr. (Washington, D.C.: The Catholic University of America Press).

13. The disputed question of contraception is treated in part 1 of *Ethics of Procreation and the Defense of Human Life*, which is arguably the most comprehensive discussion in print. Indeed, this approach has reopened a broader reconsideration of this complex question, which remains central to sexual ethics; see my "Revisiting Contraception: An Integrated Approach in Light of the Renewal of Thomistic Virtue Ethics," *Theological Studies* 72, no. 4 (December 2011): 812–47. This understanding of the Catholic teaching on contraception is based upon the definition given in no. 14 of Pope Paul VI's 1968 encyclical *Humanae vitae*, which is generally ignored by Rhonheimer's more "conservative" critics. His approach is fully consistent with the notification issued by the Congregation for the Doctrine of the Faith on December 22, 2010, which was entitled "Note on the Banalization of Sexuality Regarding Certain Interpretations of 'Light of the World.'"

poses to show the coherence of this Catholic moral tradition in serious scholarly dialogue with the broad range of interlocutors.

Locating Rhonheimer's Work in Political Philosophy

In the remainder of this section, and recognizing the insufficiency of any such attempt in a few pages, I will highlight several key themes in Martin Rhonheimer's writings in political philosophy and on Catholic social teaching, and give some preliminary indications of how his work relates to that of some other thinkers, primarily those whose works are available to English-language readers. An ongoing theme will be that his work can be seen as fostering authentic advances in political philosophy, and in the interaction with Catholic social teaching, through a painstaking engagement with the writings of ancient, modern, and contemporary thinkers, which enables him to gain a wealth of insights and make a host of illuminating distinctions. Of course, none of these preliminary indications are to be taken as sufficient in themselves; some of them, moreover, are further developed in the second part of this introduction, while all of them are to be properly understood through reference to the essays that follow. Primarily in the footnotes, I will also make some preliminary remarks—some of which will challenge the conventional wisdom found among the diverse audiences for this book—regarding how it relates to some contemporary literature.

First, whereas some contemporary virtue ethicists claim that an Aristotelian and Thomistic understanding of the common good—which necessarily includes the virtue of the citizens—cannot be reconciled with the modern state,[14] Rhonheimer—whose important role in contemporary virtue ethics was just summarized—defends their compatibility through a distinction between the "integral common good" (concerning the complete fulfillment of persons and groups) and the "political common good" (those aspects of the common good that are properly sought through the political process). Such distinctions allow Rhonheimer to hold that persons and communities living in contemporary secular states have the opportunity to pursue and promote the life of virtue ordered to true and complete fulfillment. Second, and tracing back to the New Testament and Augustine's *City of God*, Rhonheimer offers an historical-philosophical argument that many readers will find surprising, namely that secularity—the nonestablishment of religion—is the original and proper Christian position, finally recovered by Catholics at the Second Vatican Council. Third, while recognizing the medieval roots of modern

---

14. See, for example, Alasdair MacIntyre's "Politics, Philosophy and the Common Good," in *The MacIntyre Reader*, ed. Kelvin Knight (Notre Dame: University of Notre Dame Press, 1998). For a discussion and criticism of MacIntyre's position, see V. Bradley Lewis, "The Common Good against the Modern State? On MacIntyre's Political Philosophy," *Josephinum Journal of Theology* 16, no. 2 (Summer/Fall 2009): 357–78.

constitutionalism, he traces them primarily through the English tradition following the Magna Carta of 1215. Fourth, following Aquinas's distinction between the
moral law that measures all human acts and the civil law that orders the community with respect to the common good, Rhonheimer thinks that upholding the common good requires that civil law must reflect the natural law in protecting such
fundamental goods as the sanctity of human life and the procreative family unit
of husband and wife.[15] In this, he agrees with a wide range of Catholic and other
natural law thinkers, though such thinkers often differ in their understandings of
natural law; for Rhonheimer, natural law is fundamentally a matter of right reason, an emphasis that is conducive to conversation with a range of interlocutors.[16]

Fifth, Rhonheimer offers what will be taken by many as a provocative and revisionist reading of Thomas Hobbes centered on his maxim *Auctoritas non veritas
facit legem,* or "Authority, not truth, creates the law." He defends Hobbes against
the widespread charge of founding a "decisionistic arbitrariness," through a careful argument that the latter should be understood instead as a new kind of natural
law thinker, who tries to found legal positivism on natural law understood in a
strictly political way. The sixth point concerns social contract theories as introduced by modern political philosophers such as Hobbes, John Locke, and Jean-
Jacques Rousseau. Such theories *claim to establish* the social character of human
existence, without a natural basis, a claim that is criticized and rejected by Catholic thinkers. Through a historically informed study of texts, Rhonheimer argues,
on the other hand, that the "social contract" that *actually* underlies democratic
constitutional states, or constitutional democracies, is based on the preexisting
reality that human coexistence depends on respect for persons and their rights.
"Such a correction of contractualism is," he argues, "in fact no longer contractualism, given that it presupposes a naturally social individual, admitting that every
... right is inserted into a good common to all people—their social coexistence."
A "modified contractualism," as Rhonheimer calls his position, turns out to be a
more sophisticated version of the Aristotelian conception of the naturally social
nature of human beings, yet more focused on the idea that society is for the advan-

15. Here readers are referred to the previously cited *Ethics of Procreation and the Defense of Human Life.*

16. For a recent discussion of the fundamentally rational character of natural law, see part 5 of his
The Perspective of Morality, and his "Natural Law as a 'Work of Reason': Understanding the Metaphysics
of Participated Theonomy," *American Journal of Jurisprudence* 55 (2010): 41–77; and "Natural Law and
Moral Reasoning: At the Roots of Aquinas's Moral Epistemology," *Josephinum Journal of Theology* 17,
no. 2 (Summer/Fall 2010): 341–81. Although he rejects an understanding of natural law as something
like the scientific laws of nature as seen in the human body and its natural inclinations, Rhonheimer
does not follow the "new natural law" or "basic human goods" theory of Germain Grisez, John Finnis,
and Joseph Boyle. He rejects, moreover, the position of what he would categorize as "non-liberal" thinkers such as Robert P. George, who would advocate "the prohibition and punishment of sodomy committed in private between persons of the same sex." He cites George's *Making Men Moral: Civil Liberties and
Public Morality* (Oxford: Clarendon Press, 1993), 167, 228.

tage of the individual, and not the reverse. Seventh, whereas some of the scholar-ship surrounding the early works in modern Catholic social teaching—that is, that in the years surrounding the 1931 publication of Pope Pius XI's encyclical *Quad-ragesimo anno*—understood it as a "third way" between socialism and liberalism, and as based on a distinctively Catholic social philosophy, Rhonheimer explicitly criticizes these characteristics and points out that they have been superseded in the social encyclicals of Pope John Paul II. In this latter tradition, Catholic teach-ing is explained explicitly as not comprising a third way; nor should it be seen as properly philosophical, but it should instead be understood as offering insights from revelation regarding the social order, and as drawing upon philosophy as an instrument in articulating and developing these insights.

Building on the seventh point, the eighth concerns the fact that Rhonheimer is distinguished by the scholarly rigor with which he treats the philosophical ques-tions of particular interest to Catholic social teaching. His attention to the broad range of political philosophy should make his work of interest to scholars in the United States who have been part of the twentieth-century recovery of political philosophy—ancient, modern, and contemporary—and who thereby oppose the tendency to forsake philosophy for the social sciences. A helpful point of com-parison to Rhonheimer's work is found through noting how those thinkers in the United States who are attentive to political philosophy and its relationship to Catholic social teaching often approach it through the hermeneutic of a contrast, quarrel, or sharp distinction between "the ancients and the moderns." Here the former are favored for their appreciation of virtue and truth (promoted by the re-gime) while the latter are criticized for abandoning such ideals for an emphasis on structural change and rights without corresponding duties.[17] An example of Rhon-heimer's sober analysis and distinctions can be seen in engagement with the work of John Rawls. While largely critical of the early work of John Rawls as found in his *A Theory of Justice,* Rhonheimer is more appreciative of Rawls's later achieve-ment in *Political Liberalism,* acknowledging the philosophical truths about the modern state that Rawls has articulated, which explicit appreciation distinguishes

17. This hermeneutic often traces to the work of Leo Strauss, who—in helping to recover politi-cal philosophy in the United States (though not without some serious deficiencies)—influenced a wide range of thinkers. One of these was Ernest Fortin, a widely respected and longtime professor of theol-ogy at Boston College. The influence of Strauss through Fortin can be seen, for example, in the helpful new work by J. Brian Benestad's *Church, State, and Society: An Introduction to Catholic Social Doctrine,* Catholic Moral Thought Series (Washington, D.C.: The Catholic University of America Press, 2011). Ben-estad introduces the work with an introduction that quite reasonably addresses the topic of "Catholic Social Doctrine and Political Philosophy" and that includes a subsection on "the quarrel between the ancients and the moderns" (23–27). Such appreciation for this hermeneutical principle, and perhaps to a lesser extent for the work of Strauss, can be seen in a variety of other important thinkers in the United States, such as James V. Schall, S.J.. For a rare example of a scholar trained under Strauss, and therefore familiar with the broad range of political philosophy, though taking a more favorable stance toward the moderns, see the work of William A. Galston.

him from many Catholic thinkers. Rhonheimer is distinguished from many secular political philosophers, on the other hand, by his criticism of Rawls for excluding natural law reasoning from his account of "public reason," an exclusion that Rhonheimer considers arbitrary and biased.[18]

The ninth point we might mention is Rhonheimer's emphasis on what he calls "the fundamental political ethos" of the democratic constitutional state, which he picks up from the German scholar Martin Kriele, and which emphasizes the characteristics of peace, freedom, and justice. This ethos, for Rhonheimer, represents the basic ethical consensus at the roots of modern society, upon which the further ethical/legal standards can be established through the political process. Building on this ninth point about the foundational political ethos, the tenth point concerns the delicate topic of multiculturalism, regarding which he argues—in dialogue with the thought of Jürgen Habermas, Will Kymlicka, and Charles Taylor—that "multicultural citizenship" is impossible precisely because it does not accept this foundational political ethos. Eleventh, Rhonheimer considers—and finds overly ambitious, potentially subversive, and reflecting problematic assumptions about human reason—Rawls's notion of "overlapping consensus," which involves a partial convergence in the sphere of "public reason" through which policy is established. Rhonheimer finds Rawls's idea of the overlapping consensus as a freestanding moral conception unsatisfactory, however, because this "consensus" draws its support from those who disagree in ways that will never allow such a political consensus to be a really homogeneous *moral* conception. Without rejecting the idea of an overlapping consensus, Rhonheimer argues that in reality, this kind of consensus also has the characteristics of a political *modus vivendi* built on a common political will of peaceful social cooperation under the conditions of pluralism and disagreement concerning fundamental moral values. He departs, however, from Charles Larmore's understanding of the term *modus vivendi*, because he thinks that it includes a problematic notion of neutrality.

I will conclude with a twelfth point to situate Rhonheimer among contemporary thinkers, namely his approach to the questions of human rights. Because they are often asserted arbitrarily, and without reference to corresponding duties, and because they can seem to overcome a more objective appeal to natural law, a number of Catholic thinkers are critical of the modern appeal to the notion of human rights, or even reject them.[19] While he too would object to the fabrication of arbitrary rights or the neglect of corresponding duties, Rhonheimer sees the typically modern achievement of human rights as easily reconcilable with and rooted in

18. On the question of Rawls's public reason and natural law, see also Wolfe's *Natural Law Liberalism*.

19. Alasdair MacIntyre, for example, has famously objected that human rights are a fiction. In his *Church, State and Society*, Benestad is not as critical as MacIntyre but generally discusses rights as inherently problematic. Similarly, James Schall, in his *Roman Catholic Political Philosophy* (Lanham, Md.: Lexington, 2004), offers only critical remarks regarding human rights while tracing them back to Hobbes (141).

medieval thought, as a valid expression of the modern political ethos, as inseparable from constitutional democracy, and as a potential basis for broader moral
consensus based on public reason.

Regarding the Essays in this Collection

The essays in this volume are arranged in a roughly chronological order and
thereby offer the reader not only Rhonheimer's analyses and arguments regarding
the various topics addressed, but also some insights into the development of his
thought in political philosophy. As will be shown below, the topics addressed are
far-ranging. In what follows, I will offer some introductory remarks on each essay,
which—of course—can only give a general indication of their subject matter.

Why Political Philosophy Is Necessary

The first essay is entitled "Why Is Political Philosophy Necessary? Historical
Considerations and a Response," and was originally published in Italian in 1992.[20]
In two major sections it explains, respectively, the necessity of political philosophy
and how it should be understood as "fundamental political ethics," thereby linking
the present volume to Rhonheimer's work in fundamental and applied ethics. His
argument for the necessity of political philosophy includes four elements: (1) the
justification of Aristotelian political philosophy as an ethics of the *polis*—a union
of ethics and politics; (2) the justification, with respect to this classical tradition,
of modern political philosophy, which is understood as a response to the internal
contradictions of the medieval idea of the *respublica christiana;* (3) a discussion of
why the classical doctrine concerning natural law does not suffice for political philosophy; and (4) a treatment of the relation between political philosophy and the social doctrine of the Church. Similarly, the understanding of political philosophy as
"fundamental political ethics" is justified through an explanation of the following:
(1) the distinctive moral logic of political praxis; (2) the integration of the political
ethos into history and culture; (3) the founding ethos of the political culture of the
democratic constitutional state, namely the ethos of the Common Good as peace,
liberty, and justice.

Liberalism, Autonomy, and Anthropology

The second essay is entitled "The Liberal Image of Man and the Concept of
Autonomy: Beyond the Debate between Liberals and Communitarians," and was
originally published in Italian in 1997.[21] It begins with an introduction to liberal-

---

20. The Italian original was published as "Perché una filosofia politica? Elementi storici per una
risposta," *Acta Philosophica* 1, no. 1 (1992): 233–63. It was translated by Joseph T. Papa.
21. The original was published as "L'immagine dell'uomo nel liberalismo e il concetto di autono-

ism's anthropological problem, which occurs when the autonomy that is part of every form of liberalism is understood in a strong sense that is disconnected from authentic goods. In the second part, it outlines two versions of classical liberalism: the primarily political form of liberalism and the variety that includes a comprehensive ethical doctrine. While the latter includes what Rhonheimer calls a "strong concept of autonomy," which holds that free choice is valuable as such, independently from the goods chosen, that is, just because it is "my choice," and therefore should be restricted exclusively by external, political reasons, the latter does not necessarily involve such an idea but is able to recognize the intrinsic limitation of freedom by what is truly good. The essay thirdly considers the anthropological implications of recent theories of liberalism, including that of the early John Rawls (and the communitarian critique of it that he however rejects) and its "contamination" by the strong concept of autonomy, that of the later Rawls of political liberalism, and that of C. Larmore's *modus vivendi*. In the fourth and final part, after making clear the contradictions caused by the strong concept of autonomy, it explores the more promising alternative of Joseph Raz that—although raising further questions—can help to move beyond the alternatives of liberalism and antiliberalism.

The Democratic Constitutional State and the Common Good

The third essay is entitled "The Democratic Constitutional State and the Common Good," and was originally published in Italian in 1997.[22] It includes four parts. The first provides an account of the modern political ethos as an institutional one ensuring peace, freedom, and a basic level of justice. The second offers a philosophical argument for the legitimacy of the democratic constitutional state that is based on what he calls "modified contractualism," a synthesis of the Aristotelian idea of human beings as *naturally* social, and modern, mostly Lockean contractualism, which focuses on the idea that society and government are for the advantage of individuals, and not the reverse. This also enables him to found—against Nozick's idea of the libertarian minimal state—a qualified justification for redistributive measures by the state, without falling into the liberal error of claiming that the less well off have a *right* to be compensated by those who are better off, converting the state into an agency of systematic redistribution for the creation of a "just" society. In this context Rhonheimer's understanding of justice as solidarity and subsidiarity is crucial.

The third part addresses questions such as the neutrality of the state and the

---

mia: al di là del dibattito fra liberali e comunitaristi," in *Immagini dell'uomo. Percorsi antropologici nella filosofia moderna*, ed. Ignacio Yarza (Rome: Armando, 1997). It was translated by Robert A. Gahl.

22. "Lo Stato costituzionale democratico e il bene comune," in *Ripensare lo spazio politico: quale aristocrazia?* ed. E. Morandi and R. Panattoni (Padua: Il Poligrafo, 1998), 57–123 (Con-tratto. Rivista di filosofia tomista e contemporanea 6/1997). It was translated by Joseph T. Papa.

relation of public morality to the common good, arguing that the latter includes not only procedural but also substantial values. On these bases, the fourth and final part presents an understanding of the common good for a pluralistic society. This understanding relies upon the distinction between the "integral common good" and the "political common good." The former concerns the complete fulfillment of persons and groups through their own praxis, which implies that the state should neither define it nor seek to ensure its achievement. The latter concerns all those goods that are appropriately pursued through the political process, which provide necessary *conditions* (i.e., external defense, internal law and order, apt regulation of the economy, material assistance when needed, public services) so that persons and groups can pursue their complete fulfillment or integral common good.

Hobbes on Law, Authority, and Truth

The fourth essay is entitled "*Autoritas non veritas facit legem:* Thomas Hobbes, Carl Schmitt, and the Idea of the Constitutional State," and was originally published in German in 2000.[23] It proceeds through five steps. In the preliminary section it sets the stage for a consideration of the famous assertion that "authority, not truth, creates the law" by introducing the similar-sounding assertion of Carl Schmitt that "the Führer has laid down the law." This provides a point of departure for considering, in light of recent scholarship on both Hobbes and Schmitt, the reception of significant aspects the former's thought by the latter.

The second part of the essay proceeds to explore the meaning of the phrase for Hobbes. Some readers will be surprised at Rhonheimer's claim that "although he is the founder of legal positivism, Hobbes remains a true natural law thinker," who cannot be accused of promoting a "decisionistic arbitrariness." What Hobbes promotes is a pragmatic-political theory of truth in the service of peace, thus aiming at overcoming and preventing civil war. Hobbes's originality, Rhonheimer argues, is to be found in his attempt to found legal positivism on natural right and natural law. The very structure of Hobbesian political philosophy thus shows that, to be consistently founded, legal positivism needs the reference to standards of right and reasonableness *previous* to the positive legal order; therefore the very idea of legal positivism is self-contradictory. The third part then studies Carl Schmitt's interpretation of the maxim as pure decisionism, an interpretation that "consistently overlooks the pragmatic significance of the truth-claim of the Hobbesian theory" and "Hobbes' clearly stated intention ... to understand every legislative decision as clearly bound by natural right and the natural laws." The fourth further ex-

23. The original was published as "Autoritas non veritas facit legem: Thomas Hobbes, Carl Schmitt und die Idee des Verfassungsstaates," *Archiv für Rechts- und Sozialphilosophie* 86 (2000): 484–98. It was translated by Gerald Malsbary. The present volume uses the correct Latin spelling of *auctoritas* unless citing a text employing the alternative spelling of *autoritas*.

plores the thought of Hobbes and the way it is taken up by Schmitt, concluding that the latter "unintentionally, has helped us, we might say, find a therapeutic value in our study of Hobbes," because it brings to light the intrinsic paradoxes and inconsistencies of the Hobbesian solution. In the final part, Rhonheimer considers these ideas of Hobbes on law in light of his opposition to the jurists of the common law, showing that the position of the latter is more consonant with the idea of the democratic constitutional state.

Against the Soft Totalitarianism of "Laicism"

The fifth essay is entitled "The Open Society and the New Laicism: Against the Soft Totalitarianism of Certain Secularist Thinking," and was originally published, though in a shorter version, in Italian (2003).[24] As discussed in the opening "author's note," this short piece was originally written at the invitation of an Italian "secularist" (or "laicist") journal on the occasion of the hundredth anniversary of the birth of Karl R. Popper, who was perhaps most famous for his defense of the "Open Society" or constitutional democracy, which he preferred especially for its ability to transfer power without bloodshed. Popper advocated such forms of government over alternatives such as totalitarian dictatorship, theocracy, or autocratic monarchy.

For this anniversary, Rhonheimer wanted to point out, and argue against, the tendency of some secularists toward what can be called a soft totalitarianism, especially in rejecting Popper's recognition that open societies must be based on a stable system of values in some way connected with the Judeo-Christian tradition. Although some contemporary secularists consider such an understanding of absolute values to be fundamentalist, Rhonheimer shows that for Popper the fundamentalist is instead the one who thinks "ultimate and absolute criteria of truth are *immanent* to the political process." The Swiss philosopher goes on to explain that, consistent with Popper's distinction between "facts" (i.e., of legislation) and "criteria" (i.e., of values that transcend political and legal factuality and thus are able to found the distinction between "might" and "right"), Catholic objections to the legalization of elective abortion are not meant to question the legitimacy of the political procedures that led to it, but instead to say that these procedures have reached conclusions contrary to human dignity and moral truth; they should thus be opposed by the same political means that made possible the existing legislation. In this way Rhonheimer points out what he considers to be the anachronistic, argumentatively flawed, and unjust character of a kind of secularist thought that tries to exclude, on principle, determinate moral positions as politically illegitim-

---

24. As "Laici e cattolici: oltre le divisioni" in the journal *Fondazione Liberal* 17 (2003): 108–16. This present original and longer text, which was not previously published, was translated by Joseph T. Papa.

ate; at the same time, he defends the right of those believing in certain absolute truths, such as the sanctity of human life, to shape the political agenda according to its proper logic and with political arguments. He affirms that citizens should respect the political ethos (of peace, freedom, and justice) and corresponding logic of the liberal state, which is to practice "constitutional patriotism." On the other hand, Rhonheimer rejects as a myth the liberal understanding of the "neutrality of the state" that would limit the state to purely procedural and formal aspects, or that would deny that the state can reflect objective values in law and privilege certain conceptions of life. In this, he revisits a central theme also of the third essay on "The Democratic Constitutional State and the Common Good."

Centesimus Annus: Contextualization and Central Teachings

The sixth essay is entitled "The Political and Economic Realities of the Modern World and Their Ethical and Cultural Presuppositions: The Encyclical *Centesimus annus*," and was originally published in Italian in 2003.[25] It is structured in three parts: a discussion of the place of the encyclical in the history of the social doctrine of the Church; a sketch of its central themes; and some concluding observations. Rhonheimer's historical discussion of the place of *Centesimus annus* within Catholic social doctrine highlights the contrast between its teaching and the earlier understanding of the discipline. This earlier understanding, which surrounded the 1931 encyclical *Quadragesimo anno*, understood Catholic social teaching as a comprehensive "third way" between socialism and liberal capitalism, which drew upon natural law and social science—not theology—to provide a philosophical and institutional alternative. Rhonheimer discusses several weaknesses of this earlier approach, and the movement after the Second World War toward an acceptance of modern democracy. This movement was followed by what he calls the "theological turn in Catholic social teaching" that comes to fruition in John Paul II's 1987 encyclical *Solicitudo rei socialis,* which includes both the explicit denial that this social doctrine should be understood as a third way and the explicit claim that its place is to offer insights from revelation.

The essay treats the central themes of *Centesimus annus* in three subsections that address the following: first, property, the market economy, capitalism, and business; second, the constitutional state, democracy, and human rights; and third, the state and the economy. While recognizing that some formulations of the encyclical leave questions open (i.e., how the "culture of death" is related to the political and economic system), Rhonheimer's concluding observations empha-

25. This original was published as "La realtà politica ed economica del mondo moderno e i suoi presupposti etici e culturali. L'enciclica *Centesimus annus*," in *Giovanni Paolo Teologo—el segno delle encicliche,* ed. Graziano Borgonovo and Arturo Cattaneo, preface by His Eminence Camillo Cardinal Ruini (Rome: Edizioni Arnoldo Mondatori, 2003). It was translated from the Italian by Joseph T. Papa.

size the clarity of the encyclical's basic tenor in accepting the core logic or rationality of the democratic constitutional state and the free, capitalist, or market economy while criticizing the cultural and ethical lacunae that oppose human dignity.

Natural Law, Constitutional Democracy, and Rawls's "Public Reason"

The seventh essay is entitled "The Political Ethos of Constitutional Democracy and the Place of Natural Law in Public Reason: Rawls's *Political Liberalism*
Revisited." It was originally delivered as the 2005 Natural Law Lecture at the University of Notre Dame Law School[26] and proceeds through three major steps: an
argument for the historical legitimacy of the political ethos of constitutional democracy; a discussion of the relation between this ethos of constitutional democracy and John Rawls's theory of public reason; and an argument that, although
Rawls has a strong bias against the recognition of natural law in a constitutional
democracy, natural law is easily reconcilable with Rawls's understanding of "public reason." The core of the argument is to show that Rawls excludes natural law
by using a definition of society as a system of cooperation of "free and equal citizens," which—from the beginning—excludes aspects that characterize human
persons *naturally,* that is, previously from being citizens, for example, as members
of the reproductive unity of marriage and the family, or of neighborhood. From
this springs Rawls's biased understanding of the principle of reciprocity, which,
as Rhonheimer criticizes it, leads the former to unduly exclude from public reason
substantial pre-political values that are of great political relevance.

These themes are reiterated in the eighth essay, which is entitled "Rawlsian
Public Reason, Natural Law, and the Foundation of Justice: A Response to David
Crawford," and was originally published in *Communio: International Catholic Review* 36, no. 1 (Spring 2009): 138–67, as a response to Crawford's critique of Rhonheimer's "Rawls's Political Liberalism Revisited."[27] Crawford's critique centers in
the claim that Rhonheimer's "benign" interpretation of liberalism falls into the
typical errors of liberal proceduralism, especially by not rooting justice in a sound
anthropology (a theme treated philosophically in chapter 2 of this volume). Drawing on the work of von Balthasar and the *Communio* school, Crawford thinks this
sound anthropology is necessarily rooted in anthropology of "nuptiality," in an
understanding of what he calls the "familial person," and in particular understandings of Trinitarian theology and Christology. He also thinks Rhonheimer has

---

26. It was then published as "The Political Ethos of Constitutional Democracy and the Place of
Natural Law in Public Reason: Rawls's 'Political Liberalism' Revisited," *American Journal of Jurisprudence* 50 (2005): 1–70.

27. Crawford's essay is entitled "Recognizing the Roots of Society in the Family, Foundation of Justice," *Communio* 34 (Fall 2007): 379–412.

neglected the foundational role in society of natural law, and especially in laws respecting the family.

Rhonheimer's response includes, among others, the following key points: that Crawford is critiquing "the first Rawls" of *A Theory of Justice,* whereas his natural law lecture concerned "the second Rawls" of *Political Liberalism;* that both Rhonheimer and "the second Rawls" of *Political Liberalism* agree with Crawford in opposing pure proceduralism; that *Political Liberalism* explicitly accepts the Catholic view of common good as a legitimate notion that can be advanced through "public reasons"; that natural law arguments should be acceptable to Rawls based on his understandings of "empirical facts" and "public reason" but are instead excluded by him based on a bias typical of twentieth-century "liberals"; that the Rawls of *Political Liberalism,* therefore, irrationally excludes recognition of the family as a "natural institution" and thus a civil privileging of heterosexual marriage; that, by his appeal to Trinitarian theology and Christology, Crawford mistakenly makes what he thinks are natural law arguments for political ends; and that Crawford has failed to understand Rhonheimer's goal in the essay, which was to subvert "liberal" conceptions of public reason through traditional natural law thinking in order to show how the dignity of human life and the heterosexual family unit can be supported within the logic of the liberal democratic state.

Human Rights and Universal Ethics

The ninth essay, originally written in 2007 and not previously published in this form, is entitled "Can Political Ethics Be Universalized? Human Rights as a Global Project."[28] This essay begins by introducing the topic of human rights as a global political ethos, noting that although they are Western in origin, they are understood to have universal application. It continues to provide a basic description of political ethics in general, with particular attention to the human rights that are an expression of the political ethos of constitutional democracy. Political ethics are presented as "the moral base of the institutions in which the political life of a country takes place"; whether judicial, political, or social, these institutions are "an expression of political culture." Whereas natural law governs what is reasonable for human action, its reasons are not valid for the realm of political and public reason unless they are advanced by specifically political, that is, public, reasons referring to the political common good. Although this last claim may

---

28. A much more extended version of this essay with the same title was published in *Ethics and Health in the Global Village: Bioethics, Globalization and Human Rights,* ed. Emilio Mordini, preface by Franco Frattini (Rome: CIC Edizioni Internazionali, 2009), 39–58. Parts of the essay as it is published in the present book (i.e., section 2) were reworked for inclusion in Rhonheimer's "Christian Secularity, Political Ethics and the Culture of Human Rights," which was published in the *Josephinum Journal of Theology* 16, no. 2 (August 2009): 250–72.

sound problematic to antiliberals, it is consistent with Aquinas's understanding of the distinction between moral law and civil law.

From here, Rhonheimer specifies the understanding of political ethics that is implicit in the notion of human rights; as we have already seen, this understanding is centered in peace, liberty, and justice, while including related notions such as equality and solidarity. The essay concludes by exploring whether this understanding of political ethics can be universalized, especially given the way those ethics have been shaped by the particulars of history and culture. For Rhonheimer, this potential universalization of the political ethics of human rights depends on factors such as "finding an overlapping intercultural consensus that would be based on human rights and their implementation through the institutions of a constitutional democracy of the Western type." This means that "a policy of 'multicultural citizenship' (Will Kymlicka) and the 'recognition of difference' (Charles Taylor) must therefore always be also a policy of integration, of assimilation, of socialization" such that those who are welcomed into democratic constitutional states must be willing to be integrated and socialized into the political culture.

Christian Secularity

The tenth essay is entitled "Christian Secularity and the Culture of Human Rights," and was originally presented at the symposium "A Growing Gap: Living and Forgotten Christian Roots in Europe and the United States," which was held in 2006.[29] This essay sketches how Christians, and especially Catholics, should understand their identity in relation to modern political secularism, which for Rhonheimer is consistent with Augustinian dualism between the cities of God and man. The essay begins with a discussion of the distinctions between the European and American traditions of regarding religious freedom in the secular state. Whereas the European tradition—following upon the Protestant Reformation and subsequent wars of religion—has been characterized by considerable tensions with and hostility toward religion, the American tradition has been marked by a situation in which religion "developed into a constructive force in American public life," which is not to deny that significant blocks of American secularists advance a European-style hostility to religion.

Rhonheimer next treats the topic of "Christian Secularity," or the properly Christian way of living in a secular state, which involves the seeming paradox and "double identity" of being both a Christian and a citizen. In his view, Christians should fully embrace their role as citizens, accepting the logic of the political, being able, without ceasing to be citizens of faith, to cooperate with those citizens

---

29. This essay was published in a more developed form as the just-cited "Christian Secularity, Political Ethics and the Culture of Human Rights."

who do not share their values. This, as Rhonheimer emphasizes, also concerns the question of whether a merely political-pragmatic justification of the human rights that form the political ethics of such societies is sufficient, and whether a consciousness of their metaphysical and anthropological roots is not also needed. Although in the political realm these rights are articulated through properly political reasons, based on the pragmatic evidence of the advantageousness of human rights and on correspondent public reasons (which are neither religious nor bound to any special metaphysics), human rights ultimately are founded in strong metaphysical beliefs about human dignity that are decisively supported by Christian faith. While recognizing that such a foundation of natural rights will not be persuasive to fellow citizens of different beliefs, it is the proper task of Christians to foster the consciousness of these rights being rooted in the metaphysical truth about man. Only this consciousness provides an ultimate and stable cognitive basis for a culture of human rights. Rhonheimer concludes with a discussion of why "pluralism" is a healthy feature of this political ethos whereas "multiculturalism" is not, a theme that is treated more extensively in the following essay.

Multicultural Citizenship in Liberal Democracy?

The eleventh essay is entitled "Multicultural Citizenship in Liberal Democracy: The Proposals of C. Taylor, J. Habermas, and W. Kymlicka," and was originally published in Italian in 2006.[30] It treats in depth a topic broached in the preceding essay regarding the basic question of "multicultural citizenship" and the various aspects of the debate concerning "multiculturalism." These include the relation between multiculturalism and the fact of the diversity and clash of cultures, its intranational and international dimensions, the distinction between national minorities and ethnic groups, the questions of racism and of religion, and the integration of Moslem immigrants in secular states.

Three representative positions are presented and evaluated: Charles Taylor's politics of recognition, Jürgen Habermas's deliberative democracy and constitutional patriotism, and Will Kymlicka's liberal theory of minority rights. As foreshadowed in the preceding essay, this one concludes that a properly multicultural citizenship within a democratic constitutional state is impossible, precisely because such states are established by a consensus regarding the foundational political culture of peace, freedom, and justice. In its proper and strong sense, on the other hand, the acceptance of multiculturalism entails the surrender of this achievement of consensus and political culture.

---

30. The original was published as "Cittadinanza multiculturale nella democrazia liberale: le proposte di Ch. Taylor, J. Habermes e W. Kymlicka," *Acta Philosophica* 15, no. 1 (2006): 29–52. It was translated by Joseph T. Papa.

Christianity and Secularity

The twelfth essay is entitled "Christianity and Secularity: Past and Present of a Complex Relationship," and was originally published in Italian 2008.[31] It offers an extensive argument for the thesis that "Christianity introduced a clear separation between politics and religion into Western history"; this separation, moreover, affirmed "the supremacy of the spiritual with respect to the temporal" such that "political power" is subordinated to "criteria of moral truth, natural law, justice, and criteria of an eschatological nature." Nevertheless, Rhonheimer argues, "Christianity has been the condition of possibility for the development of a secular political culture," and "though it may seem paradoxical—is still one of its guarantors today." Because Christianity was characterized for several centuries by the employment of the coercive power of the state at the service of religious truth, and—until the Second Vatican Council—by its rejection of the right to religious freedom, a detailed historical explanation is required to support this thesis. It is impossible to give in a few words an adequate summary of Rhonheimer's highly complex argument.

The first of its two parts addresses "the past" by tracing the history of the relation between the Church and political power, through the encyclical *Centesimus annus* and to the present day.[32] It discusses what Rhonheimer calls the original Christian dualism between politics and religion, including its articulation by Augustine. After the collapse of the Western Roman Empire, the Church took on a new role leading to the triumph of "political Augustinianism," which—through a corruption of Augustine's thought and a departure from the original Christian dualism—involved a fusion between religion and politics by asserting the temporal power as being at the service of the spiritual power. This fusion prevailed until the loss of Christian unity and the birth of the modern primacy of the political, which eventually led to the genesis of the secular constitutional state and, later, to constitutional democracy based on the recognition of individual human rights.[33]

31. The original was published as "Cristianesimo e laicità: storia ed attualità di un rapporto complesso," in *Laicità: la ricerca dell'universale nella differenza*, ed. Pierpaolo Donati (Bologna: Il Mulino, 2008), 27–138. It was translated into English by Joseph T. Papa. A Spanish translation of this substantial essay was recently published in book form as *Cristianismo y laicidad. Historia y actualidad de una relación compleja* (Madrid: Rialp, 2009). A considerably expanded text was recently published in German as *Christentum und säkularer Staat. Geschichte—Gegenwart—Zukunft*, with a preface by Ernst-Wolfgang Böckenförde (Freiburg im Breisgau: Herder, 2012).

32. The book does not attempt to make original contributions to legal or political history; rather, its contribution is the philosophical-ethical (and also theological) interpretation. The longer German version, *Christentum und säkularer Staat*, maintains this focus while deepening it historically, philosophically, and theologically.

33. Rhonheimer recognizes the roots of constitutionalism in the Christian Middle Ages and traces it back to the Magna Carta of 1215 (which relies on the Anglo-Saxon constitutionalist tradition). He sees thinkers such as Jean Bodin (1530–96) and Thomas Hobbes (1588–1679) not as founders of a "liberalism" that aimed at neutralizing religion and religious authority but as examples of the modern "primacy of the political" and as founders of a modern idea of sovereignty that was opposed by the liberal constitutionalism that drew on medieval tradition.

Because of the weight of a centuries-old canonical and theological tradition, mainly aiming at defending the *libertas ecclesiae,* the freedom of the Church, among other factors, only slowly did the Church come to accept secular democracy and human rights, especially after the Second World War.

The second of its two parts addresses "the present," in which the Church must carry out its spiritual mission within the modern secular state. Within a state that embodies the liberal ethos of peace, freedom, justice, and equality, this context involves a "political concept of secularity" (in the words of Benedict XVI a "healthy secularity"), which implies the separation of politics from religion but not a state hostility toward religion. This is contrasted by Rhonheimer with what he calls an "integralist concept of secularity," which is characterized as a program of imposing through state power a secularist and antireligious agenda, aiming at excluding the voice of the Church and of religious citizens from the public sphere. Such unhealthy and even dangerous forms of secularity reflect what Josef Ratzinger called a "dictatorship of relativism." Among many other points, and a wealth of valuable insights, Rhonheimer discusses the widespread contemporary situation in which democratic mechanisms are employed to advance policies contrary to both the dignity of human life and the procreative family unit. He argues that—in spite of objections that the Magisterium of the Church has improperly intruded into the public sphere, thereby violating the principles of the secular state—members of the Magisterium have the right and duty to uphold the common good through arguments based on a defense of natural law. While claiming this right and duty for the Church, Rhonheimer specifies that the Church does not claim sovereignty over the political process. Instead it simply acts as a public interlocutor, addressing citizens consciences with reasons that—although perhaps grounded in revelation—are able to be understood and expressed as political reasons, referring to the political common good; in precisely this way, he thinks the Church properly influences the democratic process. He concludes that although the secular state does not derive directly from Christianity, it is essentially congruent with Christianity's "founding charism"; it can even be understood as an outgrowth of Christianity. The Church, however, will never relate to the secular state in a simply affirmative or harmonious way, but only "coexists" with it. There will always be inevitable tensions and "constructive conflict" between the Church and the secular state. This tension will necessarily follow from the Church's self-understanding as representing a higher, revealed truth, necessary for salvation and for healing earthly realities from the consequences of sin, a self-understanding that defines its very identity, which it has preserved through the centuries. In this context, Christians today must exercise their role as "salt of the earth" and "light of the world" and carry out the new evangelization while accepting wholeheartedly the secularity of the modern state, not simply for merely tactical or prudential reasons, but because they recognize its being consonant to Christianity's primary identity as rooted in the Gospel and lived by the early Christians.

Regarding the above reference to public reason, it is important to distinguish between the *public political discourse between citizens,* to which the above referred, *and the wider task of the Church and its Magisterium.* The latter obviously does not confuse its role with the teaching of political philosophy, but it does render judgments about political realities. Rhonheimer concludes the first half of his essay as follows:

The Church can give a judgment concerning political realities only from its specific doctrinal and pastoral perspective, a perspective that defends the transcendent dignity of the human person and the temporal conditions that respect that dignity. Ultimately, therefore, the Church gives its evaluation of secular democracy in the light of the two great principles that have been present from the beginning of its history: the primacy of the spiritual over the temporal, and the ordering of what is earthly and temporal to what is heavenly and eternal.

More than providing a doctrine on the nature, legitimacy, and functioning of modern democracy, the Church, in fulfillment of its pastoral task, offers—and is fully justified in doing so—its own conceptual *ideal* of democracy, full of substantial values that can be realized democratically, along with a conception of the common good.

Here again Rhonheimer stresses the continuity of the Church's self-understanding in claiming to possess, as the supreme and divinely instituted spiritual power, the right to subject any temporal power to its moral judgment, denying that there be any political power that can be the ultimate source of moral standards. This "antitotalitarian" program, Rhonheimer argues, was already the very essence of the high medieval idea of papal *plenitudo potestatis.* What the Church had to learn, however, was that it should exercise this spiritual authority without claiming juridical and thus political sovereignty over the temporal power, which ultimately means recognizing the secularity of the state.

Having offered a philosophical reflection that builds upon a reading of the history of the relations between Church and state that is solidly supported by common scholarly historical evidence, we are ready to say a few words about an intervention by Rhonheimer into a current debate among Catholics. In this debate, some Catholics have rejected the Church's reconciliation with the democratic state, based on the Second Vatican Council's recognition of fundamental rights, mainly the right to religious liberty, thinking this recognition to be a departure from established doctrine.

Benedict XVI's Hermeneutic of Reform and Religious Freedom

The thirteenth essay is written in support of Pope Benedict XVI's December 2005 Christmas message to the Roman curia, which included some remarks regarding the fortieth anniversary of the conclusion of the Second Vatican Council, and addressed especially the question of why the implementation of the council had been so difficult. The pope proposed that the answer was found in the competing hermeneutics through which the council has been interpreted, namely the mistaken "hermeneutic of discontinuity and rupture" and the correct "'hermeneutic of reform,' of renewal in the continuity," which Benedict traces to the speech of Pope John XXIII that inaugurated the council. According to the hermeneutic of reform, Benedict reads the contested Declaration on Religious Freedom, *Dignitatis humanae,* not as a rupture as had others from different ends of the ideological spectrum—mainly the so-called School of Bologna—but as the recovery of "the deepest patrimony of the Church." This claim, however, was seen as highly problematic, especially by those who took as binding the nineteenth-century declarations of Pope Pius IX that the Church could not be reconciled with the liberal, that is constitutional and secular, state. As the introductory remarks regarding Rhonheimer's essay on "Christianity and Secularity" suggest, that prior essay provides—within a very different literary context—a treatment of many of the matters at stake in the present one.

The first part of the present essay addresses these matters concisely as they pertain to the Second Vatican Council under the heading of "Continuity or Rupture: How Did Vatican II Understand the Church's Relation with the Modern World?" Here Rhonheimer acknowledges frankly a real discontinuity in Catholic teaching regarding the secular state. He follows a distinction made by Benedict XVI that first affirms a fundamental doctrinal continuity—on the level of principles—concerning the truth of Christian religion and of the Catholic Church, as for example in the requirement that each human person seek the truth and adhere to it when found. The discontinuity, on the other hand, is located in a different judgment regarding the application of doctrine to historically contingent and human matters, namely the political order and the understanding of the nature and the role of temporal power (the state). It is on this latter level that Rhonheimer, following the suggestions made by Benedict XVI, finds discontinuity—a discontinuity that, however, does not affect the *depositum fidei* or the essence and the nature of the Church. The second part of the essay is a long appendix answering a question of great concern to certain Catholics: "Does the Existence of Discontinuity Call into Question the Infallibility of the Magisterium?" It does so by treating the question itself of infallibility, the doctrinal substance of the nineteenth-century condemnation of religious freedom by Pius IX, the insight that religious freedom is a natural right, and Rhonheimer's argument that there is no discontinuity in dogmatic doctrine but only in the doctrine concerning the nature and role of the temporal power, or the state.

The Free Market and the Common Good

The fourteenth and final essay is entitled "Capitalism, Free Market Economy, and the Common Good: The Role of the State in the Economy," and should be of considerable interest in light of the global economic struggles since 2008.[34] From the perspective of moral and political philosophy, this substantial essay addresses the subject matter indicated in the title, while striving to be well informed by sound economic thinking so as to reflect the logic proper to economics.

The essay poses the fundamental question: are free markets the best institutions for fostering the common good, or is the common good something entrusted to the care of states and governments?[35] After reviewing the alternative visions of Keynes and Walter Eucken on this subject, Rhonheimer concludes that, in general, the free market and not the state is the best institution for fostering the common good, but only if it is allowed to function correctly. He argues that for this to occur, the state's activity must aim at making the market mechanisms work in an undistorted way. When governments go beyond this limit, by interfering in the business decisions of firms or in the price system, they actually damage the common good. "In the line of Ordoliberalism, but also inspired by representatives of the Austrian School of Economics, [Rhonheimer] opts for a qualified rehabilitation of *laissez faire,* and of Adam Smith's idea of the 'invisible hand,' ideas which in the wake of Keynesian analysis of economic matters are often gravely misrepresented." Based on these convictions, Rhonheimer shows why the logic of politics is different from the economic logic and how, therefore, democratic politics often lead to state solutions and subsequent state failures, falsely attributed to the market and its lack of state regulation.

He considers what he sees as a systemic conflict between economic logic and political logic. Whereas the former logic naturally looks to long-term interests that are consistent with the common good, the latter—which drives the political process—tends toward short-term and group interests, which often oppose the common good. Rhonheimer also analyzes "the history of the social teaching of the Catholic Church, pointing out that in the past, some official documents were not free of statist attitudes and did not fully comprehend the logic of capitalism and free market economies. With the encyclical *Centesimus annus* by John Paul II this has changed. *Centesimus annus* accepts the logic of modern free economy, of capitalism and democracy." The subsequent encyclical *Caritas in veritate,* by Pope Benedict XVI, though "less clear on this subject, importantly introduces in the Social Doctrine of the Church the idea of institutional ethics." By so doing Pope Benedict thus advocates "a conception of the common good" that is "not in the first place a pre-determined social pattern of just distribution of wealth and opportunities, but rather the institutional framework for free cooperation of citizens from

34. This paper was originally presented at a conference on the theme of Free Markets and the Culture of Common Good, which was held in Rome October 14–15, 2010, and has been published in *Free Markets and the Culture of Common Good,* ed. M. Schlag and J. A. Mercado (New York: Springer, 2012), 3–40.

35. The following two paragraphs are adapted from an abstract originally written by Rhonheimer and published on the first page of the essay as originally published in *Free Markets and the Culture of Common Good.*

which social justice and the common good is a result." Because, however, not all human needs are marketable and because weaker social groups must sometimes be protected from the immediately damaging effects of sound economic policy, Rhonheimer concludes that there will be always a trade-off between economic efficiency and equity. The role of the state, however necessary it may be, must be limited so it does not create—in the name of social justice—structural economic inefficiencies that in the end are unjust and damage the common good.

The essay finally shows how liberalism and Catholic social doctrine can learn from each other. The free market itself is neither good nor evil, nor is it more than a part of the common good. Still it is the most efficient way to coordinate human creativity, and the allocation of resources. Thus its basic mechanisms must be fostered and not undermined by extreme welfare-state forms of capitalism that—in the name of social justice—undermine subsidiarity, solidarity, and responsibility among citizens, while discouraging initiative through excessive bureaucracy, all of which have led Western democracies to excessive and unsustainable levels of debt.[36]

Conclusion

It is my hope that readers will find this collection of essays to make a significant contribution to the field of political philosophy and to be a valuable resource for those working in Catholic social teaching. I also hope it will receive thoughtful consideration as part of a comprehensive body of practical philosophy that not only engages at the highest level the broad range of interlocutors, but also is of service to Catholic moral theology in upholding what Pope Benedict XVI calls the "link between life ethics and social ethics," and thereby contributing to what he calls the recovery of reason.

William F. Murphy Jr.
Pontifical College Josephinum

36. At this point, some will be disappointed that Rhonheimer does not include a significant engagement with the cultural and political objections made by some contemporary critics of liberalism. Such critics object that the contemporary situation—which traces in no small part to consumerist capitalism—is impervious to the rational arguments of public reason. Although the present volume includes key elements of Rhonheimer's approach to such challenges—including the importance of virtue ethics, the importance of mediating institutions, and the indispensable role of the Church—it is not meant to provide a direct response to these cultural and political problems. Rhonheimer would perhaps also emphasize that consumerism is not essentially a consequence of capitalism or a free economy, but rather the outgrowth of the modern welfare state that systematically provides incentives for excessive spending—or better, insufficient saving—and for lack of personal responsibility.

THE
Common Good
OF
Constitutional
Democracy

ONE

Why Is Political Philosophy Necessary?

Historical Considerations and a Response

The question "Why is political philosophy necessary?" could seem strange and out of place to those familiar with the history of philosophy and with the present-day "renaissance," at the international level, of philosophical reflection on questions concerning politics. At the same time, an authentic political philosophy could easily seem superfluous to someone who considers the theme to have been sufficiently dealt with by ethics as such, by the doctrine of natural law, or by the social doctrine taught by the Church and in universities as an academic discipline. To still others, it could seem obvious that what the modern era means by "political philosophy" merely results from the ignoring of certain classical truths, whether ethical, metaphysical, or anthropological, with the consequent loss of the link between politics and morality. In this case, what would be needed is not so much a political philosophy, but an ethics, a metaphysics, and an anthropology, with a corresponding renewal of natural law thinking.

In the light of such possible objections, I would like in the following pages—the first part of this essay—to respond to the question "Why is political philosophy necessary?" with the exposition of four principal points: (1) the justification of Aristotelian political philosophy as an ethics of the *polis;* (2) the specific justification of modern political philosophy with respect to the classical tradition of the ethics of the *polis;* (3) the insufficiency for political philosophy of the classical doctrine on natural law; (4) political philosophy and the social doctrine of the Church.

Based on the exposition of these four themes, necessarily only outlined and very incomplete, I will then—in the second part of this essay—attempt to draw four conclusions regarding the nature and the justification of political philosophy as fundamental political ethics: (1) political praxis possesses its own moral logic; there exists, therefore, a properly political ethics; (2) the political ethos is integrated into history and culture; (3) the modern political culture of the democratic constitutional state possesses its own founding ethos; (4) political philosophy is "fundamental political ethics."

The Necessity of Political Philosophy

The Justification of Aristotelian Political Philosophy as an Ethics of the *Polis*

The inclusion of political philosophy in ethics is part of the classical heritage. Indeed, in Plato ethics became essentially political philosophy, though remaining metaphysical research: for him, to know in what the virtue of justice consists for the individual, one must contemplate man "writ large" which is the *polis*.[1] Justice for the individual person consists precisely in being *part* of the *polis* ordered according to justice. This justice is fully realized not as virtue but as political-social order—that is, in the structured whole of the *polis*—and only subsequently in the individual, that is, in the degree to which the latter occupies a position and a specific function in the order of the *polis*. This state of affairs, however, should not be thought of as a "totalitarian" conception; it seems rather to be the unfortunate consequence of conceiving political philosophy as metaphysics.

Aristotle—though he rejected the Platonic identification of *polis* and *oikos,* asserting the pluralistic structure of the former[2]—never truly departed from the Platonic program that we may call "ethics of the *polis*," the essence of which consists in the assertion that man arrives at perfection only as a member of the *polis*, the ultimate end of which is to make men good and virtuous. Political life and political institutions—and above all laws—have the purpose of assuring that people act virtuously, so as to attain the good life, the happy life. The unity of ethics and politics is not severed in Aristotle, even if he does separate ethics from metaphysics, emphasizing the strictly practical character of the former. For Aristotle, one no longer

1. See Plato, *Republic,* Book II, 368d–369a; see also Book IV, 434d.
2. See Aristotle, *Politics,* I,1, 1252a 8ff; II, 2–3, 1261a 10–1262a 24.

makes an inquiry into the *idea* of justice, grasped in the vision of the *polis* as *makro-anthropos,* as was the case with Plato. And for Aristotle the justice of the individual person does not consist in being—or especially in knowing oneself to be—a part of that man "writ large" that is the *polis.* Rather, political philosophy is *practical* for Aristotle: the *polis* in fact is not the *cause* but the *telos* of humanity, and therefore also of the praxis of individuals, who attain the virtuous life as citizens of the *polis.*

Aristotle's *Nicomachean Ethics,* however, declares itself from the outset to be *epistēmē politikē,* "political science."[3] Moral praxis or ethos, the attaining of a good and happy life, is conceivable for Aristotle only as political existence, that is, life *in the polis* and *by means of the polis.* (Only the "philosopher," as such, transcends political life, through an activity that is precisely not practical, but theoretical.)

Thus, to speak in precise terms and contrary to what is often claimed, in essence Aristotelian political philosophy does not *presuppose* ethics, but rather *is* ethics. Or better: Aristotelian ethics is, in essence, political philosophy. Thus from its very first pages the *Nicomachean Ethics* points toward its fulfillment in the books on politics, without which ethics itself would be incapable of responding to the most important ethical question: how does one *acquire* the moral virtues? And the response is: the moral life and the acquisition of the virtues are possible only in the *polis,* that is, in the *polis* ordered according to a constitutional structure, with laws that punish those who fail to act according to virtue, thus teaching them to live virtuously by means of the coercive power of laws—"institutionalized moral wisdom"—and through the resulting fear of punishment.[4] The only practical example of this provided by Aristotle, in the unfinished eighth book on politics, is the law concerning which musical styles, songs, and rhythms should be taught to children, and which not. The Aristotelian *polis* is an eminently pedagogical enterprise, established so that people may not merely live, but "live well."[5] The *polis* is, to adapt the Platonic expression, moral virtue "written with capitals."

---

3. Aristotle, *Nicomachean Ethics* (henceforth *EN*), I, 1, 1094a 28 ff.

4. See *EN,* X, 10, 1179b 32–1180a 24. Even if we find fragments in Aristotle for a practical moral epistemology (i.e., a theory concerning how to *know* the good of virtue), a satisfactory response to the difficult problem of the Aristotelian doctrine on the acquisition of virtue through inurement cannot be found, it seems to me, based on the texts themselves, as long as one does not consider Aristotle's *Politics* as a necessary completion of the ethical discourse of *EN.* On the difficulty of interpretation in this regard see for example: Richard Sorabji, "Aristotle and the Role of Intellect in Virtue," *Proceedings of the Aristotelian Society,* new series, 74 (1973–74): 107–29; Troels Engberg-Pedersen, *Aristotle's Theory of Moral Insight* (Oxford: Oxford University Press, 1983), 160–87.

5. *Politics,* I, 1, 1252b 30. It should be noted that for Aristotle the ideal model is not the Athenian

When confronted with the Aristotelian ethics of the *polis*, therefore, we are inclined to defend personal ethics, the ethics of the individual—especially his liberty and his responsibility to realize the good in his own life, according to truth. Ultimately, in Aristotle there is too much political philosophy, given that *everything* is political philosophy.

In reality, however, unlike Plato, Aristotle makes a first distinction between the ethics of the individual and political ethics; or, put otherwise, between an ethics of the good "for me" (as an individual) and an ethics of the "common good" (i.e., of the good common to all the individuals living in a particular political society). In Aristotle, the articulation of the individual virtues is in fact a specification of "my good," of the means "to my happiness"; this is a consequence of the truly *practical* nature of his moral philosophy. Aristotle then teaches, however (a teaching that is present from the outset): on the specification of my happiness, thus on what renders the life of the individual person good and happy, depends the knowledge of what renders "happy"—that is, good, just, and well-ordered—the *polis* as a whole.[6]

Aristotle thus works from an implicit distinction between "my good" and "the common good." He claims, however, that the latter good consists precisely in establishing the conditions whereby "I" can be good, according to the previously established articulation of individual virtue. No problem exists here, therefore, for justifying political philosophy: it is the fulfillment, the "last word," of ethics itself. "Politics," as the establishment of a constitutional structure with corresponding legislation, is none other than the realization of the ethical program: the good or happy life.

The defense of an "ethics of the common good" in the face of an "individualistic" reduction of human praxis thus appears to be a specifically modern theme, or even "post-modern" in the sense of "post-liberal."[7] This

---

polis, but that of Sparta (see *EN*, X, 10, 1180a 25 ff.), which was also the ideal, among others, considered by Rousseau in his *Discours sur les sciences et les arts*, which condemns the vices of the Athenians and exalts the virtues of Sparta and "la sagesse de ses Loix" (Jean-Jacques Rousseau, *Oeuvres complètes*, ed. B. Gagnebin and M. Raymond, III [Paris: Gallimard, 1964], 12).

6. As is asserted in the celebrated beginning of the seventh book of the *Politics:* "The student who is going to make a suitable investigation of the best form of constitution, must necessarily decide first of all what is the most desirable mode of life" (according to H. Rackham's translation, in Aristotle, *Politics*, Loeb Classical Library 264, at 533).

7. This "post-liberal" concern is typical for liberal authors such as John Rawls (*A Theory of Justice* [Oxford: Oxford University Press, 1972]) or Bruce A. Ackermann (*Social Justice in the Liberal State* [New Haven, Conn.: Yale University Press, 1980]); also in the argumentation of Charles E. Larmore (*Patterns of Moral Complexity* [Cambridge: Cambridge University Press, 1987]). In truth, the defense of the "common

was not Aristotle's objective, however, and to look for it in his philosophy would be to commit an anachronism. With respect to the classical tradition, as I have said, we are rather inclined to defend another position: the *distinction* between an ethos of the individual and an ethos of the political community, which is a typically modern distinction (as we shall see). This distinction would have been unintelligible for a member of the Greek *polis:* the *polis* formed a unity of life, in the moral and religious sense, that did not allow of the intelligibility of a separation between the good of the community and the good of the individual. It is precisely this distinction, the fruit of a long historical experience, that renders intelligible the justification of modern political philosophy.

The Specific Justification of Modern Political Philosophy with Respect to the Classical Tradition

The road to the arrival at the just-mentioned distinction would nevertheless be a long and difficult one. By the Hellenistic period, the ethics of the *polis*—political philosophy—no longer made sense. The *polis* no longer existed, either as a political actor or as a unity of life; political thought, if it existed at all, centered on the figure of the *basileus,* celebrated in the panegyric literature as an "animated law" *(nomos empsychos).* Or conversely, political thought, as in the Stoics, was impregnated with a cosmic universalism, metaphysical rather than practical, in which an individualistic morality was heralded that considered one's removal from all involvement in public affairs to be the condition of happiness, in a way not much different than Epicureanism.

The epoch of the Roman republic, with Cicero, experienced a rebirth of authentic political-juridical-ethical thought, soon, however, to be exploited by the ideology of the Roman Principate, an ideology full of fictions juridical (expressed in the *lex de imperio,* an adapted version of the ancient *lex regia,* i.e., the idea of the *translatio imperii* of the people into the hands of the *princeps*) and moral (the unification, in the person of the *princeps,* of the *potestas,* i.e., the coercive power, and the *auctoritas,* the moral charism), the purpose of which was to legitimate a power that increasingly showed itself to be a despotic rule based on simple military force. In this case the ideology of

---

good" vis-à-vis the demands of the individual is properly a "liberal" theme, in the sense that it arises *with* liberalism, i.e., from the preoccupation with the liberty of the individual and the resulting problem of how to conceive of a "common good" based on this presupposition.

the civil religion compensated for a lack of philosophical-political reflection. One can thus better understand the content of St. Augustine's great work *De civitate Dei:* it was to a large extent a polemical destruction of the civil religion of the Roman Empire.

In fact, when the *Christian* religion became the civil religion, it was Augustine himself who recognized the urgent need to dissolve the extremely dangerous ideological link between the Roman Empire and the Christian religion: the fall of Rome, taught the bishop of Hippo, is not a valid argument against Christian truth. Constantine's motto, *In hoc signo vinces*—celebrated by Eusebius of Caesarea from the perspective of a Christian adaptation of imperial political theology and of the idea of *Roma aeterna*—had to be set aside. According to Augustine, the purpose of the cult of the true God was not to make Rome great, maintaining its power and splendor, but to lead men and women to the heavenly homeland. The city of God is built not in this world, but in the hearts of men; it is an eschatological reality that does not find institutional expression in the temporal order, not even in the Church considered as a visible reality.

The ancient *polis*, therefore, was dead: a political philosophy in the tradition of the ethic of the *polis* was no longer possible on the basis of a Christian dualism as formulated by St. Augustine. The *polis,* as an existential unity, was divided on the one hand into an earthly part, aimed at the "preservation of mortal life" and thus responsible for subjecting men to an order of peace and cohabitation, legitimate to the extent that it did not impede the religion that taught the worship of the true God;[8] and on the other hand a heavenly part, that is, the kingdom of God, which becomes reality in the hearts of men. Saint Irenaeus, even before St. Augustine, clearly expressed this "residual" political thought, affirming that human beings before all else are sinful and vicious; the state, through the law, has the function of assuring by fear of punishment that the big fish don't eat the little ones.[9] The earthly city thus guarantees an orderly and peaceful survival, but it is not the guarantor of truth and virtue.

After this period, a change occurred. In so-called political Augustinianism,[10] an unfaithful reinterpretation of St. Augustine's thought, an idea

---

8. St. Augustine, *De civitate Dei,* XIX, 17.

9. See Irenaeus of Lyons, *Adversus hareses,* V, 24.

10. The term was created by Henri-Xavier Arquillière; see Arquillière, *L'Augustinisme politique. Essai sur la formation des théories politiques du Moyen Age,* 2nd ed. (Paris: J. Vrin, 1955). For a synthetic exposition see Jean-Jacques Chevalier, *Storia del pensiero politico,* vol. 1, 2nd ed. (Bologna: Il Mulino,

appeared that would endure for centuries and shape the medieval world: "power over all people has been conceded from on high to the one who governs, *such that the earthly kingdom would be a service which subordinates itself to the heavenly kingdom,*"[11] the latter represented in this world by the visible Church. The earlier Gelasian doctrine on the dualism between the temporal *potestas* of princes and the spiritual *auctoritas* of the priesthood (which implied not a dualism between two "powers," but that between the coercive power of the state and the moral authority of the Church), became a restoration of the ethic of the *polis*, based this time, however, on Christian theological premises: the Christian *polis*, the *respublica christiana* in which everything is a means to salvation.

In an initial period, this meant the consecration of the temporal power of the French emperors (thus forming a quasi-natural alliance that served to safeguard the political independence of the Apostolic See), with a consequent integration of ecclesial structures into temporal structures. This was an expression not of the superiority of the temporal power over the spiritual, but of the sacred character of every temporal power as an instrument for man's supernatural end. The spiritual authority of the Church was, under various aspects, integrated into the structure of the temporal power, conferring on the latter its highest significance as a *sacred* power, a quasi-sacramental participation in the kingship of Christ.[12] This in fact was *not* caesaropapism; rather, beginning with Charlemagne, emperors fulfilled an ecclesial-sacral function at the service of the Church's spiritual and supernatural end.

After the fight over investitures—which should be thought of not as a rupture of continuity with the establishment of the *respublica christiana*, but as a logical consequence of what had preceded it—the juridical terms were turned upside down.[13] To free the Church from its entanglement with temporal structures—which had become dangerous for the spiritual mission of the Church because of a growing "political" consciousness on the part of the Salian em-

---

1989), 256–80; and Georges de Lagarde, *La naissance de l'esprit laïque au déclin du moyen age*, 5 vols. (Louvain: Nauwelaerts, 1956–70), esp. vol. 1: *Bilan du XIIIème siècle*, 3rd ed. (1956); vol. 2: *Secteur social de la scolastique*, 2nd ed. (1958). For an orientation, including bibliographical, see Víctor de Reina, "Los términos de la polémica Sacerdocio-Reino," *Ius Canonicum* 6 (1966): 153–99.

11. Gregory the Great, *Epist. III*, 65.

12. See the classic study of Ernst Kantorowicz, *The King's Two Bodies: A Study in Medieval Political Theology*, 3rd ed. (Princeton, N.J.: Princeton University Press, 1973).

13. A true and proper "papal revolution" has even been spoken of, the origin of the modern western juridical tradition. See Harold Berman, *Recht und Revolution. Die Bildung der westlichen Rechtstradition* (Frankfurt am Main: Suhrkamp Verlag, 1991), 144ff.

perors—not only full *auctoritas* in the spiritual sense was attributed to the pope, but, reinterpreting the Roman *lex regia*,[14] also the *plenitudo potestatis*, a power from which every other power, including temporal, derived. This was in fact the first formulation of a true sovereignty, carefully elaborated in the thirteenth century by the canonists and theologians of the Roman Curia, in some cases making use precisely of the Aristotelian concept of the *polis*.[15] (This same concept of sovereignty was later used by secular jurists in the service of territorial princes to establish the sovereignty of the latter).[16]

In this period the order of the *polis* was understood as a religious-political unity in which ecclesial spiritual supremacy and feudal temporal order were intertwined.[17] It was the age not of political philosophy, but of theology and canon law.[18]

14. For a brief synthesis on the presence of the *lex regia* in medieval thought see Hanns Kurz, *Volkssouveränität und Volksrepräsentation* (Cologne: Carl Heymanns, 1965), 38–42.

15. Martin Grabmann, "Studien über den Einfluss der aristotelischen Philosophie auf die mittelalterlichen Theorien über das Verhältnis von Kirche und Staat," in *Sitzungaberichte der Bayerischen Akademie der Wissenschaften*, Phil-hist. Abt. vol. 2. (Munich: Verlag der Bayerischen Akademie der Wissenschaften, 1934), 41–60.

16. This theme has been amply studied; see among others: Sergio Mochi Onory, *Fonti cononistiche dell'idea moderna dello stato* (Milan: Vita e pensiero, 1951); Helmut Quaritsch, *Souveränität: Entstehung und Entwicklung des Begriff in Frankreich und Deutschland vom 13. Jh. bis 1806* (Berlin: Athenäum, 1986); Dieter Wyduckel, *Princeps Legibus Solutus. Eine Untersuchung zur frühmodernen Rechts- und Staatslehre* (Berlin: Duncker & Humblot, 1979); Helmut G. Walther, *Imperiales Königtum, Konziliarismus und Volkssouveränität: Studien zu den Grenzen des mittelalterlichen Souveränitätsgedankens* (Munich: Fink, 1976); Paolo Prodi, *Il Sovrano Pontefice. Un corpo e due anime: la monarchia papale nella prima età moderna* (Bologna: Il Mulino, 1982). This last study focuses on papal sovereignty within the Papal States in the early modern period, i.e., from the fifteenth century until the middle of the seventeenth, an example of modern statehood based on principles that came from medieval canon law.

17. In a famous text of Innocent III, the decretal *Novit ille* of 1204, the pope established that ecclesial judges can proceed judicially against laymen, kings included (in this case the king of France), *ratione periurii vel pacis fractae*. Despite a clear distinction between, on the one hand, what pertains to the temporal dimension of the feud, and on the other what refers to its spiritual dimension ("non enim intendimus iudicare de feudo ... sed decernere de peccato"), the peculiar character of the feudal order meant that litigation and controversies always also included the dimension of "sin" (especially against the peace). The decretal referred to Theodosius and Charlemagne ("Quicumque videlicet litem habens ... ad episcoporum iudicium cum sermone litigantium dirigatur"), with the reminder that ecclesiastical power comes from God ("non humanae constitutioni, sed divinae legi potius innitamur, quia potestas nostra non est ex homine, sed ex Deo"). The formula of an ecclesiastical competence *ratione peccati* can thus be extended to everything ("nullus, qui sit sanae mentis, ignorat, quin ad officium nostrum spectet de quocunque mortali peccato corripere quemlibet Christianum, et, si correctionem contempserit, ipsum per districtionem ecclesiasticam *coercere*"). Kings are not an exception. ("Licet autem hoc modo procedere valeamus *super quolibet criminali peccato*, ut peccatorem revocemus a vitio ad virtutem, ab errore ad veritatem, *praecipue tamen quum contra pacem peccatur*, quae est vinculum caritatis.") Text cited from Emil Friedberg, *Corpus Iuris Canonici*, vol. 2, reprinted by the Editio Lipsiensis secunda (Graz: Akademische Druck- u. Verlagsanstalt, 1955), cols. 242–44. The different curial theories in this field and their development are treated by Charles Journet, *La Juridiction de l'Église sur la cité* (Paris: Desclée, 1931). For the entire period see Walter Ullmann, *Principles of Government and Politics in the Middle Ages* (London: Methuen, 2nd ed., 1966; 3rd ed., 1973), and by the same author, *Medieval Papalism: The Political Theories of the Medieval Canonists* (London: Methuen, 1949).

18. For a study of this complex theme (and some sources), still useful is Robert Warrant Carlyle

The birth of the modern territorial state, however, could not coexist with such a limitation of its sovereignty.[19] The celebrated formula *rex imperator in regno suo, et superiorem in temporalibus non recognoscit* ("the king is emperor in his own kingdom and does not recognize a superior in temporal affairs," a phrase initially elaborated by canonists to protect feudal princes against the sovereignty claims of the emperor, and recognized for this purpose by Innocent III in his decretal *Per venerabilem*),[20] later became the formula for territorial sovereignty directed precisely against the *plenitudo potestatis* of the Roman pontiff that, through the formula *ratione peccati*, limited the independence of rulers *in temporalibus*. The well-known conception of Marsilius of Padua was in essence already modern: to assure peace and security within states, the theory and practice of the *plenitudo potestatis* of the Roman pontiffs must be opposed, and priests must limit themselves to preaching the gospel and administering the sacraments; all other power must be reserved to temporal rulers.[21]

The decisive event, however, was the rupture of the unity of the faith:

---

and Alexander James Carlyle, *A History of Mediaeval Political Theory in the West*, 6 vols. (Edinburgh/London: William Blackwood, 1903–36; last printing in 1970); especially vol. 2; a very useful tool (also for its rich bibliography) is James Henderson Burns, ed., *The Cambridge History of Medieval Political Thought c. 350–c. 1450* (Cambridge: Cambridge University Press, 1988). For a fair evaluation of the "medieval system," one must bear in mind the anarchic character of a feudal society, in which the Church's influence played a certain pacifying and "moralizing" role. The civilizing influence of the Church became superfluous and even disturbing, however, when the territorial princes themselves began to pacify feudal society. The best and, with respect to European history, most decisive example is that of England beginning with Henry II. Moreover, regarding the conception of the supremacy of the spiritual power over the temporal, in general the curial theories (in the sense of the hierocratic idea of *potestas directa*) went beyond the power that the popes actually attributed to themselves (in the sense of *potestas indirecta*). Even this latter power, however—because it claimed not only the superiority of the spiritual power over the temporal but, on the basis of the doctrine of the two swords, also the source of the temporal power in the *plenitudo potestatis* of the Roman pontiff—was nonetheless a formula of political sovereignty (which was shown to be so by the possibility of deposing rulers and of dissolving the bond of fidelity of their subjects). The spiritual power, even if always motivated by pastoral-spiritual reasons, could not thereafter avoid a certain "politicization": when the spiritual authority claims superiority over the political-temporal power, even if only for spiritual reasons, it necessarily becomes a political power.

19. Still indispensable for a study of the sources is Jean Rivière, *Le problème de l'Eglise et de l'Etat au temps de Philippe le Bel* (Louvain: Spicilegium Sacrum Lovaniense, 1926).

20. See Mochi Onory, *Fonti canonistiche*, 271ff. The sentence is not found in its entirety, however, in the mentioned decretal; see the complete text in Friedberg, *Corpus Iuris Canonici*, cols. 714–716.

21. See Marsilius of Padua, *Defensor pacis*, I, 19. Marsilius also rejected all jurisdictional power of the pope in the ecclesial domain itself, conferring even judgment concerning heresies on the temporal power. It is important to understand that the intention of such a request of the submission of the spiritual power to the temporal was in no way a "sacralization" of the temporal power; rather, it was a formula for peace, already typically "modern," i.e., a request that followed a strictly *political* logic, and not theological, not even in the sense of a "political theology." The problem with Marsilius, who as a good Aristotelian maintains the essential unity of the *polis* and thereby inverts the relationships of sovereignty, shows itself when he declares the (earthly) *civitas* to be the only *communitas perfecta* (*Defensor pacis*, I, 3), thus enclosing man in the monism of the temporal state.

with Christianity divided, every attempt to reconstruct the Christian *polis* was rendered futile. Temporal power once more needed to be legitimized on the basis not of faith, but of reason. Reenter political philosophy.[22]

This presentation is obviously simplified. I have not spoken, for example, of medieval Aristotelianism, which was present, though primarily in the universities.[23] Nor have I mentioned some extremely important institutional developments, for example, those of the medieval constitutional heritage (such as the charter of freedoms in England or in Aragon, or the development of urban culture).[24] Quite a different problem, however, disturbed the people of the sixteenth and seventeenth centuries: how to assure peaceful coexistence in a world where religious differences and contrasting convictions concerning the "good life," happiness, and justice produced conflicts and bloody wars, or at least provided "ideological" justification for the political projects of the nascent territorial powers?

The responses to such questions provided by Jean Bodin and Thomas Hobbes have a point in common: to guarantee peace, what is highest in the realm of values must be renounced in order to guarantee what is fundamental—survival, peace, and cohabitation.[25] The first theoreticians of sovereignty and of the absolute state were in fact philosophers of peace: the sovereign state is necessary in order to assure institutions of power and of law that guarantee the possibility of peaceful coexistence in a society otherwise divided by conflict. It is necessary—as the jurist Bodin wrote in an explicit polemic against Aristotle[26]—to distinguish a public-political realm from the private-personal realm, and this according to rules of law.

Individuals pursue happiness, for which there are many differing conceptions, and these differences are the cause of discord and conflicts. The state should limit itself to what regards the public interest: peace and survival. *Primum vivere, deinde philosofari* ("First one must live, only then one can start philosophizing"). As Michel de l'Hôpital, chancellor to the king

---

22. See Pierre Mesnard, *L'essor de la philosophie politique au XVIe siècle* (Paris: J. Vrin, 1951).

23. For an evaluation of the significant influence of an Aristotelian-style constitutionalism in the formation of modern political thought, see the observations in Peter Graf Kielmansegg, *Volkssouveränität: Eine Untersuchung der Bedingungen demokratischer Legitimität* (Stuttgart: Klett, 1977), 36ff. (and the bibliography cited there). See also De Lagarde, *La naissance de l'esprit*.

24. Influences sufficiently highlighted in the work of Carl Joachim Friedrich, *Constitutional Government and Democracy*, 3rd ed. (Boston: Ginn, 1951).

25. This has been optimally shown by Martin Kriele, *Einführung in die Staatslehre: Die geschichtlichen Legitimitätsgrundlagen des demokratischen Verfassungsstaates*, 4th ed. (Opladen: Westdeutscher Verlag, 1990), 48–52.

26. Jean Bodin, *Les Six Livres de la République* (Paris: Chez Iaques Du Puys, 1576), I, 1.

until 1568, asserted, and as was later reiterated by the group of jurists called the *politiques* (the fathers of the edict of tolerance of Nantes): what matters is not which is the true religion, but how is coexistence possible;[27] it does not matter for *politics,* that is, what the true religion is, even though it *is* important for the individual and for his happiness. This latter, however, is not the task of the state.

The bitter experience of the absolute state, with its claims of an undivided and, as it was experienced, unrestrained and arbitrary sovereignty, produced a consciousness of the requirements of liberty: true peace is not possible without liberty, the condition of true justice. The state does not "own" society or the individual; moreover, the latter possesses inalienable rights. The governing power is at the service of society, which latter must make possible the free development of the person. Government, as John Locke wrote, is nothing other than a "trust." The centuries-old Anglo-Saxon tradition of the Rule of Law—of government by law, based on common law (which includes an authentic constitutional law),[28] on the independence of judges, and on the division of power between parliament, king, and judges—all this inspired Montesquieu to preach to his fellow Frenchmen about that "wonderful English system discovered in the woods," which guaranteed liberty.[29]

The English juridical-political spirit—transformed into political philosophy by Locke[30] (and later into constitutional theory by Blackstone),[31] sys-

27. See Roman Schnur, *Die französischen Juristen im konfessionellen Bürgerkrieg des 16. Jahrhunderts. Ein Beitrag zur Entstehungsgeschichte des modernen Staates,* (Berlin: Duncker & Humblot, 1962), 19. Also see the important study of Joseph Lecler, *Histoire de la Tolérance au Siècle de la Réforme,* 2 vol. (Paris, 1955); reprinted as one volume under the same title (Paris: Albin Michel, 1994).

28. See the important reply to Thomas Hobbes, written by Chief Justice Sir Matthew Hale (d. 1676), *Reflections by the Lord Chief Justice Hale on Mr. Hobbes His Dialogue of the Lawe,* manuscript reprinted in William Searle Holdsworth, *History of English Law,* 13 vols., 7th ed. (London: Methuen, 1956–64), vol. 5, appendix 3, 500–513). For an evaluation: D. E. C. Yale, "Hobbes and Hale on Law, Legislation and the Sovereign," *Cambridge Law Journal* 31, no. 1 (1972): 121–56.

29. Montesquieu, *De l'esprit des lois,* ed. R. Derathé (Paris: Garnier, 1973), tome 1, livre 11, chap. 6 ("*De la constitution de l'Angleterre*"), 179.

30. Whose thought is nevertheless not properly "constitutional": the "community," which is sovereign, does not institute a constitution, but a parliamentary government (see the famous chapter 13 of the *Second Treatise of Government,* "Of the Subordination of the Powers of the Commonwealth," §149 ff.). In fact, as observes Kriele, *Einführung in die Staatslehre,* 202, in England Locke's thought promoted not so much the fundamental liberties of the individual as parliamentary sovereignty (given that in England there had never existed a written constitution). The Americans, on the other hand, read Locke from a constitutionalist perspective.

31. Sir William Blackstone, *Commentaries on the Laws of England* (4 vols., 1765, 1766, 1768, and 1769), ed. William G. Hammond (San Francisco: Bancroft-Whitney, 1890). See Herbert J. Storing, "William Blackstone," in *History of Political Philosophy,* ed. Leo Strauss and Joseph Cropsey, 3rd ed. (Chicago: University of Chicago Press, 1987), 622–34.

tematized by Montesquieu, and finally enriched by the notable communitarian sense of Presbyterian Calvinism—led the American colonies to proclaim the rights of man as *positive* rights, that is, claimable in a court of law, and to constitute themselves as a constitutional federal state.

The basic idea, already present in the Virginia Bill of Rights (1776), was to submit power and those who exercise it to law and to institutional control, thus protecting the liberty of the individual. This idea made a powerful impression across the Atlantic, and was imitated in the Declaration of the Rights of Man of the French Revolution in 1789 and in the first constitution of the Revolution in 1791.[32]

Modern constitutionalism was not the product of philosophers, but of a long development of legal institutions, promoted by political men possessed of an acute juridical spirit.[33] The ideas of Rousseau, the dreamer, were *not* followed: his notion of the "sovereignty of the people"—a true "popular absolutism"—was irreconcilable with the idea of the "rights of man," that is, with the submission of the sovereignty and of every power to

---

32. This view, called "Atlantic," is fully developed in Robert R. Palmer, *The Age of Democratic Revolution*, col. 1: *The Challenge* (Princeton, N.J.: Princeton University Press, 1959). The first to show the dependence of the French Declaration on the Rights of Man of 1789 on the "Virginia Bill of Rights" was Georg Jellinek in 1895: Jellinek, *Die Erklärung der Menschen- und Bürgerrechte*, 3rd ed. (Munich, 1919); reprint of the 4th ed. (identical to the 3rd) in *Zur Geschichte der Erklärung der Menschenrechte*, ed. R. Schnur (Darmstadt: Wissenschaftliche Buchgesellschaft, 1964), 1–77. Jellinek's work provoked a testy response from a French scholar: Emile Boutmy, "La déclaration des droits de l'homme et M. Jellinek," *Annales des sciences politiques* 17 (1902): 415–43 (reprinted in Boutmy, *Etudes Politiques* [Paris: Armand Colin, 1907], 119ff.; German translation in the cited work of Schnur, 78–112, with a reply by Jellinek). Boutmy wanted to show the originality of the French declaration, which he claimed had its roots in Rousseau's philosophy. His effort can be considered to have failed, both for reasons of its content and as shown by later research (esp. that of Otto Vossler, *Studien zur Erklärung der Menschrechte*, in Schnur, 166–201). It is thought that the plan for the French declaration was elaborated by Lafayette when Thomas Jefferson was ambassador of the United State at Paris; Lafayette and his friend Jefferson together revised the text. Some interesting observations are also found in Norberto Bobbio, "La Rivoluzione francese e i diritti dell'uomo," in Bobbio, *L'età dei diritti* (Turin: Einaudi, 1990), 89–120.

33. In fact the history of English constitutionalism begins in 1215 with the *Magna Charta Libertatis*, which, through parliamentarianism and common law and despite its initial feudal character, gradually generated the principal rights of liberty, above all the fundamental one of *habeas corpus* (which, historically, is the "original fundamental right," and not religious liberty, as Jellinek thought; see Kriele, *Einführung in die Staatslehre*, 149–59). One thing is the *institutional reality* of the rights of liberty (a legacy of English history, going back to the Middle Ages), and another the *philosophical idea* of the rights of man, which is a fruit of modern natural law doctrine. Both traditions came together in the American and French revolutions (though it is true that the latter tended more toward the declamation of philosophical ideas than toward the establishment of *positive* (enacted and written) constitutional law. In any case, it seems a grave error to limit the history of political thought to the literary history of philosophical texts; equally important is the history of the development of legal institutions and of the thought of those who were the protagonists of that history; in England, for example, Chief Justice Edward Coke, creator of the *Petition of Rights* of 1627. On Coke see Jean Beauté, *Un grand juriste Anglais: Sir Edward Coke 1552–1634. Ses idées politiques et constitutionelles, ou aux origines de la démocratie occidentale moderne* (Paris: Presses Universitaires de France, 1975).

law.[34] The constitutional state wanted to teach humanity: enough with sovereigns! Every sovereignty, including that of the people or of the "nation," must be subject to law and to the true and inalienable rights of man, and no government that fails to respect these is legitimate; indeed, the people have the right to overthrow such a regime. Constitutionalism and the right of resistance go hand in hand, and are part of a *medieval* heritage.[35]

Constitutionalism thus means the recovery of a long pre-absolutist tradition, but also the *institutionalization* of that tradition: the rights of man—natural rights—must be converted into *positive* law, claimable before independent judges.[36] Moreover, liberty left to itself does not tend to be liberty *for all*. The English parliament was, after all, an aristocratic oligarchy until the middle of the nineteenth century. And French liberals at the time of the restoration (Constant, Thiers, etc.) were convinced that democracy, meaning universal suffrage, was useless: people without property or culture could not have political power.

The nineteenth-century bourgeoisie understood itself to be the "universal class," the bearer of all progress and of a development that, in the long run, would blossom into a universally bourgeois society (which happened at a later point, but not without the active integration of the "worker class" into the political system). Economic liberalism was convinced that all problems of justice and of the distribution of riches would be resolved simply by

34. It now appears that the actual influence of Rousseau's thought on the French Revolution was very slight; see Iring Fetscher, *Rousseaus politische Philosophie: Zur Geschichte des demokratischen Freiheitsbegriffs*, 3rd ed. (Frankfurt am Main: Suhrkamp, 1975), 258–304. The extent to which the constitutional ideas of the French national assembly in fact contrasted with those of Rousseau has been shown by Karl Loewenstein, *Volk und Parlament nach der Staatstheorie der französischen Nationalversammlung von 1789* (Munich: Drei Masken Verlag, 1922; reprint, Aalen: Scientia, 1964 and 1990). The nucleus of the idea of the "sovereignty of the people," present in the thought of the first Revolution and clearly incompatible with Rousseau's thought, was the distinction of the Abbé Sieyès between *pouvoir constituant* and *pouvoir constitué*, which implies precisely the submission of the "sovereignty of the nation" to (constitutional) *law*. See *Préliminaire de la constitution, reconnaissance et exposition raisonnée des Droits de l'Homme & du citoyen. Lu les 20 & 21 Juillet 1789, au Comité de la Constitution,* German translation in Emmanuel Joseph Sieyes, *Politische Schriften 1788–1790,* trans. and edited by Eberhard Schmitt and Rolf Reichardt (Neuwied: Luchterhand, 1975), 241–57.

35. See Fritz Kern, *Gottesgnadentum und Widerstandsrecht im früheren Mittelalter. Zur Entwicklungsgeschichte der Monarchie*, 7th ed., reprint of the 2nd edition of 1954, ed. Rudolf Buchner (Darmstadt: Wissenschaftliche Buchgesellschaft, 1980); Ernst Reibstein, *Volkssouveränität und Freiheitsrechte. Texte und Studien zur politischen Theorie des 14. bis 18. Jahrhunderts,* 2 vols. (Freiburg-Munich: Alber, 1972).

36. As has been well emphasized by Kriele, the essence of the Anglo-Saxon idea of the Rule of Law is the independence of judges (an essentially constitutional idea that follows from the division of powers), as opposed to the nineteenth-century German idea deriving from Kant of the "state of law" *(Rechtsstaat),* which does not necessarily imply the independence of a jurisdictional power. We are not accustomed today to clearly differentiating these two concepts, which nevertheless are very different in both historical origin and political meaning.

the free interplay of market forces.[37] The Americans, however, demonstrated that this was not the case. Also, the French liberal Alexis de Tocqueville, diffident with respect to the democratic egalitarianism of the Americans, preached across the continent: granted, democratic equality is a danger to freedom and leads to the tyranny of the majority, but the Americans have attenuated this danger by submitting the influence of the majority to law.[38] This typical nineteenth-century liberal mistrust of democracy, with its implicit equality of rights and the consequent principle of majority and all the problems and dangers these entail, is nonetheless not sufficient to negate the experience that liberty for all, and consequently the possibility of justice, exists only where there is the participation and representation of all, that is, in representative, parliamentary democracy.

The democratic constitutional state is in fact justified by its purpose of *equality of liberty,* given that the constitutional state by itself—meaning liberty alone—does not guarantee liberty *for all* and hence, in a modern industrial society with its inherent tendency to create new socioeconomic dependencies, neither is justice guaranteed.[39] In this, however, the function of the democratic principle appears more clearly: its purpose is not to realize a presumed or homogenous "general will," or "the identity between rulers and governed," and in this sense the "government of the people" (which as a homogenous entity does not exist). Rather it is a *means,* unfortunately fragile and open to abuse, of guaranteeing a just and equal administration, in liberty, of that social power—political, economic, and cultural—which, in its plurality, is always the result of every true liberty.[40]

Thus we arrive at the "modern *polis,*" which is no longer the ancient *po-*

37. For the history of liberal thought in the nineteenth century, still indispensable is Guido de Ruggiero, *Storia del liberalismo europeo,* 3rd ed. (Bari: Laterza, 1984; 1st ed. 1925).

38. Alexis de Tocqueville, *De la Démocratie en Amérique* (first part of 1835), 2:8 ("De ce qui tempère aux États-Unis la tyrannie de la majorité: De l'esprit légiste aux États-Unis, et comment il sert de contrepoids a la Démocratie").

39. It was precisely in England where the slow but continual democratization of the parliamentary system was the fruit of the success of the capitalist economy and of the accompanying industrial revolution. It was not by chance that the deathblow for England's aristocratic parliamentary oligarchy was the abolition of the duty on grain in 1846—which meant the end of agrarian protectionism—a victory won by Richard Cobden, head of the liberal economic school of Manchester, and a reform that opened the way for the definitive triumph of the industrial revolution.

40. The destructive influence of a criticism of parliamentary democracy based on an "identificatory," and in this sense Rousseauian, conception, I have studied in my book *Politisierung und Legitimitätsentzug. Totalitäre Kritik der parlamentarischen Demokratie in Deutschland,* Reihe Praktische Philosophie 8 (Freiburg: Karl Alber Verlag, 1979). See also Hartmut Wasser, *Parlamentarismuskritik vom Kaiserreich zur Bundesrepublik: Analyse und Dokumentation* (Stuttgart-Bad Cannstatt: Fromman-Holzboog, 1974), "Problemata" 39.

lis, nor the medieval *respublica christiana,* which in any case failed, for reasons political rather than spiritual. The modern *polis* reduces the realm of political praxis to the public sphere. It guarantees the rights, both of liberty and of participation, of the individual; it does not attempt to educate men in virtue, but makes peaceful coexistence possible in mutual respect for liberty and justice, a justice that finds its limit, however, in the requirements of liberty and in a consensus attained by majority. It resolves conflicts according to the procedural logic of law; holds a monopoly of legitimate force; and distinguishes the common good of society in an integral sense from a strictly *political* common good, defined not in moral terms, but juridical: *peace, liberty, and justice,* to be realized according to the logic of an institutionalized praxis under the stipulations of constitutional law, which is the limitation and control of power.

It is thus a *polis* whose political institutions respect the pluralism in society that results from liberty, and at the same time creates the possibility of cooperation among people who are potentially in mutual conflict. The modern *polis,* however, is not simply "democracy"; it is *"constitutional democracy,"* or the "democratic constitutional state": the power of the majority is subject to and limited by law, and the so-called neutrality of the state is based on a strict non-neutrality with respect to those fundamental values that form the constitutional order, first among these the "rights of man."[41]

Obviously, at the basis of such a political culture there is a corresponding *proper* political philosophy that has the twofold task of justifying that political culture and of formulating the concrete political-moral requirements of a corresponding political praxis. We may now ask ourselves: isn't a doctrine concerning natural law in the classical sense sufficient for such a purpose, even today? Or, why is *political philosophy* necessary?

---

41. Possibly the fundamental error of the otherwise very interesting book of Charles E. Larmore (*Patterns of Moral Complexity*) is to have reduced the "neutralizing" logic of liberal (in the broad sense) political culture to the logic of Bodin, i.e., to the mere attempt to find a *modus vivendi* between people with contrasting conceptions of the good life. Larmore ignores the constitutional character of modern political culture, which is to say its foundation on the content of the rights of man. A similar error, this time on the basis of a Hobbesian-style reduction (and Schmittian), is present, in my opinion, in the well-known article of Ernst-Wolfgang Böckenförde, "Die Entstehung des Staates als Vorgang der Säkularisation," in Böckenförde, *Staat, Gesellschaft, Freiheit. Studien zur Staatstheorie und zum Verfassungsrecht* (Frankfurt: Suhrkamp, 1976), 42–64. See also, in the same volume, the article "Entstehung und Wandel des Rechtsstaatsbegriffs," 65–92. For a critical position toward Böckenförde, see Rupert Hoffmann, "Die Zumutungen des Grundgesetzes. Zur verfassungsstaatlichen Entwicklung der Bundesrepublik Deutschland am Ende der siebziger Jahre," *Zeitschrift für Politik* 27 (1980): 129–54.

The Insufficiency for Political Philosophy of
the Classical Doctrine on Natural Law

First, an initial observation: a political philosophy that is based on the recognition of a "natural law," that is, of a law that exists independently of a positive juridical structure and an institutionalized political order, is essentially different from a political philosophy that does not recognize a "natural law." Moreover, the idea of natural law concretely implies: (1) a common good of society exists that must be respected by every governmental-political power; (2) the *legitimacy* of the political power depends on such respect; (3) the political power is therefore subject to the idea of law.

Indeed, to cite the limit case, the political philosophy of Thomas Hobbes respects these requirements of the idea of natural law.[42] In this Hobbesian sense, however, "natural law" is a largely formal principle (though also capable, as with Hobbes, of founding a juridical positivism), though not without a specific material content: the implicit distinction between legitimate and illegitimate power, the supremacy of law over power, and the supremacy of non-positive law over positive, the political essence of which is the right of resistance.[43]

Such formal content is not enough for political philosophy, however. Political philosophy is a *practical* philosophy, that is, a reflection *on* praxis for the purpose of *orienting* praxis. Any praxis, political included, is essentially about *concrete means*. This is true—it should be emphasized—for every practical science. Not even Aristotelian ethics is simply a doctrine about the *ends* of action (happiness, the virtuous life); indeed, he says relatively little about these. It is above all a doctrine on the means by which such ends are attainable.

Consequently, the traditional distinction in the field of political action between "moral principles" and "technical aspects" is very problematical. "Technical aspects" are precisely those aspects that properly regard action; for action, moral principles alone are insufficient. To render moral prin-

---

42. As has been shown by Norberto Bobbio; see Bobbio, "Hobbes e il giusnaturalismo," *Rivista Critica di Storia della Filosofia* 17 (1962): 470–85.

43. This also is still true for Hobbes, as opposed to contemporary positivism (for example, that of Kelsen): Hobbes's originality is in his *identification* of the entire positive law with the natural law (self-preservation), thus leaving room for only one case of conflict between natural and positive law: the threat of death at the hands of the sovereign. Later contractualism remained faithful in substance to the *logic* of this understanding, while changing and expanding the *contents* of the "natural laws," which in turn implied a change in the legitimate contents of positive law.

ciples *operative*, "technical" means must be identified (these means thus showing themselves to be *the realm of morality made concrete and operative*), which in politics are things such as positive legislation, the creation of legal institutions, the constitutional framework, and the like.

It is therefore not enough to set up principles or ends as criteria of legitimacy for means, that is, assuring the noncontradictory character of the latter with respect to the former. Political philosophy wants to say something about how *to act* in a *really existing* world, a historically contingent world with all its peculiar characteristics. As a practical science, political philosophy does not focus on principles, but on the application of principles, on their *realization* in the realm of the means that form the proper object of praxis. And *political* praxis is precisely the establishment of institutions, constitutions (thus one reads Aristotle!), positive legislation, and so on. This is the great Aristotelian lesson, which has never been forgotten in the West.[44]

Nevertheless, departing from a single set of principles of "natural law," it is possible to arrive at political solutions that are quite diverse. This diversity is generated not by a difference in conceptions of the natural law, but by the differing political philosophies on the basis of which these principles are applied, and this precisely because a political philosophy always includes a theory about means. The best example would perhaps be religious liberty. It is a natural right of man to freely embrace religious truth as

---

44. At this level one encounters another problem that is intimately linked to Hobbes, the problem of the *authoritative interpretation* of the natural law, actually of every norm of "justice": the truth of a norm is one thing, its effective implementation in a political community is another: *non veritas, sed autoritas facit legem* (*Leviathan*, ch. 26 of the Latin edition; the English version gives a clearer idea of the sense: "For though it be naturally reasonable; yet it is by the Soveraigne Power that it is Law"). Which is to say: it is not philosophers or theologians, or even judges, who *effect* laws, but the sovereign authority (this was essentially an attack on the English system of common law, and more concretely on Edward Coke, who was named explicitly). Without legislative authority, Hobbes argued, there would only be endless disputes over what is law. The weakest interpretation of this principle, and in this sense hermeneutically more reasonable, is that Hobbes here confirms the modern principle of *legal security*, which leads to the principle of *nullum crimen et nulla poena sine lege*. I want to avoid, however, entering here into the thorny and complex problem of this Hobbesian principle. Some interesting critical comments can be found in Walter Euchner, "Auctoritas non veritas facit legem. Zur Abgrenzung von Politik und Nicht-Politik bei Thomas Hobbes," in *Furcht und Freiheit. Leviathan-Diskussion 300 Jahre nach Thomas Hobbes*, ed. U. Bermbach and K.-M. Kodalle (Opladen: Westdeutscher Verlag, 1982), 176–93: see also chapter 4 of the present volume, which is entitled *"Auctoritas non veritas facit legem*: Thomas Hobbes, Carl Schmitt, and the Idea of the Constitutional State." This was originally published as "*Autoritas non veritas facit legem*: Thomas Hobbes, Carl Schmitt und die Idee des Verfassungsstaates," *Archiv für Rechts- und Sozialphilosophie*, 86 (2000): 484–98; and also my book *La filosofia politica di Thomas Hobbes: coerenza e contraddizioni di un paradigma* (Rome: Armando, 1997), 214ff. For a defense of Hobbes see the important book of Simone Goyard-Fabre, *Le Droit et la Loi dans la Philosophie de Thomas Hobbes* (Paris: C. Klincksieck, 1975).

he sees it. From this, however, two opposite *political* consequences could result. The first of these is based on the political philosophy we have called the "ethics of the *polis*," which aims above all to establish and protect *truth*, though nevertheless tolerating persons who are in error. Such a conception presupposes a sovereign who is not submitted to any positive law and may, with discretional power, concede or not concede tolerance. The second conception entails the political philosophy of the constitutional state, which attempts to protect, not truth, but *persons* and their liberty; this liberty is limited, however, according to a strictly *political-juridical* rationale, that is, the public order and the equal liberty of citizens.[45]

Classical doctrine on "tolerance" and modern doctrine on "religious liberty" are not necessarily different at the level of natural law, but they *are* different at the level of the political philosophies presupposed by each, which leads them to draw different *political* consequences from the natural law. *Politically*, that is, "religious tolerance" is a simple discretional concession and implies a sovereignty not submitted to (positive) law; "religious liberty," on the other hand, implies a limitation of sovereignty and its submission to (positive) law, with a consequent protection of persons. The difference is therefore located at the level of political philosophy, and more specifically in their respective doctrines concerning the function of the state.[46]

45. This is precisely the position of the Second Vatican Council's decree *Dignitatis humanae*, as has been excellently shown by Amadeo de Fuenmayor, *La libertad religiosa* (Pamplona: EUNSA, 1974). The Church's position was further laid out by John Paul II in the *Message for the Celebration of the World Day of Peace 1991* of December 8, 1990, in which respect for religious liberty is even called the condition of peace, adding that "without a concomitant juridical guarantee through appropriate means, such Declarations are too often destined to remain dead letters" (VI). This strikingly juridical perspective on the problem coincides in substance with that of a "classical" liberal: Francesco Ruffini, *La libertà religiosa. Storia dell'idea* (1901), new ed., ed. Carlo Jemolo (Milan: Feltrinelli, 1991). It is significant, however, that even Ruffini thought (33) that the "intransigent" position of the Catholic Church was based on the "principle of revelation and the dogma of exclusive salvation." The conciliar confirmation of the existence of a right to religious liberty is in fact not based on the negation of these principles, but on the new political-juridical framing of the problem, which implies the abandonment of the traditional idea ("expressivist," according to Larmore, a locution also found in traditional liberalism) that the juridical-political order should, in the sense of the ancient ethic of the *polis*, express a specific truth concerning the "good life"—in this instance religious truth. Norberto Bobbio still succumbs to the old myth that the right to religious liberty presupposes the nonexistence and even the impossibility of a truth regarding religion; see Bobbio, "Sul fondamento dei diritti dell'uomo," in Bobbio, *L'età dei diritti*, 10. In reality, however, and in its political-juridical essence, the right to religious liberty means only that the public order of the state refuses to attribute to itself the task of deciding on such truth, or to protect or promote it, not because of a nonexistence of religious truth, but so as to not violate the liberty of persons in an area where liberty is essential.

46. See also Böckenförde, *Religionsfreiheit. Die Kirche in der modernen Welt (Schriften zu Staat—Gesellschaft—Kirche, III)* (Freiburg-Basel-Vienna: Herder, 1990). The state of the problem at the international level in the mid-1960s is briefly synthesized by Hans Maier, "Religionsfreiheit in den staatlichen Verfassungen" (1966), reprinted in Maier, *Kirche und Gesellschaft* (Munich: Kösel Verlag, 1972), 58–81.

Thus we can conclude: no doctrine of natural law is capable of providing criteria for political praxis, that is, criteria regarding means. Rather, a conception is needed of the moral rationality proper to political praxis (for example, legislative praxis), so as to be able to formulate a judgment on the concordance or non-concordance of such praxis with a principle of "natural law." This is also true because a plurality of such principles exists, and it is not always immediately evident with which principle the praxis in question should agree, or which principle should be considered to have priority in cases where they conflict (e.g., the two principles, at times in opposition, of the universal destination of goods and the right to private property). Without political (and economic) philosophy, the drawing of practical-political conclusions from principles of natural law could easily become an arbitrary undertaking.

Arbitrary, in short, because in reality one must always necessarily adopt one political philosophy (or morality) or another. Obviously, a natural law approach could limit itself to simply defending what is indispensable for preserving human dignity, thus restricting itself to limit-cases, without entering into the concrete problems of political praxis. In reality, however, no political thought that considers itself to be a simple explication of "natural law" restricts itself in this way; nor has Catholic natural-law thinking ever done so.[47] When natural law is made "concrete," a political philosophy will implicitly be employed, though often in a way that is not examined or reflected upon. It will easily succumb, therefore, to the apparent obviousness of what are in effect only the prejudices of an age, or convictions shared by a particular social group or religious community. In such cases, natural law becomes ideology, open to the danger of inconsistency and of argumentative gaps, when what was at one time evident to everyone no longer is so, due to changes in public consciousness.

Political Philosophy and the Social Doctrine of the Church

In this fourth point, which is similar to the third, I will propose the following thesis: the social doctrine of the Church is not capable of justifying itself as an alternative to political philosophy—understood as it will be outlined in the course of the argument—given that the Church's doctrine pre-

47. See the interesting observations in this regard by Böckenförde, "Kirchliches Naturrecht und politisches Handeln," in Böckenförde, *Kirchlicher Auftrag und politisches Handeln. Analyse und Orientierungen (Schriften zu Staat—Gesellschaft—Kirche, II)*, (Freiburg-Basel-Vienna: Herder, 1989), 173ff.

supposes and includes political philosophy, and therefore requires a philosophical-political point of view in order to be evaluated rationally.

According to the encyclical *Sollicitudo rei socialis,* the social doctrine of the Church is "the accurate formulation of the results of a careful reflection on the complex realities of human existence, in society and in the international order, in the light of faith and of the Church's tradition" (41). Moreover, according to the same encyclical, the Church's social doctrine understands itself to be "moral theology." It is therefore, according to the Magisterium's own teaching, a reflection on social and political reality in the light of faith and of Christian morality.[48]

Consequently, it might seem that Catholic social doctrine and political philosophy—or theology and human philosophical reasoning—could find themselves in competition with one another, that each plows the same field, though arriving at different and possibly contrasting results.

This cannot be the case, however. Given that Catholic social doctrine is a discipline that is developed at the level of moral theology, it necessarily presupposes, includes, and makes use of—as every theology does—concepts and categories that come from reasoning that takes place at the philosophical level. No theology, whether dogmatic or moral, orients itself directly, solely on the basis of the revealed content of the faith, to the reality of creation, of man, his action, and so on. All theological work involves the intervention of specifically human reason, that is, a philosophical rationality with its proper concepts and categories. It is simply impossible to think scientifically in theology without the mediation of a particular philosophy.

What, however, is the "philosophy"—or for our purposes the "ethical philosophy"—implicit in that moral theology which is called "Catholic social doctrine"? What type of philosophical rationality does it use to elaborate its contents?

I want to emphasize here that this question is not normally asked, to my knowledge, by representatives of the discipline "Catholic social teaching." Obviously, they have always made use of specialized knowledge regarding economics and social politics. And in fact, moral philosophy has been used, for example, Thomistic doctrine concerning natural law, or the relative doctrine on property, or generally concerning the virtue of justice. In doing so, social doctrine is distinguished by the fact that it makes a direct

48. See also Congregation for Catholic Education, *Guidelines for the Study and Teaching of the Social Doctrine of the Church in Priestly Formation* (December 30, 1988).

application of valid moral criteria—criteria of moral virtue—to the action of the individual person.

This could be sufficient, but only on the following condition: only if a political ethics other than ethics *simpliciter* does not exist. Such a strict continuity, however, between the ethics of the individual (and his "good life") and political ethics is the case only for the classical ethics of the *polis*. Thus, in the elaboration of a social doctrine as "moral theology," to use simply the rationality of the ethics of the individual and its requirements for a "good and happy life" and "moral virtue" already implies the adoption of a specific political philosophy, and this in an unreflective way: the ethics of the *polis*.

It can easily be shown, however, that developments in the Church's social doctrine have been due to changes that took place precisely at the level of political philosophy. Recall, for example, the doctrine on religious liberty. The same is true for judgments of the social Magisterium on democracy, on the economy, on the content of the common good, on the function of the state, or, in a more concrete example, on worker participation. In the formulation of its doctrine on religious liberty, moreover, the conciliar decree *Dignitatis humanae* adopts the ethical-political rationality of the constitutional state, recognizing the primacy of safeguarding the liberty of the person. And the fifth chapter of the encyclical *Centesimus annus* (entitled "Politics and Culture") begins by highlighting the importance of the doctrine of the division of powers—the backbone of modern constitutionalism—and the limitation and control of power by law, that is, the "Rule of Law" and the "state under the rule of law" *(Rechtsstaat)*.

Centesimus annus views democracy as integrated with and subject to constitutional guarantees of the fundamental rights of man. Thus, in reality, "moral theology" (= social doctrine) arrived at this development by replacing the philosophical-political presuppositions implicit in its earlier doctrine with others. And, regarding the so-called fundamental and immutable principles of Catholic social doctrine, these in fact are not exhaustively determinative for the stipulation of the concrete content of this doctrine as a *social-political* doctrine, elaborated for the purpose of orienting *praxis*.

We can conclude, then, that political philosophy does not compete—nor *can* it compete—with Catholic social doctrine, but is rather *a condition for its elaboration,* given that theology itself does not provide its own continually updated categories for the rational understanding of contemporary realities.[49] A social doctrine as "moral theology" that is not mediated by a fundamental political ethics would be similar to a moral theology without the service of philosophical ethics; such a doctrine would be rationally disoriented.

One thinks here of Marxist-style "liberation theology," which recognized the fact that a "Christian social doctrine" needs a philosophical instrument, that is, a proper philosophical rationality, so as to establish the link between faith and social-political reality. It was not incorrect to attempt to establish the link between faith and social reality through an instrument allowing a *rational* comprehension of that reality, a comprehension, moreover, oriented toward political praxis; what was mistaken was to employ a Marxist rationality that, as is quite clear today, was incapable of either comprehending that reality or of orienting political praxis toward the common good.

The Nature and Justification of Political Philosophy as Fundamental Political Ethics

Political Praxis Possesses Its Own Moral Logic; There Exists, Therefore, a Properly Political Ethics

If we abandon the presuppositions of an ethics of the *polis*, we arrive at the conclusion that political praxis is not a simple extension or application of the criteria that guide individual praxis, that is, the praxis of the search for happiness, the good life, and virtue. Political praxis, rather, obeys its own proper rationality, a rationality of peace, liberty, and justice as the common *political* or "*public*" good of society.

As was briefly mentioned above, the "*political* common good," that is, the common good of society as a political community, is thus to be differentiated from the common good in an *integral* sense, which latter includes all of the values that are realized *freely*, whether by individuals taken as single persons or by the various partial and intermediate societies that comprise society as a whole.[50] The "state"—the political or public power—does

49. See also the timely observations of Francesco D'Agostino, *Il diritto come problema teologico*, Recta Ratio 17 (Turin: G. Giapichelli, 1992), esp. 143–67.

50. For the distinction between integral common good and common good in a restricted sense, see Bernhard Sutor, *Politische Ethik: Gesamtdarstellung auf der Basis der Christlichen Gesellschaftslehre* (Paderborn: Schöningh, 1991), 34–36. Also useful is Joachim Detjen, *Neopluralismus und Naturrecht. Zur politischen Philosophie der Pluralismustheorie*. Politik- und Kommunikationswissenschaftliche Veröffentlichungen der Görres-Gesellschaft 1 (Paderborn: Schöningh, 1988).

not have the task of realizing the *integral* common good, but limits itself to the *political* common good, which is determined according to the nature of political praxis itself. This distinction, in fact, synthesizes the difference between modern political thought and that of the ethics of the *polis*. This differentiation, moreover, leaves open the possibility, and indeed the obligation, of the realization of the integral common good on the part of society, which in any case must not be subjected to the "totalizing" action of a political power that understands itself to be the bearer of all values, responsible for their integral realization.[51]

Political philosophy therefore, to speak in precise terms, does not make judgments about situations, social and political praxis, and the like, *without any morality*. In fact political praxis is not a nonmoral sphere that is only later subjected to a judgment or "limitation" (in the sense of a "curbing") according to moral criteria. Rather, because public-political action is a *specific* type of human praxis, reflection on it should bring to light its inherent and proper ethos.[52]

Political philosophy should therefore understand itself as "moral philosophy," that is, the *elaboration of an ethical doctrine*, and precisely a *political ethics*. Such a political ethics, moreover, is methodologically sub-

---

51. The distinction between "public" and "private," fundamental for modern political culture, is often questioned by *sociology*, which emphasizes, on the basis of empirical data, the mutual interpenetration of "private" and "public" and their "relationality" (see for example Pierpaolo Donati, *Teoria relazionale della società* (Milan: Franco Angeli, 1991), 298. It must be emphasized, however, that the distinction between "public" and "private" is of a *political-juridical* nature, and thus essentially *normative*. It is not sociology's task to deal with juridical-political normativity, which manifests its decisive importance precisely when it comes into conflict with *empirical reality*. The "subversion" of law, especially constitutional law (and with that also ethical-political normativity) on the part of sociological thought is a real danger (the most notable case perhaps being that of Harold Laski and his pluralistic theory of the state, which arrives at the conclusion that the state no longer exists, a thesis significantly adopted—with strange enthusiasm—by Carl Schmitt). See Ernst Fraenkel, "Der Pluralismus als Strukturelement der freiheitlich-rechtsstaatlichen Demokratie," in Fraenkel, *Deutschland und die westlichen Demokratien*, 8th ed., ed. Alexander von Brünneck (Frankfurt am Main: Suhrkamp, 1991), 297–325. On the problem of the "public sector," which concretely is the problem of the dysfunctionality between democratic processes and bureaucratic systems, useful are the various sociological, economic, and political contributions of Francis-Xavier Kaufmann, ed., *The Public Sector: Challenge for Coordination and Learning* (Berlin: De Gruyter, 1991). In the present context, see especially the second part, "The Public Sector: Constitutional and Conceptual Problems." A juridical criticism of the liberal distinction between public and private can be found in Nicola Lacey, *State Punishment: Political Principles and Community Values* (London: Routledge, 1988), 150ff. For a more in-depth historical treatment of the distinction between "state" and "society" (analogous to that between "public" and "private") see Peter Koslowski, *Gesellschaft und Staat. Ein unvermeidlicher Dualismus (Mit einer Einführung von Robert Spaemann)* (Stuttgart: Klett-Cotta, 1982).

52. The first to have seen this problem, it must be said, was Machiavelli. He resolved it, however, based on an opposition between politics and ethics. For a correct evaluation, however, one must read his *Discourses*, and not *The Prince*, an occasional work that does not express true Machiavellian republican thought.

ordinate neither to revealed morality nor to "natural morality," and there-fore neither to ethics as such, given that it itself *is* ethics—a specific field of ethics—and as such it extends, completes, and perfects individual ethics. It does, however, respect its own internal logic, which is the logic of political ethics. *Such a political ethics contains its own proper truth, which is a practical truth.*[53] As I will have occasion to say again below, I am not here proposing an absolute separation between these spheres; I am simply pointing out their specificity.

The moral logic of political praxis corresponds to a large extent to the logic of *public praxis, institutionalized according to rules of law.* It is not simply an ethics of virtue, but also an ethics of institutions and of institutional praxis—which is to say praxis *in* institutions and *by means of* institutions.

Political Ethos Is Integrated into History and Culture

The political ethos is an ethos that cannot be understood apart from the consideration of concrete historical conditionings and structures: the practical truth of political ethics reflects not a "natural" ethos, but a "cultural" ethos.[54] The historical framework provided above was intended precisely to render this affirmation intelligible. In fact, the modern democratic constitutional state is a product of civilization and of culture. It is not "nature," but a particular historical type of *realization* of human nature, that which is called "culture" or, in this case, "political culture." The ethos of political praxis is formulated in the context of this culture and reflects its moral rationality.

This perspective clearly differs from the Enlightenment illusion that with institutional progress, the moral perfection of individuals would also progress. Institutional progress does make people more civilized, however, in the sense that one who has recourse to a judge is more civilized than one who takes justice into his own hands. Also, as Hegel saw—in a modern expression of the Aristotelian *polis*—security and institutional protection are conditions for making people better, inasmuch as they make honest behavior less odious. Indeed, it seems easier to pay taxes honestly when

53. "Practical truth" in the classical understanding of the expression as "concordance between concrete action or means with right desire." At the level of political praxis, the ends with which action must agree are neither happiness nor the individual virtues in which happiness is realized, but precisely the ends of political praxis, i.e., peace, liberty, and justice in the sense in which they have just been described.

54. And in this sense also an "Ethos-ethics"; this phrase is from Wolfgang Kluxen, *Ethik des Ethos* (Freiburg: Alber, 1974).

the institutions that administer taxes function well and enjoy the trust of the people. "Political culture," then, is an accomplishment of civilization, whereas moral perfection as such is not; the former does, however, clearly facilitate the exercise of the moral virtues. Conversely, the moral corruption of a society is what corrupts institutions, culture, and the civilization itself. The fundamental problems are thus not political, but problems of society, of people.

The Modern Political Culture of the Democratic Constitutional State Possesses Its Own Founding Ethos

This third conclusion hardly needs further justification, specifying as it does the previous conclusion: the democratic constitutional state is an order of peace, liberty, and justice. These three elements form *the fundamental common good* of the political community organized in this way. Assuming the political rationality—which is an ethical rationality—of the modern democratic constitutional state, the acceptance of this state as an order that guarantees the common good of peace, liberty, and justice implies a moral *choice;* that is, such an acceptance already formulates the initial contents of a political ethics and the foundation for a further development of that ethics.

This is also true because a political ethics, as with any ethical system, must be formulated taking into account the real conditions in which human action is carried out. These real conditions are not abstract principles, and neither is the human being as such, considered as an individual person; rather, these conditions are created by people themselves, as political actors in the course of history. The modern democratic constitutional state is a cultural product of centuries, a product of human beings in which is uniquely expressed, even if *semper reformanda,* the accumulated and purified experience of these same human beings as *zōon politikon* (political/social animal).[55]

---

55. I am not, however, a supporter of a "linearly progressive" view of history. The modern democratic constitutional state, with its political culture of parliamentary representation, rule of law, participation of all citizens in the formation of a political will, institutional guarantees, etc., is certainly not the product of linear and progressive plan of history—as is still believed today, following Hegel, e.g., by Francis Fukuyama, who consequently predicts the "end of history." The constitutional state (which is the presupposition of every true modern democracy) is in a certain sense a "turning back," a turning back from the "pure" principle of modern statehood as it was realized in the absolute territorial state of the early modern period. This "turning back" recovers the inheritance of a long history, a recovery that is realized, however, on the basis of the foundation created precisely by the modern territorial state.

By understanding political philosophy—and with it political ethics—to be the expression of an ethos formed by a particular political culture in a specific historical context, one is essentially following the *spirit* of Aristotelian political science. Indeed, the latter is not a reflection on moral principles independent of the reality of the Greek *polis,* but integrates into its reflection the real conditions of practicability of any political praxis. The position espoused here, therefore, could be considered a type of "non-Aristotelian neo-Aristotelianism."

This in no way means to assert that political ethics should limit itself to formulating, historically, the ethos proper to particular periods of history. Even our own period offers different possibilities, including the choice *against* the democratic constitutional state. The political ethics I wish to argue for *already presupposes* a rational choice in favor of the democratic constitutional state, on the basis of the values that both are realized by it and are its task to realize: peace, liberty, and justice as integral and fundamental parts of the *political common good* of the earthly city, a common good that is *partial, limited,* and *incomplete.* Political philosophy has the task of explaining the *moral* rationality of such a choice.

Such a choice also implies the recognition that the democratic constitutional state lives by presuppositions that it itself has not created, but has merely allowed to flourish in a practicable and rational way: the rights of man as an expression of human dignity, that is, the dignity of a being created in the image of God.[56] The political culture of the democratic constitutional state thus lives by presuppositions it cannot guarantee, neither by its institutional, political, juridical, nor economic means.[57] Just as "the habit

---

In a certain sense, therefore, we are dealing with a *synthesis* of history in which the perennial idea of the *regimen mixtum* has been realized as never before (see St. Thomas Aquinas, *Summa Theologiae* I-II, q. 105, a.1). All of this, however, does not remove the dangers and imperfections to which every order created by human beings is exposed.

56. Against the claim of Larmore, *Patterns of Moral Complexity,* a certain expressivism is therefore inevitable. Even he, ultimately, is unable to avoid it, his "liberal state" being precisely the expression of an ideal: the ideal of the continual search for a *modus vivendi,* what in the end corresponds to the reduction of the political ethos to a "Bodinian" ethic of peace. I do not see how Larmore can avoid the consequences of a political ethos that sees in peace, and in peace alone, the one political value to be pursued, without guarantees of liberty and of justice. In truth, a truly "liberal" political culture is not *only* an expression of "neutrality" and of the will to find a *modus vivendi,* but it is always also an expression of respect for the liberty of every human person and of the commitment to justice. This does not negate Larmore's most valuable insight: that a "liberal" (still in a broad sense) political culture is not an expression of a conception of the "good life" of the individual in the Aristotelian sense, but a political-juridical understanding of political society that is open to a pluralism of conceptions concerning the "good life."

57. See Böckenförde, *Die Entstehung des Staates als Vorgang der Säkularisation,* 60. The same idea is also expressed in Joseph Ratzinger, *Wendezeit für Europa? Diagnosen und Prognosen zur Lage von Kirche und Welt* (Einsiedeln-Freiburg: Johannes Verlag, 1991), 100.

doesn't make the monk," so it is not institutions alone that bring about peace, liberty, and justice; people always play a fundamental role. Political institutions, for example, cannot make up for a corruption of the society itself and of its members, a corruption that would render unintelligible the very foundations on which the political culture is based.[58]

It is political philosophy's task, therefore, to clarify, including publicly, the foundations of modern political culture. To clarify, as well, "what belongs to God and what belongs to Caesar"—to make intelligible, that is, what is called the "legitimate autonomy of temporal realities" and, citing the encyclical *Centesimus annus* (47), the "legitimate autonomy of the democratic order." Included here would be a just moral valuation of the work of parliament (rather than cynical laments over the "shady affairs of politics"), and the proposal of moral criteria for positive legislation in a pluralistic society. Finally, political philosophy, as a *practical* philosophy, has the task that pertains to every ethics: to reflect on political praxis so as to orient it toward its proper ends: peace, liberty, and justice (which clearly also implies reflection on the moral rationality proper to the economy and its integration into the political culture of the constitutional state).[59]

With respect to this task of clarifying the foundations of modern political culture, these foundations were not, in my opinion, adequately expressed in the political philosophy that stimulated, accompanied, and interpreted the original development of this same modern political culture. Contractualism especially—the eminent philosophical formulation of a political culture of liberty and justice—is incapable of justifying social life, or the law vis-à-vis liberty, even if this doctrine undoubtedly played a very specific and important historical role.[60] Contractualism erred in thinking that the harmonization of liberty, law, and equality was the fruit of the self-

---

58. This is the case, in my opinion, with respect to the demanded "right to free choice" regarding abortion. Such a right could be claimed only if the unborn are not human persons, protected by law like all other citizens. If this were the case, then the prohibition of abortion would indeed be an illegitimate interference in *privacy* by the state. If it is not the case, however, a requested "right to free choice" in this area not only discriminates against the unborn, but is also a clear violation of the ethos that is at the foundation of the constitutional state. The fact that such a question is evaded in today's society indicates a true degeneration of society itself, dangerous for the ethos of liberty implicit in modern political culture.

59. See Peter Koslowski, "Ethics of Capitalism," in *Ethics of Capitalism and Critique of Sociobiology: Two Essays with a Comment by James M. Buchanan* (Berlin: Springer: 1996); idem, *Principles of Ethical Economy* (Berlin: Kluwer Academic Publisher/Springer, 2002); idem, *Gesellschaftliche Koordination. Eine ontologische und kulturwissenschaftliche Theorie der Marktwirtschaft* (Tübingen: J. C. B. Mohr, 1991).

60. A similar conclusion is reached in the classic historical-critical study of John Weidhofft Gough, *The Social Contract: A Critical Study of Its Developments* (London: Oxford University Press, 1936; 2nd ed. 1957/1963/1976; last reprint, Westport, Conn.: Greenwood Press, 1978).

interested individual alone, through an interest mediated by a contract. It seems, rather, that any contractual coordination of individual liberty already presupposes what the contract proposes to create: a natural will toward cooperation, law, and equality, that is, the acknowledgment of the other as equal to me, not in my own interest, but precisely in the interest of the other. The human being as *zōon politikon* therefore needs to be rearticulated on modern premises.

The rights of man seemed self-evident to the founding fathers of the United States of America. Are they? Were they not "self-evident" to those men only because they were children of a culture impregnated with the Christian idea of human dignity? If the Catholic Church itself now echoes modernity's expression of its roots in its official doctrine, perhaps the time has also come for a recognition that respect for the rights of man—said to be "inalienable"—presupposes a *truth* about man. The "inalienability" of rights and dignity are inconceivable in a culture that loses a sense of *truth*.

Even if modern political culture is no longer an order of truth in the sense of the ethics of the *polis*—meaning an order that feels itself called to realize a *specific* truth—it *is* nevertheless an order of truth with respect to the ultimate foundation on which its aspirations for peace, liberty, and justice are based. "Neutrality," respect for pluralism, and respect for liberty are founded on a truth concerning man; otherwise these could not be defended as moral demands, and indeed they could not be defended on any basis.[61]

Certainly, a position such as that of Norberto Bobbio is also thinkable, which asserts for epistemological and historical reasons that a coherent justification of the rights of man is impossible; the problem today would be "not so much to *justify* them, but to *protect* them. It is a political, rather than a philosophical problem."[62] Such an opposition seems unsatisfactory, however, given that the problem inherent in the justification—and thus in the philosophical *understanding*—of the rights of man is an eminently *political*

---

61. Thus, in defense of "liberal" political culture, Thomas A. Spragens opts precisely for a revision of the philosophical foundations of the liberal tradition, which he calls self-destructive. His main argument is that a rational society needs a commitment to truth "because rationality is by definition oriented toward the truth," Spragens, *The Irony of Liberal Reason* (Chicago: University of Chicago Press, 1981), 384. On the other hand, Ronald Dworkin claims that individual rights cannot be demonstrated as true, although this does not mean that truth does not exist. Dworkin, *Taking Rights Seriously* (London: Duckworth, 1977), 81, 279ff. Alasdair MacIntyre has concluded that the rights of man are mere fictions and that "there are no such rights, and belief in them is one with belief in witches and unicorns." Macintyre, *After Virtue. A Study in Moral Theory* (Notre Dame: University of Notre Dame Press, 1981), 69. Anti-modern neo-Aristotelianism suggests that there is an alternative to the culture of the rights of man; such a position falls apart, however, inasmuch as it has been incapable of articulating such an alternative.

62. Bobbio, "Sul fondamento dei diritti dell'uomo," 16.

one: a culture based on the rights of man and organized democratically is not imposed by a political elite, but presupposes the consensus of society, a consensus that cannot be formed and sustained without an understanding, present as culture, of how such rights are justified.

"Political culture" is not limited to a structure of institutions, but includes equally the public consciousness of the ethos corresponding to these institutions. Moreover, the rights of man are not a static achievement, but dynamic principles of political and, above all, judicial praxis—they are protected not as museum pieces, but through their use and application. Only if juridical positivism were true would this not be anymore a fundamental political-juridical problem. How, then, to apply/protect the rights of man, and according to what criteria?[63] This depends precisely on how these rights are understood and on how they are justified in the sphere of a public philosophy.[64]

Recent debates show that this is precisely where the problem lies.[65] I want here to briefly outline a response. Historically, the rights of man have been claimed as *individual* rights, and in truth they are. This fact, however, has generated the idea that both civil society and political society (or the state) are nothing other than means to the end of protecting and promoting the liberty, autonomy, and so on, of the individual. Thus, according to a "contractualistic" way of thinking, any communitarian commitment of an individual would be based, ultimately, on the rationale of "distributive advantage," that is, the rational calculation that "my" renunciation of certain natural liberties, increasing and assuring the liberty of all (thus, a communitarian commitment), would *also* increase and ensure my liberty.[66]

Recent attempts to rearticulate the concept of justice (Rawls, Ackermann) also ultimately depart from this premise: they are forced to justify

63. See the judgments of constitutional courts in cases of individual rights. Very useful for a quick overview of the mode of argumentation, e.g., of the Supreme Court of the United States, is Ralph C. Chandler, Richard A. Enslen, and Peter G. Renstrom, *The Constitutional Law Dictionary*, vol. 1: *Individual Rights* (Santa Barbara: Clio Press, 1985) (the second volume, 1987, contains judgments on questions of "governmental powers").

64. A similar concern is also present in the book of Vittorio Possenti, *Le società liberali al bivio: Lineamenti di filosofia della società* (Perugia: Marietti, 1991).

65. Two jurists can be cited in this context: Dworkin, *Taking Rights Seriously*; and an attempt at the reconstruction of the liberal ethics underlying the political culture of the rights of man, Carlos Santiago Nino, *The Ethics of Human Rights* (Oxford: Oxford University Press, 1991), in part identical to the author's preceding volume *Etica y derechos humanos* (Buenos Aires: Paidós, 1984; 2nd ed., Buenos Aires: Astrea, 1989). These books have the merit of doing justice to the political nature of a philosophical justification of the rights of man, overcoming positivistic, utilitarian, and skeptical limitations.

66. This is the case for Otfried Höffe, *Politische Gerechtigkeit: Grundlegung einer kritischen Philosophie von Recht und Staat* (Frankfurt am Main: Suhrkamp, 1989).

any non-self-interested communitarian commitment in the face of an individual who is interested only in his own advantage, which is understood as the most autonomous realization possible of his own conception of the good. It is not that these authors want to assert that man is selfish—but for them the "possibility of altruism" (Thomas Nagel) needs an explicit articulation and justification.[67]

Falling essentially outside of such a perspective is the fundamental truth, mentioned above, that "human liberty," according to the logic of the Golden Rule, means to be *equally* interested in the good of the other; and this not because it is more advantageous to me, but because it is advantageous to the other, who is recognized as a *being equal to me* and therefore possessing the same rights. This is the fundamental principle of justice[68] and of every right, different from a principle that conceives of "natural" man as a deliberately isolated individual, whose only relationship with others and with society is one of an advantageous calculation aimed at assuring the possibility of claiming his own individuality. If this latter conception is *not* true, the communitarian commitment of the individual and his social nature do not need to be rearticulated; rather these would be seen to be originary facts, given precisely with the *rational individuality* of man whose nature it is to transcend himself toward the good of others.

From this I conclude that the rights of man should be integrated within this more fundamental framework of a notion of justice that, in reality, is a "natural" sense of justice and of solidarity. This assertion, though being at a fairly abstract level that does not allow immediate political conclusions to be drawn, is nevertheless not without consequences: it is not possible to recognize the other as equal to me and as a possessor of the same rights without a *common* understanding concerning man and the meaning of such

67. Thus, very important is chapter 22 in John Rawls's *A Theory of Justice,* entitled "The Circumstances of Justice," where, referring to Hume, the author provides the anthropological presuppositions that make justice *necessary*. One of these presuppositions is the fact "that the parties take no interest in one another's interest"; they are "selves" who are solely interested in the recognition of their own conception of the good. It is precisely this "willful" and intentional isolation of the individual that is the basis of Rawls's construction, not only of justice, but of fraternity, benevolence, etc. It should be emphasized that not even Locke was this radical; he characterized the state of nature as a "State of Peace, Good Will, Mutual Assistance, and Preservation," with the only thing lacking being an authority that could judge and impose a sentence in cases of conflict (*The Second Treatise of Government* § 19). Also important for a revision of the ethical-political concept of justice is the contribution of Agnes Heller, *Beyond Justice* (Oxford: Basil Blackwell, 1987).

68. For a more detailed exposition, see my book *The Perspective of Morality: Philosophical Bases of Thomistic Virtue Ethics* (Washington, D.C.: The Catholic University of America Press, 2010), originally published in Italian as *La prospettiva della morale: Fondamenti dell'etica filosofica* (Rome: Armando, 1994).

rights. "Equal concern and respect"[69] is not possible without a fundamental, content-laden conception, which is moreover *communally shared*, concerning what *merits* "concern" and "respect," and *why* these are merited.

In other words: even a "liberal" culture based on the protection of individual rights, in order to be capable of generating authentic principles of justice, presupposes and implies a conception of the "good life," though obviously one different from Aristotelian and neo-Aristotelian conceptions. This conception, moreover, is not imposed authoritatively in the classical sense of an "ethics of the *polis*," but is rather the foundation of a political culture of liberty that conceives of liberty not only as a "good for me," but precisely as a *common* good—and for this reason also as a good involving demands of justice that don't necessarily always promote "my" freedom and "my" advantage, at least if one doesn't consider "my" advantage to also include simply being a just and good person.

Political Philosophy Is "Fundamental Political Ethics"

Based on what has been said thus far, we can state that political philosophy is, essentially, "fundamental political ethics." The entire Aristotelian ethics, being essentially an "ethics of the *polis*," can be understood as a fundamental political ethics, though simultaneously as a fundamental ethics for individual ethics. While abandoning the classical model of the ethics of the *polis*, we must nevertheless maintain that in fact we have need of *two* fundamental ethics: one for the action of individuals (an ethics of happiness, of the good life, of moral virtue), and another for political or public action. I am not by this claiming an opposition or a lack of relationship between the two; in fact, the values that form the basis of modern political culture can be understood precisely as those considered in a virtue ethics of the individual person.

Obviously, this assertion does not resolve every political-philosophical question. Nor are we forgetting the innumerable contradictions and inconsistencies of today's political culture, often in contrast with the implied ideals of that culture, which are nonetheless normative. Nor do we forget the historical contradictions, that is, the frequent illiberality of the modern "liberal" state, and the great threat of the absorption of society and of individuals by the omnipresent bureaucracy of the welfare state.[70] It was not,

---

69. Dworkin, *Taking Rights Seriously*, 273.

70. Still instructive on this problem is the perspective of F. A. von Hayek; see among others his *The Constitution of Liberty* (Chicago: University of Chicago Press, 1960). The problem with his position

however, my purpose to resolve such problems here, but to respond to the question "Why is political philosophy necessary?" This question could not be answered adequately without specifying some presuppositions of political philosophy, given that the "why?" of such a philosophical investigation cannot be justified independently of a historical position, a justification that, however, had to be set forth precisely in terms of an *ethical-political rationality*. In this, also, I believe we are in agreement with Aristotle.

Conclusion

In conclusion, a final consideration, which may at first appear provocative: with what I have outlined above, I also mean to express the conviction that it is necessary to abandon the idea that Christianity—*sic et simpliciter*—can provide the political solution for every problem of human society and of the earthly city. We again need the wisdom of St. Augustine, but this time on new premises. To wit: the specific mission of the Christian religion is not to resolve the problems of the earthly city, but to be leaven in this city that is nonetheless governed by its own legitimately autonomous rationality. This does not, however, mean that resolving the problems of the earthly city is not the task of Christians *as its citizens;* indeed, quite the opposite.

The *first* evangelization led to a Christianization of institutions that were the legacy of a pagan culture. The result was often ambiguous, and in the end contradictory. A *new* evangelization would be a Christianization in a world shaped by institutions that are the fruit of a Christian civilization. The result could be *a new type of secularity in a society of Christians*. This would be a secularized society, though fully Christian, including with regard to respect for each person's liberty: "God, in creating us, accepted the risk and the adventure of our liberty: he wanted history be a true history, made by authentic decisions, and not a fiction or a game. Every person must have an experience of his own personal autonomy, with the unforeseen events,

---

(which in the United States is not called "liberal" but rather "libertarian") is the fundamental disposition, based on the uncontestable rationality of liberty as the principle of progress, to "sacrifice" justice toward one generation for the sake of the progress of future generations. This perspective considers "humanity" to be the subject of history, a subject that in reality does not exist; only "persons" exist, each of whom lives during a relatively brief period of time. Political rationality—which is always a rationality of justice—at times demands the choice of solutions in favor of those now living that are less rational from the point of view of a "global historical progress" with a presumed single subject, "humanity." I agree with von Hayek, however, on his fundamental thesis that the principle of liberty is better at generating justice and social progress than the plans of the bureaucracy of an assistance state, and this for economic, political, and anthropological reasons.

the effort and even the uncertainties this involves."[71] A sign of authenticity of a Christian society would therefore be the existence of a political culture that respects—indeed loves—liberty, peaceful coexistence, and an impartial justice that guarantees that pluralism which will ever be the logic and the necessary consequence of liberty.

It would be neither possible nor just to omit mention in this setting of the work of Jacques Maritain, who—after his "conversion" from an antimodern position to a fair valuation of modern political culture, which took place during his exile in the United States[72]—clearly recognized the profound difference between, on the one hand a "clerical *state*, i.e. cosmetically Christian," and on the other a "Christian *society* that is vitally and really Christian."[73] Nevertheless, Maritain's vision of the relationship between Christianity and democracy perhaps cannot be upheld when faced with historical facts. His conception of democracy, moreover, following the French tradition, appears to be overly attached to the ambiguous idea of the sovereignty of the people and insufficiently aware of the importance of the Anglo-Saxon constitutional tradition, thus arriving at a new, almost utopian moralism that expects everything of "new elites, arising from the depths of the nation."[74]

It seems to me that the various stimuli, unquestionably positive, deriving from Maritain's philosophy[75] should be channeled into a more sober and realistic reflection that could be used by political philosophy to overcome its isolation from other disciplines such as history, jurisprudence, political science, and sociology. This would lead to a conception of political culture that

71. Josemaría Escrivá, *L'avventura della libertà* (Milan: Edizioni Ares, 1972), "Homily No. 6," 28.

72. He attests to this in his book *Man and the State* (Chicago: University of Chicago Press, 1951).

73. "Ce qui importe ici, c'est de distinguer l'apocryphe d'avec l'authentique, un État clérical ou décorativement chrétien d'avec une societé politique vitalement et réellement chrétienne." Jacques Maritain, *Les Droits de l'Homme et la Loi Naturelle* (New York: Éditions de la Maison Française, 1942), in Jacques Maritain and Raïssa Maritain, *Oeuvres complètes,* 7:633 (Fribourg-Paris: Éditions Universitaires Fribourg-Suisse/Éditions Saint-Paul, 1988).

74. "[L]es nouvelles élites sortent des profondeurs des nations.... Le problème essentiel de la reconstruction n'est pas un problème de plans, c'est un problème d'hommes, le problème des nouvelles élites directrices à venir." Maritain, *Christianisme et démocratie* (New York: Éditions de la Maison Française, 1943), in *Oeuvres complètes,* 7:749. The political wisdom of constitutionalism, on the other hand, consists precisely in the establishment of a political-juridical constitutional structure that guarantees, through the rule of law, the fundamental rights of persons independently of the personal qualities of rulers. The "problem of people" is not the first to be resolved; rather, it is always the last, and certainly decisive if institutions are not to become corrupt. Maritain's position could easily degenerate into an indefensible political moralism, resulting as a last resort in the call for a "secular faith" in democracy (this is the position adopted by Enrico Berti, "Momenti della rifondazione etica della democrazia." In Berti, *Le vie della ragione* (Bologna: Il Mulino, 1987), 282. Berti refers to Maritain's *The Man and the State* (108ff.).

75. Above all on the Vatican Council II; see Vittorio Possenti, *Una filosofia per la transizione: Metafisica, persona e politica in J. Maritain* (Milan: Massimo, 1984), 220ff.

reflects on the *real conditions* of liberty and democracy, which in turn would allow a more accurate grasp of the internal limitations and threats inherent in democracy, obviously so as to contribute to the survival of a political culture based on liberty and democracy.

As an illustrious historian has written recently, modern political culture was born from an illusion of liberty, that is, of an absolute liberty as the fruit of a social revolution.[76] The French Revolution in particular—as with all modern revolutions—"paradoxically produced fruits of liberty and democracy only after the failure of the myth of the illusion of total revolution, and through an agonizing process."[77] Beyond the well-known conflict between a Church linked to the *ancien regime* and the new powers, by that time already overcome, there was, and still is, a much deeper conflict between religious consciousness and a revolution oriented toward liberty: "the religious consciousness of the time denied in principle, as it still does today, every illusion of absolute liberty produced by a social revolution. Ultimately, in its conflict with the revolution, religious consciousness acted as a 'filter' to the revolution's legacy, assuring that authentic values of liberty would emerge from the experience."[78] This process was accompanied by conflicts and not-insignificant misunderstandings. "That same religious sense of a limit and of the sin which opposes the illusion of revolution as a global and definitive response to the problem of evil can also lead—and historically *has* led—to the assigning to the public power, though subject to religion, the task of establishing order."[79]

How, though, should one think of this submission of the public power to religion? The response of the Catholic thought of the Counter-Revolution (e.g., De Maistre) saw this in institutional terms, and in this sense was not proposing simply a restorative romanticism, but in fact a modern-style totalizing sociologism,[80] modern in the same sense as a certain despotism present in democracies and in some "liberal" states toward the end of the nineteenth century.[81] The submission of the public power to religion, however,

---

76. Pietro Scoppola, *La repubblica dei partiti: Profilo storico della democrazia in Italia (1945–1990)* (Bologna: Il Mulino, 1991), Introduction.

77. Ibid., 20.   78. Ibid.

79. Ibid.

80. This is true also for L. G. A. de Bonald; see the study of Robert Spaemann, *Der Ursprung der Soziologie aus dem Geist der Restauration: Studien über L. G. A. de Bonald* (Munich: Kösel, 1959).

81. The judgment of a convinced liberal, issued in the 1920s, is surprising: "One who reflects on the harshly authoritarian character of contemporary democratic civilization, cannot deny that the Church in fact represents a bulwark and a defense of liberty against state 'tyranny'—even if this latter is anything but liberal in its intimate motivation" (De Ruggiero, *Storia del liberalismo europeo*, 429).

can no longer be conceived of as realizable by means of public and political institutions, but through the conversion of the hearts of human beings. This alone can be the task of a new evangelization, in which the Church acts as a moral authority within society, though in a way not opposed to a pluralistic political culture, being "at once a sign and a safeguard of the transcendent character of the human person."[82] We thus arrive, again, at the wisdom of St. Augustine, although with an important nuance: the conversion of hearts, the genesis of the heavenly city in human hearts, involves not only an eschatological sense, but also a *temporal* sense. It is called to give the earthly city a visage consistent with human dignity.[83]

82. Vatican Council II, *Pastoral Constitution "Gaudium et spes,"* n. 76.

83. The present article is the expanded version of a paper read on the occasion of a seminar at the Roman Athenaeum of the Holy Cross, April 6, 1992. The Italian original was published as "Perché una filosofia politica? Elementi storici per una risposta" in *Acta Philosophica* 1, no. 1 (1992): 233–63.

TWO

The Liberal Image of Man and the Concept of Autonomy

Beyond the Debate between Liberals and Communitarians

Liberalism and the Anthropological Problem

More than a philosophical theory, today liberalism is a political reality. Even socialists and social-democrats in Western democracies profess a liberal political consensus. This consensus has its historical roots in those same political values and institutions by which liberal parties and movements traditionally struggled against absolutism, political and juridical arbitrariness, and every form of suppression of basic human rights. Today's liberal political consensus is inspired by those same values that have promoted the free development of the creative and innovative forces inherent in society. In a certain sense we are all "liberals." We identify ourselves with a political culture characterized by the fundamental principles of a constitutionalism whose central idea is the rule of law—the submission of raw power to a law that guarantees fundamental individual liberties. We appreciate the independence of the judiciary and the impartial justice that requires respect for the regulations (in large part procedural) of the positive law. We hold as indispensable and irreplaceable the principles of representation by a parliament elected by universal and secret vote, majority rule, and the protection of minorities. The fact that the profession and practice of this or that religious faith does not influence our conditions of citizenship seems reasonable and just to us. The fact that being born into a specific social class does not definitively determine our place and function in society also seems reasonable and just. We defend the freedom and autonomy of the individual as the fundamental value that justifies our political institutions. We defend the fundamental right of every person to live a life in accord with personal and responsible choice—even if always somewhat conditioned by different social, cultural, and economic factors—rather than simply in accord with tradition, social position, or the impositions of those in public power.

Certainly there are ideological aspects and components of classical and contemporary liberalism that are incompatible with the cultural-political order created by historical liberalism. Liberalism is not "a unitary development but a set of more or less converging tendencies."[1] It would be a simplistic error to equate liberalism with the ideals of the eighteenth-century Enlightenment. Liberalism's weakness was always a theoretical weakness, a lack of an ultimate foundation. Since the salient features of liberalism—such as individual freedom and moral rights—lack an ultimate basis, they "become the object more of faith than of knowledge. They signify a preference."[2] The contrast between liberalism's practical strength and success and its widely recognized theoretical weakness as a political theory is a paradox in need of explanation. Without such an explanation, without clarifying what some consider a lack of philosophical coherence of the "liberal idea," we can never fully understand the ultimate conceptual foundations of our liberal democracies.[3]

In the last twenty-five years, despite the historic theoretical weakness of liberalism, political philosophy has made important attempts to make explicit the major values of the liberal tradition inherent in contemporary democratic society, and in so doing has reopened the debate about liberalism as public philosophy.[4] John Rawls's influential *A Theory of Justice*[5] stimulated

1. Vittorio Possenti, *Le società liberali al bivio: Lineamenti di filosofia della società* (Perugia: Marietti, 1991), 402. Editor's translation.

2. Ibid.

3. Frans A. M. Alting von Geusau, *Die liberale Gesellschaft und der Rechtsstaat*, in *Die liberale Gesellschaft: Castelgandolfo-Gespräche, 1992*, ed. Krzysztof Michalski (Stuttgart: Klett-Cotta, 1993), 103–32, especially 128.

4. For a discussion of the debate regarding liberalism as public philosophy, see Vittorio Possenti's *Le società liberali al bivio*. For a reconstruction of a public philosophy on a non-liberal basis see William M. Sullivan, *Reconstructing Public Philosophy* (Berkeley: University of California Press, 1986).

5. John Rawls, *A Theory of Justice* (Oxford: Oxford University Press, 1972).

debate regarding liberalism's anthropological implications, that is, liberalism's "image of man." Because of important critiques advanced by the so-called communitarians and the subsequent correction of liberal theory, it is no longer clear whether liberalism implies any specific "image of man" or whether such an implication would even be desirable. One of the reasons for current confusion regarding liberalism's anthropological implications can be traced to a defect in the communitarian critique. Throughout the debate, it has never been clarified whether the communitarians meant to target the *theory* of liberalism or the *institutional reality* of the democratic, liberal, constitutional state. The fact that the communitarians have never proposed a specific political alternative has only further obscured the issue.[6]

In the following pages, while analyzing the positions of some classical and contemporary authors, I will argue that—according to its original intent—liberalism is a specifically political doctrine that, like every coherent political philosophy, inexorably implies significant anthropological presuppositions. On my account, even those liberal political philosophies that attempt to render themselves independent of any such presuppositions nonetheless conceal a hidden, implicit image of man. Although these inevitable presuppositions do not necessarily form a complete anthropological or moral doctrine, in every form of liberalism—in one way or another—the image of man is always centered on the *idea of autonomy*. In the final analysis, the form of autonomy advanced by a political theory and culturally embodied by the democratic constitutional state reflects whether that political theory may be considered truly liberal or, on the other hand, whether that autonomy has been converted into what I call the "strong concept of autonomy" and therefore reflects a specific, or even sectarian, ideology.

Two Versions of Classical Liberalism

Even though historical liberalism was meant to be a strictly political doctrine,[7] there have always been two currents within the liberal tradition.

6. Perhaps the best exposition of the diverse positions and their development may be found in Stephen Mulhall and Adam Swift, *Liberals and Communitarians* (Oxford: Blackwell, 1992). See also Alessandro Ferrara's introduction to his anthology entitled *Comunitarismo e Liberalismo* (Rome: Editori Riuniti, 1992). See also Axel Honneth's "Grenzen des Liberalismus. Zur politisch-ethischen Diskussion um den Kommunitarismus," *Philosophische Rundschau* 38 (1991): 83–102; Gino Dalle Fratte, ed., *Concezioni del bene e teoria della giustizia: Il dibattito tra liberali e comunitari in prospettiva pedagogica* (Rome: Armando, 1995).

7. An indispensable work for the history of liberalism is the classic: Guido De Ruggiero, *Storia del liberalismo europeo* (Bari: Laterza, 1925). A critical-historical analysis may be found in Anthony Arblast-

The first current is motivated primarily by political objectives. In addition to the objectives pursued by the first current, the second is also motivated by a specific vision of man and therefore forms part of a complete moral and anthropological doctrine. Montesquieu, the Founding Fathers of the United States, especially the authors of the *Federalist Papers* (Alexander Hamilton, James Madison, and John Jay), Benjamin Constant, and Alexis de Tocqueville exemplify the first current. Immanuel Kant, Wilhelm von Humboldt, and John Stuart Mill are representative of the second.

Liberalism as a Primarily Political Doctrine

The authors of the *Federalist Papers* represent that Anglo-Saxon political-legal tradition centered upon a realistic vision of man and political power. The *Federalist Papers* reflect a pessimistic universal anthropology in which both subjects and rulers are seen as inevitably inclined to evil. The corresponding political thought aims to design a government capable of achieving justice—the goal of every legitimate government—without suppressing individual freedom. Its success requires an organization of political power that is able not only to protect the individual from every other individual, but also to protect the individual from the coercive power of the state. It therefore requires both a government that controls the governed and a government that controls itself through the division of power, parliamentary control, and an independent judiciary.[8]

The Swiss-born political theorist Benjamin Constant may be included within this tradition of realistic political philosophy. In his famous discourse *The Liberty of the Ancients Compared with That of the Moderns,* Constant contrasted the more limited freedom of antiquity with that of modernity. On Constant's account, freedom in antiquity consisted in the vocal participation in public decisions along with the total subjection of the individual to the power of the collective. In contrast, the freedom of modernity consists in *the independence of the private citizen* regarding the public affairs that are performed by elected representatives of the citizen.[9] Thus, in

---

er's *The Rise and Decline of Western Liberalism* (Oxford: Blackwell, 1984). For a theory of democracy according to a liberal perspective see Giovanni Sartori, *The Theory of Democracy Revisited* (Chatham, N.J.: Chatham House, 1987). Concerning the connection between liberalism and constitutionalism see Nicola Matteucci, *Organizzazione del potere e libertà: Storia del costituzionalismo moderno* (Turin: UTET, 1988).

8. See *The Federalist* 10 and 51 (Madison); see also Montesquieu, *De l'esprit des lois*, ed. R. Derathé (Paris: Garnier, 1973), XI, 6 e XII, 2.

9. See Benjamin Constant, "The Liberty of the Ancients Compared with That of the Moderns," in *Political Writings,* trans. and ed. Biancamaria Fontana (Cambridge: Cambridge University Press, 1988),

accord with the modern notion of freedom, the person lives his *own life* and enjoys the fruits of his work according to his own preferences. In modernity, the first and most fundamental characteristic of the citizen consists in the exercise of individual freedom under the protection of the state, not in participating in public affairs. The modern notion of freedom views the person as autonomous and independent, free to choose his own plan of life. While favoring the modern notion of freedom, Constant argues that autonomy, individual independence, personal liberty—and not control, oppression, and the arbitrariness of the state—are "the aim of all societies; upon it depend both public and private morality; upon it depend the expectations of industry; without it men can enjoy neither peace, nor dignity, nor happiness."[10]

Critics of liberalism might consider Constant's defense of the modern view of freedom as a straightforward program for hedonistic, "individualistic" egoism. But Constant's analysis is a political program, directed against a well-defined adversary: a state that, while free from the control of other political powers, arbitrarily oversees the welfare of its citizens, organizes the economy, and even establishes the permissible ways of personal fulfillment.[11] The adversary and antithesis of liberal independence and personal responsibility is the absolute state, for which the individual becomes the means of attaining not so much the good of the citizen but the *salus publica:* the good of the state, and not infrequently, the good of those in power.[12]

307–28. Constant develops some of these ideas also in "The Spirit of Conquest and Usurpation," 149–69, and "The Principles of Politics Applicable to All Representative Governments," 170–307, in *Political Writings.*

10. Benjamin Constant, "The Principles of Politics Applicable to All Representative Governments," in *Political Writings,* 289–90.

11. See ibid., 290: "Arbitrary power destroys morality, for there can be no morality without security.... Arbitrariness is the enemy of all the transactions that establish the prosperity of peoples. It disrupts credit, crushes commerce, strikes at all security. When an individual suffers without having been found guilty, anyone of any intelligence feels himself threatened, and with good reason. For security is destroyed; all transactions feel the impact; the earth trembles and it is only with fear that we go on our way."

12. Stephen Holmes has pointed out the importance of contrasting the various features of liberalism with their authentic antitheses; see his *The Anatomy of Antiliberalism* (Cambridge, Mass.: Harvard University Press, 1993), 253ff. Many make the mistake of creating false antinomies. For instance, rather than seeing the right to private property as the alternative to the arbitrary confiscation of property by those who rule, they often falsely contrast it with the demands of charity. Rather than viewing instrumentalist utilitarianism as an alternative to the inefficient largess and sumptuous ostentation of a privileged few, they falsely contrast it with morality. Rather than viewing "right" as corresponding to "duty," they consider "right" the antithesis to the cruelty and even slavery of tyrannical magistrates. Mistakes have also been made in the interpretation of entire political philosophies. For instance, despite its many limitations, contractualism did not necessarily entail radical individualism. For Locke, man in the state of nature is already a social being and not an "atom." The purpose of contractualism was to give precedence to the individual's interests over those of the state. Contractualism was designed to defeat the idea that political power was an inheritance in the hands of privileged persons and classes. For contrac-

Constant's political liberalism is directed against a state that abuses power and overreaches its proper jurisdiction, thus exposing itself to corruption and bureaucratic inefficiency. The liberal is convinced that the public authority is inept at planning and organizing the economy and believes that . the state should not prescribe how its citizens pursue personal happiness.

For Constant the political freedom meant to protect the freedom of every person is not an end in itself, but only the means and necessary condition for the attainment of personal perfection, the content of which each one must be able to choose in full freedom.[13] Constant's liberalism, therefore, is a strictly political doctrine that willfully abstains from specifying the content or purpose of personal freedom and autonomy. His concept of autonomy is primarily political insofar as it reflects a view of public power rather than a full-fledged anthropology. For Constant the state is to be limited in its jurisdiction and subject to a law designed to guarantee a well-defined liberty, an autonomous space, for the individual. Such a political liberalism, being an account of the *political-juridical conditions* of civil liberty, presupposes an appreciation for personal autonomy as—to use the terminology of Isaiah Berlin—a both negative and positive freedom. Such a doctrine entails the recognition that, rather than being an instrument in the hands of others, the person acts with personal responsibility on the basis of his own choices, ideas, and purposes, to which he freely adheres.[14]

The notion of freedom entailed by Constant's political liberalism reflects the strong and weak points of his theory. As mentioned above, modern political liberalism overcame decisively the tradition of the absolute, arbitrary, and in many respects oppressive state in which individuals were often in-

---

tualism, the use of power must abide by the rule of law and therefore be based upon general consensus. The concept of contract was for the sake of mutual advantage instead of the submission of one person to the other. Contractualism therefore entailed the equality and dignity of persons. The false antitheses obfuscate the true contributions of liberal political principles throughout history. Mistakes have also been made by misinterpreting the antitheses within liberal economic theory. Adam Smith constructed his theory concerning the "wealth of the people" in order to contrast the absolute state's appropriation of the creativity and labor of its citizens and material goods under mercantilism. Where mercantilism considered the economy as a zero-sum game, the liberals were convinced that fostering individual liberty and creativity could generate wealth and all could be enriched. Today it is easy to criticize the shortcomings of the early liberal theories and disregard the enormous merits of their conceptual revolution. Those merits are still ignored by those who would address social problems solely with the mechanisms of distributive justice.

13. See Constant, "The Liberty of the Ancients Compared with That of the Moderns," 327.

14. Cf. Isaiah Berlin, "Two Concepts of Liberty," in his *Four Essays on Liberty* (Oxford: Oxford University Press, 1969), 131. For a discussion of Berlin's distinction between negative and positive freedom see Chandran Kukathas, *Liberty,* in *A Companion to Contemporary Political Philosophy,* ed. Robert E. Goodin and Philip Pettit (Oxford: Blackwell, 1993), 534–47.

strumentalized for the sake of the community. Insofar as they embody the rule of law, today's liberal democracies give proof of having achieved the original goal of liberalism. But the weak point of such a liberalism is its tendency to set aside the fundamental question of the human good, the very objective of freedom, insofar as liberalism speaks of only the political-legal conditions of freedom. One could claim that since liberalism is a purely political doctrine it need not address the question of the content of the human good. And in fact, the question of the human good becomes urgent only when criteria must be defined for the application of the coercive measures of the state and when those criteria inevitably imply a specific and controversial conception of the content of the human good. Although such controversy did not arise in the nineteenth century, it does today when, for example, the traditional juridical preference for heterosexual marriage is challenged. Nineteenth-century classical liberal thought, which focused on the problem of guaranteeing the freedom of the individual against the threat of public authority, coincided with a historical period of broad social consensus regarding the essential components of public morality, and therefore generally lacked an awareness of the problem of conflicting views of the human good. An awareness of the problem entailed by liberalism's reticence regarding of the content of the human good could mature only once the broad consensus regarding public morality broke down.[15]

Liberalism, therefore, may be considered a political doctrine centered upon the value of personal freedom, or the autonomy of the individual in the face of the coercive power of the state. As a political doctrine, liberalism attempts to answer the question of how to organize public power in order to attain the aim of government while preserving and promoting the freedom of every citizen. Liberalism holds personal freedom as the first and most indispensable condition for the development and well-being of all.

Liberalism as Moral Ideal and Comprehensive Ethical Doctrine

The second version of classical liberalism was originally developed within a comprehensive moral-philosophical theory and not simply as the solution to a contingent political problem. This second version primarily

---

15. For an informative discussion of the development of liberalism, see Thomas A. Spragens Jr., "Communitarian Liberalism," in *New Communitarian Thinking. Persons, Virtues, Institutions, and Communities,* ed. Amitai Etzioni (Charlottesville: University Press of Virginia, 1995), 37–51.

proposes a theory of the person as free and autonomous and then, only secondarily, attempts to express that theory in political principles. Its human ideal is one of rational autonomy (Kant) and the formation of one's humanity and individuality (von Humboldt and Mill). Such a comprehensive liberalism obviously does not contradict the first; rather it *can be* a philosophical complement to it, even if it seems, as in the cases of Kant and von Humboldt, to lack the philosophical realism of the first version. Like later German liberalism, these authors, on account of their naiveté and excessive confidence in the force of rational arguments, failed to fully appreciate the need for constitutional constraints on the supreme power. They failed to see the need to use power to control power. Kant's failure to recognize the danger of an expanding state is reflected in his unconditional repudiation of any right to resistance. Von Humboldt's failure is reflected in what history would show to be a politically naive chimera: the liberal state as the final product of a slow process of moral progress toward the appreciation of freedom.[16]

In Kantian philosophy man's image is that of an autonomous individual whose dignity consists in being exclusively subject to a self-imposed law. Kant's image ends up justifying the liberal state as a state of law that guarantees the coexistence of free individualism, rather than as a means of protecting the individual's autonomy from the public power. According to the Kantian image, public power is designed to establish an order in which coercive laws allow for the coexistence of competing personal autonomies. Applying to such an order the traditional adage *salus publica, suprema civitatis lex,* Kant declared illicit all resistance to public power, even if despotic. He did so because such resistance could endanger the fundamental public principle: to guarantee the individual's autonomy from potential conflict with the autonomy of others. The liberal state inspired by the Kantian image primarily promotes individual autonomy as *neutrality* concerning the various possible concepts of the human good and the ways of incorporating it in one's life. Each person is to find *his own* way to obtain happiness, provided that he does not violate the rights of others.[17] According to the

16. Friedrich Schiller forcefully expressed this same idea in his "Über die aesthetische Erziehung des Menschen in einer Reihe von Briefen," in Schiller, *Sämtliche Werke* (Munich: Carl Hanser Verlag, 1962), 5:592.

17. Concerning individual autonomy as neutrality in Kant, see his "On the Common Saying: 'This May Be True in Theory, but It Does Not Apply in Practice'"; a partial translation may be found in *Political Writings* (Cambridge: Cambridge University Press, 1991), see especially 73–86.

Kantian model, the liberal state may exercise its public power by adopting any legislative or executive measure, if compatible with autonomy and self-determination.

The concept of such a liberal state inspired Wilhelm von Humboldt's early work, significantly entitled *The Limits of State Action*.[18] The Prussian politician and philosopher stated that the true human end is the maximum and harmonious formation of all of the person's natural forces in order that he become a well-proportioned whole. Freedom is the first and indispensable condition for attaining such integral perfection. Von Humboldt defends freedom primarily for the sake of the individual's development, not to defend the individual from the dangers of abuse from an overreaching public power. Every individual must develop himself, in accord with his particularities, toward a unique and special whole. But since the state tends to suppress that which is most precious, unique, and unrepeatable in the person, it is capable of creating only uniformity. Only the liberal state that allows for a maximum of variety in individual decisions permits the creation of the diversity and individuality necessary for truly personal development.

Von Humboldt's project reflects an admirable appreciation for humanity and includes important elements of truth. His aim of "freedom, tranquility, and the happiness of every individual" compares quite favorably to those political configurations that—as he wrote—aimed to "extract from the nation every possible means for satisfying the ambitions and avarice of a single individual."[19] By reducing the aim of the state to the maintenance of security, von Humboldt positioned himself within the mainstream of liberal thought. In fact, for von Humboldt, "without security, there is no freedom."[20] Civil liberty—that liberty which is assured by law—presupposes and justifies public power. Public power is therefore limited to the task of maintaining liberty. The liberalism of Kant and von Humboldt justifies the liberal state on the basis of its task of guaranteeing the perfection of the individual. Constant had also expressed this same idea but in an importantly different way. Constant's limitation of the range of state power to that of promoting individual perfection did not imply the nature of that perfection. In Kant

---

18. Wilhelm von Humboldt, *The Limits of State Action*, trans. J. W. Burrow (Cambridge: Cambridge University Press, 1969).

19. Wilhelm von Humboldt, *Ideen über Staatsverfassung, durch die neue Französische Constitution veranlasst* (1791), in *Wilhelm Von Humboldt's Gesammelte Werke*, vol. 1 (Charlestown, S.C.: BiblioBazaar, 2008), 35. Editor's translation.

20. Von Humboldt, *The Limits of State Action*, 43.

and von Humboldt we find the enthronement of the freedom of choice in its existential singularity as the ultimate value. Their exaltation of individual autonomy leads to a conception of the state that limits the criteria for licit interference in the life of the individual to the sole purpose of conserving freedom of choice, but without any consideration of the good for which this freedom is used.[21]

In similar fashion and with explicit reference to von Humboldt, John Stuart Mill expounded his theory of individuality.[22] Mill advocated the intrinsic value of free choice, and therefore favored a life of individual responsibility rather than adherence to custom. Mill's defense of individuality included the claim that when a minimum of common sense and experience is assumed, every person's "own mode of laying out his existence is best, not because it is the best in itself, *but because it is his own mode.*"[23] Within the limits of "common sense" and "experience," there are a wide variety of life plans, some "objectively" superior to the others. Nevertheless, as Mill proposed, that life which each one lives on the basis of his own choice is for him the best inasmuch as it is precisely his. Mill, however, only superficially addressed the problem of determining the limits of "common sense" and "experience."

From the fundamental moral value of individuality, Mill derives the *harm principle,* according to which everyone must be left free to do that which he considers good provided that it does not harm others. This highly debated principle requires that the criteria regulating the public power's licit interference in the lives of individuals be established on the basis of the moral value of the autonomy of choice, an autonomy that is at the service of one's own individuality.[24] A full and accurate evaluation of Mill's liberal-

21. Once again Constant is more concerned with limiting the sovereign's power—even that of the sovereign people—than with imposing moral restrictions. See his "On the Sovereignty of the People," within the chapter entitled "Principles of Politics Applicable to All Representative Governments" in *Political Writings,* where he proposes as "the important truth" and the "eternal principle" that "sovereignty is limited, and that there are wills which neither the people, nor its delegates, have the right to have" (180). In consequence, "the will of an entire people cannot make just what is unjust" (182). Moreover, "the assent of the majority is not enough, in any case, to legitimate its acts: there are acts that nothing could possibly sanction." (177).

22. See John Stuart Mill's epigraph to *On Liberty,* in *Utilitarianism, On Liberty, and Considerations on Representative Government,* ed. H. B. Acton (London: J. M. Dent & Sons, 1972), where Mill quotes Wilhelm von Humboldt while writing: "The grand, leading principle, towards which every argument unfolded in theses pages directly converges, is the absolute and essential importance of human development in its richest diversity."

23. Emphasis added. John Stuart Mill, *On Liberty,* 116. See also 125: "If a person possesses any tolerable amount of common sense and experience, his own mode of laying out his existence is the best, not because it is the best in itself, but because it is his own mode."

24. Ibid., 114 and 136ff.

ism requires that one take into account the social context of his time: the puritan society of the Victorian age in which the public power kept itself busy watching over the integrity of the moral conduct of its subjects. Mill explicitly declares that a man who, for reasons of intemperance and extravagance, is unable to pay his creditors and thus ruins his family is perhaps justly punished, but only for his failure to fulfill his obligation to creditors and family, and not, however, for his intemperance and extravagance.[25] The *harm principle* could therefore be understood as simply the *formal* criterion of interference—in the example above by means of the criminal penal law. Mill therefore promotes a vision of the state that limits itself to guaranteeing individual freedom and a just social order without, however, assuming responsibility for the moral integrity of its subjects.

The Strong Concept of Autonomy

The problematic point, for Mill but even more so for Kant, is what I call the "strong concept of autonomy." In accord with this strong concept, personal freedom and autonomy find their ultimate justification in the free exercise of the capacity to choose and not in the good for which this capacity is being exercised. Therefore, unless the exercise of one's autonomy were to impede the exercise of another's autonomy, every interference of the state in individual freedom would be illicit. In contrast, a "weak concept of autonomy" conceives autonomy as the capacity for the free choice of substantial goods in such a way that these goods confer authentic value upon the capacity to choose. A weak concept of autonomy, which merely holds that freedom is indispensable for moral adherence to any good, does not include the criteria needed to distinguish between an exercise of autonomy that profits from its intrinsic value and one that violates it. In contrast, the strong concept of autonomy sees a substantial value in the capacity to choose among alternatives and needs no further justification for its free exercise than autonomy itself. Any use of autonomy will therefore find approval. Any choice will be intrinsically valid so long as it is a free choice.

However, like the weak concept of autonomy, the strong concept holds that only a *rational* choice can be called free. Because it sees rationality as a condition for autonomy, the strong concept requires—at least implicitly—an additional epistemological thesis. And this is a thesis that cannot but

25. Ibid., 138.

deny reason's intrinsic ordination to the truth about the good.[26] The denial of reason's tendency toward truth leads to a voluntaristic concept of choice. The strong concept of autonomy maintains that free choice—the exercise of autonomy—is the ultimate foundation of the goodness of every choice, independent of its substantial content. All things considered, it is an affirmation not so much of the autonomy of reason but of the autonomy of the *will*. It is an affirmation of an autonomy guaranteed by the formal principle of the submission of the will to the law of reason. Yet, this law of reason is a law that while not indicating any good frees us from any heteronomy; that is, from being determined by an empirical good.[27] Consequently, the weak and the strong concepts of autonomy are distinguished by the fact that only the first recognizes that freedom is intrinsically limited by the good to which it is ordered and by the truth about this good. According to the strong concept of autonomy, freedom as such is susceptible to only extrinsic and never intrinsic limitation. That is, freedom may be limited only by the coexistence of a plurality of freedoms.

The liberal might object that I misunderstand the nature of liberalism since it never intends to promote a philosophical anthropology, but only aims to promote an exclusively political doctrine.[28] In fact, there are many today who defend a liberal political philosophy who no longer see the liberal state as an expression of an anthropological and moral ideal. Instead, they see it as a mere political instrument that makes public institutions possible in a society in which there is no longer a consensus regarding the good, that is, regarding those goods that guide human freedom. Consequently, a notion such as the strong concept of autonomy would be understood not as a moral ideal but as the *political norm* of equal respect for freedom. While recogniz-

---

26. See Thomas A. Spragens Jr., *The Irony of Liberal Reason* (Chicago & London: University of Chicago Press, 1981), 384. Taking an extreme position, Bruce A. Ackermann, in *Social Justice in the Liberal State* (New Haven, Conn.: Yale University Press, 1980) speaks of a *liberal skepticism* according to which neither the universe nor the human person possess any meaning that is not conferred on them by each one of us. For Ackermann's liberal skepticism we cannot have any knowledge of the good but only some beliefs. Ackermann contends that "there is no moral meaning hidden in the bowels of the universe.... We may create our own meanings, you and I; however transient or superficial, these are the only meanings we will ever know" (368).

27. See Immanuel Kant's *Critique of Practical Reason*, where he proposes the autonomy of the will as the sole principle of every moral law and duty. For a discussion of the difference between the autonomy of reason (typical of the Thomistic tradition) and the autonomy of will, see my *The Perspective of Morality: Philosophical Bases of Thomistic Virtue Ethics* (Washington D.C.: The Catholic University of America Press, 2011). This was originally published as *La prospettiva della morale* (Roma: Armando, 1994).

28. For the claim that liberalism need not promote a philosophical anthropology, see Charles Larmore, *Patterns of Moral Complexity* (Cambridge: Cambridge University Press, 1987) and Stephen Holmes, *The Anatomy of Antiliberalism*, especially 189.

ing that the perennially valid nucleus of liberalism is an essentially political doctrine, I contend that liberalism, like all other political philosophies, remains inexorably linked to a vision of man. My claim that all political theories involve anthropological implications is not necessarily a disadvantage for liberalism. But to make the claim is to require a careful elucidation of the anthropological implications of those doctrines that claim to be "neutral." The full development of a political theory requires a description of its anthropological implications. Each version of liberalism entails its own anthropology. Recent attempts to render political liberalism independent from all pre-political conceptions of man and of the human good fail to provide a full account of their own foundation.

The Anthropological Implications of Recent Theories of Liberalism

The Early Position of Rawls

In *A Theory of Justice,* Rawls states that moral personality is characterized by the capacity to form a concept of the good and to have a sense of justice.[29] In each person the capacity to form a concept of the good is expressed in the rational plan for his personal and private life. The capacity for a sense of justice is seen in the individual's desire to act in the public sphere on the basis of specific principles of justice. Rawls formulates a theory of the liberal state in which the individual operates on two levels: the public level, which is regulated by the principles of justice, and the private or personal level, normatively regulated by those goods that the individual rationally proposes to pursue. According to Rawls, human society is an enterprise of cooperation for mutual advantage. Therefore, society must be regulated by principles that can be shared by all. For these principles to be held in common they must not favor any particular conception of the good and they must correspond to *fairness.* Rawls relegates to the individual the determination of his own personal and private fulfillment. The "just" has priority over the "good" because the principles of justice are not determined by any particular conception of the "good life," and the legitimacy of any particular conception of the good and of the corresponding life plan(s) is consequently dependent upon their compatibility with the principles of justice.

29. See, for example, *A Theory of Justice,* 561.

The principles of justice, or rules of fairness, are determined by considering the members of society as individuals who stipulate a hypothetical contract. Not knowing their position within the future society, or even their sex, color, talents, and interests, they find themselves in what Rawls calls the "original position" in which all are cloaked in a "veil of ignorance." The rules of justice thus elaborated can be accepted by all as the foundation for society. They express a political consensus unburdened from all those particular outlooks (e.g., diverse conceptions of the good life, religious beliefs, and moral doctrines) that divide a pluralist society. Within the limits established by the structural foundation, each one can live according to his concept of the good and simultaneously live and cooperate in a productive way with his fellow citizens on the basis of a publicly valid, common conception of justice. Such a community is what Rawls calls a "well-ordered society."[30]

With the first formulation of his theory, Rawls was convinced that his conception of justice as fairness, and more especially the method for determining the principles of justice from the original position, was an expression of the essential autonomy of the person according to the Kantian model.[31] Rawls's notion of autonomy entails an implication that has been criticized by communitarians. Each person finds himself in an original and quasi ontological distance with respect to the possible ends or goods chosen by him. This ontological independence of the self from any conception of the good is the anthropological foundation for the primacy of justice with respect to the adherence to any particular concept of the good. The priority of justice over the good is therefore a manifestation of a specific human ideal.[32] Rawls contends, moreover, that human reason can produce only a plurality of contradictory conceptions of the good; and therefore, in his more recent publications, defends a *reasonable pluralism*. Thus, the conception of justice as *fairness* becomes for Rawls an expression of the free and autonomous person who, in a well-ordered society and in coexistence with other autonomous individuals, can express his own diversity and singularity. It is not coincidental that Rawls refers to von Humboldt in outlining the prospect of a community whose members enjoy diversity and singularity under the coordination of, and unified by, liberal institutions.[33]

30. Ibid., 4ff.
31. See Larmore, *Patterns of Moral Complexity*, 120.
32. Larmore uses the term "expressivism" to denote those political doctrines, like that of the first Rawls, which express a specific human ideal. See *Patterns of Moral Complexity*, 76.
33. *A Theory of Justice*, 523.

The Communitarian Critique of the Liberal Image of Man

Communitarian critiques of Rawlsian liberalism have always targeted the concept of the person implicit in liberal theories of justice.[34] The communitarians claim that the liberal theory entails a concept of the person as a radically nonsituated, or unencumbered, self, whose very existence would be impossible. For the communitarians everything must begin with the existence of a relationship between the self and the society through which one's identity is constituted. Moreover, as Sandel emphasizes, the self cannot be defined independently of the ends he chooses. A person is a certain type of person according to the goods that he pursues. The communitarians therefore object to the liberal precedence of the just over the good. Given that the self is always found situated within a social context in a narrative unity of life, it is unthinkable to establish rules of justice that do not already reflect some good that is constitutive of the identity of the self. The rules of justice would be morally relevant only insofar as they reflect some good for the person. Moreover, the communitarians claim that the reasonableness implicit in Rawls's original position is fictitious and that this supposedly neutral proposal actually conceals the strong anthropological presupposition of his liberalism: an autonomous self whose identity is forged in complete independence and original indifference with regard to any concept of the good. The liberal self would generate only the mere illusion of the possibility of establishing principles of justice *independently* of a determined conception of the good.

Charles Taylor has coined the term "atomism" to describe this concept of the individual.[35] The atomist self suffers from a self-understanding that is independent and prior to the society in which he is existentially situated, a society for which he has a merely instrumental function. Taylor believes that atomism is intimately linked to that modern spirit of contractualism, which proposes "a vision of society as in some sense constituted by individuals for the fulfillment of ends which were primarily individual."[36] Ac-

---

34. The most important and brilliant text is the book of Michael J. Sandel, *Liberalism and the Limits of Justice* (Cambridge: Cambridge University Press, 1982). See also Alasdair MacIntyre, *After Virtue: A Study in Moral Theory,* 2nd ed. (Notre Dame: University of Notre Dame Press, 1984); Charles Taylor, "Identity and the Good," part 1 of *Sources of the Self: The Making of the Modern Identity* (Cambridge: Cambridge University Press, 1989).

35. Charles Taylor, "Atomism," in his *Philosophy and the Human Sciences,* Philosophical Papers 2 (Cambridge: Cambridge University Press, 1985), 187–210.

36. Ibid., 187.

cording to an atomistic conception, autonomy entails the absolute primacy of the freedom to choose one's lifestyle over any conception of the good. Such autonomy renders impossible any comparative and objective judgment about the morality of various lifestyles.[37] This concept of autonomy therefore presupposes a procedural and nonsubstantial conception of practical reason, capable of formulating principles of justice without, however, being able to make "strong evaluations" regarding the good of the person.[38]

The communitarians hold that the individual cannot be understood independently of the social picture into which he is integrated and that living in society is a necessary condition of rationality.[39] The self does not exist and cannot be articulated without presupposing some relationship with society and the corresponding experiences of the good. Sandel believes that it is not even possible to imagine ourselves as the sort of being that Rawls's theory requires us to be.[40] Taylor seems to utilize the critique not so much to attack liberalism but to establish the very real presuppositions that it implies. He concludes that the autonomous and self-determined liberal self needs the context of a society that promotes the value of autonomy as a good in the "strong" and substantial sense.[41] According to Taylor's discovery of the liberal's hidden presupposition of the promotion of autonomy as the fundamental good, it would seem that the liberal's claim to the priority of the just over the good is to be discarded. A conception of the just requires a strong appreciation of those goods that are capable of rendering justice intelligible *as a moral value*.[42]

In my opinion, this critique expresses an acute analysis of the problematic moral and anthropological presuppositions of that type of liberalism that is based on a strong concept of autonomy. Nonetheless, I also hold that the communitarian critique is mistaken about that which is most specific to

37. See ibid., 196.

38. See Taylor, *Sources of the Self,* 86–89; also Michael J. Sandel, "The Procedural Republic and the Unencumbered Self," *Political Theory* 1 (1984): 81–96.

39. This thesis was first formulated by Alasdair MacIntyre, *After Virtue,* see especially 236ff. MacIntyre has further developed it in *Whose Justice? Which Rationality?* (Notre Dame: University of Notre Dame Press, 1988), and more recently in *Dependent Rational Animals: Why Human Beings Need the Virtues* (Chicago: Open Court, 1999).

40. See Sandel, *Liberalism and the Limits of Justice,* 14.

41. See Taylor, "Atomism," 205–9. Taylor emphasizes that there is not necessarily a contrast between a liberal political culture and a communitarian one. For him it is conceivable, in the more republican-participatory tradition of civic humanism, to have a liberalism that is not "atomistic" but "holistic." See also Charles Taylor, "Cross Purposes: The Liberal-Communitarian Debate," in *Liberalism and the Moral Life,* ed. Nancy L. Rosenblum, (Cambridge, Mass.: Harvard University Press, 1991), 159–83.

42. Taylor, *Sources of the Self,* 89.

liberalism as a political doctrine. Even if the concept of the unencumbered self and the idea of a priority of procedural justice over a substantial concept of the good reflect an untenable anthropology, they express an institutional-political logic that can withstand the force of the communitarian critique. The institutional-political logic of liberalism demands a certain capacity—typical for a citizen of a liberal democracy—to distance himself from himself and the particular interests of his personal life in order to be able to act in view of the common good and according to the universally accepted norms of the public sphere.[43] Moreover, the normative and descriptive affirmations of the communitarian critique are confused insofar as they fail to distinguish between liberal theory and liberal society.[44]

In the last analysis, communitarianism embraces a very dubious vision of "community" that offers few desirable political prospects. Communitarianism seems to be blind to the value of the original intentions of liberalism: to create a juridical-political order that guarantees the control of power, the rule of the law, and the protection of fundamental liberties of the individual.

Even if the communitarian critique contains some elements of valid political anthropology and epistemology, it is founded on the idea that the constitutive element of the self, and therefore of the person as moral subject, is the insertion of the individual into a specific context of social community, traditions, and corresponding practices. The potential political deductions of such a claim are disturbing, not because of what they affirm, but because of the confusion that they can cause concerning the institutional conditions of liberty. In fact, the communitarian seems to favor a certain predisposition to despise those liberal institutions that have proven to be indispensable presuppositions of a society in which every citizen enjoys the liberty that is due him as a human being and as a person who by his nature transcends the political community in which he lives.

In other words, the communitarian critique of liberalism is a two-sided coin. The communitarians legitimately critique the concept of an individual whose freedom and autonomy are defined merely in terms of the capacity to choose one's own lifestyle, independent of any moral account for discrimi-

43. See Holmes, *The Anatomy of Antiliberalism*, 238–40; Stephen Macedo, *Liberal Virtues: Citizenship, Virtue, and Community in Liberal Constitutionalism* (Oxford: Clarendon Press, 1990), 240–51.

44. The lack of distinction between a critique of theory and society is what Stephen Holmes calls *the shifting target* of the communitarian critique. See *The Anatomy of Antiliberalism*, 181. The communitarian critique has also been criticized for a certain confusion between the literary tradition, like that which is Aristotelian, and the actual political conditions of the past. See Robert Alan Dahl, *Democracy and Its Critics* (New Haven, Conn.: Yale University Press, 1989), 299ff.

nating between right and wrong. But the communitarian critique leaves unresolved the question of its own implications for the due political and institutional form of society. In particular, the communitarian critique leaves unresolved the question, *quis interpretabitur? quis iudicabitur?*—who will decide what is good and what is bad?[45]

At this point liberalism opts for a resolute neutrality by defining itself as a political system capable of establishing a social order that does not base itself on the public and coercive influence of any specific concept of the good life. Furthermore, this liberal social order affirms, by means of the idea of fundamental rights, a primacy and independence of man *as man* over values that dominate through specific traditions, communities, or collective practices. Liberalism's appeal to fundamental rights surely does not resolve the problems raised by the critics of liberalism. Liberalism leaves these questions open so that they may be resolved in accord with the specifically political values of the liberal constitutional state.[46]

While seeming to despise the liberal universalism of human rights and to opt for a republicanism based on the idea of social integration and civic participation in a *community of virtue,* communitarianism does not really offer an institutional alternative.[47] Is liberalism possible without a strong concept of autonomy?

45. Obviously, MacIntyre's reference to the classic doctrine that the true good appears good only to the virtuous, which implies that not all humans have the same capacity for moral knowledge, is important for moral theory—see Alasdair MacIntyre, *Three Rival Versions of Moral Enquiry: Encyclopedia, Genealogy, and Tradition* (Notre Dame: University of Notre Dame Press, 1990). However, it is not clear what political consequences follow from it. For MacIntyre it seems obvious that from the fact that in order to read a book correctly one needs to have a certain moral and intellectual formation, it follows that the public order must meet corresponding standards. MacIntyre therefore asserts that the above-mentioned fact is "alien to the assumption of liberal modernity that every rational adult should be free to and is able to read every book" (133). If "liberal modernity" refers to the liberal political culture, I do not see what consequence other than censorship MacIntyre can draw from his affirmation. It would seem that MacIntyre does not intend to suggest any specific political consequence. Yet, this lack of clarity between policy and political theory makes dialogue between communitarians and liberals so difficult.

46. Undoubtedly, the so-called communitarian movement operates in large part within the tradition of the liberal, democratic, and constitutional state. Underlining personal responsibility seems to be more liberal than welfare and state-centered liberalism. See for example Amitai Etzioni, *The Spirit of Community: Rights, Responsibilities and the Communitarian Agenda* (London: Fontana Press, 1995); Mary Ann Glendon, *Rights Talk: The Impoverishment of Political Discourse* (New York: Free Press, 1991). See also Amitai Etzioni's anthology, *New Communitarian Thinking: Persons, Virtues, Institutions, and Communities* (Charlottesville: University Press of Virginia, 1995). A certain convergence between liberal and communitarian thought can be faintly seen in Amy Gutmann, "Communitarian Critics of Liberalism," *Philosophy and Public Affairs* 14 (1985): 308–22. For Michael Walzer, "The Communitarian Critique of Liberalism," in *Political Theory* 18 (1990): 6–23, the communitarian critique is nothing more than an inevitable concomitant phenomenon—the accompanying music so to speak—of the reality of the liberal state, and in this sense is perhaps one of its correctives.

47. On "community of virtue" see MacIntyre, *After Virtue,* 236.

Modifications and Nuances: The Liberal Response
to the Communitarian Critique

Neutrality and Anti-perfectionism

In various articles, brought together and synthesized in his *Political Liberalism*,[48] Rawls modified significantly his earlier theory to favor a concept of liberalism as a merely political, *freestanding view:* that is, a view that is independent of any comprehensive moral or metaphysical doctrine, while still—nonetheless—being moral. Charles Larmore, the liberal political philosopher who criticized Rawls's earlier position for its dependence on a specific vision of man, elaborated his version of a merely political concept of liberalism as a political doctrine based on the idea of a *modus vivendi,* an idea that originates more from a strategic and pragmatic consensual calculation than from a general philosophical theory. Thus, Larmore's proposal may be classified within the tradition of the political formulas for peace formulated during the European religious wars.

Both Rawls's freestanding view and Larmore's *modus vivendi* are anti-perfectionist and neutralist.[49] They maintain that public institutions, and especially the coercive power of the state, must avoid any measures that intend to influence the citizen, in the sense of promoting his moral perfection, in the direction of a determined conception of the good life. Instead, public institutions must maintain a rigorous neutrality with regard to the diverse conceptions of the good. The anti-perfectionism and neutrality of both Rawls and Larmore are designed to avoid any appeal, even implicit, to a philosophical anthropology, by limiting themselves to practical principles of an exclusively *political* nature.

The Second Rawls: Political Liberalism as a Freestanding View
and the Problem of the Concept of Reasonable Pluralism

In *Political Liberalism,* Rawls begins with the presupposition of the existence of fundamental disagreement, or political pluralism, regarding the

48. John Rawls, *Political Liberalism* (New York: Columbia University Press, 1996). This book integrates the ideas of some previous articles such as: "Kantian Constructivism in Moral Theory: The Dewey Lectures," in *Journal of Philosophy* 77 (1980); "Justice as Fairness: Political Not Metaphysical," *Philosophy and Public Affairs* 14, no. 3 (1985); "The Idea of an Overlapping Consensus," *Oxford Journal of Legal Studies* 7 (1992); "The Priority of Right and Ideas of the Good," *Philosophy and Public Affairs* 17 (1988); "Domain of the Political and Overlapping Consensus," *New York University Law Review* 64 (1989).

49. Ronald Dworkin and Bruce A. Ackermann have also developed important responses to the communitarian critiques of liberalism. But my analysis must leave them aside while concentrating on the responses of Rawls and Larmore. I must also set aside Robert Nozick's extreme libertarian individualism.

ultimate and most profound questions concerning the meaning of life. At the same time, he presupposes a need to find a solid foundation on which to base a well-ordered society in which peace and freedom coexist and all citizens cooperate for mutual advantage.[50] In contrast with his earlier *A Theory of Justice*, *Political Liberalism* no longer considers the principles of justice at the basis of social stability as an adequate expression of a "liberal" image of man; rather the principles of justice are simply an expression of a specifically political consensus regarding a partial convergence of the moral convictions of the citizens. This *overlapping consensus* is the sphere of a public reason that corresponds to the principles of fairness that are institutionalized in a basic constitutional order. Such principles are elaborated in the original position, which is no longer presented as an ideal model of practical rationality, with the corresponding anthropological implications, but simply as an "expedient of representation." The original position would now express the position of the person as citizen, responsible for generating the overlapping consensus. Rawls thereby creates a specifically political morality that is independent from but not contrary to all the licit, comprehensive moral and metaphysical doctrines that the citizens might hold.

Is Rawls successful in rendering his theory truly independent of a strong concept of autonomy and its anthropological implications? The only concept of the person that Rawls declares relevant for his theory is a political concept of the person as citizen. According to Rawls, his political concept of the person is entirely free of any anthropological or metaphysical presuppositions.[51] The notion of the person required by his political liberalism corresponds solely to the person as citizen, and not at all to the person simply as he is. It is a *normative,* juridical, and political concept and in no way descriptive, ontological, or anthropological.[52]

Nonetheless, a serious problem still remains concerning the concept of reasonable pluralism. According to Rawls, reasonable pluralism is an inevitable condition that necessitates the pursuit of an overlapping consensus.

---

50. See Rawls, *Political Liberalism,* "Introduction," xviff.

51. See Rawls, "Justice as Fairness: Political Not Metaphysical," and *Political Liberalism,* 29ff.

52. The idea of a normative, juridical, political concept of the person goes back to Thomas Hobbes: according to the ninth law of nature, the condition for being able to enter into the state of civil society is the mutual recognition of the equality among men. "If nature therefore have made men equal, that equality must be acknowledged: or if nature have made men unequal; yet because men that think themselves equal will not enter into conditions of peace, but upon equal terms, such equality must be admitted." Thomas Hobbes, *Leviathan,* chap. 15, as published in *The English Works of Thomas Hobbes,* ed. W. Molesworth (Aalen: Scientia, 1966). See also my *La filosofia politica di Thomas Hobbes: coerenza e contraddizioni di un paradigma* (Rome: Armando, 1997).

The concept of reasonable pluralism implies a strong thesis regarding human rationality, according to which human reason necessarily produces a plurality of contradictory, incompatible, and *reasonable* conceptions of the human good. With his "reasonable pluralism," Rawls does not intend only to refer to a pluralism constituted by the expression of the diversity and plurality of possibilities of adhering to certain fundamental goods and choosing fundamental plans of life: for example, the pluralism constituted by the fact that while acknowledging the goods involved in both married life and celibacy one cannot simultaneously choose both. Rather, Rawls speaks of a reasoned, contradictory affirmation of incompatible positions on the part of different persons. These positions are incompatible not simply existentially but *cognitively,* such that one person could affirm as good that which another finds to be bad, perverse, or even absurd. The term *reasonable pluralism* expresses an incompatibility of reason with itself. According to Rawls this pluralism is not the effect of ignorance, of bad affective disposition, or of prejudice, but rather the inevitable, and therefore "natural," effect of the exercise of reason in the condition of freedom.[53]

Without a doubt, Rawls's reasonable pluralism is a strong anthropological thesis, and yet it is also an indispensable presupposition for his political liberalism. Reasonable pluralism is indispensable for his political liberalism because it is only on the basis of this presupposition that he can consider his conception of political justice a *freestanding view,* independent of every moral and metaphysical conception of the good, while also considering it, nevertheless, as a kind of political morality in addition to being a pragmatic consensus. The thesis of the natural pluralism of reason regarding the truth about the good seems to be the essential presupposition of a political philosophy of overlapping consensus among persons who, while disagreeing at one level, may agree on another level of reason, that is, at the level of a public reason that is concretized in the constitutional order found at the very basis of the liberal state.

Rawls's political liberalism therefore entails limiting the sphere of public reason to topics that are independent of those comprehensive conceptions of the good to which individual citizens adhere. In a recent critique,

---

53. See Rawls, *Political Liberalism,* "Introduction," xviff., 36ff., 58, and 144. Rawls attempts to explain this inevitable condition of reasonable disagreement with what he calls *the burdens of judgment* (see 54ff.). However, the doctrine seems rather obscure and even unconvincing because Rawls never shows why the fact of pluralism in society necessarily excludes the possibility of a concept of reason that is at once intelligible, compatible with itself, and respectful of the richness and diversity of reality.

Michael Sandel uses the example of the abortion debate to demonstrate the absurdity of such a restriction of the public use of reason.[54] Sandel observes that Rawls's restriction necessarily leads to the exclusion of the most morally decisive aspects of the question and in fact favors a specific moral vision of the question.[55]

Sandel—and also Taylor—shows that even with the presuppositions of a liberal constitutional order, the intrinsic connection between publicly valid principles and a specific conception of the good remains intact. And once one acknowledges the inseparability of public principles and particular conceptions of the good, Rawls's attempt to base his idea of a liberal constitutional order, based on an overlapping consensus on the idea of reason's "natural" incompatibility with itself, is seen as highly subversive of social stability. Rawls's proposal embodies a potentially subversive impetus insofar as his "overlapping consensus" is a much more ambitious instrument than a simple *"modus vivendi."* "Overlapping consensus" is the partial convergence on the level of the just of the various comprehensive convictions of citizens regarding the good. For Rawls, this partial convergence of convictions constitutes a moral value of its own that is meant to confer unity and stability on the whole of society. Yet, how could the partial convergence of convictions, whose source is a Rawlsian type of reasoning, ever generate a consensus that could enjoy the freestanding intelligibility that is absolutely necessary in order for such a consensus to serve as the basis for the stability

54. See Michael J. Sandel's *Liberalismus und Republikanismus: Von der Notwendigkeit der Bürgertugend* (Vienna: Passagen Verlag, 1995), 45–54; partially based on his earlier "Political Liberalism," *Harvard Law Review* 107 (1994): 1765–94; and John M. Finnis, "Public Reason, Abortion, and Cloning," *Valparaiso University Law Review* 32, no. 2 (1998): 361–82; and my essay entitled "Fundamental Rights, Moral Law, and the Legal Defense of Life in a Constitutional Democracy," in chapter 7 of my *Ethics of Procreation and the Defense of Human Life*, ed. William F. Murphy Jr. (Washington, D.C.: The Catholic University of America Press, 2010), and originally published in *American Journal of Jurisprudence* 43 (1998): 135–83.

55. Moreover, Sandel states, such a restriction would attack the very ideal of liberalism that is based on the mutual respect that citizens have for their profound convictions. While liberalism allows for respect for the convictions of others by suspending them for the sake of political debate, Sandel contends that it would be more deeply respectful to take the convictions of others into serious consideration by reflecting on them. With appreciation for the first part of his critique, Sandel's final argument does not seem completely convincing. It misses its target because political liberalism does not state that we must not take into consideration the most profound convictions of all our citizens. Rather, it intends to form a public procedure to establish a consensus even when there are irreconcilable differences among members of society. Alasdair MacIntyre's acute and provocative observation (*Whose Justice? Which Rationality?* 344) concerning the greater prevalence of lawyers than philosophers in the liberal state is also insufficient as a critique of liberalism. While the prevalence of litigation is a consequence of a civilization in which the ultimate resources of public debate are the arguments of lawyers and the verdicts of judges, to my mind, a liberal polity need not exclude deeper resources for debate.

of a just society? What we are really facing here is a political morality and a public rationality created *ex nihilo.* If this is the case, then Rawls's position therefore can be justified only as a (albeit more sophisticated, but precarious) version of a *modus vivendi*-theory.[56]

The Liberalism of the *Modus Vivendi* of Larmore

I contend that in certain aspects the concept of *modus vivendi* provides a more plausible foundation for the idea of a liberal, democratic constitutionalism than Rawls's overlapping consensus with its problematic assumptions concerning human reason. The idea of *modus vivendi* is originally strategic. It is a calculation whose reasonableness is derived from the necessity of seeking an alternative to a society divided by conflict. *Modus vivendi* arises from the desire to resolve conflicts in a nonviolent manner by means of universally accepted, institutionalized political rules.[57]

But for Larmore, the idea of *modus vivendi* takes on a larger meaning and is only terminologically distinct from the Rawlsian conception of overlapping consensus.[58] For Rawls, *modus vivendi* denotes a mere strategic position, based on a Hobbesian utilitarian calculation. But political community thus founded would not be stable since it would depend on the momentary distribution of power in accord with a momentary calculus of advantage. According to Larmore, it is necessary to base the idea of *modus vivendi* on a concept of neutrality that implies a basic morality that serves as common ground.[59] This minimal morality is found in the norms of rational discourse and mutual respect. Thus, a society is brought forth in which the rights and duties of the citizen are formulated independently of controversial concep-

---

56. Another possibility would be the anti-foundationalist and postmodern position of Rorty, for whom the rationality of liberalism would reside—for us who live in a liberal culture—simply in the fact that it seems plausible to us because it is our cultural self-comprehension. Every attempt to form any ideological, philosophical foundation within a liberal political culture would be in vain. Rorty proposes such an interpretation of Rawls. See Richard Rorty, "The Priority of Democracy to Philosophy," in *Philosophical Papers,* vol. 1 (Cambridge: Cambridge University Press, 1991). See also Rorty's *Contingency, Irony and Solidarity* (Cambridge: Cambridge University Press, 1989).

57. It is strange that MacIntyre believes this to be the serious error of the liberal culture: "Modern politics is civil war carried out by other means" (*After Virtue,* 253). MacIntyre instead thinks of an ideal society that, as a whole, is based on common, first, moral principles: on a general moral consensus. I do not deny that this is an ideal. But this cannot be a political ideal if politics is meant to create and institutionalize such a consensus *that in fact does not exist.* The liberal political culture provides an answer to exactly this problem. But even if our political culture were "civil war carried out by other means," it might still be able to generate some common principles of a public and political morality and with this a set of common, first, moral principles of a peaceful, free, and just social community.

58. Charles Larmore, "Political Liberalism," *Political Theory* 3 (1990): 339–60.

59. *Political Liberalism,* 346–53.

tions. As a result, "liberalism need not be a 'philosophy of man.'"[60] The norms of rational discourse and mutual respect certainly "do make a certain individualism overriding within the political realm: the rights and duties of citizens must be specifiable in abstraction from any controversial ideals they may share with others. But the two norms do not imply that a broader individualism, concerning the sources of value, must pervade the whole of social life."[61] Therefore, within society, the violation of fundamental rights will be illegal, without, however, preventing the private sphere from being constituted, even on the level of associations, according to "illiberal" values. Thus, Larmore states, the Catholic Church as a legally recognized institution can internally apply principles in contrast with those of the liberal *modus vivendi*. "It may not burn heretics, for that is contrary to their rights as citizens, but it may still excommunicate them."[62]

Examples like this demonstrate the unquestionably positive, differentiated logic of the liberal idea of *modus vivendi*. However, serious problems remain. First, in order to avoid any shadow of "expressivism," Larmore seems to avoid basing his position on any specific conception of human reason. Nevertheless, by affirming that the *modus vivendi* is not a mere product of prudential, strategic calculation but is based on the moral norms of discourse and mutual respect—a morality of procedural neutrality—Larmore implies a substantial thesis concerning human reason. In fact, Larmore affirms that the liberalism of the *modus vivendi* is a good example for demonstrating the anthropological fact of disunity in practical reasoning. The disunity inherent to the political morality of procedural neutrality would also pertain to all the other spheres of morality. For Larmore, morality is therefore a heterogeneous set; the fonts of morality are many, and equally heterogeneous and definitely discordant.[63] It is plausible that Larmore sees no difference between his position and that of Rawls. His proposal actually contains a similar thesis on human reason and human nature and, therefore, entails the same theoretical difficulties mentioned above in my critique of Rawls.

The problem of neutrality therefore still needs to be addressed. *Modus vivendi* means neutrality of the state. Larmore proposes a neutrality of procedures, not of results.[64] According to him such neutrality is a condition of

---

60. Ibid., 351.   61. Ibid., 350.
62. Ibid.
63. Larmore, *Patterns of Moral Complexity,* 130 and 138.
64. See ibid., 44.

legitimacy for every coercive measure of the public authority. One could object that it is not obvious that the implementation of a *modus vivendi* must necessarily *coincide* with the demands of procedural neutrality. Although the democratic constitutional state can be characterized in terms of a *modus vivendi* based on a *juridical* culture of procedural neutrality, this does not entail that the whole publicly accepted *moral* content must limit itself to such a procedural neutrality. In fact the procedural neutrality of the state may be integrated into the framework of an institutional order permeated by a minimum of substantial assumptions concerning the human good so long as those assumptions meet the following criteria: They (1) support at least some ideal of autonomy and procedural equality, (2) find support in an ample consensus, and (3) safeguard the fundamental rights of liberty. Some of the communitarian proposals suggest such a solution, as do the proposals made by some antineutralist liberals.[65]

Anti-neutrality and Liberal Perfectionism

An Example: Homosexual "Marriages"

More recent currents of liberalism maintain that every form of neutrality is illusory because neutrality means selectivity; but selective neutrality is not neutral.[66] William Galston therefore concludes that "no form of political life can be justified without some view of what is good for individuals."[67] The antineutralist liberals therefore hold that liberalism ought to promote and even inevitably does promote specific moral values. Liberalism is a political system dedicated to protecting and fostering certain values, attitudes, and the corresponding virtues. The first and most fundamental of these values is autonomy, in the strong sense.

---

65. Regarding the similarities of my proposal with some communitarians', see Michael J. Perry, *Morality, Politics, and Law* (Oxford: Oxford University Press, 1988); especially 102ff. For a critical examination of the idea of neutrality contained in the liberal concept of tolerance, see Susan Mendus, *Toleration and the Limits of Liberalism* (London: Macmillan, 1989).

66. Macedo, *Liberal Virtues*, 262.

67. William A. Galston, *Liberal Purposes: Goods, Virtues, and Diversity in the Liberal State* (Cambridge: Cambridge University Press, 1991), 79. Ronald Dworkin also holds that a view of the good is necessary for political life, but proposes "equal concern and respect" as the fundamental good of the individual in order to coordinate a view of the good with political neutrality. Concerning Dworkin's "ethical individualism" see his "Freiheit, Gleichheit und Gemeinschaft," in *Die liberale Gesellschaft*, ed. Michalski, 69–102; and his "Liberal Community," *California Law Review* 77 (1989): 479–504. See also *Taking Rights Seriously* (London: Duckworth, 1977), 180ff. and 266–78, and his important article "Liberalism," in *Public and Private Morality,* ed. Stuart Hampshire (Cambridge: Cambridge University Press, 1978), 113–43.

Before further discussing this antineutralist and perfectionist variant of liberalism, I would like to highlight one of the fundamental problems of the concept of *modus vivendi* when based solely on the idea of procedural neutrality. The problem, which also exists for Rawls's theory of overlapping consensus, is that the liberal principle of equal rights cannot function in an impartial, neutral manner. It is inevitably loaded with presuppositions concerning the good. Take for example the right to freely choose one's marriage partner. This right may be duly claimed by anyone within certain legal limits. Now, imagine a homosexual couple that on the basis of the right to marry whomever they wish requests to contract a legally recognized union equivalent to marriage. A refusal of their request would be denounced as a violation of the right to freely choose one's partner. The rejection of this supposed right would be considered a pernicious form of discrimination. If, however, the right to freely choose one's marriage partner is formulated within the context of presupposed, specific, normative notions regarding the legal properties of marriage—that is, a union of lives between two persons of opposite sex, open to transmitting life, and providing education for that new life—then a homosexual couple could not appeal to this right since they do not intend to contract that which the law comprehends and recognizes as marriage. If, on the contrary, the formulation of the right to freely choose one's partner were silent regarding presuppositions such as heterosexuality and reproduction, then the homosexual couple could claim the right to contract matrimony. In this last case, it would be wrong, however, to conclude that the state is neutral. Suppose there were a new, different, and more ample definition of "marriage," the effect would be a new and different definition of traditional marriage. The publicly recognized character of marriage would no longer have anything to do with heterosexuality, or with the procreative and educational implications of heterosexuality. Whether presupposing the traditional understanding of marriage or attempting to evade any such presupposition, the state inevitably links the fundamental rights of the citizen to a specific, strong conception of the good, to an ideal for human life, and to a specific meaning for a social institution.

It is therefore impossible that, in analogous cases, the juridical order of society could remain entirely neutral. Nonetheless, the exclusion of the neutralist possibility does not necessarily lead to a perfectionist approach, because the refusal to equate homosexual and traditional heterosexual marriages need not be based on the moral perversity or repugnance of homosexual acts. The choice not to equate the two forms of union may be made on the basis of a rationality that expresses the content of an exclusively public morality. To exclusively privilege heterosexual unions may correspond to a moral judgment based merely on public interest and utility, namely, the protection of the union between man and woman that serves the transmission of life. The affective life and unions of homosexuals belong solely to the private sphere. There is no justification for conferring on them the privileges conferred on heterosexual unions for the sake of public interest, because there is no corresponding public interest proper to homosexual unions.

The distinction between the public interest involved in the child-rearing capacity of heterosexual unions and the lack thereof in homosexual unions is obviously also a distinction between the morality per se and in principle between heterosexual and homosexual love. The particular moral dignity of traditional marriage is based upon its being a procreative and educative community within the larger, public community. It is therefore impossible to always separate public morality from private morality and the just from the good, because an aspect of the human good, even a "private" aspect, involves a social dimension, which is relevant to the community and therefore also an issue of public order.[68] While recognizing the specificity of public morality, the unity of the person prevents separating morality into heterogeneous spheres.

The Impossibility of Neutrality and Impartiality:
The Liberal Response

The liberals that defend the antineutralist position attempt to relativize and minimize the difference between the public and private spheres because they are convinced that liberal political norms help structure private life according to the ideal of autonomy.[69] The choice to give homosexuals equal rights, in the example mentioned, could therefore be motivated by the ideal of strong autonomy as the most fundamental value. The right to free choice,

68. My argument for exclusively heterosexual marriage within a liberal polity proceeds in the inverse manner to Sandel's. Sandel seems to proceed from the immorality or morality of certain practices to the creation of corresponding legislation. I propose to move from the social interest or utility of certain practices to a moral appreciation for these practices that would justify their privileged public position. For Sandel's argument, see his article "Moral Argument and Liberal Toleration: Abortion and Homosexuality," *California Law Review* 77 (1989): 521–38, reprinted in *New Communitarian Thinking*, ed. Etzioni, 71–87.

69. Macedo, *Liberal Virtues*, 263–65.

or autonomy, would therefore be the trump value. Homosexual unions could, therefore, be legally equated with traditional marriage in order to increase the range of autonomy.

Even an antineutral liberalism that promotes the value of autonomy would in many cases arrive at the same conclusions as the purportedly neutral liberalism. Stephen Macedo states the case in provocative fashion. An antineutral liberalism promises, or better yet threatens, to make the whole world like California. By encouraging tolerance and sympathy for so vast an array of lifestyles and eccentricities, liberalism would create a community in which everyone could decide to abandon their career, their spouse, and their children, and enter a Buddhist sect—all within a week. Granted, such a continuously changing society would entail an exciting variety of possible choices and ways of self-fulfillment. But Macedo concludes that liberalism will not please those who are seeking an ultimate and definitive answer to the question of how to live, or to any of the other great questions of human life.[70]

Macedo's critique warns of the specter of an all-encompassing, even totalitarian liberalism, unwilling to coexist with rival conceptions of freedom. Since such a liberalism tends to consider rival viewpoints as intolerant, it therefore permits any intolerance toward that intolerance which threatens the liberal's tolerance. Such a non-neutralist liberalism openly aims to form society and human relations according to its specific vision of human perfection.

Nonetheless, it should be granted that non-neutralist liberalism takes into account some of the important gaps of previous liberal theories. For instance, non-neutralist liberalism resolves the insufficiency of the concept of a mere *modus vivendi*, the impossibility of totally separating a public political morality from those goods that are fundamental for private life, and therefore the impossibility of a public discourse entirely independent of that moral discourse which is valid at the personal level. But the problem of a strong concept of autonomy remains. All of these non-neutralist liberal theories entail, explicitly or implicitly, a strong autonomy that excludes not only the legislation of substantial goods but even their discussion in the public square.

We are therefore left with the choice between a liberalism that futilely

70. Ibid., 278 and 280.

seeks independence from any specific anthropology and a liberalism that, conscious of the futility of such an attempt, bases itself in a strong concept of autonomy and the corresponding view of human reason. The latter alternative will always be unacceptable for those who do not share its ideal, and even consider it contrary to their deepest intuitions regarding the meaning of freedom, which they understand to be the pursuit of authentic human goods and not an affirmation of freedom for freedom's sake.

Despite the philosophical difficulties internal to the various forms of liberalism, I do not intend to put into question the validity of liberalism as a whole and as an institutional reality. My argument presupposes the validity of the Western, liberal, democratic, political culture that has effected a degree of peace, freedom, and justice never before seen in history. Anyone who shares these convictions will need at least some concept of autonomy, since it is part of the fundamental rationale of liberal, democratic constitutionalism. In fact, as Robert Dahl has written, the democratic, constitutional form of government rests on "the presumption of personal autonomy,"[71] that is, the respect for the freedom of individual persons.

Is There an Alternative to the Strong Concept of Freedom?
Contradictions Caused by the Strong Concept of Autonomy

According to the opinion of many, including the communitarians with whom I agree on this point, our public political culture, which is to a large extent formed by the achievements of historical liberalism, cannot function in a stable way as a social system respecting the freedom of all, if this political culture—insofar as it is a public philosophy with all its influence upon legislative and juridical processes, public opinion, and general culture—entails the strong concept of autonomy, that is, free choice as overall trump value. Carlos Santiago Nino's defense of divorce illustrates the contradictions that inevitably follow from the foundation of society upon a political philosophy of strong autonomy. According to Nino the aim of the liberal state is to maximize the liberty and autonomy of individuals. Sometimes, however, guaranteeing the freedom of all requires limiting autonomy.[72] The

71. Dahl, *Democracy and Its Critics*, 100.
72. Carlos S. Nino, *The Ethics of Human Rights* (Oxford: Oxford University Press, 1991), 215ff.

state may therefore use coercion to impose principles of public morality, and thereby qualify the moral value of some actions on account of the secondary effects that they may have on the interests of others.[73]

I think it is possible, without violating the liberal principle of individual autonomy, to appeal to such a principle in order to formulate an objection to legalized divorce—at least for couples with children—with the argument of protecting the rights of children and other values of familial solidarity and stability that are obviously of public interest. Such an argument against divorce presupposes considering children as having interests and liberties to be protected.[74] Surprisingly, however, Nino rejects such an appeal to principles of public morality. For Nino the liberal concept of autonomy requires that all social communities, including marriage, must be "consensual" because liberalism requires maximizing the possibility to rescind any promise that limits freedom. Nino therefore claims that liberalism requires legalized divorce.

It is generally typical of liberal political philosophy that there are two levels of argumentation that are in mutual conflict, causing the kind of internal contradiction of which Nino's reflections on divorce provide an example. On one hand, one accepts that limiting autonomy is no violation of liberal principles provided it is necessary to ensure the autonomy of other persons, thus protecting their dignity as equally free persons. But when one proposes to limit some kinds of autonomy, even though that limitation is fully justifiable in liberal constitutionalistic terms, the proposed limitation is rejected as a violation of liberal principles. The only way such an attitude can be reasonably justified is by upholding a strong concept of autonomy.[75]

---

73. *The Ethics of Human Rights*, 131.

74. An analogous argument could be constructed in order to protect the unborn (I did this in my above-quoted article, "Fundamental Rights, Moral Law, and the Legal Defense of Life in a Constitutional Democracy"). It is interesting to note that the definition of the person adopted by Rawls (*Political Liberalism*, 18), as "someone who can be a citizen, that is, a normal and fully cooperating member of society over a complete life" is extremely ambiguous: "can be" includes all the possible meanings of "to be able to be something." It is not clear if this "to be able to be" is *currently* (thus it would exclude fetuses, minors, and the mentally disabled from being persons); or if it is an actualizable "to be able to be," a real but not yet actualized capacity (in this case a fetus and a minor "can be" citizens but the mentally disabled cannot). In order to have a concept of the person that is also politically complete and relevant, one needs to consider an ontology that liberal neutrality is so intent on avoiding.

75. Surprisingly, Nino does not share what he calls Rawls's relativism and skepticism of the good. According to Nino, reason may be open to a true concept of the good without being forced to abandon the primacy of the principle of autonomy. The principle assumes that the good must always be rationally chosen for it to be considered truly good. Nino, therefore, holds to a weak principle of autonomy, without, however, further developing the relationship between autonomy and the openness of reason to the truth about the good.

This contradiction, consequent upon a hidden use of strong autonomy, is the frequent target of communitarian and other antiliberal critiques. These critiques resist the usurpation of the value—considered a gain for all of humanity—of liberal constitutional democratic political culture by a very particular and specific ideology based on a determined concept of autonomy that fails against the common sense of the ordinary citizen. In fact, both in the past and today only a narrow intellectual elite is congenial to the strong concept of autonomy.[76]

"Strong-autonomy" liberals obviously presuppose that their concept of autonomy is the only one compatible with the culture of constitutional democracy based on liberal principles. But this is not necessarily so, and here lies the real problem: is there a liberal public philosophy without the presuppositions of strong autonomy? The heart of the question at hand is to determine whether liberalism is possible without those implications that are often and justly criticized. The best approach toward demonstrating such a possibility is to first provide an example of an already developed theory of liberalism without the implications of strong autonomy. Fortunately such a well-known theory already exists.

Raz's Perfectionalism

In *The Morality of Freedom*,[77] Joseph Raz proposes a liberal theory based on a non-neutral, perfectionist concept of autonomy that is very different from mainstream liberalism.[78] The distinguishing feature of Raz's liberalism is his concept of autonomy. Raz affirms that it is possible to distinguish rationally between true and false goods. Furthermore, he states that autonomy is morally valid only insofar as it is exercised in the pursuit of a true good.[79] He affirms that satisfaction based on flawed reasoning does not contribute to well-being and that the person can be mistaken about the value of that which he pursues.[80] Morality and well-being are inseparable.[81] The well-being of the person depends on the ends he chooses, yet these ends are interwoven within the forms of one's society. Sound social forms contribute

---

76. I continue to call this political culture "liberal" because historically the credit has gone to the liberal movement, even if what we call liberalism transcends many of the particularities of a movement or even a determined political party. I do not wish to deprive the liberal movement of its undisputed historical merits, and for this reason I speak of liberalism in an affirmative sense.

77. Joseph Raz, *The Morality of Freedom* (Oxford: Oxford University Press, 1986).

78. Ibid.   79. Ibid., 381.

80. Ibid., 301.   81. Ibid., 313ff.

to personal well-being.[82] Raz recognizes that an autonomous life is constituted not only by the conditions and forms of life that one chooses but also by those that, without choosing them, one voluntarily accepts, for example, one's parents and one's forming part of a determinate family. Raz's notion of personal autonomy is therefore not so much that of independence from social or axiological presuppositions—and the continual possibility of arranging the obligations that arise from them—but the idea that every man must be the author of his own life. Although Raz does not use this terminology, one could say that according to his liberalism everyone must live in such a way that they can be considered fully *responsible* for their actions.[83] Authentic responsibility of autonomous agent presupposes a pluralistic society in which it is truly possible to choose among many alternatives. Alternatives, however, that are substantially good and sound.

The difference between Raz's complex theory and other forms of liberalism is illustrated by analyses of issues such as the definition of marriage as a recognized social institution.[84] Raz responds to those who claim that the promotion of a specific kind of marriage would be a violation of autonomy. Marriage, being a form of life that involves more than one person, is a social issue. In accord with his principle that the exercise of autonomy presupposes morally valid "social forms" and coercive measures of the state to support them, monogamous marriage needs support from the surrounding culture and juridical institutions. Even though these coercive measures would restrict the field of possible choices for the individual, they would not violate the value of autonomy because they create and conserve the conditions favorable for its exercise.

But Raz is truly a liberal. He does not propose the inverse of his argument. From the possibility that the state privilege certain life styles—which always implies a certain coercion—it does not follow that the state should prohibit moral practices *simply because they are morally wrong or repugnant.* The state should intervene only when necessary to maintain public

---

82. Ibid., 319.

83. Ibid., 370. In marked contrast with the strong concept of autonomy, Raz's notion of autonomy allows for a life of self-sacrifice or a life of obedience such as that of marriage, or even a religious vocation, to be understood as an actualization of autonomy so long as one's choice remains free and voluntary. Only if such a choice were to entail the renunciation of responsibility for one's actions would it reflect a lack of autonomy. But obedience does not entail diminished responsibility for one's acts of obedience, so long as one has freely chosen to obey in such a way that every act of obedience becomes the actualization of the initial free choice to obey.

84. Ibid., 161ff.

morality, that is, only when it is necessary to protect valid forms of life required for the sake of exercising one's personal autonomy, which, in the case of Raz, implies pursuing that which is truly good. Thus, Raz attempts to reinterpret and integrate John Stuart Mill's *harm principle* into his perfectionalist theory.

Beyond Liberalism and Anti-liberalism

I do not intend to say that Raz's position solves all the problems. New problems arise. However, his argument clearly demonstrates that it is possible to have a liberal attitude based on the value of autonomy, which, without turning civil law into the simple codification of the moral law, is favorable to restrictions of autonomy in service of a public morality, containing above all the defense of and favorable legal attitude toward determined social forms and lifestyles considered intrinsically valid from the moral point of view. The most profound reason that permits Raz to come to this conclusion is precisely a concept of autonomy that is different from the strong concept and that implies a very different image of man and, logically, a politically relevant rejection of moral relativism and skepticism.[85]

Recently, Robert George, from a non-liberal point of view, but with equal respect for individual liberty, described liberal theory as being specifically characterized by restraint from prohibiting immoral practices considered to be "without victims." George would therefore go well beyond the legal limitation of marriage to heterosexual couples—a proposal that I think can be defended from within liberalism. George also advocates the prohibition and punishment of sodomy committed in private between persons of the same sex. Therefore, for non-liberal authors like George it would be very important not only to deny legal recognition of homosexual couples' attempts to marry—a denial that I think can be justified even within a liberal political position—but also to prohibit and punish by means of the law the private practice of sodomy between persons of the same sex. George advances a

85. In contrast with Raz, Otfried Höffe advances a neo-Kantian, neutralist critique of Rawls. Rather than seeking an overlapping consensus among doctrines held to be true, Höffe proposes a political rationality entirely indifferent with respect to competing *Weltanschauungen*. Public reason would not advance any pretense of the truth, neither partial nor political. Höffe's public reason would therefore be distinct from religious beliefs because they advance complete and salvific doctrines considered true. For Höffe, religious beliefs are entirely foreign to the political process. Public reason should maintain a cool indifference with respect to them. See Otfried Höffe, "Ragione pubblica o ragione politica? A proposito di Rawls II," in *Concezioni del bene e teoria della giustizia*, ed. Gino Dalle Fratte (Rome: Armando, 1995), 43–53.

legal theory that extends the sphere of penal law beyond the reach of any liberal theory because his position is based on the fundamental rights of the citizen concerning objective moral values.[86]

The liberal constitutional form of democracy was originally meant to construct a social order capable of integrating a plurality of religious beliefs and moral convictions.[87] That the liberal political project was meant to achieve the peaceful integration of various religious and moral convictions does not entail that human rights, and the other ideals intrinsic to Western liberal democratic culture, were not based on authentic values and moral truth. All of the moral values at the basis of our liberal polity do have, however, a specific political relevance. They are the values of peace, liberty, and justice. The liberal respect for the dignity and liberty of all is very much a moral value, in that it permits adherence to the rule of law and to public institutions that guarantee freedom, even for those who do not share our religious and moral convictions. Nonetheless, the liberal polity also includes the conviction that not all of that which is morally relevant needs to be regulated through the public force of political power.[88]

In addition to its intrinsic moral value, the liberal tradition also entails a certain institutional wisdom. The communitarian critique, although in

86. See Robert P. George, *Making Men Moral: Civil Liberties and Public Morality* (Oxford: Clarendon Press, 1993), 167 and 228. It is important that George considers illicit the legislative imposition of moral values unless they are *true* moral values. His proposal contrasts with a type of communitarianism that considers it licit that every society protect, through the coercion of the law, *its* constitutive morality, independently of a judgment of its veracity. Thus, for example, is the well-known position of Lord P. Devlin, *The Enforcement of Morals* (Oxford: Oxford University Press, 1965); and in the same line of thought: N. Lacey, *State Punishment: Political Principles and Community Values* (London: Routledge, 1988). Nonetheless, in a practical, political sense, George's proposal is problematic, if not impractical. A liberal political proposal could be advanced as the moderate solution between the legislative imposition of moral values for which there is no public consensus (and therefore democratically impossible) and a communitarianism for which the only valid criteria for the licit imposition, through legislative measures, of determined moral values would be that they are in fact constitutive values of *this* social community.

87. See chapter 1 of the present volume, entitled "Why Is Political Philosophy Necessary? Historical Considerations and a Response." This was originally published as "Perché una filosofia politica? Elementi storici per una risposta," *Acta Philosophica* 1 (1992): 233–63.

88. In disagreement with Rawls, Raz (*The Morality of Freedom,* 4) does not admit a simple distinction between principles of political morality and principles of personal morality. He understands his political philosophy as a moral philosophy, centered upon themes that have a special political relevance. Even if, personally, I am convinced that political morality is a specific type of morality within the moral sphere, I share with Raz the idea of continuity. That is, the idea that it is inconceivable to have a political moral value that is not also a value for personal morality. With Raz, and contrary to some currents of non-liberal thought, I think that this does not imply the justification of penal measures against determined personal practices simply on the grounds that they are morally repugnant. On the other hand, every justification of penal intervention also implies a judgment of the moral perversion of the corresponding practice. That is, such intervention can and must be morally justified, even if in certain cases it is precisely a political justification, which is also a type of moral justification.

various points illuminating and substantiated, runs the risk of rendering impossible a productive reflection on the institutional conditions for civil liberty. I maintained above that the communitarian critique of liberalism is misdirected insofar as it misunderstands liberalism's fundamentally *political* intentions. As a consequence of this misunderstanding of liberalism, the communitarian critique tends to rule out the very core of both its concept of autonomy and its political reasonableness, such as the utility of procedural justice and the priority of the fundamental rights of the individual, which is the guarantee for the spaces of autonomy required by the human dignity of a free being. These liberal political core values are, in my view, the most valuable; from the viewpoint of political morality, they are indispensable components and historical achievements of our current political culture.

On the other hand, liberals can only profit from a deeper consideration of their concept of autonomy. To do so, however, would perhaps require an even more profound change in their hearts: mainly they should lose the fear of discovering a connection between practical rationality and truth, and between freedom and truth about the good. Liberals need to recognize that the political community is always also a community of values that are expressed in not specifically political but rather social institutions such as the family, the school, and so on. It seems that the typical liberal manner of thinking, although effective on the strictly political level, often has a destructive influence when it is applied in other social spheres.

When considering liberalism as a political theory of the citizen—and not of the human person as such—the liberal can licitly withdraw to a position like that of the individual citizen who, while not sharing important fundamental convictions concerning the most profound questions of human life, desires to live with others in peace and freedom. This requires a political consensus, of which the political philosophy of liberalism intends to be the theory.

Perhaps we will never find a perfect solution to the basic problem of who judges in a politically and binding way—involving the coercive apparatus of the state—what is politically good and just. I personally believe that the only possible solution is a complex one, never free of internal tensions. The political solution for our pluralist societies must integrate the procedural justice of the rule of law within a context of substantial values defined through the constitution of the state and further articulated in law. These values cannot be *created* by a political, juridical process. They must be *rec-*

ognized by the public authority as the values of a specific society and therefore as a component of public reason. The task of the political process is to determine, here and now, the right equilibrium within this tension. Thus, all depends on the society's capacity, and therefore the capacity of its members, to adhere to authentic human values, among which without any doubt the just autonomy of the person deserves priority.[89]

89. This essay was originally published as "L'immagine dell'uomo nel liberalismo e il concetto di autonomia: al di là del dibattito fra liberali e comunitaristi," in *Immagini dell'uomo. Percorsi antropologici nella filosofia moderna*, ed. I. Yarza and trans. Robert A. Gahl (Rome: Armando 1997).

|||||||||||||||||||||||||||||||||||||||||||||||||||||||||||||||||||||||||||||||||||||||||||||||||||||||||||||||||

THREE

The Democratic Constitutional State
and the Common Good

The great majority of people living in today's so-called developed world are also participants in a culture characterized by the political-institutional reality of the *democratic constitutional state*. This type of political organization of society developed during the European history of recent centuries, up to and including the century just concluded. The most fundamental principles of constitutionalism, intimately linked to the liberal movement of the nineteenth century, are an established reality within this political culture, including the principle of parliamentary representation and the demand—though not of liberal origin—for democratization through universal suffrage.

Is it possible, in the context of the political culture of the democratic constitutional state, to still speak of the common good? This is the theme I will consider in this essay. For example, in a system characterized by guaranteed individual liberties and democratic processes subject to the principle of majority rule, isn't it superfluous to speak of a common good? Doesn't the very term "common good" derive from a context different from the modern one, which is marked by individualism, a "contractualistic" mentality, "rights" language and the reality of a *homo oeconomicus* pursuing his own interests in a market whose functioning the modern state guarantees? Isn't a market itself simply a system for the coordination of free agents, each acting without any common interest as an immediate aim of their transactions? And finally, isn't it true that a "common good" appears only as the final result of a process that is itself not guided by any common intentionality—and certainly never as a point of reference for the concrete economic or political choices of individual citizens?

It is difficult to respond "no" to these questions. Nevertheless—and somewhat surprisingly—the concept of common good *has* survived in our political discourse; indeed, it seems to continue to be indispensable. Even today politicians seek approval for their proposals and programs by referring to a presumed "common," "general," or "public" interest, with the most widely divergent interests of both individuals and groups often being promoted in the name of the common good. Likewise, we are quite ready to condemn a political player who is perceived to act only in his own interest, rather than what is called the public or common interest. The common good, as a point of reference for political debate, undoubtedly exists. It has become difficult, however, to articulate precisely the categories by which we can make the common good the object of philosophical-political reflection. The suspicion remains that the concept of the common good is merely an ideological superstructure, or even an anachronism to be cast aside.

In the following pages I wish to suggest how the concept of the common good might be reintegrated into political philosophy. I will not give a systematic and comprehensive treatment of the question, rather offering some reflections in the way of a broad outline. Moreover, my proposal will *not* take the form of a criticism or a polemic against contemporary political culture, so influenced by historical liberalism; it will instead be a reflection arising from and taking place *within* the context of this culture itself. It will therefore not be neo-Aristotelian or neo-Thomistic in the strict sense, but a rethinking, in the spirit of the great classical tradition of philosophical-political thought, of the contemporary reality of the constitutional democratic state, which is the realization of the most essential principles of the liberal movement of recent centuries and has now become a culture and a civilizing agent in its own right.

With these reflections I also hope to contribute to what has recently been defined as the "fundamental political question," that is, whether "the political bond is something *produced* or *given*; i.e. whether it is an expedient for inevitable human coexistence, or whether it is an interior bond proper to the human subject."[1] Put more plainly, the question asks whether society is

---

1. Francesco Botturi, "Per una teoria liberale del bene comune," *Vita e Pensiero* 79, no. 2 (1996): 82–94, at 83.

merely an expedient so the individual can better realize his own individual aspirations, or rather whether the individual must be considered a being who "naturally" transcends himself toward the good of others, and thus toward the common good. Our reflections will lead us to conclude that a political philosophy of the common good is also a political morality, in which individual freedom and solidarity are thought of as intimately connected.

In the first section, some specific characteristics of the modern political ethos will be examined, showing how that ethos requires a notion of the "common good" as a practical category in the aspect of its institutional praxis. The second section will show the insufficiency of contractualism as a philosophical foundation for the democratic constitutional state, *without,* however, rejecting fundamental aspects of the idea of contractualism, opting rather for a "modified" contractualism; this will provide a basis for the concept of *solidarity,* an aspect of justice and necessarily connected with the idea of the common good. In the third section I will discuss the neutrality of the state and the inevitable existence of a public morality, as part of the common good. In the fourth and final section I will attempt to show that in a pluralistic society, the common good must be understood not so much as a preestablished entity, but, in the first place as a structure of the institutions of the democratic constitutional state that makes the political process possible, and second as the *result* of this process, a result that will necessarily reflect the pluralistic structure of civil society itself.

The Modern Political Ethos as an Institutional Ethos
Material Political Order and Formal/ Functional Political Order

According to a well-known formulation of Ernst-Wolfgang Böckenförde, the democratic constitutional state is *an order of freedom and of peace* rather than *an order of truth and of virtue.*[2] With this antithetical statement Böckenförde intends to express a fundamental difference between the classical, ancient, and medieval ideal of the *polis* and modern political culture: the ancient *polis* was understood—most clearly in Aristotelian political

2. Böckenförde, "Die Entstehung des Staates als Vorgang der Säkularisation," in Böckenförde, *Staat, Gesellschaft, Freiheit. Studien zur Staatstheorie und zum Verfassungsrecht* (Frankfurt: Suhrkamp, 1976), 42–64, esp. 60.

philosophy—as an order of cooperation that expresses the truth of human nature, and whose intrinsic finality consists in making possible the good and virtuous—and as such happy—life of human beings.[3] Modern political culture, on the other hand, departing from the non-homogeneous and often conflictual nature of human society, does not attempt to realize these higher values, instead assuring those values fundamental for human coexistence: peace, freedom, and justice.[4] Accordingly, this culture leaves to each person "his truth" and "his virtue," assuming of course that these do not interfere with others' enjoyment of the same freedom. The ideal of the modern state, the "democratic ethos," therefore, is not a material ideal or ethos implying a specific content, but rather is functional and formal.

Böckenförde's thesis seems reasonable to the extent that it claims that the modern state has replaced the ancient idea of the *polis* centered on a good and happy life with a new, more formal and functional, conception of political culture. One must be careful, however: Böckenförde speaks of an order of peace and of freedom, but not of the third element, justice. Also, the sharp contraposition of the two concepts "order of freedom and peace" and "order of truth and virtue" seems unjustified; it is not clear why a political culture founded on an ethos of peace and freedom could not also express, in its own way, an aspect of human nature and the truth concerning it.

The Modern Distinction between "Public" and "Private," and between an Ethic of Virtue and an Ethic of Institutions

Based on Böckenförde's distinction, it seems difficult to grasp adequately the difference between the old idea of the *polis*—which reappeared, at least in part, in medieval political and juridical thought—and modern political culture. In fact, the difference consists not so much in the substitution of the values of truth and virtue by formal values guaranteeing peace and freedom, but in expressing in a different and more precisely articulated way the political and practical truth of the common good and the political virtues corresponding to it, virtues pertaining both to political actors in the

---

3. See chapter 1 of the present volume, which is entitled "Why Is Political Philosophy Necessary? Historical Considerations and a Response." This was originally published as my "Perché una filosofia politica? Elementi storici per una risposta," *Acta philosophica* 1, no. 2 (1992): 233–63.

4. See Martin Kriele, *Einführung in die Staatslehre: Die geschichtlichen Legitimitätsgrundlagen des demokratischen Verfassungsstaates*, 4th ed. (Opladen: Westdeutscher Verlag, 1990), 48–52.

strict sense and to ordinary citizens. This modern distinction is twofold, consisting on the one hand of the distinction between *private* and *public*, and on the other hand of that between an *ethics of virtue (of the individual person)* and an *ethics of institutions (or of institutional praxis)*.

Modern political culture sees political activity as taking place in and with reference to a public sector, to be distinguished from the "private life" of citizens. Moreover, this public activity is to a large extent action that occurs in the context of institutions of a public character, and is indeed a praxis *of* institutions, that is, an "institutional praxis"—a characteristic strictly linked to constitutionalism. Böckenförde himself does not deny that the formal ethos, especially that of the *Rechtsstaat* (the state under the rule of law) establishes a material content, that is, values of equality, freedom (i.e., liberty) and justice.[5] Precisely this fact casts doubt on the ultimate usefulness of Böckenförde's antithesis.

The two distinctions between private and public, on the one hand, and individual virtue and that of the political agent, on the other, are historically a response to a threat to an even more fundamental political good: peace in society. "Peace" as a fundamental good of civil society is a tradition of both St. Augustine's thought and Christian Aristotelianism.[6] The modern era, moreover, has had sad and bloody experience of how damaging and dangerous is the claim that a presumed moral integrity—and even religious orthodoxy—on the part of both citizens and governments is the indispensable prerequisite for peace and social order. For the primary and fundamental aspects of the peacefulness of society, these convictions are rather more apt to be harmful to peaceful coexistence. For postmedieval and modern societies, divided by profound religious and ideological conflicts, the claim that peace must be based on moral and religious truth amounts to an abstract claim that ignores the real conditions (both anthropological and historical) in which political praxis is realized, and also ignores the sad experience that such abstract doctrines easily become ideological justification for those who abuse their power.

Such experience led to the first step, taken by Bodin in his book *Six Livres de la République,* toward distinguishing between public good and private good. Whereas in the Aristotelian tradition all of the cardinal vir-

---

5. See, in Böckenförde, *Staat, Gesellschaft, Freiheit,* 65–92, the article "Entstehung und Wandel des Rechsstaatsbegriffs."

6. See e.g., St. Thomas Aquinas, *De regimine principum (De Regno)* I, 3 and 16.

tues are called "political" virtues,[7] the modern epoch tends to refer political virtues to a public sector, distinct from the private. The distinction between public and private is the foundation of the *ethos of peace.*

The absolutism that results from Bodin's position, which continued to consider everything as dependent on the person of the monarch, was corrected by the idea of the constitutional limitation of political power in favor of freedom: thus public action is introduced as an action on the basis of institutions established at the level of constitutional law. This institutionalization of public action is the basis of the *ethos of freedom* or *liberty.*

Finally, the tendency of the constitutional state to not guarantee equality of freedom and rights to all led to the demand for "democratic" participation, the participation of all, in representative institutions. Such participation, accomplished through a real representation and thus by the democratization of institutionalized public action, forms the basis of the *ethos of justice,* which of course is also guaranteed at the level of constitutional law.

This threefold process of differentiation also reflects the typically modern characteristic of political ethics: *the solution of the problem of realization,* that is, the resolution of the problem of the peaceful coexistence of human beings in freedom and in a community of justice under conditions of potentially conflictual pluralism resulting from the lack (and in a certain degree the nondesirability) of the public validity and enforcement of a homogeneous conception of the good. This leads to the famous problem of the *quis interpretabitur? quis iudicatibur?*—formulated magisterially but inadequately resolved by Hobbes—or the problem of the institutionalization of consensus in a society where disagreement exists concerning what is just. The problem of realization is therefore that of reconciling freedom with the demands of an efficacious constitutional and legal order, the problem of "how to do things" in a society in which there is no unanimity concerning "what should be done." This problem demands a specific ethical-political reflection; to a large extent, the history of modern political thought is the history of that reflection.[8]

Both Bodin and Hobbes realized that in an ideologically conflictual society, to maintain that peace can be realized only through the public enforcement of religious and moral truth leads to civil war. The reason is that the

7. They are still understood in this way by St. Thomas; see *Summa Theologiae* I-II, q. 61, a.5.

8. For some reflections on the difference between classical and modern political philosophy, see the introductory chapter to my book *La filosofia politica di Thomas Hobbes: coerenza e contraddizioni di un paradigma* (Rome: Armando, 1997), 16–25.

concept of peace itself becomes "ideologized" or "moralized," given that everyone considers as destroyers and enemies of peace—and ultimately fights against them—precisely those who have different conceptions of the human good, of the just, and of truth in the religious sphere. If peace can only be the result of a political praxis that presupposes a "truth" with respect to justice, the good, and even with respect to religion, the conflictual nature of society is even exacerbated, since every conflict, including war, can and must necessarily be justified precisely in the name of "peace." This same logic also short-circuits any attempt to seek peace in a given conflict.

The ethic of the Aristotelian *polis,* together with the acceptance of Roman law and integrated with what is called "political Augustinianism,"[9] led in the Middle Ages to the violent repression of heretics and to an extremely ambivalent concept of "just war" and "holy war." In the modern era, with its confessional and moral pluralism, that same ethic leads by the same logic to civil war.

Modernity has not concluded from this, however, that the virtues are unnecessary (in a certain sense, with the exception of Kant and Hegel). Rather, it has tried to identify in reality which political virtues—in both citizens and those who govern—make peace, freedom, and justice possible (for example Montesquieu's famous reflections on the political virtues of citizens in a republic—love for country and equality—as opposed to those in a monarchy, which is based on the love of honor). Furthermore, modernity has posed the question of what are the real conditions necessary whereby such political virtues can be exercised.

It will be helpful, therefore, to roughly sketch the virtues required for the institutional praxis that corresponds to the political culture of the contemporary democratic constitutional state. From there we can begin to formulate an adequate conception of the common good, leaving for later the question of the possible foundation—contractualistic? individualistic? Aristotelian? communitarian?—of a political praxis directed toward that common good.

The Political Virtues of Public and Institutional Praxis

The political virtues that pertain to the ethos of peace, freedom, and justice, are, for example, virtues such as *tolerance;* the use of *force of argument*

---

9. H.-X. Arquillière, *L'Augustinisme politique. Essai sur la formation des théories politiques du Moyen Age,* 2nd ed. (Paris: J. Vrin, 1955).

(in parliament, in the formation of public opinion, etc.) rather than physical force; the *disposition toward compromise;* the submission of disputes and conflicts to the *observance of formal and procedural rules of law* that guarantee an equal and impartial treatment for all, giving solutions to these disputes a maximum of independence from the personal qualities, prejudices, or political or religious (etc.) convictions of the persons charged with resolving the disputes.

The concrete conditions guaranteeing that action consistent with these virtues will predominate are formulated by the idea of the democratic constitutional state; such a political order creates a structure of institutions making it possible for human coexistence to be regulated precisely by actions of this type.

One could object, obviously, that such a set of values is attractive, but is not presently realized and perhaps never will be. Indeed, the case could easily be made that in fact what often counts are not arguments but demagogic seduction, or how frequently abuses by representatives of public institutions occur, or how often legal arrangements are manipulated, and so on. These are not arguments *against* what I affirmed above—in fact they are a confirmation! Such criticisms presuppose and confirm the fact that our political culture possesses a well-defined ethos that is considered—and indeed precisely by the critic—an expression of a morality, both political and public, which is used as a measure in the criticism itself, and as such is both presupposed and confirmed by it.

Criticisms like those just mentioned, therefore, point out at which level conflicts are dealt with in a democratic constitutional state: conflicts between people are converted into conflicts regulated by processes, political propaganda, votes and elections, and the like. The antagonisms, abuses, injustices, and so on that always exist in a society, as well as their hoped-for resolution, take place at an institutional level, in such a way that peace, coexistence, fundamental liberties, and so on are not jeopardized. From this one can understand that the institutional ethos of the constitutional state is precisely a political culture, an accomplishment of civilization—the value of which can be adequately evaluated in comparison with those societies not possessing such a political culture.[10] This is not to say that the citizens of

---

10. For this reason, the following observation of Alasdair MacIntyre seems to me to be somewhat inaccurate: "Modern politics is civil war carried on by other means" (*After Virtue: A Study in Moral The-*

the latter type of society are necessarily "worse" than those of the former, or that, conversely, the citizens of a democratic constitutional state are necessarily better; the citizen of a democratic constitutional state is, however, more "civilized," at least in the sense that he is more restrained, controlled, and protected, has less fear, feels himself to be secure, and knows himself to be free—indeed, it is possible to become accustomed to such freedom and security, while no longer appreciating its value. Montesquieu was correct in saying that there is a strict relation between political freedom and security, or at least with the opinion one has of one's own security.[11]

I will conclude with the observation that institutions, whether juridical, political, or social, are not meant to create the good of man *simpliciter*, but only to assure that minimum of morality necessary so that people can live together in peace and in equality of freedom (the latter also implying "social justice," i.e., the promotion of the basic rights of those who due to their social or economic situation cannot make use of those rights—i.e., of those for whom "freedom" means weakness and powerlessness, and who consequently don't feel themselves to be free.)

To articulate the ethos of institutional praxis in more detail, however, it is first necessary to discuss the function of political institutions in general. Generally speaking, such "institutions" have multiple functions, exercising both a *regulative function and a function of exoneration*. Institutions compensate for human defects, and as such they tend to diminish, or at least to control, rather than to amplify conflicts.

According to Bernhard Sutor's helpful list,[12] which I include here with some modifications, political institutions fulfill the following functions (among others), especially relevant from the point of view of political morality:

1. Institutions "incarnate" a shared framework of "meaning" in a prejudicial way, based on which the members of the political community exist in fundamental agreement (as, e.g., the protection of the rights of man, modes of political participation, division of power); this framework of meaning

---

ory, 2nd ed. [Notre Dame: Notre Dame University Press, 1984], 253). Precisely these "other means" for the resolution of conflicts are a significant cultural accomplishment, making it possible for conflicts to no longer have to assume the character of war—even if some of these means are abused, as if a state of war in fact existed.

11. See Book 12 of Montesquieu's *De l'ésprit des lois*, 2nd ed. (Paris: Garnier, 1973), 1:202.

12. Bernhard Sutor, *Politische Ethik: Gesamtdarstellung auf der Basis der Christlichen Gesellschaftslehre* (Paderborn: Schöningh, 1991), 67ff.

serves as the presupposition and orientation for political decisions, assuring such decisions social coordination, security, and stability.

2. Institutions compensate for the *deficit* in individual morality. They moreover facilitate (exterior) moral, and perhaps even virtuous, behavior (for example, paying taxes or dealing honestly in economic matters), even making such behavior rationally advantageous, or at least not onerous.

3. Institutions are capable of coordinating divergent interests and regulating conflicts in a way compatible with the common good.

4. Institutions render more superfluous isolated and arbitrary interventions, promoting transparent decisions that can be monitored with broad participation and consent.

5. Institutions based on a broad consent, that is, on the moral will to submit to these institutions—a will expressed precisely in such consent— unify the diversity of wills on specific questions toward a common political rationality, consistent with the meaning of such institutions. They establish, and at the same time facilitate as a moral obligation, obedience to legitimately enacted laws, dispositions, and decisions, that is, enacted according to the requisite procedural forms.

6. In this sense institutions tend to de-ideologize and remove both the political process and individual decisions from that "moral burden" that would cause the citizen to feel continually obligated at the level of his fundamental moral convictions, which would ultimately be a motive for conflict.[13]

7. Finally, institutionalized political praxis allows a judgment concerning the moral content of a concrete policy independently of the personal moral qualities of those promoting the policy. As such, people accept judges or legal procedures for resolving conflicts to the extent to which they pos-

---

13. In this way, for example, one who belongs to a political minority could nevertheless behave loyally with respect to the institution in question, given that he is not constrained to identify himself personally with the content of the majority's decision; he must only support the rules of such a decision. To withdraw support for the institution itself because one is subjected as a minority to an unfavorable decision would be an infraction of the ethos of institutional praxis. Precisely for this reason Rousseau should not be considered a precursor of the ethos of constitutional democracy, given that he claimed that the majority always expresses the "general will," which is the truth or the true "common interest." As such, the minority, simply because it is the minority, must consider itself to be in error and as only pursuing a "particular interest," which according to Rousseau would be illegitimate ("Quand donc l'avis contraire au mien l'emporte, cela ne prouve autre chose sinon que je m'étois trompé, et ce que j'estimois être la volonté générale ne l'étoit pas": Jean-Jacques Rousseau, *Du contrat social*, bk. 4, chap. 2, in *Oeuvres complètes*, ed. Bernard Gagnebin and Marcel Raymond, vol. 3, Bibliothèque de la Pléiade [Paris: Gallimard, 1964], 441). The good citizen must therefore make the decision of the majority his own, i.e., submit himself, including interiorly, to the "general will." This position is obviously a specifically modern form of the "ethic of the *polis*," open to a totalitarian interpretation.

sess institutional legitimacy (and thus formal, functional, or procedural legitimacy), and not insofar as the people are considered to be good or not, Catholic, Protestant, Jewish, or Moslem, or a member of this or that political party. The extent to which this principle is the case indicates precisely the level of political culture and pacification of a society.

The Multi-Dimensional Ethos Implicit in Institutional Political Praxis

The most common arguments and criticisms advanced against the political culture of the constitutional democratic state are usually based precisely on a lack of appreciation for, or even ignorance of, the positive function of the just-mentioned characteristics of a political culture based on an institutional ethos. The distinction between institutional ethos and institutional praxis, on the one hand, and the individual's virtue and his conception of truth, on the other, bring it about that in the political culture of the democratic constitutional state, moral judgment and even ethics itself become a "multidimensional" morality, that is, a morality "at many levels."

This is not meant, obviously, in the sense of a "double morality," but in the sense in which, in the terminology of Rawls, the "basic structure" of the political system on which the society organizes itself—the institutions that formulate constitutional rules and the basic principles of distribution—must be distinguished from the mechanisms that generate subsequent decisions on the basis and within the context of this underlying structure. It is entirely possible to adhere to the basic structure of the political-juridical system—and to defend it—even if one simultaneously finds oneself in profound disagreement with decisions and concrete policies carried out by the system. From the perspective of the ethos of institutional praxis, to accept institutions and their corresponding rules only and on the condition that these are desirable would be profoundly immoral (obviously without excluding limits, in that a constitutional structure could be abused to such an extent that it loses its legitimacy). At the same time, from the point of view of a multidimensional ethos, the position is entirely coherent when someone, remaining firm in his moral convictions on the personal level, uses every legal means to fight for the abolition or the introduction of certain statutes or reforms he believes necessary; one can, for example, remain a loyal and convinced defender of a political system even if it is capable of a general legalization of abortion, or if it is incapable (like any other political system) of eliminating corrupt politicians.

I will here propose a brief list of these "moral levels" and their relative presuppositions, to then arrive at an overall view of the ethos implicit in the democratic constitutional state:

1. Institutions, and political praxis based on them, develop their own *internal ethic* (we could speak here of the "virtues of institutional action"), which is nothing other than the aggregate of the presuppositions necessary for the good functioning of the institutions themselves: for instance, *collegiality* or *participatory humility*, that is, the disposition to accept the fact of having only one vote along with everyone else, even if one is convinced one is correct, and to submit to the decisions of the majority or be open to compromise; *communicative justice*, that is, the disposition to influence the formation of majorities by means of truthful arguments, as well as to listen to and evaluate the arguments of others; *procedural justice*, that is, respect for the equality of every participant in institutional praxis, expressed by respect for the procedural rules proper to each institution; etc.

As can easily be seen, such an internal ethic of institutions does not replace personal moral virtues; rather, such an ethic is formed by virtue—by virtues, however, that are a product of a political culture based on institutional praxis and that are fostered by this same political culture. It is characteristic of an internal institutional ethic, however, that it exists not on the basis of a moral choice of the individual, but on the basis of rules that define the institution in question. Such an ethos is therefore in principle present and active independently of the other moral qualities of individual participants (even if, due to the *connexio virtutum,* this cannot function perfectly).

2. This last observation brings us to the second "moral level": reflection on the properties of an internal ethic of institutions shows that these have need of another morality, an *external* morality, understood in two senses:

 a. A morality is needed not only for action *within* the institution, but also for the preservation, protection, and maintenance of the institution itself. Thus, qualities such as *loyalty* and *love of peace.*

 b. To the same end, institutional praxis requires that its internal ethic be followed not solely for utilitarian reasons, that is, in a calculated self-interest, but truly as virtue, specifically aspects of the virtue of justice, respect for others, and respect for the legitimate interests of others.

As we have seen, it is typical of an internal institutional ethic that its existence or nonexistence is due not to the moral choices of participating individuals, but to the rules that define such institutions: such an ethos is present and active independently of the moral qualities of individuals. If within a particular institution, however, all participants observe the internal ethic—including the rules defining the institution—solely on the basis of a calculated interest, the institution will not be able in the long run to exercise its primary function of integration, exoneration, and pacification. The reason for this is that to the extent that an institutional praxis is seen as disadvantageous for a particular participant, he will no longer feel rationally motivated to support the practice, and ultimately the institution in question would be rendered pointless.

Put otherwise: an external ethic is needed that would support the institution independently of "my" own interest, that is, independently of whether or not the results of institutional processes are favorable to my interests. An ethos is needed requiring support of institutional praxis not on the basis of self-interest, but on the basis of a common or public interest, which is precisely an interest in the existence of the institution itself. And here we encounter—for the first time—the notion of the common good.[14]

In essence, we have arrived at the problem proposed by Hobbes. According to his philosophy, the only rational motivation for submitting oneself to communal institutional rules is self-interest and the accompanying rational hope, guaranteed by a coercive power, that others will do the same.[15] The logical consequence, however, is that once the state is created, such an interest is not replaced by an interest in the common good. According to Hobbes, the basis of the preservation of the state is its power and its ability to inflict punishments, making disobedience to positive laws disadvantageous for the individual; the institutions of the state would thus rely solely on the sovereign power of the state and on the self-interest of subjects. The institutional

---

14. An example that might illustrate this type of ethos was the attitude of the liberal Englishman Walter Bagehot, famous economist and journalist, who in 1867 defended the majority elective system for institutional reasons of principle, even though throughout his entire life he was constrained to vote in parliamentary elections for the liberal candidate in his district who never stood a chance of being elected—precisely because of the majority electoral system. This notwithstanding, Bagehot continued to defend the system, convinced that it was the best for his country. See Walter Bagehot, *The English Constitution* (1867) (Oxford: Oxford University Press, 2009). See also Carl J. Friedrich, *Der Verfassungsstaat der Neuzeit* (orig. *Constitutional Government and Democracy*) (Berlin/Göttingen/Heidelberg: Springer 1953), 319ff.

15. See the coherent reconstruction of Hobbes's logic in Gregory S. Kavka, *Hobbesian Moral and Political Theory* (Princeton, N.J.: Princeton University Press, 1986).

ethos of a constitutional state cannot be interpreted in this way, however, given that submission to rules by those participating in institutional praxis is ordinarily not enforced by punishments. Such a practice is valid at the most for the relation between laws and the individual, but not for that between institutional rules and participants in institutional praxis. A member of parliament or even an entire political party, for example, could withdraw from parliamentary participation because it does not seem possible to realize its political goals through the institution (being continually in the minority, or lacking electoral support)—even to the point of publicly casting doubt on the institution of parliament itself. Such behavior, though not sanctioned by any punishment, is nonetheless ruinous for a parliamentary system.

Consequently, loyal support for an institutional praxis cannot be sufficiently explained on the basis of a morality based simply on self-interest. An ethos of the common good is necessary. At a minimum, the following "calculation" is needed: "To loyally support institutional praxis for the common good is also ultimately in my own interest." Or: "The promotion of the common good promotes, in the best realizable way, my personal good as well." Even though this is a calculated interest, it is not the same as a Hobbesian calculation, given that it requires adherence to the common good based on a rationale that is precisely *not* that of self-interest, even if one does so because one is convinced that in the long run it is also in one's own personal interest. *Yet, the "common good" appears as an independent and proper entity in such a calculation, not directly deducible from mere self-interest.* Moreover, the calculation seems legitimate and in a certain sense even inevitable, given that the common good, to be properly a *common* good, must also include *my* interest. Supposing my interests are licit, a system in which they are excluded a priori would be intrinsically unjust. A common good not promoting the particular good of each individual, but sought in an absolutely "disinterested" way, would only with difficulty be a *common* good (or some individuals would be constrained to consider themselves as being outside the community whose good is sought). Such a calculation, therefore, considered in itself, supports and promotes the stability of institutions. As opposed to a "Hobbesian" ethic, a political ethic of the common good allows one to act rationally for the good of others; consequently, it is an ethic of solidarity.

3. A third level is necessary, however: in a democratic constitutional state, the ultimate legitimacy and justification for every kind of institutional praxis depends, obviously, on the legitimacy of the constitutional structure

of the state. This in turn presupposes an ethos of peace, along with an ethos that includes the protection and promotion of human rights equally for everyone, that is, according to justice. Such an ethos, however, cannot be supported and ultimately legitimated by the calculation minimally required to support institutional praxis within the democratic constitutional state, that is, by the calculation that pursues the common good only for one's own interest. Note that we are claiming here not only that the Hobbesian calculation is insufficient (which we have already shown), but also that a position like Locke's seems insufficient, that is, incapable of legitimizing the constitutional state (in fact Locke never speaks of the constitutional state, but only of a parliamentary government).

The insufficiency of Locke's position is due to the fact that his philosophy, which legitimizes the parliamentary representation of "rights" or individual interests as the foundation of a legitimate government, presupposes rights or material interests of a homogeneous content: life, freedom, and property. The Lockean parliament, therefore, is an assembly with a homogeneous structure of interests, and can function only insofar as it is homogeneous—to the extent that if a government attempted to violate *property* (of owners) it would be rendered illegitimate, something Locke himself expressly states. This position reflected the structure of the English parliament of his time, which in fact simply excluded those having a heterogeneous interest (non-Anglicans, Protestant sects, Calvinists, Catholics, women)—that is, the parliament had an oligarchic structure.

The contemporary constitutional state, on the other hand, assumes a maximum heterogeneity of personal interests (as well as beliefs, confessions, and moral options), while at the same time establishing the protection of what is in the common interest of all as people and as citizens (and not insofar as they are owners, entrepreneurs, white, Anglicans, male, etc.). Thus, at the level of the rights of man and of the citizen, upholding the rights of others (for example, their religious freedom) may well be in contrast with "my" personal interest. I must nevertheless respect my neighbor's freedom as a person and a citizen because, as a person and a citizen, he is equal to me, and respect for that equality is an essential content of the constitutional state. This, however, *cannot* be explained on the basis of a calculation aimed at self-interest. Indeed, in the context of the constitutional state, the only thing that can be explained solely on the basis of self-interest is discrimination (e.g., against a race or the unborn).

To found an entire political culture on the idea of the rights of man, therefore, implies and presupposes a *disinterested* moral attitude, that is, an attitude that fundamentally recognizes other people, without exception, as being equal to me. This is a fundamental act of justice, not deducible from any self-interest; rather it is precisely the first step in transcending mere self-interest, opening one's will to the good of others and through this also to the common good.

Thus appears the fundamental dimension of the ethos on which the political culture of the democratic constitutional state is based. This ethos, however, is not created by constitutional institutions, nor is it sufficiently guaranteed and protected by them, given that such institutions *presuppose* the ethos. At this level, therefore, it becomes evidently clear that all basic institutional structures require a specific type of fundamental moral rectitude among citizens: that fundamental justice expressed in the "Golden Rule," a formulation of the moral precept of loving one's neighbor as oneself.

Even Hobbes states explicitly that his "pacifying calculation" is nothing other than a summary of the Golden Rule.[16] It must be said, however—and I have attempted to show this in detail elsewhere[17]—that Hobbes falsifies the sense of this rule. For him, the Golden Rule is identified with the interested calculation of mutual self-renunciation of the defense of one's own life in favor of a more peaceful situation, which in turn is even more advantageous for the individual. The Golden Rule is thus interpreted based on self-interest. The authentic sense of the Golden Rule, however, is not calculated interest, but the formulation of the first step toward transcending the seeking of one's own interest alone, opening oneself to the good of others; and this not because it is more advantageous to me, but because the other is recognized as a human being, "equal to me," and as such possesses the same fundamental interests I do. These interests are recognized in a fundamental act of justice that occurs not in my own interest, but precisely in the interest of the other. It is here that one finds the point of departure for the formation of the virtue of justice.[18]

As we have seen to this point, the democratic constitutional state presupposes a fundamental ethos requiring a fundamental goodness in peo-

16. Hobbes, *Leviathan,* chapter 15 (page 214 in the easy available Penguin Books edition, edited by C. B. Macpherson, which reproduces the 1651 *Head* edition of the Leviathan).

17. Rhonheimer, *La filosofia politica di Thomas Hobbes,* 122ff. and 138ff.

18. See also Rhonheimer, *The Perspective of Morality: Philosophical Bases of Thomistic Virtue Ethics* (Washington, D.C.: The Catholic University of America Press, 2011). This was originally published as *La prospettiva della morale. Fondamenti dell'etica filosofica* (Rome: Armando, 1994), 242–45.

ple, at the level of basic justice. The ultimate raison d'être and legitimization of the democratic constitutional state can therefore be neither created nor guaranteed by any institutional praxis or institutional ethos, given that these latter already presuppose the acceptance of the democratic constitutional state. The presupposition of the political culture of the democratic constitutional state is precisely that which we have called a fundamental ethos of justice, which is in fact an ethos of solidarity.

This minimal moral foundation required by the democratic constitutional state nevertheless leaves ample space for freedom: contemporary political culture can ultimately be corrupted by the fundamental injustice of participants. Similarly, one can also say that the moral quality of the people who compose a political community will influence the ability of a democratic constitutional state to attain a greater or lesser degree of humanity.

The political culture of the democratic constitutional state does not attempt to guarantee the good *simpliciter* of people—indeed it explicitly abstains from this effort. Thus, it does not pursue a "pedagogical" or "perfective" purpose at the personal-private level. This in no way implies, however, that the moral virtues of the citizens are not determinative both for the survival itself of the democratic constitutional state and for the level of humanity attainable within that state. Nor does this imply that the state must or should be "neutral" with respect to all conceptions of the good and that no relationship exists between private and public morality, or between what is good and what is just.

4. We thus arrive at a fourth and final level of morality, one that is not presupposed by the constitutional state, but that does contribute to its greater or lesser perfection—the virtuousness and moral goodness of the citizens, especially with respect to those virtues that, by their nature, cannot be the content of properly institutional praxis: *personal solidarity* (as a complement and corrective to that solidarity which can be guaranteed institutionally, e.g., through a system of funds for the sick whereby the healthy pay for the sick or the richest for the poorest, and other similar redistributive mechanisms), and above all *mercy, piety, generosity, industriousness,* and the like. I would also see precisely at this level the decisive influence of every possible Christianization of society: in a truly Christian society, that is, one that is permeated by Christian behavior—which is defined by the perfection of virtue—a democratic state can and indeed must arrive at a higher and more perfect level of humanity.

With respect to Böckenförde's thesis mentioned at the outset, then, we can conclude that it seems incorrect to maintain that the democratic constitutional state is only an order of freedom and security, and not *also* an order of truth and virtue. The contraposition itself is nonsensical. The modern democratic constitutional state is also an order of truth and virtue, even if this is so in a very different way than in the classical ethic of the *polis*; which is to say it *is* such an order, mediated by the functionality of institutional praxis that limits, restricts, and conditions political praxis according to criteria of peace, freedom, and justice. A concept of the common good derives from this, as well as a more precisely articulated, multidimensional concept of a political ethos.

We will now investigate whether and to what extent this ethos can be based on contractualism and modern individualism.

The Philosophical Legitimization of the Democratic Constitutional State

"Zōon Politikon," Individualism, and Contractualism

The most important political thinkers of the seventeenth and eighteenth centuries attempted to justify the legitimacy of the state and its functions, as well as the relation between state and citizens and the rights of citizens, with the theory of contractualism. Without entering here into the extremely complex and rich history of contractualism,[19] contractualistic theories of the 1600s and 1700s depart from the notion of a pre-social individual who, as an individual, possesses certain fundamental interests that are his rights. This individual is nevertheless aware of the fact that he, as an individual, is incapable of effectively protecting and promoting these interests or "natural" rights. He therefore forms an association with his fellow-citizens (a society) based on a contractual bond, entrusting the protection of his natural rights to a governing power, which is legitimized precisely by the function of guaranteeing and promoting the natural rights of the individual person. In

---

19. See for example the classic study of John W. Gough, *Il contratto sociale. Storia critica di una teoria* (Bologna: Il Mulino, 1986), and Wolfgang Kersting, *Die politische Philosophie des Gesellschaftsvertrags* (Darmstadt: Wissenschaftliche Buchgesellschaft, 1994). This is also useful for the distinction, though not always clear, between a contractualism that serves to explain and legitimize the origin of the state and of sovereign power (e.g., Hobbes, Locke), and another, more modern contractualism along the lines of Kant, which limits itself to founding and justifying some principles of justice, political ethics, or public morality with the idea of the contract (e.g., Rawls, Buchanan).

this way the state comes into existence, with its common good as a function of the interests of the pre-political individual. The most recent contractualistic theories (e.g., that of Rawls) adopt the idea of the hypothetical contract (Rousseau, Kant): the members of a society are, in a fictitious way, imagined as stipulating a contract in a situation of originary equality. Thus we have an expedient for reconstituting the public principles of justice to which all citizens can give their assent, precisely as stipulators of the contract and subject to its respective conditions.

Despite the obvious utilitarian reasoning implicit in such a conception, nineteenth-century utilitarian philosophers, especially Jeremy Bentham and James Mill, formulated an antithesis to the doctrine of contractualism: they claimed that any political government is legitimized by its function of guaranteeing "the maximum happiness for the greatest number of people." According to this conception, the criterion of legitimacy for legislative and governmental measures is not the individual, but the community of individuals: it is not so important whether this or that individual, taken as an individual, fails to realize himself—what matters rather is that the society considered as a whole arrives at a higher level of "happiness." As such the English utilitarians—especially Bentham and Mill—were not only the adversaries of contractualistic individualism, but also the most conspicuous opponents of constitutionalist traditions (with their sense of the limitation of power and in favor of individual rights of freedom), instead favoring a social and "welfare" rationale for legislation.

A contemporary American liberal, Bruce A. Ackermann, has correctly noted that to the false individualism of contractualism, the utilitarians have responded with a false idea of community.[20] Contractualism, on the one hand, requires respect for the self-interest of the individual, basing the significance of the political community on such respect; utilitarianism, on the other hand, claims that the interest of the individual doesn't matter, but rather that of the group: what must be promoted is the "maximum degree of happiness for the maximum number of individuals." Self-interest in the latter is thus submitted to the common interest of promoting the most "satisfied" social community possible. According to Ackermann, both positions are erroneous because they attempt to make the partial truths of their respective positions into the whole truth.

20. Bruce A. Ackermann, *Social Justice in the Liberal State* (New Haven, Conn.: Yale University Press 1980), 345ff.

Without sharing Ackermann's solution, we can agree with his analysis, although not without adding an important historical qualification: it was individualism, and not utilitarianism, that promoted the idea of the constitutional state. Moreover, while individualism, considered in itself, provides legitimization for the constitutional state, utilitarianism conversely has a negative effect with respect to that state. Utilitarianism is perhaps "democratic" and "social," but it is nevertheless incapable of promoting a consciousness of the importance of the fundamental rights of man. With respect to the reality of the democratic constitutional state, therefore, contractualistic individualism seems more suitable than utilitarianism, precisely because we consider democracy to be legitimate only to the extent that it is integrated into the constitutional state, which protects and guarantees the individual rights of persons.

Prima facie then, we are inclined to reject utilitarianism in favor of individualism. We consider it more important to guarantee the rights of man than the perfection of the community in the sense of the maximum possible happiness for the maximum number of people. We would not under any circumstances want to sacrifice freedom to "social justice," if such an alternative indeed existed. We prefer less happiness for a smaller number of people, supposing that the alternative would be to violate the basic rights of some.

Thus, our task would seem to be to overcome the unilateralness and limits of individualism, rather than to abandon it. Indeed the problem with the classical conception of "individualism," as expressed in contractualism, becomes clear precisely when we analyze the concept of contract: a contract establishes a union between particular individuals who had to this point not been united with respect to the contents of the contract, a union that is based on a mutual recognition of rights and duties. The idea that the social bond between individuals—and with that political society and the political existence of the individual—is created through a contract implies the idea that the individual does not *naturally* possess such a bond; or rather, that he is not naturally a "political" being, one oriented toward the needs, interests, and good of others, and therefore not oriented toward a "common good." As such, contractualistic individualism seems to be an antithesis to the Aristotelian doctrine of man as *zōon politikon*, a being who is naturally political and social.[21]

21. According to Hannah Arendt (*The Human Condition* [Chicago: University of Chicago Press, 1958], 22) it would be erroneous, in the medieval tradition and especially that of St. Thomas Aquinas, to

Thus we can ask: is contractualism an antithetical position to the classical doctrine of man as a naturally political being, or is it simply a transformation of this doctrine? In what follows I would like to show that the latter is actually the case, which offers the possibility of arriving at an internal constructive criticism of the individualism implied in contractualism.

In fact, according to my thesis, contractualism can be understood as a mode of reasoning that tries to show why and in what sense man is naturally a social being, given that its doctrine claims that man on his own is unable to realize his individuality or to promote his rights. Precisely this incapacity to realize his individuality moves man "naturally" to associate with others in social and political life. Theories that posit a *rationally necessary* passage from a state of nature to a social state would thus be *sui generis* "proofs" of the social nature of man. This sociality is not natural in the sense of "given by nature," but in the sense of what is inexorably required according to the dictates of natural reason.

In this sense, therefore, the doctrine of contractualism can be understood as an attempt to rearticulate and rationally justify man's political nature. This rearticulation, however, possesses an essential characteristic: it sees in society and in politics, as well as in the very "common good" that it seeks, a mere instrument for the realization of individuality. Man, that is, needs the social community only so as to realize his individuality. Social life is thus understood not as a perfection of man, but as a condition of possibility of the realization of his nature, which is individuality. Even in the social state man would remain essentially an individual, with society, the political

---

identify Aristotle's *zōon politikon* with the idea that man is a naturally *social* being. According to Arendt, Aristotle saw the peculiarity of man precisely in political existence, meaning properly political life and activity, characterized by his existence as a citizen, magistrate, governor, etc. It is certainly true that for Aristotle—as Benjamin Constant later emphasized—the freedom of the citizen consisted in participation in public affairs, and not in the guaranteed security of a private sphere. Arendt is incorrect, however, in her criticism of St. Thomas and the tradition following him. Her citations are incorrect—the following formulation is not found in St. Thomas: "homo est naturaliter politcus, *id est*, socialis"; Thomas translates *zoon politikon* correctly as *civile animal* (*In I Politicorum*, lect. 1) or *animal politicum* (*ST* I-II, q. 61, a. 5), or speaks of *animal domesticum et civile* (*In I Politicorum*, lect. 1, see Aristotle, *Politica* 1253a 18). To speak in the context of the Aristotelian tradition of the "political and social animal" is therefore entirely justified from Aristotle's texts, and moreover because Aristotle considers the political sphere as the perfection and culmination of the phenomenon of *koinônia*, the social phenomenon: marriage, the *oikos*, and the *polis* are all types of social community: *koinônia hê politikê* (*Pol.* I, 1 1252a 7). The expression of St. Thomas in *ST* I, q. 96, a, 4—the citation indicated by Arendt—"homo naturaliter est animal sociale," refers to the *Nicomachean Ethics* IX, 9, 1169b 18: "politikon gar ho anthrôpos kai *syzên* pephykos" ("Man is in fact a political being and naturally drawn to life in society") and *NE* I, 7 1097b 9-12 where *politikos* is referred to all aspects of social life: relatives, wives, children, friends, fellow citizens. Even if for Aristotle political life, the existence of the citizen, is something very specific, the phenomenon of the *polis* is thought of in the context of, and as the culmination of, the natural sociability of man in general.

community, and institutions being only instruments for preserving his autonomy and natural individuality.

According to this conception it is clear that even after the contract, man remains in the "state of nature," or rather he finds himself in a social state without any change to his "nature" as man: he remains the same (individuality), though now inserted into the context of a legal bond with his neighbors advantageous for the realization of his individuality. As such, the legitimacy of these social bonds would depend on the extent to which they are experienced as advantageous for man as an individual.

Is it possible to legitimate the constitutional state on this basis? We have seen above that this does not seem possible, especially with respect to the ethos of peace, freedom, and justice implied in a constitutional democracy. Such an ethos includes, as we have seen, a conception of peace, freedom, and justice that are not simply goods "for me" as an individual, but goods pertaining to the content of a common good that is not a simple instrument for "my" own good.

To conceive of peace, freedom, and justice as components of a common good, however, presupposes a fundamental act of recognition of the other as "equal to me," that is, a fundamental act of justice, a justice consisting essentially in equality—an equality based on a common humanity. Indeed, without this equality and its acknowledgment, a contract would not even be possible. This in turn implies that the state of nature is in reality already a "social" state, in that to arrive at a social contract, a relation between "individuals of the social type" is necessary; individuality as such is not sufficient.

In what follows I will attempt to demonstrate this thesis in more detail. First, however, a brief observation: what has just been characterized as the essence of contractualism, especially the idea that society is conceived of only as an instrument so individuals may better pursue their individual interests, is strongly contested at present not only by the representatives of communitarianism, but also by adherents of neo-contractualism, as for example Rawls, and in general by liberals in the American sense of the term. All these offer theories that attempt to give a central role to the idea of solidarity among citizens, especially through redistributive measures. We will consider later whether and in what way the political philosophy of redistributive liberalism can overcome the limitations of contractualistic individualism.[22]

22. As has been correctly noted by Kersting, *Die politische Philosophie des Gesellschaftsvertrags*, 262ff., generally in Anglo-Saxon political philosophy the theme of the legitimization of sovereign power

The Insufficiency of Contractualism

The idea of contractualism, then, is insufficient for the rearticulation of the political nature of man; indeed it is a *petitio principii*, that is, it presupposes what it intends to establish. Concretely, contractualism presupposes the recognition of the other as equal to me, and with that the recognition of the interests of the other as equally honorable with respect to my own. Otherwise, the "contract" would not be a contract, but simply a tactical measure—essentially deceptive—that induces the other to renounce what is to my disadvantage so that I might better reach what is to my own personal advantage.

Obviously, in the case of Hobbes, the social contract asks no more than this; herein lies the astuteness of Hobbes's argument. His argument, however, does not lead to a state that protects the freedom of the individual in the sense in which the constitutional state intends. Rather, it results in a near-unconditional submission to a sovereign power, which secures and maintains submission to the contract through force and fear. The contract that produces the Hobbesian state guarantees that individuals will no longer be troublesome or harmful to one another, but it also ensures that subjects will never join in effective social and political cooperation. Hobbesian society exists not because human beings have become social, rather merely because a sovereign power already exists that constrains the subjects not to mutually harm one another. In the final analysis, politics is not the affair of citizens in the Hobbesian state, but of the sovereign. The subject is not a political subject, but only "subject" with respect to the only extant *political* subject, the sovereign.

Leaving aside for the moment a similar analysis of the more-refined thought of Locke, we can go straight to the question of whether the genuine ideal of the constitutional state, and even more so that of the democratic constitutional state, can be founded on an individualism centered exclusively on self-interest. The response clearly appears to be negative, given that such a political culture intends to found an environment of social and political cooperation based on a fundamental respect for the freedom of

---

is no longer central, though it was the initial theme of classical contractualism. The theme of contemporary contractualism is, almost exclusively, that of (social) justice. This is also true in a negative sense, as in the case of authors espousing *libertarianism* (e.g., Robert Nozick, *Anarchy, State, and Utopia*, New York: Basic Books 1974), i.e., to contest the legitimacy of a policy of redistribution and the meaning of the term "social justice."

each person. "Cooperation," by its nature, cannot be legitimized solely as a function of individuality, but only on the basis of a conception of the intrinsic value of social life itself, inasmuch as it surpasses mere individuality.

Contractualism is an abstraction that considers things "upside down": the truth is that man is a being who naturally needs cooperation, for a variety of reasons. The first of these, adduced by Aristotle, is reproduction, which requires two people. Second, because man is an intelligent being who transcends the limits of his personal needs in his every activity, yet at the same time a finite being unable to satisfy all his needs by himself. The words of Genesis, "It is not good for the man to be alone," express the fact that man is not sufficient unto himself. He therefore enters into relationships with those like him, relationships of exchange of both material and spiritual goods—his entire being has need of the human "thou." Finally, human beings face the fact that resources are generally scarce, and they must consequently make agreements with others on the common use of these goods.[23]

Obviously, neither Hobbes nor Locke could ignore all of these factors. And this is indeed the strongest argument against their thesis of a "natural state" that precedes, at least conceptually—as an anthropological "nucleus"—man's social condition. In fact it is clear in Hobbes that this "state of nature" is already a social state; he is unable to describe the natural state without making reference to essentially social relationships. He describes a society, but in conflict; humans fight with one another, and infidelity, aggression, and thus war reign. Hobbes does not present a solitary person—in fact Rousseau's thought is more coherent on this point—but human beings who find themselves essentially in relation to other human beings; otherwise the social contract wouldn't be necessary! The state of nature in both Hobbes and Locke demonstrates clearly that man is, as it were, "condemned" to live in society, or that he is naturally a social being, even if the principles for coexistence and cooperation are not found "in nature." For man, in contrast with animals, such principles are the fruit of free action, that is, a *cultural* product and not "given" with nature.

With this assertion, however, we are already very close to Aristotle, given that sociality and cooperation are seen as a need of man. We can never-

---

23. In contrast to this, Rousseau's conception of the "state of nature" is characterized by a superabundance of goods; Rousseau's isolated natural man is self-sufficient. For Rousseau, however, man in the state of nature is a hypothetical character, a fiction corresponding to no empirical situation.

theless go further in our analysis. If Hobbes and Locke speak of the "natural rights" of man, we must ask: where does this concept of "rights" come from? For both philosophers the concept of "rights" is prior to the concept of "contract," which latter presupposes the existence of "rights" (otherwise no "Right of nature" would exist). As such, to possess a "right" presupposes another person with respect to whom one holds this "right." Man as an isolated individual would not have "rights"—he would have tendencies, aspirations, needs, and the like, but he clearly could not have "rights." The concept of rights *presupposes* a social context, or at a minimum a relation to another person.

An isolated individual who possesses "rights" is therefore inconceivable. If, to consider the most extreme case, Hobbes claims that man has the "natural right of self-preservation," this does not mean simply that he has the tendency or the empirical will to preserve his life, but that he must be able to claim that this will or tendency must be respected. The same is true with respect to physical integrity, freedom, and property in a Lockean sense.

It is clear that Hobbes's philosophy carefully avoids this conclusion, first because his "Right of nature" is identified with the empirical inclination to self-preservation (which presupposes no recognition on the part of others), and second because Hobbes attempts to base the rationale of the contract solely on self-interest. The price he pays, however, is that (1) the "Right of nature" is in fact not a "right" in the proper sense, and (2) the Hobbesian contract is in reality not a contract, but simply a mutual, irrevocable renunciation. In reality, we are dealing with the pure submission of the two parties to the contract to the power of a third, resulting in something entirely different than a constitutional state (for Hobbes, the freedom of the citizen consists essentially in his submission to the sovereign, and not, as for Locke, a freedom guaranteed and maintained by political society). The seventeenth-century German social philosopher and lawyer Samuel von Pufendorf wasn't alone in wanting to correct this conclusion (introducing a double contract, one social and the other of submission); Locke also saw things differently, with the social contract generating the *community,* or the society, and not the political power per se. This latter, and only in a later phase, is instituted by the community.

If this is the case, however, the social contract in fact creates nothing—it rather confirms what already exists, that is, precisely that man is naturally a social being. The contract therefore does not found society, but is rather a form of expression of the mutual recognition, both public and legal, of an already existing social fact: that human beings cannot live together without mutual recognition of and respect for the individuality of each member of society. That coexistence is in fact unavoidable is already clearly shown by the descriptions of the state of nature found in both Hobbes and Locke. *The social contract does not establish the "social" character of human coexistence, but only the conditions under which that coexistence does not become the destruction of the individual by the power of the strongest.* Thus the contract is the intersubjective and public confirmation of something that *must* be recognized by all, on the basis of human nature itself. Seen in this way, the contract does not introduce man into a social state; *rather it introduces him into a social state regulated by law,* that is, a social state that respects the rights of the individual. It changes the mode and the quality of his social coexistence, without, however, implying that man is not *naturally* a social being.

It seems obvious that, with this interpretation, the nature of contractualism becomes less "dramatic." Indeed, what is most dear to supporters of the doctrine is not lost—the idea that every social and political organization must be legitimized on the basis of respect for the fundamental rights of the individual person. Something essential is gained, however, or rather the most serious defect of contractualism is avoided, the strange idea that society and its common good are exclusively an instrument for satisfying the interest of the individual as such, and nothing more. Such a correction of contractualism is, however, in fact no longer contractualism, given that it presupposes a naturally social individual, admitting that every individual right is inserted into a good common to all people—their social coexistence. At the same time, such an interpretation continues to insist that any organization of human coexistence is legitimate only if it respects the rights of the individual.

"Modified Contractualism": Some Historical Models

The first conclusion we can draw is that the conception underlying the actual development of the constitutional state was in fact rather a type of "modified contractualism." Such a modified kind of contractualism seems at least sufficient for understanding this development. It is also confirmed by history. To this end, I want to briefly consider three classical documents that express the self-understanding of modern constitutionalism: the Virginia Bill of Rights of 1771, the *Déclaration des droits de l'homme et du citoyen* of 1789, and an explanatory commentary by the Abbé Siéyès on his own proposal for such a declaration.

The Virginia Bill of Rights in fact does *not* claim that society or political government is legitimized for the sole function of protecting the rights of the individual.[24] Rather, the text asserts that all men are equally free and independent, and possess certain inalienable rights of which citizens cannot be deprived. The document, therefore, does not legitimize the existence of society on the basis of the rights of the individual, but seeks to protect the rights of the individual with respect to an already extant society. Society cannot deprive man of his right to life and liberty, of the means of acquiring property and pursuing and attaining his happiness and security. This is not a principle of legitimization for the existence of the power of the state— rather, it is a principle for establishing the limits of *any* power, whether social or governmental. Indeed, instead of legitimizing society or political government, the document legitimizes the individual with respect to society and the political power.

In establishing the purpose of government, then, the document claims that this consists not in assuring the rights or freedoms of individuals, but in reaching the "common benefit, protection and security of the people, nation or community."[25] The basic idea is one of protecting the individual from a possible abuse of power, "the danger of maladministration."

It therefore seems obvious that the Virginia declaration does not justify the existence of society by an appeal to the demands of individual freedom. Indeed, the document recognizes the social phenomenon as one that transcends individual freedom. The "common good" consists not simply in the protection of the rights of the individual, but in certain goods that are proper to the social community, and that are attainable only in the context of the community. These goods consist specifically in coexistence in peace and solidarity, the internal security of the society, and the protection of individuals from external enemies.

Thus, according to the spirit of the Virginia Bill of Rights, it would be in-

---

24. For the original text see Günther Franz, ed., *Staatsverfassungen: Eine Sammlung wichtiger Verfassungen der Vergangenheit und Gegenwart in Urtext und Übersetzung* (Munich: R. Oldenbourg 1975), 6ff.

25. See also the famous article No. 51 of the *Federalist Papers* (written by Alexander Hamilton): "Justice is the end of government. It is the end of civil society."

correct to say that individuality is the raison d'être of society or of the power of the state. The document merely claims that the protection of the rights of individuals is the condition of legitimacy of every governmental power. Therefore, a precise formulation of the "modified contractualism" implicit in the Virginia Bill of Rights would *not* be that the existence of the state is legitimized on the basis of its function of protecting the rights of individuals; or, put otherwise, the document does not propose a legitimization of the power of the state based on a pre-social concept of the individual. Rather, a precise formulation would be that a concrete state power is legitimate only if it respects particular rights or freedoms of individuals. Thus, the document does not attempt to justify the existence itself of the sovereign power, but only the legitimacy of such power and its exercise.

Classical contractualism confuses what is merely a *condition of legitimacy* of a governmental power with the basis of the raison d'être of such power. Nevertheless, the power of the state, as the governing part of society, is not "made" by individuals. Rather, it is a "natural" demand of human nature, which needs an ordered life in society to avoid falling into a deplorable condition. Thus a modified contractualism, capable of demonstrating the conditions of legitimacy of every state power, and the classical idea of man as *zōon politikon,* which emphasizes that such power is a "natural" requirement of the human condition, are seen to be compatible.[26]

We will now consider the *Déclaration des droits de l'homme et du citoyen* of 1789, placed as a preamble to the French constitution of 1791. In this preamble, the document declares that "forgetting or despising the rights of man are the only causes of public disasters and of the corruption of governments."[27] It is already clear from this statement that, again, respect for the rights of man is seen not as a reason for the existence of the government,

26. It is necessary also to distinguish between the political significance of contractualism and its concrete philosophical formulation. As Stephen Holmes has pointed out, in *The Anatomy of Antiliberalism* (Cambridge, Mass.: Harvard University Press, 1993), 193ff. and 254–55, the original political meaning of contractualism can be understood only in contraposition with the absolutism in which the monarch considered himself to be the owner of state power, with the citizens being considered instruments for pursuing the goals of the state. Against this, contractualism expressed the programmatic idea that it is part of man's dignity to have personal ends—the famous self-interest—which cannot be sacrificed to the interests of the community as these interests are interpreted by an unfettered monarch, and that every legitimate exercise of power must, ultimately, be based both in law and in fact on the consent of the governed. The concept of contract also implied the notion of mutual advantage—which is essential for any contract—instead of service and submission of one to the other, and with this also the idea of equality of dignity.

27. Franz, *Staatsverfassungen,* 302 ("l'oubli ou le mépris des droits de l'homme sont les seules causes des malheurs publics et de la corruption des gouvernements").

but as a condition by which governments can be both legitimate and safe from corruption.

The second article of the declaration, however, seems to contradict this first claim, where it says: "The purpose of any political association is the preservation of the natural and inalienable rights of man. These rights are freedom, property, security and resistance to oppression." And as the twelfth article says, to such an end it is necessary to institute a "public power," "for the advantage of all and not for the utility of those to whom such power is entrusted."

The language of the French declaration in fact seems more individualistic than that of its American model. We must not forget, however, that this language is employed against the background of the idea that the source of the state is the nation, in which sovereignty resides: the "nation," which is identified with the "third state"—bourgeois society—exists independently of any political community, and indeed is its source. The thought of the French declaration starts therefore not from a "natural," "isolated" man, but from a man who is part of a social organism, the nation, that is, bourgeois society. This society, however, can legitimately organize itself as a political society with a public power only to the extent that it respects the fundamental rights of man (which are the rights of the "bourgeoisie"). Again, these rights are not the raison d'être of the society (or rather, of the "nation"), which is a reality that requires no ulterior foundation given that it is already a fact, but rather the criterion of legitimacy of a public power capable of organizing the nation as a political society. As such, law is considered to be an expression of the "general will" (which is that of the "nation"), and not of the will of individuals. Contractualism is of no help, therefore, in this perspective, as it cannot account for what is the origin of everything: the nation.

This ideological background becomes even more clear if we examine a commentary of the Abbé Siéyès on a proposal for a declaration of the rights of man, read before the "Committee for the Constitution" on June 21–22, 1789.[28] The text is nothing other than a brief treatise of political philosophy, attempting to explain the origin and meaning of such rights. (The final declaration was not the work of Siéyès; he did have much influence in the

28. *Préliminaire de la constitution. Reconnaissance et exposition raisonnée des Droits de l'Homme & du Citoyen* (Paris: Baudouin, 1789); I have referred to the German translation, *Einleitung zur Verfassung. Anerkennung und erklärende Darstellung*, in E.-J. Siéyès, *Politische Schriften 1788–1790*, trans. and ed. E. Schmitt and R. Reichardt (Darmstadt und Neuwied: Luchterhand, 1975), 239–57.

elaboration of the first revolutionary constitution of 1791, of which the declaration of 1789 formed the preamble.)

According to this comment, man is a free being, but limited by many
needs. Human beings are naturally equal in freedom and rights, but unequal with respect to the means they possess for realizing their freedom. For
this reason, man needs society. In life in society, man is able to perfect himself because his means for realizing his freedom are greater. Society, however, must continually protect the equality of *rights* in light of the inequality
of *means* (people have different capacities, intelligence, wealth, etc.). Thus,
man does not lose his freedom upon entering society; rather, it increases.

The central idea of Siéyès's thought is the affirmation that not only does
the state of society protect man's natural freedom, but that through it his
freedom is increased, empowered, and perfected. Moreover, by one's assuming human obligations as a citizen, freedom is not lost—rather, it is realized according to justice.

Implicit in such a perspective, which is the nucleus of a liberal-bourgeois
conception, is the idea that the so-called rights of man—"natural rights"—
need the support of life in society in order to be truly valid. The thought of
Siéyès exquisitely expresses the "dialectic" that exists between the "rights
of the individual" and the "political (or social) existence" of that individual:
man needs society in order to be fully man. Human nature fully becomes
"human nature" only when a person lives in society. For this reason Siéyès
claims that the social order is almost a consequence, a completion of the natural order, spontaneously created by reason.

With this we arrive at a final conclusion: the idea of the natural rights
of man as properly *pre-social* or *pre-political* rights is somewhat of a fiction.
That said, it might be considered a conceptual fiction, that is, a necessary
abstraction so as to be able to defend the individual, or the dignity of the
person, in the face of possible oppression on the part of the political community, the majority, or a public power. And this defense is the essence of the
"liberal" program, which underlies the genesis of modern constitutionalism.

For the philosophical foundation of this idea it is necessary, in part, to
sacrifice the idea of the political nature of man in the Aristotelian sense. Aristotelianism is incapable of rendering individual freedom intelligible with respect to the demands of the *polis*, that is, in light of man's communal-political
existence. A fundamental preoccupation with individual freedom forced constitutional liberalism to rearticulate the social nature of man on the basis of a

fictitious "state of nature" and his "individual freedom," precisely pre-social and pre-political. Lost in this formulation, however, is the fundamental idea that every individual's freedom is from the outset inexorably integrated into a social fabric: man's freedom, or his will, is confronted with the necessity of recognizing other men and women as "equal to himself," with justice itself being founded on this recognition. This equality of rights, of freedom, and ultimately of dignity between people cannot, however, be articulated according to the idea of a contract, precisely because the possibility of any contract (if one really intends to found a "society" or a "social community") *already presupposes* such an equality of rights; thus, a contract can only confirm this relationship of justice, integrating it into a positive legal order.

Aristotelianism and contractualism, therefore, each express a part of the truth. Aristotelianism teaches us that freedom has the capacity and the need to transcend itself toward life in community, without which the individual person cannot fully realize his humanity; from contractualism, on the other hand, we learn that every human community is a community of individual beings having dignity and interests not identifiable with the community itself, so that every social and political body must justify itself, in a certain way, by being at the service of the individual.

Aristotelianism and contractualism could be combined based on a deeper reflection on the intrinsic auto-transcendence of individual freedom, that is, on its intrinsic ordering toward the "good of others," expressed in the fundamental principle of justice, the Golden Rule. This rule, as we have seen, presupposes respect and recognition of the other as "a being equal to me"; thus, at the very foundation of human freedom we find equality between persons. This fundamental equality has no need for articulation through a contract, as it *cannot* be the result of a contractual agreement between free individuals; rather, it is *already inherent* in individual freedom, which latter thus manifests itself as a principle of sociability and solidarity.

My argument has shown with even greater clarity how everything depends on the concepts of individual (or human person) and freedom one uses. To think of social bonds contractualistically can mean many different things, according to the concept we have of the *parties* to the contract. Ultimately, an anthropological question is implicit in the question we have addressed, on which the existence or conception of a "common good" essentially depends.

The Legitimate Primacy of Freedom and the Demands of Justice: the Parallelism between Rights and Duties

The centrality of the concept of the individual leads us to consider how some contemporary liberal doctrines—philosophically, heirs of classical contractualism—articulate the bond between individual, society, and political system, and how they deal with compatibility between freedom and solidarity, and between individual rights and the demands of social life. Unquestionably, liberalism is a doctrine that gives priority to freedom. We can also state with confidence that, in its political essence, the classical liberal program has to a large extent become the fundamental reality in our modern constitutional democracies. The great problems of political legitimacy and justice are considered today in the context of specific principles and institutional realities that are genuinely liberal, and that represent a cultural accomplishment questioned only by a few extremist groups.

This priority of freedom means that the freedom of the individual is given a privileged place with respect to every other social value. What was said above concerning the difference between individualism and utilitarianism is also valid here: the primacy of freedom implies that we are unwilling to accept that the rights of particular individuals be sacrificed in favor of an eventual greater utility to the community. We see the freedom and autonomy of the individual as a "zone of noninterference," necessarily impervious to any attempt at utilitarian instrumentalization of the individual for ends beyond himself.

Obviously, the concepts of political society, justice, and common good that can be justified on the basis of these presuppositions depend on the conceptions of the individual and of freedom that are used. Along these lines, two typical currents in contemporary liberal political philosophy (liberal in a broad sense), practically antithetical to each other, are represented by the thought of Robert Nozick and John Rawls. I will now show how these two philosophers operate with two different conceptions of the individual. This will allow us, in contrast with their positions, to clearly distinguish our concept of the individual, which, as noted, includes self-transcendence toward the good of others as a constitutive component.[29]

---

29. It must be borne in mind that Nozick's theory and even more so Rawls's are primarily theories of distributive justice. The classical questions of political legitimacy are posed by these authors largely in the context of this discussion.

The Person and His Self-transcendence toward the Good of Others

To be more specific, our conception of the individual sees him as a rational being for whom sociability is constitutive, in the sense that the individual cannot be conceived, precisely as an individual, without a relationship to the other. By this I do not mean that the other is, so to speak, an "ontological" part of the self, but that, supposing the existence of the other, the relationship of the self to the other—his self-transcendence toward the good of this other—is an ineluctable act, and in this sense "natural" to every individual self[30] (which does not exclude the possibility of freely resisting this inclination, closing oneself in oneself). This constitutive self-transcendence toward the good of others is based (to repeat) on that act basic to all justice, the fundamental recognition of the other as equal to me, with the denial of this recognition being in turn the fundamental act of injustice.

Individuals, as we have just defined them, we call "persons." A personalistic conception of the individual, however, *always treats the person as an individual,* that is, as a separate and autonomous existence. According to the classical definition of Boethius, the person is *individua substantia,* but an individual substance precisely of a *rationalis naturae:* spirituality is the basis of the self-transcendence of the individual toward the good of others, the latter expressed, as a norm of justice, by the Golden Rule. "Individualism," "individual freedoms," and "individual rights" thus acquire a richer significance, in which the relationship to the good of the other—and thus to a *common* good—is already implicit. Such an "individual-person" experiences the demands of solidarity as constitutive of his practical intentionalities.

Clearly, the implications of such concepts of human individuality, freedom, and autonomy are significant. Not only so as to be able to distinguish, as I have done elsewhere, between autonomy in a strong and in a weak sense,[31] but above all to be able to construct a political philosophy in which

30. See on this the beginning of the eighth book of Aristotle's *Nicomachaean Ethics,* where he speaks of the natural familiarity and friendship between man and man which especially shows itself "during trips" (1155a 22)—i.e., in foreign lands—an idea taken up again by St. Thomas Aquinas to illustrate the social nature of man which shows itself precisely in cases of necessity with respect to complete strangers: "ac si omnis homo omni homini esset naturaliter familiaris et amicus" (*Summa Contra Gentiles* III, 117).

31. See chapter 2 of the present volume, which is entitled "The Liberal Image of Man and the Concept of Autonomy: Beyond the Debate between Liberals and Communitarians." This was originally published as my "L'immagine dell'uomo nel liberalismo e il concetto di autonomia: al di là del dibattito fra liberali e comunitaristi," in *Immagini dell'uomo. Percorsi antropologici nella filosofia moderna,* ed. Ignacio Yarza (Rome: Armando, 1997), 95–133.

the primacy of the individual and his freedom not only are not impediments to, but, on the contrary, are fundamental elements of a sociability that is no longer merely self-interest, but solidarity—which is to say interest in the good of others *precisely as* the good of others.

The Individual as Possessor of Himself, of Entitlements and of Rights (R. Nozick)

In contrast with this concept of individual-person, Robert Nozick—a representative of what in the United States is called not *liberalism*, but *libertarianism*—includes in his libertarian theory his interpretation of the Kantian idea that individuals are ends in themselves, and must never be treated as a means to other ends. "Individuals are inviolable,"[32] and are the only realities that exist. There is no "social entity," with a good proper to it, for which a good of the individual could legitimately be sacrificed. No "overall *social* good" exists, no social good of a higher order—only the good of separate persons, "indifferent individual people,"[33] with every person being the exclusive possessor of himself. From this principle of separateness and self-possession Nozick derives what he calls the "root idea" of his theory of justice: "There is no justified sacrifice of some of us for others." No person may ever be considered to be a resource for other persons, which would be precisely the case if a redistributive policy were adopted with coercive measures. This would be akin to constraining some to forced labor for the sake of others, and thus the same as an aggression or a theft.[34]

On this basis, Nozick elaborates a theory of justice that above all seeks to avoid any proposal of desirable "patterns" according to which society should be organized. The only thing Nozick's theory offers are some guidelines for establishing the just acquisition and transmission of goods, that is, for a title ("entitlement") of just possession. Supposing a legitimate original appropriation and a corresponding title, according to Nozick an actual distribution of goods can be considered just if it results from the mechanism of transfer that is the free market. "A distribution is just if it arises from another just distribution by legitimate means."[35] Outside of these rules, no obligation and no right toward other persons can be justified. Given that every individual is a separate existence and the exclusive possessor of himself,

---

32. Nozick, *Anarchy, State, and Utopia*, 31.   33. Ibid., 32f.
34. Ibid.   35. Ibid., 151.

his position in society and his titles to possession are legitimized exclusively by the justice of the mechanisms of acquisition and transfer. Redistributive measures would be intrinsically unjust, a violation of the freedom and integrity of the individual. One who possesses much—for example, because he has received an inheritance, or because he is talented and has worked hard with ingenuity and good fortune, and so on—has no obligation toward one who is not well off due to lack of talent, ingenuity, luck, or opportunity. And this latter has no right to be helped and "compensated," in some way or another, by those who are well off.

This theory is interesting in that it shows exactly the extent to which a theory of political justice depends on the concept of individual it employs. Nozick's arguments, which are blatantly anti-utilitarian, *are* effective in showing, as contrary to the anthropological fact of the ontological autonomy of man and of his freedom and responsibility, the inadequacy of the idea that the riches of some confer on the worse-off a right, so to speak, to a partial expropriation through redistribution from the owners of such riches. Nevertheless, Nozick's arguments are valid only in opposing this specific motivation for redistributive measures. *They do not prove that no obligation of the better-off exists toward the worse-off,* and consequently they also fail to prove that a redistributive policy would necessarily imply the instrumentalization of persons for ends other than those persons themselves, illegitimately imposing burdens and sacrifices on them. We will now examine this in more detail.[36]

The principle just cited, "A distribution is just if it arises from another just distribution by legitimate means," is in fact extremely ambiguous. In a certain sense it is also tautological, because in essence it merely says: "*The origin* of a specific distribution is just, if it arises from another just distribution by legitimate means." To affirm that the origin of a distribution is just, however, is not yet the same as saying that the distribution itself is just.[37] The legitimacy of the *origin* of a specific distribution is not a sufficient condition for declaring the structuring of a society on the basis of this type of distribution also to be just. To be able to claim that the distributive structure of a society is just simply because the origin of its various distributions occurs according to rules in themselves considered just, another premise

36. Other weak points in Nozick's theory are well explicated by Will Kymlicka, *Contemporary Political Philosophy: An Introduction* (Oxford: Clarendon Press 1990), 95–125.

37. My intent here is not to speak only of the distribution of material goods, but also of social goods such as rights to participation in political decisions, to formation, to opportunity, etc.

is necessary. This premise would be the impossibility that there be—other than the existence of a legitimate title of ownership and a corresponding absence of rights of other persons who are perhaps less fortunate—another factor from which it could result that a specific distribution of goods, even though initiated justly, could nevertheless be unjust.

And indeed such a factor does exist. We see this precisely once we admit that the individual, even when conceived of as a person with a separate, inviolable existence who can never be used for other ends, possesses not only rights that must be respected by others, but also duties toward others. Such duties, however—and this is key—do *not* result from a "right" of these others toward those who have the duty and consequently do not limit the latter's rights, such that "duty" would be equivalent to "limitation of right," converting one who has a duty toward X into a resource *for* X (precisely what Nozick correctly considers to be morally unacceptable). Rather, we must think of these duties toward other persons as originating from the *need* of these others, from an insufficiency of goods due them in virtue of their dignity as persons "equal to me." Without violating the principle of the separateness and autonomy of persons, as well as their right to be "possessor of themselves" and to not be used for other ends, it is nevertheless conceivable that the individual, in the depth of his freedom as guided by reason, may perceive an obligation of solidarity toward those concerning whom he must recognize an equal dignity as persons. This self-transcendence toward the good of the other is specifically *not* the use of an autonomous individual for an end external to himself; rather it is precisely an act of freedom of this same autonomous individual. This obligation of solidarity, however, is recognizable as originating from an act of freedom only to the extent that it is understood not as the simple correlate of the right of another toward me—given that the rights of others toward me are a limitation of my freedom and as such generate an obligation—but as truly an act of turning oneself toward the other and his need, again on the basis of recognizing him, in a fundamental act of justice, as equal to myself.

Nozick knows only the language of rights, as is generally the case for modern political philosophy in the contractualistic tradition. He has forgotten the language of man as a being with needs, that is, the fact that people seek cooperation in society not only so as to more effectively claim their rights, but, even more fundamentally, to effectively address their needs. One who attempts to integrate the needy character of human existence into political philosophy according to the contractualist tradition would thus be inclined to interpret every need as the source of specific rights toward others, and every duty as generated by a corresponding right of another.[38]

Once the idea is admitted that the human individual is a being characterized by concrete needs—different in each case because of natural and historical contingencies—which create not *rights* of the needy but *duties* of solidarity toward them, then Nozick's argument for proving the intrinsic justice of a distribution according to criteria he has established becomes weak. Nozick only defends the individual against coercive measures that use him for extrinsic ends, violating his rights as an individual and necessarily turning him into a resource for others according to a utilitarian logic, in light of a presumed "overall social good." Nozick fails to take into account the fact that, precisely as a "separate" individual, man "naturally" transcends himself toward the good of others, according to their needs. Even if rights in general, along with the rules for the just transfer of titles of ownership in the market, are the same for everyone—*nevertheless concrete needs generated by such an economic structure are not equal for all.* In fact, justice pertains not only to what we owe others based on their rights, but also to what we owe them in consideration of their needs.[39] We owe our neighbor not only what is his right, but also that which corresponds to his needs—even if he does not properly possess a legal title to such a "debt." In this way a duty of solidarity is added to our rights and the freedom that corresponds to them. Rights of freedom and duties of solidarity run parallel to each other and must be taken together. It is *not* a case, however, of preferring or subordinating one to the other—our rights are not diminished, but *accompanied,*

38. Author's note, 2008: In his recent book *Justice: Rights and Wrongs* (Princeton, N.J.: Princeton University Press, 2008), Nicholas Wolterstorff defends a brilliantly argued strict correlation between rights and duties. I am not sure the extent to which Wolterstorff's account contradicts the idea expressed above and might be a challenge to my view. I think that Wolterstorff's argument is situated on a different, more fundamental level. What he says actually is that every human person has a moral right to having his neediness acknowledged by others. Yet, this does not imply—and this was my point—that they also have a right to some portion of the possessions of others, in the sense of what Aquinas calls properly a legal right, a right that in turn *diminishes* correspondingly the equally legal right of the possessor toward his possessions.

39. The discussion becomes somewhat complicated here because when modernity speaks of "rights," it speaks of *subjective* rights. Although (as it is nowadays more and more acknowledged) the concept of subjective rights has its roots in medieval canon law and perhaps is not totally alien to Roman law, pre-modern jurisprudence, as well as ethics in the Aristotelian tradition and that of St. Thomas Aquinas, it is generally considered that the object of the virtue of justice was *ius*, considered, however, precisely as that which is due someone according to justice. A (subjective) right is only a special case of *ius* understood in this way. Obviously, when speaking of *ius* in an objective sense, we can maintain that "right" and "duty" are strictly correlates.

by our duties. We should thus opt for a political philosophy of a solidarity that does not relativize the primacy of freedom and its corresponding rights, but is inseparably bound to them.

We thus arrive at the following conclusion: even if the origin of a concrete distribution is just according to Nozick's criteria, that same distribution might nevertheless be unjust, relatively or in certain aspects, if we consider the actual needs of persons living in a society structured on this distributive pattern. A certain concrete distribution, even if just from the point of view of its origin, could require a correction or adjustment for reasons of solidarity—and to omit such a correction would in fact be unjust. To be clear, it is not unjust that some people have more than others—we can continue to hold that the better-off are fully entitled to their possessions (supposing the criteria of legitimacy proposed by Nozick). What *would* be unjust in such a situation would be to deny that the well-off have a certain duty to help meet the needs of the worse-off, so that these latter would be enabled to improve their situation through the exercise of their rights and their own efforts. The presence of needy persons may create a duty in one who legitimately owns possessions—precisely a duty of solidarity—to make a part of his own resources available to the worse-off; again, resources he rightly possesses. This calls into question not the legitimacy of the title of acquisition, according to Nozick's criteria, but rather his implication that such a title implies the non-existence of any duty of solidarity with respect to the needs of others. Such an obligation of solidarity is precisely an aspect of the demands of justice.

Parallelism between Rights and Duties

I have strongly insisted on the fact that the duty of solidarity toward the worse-off is not based on the existence of a right of the needy toward the well-off, nor is this duty created by a diminution of the rights of the more fortunate (with the exception of the case, which Mill also considers, of resources—especially land—held in an unproductive manner, and therefore unjustly; but here no legitimate title exists in the first place).[40] Furthermore, I have emphasized that the obligation of solidarity of the more fortunate toward those who are worse off *simply coexists* with the rights of the more fortunate; it is part of the intrinsic structure of the person as a moral sub-

---

40. See John Stuart Mill, *Principles of Political Economy,* bk. 2, ch. 2, sec. 6, in *Collected Works of John Stuart Mill,* ed. J. M. Robson (Toronto: University of Toronto Press, 1965), 2:230: "No man made the land. It is the original inheritance of the whole species. Its appropriation is wholly a question of general expediency. When private property in land is not expedient, it is unjust."

ject, for whom self-transcendence toward the good of others is constitutive. More than a limitation of his rights, this duty appeals to his responsibility as a being who must recognize in those who are less well off beings equal to himself, in that they too are human persons.

If this distinction seems an unnecessary subtlety, it seems important to me for two reasons. The first becomes clear if we consider that, theoretically, another possibility exists within the liberal tradition for opposing Nozick's position: we could simply assert that an individual possesses only those rights compatible with the needs of others; or vice versa, that the needs of a needy person would create a right on his part to a portion of the goods of the well-off, that is, *that the actual needs of some persons would restrict the actual rights of others.* I would grant that this is true in a certain sense, that is, in the sense that the goods of this earth are given by God to all in common (as Locke affirmed).[41] An imagined "originary" act of appropriation would then not be the acquisition of something that simply belonged to "no one," but the appropriation as personal property of a portion of what was originally destined to provide for the needs of all. This idea, however, does not resolve our problem. Once we have admitted—for various reasons we will not address here—that the institution of private property with its juridical consequences is the most suitable and just way of putting the goods of this world at the disposition of all,[42] then ordinarily we must argue without reference to the fact that the goods of this world were created by God for the benefit of all.

Many liberals who reject Nozick's libertarian views rightly hold that a concept of the right to property that would exclude in principle any redistributive measures is indeed contrary to justice, thinking that it is not just to claim that the more fortunate simply have no duty toward the less fortunate. From this they infer that, supposing such a duty exists, it could derive only from a corresponding right of the less fortunate, a right that obviously implies a real diminution of the rights—the title of ownership—of the more prosperous (and thus one easily arrives at that typically American liberalism which inclines to the welfare state). But this is precisely what Nozick, not without reason, declares to be unjust: the idea that those who are less fortunate have rights of property, at least in part, with respect to other per-

---

41. John Locke, *Two Treatises of Government, Second Treatise,* chap. 5, sec. 25.
42. Ibid. (26): "God, who has given the World to Men in common, hath also given them reason to make use of it to the best advantage of Life, and convenience."

sons, rights that would be put into effect through redistributive measures imposed by the state.[43]

According to our understanding, rather, a right—a legitimate title—is not properly limited or diminished by the needs of others. No person may claim a right to the property of other persons.[44] Nevertheless, these needs generate on our part a duty of solidarity with persons who are less fortunate. Rather than saying—not without risk—that our rights diminish to the extent that the needs of others increase, we can more reasonably say that to the degree our titles of ownership increase—that is, to the degree that one possesses resources, both material and of every kind of opportunity—*so does our duty of solidarity toward the more needy increase.* (So as not to be misunderstood, this principle is still very general, and must be applied according to further criteria of justice: it is not *need as such* and without any ulterior qualification that generates a duty of solidarity in others. We must distinguish between culpable and inculpable needs; one must also evaluate the situation and the possibilities of the needy person, who possesses a duty to better his situation, with corresponding rights. The duty of solidarity of the more fortunate is generated by a *legitimate* need, according to criteria of justice.)

We thus arrive at the second reason why it was important to emphasize that the duty of solidarity does not result from a diminution of our rights, but originarily coexists with and simply "accompanies" our rights. This would be the establishment of a correct foundation for legitimate redistributive measures by the state, consistent with the primacy of freedom. One could conclude—prematurely—from what has just been asserted that solidarity must be restricted to individual, free charity and that it would be illicit on the part of the state to intervene in society with its coercive power to enact redistributive measures. This conclusion would be incorrect—first, because the duty of solidarity is not a duty of charity, but truly one of justice (though perhaps not always perfect or legal justice, yet it belongs to the sphere of the virtue of justice). Second, and as a consequence of the first, the conclusion would be mistaken because, as we have seen, men create the

---

43. See Nozick, *Anarchy, State, and Utopia,* 172.

44. The exception to this, commonly upheld by the tradition, is theft for the motive of mere survival, i.e., in cases of extreme necessity. The reason for this is that no title of property can be considered "just" and so to speak "air-tight" when confronted with this kind of urgent necessity. We could also say, however, that in such a case the duty of solidarity is so strong and urgent that the needy person could legitimately presume the owner's consent, or, if such consent were not explicitly given, he could appeal to the right to legitimate defense (given that one is dealing with a question of life or death).

state, which receives its legitimacy among other reasons precisely for the purpose of justice. Once we have accepted our presupposition of an anthropology of the individual-person who is characterized by self-transcendence toward the good of others, with a corresponding interest in their good—the source of the duty of solidarity—*we can now conceive of a state, still in a contractualistic context, that considers among its duties not only the maintenance of peace and the protection of the freedoms and rights of its citizens, but also the promotion of solidarity—and this precisely as representing the interests and concerns of its citizens.*

Considering that, in a contractualistic context, political society and state institutions with coercive power are created by men, one could readily see how such institutions can also be understood as *instruments of solidarity*, and not only of *protection of rights*. Once we admit that individuals have not only rights, but also duties of solidarity toward their neighbor, and the impossibility that these obligations would be fulfilled effectively merely through the interplay of the free forces of society, contractualistic reasoning would then require that the state, legitimized by an at least hypothetical contract, would become not only the protector of my rights, but also the authorized representative of my duties of solidarity—to the exact degree, however, that this is reconcilable with the primacy of freedom, and desirable for other reasons such as efficiency and economic reasonableness. The underlying idea is that such a state is not—as in the conception of the welfare state—conceived of as a preexistent entity, originarily "above" the citizens and concerned with an overarching common good, giving it the right to limit and condition the rights of citizens according to these "higher" demands of the common good—that is, an authoritarian, bureaucratic, "planning" state. Rather, it is seen as *a state "created" by the citizens themselves for the citizens* (note here the contractualistic element), with the task of accomplishing communally what is in the citizens' common interest but which nevertheless cannot be accomplished individually, even as individuals working in common, without the support of coercive state institutions. Thus, consistent with our anthropology of an "unselfish" individualism, we also consider among the interests of the citizen the interest for the good—the advantage—of the other, with a corresponding interest in fulfilling the practical duties of solidarity pertaining to such an interest. As such, we have arrived at a properly *noneconomic* concept of self-interest; according to this conception, freedom is thought of as a faculty intrinsically limited by the duty of solidarity. Even if one's rights—entitlements—are not affected by the needs of others, the morally legitimate exercise of freedom by one who possesses a specific right could be profoundly affected by the duty of solidarity. If we include this aspect in contractualistic logic, we arrive at a contract in which the reciprocal auto-limitation of freedom would give rise precisely to a state possessing redistributive rights, *conferred on it by its citizens,* for the carrying out of the duty of solidarity originarily inscribed in their freedom as individual-persons. And on such a basis, Nozick's argument clearly could no longer be sustained, not even on the basis of contractualist thinking.

Basing solidarity on self-interest (Rawls)

At this point new horizons of discourse about political justice open, discourses that obviously also belong to the liberal tradition. I refer to the discussion initiated in 1971 by John Rawls by his landmark and meanwhile classical *A Theory of Justice,*[45] a book that provoked a genuine rebirth of contractualism and generally of political philosophy. With his "difference principle," Rawls proposed that inequalities—and in general every improvement of the position of the well-off with respect to the worse-off—can be justified only to the extent that they also improve the position of the less-fortunate. This is clearly a principle of solidarity, and even, in Rawls's terms, brotherhood.[46] This appears, however, to be a solidarity based on a relative diminution of the rights of the more fortunate, who according to Rawls would implicitly not have a right to what they possess, supposing there is not a simultaneous improvement of the situation of the less fortunate. Without such an improvement, the state would take redistributive measures.

In Rawls's theory, the "difference principle"—a principle of justice made operative through the basic structure of society—is chosen in a hypothetical situation that he calls the "original position." It is interesting to note that the idea of the "original position" has the effect (among other things) of *homogenizing* the parties to the contract—of putting them in a fictitious state of equality by means of a "veil of ignorance"—in such a way that each of the parties to the contract could *potentially* be any of the other parties. This perspective inclines all parties to choose principles advantageous to the worse-off, given that each party, according to the theory, could be that worse-off.

45. Cambridge, Mass.: Harvard University Press, 1971; Oxford: Oxford University Press, 1972. For the sake of exactness, Nozick's book, which we have treated first, was actually written as a response to that of Rawls.

46. Ibid., 105.

The originary position is therefore a situation in which everyone is in solidarity with the less-fortunate, but only because the less-fortunate one could possibly be himself. The self-interested subject—the perfectly rational selfish person—would then adopt a strategy according to the "maximin rule," that is, a preference for a situation in which one can earn only a little, but still be relatively well off even if unable to earn anything at all, over one in which a person can earn a lot, but in the case of a general downturn would be left with nothing. It is therefore a strategy for minimizing risks and anticipating the worst case—a type of preventive pessimism—and of choosing guiding principles most advantageous in the worst case, that is, the maximum of the minimum. And as such, from a collective "selfish" choice derive principles of justice and corresponding institutions that overcome this original selfishness, functioning with solidarity.

Obviously, the originary position is a hypothetical one, an ideal of practical deliberation and thus a privileged cognitive or "epistemic" position used to render the demands of justice intelligible. According to Rawls, these demands become intelligible precisely when we find ourselves in an imaginary state of equal freedom in which everyone could be the most needy. It is a state, moreover, requiring hypothetical abstractions from any actual natural or social circumstance, from talents, capacities, psychological inclinations, moral conceptions, and so on. Principles of justice would be those that any individual, conceived of as a perfectly rational selfish person, would choose in such a cognitive position of fictitious equality created by a veil of ignorance.

As has been correctly observed by Will Kymlicka, the parties to such a contract would be adopting a perspective in which the good of others simply becomes a component of their own good, either actual or possible.[47] As in the utilitarian strategy of universalization or of the "ideal sympathizer," everyone is forced to take the good of other concrete persons into consideration, but precisely in such a way that every one of these concrete others is potentially oneself. Consequently, a true alterity does not seem to exist. Even solidarity itself, at least with respect to its motivation, is reduced to an interest in one's own good.

Rawls's theory, then, is an attempt to reconstruct the demands of justice and solidarity starting from the self-interested subject. He is aware, how-

---

47. Kymlicka, *Contemporary Political Philosophy*, 69.

ever, that such a reconstruction would merely be a vicious circle—of the Hobbesian variety—if principles were not present in the original position that, in a certain sense, imply the existence of a true alterity. Rawls calls these principles "natural duties"; these principles, like the principle of fairness, govern not the functioning of institutions, but the behavior of individuals.[48]

While the principle of fairness generates the obligation to fulfill the rules of those institutions that exist as a result of the agreement of the parties to the contract,[49] natural duties would be obligations that we have independently and prior to the existence of such institutions, and also independently of any of our voluntary acts founding such institutions. The first and fundamental natural duty, according to Rawls, is precisely the "natural duty of justice," implying that, assuming the basic structure of a society is just, everyone has the duty to give their support to the respective institutions. This natural duty of justice is thus the expression of a type of natural obligation to give one's assent to, and consequently to promote, the establishment of a just basic structure, according to which a multitude of individuals can organize themselves politically. According to Rawls, this principle is preferable to a utilitarian principle in the originary position, because it resolves the fundamental problem that without such a principle citizens would not feel themselves obligated toward a just constitution before they had benefited from it.[50] This is even more true if we ask the question: why feel obligated to a political system simply because we are born into it? Supposing the self-interested mechanism of the originary position that confers legitimacy on the system, once the veil of ignorance is removed it is precisely the well-off—for whom redistributive measures are not a benefit, but a burden—who would no longer have a reason to support the system. A principle is therefore necessary that transcends or compensates the mere self-interested calculation. Rawls sees this principle in a natural duty of justice—which obviously is itself chosen by selfish individuals in an originary position, to avoid something worse!

Other examples of natural duties mentioned by Rawls demonstrate that he senses the need to establish principles that genuinely lead individuals to act in relationship with a true and proper alterity: the duty to recipro-

48. See Rawls, *A Theory of Justice*, 114–17; 333–42.
49. Ibid., 111ff.
50. Ibid., 336–37.

cal help in situations of need or danger, the obligation to avoid cruelty, the obligation of mutual respect. Rawls attempts in this way to resolve the not-insignificant "assurance problem,"[51] resolved by Hobbes by the institution of the absolute sovereign who guarantees the fulfillment of the contract through fear of punishment. We have already seen that free societies like our constitutional democracies are inconceivable without citizens who count among their interests precisely the interest for the institutional structure as a common good, independently of whether these institutions favor their immediate advantage in terms of their own personal good.

This seems to be precisely the significance of Rawls's natural duties, and he thus admits that the self-interested logic of the originary position cannot found itself. Rawls's natural duty of justice has as its object precisely a common good. From an anthropological point of view, however, the admission of these natural duties seems to introduce a strange hybrid into Rawls's theory: the assertion that the natural duty of justice must necessarily be conceived of as an inclination toward a common good renders fragile, from an anthropological point of view, Rawls's dichotomy between the good and the just.

With his natural duties, Rawls in some way integrates the *zōon politikon* into his contractualism, that is, a certain naturality of human sociality. Rawls claims that, even in a position of originary equality, the self-interested individual must be thought of as a subject obligated to transcend a mere interest in his own good, toward a common good. The common good—and with that the idea itself of justice—cannot therefore be constructed on the basis of mere self-interest, which can be part of a theory of justice only if it is integrated into the larger dimension of the community of good.

One sees here a certain contrast with a liberal ideal of autonomy that would be the source of a respective pluralism of goods, given that natural duties are logically prior to any principle of justice and to any institution oriented to the realization of justice; these duties are in fact part of the autonomous self. A conception of the good that is not rooted in these duties is unthinkable; thus, the division between the good and the just is no longer sustainable. Every principle of justice must be an at least partial expression of a basic "natural" conception concerning the good. Justice and the institu-

---

51. Ibid., 336. Habermas speaks, in an analogous context, of a *Solidaritätslücke* ("lacuna of solidarity"). Habermas, *Faktizität und Geltung. Beiträge zur Diskurstheorie des Rechts und des demokratischen Rechtsstaats* (Frankfurt am Main: Suhrkamp, 1992), 51.

tions created by men to assure justice are a common good; put otherwise, they are part of that good which is common to men in virtue of their being human beings.

Therefore, a distinction between the "just" and the "good" doesn't make sense as a dichotomy, that is, as the objects of two different moral capacities, a sense of justice on the one hand and the capacity to have a proper conception concerning the good on the other, as Rawls holds.[52] Truthfully, every conception of justice implies a position, even if partial and qualified, with respect to the good. Otherwise one cannot understand why, within a particular conception of the good, that is, in the framework of a particular rational pattern of "private" life, certain principles of justice might be lacking that—so as not to be required to assume that every person has two different senses of justice—nevertheless must have a connection with that same sense of justice constitutive of the public sphere. This does not mean that every distinction between individual personal morality and political morality—the morality of public and institutional action with its respective conception of justice—must be denied, or that between "private" moral reasoning and the public reasoning of which Rawls speaks in his most recent works.[53] We have already spoken about this multidimensional morality. Nevertheless, the decisive point seems to be that these two moralities, even if we can distinguish between them, cannot simply correlate to two different moral capacities; we must not undervalue their intimate reciprocal connection.

We can therefore see that individual patterns of life and conceptions of the good are in close "contact" with that common good that gives origin to principles of justice. The "second" Rawls in a certain way admits this when he says that the principles of justice and public reasoning are the result of an "overlapping consensus"[54] that expresses, as public reasoning, a partial convergence between the moral convictions and doctrines that citizens hold privately, which of course differ among themselves. Rawls insists that this is not a simple *modus vivendi* but a moral conception, held publicly for more or less moral reasons[55]—and as such including precisely a consensus on aspects of the good. With this—though Rawls does not say it—the relationship between the just and the good can no longer be adequately understood by

52. Rawls, *A Theory of Justice*, 561; Rawls, *Political Liberalism* (New York: Columbia University Press, 1993), 19.

53. See Rawls, *Political Liberalism*, 212ff.

54. Ibid., 133ff.

55. Ibid., 147. See also chapter 2 of this book and *L'immagine dell'uomo nel liberalismo*, 116ff.

the idea that they are respectively the objects of two different moral capacities; rather, it is more appropriate to say that the sense of justice is a specific application, precisely in the public sphere, of the capacity of having a particular conception of the good. As such, "private" and "public" morality would not be simply different, but the latter would be a specific and peculiar case of the former, not in the sense of an application of morality *simpliciter* by the coercive power of the state—and thus the public institutionalization of a specific concept of morality—but in the sense of the application of moral principles in a sphere different than the "private," that of public or political action. Thus, as has been well said: "In reality personal ethics and political ethics judge different actions: the actions of the individual and the actions proper to the political whole."[56]

This, however, has consequences for the question of the relationship between law and morality, and that of the neutrality of the state with respect to differing concepts of the good.

Neutrality of the State, Public Morality, and the Common Good

The theories of both Nozick and Rawls are typical liberal, in that they justify and systematize a clear distinction between public principles of justice and the principles governing private choices of individual citizens, with the latter being based on the conception of the good that each person follows. The state cannot privilege or make its own a particular conception of the good; it must limit itself to the principles of justice that govern the basic structure of society, at the service of a cooperation mutually advantageous for individuals. A fortiori, nor can it be the public power's function to make obligatory, through legal measures, that for which the individual person possesses an inalienable responsibility: the orientation of his life according to moral and religious truth.

Two Conceptions of the Neutrality of the State

We touch here on a delicate point in our effort to understand the idea of a common good in the context of the modern democratic constitutional state,

---

56. Angel Rodríguez Luño, "Le ragioni del liberalismo," in *I cattolici e la società pluralista. Il caso delle "leggi imperfette,"* ed. J. Joblin and R. Tremblay (Bologna: Edizioni Studio Domenicano, 1996), 225–38; the quotation is from 235n21.

given that the notion of the neutrality of the state can be understood in at least two essentially different ways. The first is the typically "liberal" understanding. In this sense, the "neutrality" of the state would mean to reduce the legitimate range of action of the government, legislature, and the like to a peaceful regulation of all the currents present in a pluralistic society. Where consensus is lacking, the public authority must withdraw to that "neutral" ground on which everyone, or at least the majority, agrees, proceeding according to principles of an exclusively procedural justice from that point on. In this way the equality and the autonomy and self-determination of individual citizens is respected. From this perspective, for example, it would be logical that state prohibition of abortion be illicit—that is, contrary to freedom—provided a considerable minority of citizens actually favor its legalization. Likewise with the denial of a legal status to homosexual couples equal to that of traditional marriage between a man and a woman. In this way, the proceduralism of the law is at the service of an equal public respect for every conception of the good and the respective autonomy of citizens.

The second way of understanding the neutrality of the state would be to consider only the mechanisms of procedural justice as neutral, that is, to treat all persons according to the same rules of law, without partiality deriving from juridically nonrelevant factors (the first interpretation of neutrality, as we have seen, also accepts procedural justice, but affirms much more given that it elevates procedural justice to the highest and ultimate criterion of justice). Such a procedural justice, which is referred to and applies concrete rules and principles of law, can in this second case be perfectly inserted, however, into a juridical-political culture that accepts the public efficacy of principles that correspond to a specific conception of the good, and as such cannot be morally neutral. Herein lies the difference from the first conception.

This second mode of speaking of the "neutrality" of the state is the only reasonable and sincere one in the political culture of the democratic constitutional state. Indeed, various liberal thinkers have recognized this and consequently hold an antineutralist position, asserting for example that the state must promote the moral value of the autonomy of the person through political measures.[57] The "second" Rawls also understood this, to the extent

---

57. See, for example, William A. Galston, *Liberal Purposes: Goods, Virtues, and Diversity in the Liberal State* (Cambridge: Cambridge University Press, 1991), 79: "No form of political life can be justified without some view of what is good for individuals"; Stephen Macedo, *Liberal Virtues. Citizenship, Vir-*

that he understood public reason as the product of an "overlapping consensus," rooted in the conceptions of the good adhered to by individual citizens.

Certainly, the theme of the neutrality of the state is a vast and complex one. For the present I will limit myself to a brief comment on a single aspect: *the question of whether and in what sense conceptions of the good must enter into the formulation of the common good of a society, so that such conceptions become a part of the principles of justice publicly effected and protected by the state.* I believe that this problem of a public morality—of which we have already treated the ethical-institutional aspect in the first part of this essay—can be resolved properly within the logic of the democratic constitutional state. At the same time, I do not intend to adopt a "communitarian" position against what I consider to be a mistaken liberal neutrality. Rather, I hope to demonstrate that in the constitutionalistic tradition—and in this sense also in the liberal tradition—it is not possible to sustain a neutrality of the state with respect to any and every concept of the good: first, because the democratic constitutional state itself implies an option for specific goods that form its public conception of justice; and second, because society needs institutions, supported by law, that cannot themselves be neutral with respect to every conception of the good.

Fundamental Rights, Moral Conflict, and Public Morality

The purpose of the modern constitutional state is *not* the education of its citizens in the practice of the virtue of justice, but the protection of citizens from others' injustices so as to assure a foundation for the free action of citizens (of which the practice of the virtue of justice is a part). The constitutional state does not base itself on a specific conception of moral truth or of justice, which it declares a priori to be a common good. In this respect it is "neutral" and, as democratic, open to the political process according to constitutional rules. Rather, the constitutional state bases itself on a clear delimitation regarding certain acts it considers to be unjust; that is, it seeks to protect the individual from specific fundamental injustices, a protection expressed positively in the human rights as positively enacted civil law. Additionally, such a state seeks to establish that equality of rights and freedom

---

tue, and Community in Liberal Constitutionalism (Oxford: Clarendon Press, 1990), 26off.; and in another way, more convincing, Joseph Raz, *The Morality of Freedom* (Oxford: Oxford University Press, 1986). I have dealt with this more broadly in chapter 2 of this book and in my original essay, *L'immagine liberale dell'uomo*, 124–25 and 128ff.

necessary among its citizens so that everyone may truly exercise their rights.

The entire political culture of the democratic constitutional state is based on the fundamental consensus that is expressed in the notion of human rights. Even if in policies and legislation it tends to establish a possible consensus or *modus vivendi,* the institutions that are created for this purpose are on their part legitimized on the basis of the protection of the fundamental human rights. These rights, however—and this is important—do not express neutrality, but possess a specific material content. Freedom, when expressed as a fundamental right, is not merely a formal value, to be continuously filled by what the majority considers worthy of consensus; rather, it is a material value that limits legislation, policies, and as such also the power of the majority in its possibilities of imposing on other human beings (this is most evident in the case of the right of life and to physical integrity). Furthermore, as we have seen, freedom and its respective rights introduce a field of obligation with respect to solidarity, which is exercised in part through public and state institutions, with the consent of the citizens.

It is true that fundamental rights, as they have always been understood in the liberal tradition, serve not so much to charge the state power with the promotion of specific material contents, but above all else to limit the legitimate activity of the state. Such rights are principles of preclusion excluding certain matters from the political agenda, and in this sense they are negative and "against the State."[58] The classic example is the right to physical immunity and *habeas corpus;* other examples are freedom of religion and conscience, freedom of expression, and freedom of the press and of association. Liberals have thus defended society as a sphere of freedom, personal autonomy, and free, creative entrepreneurial initiative, against the power and interference of an authoritative, bureaucratic, and religiously intolerant state. Separation between the state and civil society, defense of the autonomy of society, and defense of the moral and economic independence of citizens with respect to the political sphere of the state and of the corresponding creativity and responsibility of the individual have thus become the nucleus of liberal self-understanding. This explains how contem-

---

58. This liberal lack of trust with respect to the state in general, and toward governing entities in particular, is not, however, to be understood in an anarchic sense. Liberalism is not opposed to the existence of a strong, well-functioning state, with an efficiently organized government and bureaucracy. Indeed, both historically and conceptually, liberalism presumes the state and its power, though claiming the rights of the individual with respect to the state, as well as the freedom of society with respect to state power. This has been convincingly shown, from the liberal point of view, by Stephen Holmes, *Passions and Constraint: On the Theory of Liberal Democracy* (Chicago: University of Chicago Press, 1995).

porary liberalism has become inclined to assert—and necessarily so to be consistent with its past—that in general everything that could become the matter of a moral disagreement must be removed from the public agenda of the state (or of legislative bodies) and left to the free decision of the society, which is to say to the private sphere of the individual citizen.

Formulated thus absolutely, however, this is not possible; nor is it deducible, strictly speaking, from liberal principles. Nineteenth-century liberals were perhaps not aware of how institutions like marriage and the family, though implying clear moral choices, need support by the political-public sphere in order to be in reality what they are. As staunch a defender of individual autonomy as J. S. Mill, for example, was extremely cautious and skeptical toward approving divorce in the case of a marriage with children.[59] The illegality of abortion, that is, the protection by law of human life from the moment of conception, was never contested by liberals with the argument that such a choice belonged to the individual citizen. Today, obviously, consensus on these and other similar issues no longer exists. From the existence of such morally conflictive issues, however, *one cannot infer the necessity of excluding the conflict from the public agenda,* simply removing the issue and leaving the respective choices to the freedom of individual persons, thus restricting the common good to what, avoiding conflict and dissent, can be commonly held by all. Indeed this latter is in reality impossible, insofar as it is precisely such freedom of choice that is unacceptable to those who consider it intrinsically damaging to the common good.

In a lucid essay, Amy Gutmann and Dennis Thompson show as unreasonable, from an otherwise perfectly liberal perspective, the liberal attempt to exclude from the public sphere—and thus from political and legislative regulation—any issue apt to cause a moral conflict.[60] They assert that the political agenda must necessarily include issues that require choices with moral implications, and that are thus not neutral with regard to particular conceptions of the good.

To this end, Gutmann and Thompson helpfully distinguish between two types or levels of principles. The first are "principles of preclusion": these establish which are the issues that should be removed from the political

59. John Stuart Mill, *On Liberty,* in Mill, *Utilitarianism, On Liberty, and Considerations on Representative Government,* ed. H. B. Acton (London: J. M. Dent, 1972), 158ff.

60. Amy Gutmann and Dennis Thompson, "Moral Conflict and Political Consensus," in *Liberalism and the Good,* ed. R. Bruce Douglass, Gerald M. Mara, and Henry S. Richardson (New York: Routledge, 1990), 125–47.

agenda and reserved to the discretion of individual citizens; formulated inversely, these principles determine what matters are apt to be legitimately
regulated by law. Principles of preclusion therefore determine where the
state must remain inactive. Clearly, many fundamental rights of freedom are
the juridical expression of such preclusion, expressing a fundamental incompetence of the state, as well as a clear mistrust with respect to the public power's capacity to regulate such issues; they thus impose the obligation
of inactivity on the state. A typical instance of such a preclusion is the right
to religious freedom.[61]

The second type of principle would be "principles of accommodation."
These are principles that regulate the management of conflicts and moral
differences regarding issues that are part of the political agenda, and thus
part of the competence of governments, legislatures, and the state. Precisely at this level, moral differences *must not* be excluded. The fact that such
a difference exists—for example regarding abortion, or treating homosexual unions as equal to marriage—does not imply that it must be resolved
through a simple exclusion of the issue from the political agenda (creating,
e.g., a "right to abortion" as part of a "right to privacy"). Rather, it would
require that once it is recognized that a contested position is truly a *moral*
position, a political (i.e., legislative) solution must be found (in the case of
abortion, for example, including the unborn in the general protection of life
guaranteed by the state). This solution would necessarily include a moral
option, according to the vote of the majority. Consequently, once it is admitted that a pro-life position is a morally respectable one, and that every
abortion involves a human life, there is no longer any reason to obligate the
state to inactivity in this regard: it can and must intervene in the actions of
citizens to protect these lives.

Once the unborn human being is recognized as a person with a right
to life equal to those already born, the right to life of fetuses would then be
recognizable as part of the fundamental right to life that all citizens enjoy.
This right, as specialists in constitutional law now recognize, is not only a
right of immunity from acts by the state attacking life, but also a right to the
state's protection from threats to life originating from other citizens.[62]

---

61. This idea is similar to what Stephen Holmes calls *gag rules* and *politics of omission*; see Holmes,
Passions and Constraint, 202ff.

62. Important in this context is Joseph Isensee, *Das Grundrecht auf Sicherheit. Zu den Schutzpflichten des freiheitlichen Verfassungsstaates* (Berlin: Walter de Gruyter, 1983); and Peter Häberle, *Le
libertà fondamentali nello Stato costituzionale,* ed. P. Ridola (Rome: Nuova Italia Scientifica, 1993). I refer

Public Morality, Common Good, and
the Question of Discrimination

The distinction between principles of preclusion and accommodation is certainly a useful one; nevertheless, it does not resolve every problem. The serious question remains, precisely at the level of the principles of accommodation, of which moral differences are legitimate, and which not. The question is important because at this level both political (including constitutional) and legislative decisions are made according to the principle of majority. Thus, in virtue of a democratic process of accommodation, there will ordinarily be minorities or individual social groups whose values or conceptions of the good will not form part—and this legitimately, according to justice and without discrimination—of the structure of values that are publically recognized and juridically normative for the society.

According to Gutmann and Thompson, which moral differences are legitimate depends on whether the positions held in a situation of conflict can be considered to be "morally respectable" positions, as opposed, for example, to unacceptable strategies of discrimination contrary to the demands of mutual respect of persons. Thus, according to the authors, a position defending slavery would not be morally respectable; similarly, a position allowing the legal persecution of consensual homosexual practices between adults would be akin to one promoting racial discrimination. At the same time, the defense of the prohibition of abortion *would* be morally respectable if it is based on the conviction that the human fetus is a person whose life merits protection.[63]

The difficulty with such a position becomes clear when we recognize that, arguing precisely on liberal grounds, we can go even further. We can hold that all those positions that do not respect the principle of autonomy, of self-determination of the individual, and so on are morally unrespectable. We would thus find ourselves back at the "strong" neutralism of the first kind, or at a liberal antineutralism that attempts to promote the value of autonomy as the primary and absolute value.

---

the reader also to my extensive essay "The Legal Defense of Prenatal Life in Constitutional Democracies," which is published as chapter 7 of my *Ethics of Procreation and the Defense of Human Life*, ed. William F. Murphy Jr. (Washington, D.C.: The Catholic Uuniversity of America Press, 2010). This was originally published as "Fundamental Rights, Moral Law, and the Legal Defense of Life in a Constitutional Democracy: A Constitutionalist Approach to the Encyclical *Evangelium Vitae*," in the *American Journal of Jurisprudence* 43 (1998): 135–83.

63. See Gutmann and Thompson, "Moral Conflict and Political Consensus," 131ff.

The position is also incoherent, at least in this absolute formulation. To be practicable in the case of abortion, for example, the question of the status of the human fetus as a person must be excluded from the discussion. If it were not excluded, the position would have to allow that individual autonomy implies the freedom to kill in certain cases—a position that would cause the prohibition of killing, guaranteed by the constitutional state, to collapse. It seems absurd, in fact, to include as part of the autonomy of the citizen the right to kill human individuals publically recognized as persons. The truth is that it would be discriminatory to exclude from the discussion the question of whether particular beings belonging to the species *homo sapiens* are persons; this would be precisely a *non*–morally respectable position.

It does not seem possible, therefore, to establish—still in the context of the political-legislative solution to questions of public morality—a distinction between positions that are morally respectable and those that are not so based on a judgment of whether or not they promote the autonomy of the citizen, at least if one uses a qualified concept of autonomy such as, for example, that of Joseph Raz; according to Raz, autonomy is morally valid only to the degree that it is exercised in the pursuit of what is truly good.[64] We can say, generally, that moral positions contrary to the fundamental rights of citizens are excluded from any possible public relevance in a democratic constitutional state. This could nevertheless be a vicious circle, as the application of this criterion also depends on how these rights are interpreted, and this interpretation may already contain a distinction between what is considered morally acceptable or not.

It is thus inevitable that the criteria for what we consider to be a morally acceptable position—and thus capable of legitimately being the content of possible legislation and institutionalization, and therefore part of public morality—derive *also* from content-oriented choices on the intrinsic value of both specific goals and ways of life, and of the respective "social forms"[65] that make possible and sustain the pursuit of these goals and ways of life. Indeed, in some cases the intrinsic value of certain forms of life is intimately tied up with interests and functions belonging to society as such—the community of citizens—in such a way that it would be impossible to correctly appreciate that intrinsic value without seeing it at the same time precisely in its aspect of being part of a *common* good. This is exactly the case with mar-

64. Raz, *The Morality of Freedom*, 381.
65. See ibid., 307ff.; see also 161–62.

riage, and family based on the community of life between man and woman, which are simultaneously social forms of life *and* social institutions that are publicly recognized and in certain aspects privileged by the law. This question becomes interesting precisely at a time when in all liberal societies we are confronted with the demand to make homosexual unions equal in the law to traditional marriage.

Private Morality and Public Relevance:
The Case of Marriage and of Homosexual Unions

It will be useful to pause briefly on this theme, taking it as an exemplary case because of its unquestionable contemporary relevance. I do not wish to defend the type of legislation—employed for the most part in Anglo-Saxon countries—that criminalizes consensual homosexual behavior between adults in private.[66] Nor do I wish to defend the idea that the state must prescribe to its citizens how they should live in order to be happy. Such extreme formulations, which offer an easy target to liberals in debate, tend only to further complicate the discussion. The question, rather, is this: Do homosexual couples wishing to establish a stable community of life have a right to equality in the law, and thus publicly, to traditional marriage between a man and a woman? Would they be discriminated against based on their sexual orientation if such a right were denied them?

I have written elsewhere that I see no reason, based on liberal constitutional principles, why such an equalization would be defensible as a demand of nondiscrimination.[67] In this essay I wish to demonstrate that such an equalization can be defended *only* by (a) recourse to a redefinition of the public reasons for which all communities of life, *including* marriage, receive a privileged legal status, and (b) the proposal of a corresponding redefinition of marriage itself. Only based on such a redefinition would the exclusion of homosexual unions be discriminatory, with the equalization of such unions to traditional marriage then becoming a reasonable claim.

First, we must consider that the public recognition of marriage between a man and a woman is not simply the public promotion of a particular moral choice, much less an imposition on those who would prefer to make differ-

---

66. This type of *morals legislation* seems in fact to be defended by Robert George, *Making Men Moral: Civil Liberties and Public Morality* (Oxford: Clarendon Press, 1993).

67. See chapter 2 of the present volume, which was originally published as *L'immagine dell'uomo nel liberalismo*, 122ff.

ent choices; neither is it a prescription to citizens on how they should live in order to be happy. Public recognition of heterosexual marriage is based rather on the fact that *this* community of life, while having its origin in private choices and in the autonomy of two citizens (in which the state does not interfere), is the fundamental institution by which the society—as a community of citizens—is formed: marriage is a community of reproduction, education, and socialization, with specific social functions and effects—such as the creation of wealth and of distributive structures through inheritance— which must in some way be regulated by law in the interest of all. Therefore what the state recognizes in a special way, conferring on it a special status, is a *specific* community of life, that is, a community open to the transmission of life and thus possible only between persons of different sex, and having a corresponding socializing and educational mission.

It would therefore not seem possible that a homosexual couple could claim the same status, inasmuch as their union is something entirely different. A homosexual "community of life" is a union with exclusively private relevance. Making it equivalent to marriage would thus be a grave injustice and discrimination *toward marriages,* who bear the burden of the transmission of life and the education and socialization of society's citizens. By denying an equal status, moreover, the state makes no moral qualification on the homosexual way of life. It simply does not confer that legal status on their unions conferred on marriage, in virtue of the properties and functions of the latter that homosexual unions precisely lack. Thus, the state does not discriminate against them; rather, it remains entirely indifferent in their regard. It would *not,* however, remain neutral if it made homosexual unions equal to marriage, given that in such a case it would give public support to a particular style of life without being able to adduce reasons for a common and public interest.

The establishment of a right to the choice of a same-sex partner so as to live in a union of life legally equal to marriage would also imply a clear non-neutrality of the state for another reason: it would discredit the specific task of traditional marriage. Clearly, the privileged status of marriage both implies and protects the public recognition of a particular conception of the good: that of the desirability of heterosexual unions with a procreative and educative task. Any attempt at neutrality at this level is frankly impossible. Making homosexual unions equivalent to marriage would distort the public understanding of marriage, which would no longer be seen as a community essentially characterized by its procreative and educative task; rather it would be reduced to a pure social fact, essentially private, with the question of whether two participants in a community of life are of different sex becoming publically irrelevant. The begetting of children and its respective educative tasks would then enter in only as possible options—of a purely private relevance[68]—but no longer as the reason for which such public recognition was granted in the first place. It is difficult to say what would be the long-term legal effects; it is foreseeable that grave injustices and discriminations would develop against the vast number of couples burdened with the responsibility of procreation and education. Such consequences would certainly be damaging for society, for the community of citizens, and thus for the common good.[69]

While we consider a simply "neutral" attitude on the part of the juridical order of society to be impossible, this does not require that we opt for the opposite, a mere "perfectionism" that attempts to use the law to promote virtue in citizens, and to repress their vices. Our conclusion that homosexual unions and marriage should not be considered equal is not based on a judgment concerning the perversity or moral repugnance of homosexual practices. Rather, it is based on reasoning belonging to an exclusively public morality or moral reasoning: the exclusive privileging of heterosexual unions—traditional marriage—follows from a moral judgment based on an interest and usefulness both public and common, that is, protecting the union between man and woman that serves the transmission of life. Conversely, the affective life and union of homosexual couples pertain to the sphere of merely private life. It makes no sense to confer on these a privilege that is conferred on heterosexual unions precisely on the basis of a public and communitarian interest, given that in the case of unions between homosexuals such an interest clearly does not exist.

It is nevertheless inevitable that such a judgment, in the sphere of public

68. This corresponds to the tendency, already quite common, to consider the having of children and their education as the fulfillment of a desire of the parents, rather than a task of service to other persons and to society (i.e., to the common good). According to this logic, the right to adopt children or even to have children of their own through artificial procreation cannot be denied to homosexual couples.

69. The fact that many married couples are unable or do not want to have children would not be a valid objection here. To respect the freedom and intimacy of spouses, public reasoning must only take into consideration the normal case: normally, marriage is a union that is both procreative and educative. Even if this were statistically not the case, marriage as a procreative and educative union would still be what is normal, and such statistical data would indicate not merely a fact, but a problem and indeed a grave crisis for society (notice that in this context "normal" has also a properly *normative* implication).

morality, would also be (or become) a judgment on the moral difference in itself and in principle between heterosexual and homosexual love. Indeed, the insertion of marriage as a procreative and educative community into a larger social, public, and communitarian context confers on it a special moral dignity. In fact it is impossible in every case to separate public and "private" moral values, the just and the good—precisely because a component of the human good, though "private," also possesses a dimension that is social, communitarian, and thus in this sense relevant for the public order.[70]

And here, once again, we encounter the common good as an existential reality of society and a normative factor of political praxis. Even if we opt for a procedural neutrality of the state, such a proceduralism either will be explicitly based on substantial conceptions concerning the good, promoted according to criteria of a public moral reasoning, or it will be a proceduralism apparently lacking such presuppositions and neutral with respect to any substantial conception of the good, while nevertheless promoting specific axiological choices, albeit implicitly and hiddenly, as we have just seen.[71] Charles Larmore's formula according to which liberal neutrality "is not a neutrality of results, but of procedure"[72] is certainly correct and useful, provided it is understood in a restricted sense, that is, in reference to a proceduralism based on and integrated into a publicly enforced institutional structure already impregnated by specific principles expressing substantial conceptions of the good. If, on the other hand, the formula refers to a proceduralism that attempts to supplant such substantial conceptions, then a dynamic would necessarily unfold producing quite predictable results, that is, "liberal" results in a problematic sense, promoting, for example, pro-choice solutions (as the process tends to suppress the question of the personality and the respective rights of the unborn as moral-religious beliefs, thus enshrining the formal principle of the freedom of choice of the strongest in

---

70. This argumentation proceeds in the opposite direction than that of Michael Sandel: it seems to me that Sandel attempts, at least in part, to derive the appropriateness of a particular law from the morality or immorality of the practice in question; what I have proposed, on the other hand, is to derive an increase in the moral value of certain practices or ways of life from their interest and utility for society, which precisely justifies their privileged public position. See Sandel, "Moral Argument and Liberal Toleration: Abortion and Homosexuality," *California Law Review* 77 (1989): 521–38; reprinted in *New Communitarian Thinking: Persons, Virtues, Institutions, and Communities*, ed. A. Etzioni (Charlottesville: University Press of Virgina, 1995), 71–87.

71. Charles Taylor's criticism of liberalism also points in this direction; the term he uses in this context is *ethics of inarticulacy.* See Taylor, *Sources of the Self: The Making of the Modern Identity* (Cambridge: Cambridge University Press, 1989), 89.

72. Charles Larmore, *Patterns of Moral Complexity* (Cambridge: Cambridge University Press, 1987), 44.

questions of life and death), or the weakening of the institution of marriage (with the accusation that its privileged status discriminates against those who choose to live according to a different sexual orientation).

Self-Determination, Moral Truth, and Common Good

Liberalism rejects what in politics is often called "paternalism," that is, the idea that the state, the government, or the public power can legitimately prescribe to its citizens what life would be best for them. Rather than paternalistic measures, a liberal state should promote the conditions by which every citizen can make his or her own choices, and live according to them.

The Canadian philosopher Will Kymlicka has properly emphasized that this liberal primacy of self-determination is not necessarily based on moral or religious skepticism.[73] Perhaps Kymlicka was mistaken with respect to many nineteenth-century liberals—some of whom still lingered at the end of the twentieth—who based the right to religious freedom on the claim that no religious truth exists.[74] But others, confirming Kymlicka's thesis, claimed that such freedom is justified by the need for a free adherence to the truth, without any kind of intervention by the state, and by the corresponding need for self-determination and to act according to one's conscience.[75] This principle of interiority is, according to Kymlicka, a genuinely liberal principle:[76] the value of self-determination, after all, does not mean that we are only interested in living a life that we *believe* to be good. Rather, in general, we are convinced that there are some things that are worthy of being done, and others not. Put otherwise, we are convinced that living a good life is not simply the same as living a life that one believes to be good: one can be mistaken. This would not, however—still according to Kymlicka—be an argument for implementing a form of paternalism, the idea of a state that promotes what is truly good, discouraging citizens from pursuing activities and forms of life erroneously judged to be good; this is also true because it is difficult to imagine that governments would be able to judge, better than citizens themselves, what is good for them.

The principal reason for this liberal antipaternalism is, according to Kymlicka, that life must be lived "from the inside": following moral and

---

73. Kymlicka, *Contemporary Political Philosophy*, 201ff.

74. This is still held today, surprisingly, by Bobbio, *L'età dei diritti* (Turin: Einaudi, 1990), 10.

75. Also along these lines is the "liberal" justification for the separation of church and state offered by Guido de Ruggiero, *Storia del liberalismo europeo* (1925) (Bari: Laterza, 1984), 428–31.

76. Kymlicka, *Contemporary Political Philosophy*, 202–5.

religious practices is pointless if not the fruit of a personal and interior choice, that is, on the basis of one's own convictions. A society morally and religiously oriented toward the truth would be one in which the activity of citizens would be carried out in a merely exterior, conformist way, and thus without meaning. It is important not only that we *do* what is good according to the truth, but also that we do what we do because we truly *believe* it to be good, and choose it as such.

I don't think it can be denied that Kymlicka is for the most part correct. His principle is valid for human activity generally: the goodness of an act—and its value as part of an authentically moral life—depends not only on whether the activity is just and good, but also on whether it is a truly human activity, chosen by the agent as something he believes to be just and good;[77] this is immediately obvious with respect to religious practice. Nevertheless, Kymlicka's assertion can have public and political relevance only for that sphere circumscribed by what we above termed principles of preclusion, where the state must remain inactive; it cannot be valid, however, for those aspects of the public order that must necessarily be informed by specific substantial moral principles.

Surprisingly, Kymlicka argues as if the question were not a political question at all, but only a moral one. Or as if the problem of the relationship between morality and politics were reduced to the question of whether and to what extent the state is responsible for the moral life of its citizens. Once the question is formulated in this way, however, the response seems obvious: the state *cannot* be the guarantor of the moral integrity of its citizens, nor is it the state's duty to keep vigil over their happiness. Nevertheless, formulated thusly, the question is a trap: isn't liberalism, after all, a political doctrine? Why then is the problem of the good life of the individual placed so much at the center, with the suggestion that one must pronounce either in favor of or against a respective responsibility of the state? Why address the question at all, and for that matter somewhat simplistically, of whether or not the state has the task of leading citizens via political measures to a life that would make them truly happy—and thus of being responsible for the morality of their choices?

---

77. A genuinely Aristotelian principle; see *Nicomachean Ethics* VI, 12, 1144a 15-20: actions that correspond to virtue are good and virtuous not because, for example, they are prescribed by the law, but because they are chosen precisely because they are considered good and virtuous. This principle of interiority does not keep Aristotle from maintaining that, for the vicious, the coercion of the law with its respective penalties is necessary for bringing them back to the path of virtue (ibid., X, 9, 1180a 1ff.).

The response to these questions—one that does not violate the central principles of liberal constitutionalism—is that in truth the problem before us is a different, more specifically political one. It is a problem, that is, at the level not of the good of the individual, but of the *common* good, which can be characterized by the following two questions:

1. Which *social or communitarian and institutional conditions* are necessary for the individual to realize what is truly good and morally valid (assuming that some aspects of the good life can be realized only if adequate social conditions and institutions exist)?

2. Which *public interests*—and in this sense also common interests—exist therefore with respect to the good life of individual citizens, of social groups and of the political community as a whole?

These are not two entirely unrelated questions, but two aspects of a single problem. I do not wish to claim, as the communitarian criticism of liberalism does, that liberals do not see this specific political problem. Liberals—except perhaps for an extreme libertarian, who would reduce the function of the state to a merely protective one—would opt for a state that creates the social and institutional conditions necessary for the good life of its citizens, in this sense recognizing the existence of public and common interests. This is not the point. The problem is that many liberals of the "neutralist" stripe tend not to see that the policies, legislative measures, and institutional structures that correspond to such an aim must inevitably be based on substantial principles that can never be morally "neutral." A common good can never be assured without simultaneously promoting at least some substantial moral values. The attempt to resolve the two questions posed in a strictly "neutral" way is in fact likely to undermine the very solution to the problem. A neutrality thus understood would exercise a destructive influence on these social and institutional conditions, which in any case receive their vitality precisely from the substantial moral "elements" present in them.[78]

---

78. Principally in the Anglo-Saxon context, the discussion on the relationship between morality and law is also invalidated by a commonly held false dichotomy between *moral reasons* and *utilitarian reasons*, a dichotomy used by authors who in other respects are quite diverse, such as Lord Devlin and H. L. A. Hart; see Devlin, *The Enforcement of Morals* (Oxford: Oxford University Press, 1965); Hart, *Law, Liberty and Morality* (Oxford: Oxford University Press, 1963). Adopting a totally "privatistic" concept of morality, so-called moral reasons would refer only to those dimensions of morality having no social relevance. On the other hand, those reasons that refer to what has social relevance would be utilitarian reasons. This dichotomy, however, doesn't make sense, first because utilitarianism is also a form of mo-

We have here a vicious circle: an erroneous liberal neutralism tends to convert what should be the social and institutional presuppositions of the good life of citizens—good examples would be marriage and schools—into a tool that essentially serves the citizen's self-determination. Self-determination undeniably being an essential part of the good life, its realization nevertheless depends on the existence of the referred-to presuppositions, whose function therefore cannot be defined in instrumental terms with respect to self-determination itself. This is also why education in self-determination, in a responsible exercise of personal freedom, cannot be realized except on the basis of the transmission of values and of a concrete style of life, something that normally occurs in the context of the family. As such, every exercise of self-determination will always be impregnated with values and with concrete experiences and an entire personal biography. In any case it is clear that the interiorization of the value of self-determination is not all that is necessary for learning to live a self-determined life.

The first aspect mentioned above—the existence of social, legal, and institutional conditions whereby citizens can realize the good life—is not the same as what liberals criticize as paternalism. We are not dealing here with "educating" citizens in virtue, deciding for them concerning what is good. Rather we are dealing with *creating or promoting certain necessary conditions without which, in the social context, no good can be effectively pursued, and no good life realized.* We must bear in mind that the largest communities, and ultimately the political community and the state themselves, receive their legitimacy from being at the service of the realization of vital goals on the part of their citizens, which nevertheless the citizens, as individuals or as families, could not effectively realize without the support of the institutions of civil society and the state. This is a common assumption, which I don't think even liberals would deny. At the same time, it does not seem possible to promote such conditions and institutions in a way rigidly neutral toward any conception of the good. Furthermore, a liberal antineutralism that enshrines the maximum autonomy of citizens as the ultimate criterion would also be harmful.[79]

The difficult question, then—given that my position, while not simply

---

rality, and second because utilitarian reasons also exist for a non-utilitarian morality. The social "utility" of marriage, as an affective union with a procreative and educative function, precisely contributes to the establishment of its value and moral dignity.

79. An example is Macedo, *Liberal Virtues*, 278ff.

"liberal," does not in any way intend to be antiliberal—is to reconcile the necessary public promotion of *privileged* institutions and social forms, considered as part of an indispensable common good such that citizens may attain their goal of realizing the good life, with the demands of freedom and self-determination, and with respect for those citizens who wish to make choices different from what the public culture of the good promotes as the common good. It is not necessary to embrace a communitarian program to resolve this question. According to such a program, at least in its radical form, a common good is required which defines, so to speak, the moral life of the community, and of which the individual is considered a part. The good and moral life of citizens would thus be explained as a participation in, and as such the individualized realization of, the structure of values provided by the community. In our treatment, rather, we have understood the common good not as the "good of the community" that also defines the good of individual citizens, but as a good common to citizens as persons and individuals, who nevertheless need social and communitarian life so as to be able to attain this good.

Common Good and Pluralistic Society

Integral Common Good and Political Common Good

In summary, we can say that the common good is at one and the same time (a) an underlying constitutional structure of all political praxis, (b) an aggregate of substantial values that are publicly recognized as important for the society, and (c) a result of the political process that unfolds within the context of these institutional and axiological presuppositions. With respect to the political process it is correct to say that the common good is not a pre-established "good," a materially well defined goal simply to be attained by a state having a kind of privileged knowledge of the common good. It is rather the result of a praxis of groups and individuals, coordinated by the rules established by the basic political structure of the society, each pursuing their own interests—their good—in solidarity with the interest of those who need such solidarity so that they too may pursue their own good.

Thus, the common good also includes the following goods, attainable only in community and through institutions common to all: peace; the freedom of individuals with respect to the coercive and pacifying power of the state, but also with respect to certain social forces or the power of third parties; justice, including the public organization of the demands of solidarity according to the principle of subsidiarity; the promotion of the social conditions and institutions necessary for the realization of the good life, so that citizens may reach their morally valid goals as beings living in society.

The following distinction will nevertheless be helpful: *in an integrated or strong sense,* the "common good" is the good of all members of society, taken as a whole. It includes the strictly personal good, the good of the family community, of associations, and so on; it contains both material and spiritual aspects. It in fact includes the ultimate realization of every good, as well as the conditions facilitating such a realization. Understood in this way, the common good of society includes everything, from physical integrity to the moral good of the person, from simple respect for the basic physical life of one's neighbor to the highest realization of charity. The common good, understood as such, would be the integral concept of all the values attainable by human beings living together in society.

Understood in this way, however, the concept of common good is not useful. It would remain a moral and metaphysical category without political relevance, unless we were to claim that human and political society is a complete unity of life, perfect, whole, with the political authority responsible for everything. We need therefore to specify and delimit a concept of the *common good in a political sense,* that is, a concept of the "political common good," of the "common good of political society."

The realization of the common good in an integral sense is an aim not of political action, but of the freedom of the individual persons living in society: through their actions as free citizens, as members of various social groups, as believers, members of churches, parents, businesspeople, and so on. The state, politics, public authorities must not try to usurp the place of society. Respecting the principle of subsidiarity, they must stimulate and regulate social forces and the initiative of individuals, while guaranteeing fundamental respect for the rights of all. To confuse the integral common good with the political common good would be, in the best case, to convert the state into an assistance agency; in reality it would be an essentially totalitarian option.

The task of politics is to assure the necessary conditions such that society, or rather every individual person, may freely arrive at his or her integral good. Thus: legal protection and juridical security; the guarantee of social peace and external defense; material assistance and social promotion according to need; regulation of economic activity, mainly to control and if necessary deal with illegitimate economic forces threatening the market; assurance of specific goods and public services necessary to the community; and so on. Each of these areas implies a great variety of options, opinions, and political concepts, represented by the various political parties competing democratically.

Political Process and Pluralistic Concept of the Common Good

Returning now to what we saw in the first section of this essay, we can say that there exists—at a minimum—a twofold moral dimension to every political action: one that is so to speak "founding," and the other "founded" or "constructive." The founding dimension consists in the moral dimension of the political rationality on which the democratic constitutional state is based, that is, the ethos of peace, freedom, and justice. This dimension forms the fundamental sphere of consensus among participants in the political process. This is not to say that dissent is not possible with respect to the concrete demands of a policy aimed at the realization of peace, freedom, and justice; what is important is that the institutional and legal structures of the basic constitutional structure be respected as the foundation of the political process. In other words, "founding" political morality consists in a respect for constitutional institutions as an expression of the common search for peace, freedom, and justice, these latter being the contents of the fundamental political common good.

Obviously, no concrete policy can be implemented solely on the basis of this political reasoning—it merely provides the presuppositions. The concrete common good must then be built on the basis of the fundamental structure of the state, a common good that must be attained, assured, and adjusted according to ever-new circumstances. This is precisely the task of concrete political processes. The second dimension of political morality is therefore a "constructive" dimension: it is the morality of normal political praxis in the strict sense, a praxis that takes place in the context of political institutions. Opinions, programs, and interests, as well as political parties and social groups, compete in this process for the attainment of their goals, as well as for the power necessary for such attainment. Power in turn consists in votes: votes of electors, votes in parliament, and so on, which are decisive with respect to the realization of programs, the issuing of laws, the formation of governments, and other such matters. The battle for power is thus a battle to attain a majority for one's political projects.

In modern constitutional democracies, a parliament and a government typically are at the center of this process, with either the government being "formed" or controlled by parliament (thus a parliamentary, or cabinet, system of government), or the government (administration) functioning independently of the parliament (which has a legislative function), but balanced and controlled by parliament (presidential system).[80]

The parliament is a representation of society. This does not mean that it is an organism that acts with an "imperative mandate" from society; that is, it is not an executive organ of a presumed "general will." Rather, it acts in the place of society. A parliament is a limited group of men and women who act representing everyone, having its own proper competence and responsibility. A parliament always reflects the reality of the society, which is divided by interests that are to some degree antagonistic and pluralistic, and seeks to construct a viable political will.

Society itself, however, is a plurality: a plurality of groups, of interests, of points of view, and more. The first to defend the pluralistic nature of the *polis,* against Plato, was Aristotle: "For a State essentially consists of a multitude of persons, and if its unification is carried beyond a certain point, city will be reduced to family and family to individual."[81] The modern rediscovery of this pluralistic nature of society was the work of Otto von Gierke,[82] which was broadly accepted in England. Gierke's theory is a response to a radical insufficiency of modern liberalism: he claimed that society is formed not simply by individuals uniting in civil society, but of social groups (family, professional corporations, economic, local, and ethnic communities); or rather, the individual is a member of society precisely as a member of a specific social group (or of various groups).

The pluralistic theory of the state had its most radical expression in the claim of the British laborist Harold Laski that, in essence, a sovereign state does not exist.[83] According to Laski, only social groups exist. The most mod-

---

80. It is not necessary in this context to also consider the various mixed forms of parliamentary and presidential government, such as for example the French system.

81. Aristotele, *Politics* II, 2, 1261a 19–20, trans. by H. Rackham, Loeb Classical Library 264 (Cambridge, Mass.: Harvard University Press, 1932).

82. *Das deutsche Genossenschaftsrecht* (1868), vol 1.: *Rechtsgeschichte der deutschen Genossenschaft* (Darmstadt: Wissenschaftliche Buchgesellschaft, 1954).

83. See for example *Studies in the Problem of Sovereignty* (New Haven, Conn.: Yale University Press, 1917) and *Authority in the Modern State* (New Haven, Conn.: Yale University Press, 1919).

erate neo-pluralism, however, acknowledges that every society is formed of groups with specific legitimate interests.[84] This latter idea was especially well received in England because in essence English parliamentarianism, which from the beginning derived from a representation not of individuals but of states or classes, has always functioned according to this logic. Thus on March 22, 1775, in a famous speech in the lower house, Edmund Burke said: "All government, indeed every human benefit and enjoyment, every virtue and every prudent act, is founded on compromise and barter. We balance inconvieniences; we give and take; we remit some rights, that we may enjoy others."[85] Even if we don't accept such an approach in our personal lives, it does express the logic of parliamentary political practice and of a democratically legitimated governmental praxis.[86]

It seems obvious that this kind of political process is open to every kind of decay and abuse; it requires political agents with a sense of responsibility and integrity. In modern democracies, however, there are control mechanisms capable of being an effective counterbalance to the worst abuses, at least in the long run; an example would be public opinion, manifest primarily in elections and opinion polls. Nevertheless, referring again to what I said in the first part of this essay, it is clear that specific virtues corresponding to the internal ethos of institutions are required of the political actor.

Normally, a parliament does not arrive at optimal solutions; at times it even seems incapable of accomplishing truly satisfactory objectives. If a parliament is indeed more "pluralistic" or antagonistic than the society itself, this would truly be a symptom of inefficiency, or even of dysfunctionalism or a lack of seriousness. Normally such a situation is due to structural defects, for example, an inadequate electoral system that does not allow the formation of clear majorities. Usually, however, parliament's apparent inef-

---

84. On pluralism, see Iring Fetscher and Herfried Münkler, eds., *Pipers Handbuch der politischen Ideen* (Munich-Zürich, Piper 1987), 5:421–36. On neo-pluralism: Joachim Detjen, *Neopluralismus und Naturrecht: Zur politischen Philosophie der Pluralismustheorie*, Politik- und Kommunikationswissenschaftliche Veröffentlichungen der Görres-Gesellschaft 1 (Paderborn: Schöningh, 1988).

85. "Speech on Conciliation with the Colonies (22 March 1775)," in Edmund Burke, *On Government, Politics and Society*, ed. B. W. Hill (Glasgow: Fontana/ Harvester Press 1975), 185.

86. At the same time one must not forget that Burke himself, in his equally famous "Speech to the Electors of Bristol" (see Burke, *On Government, Politics and Society*, 158), defends a very idealistic version of parliamentary representation, i.e., that a parliament is a "*deliberative* assembly of *a* nation, with *an* interest, the interest of the whole—in which must act as guide, not local interests or local prejudices, but the general good, resulting from the common reasoning of all," in such a way that a member elected by the people of Bristol would not be "a member of Bristol, but he is a member of *Parliament*." Nevertheless, this idea of a parliament obligated to seek the common good is not necessarily opposed to the need, expressed in the first citation, for "compromise and barter."

ficiency is the expression of a need to yield to compromises and concessions that express the reality of the pluralism of the society. In doing so, parliament would truly represent society and its common good, in a way corresponding to the ethos of peace and freedom.

Some think that a technocratic regime would be more effective. If such were the case, however, the problem would exist of a lack of consensus concerning the procedures and measures adopted by the regime. There would be no representation of dissent, meaning that a technocratic government would necessarily be authoritarian and would create disunity at the founding level of political institutions. Thus, the relative inefficiency of a parliament arises from a properly political rationality: the rationality of consensus, of compromise, of attainability. This is ultimately not a defect, but one of the most important characteristics of modern parliamentarism—and in this sense too a kind of "political efficiency."

From what we have seen to this point, it is now perhaps more clear how we should define the notion of the "common good" in a parliamentary democracy. If we depart from a recognition of the pluralistic structure of society, we cannot speak of a "will of the society" or of the people, or of a "common will" that must be represented by parliament. Similarly, it is not possible to specify a substantial, pre-defined "common good," a fixed goal to be attained, which either is or should be the content of a common will. The "common good" consists rather in the coordination of various aspects of the good as they are articulated, principally in parliament, as "interests of groups," but articulated also in a different way by so-called pressure groups, business and cultural associations, unions, and the like. The mode of action of these latter is different, as well—acting from outside parliament, they seek alliances with members of parliament and especially attempt to form public opinion.

This pluralistic notion of the "common good," however, presupposes and implies two things: first, a certain consensus among the members of parliament concerning the *formal content* of the common good. By "formal content of the common good" is meant a fundamental conception on the ends to be reached by political institutions, as for example: legal security, effective functioning of the economy, currency stability, possibilities for employment, distributive and "contributive" justice (the latter regarding a just distribution of fiscal burdens: fiscal justice), the protection of minorities and the marginalized, equality before the law, public morality, control and restraint of criminality, and the functioning of public services.

These formal contents of the common good are widely shared; conceptions concerning the concrete means to be adopted to reach such ends are what vary. Prioritization of the relative importance of these ends also varies, given that some of them conflict (for example, is currency stability—the battle against inflation—more important, or a policy of full employment?) There could also be disagreement over whether this or that end should be the aim of the formal structure of the common good at all, as for example with the promotion of "equal opportunity," or the protection and promotion of the family. The important point is that a pluralistic concept of the common good and political praxis presupposes some "formal" conception of the common good (which will vary according to different political positions, or by party), given that, without such a formal conception, a political strategy capable of effectively coordinating the various interests toward a common good or interest would not be possible.

The second presupposition in a pluralistic conception of the common good, however, would be a sphere of consensus concerning a *material content* of the common good, a consensus that expresses precisely the "founding" level of all political praxis—this is expressed primarily through the constitutional structure. A constitution may include various things: first, the guarantee of certain fundamental rights, primarily rights of freedom, that is, protection of the individual before the public power, and rights to participation in the political process (e.g., the right to vote). Second, a constitution establishes the institutional structure of the political process: the good functioning of these institutions forms an essential part of the common good. Third, a constitution normally (even if not necessarily) contains the formulation of the fundamental tasks of the public power: juridical tasks, economic, social, educative, cultural, military, and so on. In fact, at this point the "formal" part of the common good and the material foundation, guaranteed by the constitution, overlap. In any case, a constitution always formulates obligations to be carried out by the public power. Finally, it constitutes every constitutional state as a historical singularity with its specific character, and as such a singularity about which it is not possible to offer a universally valid theory.[87]

---

87. That the basic institutional structure of the political organization of a society is to be considered a substantial element of the common good is also the opinion of Robert A. Dahl, *Democracy and Its Critics* (New Haven, Conn.: Yale University Press, 1989), 306ff. Lacking in Dahl, however, is a deeper investigation into the content of the values implied in these institutions.

It becomes clear, then, that a pluralistic concept of the common good is not a "relativistic" or arbitrary conception of that good. Rather, it is a conception full of substantial contents, but also respectful of the legitimate pluralism of the society that must actuate itself through the political process. The political process itself is perhaps not oriented toward "perfect" and "limpid" solutions (in fact, members of society typically have very different conceptions concerning what a perfect or limpid solution to a particular problem would be); rather, such a process guarantees a political praxis that takes place in freedom and is realistic, based on consensus and viability. And finally, it is a political praxis and a conception of the common good not disposed to sacrifice freedom to a presumed homogeneity of society and of the common good, the latter determinable a priori or on the basis of pre-formulated conceptions of political truth.

Speaking in this way of the common good and of the political praxis that tries to attain it makes obvious again how everything depends, ultimately, not on political institutions and the public power, but on society and the people who comprise it. Conceptions concerning the good, the interests to be realized, and thus also political and moral strength, come from society itself, from real people. And it belongs to the society, not to political institutions, to realize the common good in an integral sense. To deny this would be again to opt for a totalizing model of the state or the political community, a *polis* having the task of "building" both individual persons and the entire society. Yet, the political and public power is only a part of society, of which it is always an expression.[88]

---

88. This essay was originally published as "Lo Stato costituzionale democratico e il bene comune," in *Ripensare lo spazio politico: quale aristocrazia?* ed. E. Morandi and R. Panattoni (Padua: Il Poligrafo, 1998), 57–123 (*Con-tratto. Rivista di filosofia tomista e contemporanea* 6/1997). Translation by Joseph T. Papa.

||||||||||||||||||||||||||||||||||||||||||||||||||||||||||||||||||||||||||||||||||||||||||||||||||||||||||||||||

FOUR

Auctoritas non veritas facit legem

Thomas Hobbes, Carl Schmitt, and the
Idea of the Constitutional State

Preliminary Considerations

The Hobbesian maxim *Auctoritas non veritas facit legem* ("Authority, not truth creates the law") certainly has the character of a hackneyed phrase, a commonplace of political philosophy, but it has the advantage that it not only brings out the English philosopher's political theory concisely and in all of its fullness, but also points out one of the decisive elements connecting Hobbes with the German constitutional law professor Carl Schmitt, active three hundred years later. *Decisionism* is the word for it. Since the studies of Michel Villey[1] and Simone Goyard-Fabre[2] especially, it has been recognized for some time now how deeply Hobbes was committed in his thinking to juristic categories, despite his fundamentally political intentions. For Hobbes, political and juristic thinking are most closely intertwined, and in this very respect Carl Schmitt is at one with him, but almost three hundred later.

The following discussion is concerned with answering the question, "Was Schmitt a 'genuine' Hobbesian?" Or (to ask the same question in reverse): "Was Hobbes in fact a Schmittian before his time?" Anyone familiar with the role played by Schmitt's constitutional philosophy in the con-

1. *La formation de la pensée juridique moderne: Cours d'histoire de la philosophie du Droit*, new rev. ed. (Paris: Éditions Montchrétien, 1975) ("Deuxième partie: Thomas Hobbes et la foundation du positivisme juridique"). This chapter uses correct Latin spelling of *auctoritas* unless a text using Hobbes's *autoritas* is cited.

2. *Le Droit et la Loi dans la Philosophie de Thomas Hobbes* (Paris: C. Klincksieck 1975).

text of the constitutional-ideological justification of the National Socialist seizure of power will hardly miss the explosive potential of the question. The ominous words of Schmitt, stated in response to the so-called Röhm Revolt of 1934 and the liquidation of the SA (the Nazi party militia) hierarchy: *"Der Führer hat das Recht gesetzt"* ("The *Führer* has laid down the law"), echo in the ears of many. But reference to such "derailments," by no means coincidental, serve rather to conceal than to reveal the deeper problematic of Schmittian legal thought. As has long been demonstrated by the studies of Jürgen Fijalkowski,[3] Hasso Hofmann,[4] Mathias Schmitz,[5] or Peter Schneider,[6] as a constitutional legal theorist, Schmitt was no more a National Socialist ideologue than Hobbes wrote his *De Cive* in support of King Charles I or his *Leviathan* for Oliver Cromwell—the accusations directed at him by his contemporaries, of course. To characterize Schmitt's position exclusively on the basis of his open affinity for National Socialism would not reveal anything new but only downplay, by the use of a false label, how problematic, serious, and indeed dangerous it was, consequently allowing it to be lost in the archives of dead slogans, discarded in the trashcan of history.[7] The *topos* of "totalitarianism" as the alleged essence of Hobbesian political philosophy has similarly been superseded by the Hobbes research and interpretation of recent decades.[8] For his part, Carl Schmitt's reputation has finally been restored through a postwar "Schmitt School"—the liberal "Schmittians of the Left" *(Linksschmittianer)*. Not only Hobbes, but occasionally even Schmitt has been rediscovered today as the representative of liberal constitutional thought (Schmitt's later Hobbes-interpretation has contributed much to this), and in this connection "decisionism" has also climbed to a new position of honor, despite its peculiar status as a "compromised political theory."[9] Here a certain amount of political hermeneutic is at

---

3. *Die Wendung zum Führerstaat: Ideologische Komponenten in der Philosophie Carl Schmitts* (Cologne-Opladen: Westdeutscher Verlag, 1958).

4. *Legitimität gegen Legalität* (Neuwied: Luchterhand, 1964; 4th ed., Berlin: Duncker & Humblot, 2002).

5. *Die Freund-Feind Theorie Carl Schmitts: Entwurf und Entfaltung* (Cologne-Opladen: Westdeutscher Verlag, 1965).

6. *Ausnahmezustand und Norm: Eine Studie zur Rechtslehre von Carl Schmitt* (Stuttgart: DVA, 1957).

7. For an attempt at establishing Schmitt's political and ideological context in the period of the Weimar Republic, see Martin Rhonheimer, *Politisierung und Legitimitätsentzug: Totalitäre Kritik der parlamentarisch Demokratie in Deutschland* (Freiburg/Munich: Karl Alber Verlag, 1979), 103ff.

8. See Joseph Vialatoux, *La Cité de Hobbes: Théorie de l' état totalitaire* (Paris: Lecoffre, 1935; reprinted under the title *La Cité totalitaire de Hobbes*, Lyon: Chronique sociale de la France, 1952).

9. Hermann Lübbe, "Dezisionismus—eine kompromettierte politische Theorie," in Lübbe, *Praxis der Philosophie, praktische Philosophie, Geschichtsthéorie* (Stuttgart: Reclam, 1978), 61–77.

work, or even a natural outgrowth of the ambivalence and many-sidedness of both Hobbes's and Schmitt's positions. Nevertheless the question arises: Was Schmitt a "genuine" Hobbesian, or did he only call upon Hobbes, in order to find legitimacy for his own thought in the shadow of a great figure? That the relationship between Schmitt and Hobbes was not a coincidence, and indeed that Hobbes must be seen as "a key figure in Schmitt's political philosophical doctrine,"[10] is no longer disputed today. Nevertheless, the answer to the question, just how this relationship is to be understood, is more complex than first meets the eye. Here I will attempt to answer this question in part, by considering a significant aspect of Hobbes's thought and its reception by Carl Schmitt.[11]

In the following presentation of the Schmittian reception of the Hobbesian maxim *Auctoritas non veritas facit legem*, the first step will consist of a brief analysis of its function for Hobbes—a function that has by no means been settled by the research. In fact, the dictum has a double function that is not seldom overlooked.[12] Next, I will show how Schmitt's understanding of the statement departs from that of Hobbes. Third, and finally, we return to Hobbes, and the result is a discovery that his position involves a problematic, for which a possible and yet most undesirable solution, with regard to modern social and constitutional reality, is the one offered by Schmitt's philosophy. The thesis proposed in these three steps, then, is this: Schmitt is no Hobbesian, and yet he is one; that is to say, in a decisive way he goes beyond the historical Hobbes, in order to carry his ideas further under the conditions of a different age. The return of attention back to Hobbes is meant to point out the potential for conflict of Hobbes's political theory—a theory that was really meant to be a formula for peace. Finally, in a brief treatment of the debate between Hobbes and the common law jurists (the "authority-not-truth" thesis was coined for their benefit), will be shown the real alternative to the Hobbesian concept of sovereignty and peace: the idea of the constitutional state.

---

10. Martin Jänicke, "Die 'abgründige Wissenschaft' vom Leviathan—Zur Hobbes-Deutung Carl Schmitts im Dritten Reich," *Zeitschrift für Politik* 16 (1969): 401–15, at 401.

11. An attempt at a comprehensive account of the connections between Hobbes and Carl Schmitt is provided by Helmut Rumpf, *Carl Schmitt und Thomas Hobbes* (Berlin: Duncker & Humblot, 1972).

12. See also Rhonheimer, *La filosofia politica di Thomas Hobbes: coerenza e contradizzioni di un paradigma* (Rome: Armando, 1997), 214ff.

Auctoritas non veritas facit legem
in Thomas Hobbes

The classical formula *auctoritas non veritas facit legem* appears, to be sure, only once in his corpus: in the twenty-sixth chapter of the *Leviathan*, "Of Civill Lawes," and only in the subsequent Latin version.[13] The maxim in the original, English version[14] lacks the air of a legal sentence, and in the later "Dialogue between a Philosopher and a Student of the Common Laws of England"[15] we have a variant formulation: "It is not wisdom, but authority that makes a law"—with "wisdom" set against "authority." What comes to the surface here is, first, a determination of the meaning of the Latin sentence that is orientated to his other texts, and second, an interpretation of it in the context of Hobbes's whole philosophy.

But first a few summarizing remarks about the Hobbes's whole design. For Hobbes, civil laws exist only as commands of a sovereign. The sovereignty of a lawgiver is founded on a contract, by which individual subjects relinquish their *individually* carrying through their natural rights to self-preservation and prosperity, and hand them over to a sovereign individual or body. The reasoned conclusions *(dictates of reason, conclusions, theoremes)* which, as a kind of moving mechanism, bring about peace in the service of efficient self-preservation and (along with that) the contract that leads to the existing form of civil society, are known as *natural laws*. The laws that are created for the conditions of the artificial product known as the "state" have no other function than to interpret these *natural laws* and to guarantee the efficient application of such binding interpretations in an institutional form. The content of civil laws, as Hobbes emphasizes again and again, is nothing other than the natural law. Self-preservation, safety, peace, and welfare—that is, the natural desire and *right* of the individual—is the purpose of all sovereignty and of every law. The individual living in a civil society under a sovereign does not in any way give up his natural rights; he only *authorizes* a public person to realize them. Obedience, and thereby

---

13. *Thomas Hobbes Malmesburiensis, Opera Philosophica quae Latine scripsit Omnia in Unum Corpus Nunc Primum Collectae studio et labore Gulielmi Molesworth,* 5 vols., ed. W. Molesworth (London, 1839–45; reprint, Aalen: Scientia, 1962–66), 3:202.

14. *The English Works of Thomas Hobbes of Malmesbury,* 11 vols., ed. W. Molesworth (London 1839–45; reprint, Aalen: Scientia, 1962), vol. 3; more readily available (and containing the reliable Head edition of 1651) is Hobbes, *Leviathan,* ed. C. B. Macpherson (Harmondsworth: Penguin, 1986), 317.

15. Hobbes, *English Works,* 6:5.

self-limitation and self-commitment—the essence of "law," as opposed to "right" or freedom—is the price that the individual pays for it. The artificial product called the "state," the *artificial man,* and *mortall God,* "to which we owe under the *Immortal God* our peace and defence,"[16] comes into being from the realization that the individual and particular pursuit of the right to self-preservation leads to a war of all against all, a war that operates in a direction precisely opposite to self-preservation. The waiving of carrying through particular interests and their delegation to a sovereign power is at its best in the service of individual, natural rights—but it must always *serve* them. The sovereign power finds its own meaning and limits in carrying out this work: the limit is, in modern terminology, the "pre-political" and subjective natural right to self-preservation and thereby the protection of the individual. No law can abrogate this. If it should attempt it, the person affected is no longer bound to the contract. In this precise sense, Leviathan is a "constitutional state."

The rule that authority and not truth "makes" the law is often interpreted in a one-sided way, and, also in connection Carl Schmitt, as a formula for peace as opposed to confessional or sectarian claims to truth that destroy peace. That the maxim can also have this meaning follows naturally from the historical situation and from the fact that, as events turned out, the confessional problem associated with this principle was in fact solved through it, and that even Hobbes may have seen there its most decisive relevance. The original meaning and the immediate context in which the saying occurs and to which it is connected is nevertheless a more general one and at the same time a more precise one in terms of legal philosophy. This can be seen clearly when we inspect the text.

First, looking at a translation of the Latin version, we have:

In a state, the interpretation of the natural law does not depend on the teachers or writers of books about moral philosophy, but on the state itself. Those teachings may be true, but it is not truth but authority that makes something into a law [*authoritas non veritas facit legem*].

At first this can be understood as merely a legal-technical triviality: a competent lawgiver is required for a law to be *valid.* That is what Hobbes had already said in *De Cive,*[17] and he would insist on it again, as cited above, in

---

16. Hobbes, *Leviathan*, ch. 17 (Macpherson, ed.).

17. Ch. 14, § 15; see Hobbes, *Man and Citizen: "De Homine" and "De Cive"*, ed. B. Gert (Indianapolis: Hackett 1991) 281.

his "Dialogue": the "correctness" of a law or the "wisdom" of legal experts does not make something a law, but only the authoritative command of the sovereign law-giving power (according to Hobbes, this applies to customary law as well: only in virtue of the "will of the highest ruler" does it become law).[18] But if we limit ourselves to this trivial and "weaker" interpretation, we fall short, I think, of what really matters. Because Hobbes adds the following: "This interpretation is not valid because it is the word of the person of the sovereign, but because it is the word of the state." What counts is not the mere competence of the reigning sovereign to decide, apply, and enforce laws, but rather the fact that whoever makes laws does this not as a private person—even though a person with power: as Hobbes puts it, "as a natural person"—but rather as a *public* person who is *authorized* to carry out a task that is clearly defined by contract.

In order to unpack the meaning of this statement, we must look at the English edition of the *Leviathan,* which is more developed on this point. For here, the statement occurs in a context of confrontation not with moral philosophers but with common law jurists, whose ultimately constitutional status Hobbes would never sufficiently appreciate (a point to which I will return). I will cite now a crucial sentence, aimed above all at the (explicitly named) Chief Justice Sir Edward Coke:

That Law can never be against Reason, our Lawyers are agreed.... And [that] is true: but the doubt is, of whose Reason it is, that shall be received for Law. It is not meant of any private Reason; for then there would be as much contradiction in the Lawes, as there is in the Schooles.[19]

So it is not simply a question of validity of law and its enforcement, but rather the question of the *right reason:* Whose reason is right? Whose wisdom, whose truth will hold sway? Is it going to be that of private persons, who often go astray and differ among themselves, leading to divisions in society, or is it to be a *public* reason, wisdom, or truth, which promises unity of reason and consistency in legislation, leading to peace? Hobbes concludes:

Therefore it is not that *Juris prudentia,* or wisedom of subordinate Judges; but the Reason of this our artificiall Man the Common-wealth, and his Command, that maketh law: And the Commonwealth being in their Representative but one Person, there cannot easily arise any contradiction in the Lawes; and when there doth, the same

18. Ibid.
19. Hobbes, *Leviathan* (Macpherson, ed.), 316.

Reason is able, by interpretation, or alteration, to take it away. In all Courts of Justice, the Sovereign (which is the Person of the Common-wealth) is he that Judgeth.[20]

What is decisive here is the demand for consistency: what is needed is a reason characterized by non-contradictoriness and continuous, uniform validity—and this can only be secured by a public person and the command of such a person. Only a few pages later comes the dig against moral philosophers, and the more trivial element in terms of legal technicality:

The Authority of writers, without the Authority of the Common-wealth, maketh not their opinions Law, be they never so true.[21]

Law is only valid as part of the civil law.

For though it be naturally reasonable; yet it is by the Sovereign Power that it is Law.[22]

But this argument is subordinated and subsequent to the one mentioned before, and has the function of supporting it, and proving that it works. The complete argument when read in its context goes as follows: "Right" and (politically) "true" reason is only that which can secure peace. And this is only the public reason of the artificial person known as "the state," and therefore, because a law is a law not by its claim to be true, but only because it is enacted by a sovereign power with "ability to enforce obedience" (Max Weber's *Gehorsamserzwingungschance*) and thereby attains its validity— law is based not on intelligence but on fear of punishment. Only what is "valid" in this way can guarantee peace and therefore self-preservation (which was the original reason why the sovereign power came into being). This is also why private-particular claims to truth and validity are in principle rejected as irrational—just because they are private and particular. Only the *auctoritas* that is tied to, and identified with, *potestas* provides the reason, wisdom, and truth that is called for.[23]

This means, then, that in the sentence *Auctoritas non veritas facit legem,* it is not primarily the power of the state that is being played off against truth. Hobbes is not just dismissing "truth" in a cynical or "Machiavellian" way as politically irrelevant, as if he meant that it is just a question of making laws, no matter what. Rather, he is maintaining that there is a specific reason, wisdom, and truth that is proper to the sovereign public law-making authority. For Hobbes, the student of Bacon, private "truth" is always an expression of the interests and passions of individuals or groups, of the "De-

---

20. Ibid., 317.   21. Ibid., 322.
22. Ibid., 323.   23. See Goyard-Fabre, *Le Droit et la Loi*, 136.

sire of Power, of Riches, of Knowledge and of Honour."[24] In a political and social context there is no right reason "established by nature," but only an artificially created one. The contrast here is not authority versus truth, but rather the uniformly consistent peace-guaranteeing truth, wisdom, and reason of the artificially created, sovereign, universal, public power versus the contradiction-laden, pluralistic claims to truth and "rationalities" of private individuals, which, precisely because of their particularity and interestedness, only undermine peace. This naturally pertains as well to truth-claims made for religious-confessional purposes, but it is first and foremost intended for a fundamental, constitutional legality: a theory of sovereignty and the foundation of public law.

For Hobbes, then, public truth stands over against private truth. And with his theory of sovereignty, Hobbes founds a new theory of political-pragmatic truth. The criterion of truth is effective peace-keeping. Private "truths," reason, or wisdom is distinguished from the truth, wisdom, and reason of civil law. Hobbes demonstrates this in his justification of the civil governance and direction of the opinions and doctrines of the citizens in the eighteenth chapter of the *Leviathan*: it has to do, naturally, with finding the truth; but a doctrine that contradicts peace, says Hobbes, *cannot* be true. This is because all truth—and every law as well—must agree with the natural law and be an interpretation of the same. But the natural law requires peace in the service of self-preservation. Whatever endangers and destroys peace is, accordingly, untrue in a political and natural-legal sense. In general, therefore: "And though in matter of Doctrine, nothing ought to be regarded but the truth; yet this is not repugnant to regulating of the same by Peace. For Doctrine repugnant to Peace, can no more be True, than Peace and Concord can be against the Law of Nature."[25] And the consequence of this is: "It belongeth therefore to him that hath the Sovereign Power, to be Judge, or constitute all Judges of Opinions and Doctrines, as a thing necessary to Peace, thereby to prevent Discord and Civill Warre."[26]

A truth maintained by private persons or particular groups *cannot* raise any claim to universality. Only what is commanded by law can be *universally* true. According to Hobbes's intention, truth can never be made comparative or subordinate, but only supremely universal, and that means to be

24. Hobbes, *Leviathan*, Chapter 8 (Macpherson, ed.), 139.
25. Ibid., 233.
26. Ibid.

made into political reasoning for peace. In his first monograph on Hobbes, Bernard Willms rightly notes that a "breakthrough to a new conception of truth" is here achieved.[27] This position could, I suggest, be called "political nominalism" and could be described as "pragmatic-constructive." It aims for the establishment of public security and tranquility. Because—as Hobbes says in chapter 5 of the *Leviathan*—"no one mans Reason, nor the Reason of any one number of men, makes the certainty."[28] It must instead be "introduced"—through civil laws, which thereby give authoritative interpretation of the "natural law," and consequently the holy Scriptures and will of God—since the will of God is clearly that peace should reign.

This new "concept of truth" that goes far beyond what has customarily been termed "decisionism" fits immediately into Hobbes's total philosophy: just as in the state of nature there is neither justice nor injustice nor good nor evil, so likewise there is no "true and untrue" that is permanently valid. Even claims to truth, such as every act and feeling in the state of nature, are functions of the dominant passion: the fear of death and the striving for self-preservation. Everyone's right to do everything necessary for self-preservation is here the single universal truth. But the reasoning that is driven by this passion leads—by way of the theorem of *the natural laws*—to a contractual agreement. Only now is there such a thing as a universally binding truth that limits and binds the right of the individual. But this can only be the peace-furthering content of the civil laws, which by definition can correspond not to the truth-claims of private persons, but only to the content of the decisions made by the sovereign, which in turn are to be understood as the valid interpretations of natural laws bringing society into existence. This is of course not to be taken as some decisionistic arbitrariness, but rather in the sense of a new kind of "truth," "wisdom," and "reason," as pragmatic efficiency in the service of peace and thereby of individual self-preservation and welfare, so that citizens can pursue their private business-trades and other activities in peace and quiet, under the legislative protection of the "Leviathan." This pragmatic-political truth of civil law in the service of civic security and freedom thus remains anchored in the more fundamental truth of natural right, from which it acquires its justification and by which it is limited. Likewise the unconditional validity of the posi-

27. Bernard Willms, *Die Antwort des Leviathan: Thomas Hobbes' Politische Theorie* (Neuwied u. Berlin: Luchterhand, 1970), 69.
28. Hobbes, *Leviathan* (Macpherson, ed.), 111.

tive civil law is derived from the natural law, since the latter "which forbids breach of covenant ... commands us to keep all the civil laws."[29] Although he is the founder of legal positivism, Hobbes remains a true natural law thinker. And herein also consists, no doubt, the "ideological" power of his thought.[30]

Carl Schmitt's Interpretation of the Maxim

We can understand Hobbes in the context of his times, when the fanaticism of civil strife was rampant. Carl Schmitt certainly did as well. But he did not pay quite as close attention to the text.[31] Schmitt consistently overlooks the pragmatic significance of the truth-claim of the Hobbesian theory of legislation, that is, its recourse to the natural *right* of the individual and the distinction between right and law that is thereby established. For Schmitt, the essence of law consists exclusively in its being determined by the decision of a supreme authority (i.e., one that is not necessarily a juridical authority but perhaps a merely political one). This is the key statement: "Decision, considered normatively, is born out of nothing."[32] Objecting to Hans Kelsen's doctrine of a fundamental norm, Schmitt maintains that Hobbes, as a "classical representative of the decisionist type,"[33] uses the formula *auctoritas non veritas facit legem* to clarify the question about competence: what brings into being the most primary norm "out of nothing," from which all subsequent normativity is derived? This becomes even more evident in Schmitt's *Über die drei Arten des rechtswissenschaftlichen Denkens* (1934), where Hobbes is ideally depicted as "the classical case of decisionist thought": "All justice, every norm and every law, all interpreta-

29. Hobbes, *De cive*, ch. 14, § 10 (Bernard Gert, ed.), 278.

30. This bond of justification between natural law and legal positivism was clearly seen by Bobbio, "Hobbes e il giusnaturalismo," *Rivista Critica di Storia della Filosofia* 17 (1962), 470–85. See also Rhonheimer, *La filosofia politica di Thomas Hobbes*, 229ff.

31. The relevant references to Hobbes can be found in the following works by Schmitt: *Die Diktatur: Von den Anfängen des modernen Souveranitätsgedankens bis zum proletarischen Klassenkampf* (Munich: Duncker & Humblot, 1921); *Politische Theologie: Vier Kapitel zur Lehre von der Souveranität* (1922), 2nd ed. (Munich: Duncker & Humblot 1934); *Über die drei Arten des rechtswissenschaftlichen Denkens* Schriften der Akademie für Deutsches Recht 3 (Hamburg: Hanseatische Verlagsanstalt, 1934); *Verfassungslehre* (Munich: Duncker & Humblot, 1928); *Der Leviathan in der Staatslehre des Thomas Hobbes: Sinn und Fehlschlag eines politischen Symbols* (1938), ed. G. Maschke (Cologne: Hohenheim, 1982); *Der Begriff des Politischen* [1927]: *Text von 1932 mit einem Vorwort und drei Corollarien* (Berlin: Duncker & Humblot, 1963; in this last work is included "Hobbes-Kristall" as a supplement, which is too one-sidedly concerned with the question of pacifying religious sectarianism).

32. Schmitt, *Politische Theologie*, 42.

33. Ibid., 44.

tions of the law, all ordinances, are for Hobbes essentially decisions of the sovereign, and what is sovereign is neither a legitimate monarch nor a competent authority, but just that which the sovereign decides. Justice is law, and law is the deciding command that quells any conflict about what is just; *autoritas non veritas facit legem.*"[34]

Now, since it has been observed that in his constitutional theory as well, Schmitt understands his "positive constitution concept" as an order of justice arising out of normative nothingness through an original decision, and that he treats (as in his *Politische Theologie*) the sovereign as one who decides about the state of emergency, so here, too, it becomes clear that he includes the very coming-into-being of the sovereign power and its logic of justification under the formula *auctoritas non veritas facit legem.* What is central for Hobbes—the authorization, by way of free, self-binding, and rational agreement, of a public legal person with a clearly defined sphere of legal responsibility—has naturally fallen completely out of the picture here. The constituting of a sovereign power is for Schmitt essentially a self-constituting of the one who succeeds in deciding about the state of emergency. He considers it a "genuine and pure decision" of the actual sovereign himself, and not as an authorization by free legal subjects in a contract.[35] The Hobbesian concept of contract, in fact, essentially refers back to a normative order of reason that consists in the natural laws that follow from natural right. The Hobbesian sovereign does not stand before a "normative nothingness." His legislative task is not the *creation* of justice but its *preservation* and *realization* through laws. Only the laws—and the justice established through them—are the creation of the sovereign. Carl Schmitt, by contrast, holds that "The sovereign's decision is the absolute beginning, and the beginning ... is nothing other than a sovereign decision. It springs out of a normative nothingness and concrete disorder."[36]

For Hobbes the constitution of the sovereign power through a contract is by no means "the absolute beginning"; it is only the beginning of the civil law and thereby of the legally binding difference between "right"

34. Schmitt, *Über die drei Arten des rechtswissenschaftlichen Denkens*, 27. See also 41.

35. To be sure, Schmitt refers in his *Über die drei Arten des rechtswissenschaftlichen Denkens* to a "state-making 'contract'" (41), and more precisely to "consensus of individuals"; but this consensus is in turn possible only through the state: "The sovereign is almighty through the consensus which he himself makes through his decision and public plenitude of power [*die staatliche Allmacht und Entscheidung*]." Practically nothing more than this survives of the ideas of authorization or contract. It is instead an idea of a "plebiscitic" structure of the totalitarian state.

36. Ibid., 28.

and "wrong," between "mine and "yours." But it is not the beginning of
law [Recht] as such. This was in existence from the beginning in the state
of nature that remains normatively present as a kind of original source
of right, even under the conditions of socialization and subjection to a sovereign. Right as subjective right, and its realization by individuals, is the
point of departure, content, and limiting framework of the civil law. The
insight of the Hobbesian sovereignty doctrine consists precisely in the understanding that natural right, in order to be free to realize itself optimally,
needs the self-limitation and self-binding of law. In his theoretical analysis
at least, Hobbes was consistent with regard to the distinction between right
and law.

So then it is not to be wondered at that, as a consequence of Schmitt's interpretation, Hobbes's state of nature was understood as a mere "absence of
law and order." There is no mention of the natural *right* to self-preservation,
nor of the pre-political *natural laws* that are oriented to order and dictated by
natural reason, to which all the truth, wisdom, and reason of the legislator
remains obligated, and which he must interpret. Hobbes's clearly stated intention is to understand every legislative decision as clearly *bound by natural right and the natural laws,* to a right to self-preservation and peace, that
endows every law with content and limits, and every citizen with a marginal
right of opposition to the sovereign.[37]

Reconsidering Hobbes and the
Hobbesianism of Schmitt

Hobbes has been purposely contrasted with Schmitt in order to bring
into the open just what the philosopher from Malmesbury was undertaking to claim—and obliging himself to justify—in his doctrine. His political
theory is traditional in the sense that it claims to be a theory of a political
order that puts natural law into effect.[38] To this extent, as Michael Oakeshott emphasized in his now classic "Introduction to *Leviathan*," Hobbes
belongs to a long-standing tradition.[39] In contrast with Schmitt, Hobbes

37. See on this also the classical study by Peter C. Mayer-Tasch, *Thomas Hobbes und das Widerstandsrecht* (Tübingen: J. C. B. Mohr [Paul Siebeck], 1965).

38. See for this my remarks in Martin Rhonheimer, G. B. Sadler, M. Zuckert, "Forum: Hobbes on
Laws of Nature and Moral Norms," *Acta Philosophica* 16, no. 1 (2007): 125–31 and 139–41.

39. Reprinted under the title "Introduction to *Leviathan*" in Michael Oakeshott, *Hobbes on Civil Association* (Oxford: Oxford University Press, 1975).

is a natural-law thinker. At the same time, he combines this, in contrast to Bodin, in a methodical-systematic way with the modern conception of the institutional and public guarantee of the realization of subjective right. As already mentioned, we discover in Hobbes a legal positivism, grounded in natural law—which will not seem so paradoxical if we fully understand the special character of Hobbes's natural law philosophy.

For Hobbes, despite all the fullness of the sovereign's power and law-making competence, the burning question nevertheless remains, whether or not this sovereignty and legislation actually safeguards the subjective right of the individual. And right here is where the problems begin: Hobbes can never dispel the ghosts he has conjured up. Contradictions and inco-herence are inescapable and everywhere. There is no institutional place in the Leviathan for this question to be posed legitimately and efficiently—just as today's "decisionists," oriented toward Schmitt and Hobbes, speak out against the attempts of constitutional lawyers to justify their existence. Hobbes assumes that it is not an important question to pose, or that it is enough to pose it inwardly, before the forum of one's own conscience, in order to answer it. That the individual conscience must also be articulated socially or publicly seems to him existentially unnecessary and politically dangerous to boot—no doubt because of the impact of the Puritan fanati-cism of his day (i.e., the English or Scottish Puritans who then emigrated to America). It is also quite conceivable for him that one might give spoken al-legiance to a religious creed opposite to what one holds in conscience, if the sovereign should command it. The legal-right underpinnings of law, and the difference between *ius* and *lex,* even though it is thoroughly established in theory, becomes meaningless in practice, and an ideology of justification in the hands of the lawgiver. The question about the legitimacy of the sover-eignty is in practice reduced to the question whether the power of the state can provide efficient protection against physical threats. Consequently it is exactly to this that Schmitt reduces Hobbes's position: to the fundamental relationship between protection and obedience; and this is why, although he is no Hobbesian, nevertheless he is a genuine follower of Hobbes. He simply drops what is practically irrelevant from any theoretical justifica-tion. For only then can "pure" decisionism appear: "That it was the relevant point for a decision to be made, makes the decision relatively—and under some circumstances, absolutely—independent of the correctness of its con-tent, and stops all further discussion about whether any doubts could arise.

The decision is instantly independent of the reasoned justification and has self-standing value."[40]

It is the paradox of the Hobbesian peace formula that in an emergency, subjective right can be exercised only as revolt and rebellion (or as flight from state coercion), but not in the form of a peaceful exertion of influence or even an institutionalized monitoring of government power. The result is that even the Leviathan is subject to the logic of *bellum omnium contra omnes* (war of all against all) when the individual conscience is stirred. The state necessarily becomes an instrument of repression, the most ravenous of the ravenous wolves. For Hobbes, the conscience of the individual was a *quantité négligeable* for politically existing citizens. This was a misjudgment that turns every Leviathan into a time bomb. It provokes ideological, instead of sectarian, civil war.

The logic of the Leviathan—and, to no small degree, also the insight into the detonating effect of the right Hobbes grants the individual citizen to have a reservation of conscience—leads Schmitt to the following consequence: while Hobbes's construction lives totally on the fiction of a clean separation between the sphere of sovereign state power and the social praxis of private persons, Schmitt sees very clearly that such a separation is no longer possible, given the realities of modern society and politics. Whereas Hobbes's theory could neutralize and turn aside the so-called indirect powers—that is, that of the jurists, the special interest–bound parliament, the clergy, and universities—in the pluralistic reality of contemporary society (so goes Schmitt's critical diagnosis), it is these same indirect powers that reappear in a new form as social forces (i.e., political, economic, cultural forces) that functionalize the state to their own interests. The state thereby faces two alternatives: either act as the mere agent, caretaker, and manager of such social-pluralistic forces—to become, as Schmitt has it, a "total state from weakness"—and lose its sovereignty, or alternatively, rise above all these interests and become total by strength:

Such a state does not permit any forces to arise within it which are hostile to it, inhibit it, or divide it. It has no thought of surrendering the new means of power to its enemies and would-be destroyers, and allow its own power to be undermined by such labels as "liberalism" or "state under the rule of law" [German: *Rechtsstaat*] or what-

---

40. Schmitt, *Politische Theologie*, 42. Exceptionally, when the "essence of political authority is revealed most clearly … the decision separates itself from the legal norm, and (to put it in a paradoxical way) authority proves, that it does not need to have a legal right to create a legal right" (ibid., 20).

ever one chooses to name them. This kind of state knows how to distinguish friends from enemies. In this sense, as I have said, every genuine state is a total state; and it is that as a *societas perfecta* in this world, and for all time. Political theorists have long known that the political is the total; what is new is only the technical means, whose political effects need to be understood.[41]

That we have in the meantime come to understand these effects is self-evident. But what is decisive here is this: a state understood in these terms can no longer understand itself as the preserver of the rights of individuals, but must rather formulate these rights out of its own substance and legitimacy. It should not be surprising that Schmitt (especially in his 1938 Hobbes monograph) begins to see the quintessence of Hobbes's thought to consist in his struggle against the "indirect forces." But since these new forces are nothing other than the socially organized interests of those private persons whose protection and security Hobbes wanted to guarantee through his Leviathan, the Hobbesian link between law and justice is shattered. If the ancient and original connection between protection and obedience is to be retained, if the *protego ergo obligo* is to become the *cogito ergo sum* of the state,[42] then it must understand itself as the creator of order out of normative nothingness, and no longer as the defense attorney for individual rights. What that can mean needs no special illustration today.

In this way Hobbes, probably without intending it, brought conceptual clarity to the problem of modern statecraft and sovereignty. Schmitt, on the other hand, and just as unintentionally, has helped us, we might say, find a therapeutic value in our study of Hobbes. In order for this study to be fruitful for political philosophy, it is important that we consider Hobbes's imposing and consistent theory of the link between natural right and civil laws not only in comparison with the theoreticians of the common law (who are in many respects more intelligent and also justified by the progress or subsequent events of English history), but also by taking seriously its inner, anthropological truth—a truth that Hobbes fully claimed for his hedonistic-sensual picture of man.[43] For, just as it is certainly correct that laws do not come into being so much through "truth" as through sovereign fiat, just as

41. Carl Schmitt, "Weiterentwicklung des totalen Staats in Deutschland" (1933), in Schmitt, *Verfassungsrechtliche Aufsätze aus den Jahren 1924–1954: Materialien zu einer Verfassungslehre* (Berlin: Duncker & Humblot, 1958), 359–65, at 361.

42. Schmitt, *Der Begriff des Politischen*, 53.

43. An important interpretation of Hobbes that consistently studies the "Hobbesian deduction of politics from anthropology" is that of Ulrich Weiss, *Das philosophische System von Thomas Hobbes* (Stuttgart-Bad Canstatt: Fromman-Holzboog, 1980).

certainly can sovereignty and public authority be legitimated in their function only through their ultimate anthropological truth. Thomas Hobbes himself would be the last to deny this, since he does everything he can to persuade his reader (each one a potential sovereign legislator at the top of a Hobbesian Leviathan) that his philosophy is "true." To ask the question of whether this is really the case is precisely the kind of task we would never agree to waive or to put into the hands of a legislator.

Hobbes, the *Common Law,* and the Idea of the Constitutional State

That Hobbes's doctrine of the political pragmatic truth of positive legality as laid down by the sovereign was developed in opposition to the common law jurists of his time arises immediately from the texts—not only from *Leviathan* but also from the *Dialogue* that from beginning to end is presented as an attack against the common law. In the twenty-sixth chapter of *Leviathan* both Edward Coke and his conception of the common law as *artificial reason* are mentioned by name. It is a mark against Hobbes that he—herein as well a student of Bacon—completely misrepresents the proper character of common law and Coke's idea of an *artificial reason.*[44] Hobbes takes what Coke calls "artificial reason"—the ensemble of written law and acts of Parliament, the judicial prejudices bound up with this, the growth of legal wisdom over the centuries—and quite wrongly interprets it as a "private reason" that is opposed to the sovereign political power, and that, as private law, can only be a source of disorder and conflict. But in reality the common law hailed by Coke as "artificial reason" means an *institution* that relieves the burdens of individual reason by raising itself above the private opinions of individuals—not, however, in the arbitrary fashion of Hobbesian sovereignty, but by being bound up with a body of law that is ever present, if not unchangeable. For Coke and his successors, common law has the character of *constitutional law*: it embodies a reason that stands above private reason—even that of any possible law-giver—and provides guidance for that reason by limiting it. As a quasi-constitutional institution, the common

---

44. On this see also Kriele, *Die Herausforderung des Verfassungsstaates: Hobbes und die englischen Juristen* (Berlin: Luchterhand, 1970); Rhonheimer, *La filosofia politica di Thomas Hobbes*, 221. On Edward Coke see Jean Beauté, *Un grand juriste Anglais: Sir Edward Coke (1552–1634): Ses idées politiques et constitutionelles, ou aux origines de la démocratie occidentale moderne* (Paris: Presses Universitaires de France, 1975).

law entails thereby the *limitation* of sovereignty, at least according to a logic that goes far beyond the categorical horizon of Hobbes's thought. It is the logic of the modern constitutional state.

Hobbes thinks that his conception of positive law is superior to that of the common law jurists because it legitimizes positive law through its practical and pragmatic truth. All he sees in Coke's concept is the position of the theoretically disputing, constantly contradicting, and quarrel-plagued reason of the "Scholastics," the private conflicts driven by jurisprudential "one-up-man-ship" that, consequently, could never become a closed, contradiction-free corpus of valid law.[45]

In reality, when it comes to avoiding conflict and contradiction, the position of the common law jurists, with their practical-pragmatic conception of law, is an especially strong one. This is because they argue with the validity-claims of traditional and thereby actually established law. To concede institutional primacy to this in the face of any overreaching on the part of the sovereign (one thinks of the *Petition of Right* drafted by Coke himself or the right of habeas corpus going back to the *Magna Carta*) is a very practical-pragmatic use of reason and a correspondingly practical truth with regard to the common good—the *salus populi* proclaimed over and again by Hobbes—which every law should serve. The common law jurists did not claim that common law was rational, because it was "true" in a theoretical sense. Rather, they saw in it just what Coke wanted to express with the name *artificial reason*—a pragmatic, actually existing, historically effective "artificial completion" of reason, "the fruit of long study, observation and experience, and not the natural reason of each single man," so that the old rule is confirmed, "according to which no single man on the basis of his individual reason can be wiser than the law, which is the perfection of reason."[46]

Nevertheless: Coke's position was by no means the final word in every respect. Its strongly traditional and customary character is too one-sided. And because it lacks any theory of sovereignty, it has no answer to the Hobbesian objection in the *De cive* that even customary law can be *valid* law only through approval by the existing power (although Coke would not accept that argument, since he considers customary right as itself a sovereign power with its own built-in justification). But that such a lack would have

---

45. See again Hobbes, *Leviathan*, ch. 26 (Macpherson ed.), 316.

46. Edward Coke, *Reports* 64–65, as cited by Beauté, *Un grand juriste anglais*, 63. The English is the author's translation from the French.

to be overcome, and that it could be overcome on the basis of common law, was made manifest in the (unfinished) answer to Hobbes's *Dialogue* written by Coke's successor in the office of chief justice, Sir Matthew Hale.[47] Hale brings out clearly the institutional and thereby sovereignty-limiting character of precedent law (written laws and acts of parliament), and he does so rather provocatively, with a justification recalling Hobbes: "It is Sufficient that they are Instituted Laws that give a Certainty to us, and it is reasonable for us to observe them though the particular reason of the Institution appeare not."[48] There is no cause for surprise that it was Hale who was able to recover something of the pro-sovereignty side from Hobbes. In that way, Hale became the theorist of the royal prerogative, whereby he maintained, in the tradition of Bracton, that the king was always *Rex in parlamento*. And the royal prerogative is treated in turn as a component of the common law. Royal sovereignty-claims, according to Hale, have their own legal grounding in the common law.

The formula for the modern constitutional state is sovereignty, but constitutionally bound, and hence partitioned and controlled sovereignty: Hobbes did not have the formula, and Carl Schmitt tried to discredit it. For Hobbes, partition and control of sovereignty was a contradiction in terms, the very destruction of sovereignty, whose existence he rightly saw, along with Bodin, as the necessary condition for a peaceful society. Perhaps we should not think so ill of him for not finding the right formula, since his times were evil times. They explain, and appear to demand some respect for, his exaggerated sovereigntist dogmatism, his "law-and-order fanaticism." But Carl Schmitt, through his constitutional theory of decisionism feeding into the idea of the "total state," made his equally evil times decidedly more evil than they already were (to the extent that he did have some influence).

In any case, the justification for law is not found in mere self-preservation desperately sought in times of civil strife. And the starting point for the creation of law is not the exceptional condition, and "normative nothingness." Justice and the law and order of society are bound up with the historical pro-

---

47. Matthew Hale, "Reflections by the Lord Chief Justice Hale on Mr. Hobbes His Dialogue of the Lawe," in *History of English Law*, ed. W. S. Holdsworth, 7th ed., 13 vols. (London: Sweet & Maxwell, 1956–64), vol. 5, app. 3, 500–513. See also D. E.C. Yale, "Hobbes and Hale on Law, Legislation and the Sovereign," *Cambridge Law Journal* 31, no. 1 (1972): 121–56.

48. Hale, "Reflections," 505.

cess determined by human beings: a process that has revealed the rationality of law over and over again, even if this alone is not capable of legitimizing law and the legal order as *rational* in a concluding and definitive way. But that is another theme.[49]

49. The original was published as "Autoritas non veritas facit legem: Thomas Hobbes, Carl Schmitt und die Idee des Verfassungsstaates," *Archiv für Rechts- und Sozialphilosophie* 86 (2000): 484–498. It was translated by Gerald Malsbary.

‖‖‖

FIVE

The Open Society and the New Laicism

Against the Soft Totalitarianism of Certain Secularist Thinking

Author's note: This essay was written by invitation of the Italian "laicist" ("secularist") and leftish-liberal journal *Reset* for a monographic issue on the occasion of the hundredth anniversary of Karl R. Popper. After having received the manuscript, the editors denied the publication of the text in the form presented here. But even a shorter text, which had been purged by the author of some—in the ears of Italian liberal secularists—politically incorrect affirmations, never made it to publication in *Reset*. The author then offered the "purged" text to the more conservative journal *Liberal* of the "Fondazione Liberal," where it appeared under the title "Laici e cattolici: oltre le divisioni" (Secularists and Catholics: beyond the divisions).[1] The following translation presents the integral original text, including the original title (shortened, primarily by removing a reference to Karl Popper), as it was first submitted to *Reset* and has never before been published. Only some minor changes have been introduced to render the text more comprehensible for Anglo-Saxon readers.

The Open Society and Its Foundations

Karl Popper wrote in 1987 that, despite the fact that his book *The Open Society and Its Enemies* had been continually in print since 1945, only rarely had the book's most important idea been well understood: that the essential thing is not *who* governs, but the fact that there can be a transition from one government to another without bloodshed. This, and not a hypothetical "sover-

---

1. No. 17 (2003): 108–16.

eignty of the people,"[2] is for Popper the essence of a democracy, precisely as the form of political organization of an open society, a society distinguished by the fact that it is comprised of individuals who can make personal choices and are free to express themselves on the basis of subjective values. Open societies are dynamic and innovative precisely because they allow criticism on the part of public opinion, leading to a continual process of reform.

Popper's open society nevertheless possesses two pillars that sustain it, as it were, from without. The first—as Popper explains in the addenda to his principal work of political philosophy—is "the dualism of facts and standards" or "facts and policies,"[3] meaning that "policies" (e.g., concrete laws, the legal system, institutions) may in an open society be established in such a way that they do not conform to just, valid or true moral standards. A dualism between facts and standards thus implies that any political or social fact—including the results of democratic processes—can be measured against higher moral criteria. To deny this dualism is the same for Popper as identifying the political power with the law.

The second external pillar of the open society appears in *Conjectures and Refutations: The Growth of Scientific Knowledge*,[4] where the theoretician of the open society articulates his reasons why our contemporary society can be considered the best that has ever existed. If this is true, writes Popper, it is certainly not due to technological advances, but because of "the standards and values which have come down to us through Christianity from Greece and from the Holy Land; from Socrates, and from the Old and New Testaments."[5] These values, for Popper, mean above all respect for the individual and for his inalienable dignity.

It is clear, therefore, that in Popper's opinion even an open society must be based on a stable system of values that not only is the society not able to produce of itself, but that indeed represents the criteria against which the society's results and performance are to be measured. Such a system of values has the authority of a fundamental "truth" with respect to democratic procedures, and is therefore in this sense "absolute"; it represents the founding premise of these procedures, and is independent of them. Moreover, this system of values is in some way connected with the moral standards derived from the Judeo-Christian tradition.

2. *The Open Society and Its Enemies*, 5th ed. (Princeton, N.J.: Princeton University Press, 1971), 60.
3. Ibid. Within the addenda, section 12 on "The Dualism of Facts and Standards" is at 383–84.
4. London: Routledge, 2002.
5. *Conjectures and Refutations*, 496.

Today, however, some think that one who believes in such absolute founding "truths" is not in conformity with the spirit of democracy and is therefore, in this sense, a "fundamentalist." Popper himself, however, shows the falsity of this position. A political fundamentalist would rather be one who holds that ultimate and absolute criteria of truth are *immanent* to the political process. The fundamentalist denies not only political and procedural autonomy, but also the legitimacy of the decisional openness of the democratic political process. As such, he measures the legitimacy of political decision-making processes based on whether or not their results conform to particular standards of content. For example, he would consider a system that could make possible the legalization of abortion—such as "procedural" democracy—to be illegitimate, claiming in this case that the procedures themselves should be changed.

It is another thing, however, to hold that the results of legitimate democratic processes, or of democratic decisions arrived at by the majority, can be *mistaken* or even *immoral*, based on criteria that are transcendent with respect to the processes themselves. Those who criticize the results of such processes in the name of a truth about man and his nature do not for this reason deny the instrumental-pragmatic logic of democracy. In any case, the claim that the legalization of abortion is mistaken, immoral, or unjust should be permissible, just as one should be allowed to oppose such a decision with every available argument—of course within the rules of a democracy—seeking to overturn it.

"Laicism": Auto-Censorship of Democracy?

Some contemporary liberal democratic and laicist thinkers would seem to contradict this point. Indeed this is exactly what Gian Enrico Rusconi does in his lucid and stimulating book *Come se Dio non ci fosse* (As if God did not exist),[6] when he criticizes the fact that Pope John Paul II claimed that Polish laws concerning abortion are "lacking in authentic juridical validity."[7] From a secularist point of view, this claim would be pure fundamentalism or dogmatism. The same would be true for Cardinal Ratzinger's attempt to defend the pope when, speaking out against the absolute value of democratic majorities, Ratzinger asserted that there is a truth that sur-

6. *Come se Dio non ci fosse: I laici, i cattolici e la democrazia* (Turin: Einaudi, 2000).
7. See ibid., 8.

passes the range of factual implementations of decisions made by democratic majorities. For Rusconi, such an argument is irreconcilable with the
idea of a "secular democracy," given that it includes the "claim of a transcendent truth, set up as judge of any political regime considered to be
damaging to human dignity."[8] But isn't this precisely an example of what
Popper had in mind with his distinction between facts and moral criteria?

Naturally, such a criticism would be justified if the pope and Ratzinger
had meant that such laws concerning abortion were not *valid positive laws,*
that they must be immediately removed from the legal system, and that
democratic procedures based on majority decisions that could lead to the
approval of such laws are illegitimate. I think, however, that they meant
something different, namely that these laws to some degree contradict
certain moral criteria and anthropological truths, that they are opposed to
justice and, as such, are unjust, in this sense unlawful and in need of revision. Seen in this way, the claim that a truth exists that surpasses political
majorities is in fact nothing other than the application of Popper's principle
of the dualism between facts and criteria. The claim of a transcendent truth,
by which one criticizes the facts of certain legislative or institutional regulations, is thus in no way in contradiction to the recognition of the legitimacy and autonomy of the democratic process that generated the fact being
criticized. That a criticism based on transcendent criteria is possible even in
a democracy prevents precisely the possibility that the political power and
the law—in this case, the majority and the law—come to be identified.

It is so obvious that here we are dealing with the distinction between
the political power and the law that it is surprising that an attentive author
such as Rusconi could make such a mistake. A reason for this can perhaps
be found in the deep historical mistrust toward both the official Church and
Catholic citizens who feel obligated in conscience to follow the Church and
its teachings. This type of mistrust nevertheless seems to me anachronistic and, viewed from the perspective of democracy, also unjust. Indeed for
nineteenth-century secularism it was enough to limit the Church's influence
over people's consciences. Is this perhaps considered insufficient today, out
of fear of the Catholic conscience of citizens who now enjoy complete political freedom?

It is difficult for me to conclude that this could be the case for an au-

---

8. Ibid., 9.

thor such as Rusconi. Yet it also seems clear to me that he goes well beyond what Popper asked of a democracy. According to Rusconi, Popper's premise is not only the nonviolent transition between governments, but also the exclusion of a certain type of argumentation. In effect, this latter means that in the "public democratic space,"[9] arguments referring to an authority external to the consensual logic of the debate itself should not be permitted. "What matters is the reciprocal capacity of persuasion and loyal observance of procedures."[10] It is impermissible, therefore, to refer either to the Bible or to a doctrine of the Church (and therefore obviously nor to those standards and values based on which, in Popper's judgment, our contemporary world is the best in history). And this is forbidden because the Bible and the doctrine of the Church—and thus also believing Catholics—represent an absolute "truth which cannot err,"[11] a truth that "by definition does not take into account the possibility of being mistaken."[12]

Frankly, I don't see the problem. That is, I see no problem with the fact that there may be actors in a democracy who are convinced that some of their convictions are absolutely true—at least as long as these actors abide by the rules of democracy. One of the obvious things about a democracy is precisely the fact that its decisions have *absolutely no* claim to absolute truth, and that within its structures there can be no attempt to institutionally guarantee such a claim to absoluteness. Isn't this enough? Where is the problem if someone, in his role as a member of parliament, votes against a law (or against a change in the constitution) providing for the introduction of racial discrimination, simply because he is convinced (perhaps based on biblical revelation or influenced by the latest papal encyclical) that it is an absolute truth that all people have been created in the image and likeness of God? Would it be permitted to express such an opinion only on the condition that the one who held it *also* admitted "the possibility of being mistaken"?

In fact, anyone referring to the Bible (or to the Koran) or to a papal encyclical in a political debate usually doesn't have much chance of winning a majority. He must rather—even if his conscience is in some way guided by the Church—defend his positions and seek to convince others with arguments of a political-ethical nature. Consequently, it is difficult to dismiss the idea that Rusconi's verdict is nothing other than an effort at intimidation, aimed

9. Ibid., 7.
10. Ibid.
11. Ibid., 10.
12. Ibid., 164.

at characterizing *certain* arguments as unsuitable for debate or illegitimate insofar as they are in conformity with the Church's teaching or because they are conducted along philosophical-metaphysical lines, which Rusconi frequently rejects as unacceptable. Certainly, one can always cite this or that monsignor who puts himself forward with tedious "bio-theological" arguments, as Rusconi calls them. On the other hand, I feel rather uncomfortable when laicists propose as a characteristic element of their position the allegedly more enlightened disposition to "learn critically, from science, to redefine life and nature."[13] Certainly the disposition to learn from science is not mistaken a priori. (Haven't we fortunately learned from modern embryology—roughly since the beginning of the nineteenth century—that human life exists from the moment of conception and not only forty days afterward, as St. Thomas Aquinas, according to a general prejudice of his time, held?) Why should resolute opposition to certain rather highly problematic attempts to redefine human nature not also be capable of being an expression of a truly *secular*—that is, not specifically religious or even catholic—position and of a sense of civil responsibility? In the final analysis, science has many times in the past attempted to redefine human nature—with disastrous consequences for the respect of human dignity.

I think, therefore, that a democracy should not censure itself by fixing in advance what types of argumentation or truth-claims are acceptable in the public space. Even the principles of Habermas's discourse ethics, which are very dear to Rusconi, clearly do not represent a truth that is binding for democratic public opinion, even if they do contain some truths. Democratic processes are not philosophy seminars, but institutions in which power is exercised in a responsible and ordered way, according to law and based on decisions made by the majority. Ultimately, each person must weigh in his conscience whether or not this power has been exercised for the good of his fellow citizens. It therefore seems superfluous to me that Catholics be asked to comport themselves "as if God didn't exist."[14] The only important thing is that they act *in freedom and with a personal sense of responsibility*—and thus not as a "secular branch" of the ecclesial hierarchy—ready to collaborate with all on the basis of their Catholic conscience.

13. Ibid., 18.
14. See especially ibid., 19–21.

Political Ethos, Pluralistic Society,
and "Constitutional Patriotism"

Nevertheless, on an essential point—and indeed not the only one—I agree with Rusconi: that the modern secular political culture of constitutional democracy—of "secular democracy"—possesses a proper, specific, and autonomous structure of values, which must be defended as the common platform of the collective life of human beings in the face of all claims to a "higher" truth, irrespective of how important and decisive such a truth might be for the lives of individuals.

The modern political culture of the democratic constitutional state is clearly a response to the need for the creation of institutions of cooperation and common life in a pluralistic world that is marked by religious, economic, and social conflicts, not to mention antagonistic interests. These institutions are characterized by a *political* ethos, one that obeys a specific ethical-political logic. This logic aims at the maintenance of peace (the state), the guarantee of freedom (constitutional state), and the guarantee of justice and of solidarity understood as the equality of freedom (democratic constitutional state). For this reason I appreciate the fact that Rusconi, in *Possiamo fare a meno di una religione civile?* (Can we do without a civil religion?),[15] distinguished between the concepts of "secularity" and "multiculturalism." "The principle of secularity ... does not limit itself to asserting the principle of a benevolent tolerance, but positively demands a *reciprocal bond* on which a political community is built, which is solidaristic in that it consistently recognizes, in principle, rules and institutions which prescind from particular cultural roots, and which are not generalizable."

But what exactly does this mean? In my opinion, it means that this type of political culture has its own specific criteria of value from the ethical-political point of view. This secular ethos, which is in large part a procedural ethos, is capable of providing a common platform for collective civil life and a reciprocally advantageous cooperation precisely to the extent that it does not propose to realize *ultimate values* for the individual (e.g., moral perfection, holiness, specific concepts of happiness or of the "good life"), but limits itself to that which is *fundamental* for human cohabitation. As an example, German Catholics acted against this principle of the political

---

15. *Possiamo fare a meno di una religione civile?* (Rome: Laterza, 1999).

priority of what is fundamental with respect to higher values when, in 1933, the party of the Center (under the guidance of Msgr. Kaas and with the support of the bishops) voted for the law that gave full powers to Hitler; they did so—with disastrous consequences—because they were willing to sacrifice the liberal-democratic constitution of the Weimar Republic under the prospect of concessions on the ecclesiastical-political level and in hopes of obtaining public support for Catholic schools. They should have instead defended what was fundamental, renouncing the "higher," along with some other things more important from a Catholic perspective. What is asked of everyone, Catholics included, is what Rusconi terms "constitutional patriotism," a concept that originated in Germany. The foundation of this constitutional patriotism is the political ethos of peace, freedom, and justice.

The recognition of this political ethos of the democratic constitutional state has as its presupposition the religious and confessional neutrality of the state. The official institutions of the secular state are blind, so to speak, with respect to claims to religious truth. But in order that this confessional neutrality not result in an aggressive, antireligious secularism (like that of the nineteenth and early twentieth centuries, which in certain respects was understandable), often nourished by various and dubious ideologies, this legitimate secularity of the state must be founded on the consciousness that the reference to transcendence, and thus the search for religious truth, is essential for human beings. The assertion of German constitutionalist Ernst-Wolfgang Böckenförde, often justly cited by Rusconi, that the "liberal secularized state is nourished by presuppositions that it cannot itself guarantee,"[16] expresses precisely this, with the consequence that for the individual citizen participating in the public democratic debate, the recognition of this truth in his conscience must be an essential source of inspiration for his argument. The affirmation of values reaches the democratic public space through the religious and moral substance of citizens, not by the authoritarian proclamation of the state. To desire to prevent this with the type of argumentative barriers Rusconi proposes would ultimately lead to the "soft totalitarianism" of a new secularism that, instead of being content with the open, pragmatic ethos of peace and freedom that has developed through history and is typical of the constitutional democratic state, would subordinate this ethos to the claims of the presumed absolute truth of a Habermasian discourse ethic.

16. Emphasis as in original. See Böckenförde's *State, Society and Liberty* (New York: Berg, 1991), 45.

In my opinion, two things are necessary today: in the first place, from the Catholic side, the recognition of the secular political ethos immanent to the democratic constitutional state as a fundamental *bonum comune*, meaning the acknowledgment of its legitimacy independent of the concrete results of elections, referenda, and other legitimate democratic procedures—thus what the Germans call "constitutional patriotism"—and also the willingness to adhere to a state and behave loyally with respect to its constitutional order, even if that state fails to realize (or does not yet realize, or no longer realizes) much of what is demanded by a Catholic conscience. Second, on the part of secularists, it is necessary that they be willing to accept that "Catholic positions"—whether influenced by the Church's teaching or not—can also win a majority in the democratic process. If both of these conditions were respected, it would no longer make sense to distinguish between "secularists" and "Catholics" in the context of the democratic public space, much less for them to mutually denigrate one another.

The Myth of the Neutrality of the State

To this point we have put an important problem between parentheses. According to the standard political philosophy of liberalism (though important exceptions exist, for example Oxford philosopher Joseph Raz), the modern democratic constitutional state is based on the principle of the neutrality of the state, of procedural justice, and of the impossibility of tying specific substantial conceptions regarding the good of man to the public juridical order. The only absolute criterion of value is the autonomy of the individual— in particular, equal respect for every style of life—along with the possibility for everyone to live according to their vision of the world to the maximum extent possible.

The neutrality of the state is nevertheless a myth. Of course, I am not referring here to the equal procedural justice of the state under the rule of law, rightly desired by all, nor to the procedural legitimacy of the democratic decision-making process, both of which possess substantial ethical-political value. That neutrality *is* a myth, however, which consists in the claim that both the theory and the practice of justice of a democratic constitutional state must limit themselves to purely procedural and formal aspects; also a myth is the opinion that such a state can avoid declaring, as part of its juridical public order, specific content-laden conceptions that are binding for all, and promoting specific conceptions of life, thus privileging them juridically.

Here, of course, it becomes more difficult to find direct support in Popper. According to him, the open society is in effect based on a conception of man similar to that of Kant, Humboldt, and John Stuart Mill. For Popper, the ultimate purpose of the state is to make possible the development of the autonomy and the individuality of each person, in such a way that the rights of other persons are not impinged upon. The state should not be paternalistic, and therefore it cannot prescribe to individuals how they are to be happy. Popper accepts this principle with a proviso: "the State is responsible when its citizens are not apprised of and thus run avoidable risks, which they themselves are incapable of judging."[17] And Popper admits that, following this path, it is possible that a significant amount of "paternalism" would arise. One appreciates in Popper, however, the fact that he is not a dogmatist, much less a liberal dogmatist.

On the basis of this principle, the radical liberal John Stuart Mill, for example, sees certain difficulties in divorce for marriages with children, inasmuch as this would represent the realization of personal freedom and autonomy (i.e., that of the parents) at the expense of others (i.e., the children, who often are seriously damaged when their parents divorce). Moreover, neither Kant, nor Humboldt, nor Mill—as far as I can see—would have ever arrived at the idea of putting homosexual unions on the same juridical plane as marriage, simply because they knew that marriage has to do with the biological, social, and cultural reproduction of society, and thus is not only a question that regards the form of private life—as does the cohabitation of persons of the same sex—but a social reality, a public interest, and a social function that require commensurate moral recognition, state support, and juridical and moral privileging, for example, through regulation by law.

My conviction—which I have already expressed more extensively elsewhere—is as follows: a liberalism that proposes to be purely procedural and neutral with respect to different content-laden conceptions regarding the good, and that in the final analysis raises the autonomy of the individual to be the ultimate criterion—claiming, for example, the juridical equality of homosexual unions, or the desire to procreate through artificial methods without also addressing the problem of the huge number of frozen human

17. Karl R. Popper, "Bemerkungen zur Theorie und Praxis des demokratischen Staates" (lecture delivered June 9, 1988, in Munich), in Popper, *Alles Leben ist Problemlösen. Über Erkenntnis, Geschichte und Politik* (München-Zürich: Pieper, 1996), 215–38, at 234.

embryos—such a liberalism leads to absurdity, in that it destroys precisely the human foundation on which it rests. One dimension of this foundation is the link that exists between family (as a reproductive community) and marriage (the publicly recognized community of life of a man and a woman). The pope, of course, says the same thing—but this conclusion can also be arrived at through one's own reflection.

Rusconi in fact holds that a broad legalization of abortion, the juridical making-equivalent of homosexual unions, or destructive research on human embryos would damage no one's fundamental rights, much less those of believers. But in reality this is not so clear. The legalization of abortion could also be considered discrimination against the unborn, or the recognition of homosexual couples as discrimination against parents, who bear the burden of raising, educating, and socializing society's new generation (which latter benefits those who do not want to or cannot have children, through social security and other benefits). Moreover, if the state were to equate in its legal system nonreproductive unions with marriage, it would not be behaving "neutrally," but would *transform* the institution of marriage into a mere "form of life" among others, thus discriminating against those who dedicate themselves precisely to that task on the basis of which heterosexual marriage was juridically privileged in the first place! Finally, destructive research on embryos—along with other things such as euthanasia —could perhaps little by little destroy that respect for human life that is necessary so as to be convinced of the absolute importance of fundamental rights as *human rights*. One who asks that we "learn critically from science to redefine life and nature"[18] would thus begin to redefine to whom such human rights can be attributed. In the future, should it be left to science to decide these questions?

Rusconi is entirely correct to note that today we face a range of problems that "do not allow us to refer only to the subjective category of mutual tolerance,"[19] but rather need public-juridical regulation, for example the bioethical questions concerning the beginning and the end of life and the questions of the biotechnologies. And he sees, correctly, that here we encounter fundamental problems that regard both our conception of ourselves as human beings and our human nature. But he again takes a position that favors an "autonomy of secular thought,"[20] wanting to reserve this field to his

---

18. Rusconi, *Come se Dio non ci fosse*, 18.   19. Ibid., 160.
20. Ibid., 163–65.

"secular democracy," "because Catholics seem to rely upon their certainties regarding nature and truth."[21] Perhaps one day he will thank God that they have done so. In this case, however, what does "certainty" mean? Perhaps what we have here is rather a conscious and responsible resistance to the certainties of a science that has been elevated in our day to be the ultimate criterion. Therefore: it is not by the fact itself of taking a position on something that the Church's doctrine belongs to the realm of "religious truths." The Church, as everyone knows, also defends natural law. Has opposition to racism become a "religious truth"—and even part of a "biotheology" (to use Rusconi's term)—and thus incompatible with democratic discourse, because of the Church's condemnation of Nazi racism? And aren't there many who believe—perhaps not incorrectly—that the Church should have been a bit more explicit in its judgment on racism, especially with respect to anti-Semitism?

I arrive here at the conclusion. Today, all of us—Catholics, Protestants, Jews, Muslims, agnostics, and "secularists"—live in a pluralist, secularized, and (thanks be to God!) de-clericalized society, and we are citizens of a state whose political culture has been shaped by the ethos of the democratic constitutional state. In this sense we are all *secular,* inasmuch as we abide by the rules of this political culture and foster a healthy constitutional patriotism. Precisely for this reason—and I think Popper would agree with this—within the democratic public space we can all remain Catholics, Protestants, Jews, Muslims, agnostics, and secularists respecting each other precisely as such and, *in spite of everything,* seeking to collaborate. Naturally, the possibility exists for every citizen that decisions made by the majority will result in principles or even whole governments not to his liking. But everyone remains free to take whatever actions he wishes within the law to replace faulty principles with better ones, and to see that inadequate governments are not reelected. And precisely in this consists—as Popper, born a century ago, taught—the essence of democracy and of the open society.[22]

21. Ibid., 163.
22. Translation of this essay from the Italian by Joseph T. Papa.

|||||||||||||||||||||||||||||||||||||||||||||||||||||||||||||||||||||||||||||||||||||||||||||||||||||||||||||||||||||||||||||

SIX

The Political and Economic Realities of the Modern World and Their Ethical and Cultural Presuppositions

The Encyclical *Centesimus annus*

The Place of *Centesimus annus* in the History of the Social Doctrine of the Church

Centesimus annus,[1] the third social encyclical of John Paul II, was published in 1991 on the occasion of the centenary of Leo XIII's *Rerum novarum.*[2] The latter was the first of the social encyclicals of the popes; with it the Church's social doctrine began to take form as a more or less systematic body of teaching, adaptable to contemporary problems with the passage of the years. The compilation of the encyclical coincided with the epochal events of 1989: the fall of communist regimes, the failure of planned socialist economies, and the resulting "triumph" of constitutionalism, liberal democracy, and the capitalist market economy.

To better understand the place of *Centesimus annus* in the whole of Catholic social teaching, some (necessarily brief) historical background would

---

1. Pope John Paul II, *Centesimus annus: On the Hundredth Anniversary of "Rerum Novarum"* (1991). Citations from the encyclicals and conciliar documents in this chapter—namely, *Centesimus annus, Rerum novarum, Quadragesimo anno, Pacem in terris Gaudium et spes, Laborem exercens, Sollicitudo rei socialis,* and *Evangelium vitae*—are taken from the official Vatican translations found at www.vatican.va. After the first reference to a given document, paragraph numbers are indicated in parentheses.
2. Pope Leo XII, *Rerum novarum* (1891).

be useful. The first social encyclical of 1891 began a process of a systematic elaboration of the Church's social doctrine. In the first thirty years of the twentieth century, the decisive contributions to this doctrine were made by the Jesuit Heinrich Pesch (1854–1926) and his students and confreres Gustav Gundlach and Oswald Nell-Breuning. The "solidarism" proposed by these authors was presented as a kind of specifically Christian "third way" between liberalism and socialism, both viewed at the time as the unhealthy fruit of modernity, and intimately linked to each other. The culminating point of this tendency was Pius XI's 1931 encyclical *Quadragesimo anno: On Reconstruction of the Social Order,* Fr. Nell-Breuning having a fundamental role in its redaction. The encyclical presents the social doctrine of the Church as a real alternative with respect to both "individualistic" liberalism and collectivist socialism. The Church's traditional antimodernism, but probably also the alarming experience of the world economic crisis, with the failure of large credit institutions and the resulting poverty of the masses, convinced the Church of the necessity to propose an alternative conception of the ordering of social and economic life, based on the eternal principles of its moral and anthropological teaching and capable of offering a practical orientation to believers. Against socialism, the Church's social doctrine beginning with *Rerum novarum* had emphasized the dignity and transcendent destiny of the person, and in particular the right to private property (including ownership of the means of production) as a right founded on human nature. Against liberalism—accused of being based on an "individualistic" conception of the person—the state's function of regulating and organizing economic life was emphasized, as was the concept of "social justice," an expression used in *Quadragesimo anno* to indicate that justice that regards, not the good of individuals, but the common good, and that must be capable of constructing "a juridical and social order which will, as it were, give form and shape to all economic life" (no. 88). Added to this was the increasing tendency of Catholic social doctrine to base itself on natural law and on the social sciences: theological reflections were not seen as useful for the eradication of society's evils at their roots; rather, a comprehensive natural law vision of society and the economy was seen to be necessary.

This Catholic social doctrine based on the social sciences and natural law certainly had great merit. In *Quadragesimo anno*, Pius XI emphasized above all how the duty to fight against the misery of the great mass of humanity derived not only from Christian charity, but was also suggested—

and this indeed primarily—by the demands of justice. Also important was the idea that the capitalist form of the economy—in fact not rejected in principle in *Quadragesimo anno*—requires an adequate juridical-political order, which is provided by the state. Nevertheless, the solidaristic inheritance of Heinrich Pesch at work in the social doctrine of that time bore with it a substantial incomprehension of the significance and function of the institutions of the liberal constitutional state, of democracy, and above all of the regulating function of the market. The establishment of "social justice" (nos. 57, 101, 110, 126)—which in the eyes of solidarism was equivalent to responsibility for the common good—was seen as primarily a task of the state, lending Catholic social doctrine a certain tendency toward a blind trust in the state and toward a directive and interventionist statism.[3] At this stage, moreover, Catholic doctrine did not deepen its reflection on political structures; in this regard everything remained where it had been left by Leo XIII.

A gradual process toward a new orientation had already begun with the prudent acceptance of the modern idea of democracy by Pius XII. A further impulse in the same direction was given by the teaching of John XXIII on the importance of human rights. In the pastoral constitution *Gaudium et spes,* Vatican Council II then proposed a sort of compendium of "some of the more basic truths" of the "Christian doctrine about human society," the "foundations" of which are set forth "under the light of revelation."[4] A decisive step, however, toward a new way of understanding the social doctrine of the Church is found in John Paul II's encyclical *Sollicitudo rei socialis,* where it is stated that "The Church's social doctrine is not a 'third way' between liberal capitalism and Marxist collectivism, nor even a possible alternative to other solutions less radically opposed to one another; rather, it constitutes a category of its own."[5] Thus, while the two ideas of the social doctrine of the Church as "a category of its own" and its equidistance with respect to "liberalism" and "Marxism" are firmly maintained, clearly rejected is the idea of a "third way" based on natural law, that is, the Church's own conception of society or of political economy proposed as an alternative to liberalism or socialism, according to a vision of Christian solidarism.

3. See on this point the volume, perhaps a bit unilateral but nevertheless useful, of Michael Novak, *Catholic Social Thought and Liberal Institutions: Freedom with Justice* (New Brunswick: Transaction Publishers, 1989). The first edition of this book was published in 1984 by Harper & Row under the title *Freedom with Justice.*

4. *Gaudium et spes* 23, § 2.

5. John Paul II, *Sollicitudo rei socialis*, no. 41.

What is surprising, however, is how *Sollicitudo rei socialis* affirms the explicitly *theological* character of Catholic social doctrine: it is precisely for this reason that it constitutes a "category of its own." The Church's social teaching is now understood as a discipline pertaining to moral theology, as "the accurate formulation of the results of a careful reflection on the complex realities of human existence, in society and in the international order, in the light of faith and of the church's tradition."[6] Natural law is no longer explicitly referred to, though it is obviously part of the Church's tradition. The idea of the Church's own conception of society, based on natural law and offering an alternative with respect to liberalism or Marxism, is thus set aside in favor of a specifically Christian theological reflection on the "realities" of social and political life.

This could not fail to be an epochal change, the consequences of which were evident in *Centesimus annus*. The necessary presupposition of this new orientation was the "discovery," already suggested by Vatican II, of the legitimacy of modernity, a fundamentally positive vision of the realities established in the course of the nineteenth century in the areas of politics and the economy. This was particularly true with respect to the idea of the rights of man and of the egalitarian ideal connected with it, the latter being ultimately irreconcilable with the ideal model of society traditionally longed for by the Church. No longer is the ideal that of a Christian state, structured in an organic and perhaps even a cooperative way, but, as can be clearly seen in the fifth chapter of *Centesimus annus*, the modern constitutional democracy, based on the "rule of law," on human rights and on majority rule. This fifth chapter often has not received the attention it deserves; it could be said that with it, the political culture of modernity has been definitively accepted into Catholic social doctrine. This "acceptance of modernity," which surpasses that of *Gaudium et spes* in some important respects, seems to be the common thread running through the entire encyclical. This substantially positive judgment on modernity is accompanied, however, by an anthropological foundation and an ethical evaluation of this reality, based on the classical principles of Catholic social teaching (such as personalism, the principle of solidarity, and the principle of subsidiarity). *This* evaluation is what specifically characterizes Catholic social doctrine; the Church no longer presumes in any way to offer its own conception of society, or to ne-

6. Ibid.

gate the importance of, or the logic proper to, constitutional and democratic modern political culture or the capitalist-style market. This "theological turn" of the Church's social doctrine—which passes from a specific conception of society, based on natural law and developed with the tools of the social sciences and understood as an *institutional* alternative to liberalism or socialism, to a reflection of moral theology on social realities "in the light of faith and of the church's tradition"—paradoxically opens the way to a more profound understanding and a substantial acceptance of the *institutional reality* of the modern constitutional state, democracy, and the rationality of the market, without for this abandoning the perennial concerns and traditional principles of the Church's social teaching.

Centesimus annus also abandons the still-prevalent idea in *Sollicitudo rei socialis* of an equidistance of the Church's social doctrine with respect to "liberal capitalism and Marxist collectivism." This point is decisive. Certainly, the encyclical does not ingenuously proclaim the triumph of the market and of liberal democracy, and thus the "end of history" (F. Fukuyama). Nevertheless, propelled by the events of 1989, the idea of the Church's doctrine occupying an intermediate position between these two poles completely disappears. Socialism (or communism, or Marxist-inspired collectivism) has clearly failed, condemned by history itself as an anthropological error.[7] Liberalism, capitalism, the market economy, and democracy, on the other hand, have prevailed: not only has history not condemned them, they have in a certain sense been made victorious; nor therefore should the Church condemn them. The Church feels only the duty to express some cautions in their regard. It is clear that, save perhaps in a few instances, the Church's instructions do not cast doubt on the value of these institutions; rather they aim at sustaining such institutions and ensuring their political, social, economic, and above all moral effectiveness. It should also be recognized that for the most part the Church proposes juridical, ethical, and political correctives that are "beyond supply and demand " (Wilhelm Röpke), correctives considered to be equally or similarly indispensable by many proponents of economic and political liberalism who are not Catholic, and thus start from different concerns than those of the Magisterium.

This orientation, moreover, is facilitated by the fact that certain fundamental principles of Catholic social doctrine are from the outset not strang-

---

7. See *Centesimus annus*, ch. 2, nos. 12–21.

ers to the tradition of liberal thought. Not only is the fundamental importance of private property emphasized in this tradition, but one also finds in it the principle of the universal destination of goods (to which private property itself is subordinated) and the principle of subsidiarity. When *Centesimus annus* states in chapter 4 that "God gave the earth to the whole human race for the sustenance of all its members, without excluding or favoring anyone," but that man by his work "makes part of the earth his own" and that on this is based the right to private property (no. 31), one seems almost to hear the English philosopher John Locke, who in effect said substantially the same things.[8] Similarly with the statement that "the possession of material goods is not an absolute right" (n. 30; see Locke, *Second Treatise*, V, § 27), and that "Ownership of the means of production, whether in industry or agriculture, is just and legitimate [only] if it serves useful work. It becomes illegitimate, however, when it is not utilized" (n. 43). This latter idea had already been proposed in the nineteenth century by John Stuart Mill in his *Principles of Political Economy* (II, ch. 2, § 6); in such cases, Mill called for state redistribution of uncultivated lands (and for this reason, frankly, he is accused by "libertarian" liberals of being a precursor of socialism). Mill also offered some basic reasons in support of the principle of subsidiarity (*Principles*, V, ch. 1), a principle later incorporated into Catholic social doctrine in *Quadragesimo anno* in the formulation of Gustav Gundlach, though it must be recognized that the context and the spirit in which these two texts address the question is not entirely the same. The strong emphasis on the fact that the market does not guarantee the availability of all goods, something particularly true regarding public goods, is based on an idea already found in Adam Smith, the father of economic liberalism, that is, the idea that the state has the duty not only to create an effective judicial system, but also "to found and maintain those public institutions and works which, though they may be of the highest usefulness to a great society, nevertheless are of such a nature that the profits would never be able to compensate the expenses sustained by an individual or a small number of individuals, and thus for which it could not be expected that an individual or a small number of individuals would found and maintain them."[9] It must be remembered that Adam Smith's fundamental purpose was to oppose the absolutist-mercantilist economic system, in which the state organized and

---

8. *Second Treatise of Government*, V, § 25–26.
9. Adam Smith, *An Inquiry into the Nature and Causes of the Wealth of Nations*, book 5, ch. 1.

directed economic life in its entirety, providing paternalistically for the welfare of its subjects.

The only period in history predominantly characterized by economic liberalism and the free exchange of goods (i.e., the years between 1850 and 1870) was also the period during which, due to the explosion of the process of industrialization, modern public infrastructures were created (streets, railroads, canals, streetlights, sewer systems and running water in large cities, etc.) to a degree vastly exceeding any previous period, with a corresponding radical change in people's daily lives. The beginnings of the industrial revolution and the pauperism caused by shortages and by untransparent and inflexible social structures were phenomena that, depending on the country, had already been overcome for some decades. The widespread poverty was not a consequence of capitalism but rather a problem to which capitalism was able to respond in a way that can only be called extraordinary. It is true that early on England, then the dominant nation, was able to exploit the economy of free exchange more than any other country (and in some cases at other countries' expense). It is also true that with the success of the sciences and their technical application came a growing materialistic outlook, along with an ingenuous and at times cynical confidence in progress, to the extent that insensitivity, selfishness, and indifference regarding the needs of workers—attitudes justified by the idea that the poverty of the mass of workers corresponded to the "natural order of things"—made for a very hard life for large segments of the population. It must nevertheless be remembered that, especially due to periodic famines, conditions of life in the pre-industrial period were certainly no less miserable, and indeed probably much worse, and that in the end industrialization, capitalism, and free exchange brought about an enduring improvement in the quality of life of the majority of people, making their lives more human, for the first time in history.

The response of capitalism and the market economy to the problems that accompanied the industrial revolution was based on the premise that the well-being of nations, societies, and people in general is the fruit not of state organization and bureaucratic regulation, but of the work, freedom, and creativity of individuals, who form relationships of mutual exchange of both spiritual and material goods (a market). There is no actor or coordinator in society possessing a superior knowledge that allows him to effectively pursue the common good via a centrally planned economy; this good can result only from the interplay of supply and demand, as a result of which it is consumers who ultimately determine what is produced. As such, the coordination of individual interests results not from state planning, but from the interaction of free subjects who do not have a universal good in mind in their individual actions (something that in any case is impossible), but pursue their own legitimate ends.[10] The principle of coordination and order that must exist for this to occur—the famous "invisible hand," which is precisely *not* a hand—is not the power of the state, but of the market. Only with time, however, was it recognized that the correct functioning of the market requires an adequate juridical order, an effective judicial system, and the availability of public services and infrastructures, and thus in this sense also a strong state: the market *is* the regulative principle of economic life, but it does not possess the power necessary to maintain itself in that role.

This idea is accepted in its fundamental aspects in *Centesimus annus,* along with the essential institutions of the liberal and democratic constitutional state. Today, obviously, we have the advantage of over two centuries of experience, and we therefore know much more than did Adam Smith, whose point of reference was a society that was still pre-industrial. Some of his ideas, in particular that of the infallibility of the regulatory forces of the free market (which is based on a mechanistic-naturalistic conception inadequate from an anthropological point of view), must be corrected, made more precise, and above all completed. But his basic idea remains ingenious—that of the regulative function of the market that coordinates the goals and interests of individual subjects and produces an overall positive result (the "market economy"), inasmuch as in the market individuals offer their abilities, ideas, products, and the like, and take the risk of making their own capital available to others so as to give these others the possibility of producing goods by their own work, thanks to which the needs of all may be satisfied ("capitalism").

Fundamental Themes of the Encyclical
Property, Market Economy, Capitalism, and Business

It is interesting to note how the substantial acceptance of the ideas of "market" and "capitalism" that we have just outlined underlies the encyc-

10. See ibid., book 4, ch. 2.

lical's argumentation precisely at that point where it expresses a positive judgment concerning a "capitalism" understood as an "economic system which recognizes the fundamental and positive role of business, the market, private property and the resulting responsibility for the means of production, as well as free human creativity in the economic sector" (no. 42). Consequently—adds the encyclical—when referring to such an economic system it would be better to speak not of capitalism, but "of a 'business economy,' a 'market economy' or simply a 'free economy.'"

Certainly, *Centesimus annus* also warns against "an 'idolatry' of the market" (no. 40) and an ideology that "fideistically" entrusts the solution of problems "to the free development of market forces" (no. 42), also rejecting a vision of the market economy and of "capitalism" that claims that these could do without a "juridical framework" (ibid.). Eminent representatives of economic liberalism, for example, representatives of classical neoliberalism or what is also called the school of Ordo-liberalism (W. Eucken, F. Böhm, F. von Hayek, A. Müller-Armack, G. Briefs, W. Röpke, and many others) of the postwar period, also hold that the market cannot survive without a strong state preserving it from its own self-destruction by means of an adequate juridical order, at times also intervening in the economy, though in a way respectful of the market itself. These thinkers maintain that the market is incapable of performing the function proper to it without the political-regulative intervention of the state.[11]

Decisive in this regard is the encyclical's statement that it seems "the free market is the most efficient instrument for utilizing resources and effectively responding to needs" (no. 34). At the same time, the market should "be appropriately controlled by the forces of society and by the state, so as to guarantee that the basic needs of the whole of society are satisfied" (no. 35). It must be said that it is not entirely clear if this last statement is to be understood as a limitation of the idea of the market itself, or if it means simply to restate the necessity we have just referred to, that is, not of a regulation of the market, but its juridical oversight, and state intervention that respects the market and aims at ensuring its functioning. While this second interpretation is entirely compatible with the idea of a market economy, the first in-

---

11. See, e.g., Walter Eucken, *Grundsätze der Wirtschaftspolitik* (1952) (Tübingen: J. C. B. Mohr [Paul Siebeck], 1968), especially 26ff. and 356ff. This current after the Second World War, to differentiate itself from the classical liberalism of *laisser-faire,* called itself "neoliberalism," a term that today has unfortunately assumed exactly the opposite meaning.

terpretation would not be. Limitation of the market as a matter of principle would in fact mean, in general, the destruction of its regulative capacity, as with the case of a social state that encourages laziness, incompetence, and inefficiency, thus aggravating and perpetuating the problems it had hoped to resolve by intervening.

Also significant from this point of view is the positive valuation of profit that we find in the encyclical (see no. 35). With it, the economic function of profit is both expressly emphasized and positively judged for the first time in Catholic social teaching. Profit is an indispensable "indication that a business is functioning well"; it is also a "regulator" and a legitimate goal of economic activity, the economy in fact serving the increase of a society's wealth, and therefore the efficient allocation of its resources. And business risks must be rewarded. But profit must not be the sole goal and criterion. Also important is the business's "very existence as a community of persons": in fact "business culture" is a decisive factor from the perspective of economic efficiency, as is commonly recognized today. It is opportune that *Centesimus annus* emphasizes this point so strongly: there are "human and moral factors" that must be considered if a business is going to be successful. Of course, all of this is perfectly consistent with the principle, set forth in *Laborem exercens* and confirmed in *Centesimus annus,* of the primacy of labor over capital, a principle that manifests the primacy of the human person and thus the "subjectivity" of work, which is not a mere commodity.

Important in this context is the observation that many people, due to a lack of material resources, education, and technical know-how, are incapable of inserting themselves in the process of the market and thus of participating in it as agents with the same rights as others. The encyclical here speaks of "human needs which find no place on the market" (no. 34), which cannot be satisfied by the free market because they belong to those who must be "[helped] to acquire expertise, to enter the circle of exchange, and to develop their skills in order to make the best use of their capacities and resources" (ibid.). Structures of solidarity must be created to supply these needs (whether these structures are the task of the state or of the free initiative of society remains an open question at this point and is clarified in the fifth chapter). It thus becomes clear in this and other passages of the encyclical how John Paul II, while valuing the structures of the market economy, is preoccupied above all with man in his entirety, given that "besides the earth, man's principal resource is man himself" (no. 32). Economic decisions always also imply options of an ethical and cultural character. As an example, the democratic idea that underlies the market, that is, that it is the consumer who decides what is produced, becomes corrupted by a consumerism that makes people responsive to artificially induced needs (e.g., drugs), thus impeding "the formation of a mature personality." Here also the logic of the market must be combined with the education of consumers, with an appeal to the sense of responsibility of producers and to those working in the means of communication, and if need be with state intervention (see no. 36).

An analogous discussion could be had with respect to the access of less-developed countries to the international market. Access to the market must not be based "on the unilateral principle of the exploitation of the natural resources of these countries but on the proper use of human resources" (no. 33). At the same time, the encyclical resolutely rejects the idea that protectionism is a recipe for development, that is, "that the poorest countries would develop by isolating themselves from the world market" (ibid.). According to *Centesimus annus,* the solution is rather to expand free trade. In this context, however, it is necessary to bear in mind the still-unresolved problem of the international financial markets. Experience shows that, unlike the markets for goods, financial markets are often a theater of speculative manipulation, dangerously manipulating international monetary flows in a way that imperils the market's regulating principles. The encyclical does not address this, however; nor does it mention the question of globalization. The biggest problem in this arena, however, also not addressed in the encyclical, is selfish protectionism on the part of industrialized nations, who close their markets to more suitable products from less-developed countries, thus defending their own quality of life at the expense of poorer nations—with well-intended appeals to "social" motives, to be sure, and with the powerful support of trade unions and politicians seeking reelection.

Constitutional State, Democracy, Human Rights

The fifth chapter of the encyclical, which treats of "State and Culture," is important and has often not received adequate attention: it presents, for the first time in this past century, a doctrine of the Church on the state and on politics. There are significant differences, however, with respect to the doctrine of Leo XIII on the "Christian state" and the "Christian statesman." Here also, the decisive novelty in *Centesimus annus* is in the fact that it no

longer attempts to delineate a doctrine peculiar to the Church, or to articulate a third way. Rather, the encyclical substantially accepts the reality of
the modern constitutional state—based on the principle of the division of
powers and the rule of law, recognizing human rights, and organized democratically—and aims to deepen its reflection on this reality. This reality is understood and explained on the basis of the anthropology, perennially valid
for the Church, according to which man is the image of God, freedom is not
severed from truth, and the human person has a transcendent frame of reference, with freedom of religion thus being given a primary role (no. 44).

According to John Paul II, the dignity of the person, which is based on
the fact that he is created in the image of God, is radically denied by *totalitarianism*. Man is "the visible image of the invisible God, [and] is therefore by his very nature the subject of rights which no one may violate"; "not
even the majority of a social body may violate these rights" (no. 44). The encyclical therefore opposes all totalitarian attempts "to lead history toward
perfect goodness" (no. 45).

With this the principal theme of the following chapters is announced:
the state itself is not "the visible image of the invisible God," and thus the
dignity pertaining to that image does not belong to the state, but only to
the individual person. Frequently in the past, traditional Catholic doctrine
had unilaterally emphasized the "dignity of the state" and the fact that "the
dignity of political authority is the dignity of its participation in the authority of God" (according to an expression of Pius XII, used again by John XXIII
in *Pacem in terris*). The Church thus made a superior and privileged actor
of the political authority, which in some way, as the "image of the invisible
God," also possessed a superior moral authority. This fact explains certain
affinities in the past between the Church's social teaching and authoritarian
conceptions of the state, as well as the Church's skepticism with respect to
democracy. In *Centesimus annus*, this vision of political authority—and thus
of the state as a power above the citizens, participating in the authority of
God and invested with special dignity—disappears completely.[12] Rather, the
power of the state is seen as an institution that has been created by men,
and must be monitored by citizens so as to not fall into the hands of "narrow ruling groups," becoming corrupted by particular interests and ideological manipulation (no. 46). Dignity, then, is a prerogative of the human

---

12. See Russell Hittinger, "The Pope and the Liberal State," *First Things* 28 (December 1992): 33–41.

person, and it is into the hands of persons that the state and its institutions are entrusted. (This changes nothing with respect to the traditional doctrine that power comes from God: what has changed is only how this fact is explained.)

According to *Centesimus annus,* a true democracy can be realized only in a state subject to the rule of law. The foundation of democracy is human rights, to which even the principle of majority rule is subordinated—this latter being a characteristic of the modern constitutional state and of its notion of the supremacy of the law. The principle of democracy and the principle of the constitutional state mutually complete one another, together forming the reality of the democratic constitutional state. The encyclical further states that a democracy is possible only "on the basis of a correct conception of the human person"; indeed, it cannot itself continue to exist if it denies the existence of ultimate truths. This claim can be understood if one considers that human rights themselves are based on "ultimate truths" about man and that, especially with respect to religious freedom, these rights are what ensures that man can open himself to his transcendent destiny. For this reason "as history demonstrates, a democracy without values easily turns into open or thinly disguised totalitarianism" (n. 46).

Even though freedom always bears within it an orientation to truth, the encyclical takes a strong position against "the danger of fanaticism or fundamentalism among those who, in the name of an ideology which purports to be scientific or religious, claim the right to impose on others their own concept of what is true and good" (ibid.). The Church's way of acting, rather, presupposes "respect for freedom," even if "freedom attains its full development only by accepting the truth" (ibid.).

None of these statements must be isolated from its context if one does not wish to distort its meaning. Clearly, freedom has its full value only when it is *not* severed from truth. Nevertheless the Church today recognizes, as it did not in the past, freedom in its specifically *political* dimension, along with the individual rights that follow from it, maintaining that civil liberty and legitimate rights must be respected and defended even apart from any reference to truth. It is not truth, as opposed to error, that has rights, but *persons,* even when these persons err based on objective criteria of truth taught by the Church. This was proclaimed by the Church for the first time in the teaching of the Second Vatican Council on the right to freedom of religion as a civil right that must be recognized by the state. Thus the link between freedom and truth must not be established on the state-institutional or juridical-political levels, where the coercive means of the public power come into play, but must be seen as a task of individuals and of the forces freely operating in society. Here questions of pluralism and the pluralistic society also come into play, but these are not addressed in the encyclical.[13]

The claim that democracy is possible only "on the basis of a correct conception of the human person," and thus based on ultimate truths, must therefore not be understood as if to say that there exist certain truths that must be excluded in principle from democratic decision-making processes by means of institutional guarantees (which would in fact themselves be foreign to democracy), or that in certain cases the validity of the principle of majority rule must be suspended.[14] Nor does it mean that there are specific truths that must be accepted such that a democracy may be established and considered legitimate. The statements of Pius XII on the relationship between democracy, natural law, and truth still tended in this direction. With *Centesimus annus*, the pertinent questions no longer concern the criteria by which to measure the legitimacy of a democracy and the conditions that allow it to come about in the first place, but the *conditions that allow it to function effectively*. John Paul II is clearly thinking above all here of questions related to the family and the right to life,[15] but also "different aspects of a crisis within democracies themselves, which seem at times to have lost the ability to make decisions aimed at the common good" (no. 47).

Important in this context, therefore, is the statement that "the Church respects the legitimate autonomy of the democratic order" (ibid.). It knows the limits of democracy and the dangers inherent in it, but criticizes these not so as to cast doubt on the legitimacy of democratic processes, but to show what are the optimal conditions for their functioning. Decisive here is the distinction, already implicit in what was said concerning the market economy and

---

13. Nor has this problem been addressed in the *Doctrinal Note on Some Questions Regarding the Participation Of Catholics in Political Life* published by the Congregation for the Doctrine of the Faith on November 24, 2002; the question that this document addresses is only that of pluralism among Christians, within the confines established by the Magisterium and by the Catholic faith; some of these questions are discussed, however, in Joseph Joblin and Réal Tremblay, eds., *I cattolici e la società pluralista. Il caso delle "leggi imperfette"* (Bologna: ESD, 1996).

14. I have explained why this interpretation is unacceptable in chapter 2 of the present volume, entitled "The Liberal Image of Man and the Concept of Autonomy: Beyond the Debate between Liberals and Communitarians." This was originally published as "Laici e cattolici: oltre le divisioni. Riflessioni sull'essenza della democrazia e della società aperta," *Fondazione Liberal* 17 (2003): 108–16.

15. See in this regard my comment on the encyclical *Evangelium vitae* in chapter 7 of my *Ethics of Procreation and the Defense of Human Life*, ed. William F. Murphy Jr. (Washington, D.C.: The Catholic University of America Press, 2010).

capitalism, between *institutions* and the *personal behavior* of those who act in the context of such institutions. From this derives the important distinction, not mentioned in *Centesimus annus*, between "institutional ethics" and "personal ethics": while the latter speaks of virtue, the former speaks rather of the political and juridical *ethos* of institutions, structures, and procedures. The immoral behavior of persons, citizens, and politicians, as well as that of groups such as parties, associations, and unions, can in fact destroy the political and juridical institutions of a democratic constitutional state, or at least seriously damage them.

Centesimus annus speaks therefore of the "legitimate autonomy of the democratic order," adding that the Church "is not entitled to express preferences for this or that institutional or constitutional solution," given that its specific contribution consists in offering the political order "her vision of the dignity of the person revealed in all its fullness in the mystery of the Incarnate Word." In this way the encyclical profoundly modifies the traditional doctrine based on which the Church is indifferent with respect to the various forms of state organization, as long as the latter respect what were called "the fundamental requirements of the natural law." Based on this traditional doctrine, it was possible for the German bishops in March 1933 to ask the faithful to respect the authority of the National-Socialist state, and in the same month for the Catholic party of the Center to vote in favor of the laws that gave full power to Hitler. The Nazi regime in fact had promised substantial concessions in the political-ecclesiastical arena that pertained, in the eyes of the Church, to the fundamental requirements of natural law (though these promises were later not maintained), and a dictator was not considered *as such* incompatible with the principles of Catholic social teaching.

With *Centesimus annus*, the governing principle now seems to be not that *any* ordering of the state is acceptable, but that any *democratic* ordering is acceptable, as long as it respects the rights of man, defending them also as fundamental positive rights. This distinction is decisive. If this were the doctrine guiding the behavior of Catholics in 1933, the German bishops and the Centrist party led by Monsignor Kaas would not have been able to approve the Nazis' taking power and, rather than aiming at the satisfaction of certain "requirements of the natural law" particularly dear to the Church (e.g., the right to Catholic schools), they would have felt the duty to defend the democratic constitutional state, along with the social-democrats and the liberals.

State and Economy

Finally, the encyclical, in the important paragraph 48 of the fifth chapter, speaks of the relationship between the state and the economy. In a certain sense the doctrine articulated here completes the affirmations of the fourth chapter on the market economy and capitalism, and is indeed indispensable for their correct interpretation. Here it is clear that for *Centesimus annus* it is not the duty of the state to organize economic life, a function that is properly the task of the free initiative of businesspeople. The state's task, rather, is to create a juridical and institutional context in which this initiative can be exercised (no. 48). Economic life requires "sure guarantees of individual freedom and private property, as well as stable currency and efficient public services" and "hence the principal task of the State is to guarantee this security, so that those who work and produce can enjoy the fruits of their labors and thus feel encouraged to work efficiently and honestly." To this is added the task of "overseeing and directing the exercise of human rights in the economic sector," even though "the primary responsibility" in this regard belongs not to the state, but "to individuals and to the various groups and associations which make up society." The state must also promote a climate favorable to the creation of new jobs, stimulate enterprise when necessary, and intervene to correct situations of monopoly that threaten the market (ibid.).

All of this is perfectly consonant with a classical political economy of a liberal or neoliberal stripe. Contrary to what many believe, both political liberalism and various forms of economic liberalism do *not* hold that the state must refrain from all activity; rather they favor a strong state, capable of imposing respect for laws that protect the market from those who would dominate or destroy it. What is decisive in this view, however, is that the state must never seek to *replace* the regulating and coordinating function of the market with its own organizing activity, even though at times an intervention that supplements or corrects the action of the market and gives it a juridical ordering (especially incentivizing effectiveness) is obviously necessary. It is precisely here where this understanding of the state is distinguished from the increasingly widespread "welfare state" or "assistance state," which *Centesimus annus* expressly rejects. Here the encyclical again refers to the principle of subsidiarity: "By intervening directly and depriving society of its responsibility, the social assistance state leads to a loss of human energies and an inordinate increase of public agencies, which are dominated more by bureaucratic ways of thinking than by concern for serving their clients" (no. 48). This theme is of great contemporary importance, if only for the fact that the social state is becoming more and more impossible to finance. This is not the place, however, to pursue this discussion further.

The encyclical further indicates that this is the course to be followed by emphasizing the importance of so-called intermediate bodies—the first among these being the family—and the importance of a commitment to solidarity on the part of volunteers in the various sectors of society. Only in this way can authentic networks of solidarity be built that are not ultimately destined to founder in inefficiency at the hands of state bureaucracies. Observing the principle of subsidiarity, the free initiatives of intermediate bodies must be assisted by the state with appropriate family and social policy measures (see no. 49). (Certainly on this point the principle of subsidiarity as it is understood by Catholics involves a more decisive intervention by the state than what liberals espousing the principle would recommend.) The encyclical then emphasizes the importance of the cultural context and asks for an adequate order of values; the theme of the family, already referred to in the fourth chapter, is taken up again here. The encyclical thus arrives at a question that is among those closest to the Church's heart, and that is ultimately the key to every authentically human ordering of society.

Concluding Observations

The purpose of our brief survey of the essential themes of *Centesimus annus* has been above all to call attention to those aspects of the encyclical that indicate its basic orientation and its originality. As always with documents of the Magisterium, some of its judgments are formulated in such a way as to leave open some questions and to allow differing interpretations.[16] In the case of *Centesimus annus,* this lack of clarity is due in some cases to the fact that one cannot distinguish with the necessary clarity statements regarding the economic and political system as such from those regarding the system's concrete implementation, or the *ethos* implied therein. More in a general way true is what the encyclical states concerning the "culture

---

16. See regarding some questions that remain open: Jean-Yves Calvez, *Les silences de la doctrine sociale catholique* (Paris: Les Éditions de l'Atelier et Éditions Ouvrières, 1999).

of death" that threatens the family today, or that the criticisms contained in the encyclical "are directed not so much against an economic system as against an ethical and cultural system" (n. 39). In any case it is clear that the basic tenor of the encyclical is as we have said: the Church accepts the fundamental logic of the modern market economy and the rationality proper to it, along with the political-institutional reality of democracy and of the freedom guaranteed by the constitutional state, but at the same time—in continuity with the tradition of *Rerum novarum* and *Quadragesimo anno,* though also using new means—criticizes the cultural and ethical lacunae that bear destructive effects both for economic rationality itself and for political institutions, leading to situations opposed to human dignity. For this type of criticism, because of its vision inspired by the Gospel and the commission it has received to teach all nations, the Church surely has a unique competence.[17]

17. This original was published as "La realtà politica ed economica del mondo moderno e i suoi presupposti etici e culturali. L'enciclica *Centesimus annus,*" in *Giovanni Paolo Teologo—Nel segno delle encicliche,* ed. Graziano Borgonovo and Arturo Cattaneo, preface by His Eminence Camillo Cardinal Ruini (Rome: Edizioni Arnoldo Mondatori, 2003), 83–94. It was translated by Joseph T. Papa.

SEVEN

The Political Ethos of Constitutional Democracy and the Place of Natural Law in Public Reason

Rawls's "*Political Liberalism*" Revisited

Constitutional Democracy: The Historical Legitimacy of Its Political Ethos

Constitutional Democracy and Liberalism: A Specific Political Expression of the Natural Law Tradition

The main concern of this essay, and the principal aim of my argument that runs through all parts of it, is to answer the question: "How in liberal constitutional democracy as it actually exists in most free and developed countries is natural law in the classical sense a *legitimate* and *politically workable* standard of reasonableness and objective moral value?" In order to answer this question, I will have to talk extensively about history (in this part). Moreover, I will develop my argument in a partly sympathetic confrontation with what I consider to be the main and most valid contemporary philosophical theory of liberal constitutionalism: John Rawls's *Political Liberalism*[1] and its conception of public reason and liberal legitimacy (in the second part). In my view, this theory contains sufficient truth to be worthy of being continuously and fruitfully revisited, but also sufficient *evident* untruth as to be a useful contrast-background for a political-philosophical

---

1. John Rawls, *Political Liberalism* (New York: Columbia University Press, 1996).

191

argument in favor of the relevance of natural law for public reason (in the third part).

The nearly unquestioned framework for normative thinking on political matters today seems to be constitutional democracy of *some* kind. The democratic constitutional state is the expression of a complex ethos, formed in the course of a long history. This ethos forms a specific conception of public reason that is embedded in a framework of pre-political reasonableness that we refer to as "natural law." Being "natural" and, thus, pre-political, it is not to be identified with public reason.

"Public reason" can be defined as the kind of reasonableness by which the basic political institutions of political society, its legal system and, based on them, concrete lawmaking—legitimately imposed by coercive state power on the multitude of citizens—can be justified in a way that is able to command general consensus and that therefore will not undermine but rather will promote social cooperation and assure stability of these basic political and legal institutions. It is the reasonableness that refers to the political common good of human society.

As I propose to point out in the following, natural-law reasons belong to public reason insofar as they *precede* public reason and, thus, shape it in a fundamental way. They, however, cannot claim to be *public* reasons, adequate for constitutional democracy, only because they are *natural-law reasons,* that is, because they are open to anyone's understanding. This is impossible because, first, natural law embraces more than what is politically relevant and can be reasonably enforced by legal coercion, and second, natural law is not positive, written law. Public reason is based in, and expressed by, political institutions and a positive legal system that define the publicly endorsed standards and rules of justice by which citizens in a constitutional democracy make binding political decisions that are legitimately enforced by the coercive apparatus of the state.

As I will argue, rather than providing properly public reasons, natural law works as a standard of public reason's own intrinsic practical truth, though this standard may be controversial and must therefore achieve legitimacy partly in and through the political process itself, as a valid standard of "truth" within that society. Thus, though natural law *as such* cannot claim to be *public* reason, the correspondence of public reason with natural law, as far as it is politically relevant, is nonetheless a condition for public reason to be fully reasonable. With this I do not mean to say that the "truth" of natural-law reasons depends on their public acceptance, but only that their recognition as politically legitimate reasons does. The more such public recognition corresponds to the requirements of natural law, the more such recognition is reasonable.

By speaking of "*constitutional* democracy" I deliberately avoid the more familiar term of "liberal democracy," though during the last two hundred years constitutionalism has been promoted mostly and on the whole very successfully by the political movement that from the early nineteenth century has been called "liberalism."[2] Yet nineteenth-century continental liberals have not always been very keen on promoting democracy. Only in consequence of the social transformation caused by the industrial revolution and under the pressure of democratic radicalism—thus, rather unwillingly—the politics of classical liberalism during the nineteenth century has gradually adapted itself to new realities.[3]

But it undoubtedly is part of the nature of liberal constitutionalism to have allowed such a development toward democratic reforms and political equality. By espousing the idea of democracy—rule by the people through universal suffrage—perhaps for the first time in history liberal constitutionalism, which from its beginning was linked to the medieval tradition of representative government, has also given to the idea of democracy a practicable form. It is based on the constitutional guarantees of fundamental rights and, therefore, on the idea and practice of government limited by the *rule of law* and through representative legislative bodies. Modern constitutional democracy is thus *limited* democracy, limited in favor of rights, liberties, and a shared conception of the politically relevant good that consists primarily in the maintenance of these liberties and rights and the basic political and legal institutions and procedures that render possible peaceful cooperation according to generally acknowledged standards of justice.

Modern constitutionalism, however, is not just "liberal." Liberal constitutionalism has reactivated and developed a tradition that is much older than liberalism.[4] Not only the Anglo-Saxon "rule of law" has its root in late

2. See the classical work by Guido de Ruggiero, *Storia del liberalismo europeo* (Bari: Laterza, 1984), first published in 1925, and translated into English by R.G. Collingwood as *History of European Liberalism* (Boston: Beacon Press, 1959).

3. Some of these aspects are treated in Richard Bellamy, *Liberalism and Modern Society: An Historical Argument* (Cambridge: Polity Press, 1992).

4. See for this the still unequaled, nearly encyclopedic presentation by Carl J. Friedrich, *Constitutional Government and Democracy* (New York: Blaisdell, 1950), which I know in its German version *Der*

medieval times. Constitutionalism is also intimately linked to the medieval doctrine of the right to resistance[5]—not surprisingly denied by Kant—which in turn presupposes the idea that the exercise of political power is in the service not of this power and its interests, but of a good common to the totality of citizens. Such doctrines survived and were further developed by the Spanish early modern theorists of natural law such as Suárez, Vázquez, and mainly Vitoria. To a perhaps even more important extent, modern constitutionalism is also the offspring of medieval conciliarism.[6] The idea that the authority of the pope depends on the consent of the totality of bishops united in a council, that he is elected by them and therefore responsible to them, was theologically unorthodox and finally rejected as heretical. Yet, through its transformation into a political doctrine of legitimate resistance by the French Huguenots, adopted later also by Lutherans, this originally theological and canonistic doctrine became an additional ferment in modern development of constitutionalism and representative government.[7] Meanwhile, Catholic political thought was unfortunately more and more influenced by the absolutist idea of the state, which conceived its authority and power as representing on earth the supreme authority of the Creator to the extent of feeling responsible not to citizens, but only to God.

Undoubtedly, Locke's idea of government as a trust and his idea of its being dependent on the constituent power of civil society are unthinkable without the presence of this late medieval tradition. Yet, Locke was not what we would call a "liberal" or a constitutionalist as, for example, was Benjamin Constant later. As far as England is concerned, Locke—and after him Bolingbroke—in fact promoted parliamentary sovereignty, which turned out not to be very respectful of fundamental rights. The tyranny of the English parliament even went so far as to temporarily suspend in the early nineteenth century the right of habeas corpus, which, as the most basic and cherished right of citizens, was supposed to have its roots in the Magna Carta of 1215. Edward Coke's idea that the Magna Carta and the rights

---

Verfassungsstaat der Neuzeit (Berlin/Göttingen/Heidelberg: Springer, 1953). Further: Nicola Matteucci, *Organizzazione del potere e libertà: Storia del costituzionalismo moderno* (Turin: UTET, 1988).

5. See the classical study by Fritz Kern, *Gottesgnadentum und Widerstandsrecht im früheren Mittelalter. Zur Entwicklungsgeschichte der Monarchie*, 7th ed., reprinted from the 2nd ed. of 1954, ed. Rudolf Buchner (Darmstadt: Wissenschaftliche Buchgesellschaft, 1980).

6. For a concise overview of this doctrine see George H. Sabine, *A History of Political Thought*, 4th ed., rev. Thomas Landon Thorson (Hinsdale: Dryden Press, 1973), chap. 17, 294ff.

7. See Quentin Skinner, *The Foundations of Modern Political Thought*, vol. 2: *The Age of Reformation* (Cambridge: Cambridge University Press, 1978).

rooted in it were a "sovereign"—that is, the idea of rule of law—was not easily compatible with Locke's idea of parliamentary sovereignty.[8]

English parliamentarianism has finally been preserved from degeneration into ever-increasing parliamentary tyranny by the ongoing process of democratization. In the American colonies, however, with their puritan background and under the influence of Montesquieu, Locke was right from the beginning read in a different way. Montesquieu developed his idea of representative government as a system of separated powers from an interpretation of what he called in the corresponding chapter of his *De l'esprit des lois* the "constitution of England."[9] In the form Montesquieu described it, such a constitution in fact never existed except in Montesquieu's interpretation of it. It was this description of a system of checks and balances that, through William Blackstone's later commentaries on the English "constitution," formed the spirit of American constitutionalism. Interestingly, Montesquieu was not a "liberal" either, but rather an aristocratic anti-monarchist; his ideas had been very much influenced by the same older traditions that gave rise to the Anglo-Saxon idea of *rule of law*, which includes the essential idea of an independent judiciary. Things are, thus, rather complexly interrelated and linked by transformations and feedbacks. History is a multifaceted continuum; nobody should appropriate it for ideological reasons exclusively for his own side.

Therefore, to understand classical political liberalism properly and to protect it from self-destruction by a partial self-interpretation, we have to acknowledge that not everything in liberalism is genetically "liberal." Classical liberalism is embedded in cultural traditions and presupposes the recognition of some truths about human persons, society, and the reality of sovereign state power. Classical political liberalism, the basic political ideas of which have fully triumphed in our times, though without causing thereby the "end of history," was from the eighteenth century, if not before, the movement opposed to abuse of power by absolutist regimes and their oppression of freedom and human dignity. Classical political liberalism has reactivated and revindicated the older tradition of limited government, the right of resistance, and popular sovereignty. Moreover and most importantly, it presupposes the tradition of representative government, unknown

---

8. For Coke see the valuable study by Jean Beauté, *Un grand juriste Anglais: Sir Edward Coke 1552–1634. Ses idées politiques et constitutionelles, ou aux origines de la démocratie occidentale moderne* (Paris: Presses Universitaires de France, 1975).

9. *De l'esprit des lois*, ed. R. Derathé (Paris: Garnier 1973).

to Greek and Roman antiquity but stemming from medieval (feudal) traditions, medieval urban political culture and parliamentarianism, and the practice of religious orders being ruled by representative bodies (the chapters). This rich inheritance would hardly have survived without the traditions of Roman law and medieval natural law in its different forms. Liberal constitutionalism, after all, has always been a specifically *political* form of expression of the natural law tradition.[10] The historical enemy of liberalism was not the medieval political world, which had long vanished by the time liberalism emerged. Liberalism's enemy was rather the modern absolutist territorial state, which was based on uncontrolled power and which arbitrarily privileged a socially and economically incompetent *noblesse de robe,* a state that, in consequence of the spiritual-religious rupture of occidental society, had extended its power, taking more and more a kind of paternalistic control over the life of its citizens.

Thus, classical political liberalism has its roots in cultural premises that cannot be understood independently from the history of the Christian occident with its Hebraic biblical and Greek, Hellenistic, and Roman background. I therefore agree with Charles Taylor that "Western liberalism is not so much an expression of the secular, postreligious outlook that happens to be popular among liberal *intellectuals* as a more organic outgrowth of Christianity" and therefore share his view that it is not "a possible meeting ground for all cultures" and "shouldn't claim complete cultural neutrality."[11] Of course, Taylor himself is a believing Christian. Yet, it might be revealing to recall in Taylor's support the famous words of a secularist and agnostic liberal like Karl Popper, who famously wrote: "When I call our social world 'the best,' ... I have in mind the standards and values which have come down to us through Christianity from Greece and the Holy Land; from Socrates, and from the Old and New Testament."[12]

It is important to keep these things in mind in order to correctly approach the issue of public reason, common good, and natural law as it has

10. See Brian Tierney, *The Idea of Natural Rights: Studies on Natural Rights, Natural Law, and Church Law 1150–1625* (Grand Rapids, Mich.: William B. Eerdmans, 1997). Tierney convincingly challenges the view of Michel Villey, for whom the idea of "rights" (as subjective rights) is specifically modern. For the roots of modern political thinking in medieval sources of legal thinking see Skinner, *The Age of Reformation.*

11. Charles Taylor et al., *Multiculturalism: Examining the Politics of Recognition,* ed. Amy Gutmann (Princeton, N.J.: Princeton University Press, 1994), 62.

12. Karl R. Popper, *Conjectures and Refutations: The Growth of Scientific Knowledge,* 3d ed. (London: Routledge and Kegan Paul, 1969), 369.

continually evolved up to today. If we trace back the genesis of this modern political culture to its roots and original motivations we come to understand why certain contemporary interpretations of public reason—or some specific aspects of these interpretations—like, for example, the one expressed by John Rawls, in my view tend to fall short of a sound understanding of the ethos of constitutional democracy.

Although Rawls's "political liberalism" claims to be an adequate expression of the intrinsic ethos of modern liberal constitutional democracy, this is only partly true. If I say "partly," I do so because I think that Rawls's mature theory of political liberalism, which I read independently from some of his questionable egalitarian views on justice, is in fact *very close* to being an adequate, even very powerful, expression of the ethos of constitutional democracy. So, my goal in criticizing Rawls is not to refute political liberalism, but rather to put into evidence shortcomings of the Rawlsian version of it and make some proposals to amend it (which, understandably, some might consider to be something futile to attempt).

In important aspects, mostly because of what Rawls himself calls its extreme "Kantian" constructivism, Rawls's political liberalism actually departs from the liberal constitutionalist—and even contractarian—tradition by substituting for its foundation in natural law the simple idea of reciprocal acknowledgment of "free and equal citizens." This, I think, is a mistake that has roots in a confusion concerning the relation between public reason and natural law, a confusion by which Rawls is led to ignore natural law entirely, holding the idea of natural law to be incompatible with his ideal of public reason. So though Rawls is close to being right, in the sense that his mistake is compact and definite, correcting it nevertheless implies a sizable adjustment to his account of how natural law and his restricted "public reason" are related.

In the following I shall first present a brief epistemological and then a more extensive historical argument in favor of the legitimacy of the political ethos of modern constitutional democracy. Secondly, I will characterize the essential features of this ethos. After that I will show why in my view Rawls's theory of Political Liberalism only partly succeeds in being a true expression of the political ethos of constitutional democracy, why he delivers a biased account of it, and why he fails to render justice to important aspects of that ethos, aspects that refer to natural law and corresponding basic political values. After this, I will try to clarify the relationship between natural law and public reason and finally turn to the political problem of natural law in a pluralistic society. I will conclude this essay by showing how what I call "Rawls's immunization strategy" against the validity of natural-law reasons in public reason necessarily breaks down in consequence of the inner logic of his own approach ("Postscript").[13]

Political Philosophy as Practical Philosophy and the Importance of History

It is a fundamental feature of political philosophy to be part of *practical* philosophy. Political philosophy belongs to ethics, which is practical, for it both reflects on practical knowledge and aims at action. Therefore, it is not only normative, but must consider the concrete conditions of realization. The rationale of political institutions and action must be understood as embedded in concrete cultural and, therefore, historical contexts and as meeting with problems that only in these contexts are understandable. A normative political philosophy that would abstract from the conditions of realizability would be trying to establish norms for realizing the "idea of the good" or of "the just" (as Plato, in fact, tried to do in his *Republic*). Such a purely metaphysical view, however, is doomed to failure. As a theory of political praxis, political philosophy must include in its reflection the concrete historical context, historical experiences, and the corresponding knowledge of the proper logic of the political.[14] Briefly: political philosophy is not metaphysics, which contemplates the necessary order of being, but practical philosophy, which deals with partly contingent matters and aims at action.

Moreover, unlike moral norms in general—natural law included—which rule the actions of a person ("my acting" and pursuing the good), the logic of the political is characterized by acts such as framing institutions and establishing legal rules by which not only personal actions but the actions of a multitude of persons are regulated by the coercive force of state power, according to which a part of the citizenry exercises power over others. Political actions, thus, are both actions of the whole of the body politic and refer to the whole of the community of citizens.[15]

---

13. Readers exclusively interested in my views on Rawls might wish to skip the epistemological and historical part and directly proceed to the section "Rawls's Idea of 'Political Liberalism' and Its Mistaken Premise: An Inadequate Concept of 'Human Society.'"

14. See chapter 1 of the present volume, which is entitled "Why Is Political Philosophy Necessary? Historical Considerations and a Response." This was originally published as "Perché una filosofia politica? Elementi storici per una risposta," *Acta philosophica* 1 (1992): 233–63.

15. See for a similar, though not in all regards identical, view see the essay by Ángel Rodríguez

Unless we wish to espouse a Platonic view according to which some persons are by nature rulers while others are by nature subjects, we will stick to the Aristotelian differentiation between the "domestic" and the "political" kind of rule:[16] unlike domestic rule, which is over people who have a common interest who are striving harmoniously after the same good and, therefore, according to Aristotle is essentially "despotic," political rule is exercised over free persons who represent a plurality of interests and pursue, in the common context of the *polis,* different goods. The exercise of such political rule, therefore, needs justification and is continuously in search of consent among those who are ruled, but who potentially at the same time are also the rulers.

Thus, unlike individual ethics, which is concerned with the goodness, fulfillment, and flourishing of human persons, political ethics and philosophy—as a conception of political action and the political, that is, the *common,* good—must be right from the beginning, and even on the level of basic principles, be prudential in a specific way: it is a *principled* kind of prudence, based on the specific subject matter of the political, that guides actions—for example, lawmaking—chosen for, and in many cases in behalf of, a multitude of free persons, the results of which are enforced by means of the coercive apparatus of what we nowadays call "the state." This principled kind of political prudence and its inherent logic of specifically political justification constitute "public reason." Therefore, *public reasons* cannot be simply identical with *natural-law reasons* as such, because natural law, as such, does not distinguish moral actions generally from the specifically political. By its very nature, natural law encompasses the whole of human life and, inasmuch as it is *natural* law, it therefore cannot be a criterion for what is to be counted as *politically* reasonable. Natural-law reasons do not distinguish between the moral norms a person is obliged to impose on her own actions and what she legitimately may impose on the actions of others. Although natural law may always work as a criterion for recognizing specific laws as unjust, it is not a criterion sufficient for making out what belongs to the *political* common good and therefore is to be *imposed* by law and the coercive apparatus of the state on the totality of citizens.[17] For natural-law reasons to

---

Luño, "Etica personale ed etica politica," in Rodríguez Luño, *"Cittadini degni del vangelo" (Fil 1, 27).* *Saggi di etica politica* (Rome: Edizioni Università della Santa Croce, 2005), 23–33.

16. Aristotle, *Politics* 1.7.1255b16ff.

17. For example: a positive law that for demographic reasons imposes on women the obligation to abort or otherwise eliminate (i.e., by infanticide, now also euphemistically called "postnatal abortion")

be valid reasons in the sphere of the political and public reason they must be a political *application, restriction, or concretization* of natural law, according to the logic of the political. This logic is not contained in the concept of natural law as such, but is specifically political, that is, it is proper to reason as *public* reason.

Finally and most importantly, unlike natural-law reasons, public reason is based on the logic of realizability, that is, on the conditions of possible consensus and cooperation under conditions of disagreement and conflict. Natural-law reasons, which appeal to normative moral truth, precisely are not the kind of reasons that are able to settle social conflicts and ideological divergence. On the contrary, they are rather part of these conflicts, and in some cases they are their cause. For those who believe in the existence of natural law—as I definitely do—natural-law reasons are rather a measure of truth, but in many cases they are also controversial. And this is a major *political* problem that cannot be settled by invoking that natural-law reasons are open to everyone's understanding. I will come back to this in more detail later in this essay.

From Aristotle to Marsilius of Padua and Early Modernity: The Experiences and Burdens of History Revisited

In one important sense, then, the spirit of my argument is clearly Aristotelian. Aristotle has taught us to reflect upon politics in this historically contextualized and essentially practical manner, which always includes the reflection on the conditions of realization of an action. He also conceived of political society as a system of cooperation between essentially free citizens who are potentially in conflict and establish between them mutual relations on the grounds of rules of reciprocity and equity. In this Aristotle deeply

---

after the third baby, or to do so generally with genetically handicapped offspring, would be clearly contrary to natural law. To show such contrariety, no additional argument is necessary. But why is it a violation of natural law for abortion to be permitted (that is, not forbidden by law) and thus left to the free choice of the citizen? Of course, also in this case, the practice of abortion would still be contrary to natural law. Yet, the question is whether the legislator's not punishing these actions is contrary to natural law. If one wants to avoid the conclusion that everything natural law demands or forbids has to be enforced by positive law, an additional argument is required to show why the legislator should protect unborn life (e.g., that also unborn human persons have a right to life, which must be legally protected, and that it would be contrary to publicly recognized standards of justice not to do so). I have tried to develop such an argument in my "Fundamental Rights, Moral Law, and the Legal Defense of Life in a Constitutional Democracy: A Constitutionalist Approach to the Encyclical *Evangelium Vitae*," chap. 7 of my *Ethics of Procreation and the Defense of Human Life*, ed. William F. Murphy Jr. (Washington, D.C.: The Catholic University of America Press, 2010); it was originally published in the *American Journal of Jurisprudence* 43 (1998): 135–83.

contrasts with Plato, for whom the just order of the *polis* aims at eliminating conflicts by establishing the *polis* as a harmoniously structured social organism, which is, as Aristotle criticized, domestic and despotic rather than political. A *political* community is an order of free citizens who, although pursuing different aims and having often conflicting interests, create an institutional and legal framework for cooperation.

In another regard, however, my position is rather un- or anti-Aristotelian. History has taught us that the way Aristotle typically conceived politics to be a part of ethics is mistaken or at least unrealistic. The way Aristotle thought of politics as belonging to ethics is precisely that he considered politics to be the consummation of the ethical, and this in two senses: that the political life, which consists of active participation in public affairs, is the most excellent life for ordinary people—that is, for all except the philosophers, who achieve first-rate happiness in contemplating truth—and that for non-philosophers political or civic involvement is therefore necessary for human fulfillment and happiness; and, secondly, that the *polis*, especially its laws, have the task to make people live the virtues and educate them accordingly by the power of legal coercion.[18]

Unsurprisingly, then, right from its beginning Aristotle calls his lectures on ethics "political science."[19] The books of the *Politics* are nothing other than the completion of the previous *Nicomachean Ethics,* which, thus, form the first part of Aristotelian *Politics.* So, in reality, Aristotle's ethics is essentially a *"polis*-ethic"; it is political philosophy in the form of comprehensive moral philosophy the central aim of which is to build politics on human virtue and which sees human virtue—moral excellence—as the principal aim of the *polis* and its laws. The virtues are to be lived in the context of the *polis,* and it is the laws of the *polis* that have the task of making citizens live the virtues or at least refrain from vices. In conceiving ethics and political philosophy in such a way as a *polis*-ethic, Aristotle is still a faithful disciple of Plato. The Aristotelian *polis* remains an eminently pedagogical undertaking. A Macedonian immigrant and despiser of the Athenian political system, Aristotle repeatedly insists, talking to the—in his view—decadent Athenians, that for him the exemplary city is the capital of Laconia, Sparta. So-called neo-Aristotelians hardly ever mention this rather problematic feature of Aristotelian political thinking.

18. *Nicomachean Ethics* 10.9.
19. Ibid., 1.2 and 3.

Yet, what happened between Aristotle and the rise of early modern political thought? Let me outline some basic features of this history, focusing on what seems to me important for understanding the proper legitimacy of the political ethos of modernity.

In Hellenistic times, with its numbers of territorially vast *basileia* and the exaltation of kingship, the traditional Greek city-state sank into insignificance, and so the Aristotelian conception of a *polis*-ethic lost its practical appeal. Finally, ancient Roman political thinking, after its temporarily republican Ciceronian and Polybian phase, was more and more centered on the empire and replaced by Roman public law, eager to confer on the principate of the first emperors republican legitimacy. Thereby the different famous juridical-political formulas—belonging to the *lex regia*—were created, such as *quod principi placuit legis habet vigorem*, "everything that pleases the Prince has force of law."[20] This formula was transmitted though medieval canon law to those who in early modern times used it, as did the Roman emperors, to justify absolute power.[21] It was based on the fiction that the people had transferred its ruling power entirely onto the emperor. Hence, every law issued by him was to be considered as just and ratified, as if it had been made by the people itself.

The corresponding absence of public political philosophy in the Roman Empire was compensated for not only by public law but even more importantly by civil religion.[22] The favor of the gods obtained by worshipping them was held to be the condition for the flourishing of the empire. When the empire and its power through Constantine, and even more, with Theodosius the Great, became Christianized and the Catholic religion was established as state religion, the Roman mentality did not change: the upholding of the Christian religion—which unlike paganism was monotheistic and, thus, increasingly unwilling to tolerate alternative cults—was thought to be the guarantee for the well-being of the empire. Constantine's vision of the Christian cross—*in hoc signo vinces*—before his decisive victory over his rival Licinius at the Ponte Milvio, a vision that assured him of his imminent victory, was a typically Roman way of adhering to the Christian God: to be

20. About the presence of the *lex regia* in medieval thought see Hanns Kurz, *Volkssouveränität und Volksrepräsentation* (Cologne: Carl Heymanns, 1965), 38–42.

21. See Sergio Mochi Onory, *Fonti canonistiche dell'idea moderna dello stato* (Milan: Vita e pensiero, 1951); Dieter Wyduckel, *Princeps legibus solutus: Eine Untersuchung zur frühmodernen Rechts- und Staatslehre* (Berlin: Duncker & Humblot, 1979).

22. For this and the following see also chaps. 2 and 3 of the second edition of Peter Brown's *The Rise of Western Christendom: Triumph and Diversity, A.D. 200–1000* (Oxford: Blackwell, 2003).

protected by him in the struggle for supremacy and for the good of the empire. This was already the reason why Constantine's immediate predecessor, Galerius—a wholehearted pagan—issued the first edict of toleration of
the Christian religion. Constantine's famous "Edict of Milan" from 313 was
only a confirmation, though a definitive one, of this previous edict.

A radical change in Christian political thinking, however, came about
when Rome a century later fell under the force of Alaric's invasion. The remaining pagans accused Christianity and its hostility to the traditional Roman gods of being the cause of this disaster. It was the moment in which
St. Augustine in his epochal work *The City of God* severed the bonds between Christian religion and the Roman Empire: the fall of Rome, Augustine
famously argued, is not an argument against the truth of the Christian religion. The worshipping of the true God is not a means to maintain the glory
of Rome, but to lead citizens of the earthly city to their heavenly fatherland.
The City of God is not to be built on this earth, but it must take shape in the
hearts of human beings.

From this moment Christian social and political thinking in the occident
began to be dualistic. The Aristotelian idea of a *polis*-ethic, with its monistic
conception of moral perfection linked to life in the *polis,* had become impossible. The *polis* was now existentially divided into two parts: the earthly
part is orientated, as Augustine writes, toward the "conservation of mortal
life" and has the task of subjecting citizens to an order that guarantees true
peace. The order of earthly state power, according to Augustine, was legitimate as long as it did not impede worshipping the true God.[23] The second
part is the City of God, which is established in the hearts of men and which
does not find its completion, not even its representation, in present history
and the actual world, but is spiritual and eschatological. This typical Christian dualism was well expressed in the formula of Pope Gelasius I (492–96):
"There are two powers by which this world is chiefly ruled: the sacred authority of the priesthood and the authority of kings." While earthly rulers
had *potestas,* coercive power, the spiritual power of the priesthood was *auctoritas,* which is charisma.[24] Dealing with matters of moral perfection and
integral salvation, the latter imposes itself by force of moral guidance, ex-

---

23. *De civitate Dei* 19.17.

24. The doctrine—first formulated in his Ep. 12 to Emperor Anastasius I—is contained in its definitive form in Tractatus 4 (printed in *Sources chrétiennes,* ed. Henri de Lubac and Jean Daniélou, vol. 65
[Paris: Cerf, 1960]). See also Wilhelm Ensslin, "Auctoritas und Potestas. Zur Zweigewaltenlehre des Papstes Gelasius I," *Historisches Jahrbuch* 75 (1955): 661–68.

cellence of doctrine, and superiority of dignity. Both *potestas* and *auctoritas* had been, in pagan times, jointly attributed to the *Augustus,* the emperor. Christianity split them into two, attributing them to two separate forces. Thus the political autonomy of coercive temporal power (the *regnum*) was established, but simultaneously, it was subordinated to the moral authority of the spiritual power (the *sacerdotium*), which, however, was not conceived as being politically coercive.

In a way, the Augustinian dualism—based on the distinction between the "political" task of coercive state power of securing the peaceful coexistence of citizens and promoting the temporal well-being of citizens without pretending to achieve their moral perfection on one side, and the spiritual task of the Church of promoting in the hearts of human persons the City of God, which consists in holiness and eternal salvation, on the other—already implied a concept of "public reason." The distinction specifies the realm of the political by conferring on it a certain autonomy and indifference to the realization of higher values. It also legitimates the use of coercive political power by a specific logic of the temporal and political common good. This is the logic of peacekeeping, social order, temporal well-being, and noninterference in religious matters. The public recognition of religious truth is no longer the condition for the flourishing of the political realm. The temporal power simply must abstain from hindering this truth from being announced by the Church and the true religion from being practiced by its citizens.

During Christian antiquity, this typically Augustinian "residual" or "minimalist" political thinking had not, however, persisted for long. What followed was rather a turn that centuries later would cause the reaction from which political modernity would take its origin. This first, and I would say fatal, turn was "political Augustinism."[25] Political Augustinism stems from a misreading of Augustine's idea of the duality of the two cities and the corresponding superiority of the spiritual over the temporal. The fundamental idea of political Augustinism was, expressed in the famous words of Pope Gregory the Great (590–604), that "who governs has received his power over all men from above, *so that the earthly city be in service of the heavenly.*"[26] In a cruder form the idea that state power had to serve the City of God and, therefore, the aims of the Church was expressed by Isidore of

---

25. See the landmark study by H.-X. Arquillière, *L'Augustinisme politique. Essai sur la formation des théories politiques du Moyen Age,* 2nd ed. (Paris: J. Vrin, 1955).

26. Epist. 3.65.

Seville, who wrote that the "powers of the earthly princes would not have been necessary if they could not impose with the terror of coercive power what the clergy has been unable to impose with his word alone."[27] This, and not Augustine's plea to the emperor—totally untypical for the saint Bishop of Hippo, who always believed in the force of dialogue—to use state force against the Donatists, was the origin of a long tradition that considered the coercive power of the state to be the secular arm of the spiritual power of the Church.

Now, Pope Gregory's intentions obviously were not political in the sense of aiming at an increase of Church power by putting the secular power at its service. On the contrary, originally, and in his spirit always remaining, a monk, Pope Gregory was a man of spirituality and prayer. Gregory rather wanted to exalt the power of secular rulers by reminding them of their task of being servants of the city of God and, therefore, of the dignity of the power they held in their hands. It was an essential implication of this Gregorian doctrine to deny any right of resistance whatsoever against earthly rulers, seeing in them a representation of divine authority on earth. In consequence, earthly *potestas,* seen as serving the higher ends of eternal salvation, now more and more acquired a kind of religious consecration (no wonder that later his teaching was so eagerly referred to by Luther, and in England used by James I, who considered himself as God's "lieutenant," in his confrontation with Catholics and Presbyterian dissenters and generally, in the formulation of sixteenth- and early-seventeenth-century doctrines of the "Divine Right of Kings"). This religiously exalted view of temporal power—very much in continuity with the self-understanding of late ancient Roman imperial thought—culminated in the Carolingian renewal of the Roman Empire. The Carolingian emperors called themselves *vicarius Christi*—the traditional title generally used for bishops and even priests—and considered the emperor's consecration as a proper sacrament.[28] This finally led under the Ottonian emperors to the system of the imperial Church, which integrated bishops as territorial rulers into the political and administrative structure of the empire. A *respublica christiana* was created, a new *polis* in which political ethics now coincided with the Christian ethics of salvation and the Christian

---

27. *Sententiae* 3.51 (Migne P.L. 83, 723–24; the entire Latin text is to be found in Arquillière, *L'Augustinisme politique,* 142.

28. See Ernst Kantorowicz, *The King's Two Bodies: A Study in Medieval Political Theology,* 3rd ed. (Princeton, N.J.: Princeton University Press, 1973).

Faith underlying it and in which, consequently, heresy was conceived of as opposed to what we would call today "constitutional essentials," and thus as undermining the political system and social order, and to be repelled by state power.[29] Though the distinction of the two powers, temporal and spiritual, survived, in practice Augustinian dualism was replaced by a political-ecclesiastical monism in which secular power had the Church at its service.

From this integration into, and subordination under, the political system the Church, defending its freedom—the *libertas ecclesiae*—liberated itself though long struggles from which, ironically, in high medieval times the papacy ended up as the only remaining sovereign power. Under the guidance of papal supremacy, now a *respublica christiana*, understood in feudalist terms and containing its proper *polis*-ethic, was created. Thus, the existential unity of the *polis*, typical for Platonic and Aristotelian political thinking, was renewed, but now defined in clericalist terms. The project was never really realized and, from the outset, was doomed to failure. It broke down for a whole series of reasons, internal and external.

The project indeed contradicted the very essence of what Christianity brought into occidental political thinking: the originally Augustinian dualism, not in its medieval form of superposing the secular and sacred orders hierarchically in the one or the other way, putting the one in the service of the other, but distinguishing them as belonging to different *institutional* orders: one political, characterized by the need of using earthly coercive power for the sake of the temporal well-being of society, and the other spiritual, characterized by authority and moral charisma, acting not by coercive power and in the name of temporal and earthly goods, but on the basis of influencing man's conscience and in the name of truth and eternal salvation.

In contrast, from the high Middle Ages, the pope now claimed to possess not only the supreme *auctoritas* proper to the priesthood, but also the *plenitudo potestatis,* with the right to consider worldly princes, including the emperor, as subjected to his jurisdiction, which, *ratione peccati*—that is, by moral reasons—was considered to extend to temporal affairs.[30] The

29. Conversely it was seen as licit to force heretics by coercive public power to salvation (actually a rather strange idea) as it was contained in the Decretum Gratianum (38, 23, 4): "haeretici ad salutem etiam inviti sunt trahendi." According to the later reception of Roman law in the occident, heresy was conceived of as the crime of *laesa maiestatis,* which demanded capital punishment.

30. See the important decretal *Novit ille* (1204) by Innocent III. Text in Emil Friedberg, *Corpus Iuris Canonici,* vol. 2, reprint of the Editio Lipsiensis secunda (Graz: Akademische Druck- u. Verlagsanstalt, 1955), cols. 242–44. Some passages of the decretal can be found in my "Perché una filosofia politica?" 239. For the whole period still very valuable is Robert Warrant Carlyle and Alexander James Carlyle, *A*

title of *vicarius Christi* passed from the emperor to the pope.[31] Though this plenitude of power and jurisdictional sovereignty was justified morally and pastorally rather than politically, it was impossible that a spiritual power claiming juridical—that is, institutional—superiority over political power would not become political itself (not to speak of medieval and, until the nineteenth century, also modern popes, who in their own pontifical states were also temporal princes and, therefore, players on the political scene). To oppose and weaken the emperor in his struggle for supremacy, the popes in the high Middle Ages promoted the independence of Italian city-states and territorial princes.[32] Therewith they ironically promoted those who less than a century later would oppose in the name of territorial sovereignty the papal *plenitudo potestatis* that they perceived to be the main obstacle to their own power and to the peaceful coexistence of citizens in their territories.[33]

This was exactly the opinion of the first "modern" political thinker, though he lived and wrote in the fourteenth century: Marsilius of Padua, a pure Aristotelian. Marsilius challenged the subordination of temporal power under papal spiritual supremacy—and the idea of clerical supremacy over worldly affairs altogether—and its concept of *plenitudo potestatis* by opposing to it an Aristotelian view of monistic *political* ethics of the *polis*. The Church and its ministers should not exercise any power, not even spiritual, but be confined to preaching the Gospel and administering the sacraments. The crucial point is Marsilius's unorthodox denial of the Church's right to exercise any form of even merely ecclesiastical jurisdiction and his assertion that it had not even the right to determine whether a theological doctrine was heretical, and in case it was, to condemn it. For Marsilius this was the task of the secular power, which, so he was convinced, was the only one that legitimately could possess *plenitudo potestatis*.

Now, the point of this kind of Erastianism—which reminds us of Hobbes's

---

History of Mediaeval Political Theory in the West, 6 vols. (Edinburgh/ London: William Blackwood, 1903–36), especially vol. 2. See also *The Cambridge History of Medieval Political Thought c. 350–c.1450*, edited by J. H. Burns (Cambridge: Cambridge University Press, 1988); Walter Ullmann, *Principles of Government and Politics in the Middle Ages*, 3rd ed. (London: Methuen, 1973).

31. Harold J. Berman has called this a "Papal Revolution"; see his *Law and Revolution: The Formation of the Western Legal Tradition* (Cambridge, Mass.: Harvard University Press, 1983).

32. See Quentin Skinner, *The Foundations of Modern Political Thought*, vol. 1, *The Renaissance* (Cambridge: Cambridge University Press, 1978), ch. 1.

33. About the ideological and theological implications see the classical study by Jean Rivière, *Le Problème de l'Église et de l'État au temps de Philippe le Bel* (Louvain: Champion, 1926).

later view—is not spiritual or religious, that is, the attempt to confer on the state a sort of higher religious consecration. The essential novelty of Marsilius's view, and what makes it so modern, is that it follows a strictly *political* logic, which is perfectly expressed in the title of his main work, *Defensor pacis* (Defender of peace). Marsilius argues, as Hobbes would two centuries later, in favor of civil peace. Thus, Marsilius's anticlericalism expresses a strictly political claim. Marsilius's is a pragmatic-political approach, and a secular one, which already points forward to what two centuries later will be the proper starting point of modern political thinking: the quest for peace in a society cruelly divided by religious and ideological controversies. Perhaps in Marsilius we find the first appearance of a modern idea of public reason. Most interestingly, but not surprisingly, it is much closer to Augustine's original Christian dualism, never entirely forgotten through the Middle Ages, than were the curialist and "papalist" ideas of Giacomo di Viterbo—a disciple of Aquinas—and Aegidius Romanus about papal supremacy and *potestas directa*, a doctrine based on a mixture of a certain brand of Aristotelianism and Roman public law, which, however, was never put into practice.[34] Ironically, medieval curialist theories on papal *plenitudo potestatis* prepared the modern political formulas of state sovereignty and absolute political power that later were adapted to needs of the rising territorial state and its secular interests.[35]

According to Marsilius it is only the civil laws that are to rule in a state, and the authority and force of the government is entirely derived from the will of the people.[36] Marsilius shows us that Aristotelian political thinking had vigorously survived during the Middle Ages, not only in the already mentioned theories of curialist theoreticians of a papal hierocracy, but in a much more fruitful and decisive way in what Georges de Lagarde has called medieval "political naturalism," which was most prominently represented by Thomas Aquinas.[37] "Political naturalism" was to assert—this time *against*

---

34. This was classically explored by Martin Grabmann, *Studien über den Einfluss der aristotelischen Philosophie auf die mittelalterlichen Theorien über das Verhältnis von Kirche und Staat* (Sitzungsberichte der Bayerischen Akademie der Wissenschaften, Phil.-hist. Klasse, 1934, Heft 2) (Munich: Verlag der Bayerischen Akademie der Wissenschaften, 1934), 41–60. See also Walter Ullmann, *Medieval Papalism: The Political Theories of the Medieval Canonists* (London: Methuen, 1949). The doctrine, which was followed in practice and which finally became the dominant one, was the doctrine of *potestas indirecta*. See the classical exposition of that doctrine by Charles Journet, *La Juridiction de l'Église sur la cité* (Paris: Desclée, 1931).

35. See Helmut Quaritsch, *Souveränität: Entstehung und Entwicklung des Begriff in Frankreich und Deutschland vom 13. Jh. bis 1806* (Berlin: Athenäum, 1986).

36. *Defensor pacis* 3.3.

37. Georges de Lagarde, *La naissance de l'esprit laïque au déclin du moyen age*, vol. 2, *Secteur social de la scolastique* (Louvain: Nauvelaerts, 1958), 51ff.

Augustinian traditions—that human society and the *polis*, rather than being a consequence of original sin, was part of the order of creation and that, therefore, it is natural for human beings to live in society and establish political forms of government.[38]

Marsilius's legacy is twofold. He is the testimony and a transmitter of what we can call Aristotelian "constitutionalism" and the first advocate of modern "public reason" in the sense of discovering the "political" as a specific kind of reasonableness. We certainly find a similar combination of both features in Machiavelli, though not so much in the Machiavelli of the *Principe*, but the one of the *Discorsi*.[39] Here he expresses the conviction that the ideal state is a republic in which through the rule of law citizens are free, while where legal institutions do not prevail, public power will fall into the hands of tyrannical princely power. In different ways, Marsilius of Padua and Machiavelli announce a new era of political thought. Yet, before it definitively broke through, Europe underwent a fundamental transformation by the breakdown of the religious unity of Christianity by the different Protestant reformations and the subsequent confessional conflicts and wars.

The Ethos of Pacification at the Root of the Political Ethos of Constitutional Democracy

The political ethos of constitutional democracy is the product of a long history of conflicts and struggles, in which much blood was shed and which left tracks of misery and hatred. Postmedieval Europe, already characterized by the emergence of territorial states with sovereign rulers, had suffered a fundamental transformation by the breakdown of the religious unity of Christianity, by the different Protestant reformations, and by the subsequent confessional conflicts and wars. It was this experience of social conflict, shared in a different context in the fourteenth century already by Marsilius of Padua and in the sixteenth by Machiavelli, which made people believe that the main task of public power was to promote not the achievement of a supreme good,

---

38. Medieval Aristotelianism has transmitted a series of essential features to subsequent ages that are crucial for modern political thinking: among these namely the idea of a common good to be realized by political and legal institutions; the idea of government by law; the conviction that any system of government is manmade and must therefore serve human interests and goods; and that, consequently, any system of government is liable to be put into question, reformed, and changed; and finally the belief that the legitimacy of any government depends on its being capable of guaranteeing a minimum of justice and common utility. See for this Peter Graf Kielmansegg, *Volkssouveränität, Eine Untersuchung der Bedingungen demokratischer Legitimität* (Stuttgart: Klett, 1977), 38ff.

39. *Discorsi sopra la prima Deca di Tito Livio*, 1.2–10.

but the avoidance of the supreme evil: civil war. This insight—typical not only for Marsilius and Machiavelli, but also for Thomas Hobbes and Jean Bodin— that for politics there was primarily not a *summum bonum* to achieve, but a *summum malum* to avoid is, as it were, the *cantus firmus* of early modern political thought.

It is Jean Bodin (1529–96) whom we can call the first outstanding champion of modern political thinking and the progenitor of "public reason" in its modern form. Not surprisingly, Bodin was a jurist, forming part of an entire group of French legal thinkers who, in the middle of the wars between Catholics and Huguenots, became known as the "politiques" or "politicians" because they advocated a strictly political solution for the problem of religious diversity. Their ideas are famously summarized in the French king's chancellor Michel de l'Hôpital's assertion that the important thing is not which one is the true religion, but how people can live together in peace.[40]

In his enormously learned and voluminous work *Six Livres sur la République* (1576), Bodin developed his doctrine of sovereignty, which for him was of the essence of the state. Far from advocating absolute power, however, this doctrine follows a specifically political logic. It is the logic of a *modus vivendi* grounded on assuring "public goods," as distinguished from private ones, which aims at creating the political conditions of civil coexistence and cooperation in a world characterized by conflict and disagreement on matters of fundamental existential relevance.

Bodin's idea of a *modus vivendi* rests upon the distinction between (1) values that are, in an existential and absolute sense, higher and (2) values that, though being of lesser moral and religious dignity, are more fundamental *politically*.[41] This distinction marks, I think, the debut of modern public reason. It is significant that the political philosopher who in our days has initiated the revival of the concept of "public reason," John Rawls, precisely draws, without explicitly referring to Bodin, upon this distinction.[42]

This distinction actually includes a nuclear *political ethic* that is an ethic

---

40. About the role of French lawyers in sixteenth-century civil war see Roman Schnur, *Die französischen Juristen im konfessionellen Bürgerkrieg des 16. Jahrhunderts: Ein Beitrag zur Entstehungsgeschichte des modernen Staates* (Berlin: Duncker & Humblot, 1962). See also Matteucci, *Organizzazione del potere e libertà*, 37ff.; and Joseph Lecler, *Histoire de la tolérance au siècle de la Réforme* (1955) (Paris: Albin Michel, 1994), 479ff.

41. For understanding the importance of Bodin in this respect I am much indebted to Martin Kriele, *Einführung in die Staatslehre: Die geschichtlichen Legitimitätsgrundlagen des demokratischen Verfassungsstaates*, 4th ed. (Opladen: Westdeutscher Verlag, 1990), 50–52.

42. See e.g., John Rawls, "The Idea of Public Reason Revisited," § 6.3, in *The Law of Peoples, with "The Idea of Public Reason Revisited"* (Cambridge, Mass.: Harvard University Press, 1999), 173.

of responsibility: the readiness to renounce political implementation of what one considers the higher values in favor of what is *politically* more funda-mental because it is supported by general interest and consensus. It estab-lishes the priority of the politically indispensable over what, from a moral and religious point of view, is higher. This distinction was necessary to rees-tablish, in a way, the original Augustinian and Gelasian dualism—and paral-lelism—between the temporal, coercive power of the state and the spiritual authority of the Church, which, mainly because of the canonical doctrine of papal *plenitudo potestatis,* had been abandoned during medieval times.

Bodin's main idea was to create an ethos of pacification, an ethos of peace that aims at securing the stability of public goods and institutions. In Bodin's eyes, the indispensable guarantee for this was the sovereignty of state power. Similarly to Hobbes, for Bodin the essential task of the public reason of the sovereign is to maintain peaceful coexistence and cooperation between citizens. Of course, this ethos of social peace is essentially linked to the rise of the modern territorial state.

It is, to put it more precisely, a political ethos that is focused on the question of how to establish, in a society lacking consensus about highest values including about what is good and just, a basis for peaceful coexis-tence and cooperation, as well as institutions to which all citizens can ad-here despite their disagreement on fundamental matters of human fulfill-ment, the sense of life, the good, and even matters of basic justice. This was the inner logic not only of Bodin's ethos of peace, but also of subsequent liberal constitutionalism.[43]

The Ethos of Liberty, Contractarianism, and Liberal Constitutionalism

Bodin's theory was one-sided, seeing the solution in undivided state sovereignty—not to speak of Hobbes's contradictory intent to base abso-lute sovereignty on extreme individualism.[44] The main defect of Bodin's

43. England is a special case because here, as in some other cases, not only does the formation of modern state power go back to the twelfth century (Henry II), but its successive constitutionalist challenge has accompanied it since then continuously, at least since the Magna Carta of 1215 and the fourteenth-century principles of *rex in parlamento* and *rex infra regem* (Bracton), as well as through the development of common law and an independent judiciary. This is another reason why it is correct to say that modern constitutionalism has medieval roots (this, of course, also applies to medieval Aragon, the constitutionalism of which, however, did not survive and develop the wide and decisive influence of English constitutionalism).

44. See my *La filosofia politica di Thomas Hobbes: coerenza e contraddizioni di un paradigma* (Roma: Armando, 1997).

view—and generally all views stressing only the need of an unquestioned sovereign power to maintain peace and secure progress—was its lack of institutional guarantees to limit state power and to put it effectively into the service of the common good, understood as including the good of individuals, and not only the good of the whole of society, understood as the "public sector," which actually turned out to be the good of the maintenance of the sovereign's power. In front of the rise of state absolutism, justifying itself by using the traditional formula of Roman public law transmitted by medieval canon law, the ethos of pacification by sovereign power had to be complemented by an ethos of civil liberty, security, and political autonomy of the individual.

Liberal constitutionalism, thus, essentially includes an ethos of liberty that comes to complement the ethos of peace. Together they form a specific kind of public reason. Liberal constitutionalism presupposes the modern sovereign state, the facts of society and government.[45] Constitutionalism in the liberal tradition and, thus, liberal democracy is not anarchic, but only wants to subordinate power to the rule of law and thereby secure the primacy of the citizen as an individual person who pursues her own interests. Liberalism is hostile to undeserved privileges and believes in the creative power of freedom of individual citizens pursuing their legitimate interests; it is skeptical toward bureaucracies, "big government," and centralized planning. Liberalism generally holds that citizens know their own interest better than state officials do, although these interests are not simply the interests of "individuality," but also those of social units, first of all those that naturally define human beings' social dimension.

The great achievements of modern constitutionalism have been to subordinate absolute power to legal restrictions and controls; to institutionalize certain natural rights and personal liberty, securing them as positive law; and to develop an independent judiciary. Theorists of modern constitutionalism based it on the idea that society and government were to be thought of as the product of a social contract. Modern contractarianism was an ingenious idea, understandable against the background of absolutism. Contractarianism opposed this with the radical claim that government was to promote not the interests of the public sphere—the state and their rulers— but rather those of individual citizens.

45. This is one of the major points made by Stephen Holmes in his *Passions and Constraint: On the Theory of Liberal Democracy* (Chicago: University of Chicago Press, 1995), especially chap. 4.

Contractarianism is commonly held to be the opposite of the Aristotelian idea that life in society and political existence are natural to man. Yet, this seems to me to be exaggerated. All contractarian theories are in fact an explanation of man's social nature because all these theories show the necessity for man of an ordered life in society and of government. Moreover, they all try to make out the precise reasons why it is intrinsically reasonable and thus natural for man to enter into a state of society and government. Modern social-contract theories, thus, can be understood as a *determinate kind of argument* in favor of the naturally social character of man.[46] Yet, this argument possesses a problematic feature: it implies the idea that society is essentially a means to realizing man's individuality. I do not want to reject this idea from the outset. It seems to me to express licitly the antiabsolutist intention of this thought mentioned above. But this idea is one-sided, and in an important way it is wrong because it erroneously seems to imply that "society" is a product of a contract between originally nonsocial individuals. This cannot be true because in order to stipulate a contract the essentials of society must already exist, although—as both Hobbes and Locke in different ways describe—it may exist in a depraved, conflictive, and unsatisfactory way.

Provided we do not want to espouse the Hobbesian view of the creation of state authority by auto-submission under a sovereign absolute power, we must reject a basic assumption of social-contract theories: we must reject the strange idea that there can be any "natural rights" independently from man's existing as a social being.[47] This means to reject equally the assumption, implied in classical contractarianism, that before a contract is stipu-

---

46. I have argued for this in chapter 3 of the present volume, entitled "The Democratic Constitutional State and the Common Good." This was originally published as "Lo Stato costituzionale democratico e il bene comune," in *Ripensare lo spazio politico: quale aristocrazia?*, ed. E. Morandi and R. Panattoni (Padua: Il Poligrafo, 1998), 57–123 (Con-tratto. Rivista di filosofia tomista e contemporanea 6/1997).

47. The idea that not only "natural rights" but "rights" altogether are previous to "society"—"society" understood in the basic sense of coexistence of individuals that relate to each other in different forms of cooperation, communication, exchange, affection, etc.—is obviously absurd because the very notion of "having a right" implies to have a claim toward *someone else*. Natural rights are not simply natural tendencies as Hobbes claimed for the natural right to use all means for self-preservation (which he simply derived from the *natural compulsion* toward self-preservation and the corresponding dominant passion, the fear of violent death). This is why I think that any "right" *(ius, iustum)* is intrinsically also a subjective right, that is, a claim toward others. The concept of subjective rights is not a modern invention as famously argued by Michel Villey, for example, in his *La formation de la pensée juridique moderne*, new rev. ed. (Paris: Éditions Montchrétien, 1975), 215–62, and his disciple Michel Bastit, *Naissance de la loi moderne: La pensée de la loi de saint Thomas à Suarez* (Paris: Presses Universitaires de France, 1990). Against Villey's view see Brian Tierney, *The Idea of Natural Rights*. I am much indebted to Tierney for a better understanding of the medieval roots of the notion of subjective rights.

lated there exist only the individuals who stipulate it and that what a social contract refers to is exclusively the interests of these pre-social individuals. As I will try to show, nowhere has this basic assumption become clearer than in John Rawls's neo-contractualist conception of an original position. By rejecting this, we need not abandon the truth of contractarian individualism, which under the conditions of political modernity, its specific problems and needs, helpfully comes in to compensate the one-sidedness of Aristotelian— and neo-Aristotelian—communitarianism.

The rejection of the idea that there are "natural rights" independent of, and previous to, man's existence as a social being implies that we also reject the assumption, implicit in contemporary contractarianism, that before a contract is stipulated there are only individuals who stipulate it, and that the social contract properly refers exclusively to the interests and preferences of these pre-social individuals. This is exactly the basic assumption of Rawls's theory of justice; see especially the design of his "original position." Yet, a social contract cannot *create* society; it can only express a determinate and qualified way of existing *in* society. Most social-contract theories in the past have acknowledged this. A social contract, mostly in the liberal understanding of its Lockean version, legitimates political power by establishing—and this is the truth of contractarianism—the legally secured priority of the individual over the collective, of the private (one might say) over the public.

Once we have abandoned the mistaken idea that society and the state are entirely to be understood as means of promoting individual interests and preferences, we can reconcile Aristotle with the central insight of modern contractarianism. Contractarianism basically expresses the idea that any form of government that does not promote the true interest of individual persons but, conversely, puts individual persons into the service of the political community, is illegitimate.[48] This, however, does not signify that society and its political organization are simply and exclusively a means to promote the interests and preferences of *individual citizens*. "Society" is a reality that naturally coexists with the individual human person, and a person's interests are also defined respecting his or her existence as an individual embedded in society. In this respect we need to return to Aristotle, who

---

48. It is crucial to understand the correct historical antonym of contractarianism; see for this the valuable remarks on "antonym substitution" in Stephen Holmes, *The Anatomy of Antiliberalism* (Cambridge, Mass.: Harvard University Press, 1993), 253ff.

teaches us what society is, and therefore also what it means for a person to be naturally a social being.

Yet, modern contractarianism and nineteenth-century liberalism were not really as individualistic as they theoretically could have been. In reality it was very clear both in theory (excepting the special case of Rousseau) and in practice that society was not something created by man simply to promote the interests of the individual. It is easy to show this. On the level of theory, Hobbes's description of the state of nature is in reality a description of a social state, although of society in conflict and war. Locke's state of nature is social in the sense that man lives in natural communities and by no means in an isolated way; the state of war, then, is the degeneration of the natural social bonds, rooted in natural law, because of lack of independent judges able to settle conflicts.[49] Locke's "life," "liberty," and "property," which government is entrusted to secure, are not simply values of individuals, but also of social unities; they presuppose the family and a social order in which land owners and working people dependent on them share—until industrialization—common interests. Similar things can be said of Kant and, of course, of previous social-contract theorists of the German enlightenment, and even more clearly of the early modern social theorist Johannes Althusius.[50]

The same applies to political documents of early constitutionalism both in the American colonies and in France: for example, in the declaration of the Virginia Bill of Rights or in the French Declaration of the Rights of Men and Citizens from 1789, constitutions and governments are understood not as creating society (or the "nation"), but as securing rights that are inherent to man as an already social being. The concept of a society as protecting individual rights but pursuing also a "common benefit" is presupposed, and in no way do these documents promote the kind of mistaken individualism that is inherent in the contractarian idea that society is created by a social contract just to promote the interests and preferences of individuals.[51] Also for nineteenth-century liberals generally there were some unquestioned social

49. That Locke's state of nature is not asocial is argued also by John Dunn, *The Political Thought of John Locke: An Historical Account of the Argument of the "Two Treatises of Government"* (Cambridge: Cambridge University Press, 1969), 103ff. It is most important not to forget that Locke's argument is mainly directed against Sir Robert Filmer's patriarchal conception of the state.

50. "Rediscovered" by Otto von Gierke at the end of the nineteenth century; see his *Johannes Althusius und die Entwicklung der naturrechtlichen Staatstheorie: Zugleich ein Beitrag zur Geschichte der Rechtssystematik*, 2nd ed. (Breslau: Verlag Marcus, 1902).

51. See, for example, section 3 of the *Virginia Bill of Rights*: "That government is or ought to be instituted for the common benefit, protection and security of the people, nation or community." "People," "nation," "community" are, thus, thought of as *preceding* the institution of government.

presuppositions for the legitimate exercise of individual freedom. A famous example is John Stuart Mill, who, though advocating divorce, declares it much more difficult and problematic for spouses with children, the existence of whom, according to Mill, decisively restricts their parents' autonomy.[52]

Far from being anarchical, classical liberalism was embedded in the evidences of social reality, like the values of marriage and the family, the importance of education, cultural values, and the value of human life. It was exactly the enlightenment's codification of civil and penal law that extended at the end of the eighteenth and at the beginning of the nineteenth century the protection of human life back to the moment of conception. So, classical liberalism conceived society as promoting the interests not only of individual persons but also of natural, pre-political, basic social unities. It is only a more recent phenomenon that—as a consequence of a pluralism and a new kind of solipsistic, sometimes even egomaniac, preference-individualism that puts into question the very bases of society—principles of political liberalism are applied to the nonpolitical presuppositions of society. This contributes to the corruption of the very social basis of liberal constitutionalism itself and its public philosophy.

Historically, thus, liberal constitutionalism and its ethos of freedom presupposed a certain consensus about the basics of a human society. Though liberal constitutionalism had yet to be complemented by the ethos of *equality* of basic liberties and opportunities through democratization, liberal constitutionalism was in practice never an ideology of simple individualistic self-realization. Individualism was, in its historical context, a valuable idea directed against the idea of a state whose power was not under control and that not only considered citizens as its property but also purported to paternalistically know their interests and to provide—in most cases, ineffectively—for their felicity.

The Ethos of Constitutional Democracy and Rawls's Theory of Public Reason

Rawls's Idea of "Political Liberalism" and Its Mistaken Premise: An Inadequate Concept of "Human Society"

As I have argued in the preceding section, the political ethos of modernity is an ethos of peaceful coexistence, of liberty, and of justice in the sense

---

52. *On Liberty,* ch. 5 (London: J. M. Dent, 1972), 158ff.

of equality of liberty. It is essential for this kind of political ethos and for a public reason shaped by it that, first, questions and doctrines about the realization of the highest moral values, such as the attainment of happiness, religious truth, and eternal salvation, are excluded from the realm of the political, so that their conflictive potential is neutralized.

Secondly, it is part of this ethos that it contains (1) a moral obligation of citizens to accept the outcomes of the legitimate political process even where they contradict their wishes, their personal interests, or even their convictions, not about the good in the comprehensive and higher sense, but also about those matters that are included in the political agenda, and (2) the disposition to reverse such decisions only and exclusively by the peaceful and legal means provided by the constitution.

It is not, however, a part of this ethos—but rather contradicts it—to exclude, on principle, from public reason basic questions *about the nature of society* and, therefore, about what *naturally* makes human persons to be social beings; these are not genuinely "metaphysical" but empirical questions. At least *some* basic affirmations about human beings and the nature of human society necessarily do not interfere with the logic of public justification and public reason; they do not, as comprehensive doctrine may, compete with political conceptions of justice. They express what *naturally* forms the basic structure of society and, therefore, is at the root of the phenomenon of the political. Consequently, a priori there can be no valid public reason why corresponding values should not be politically privileged or publicly endorsed. Such are the value of human life in every stage of its development, the dignity of the person, the reproductive marital union of male and female and the family rooted in it, and also basic local communities that spring from the natural need of division of labor and communication. They are natural in the sense that the very possibility of political society depends on them, and any sound political conception of justice must include and serve them.

To put what has been outlined so far in a schematic order, the political ethos of modernity is shaped by the following two basic features, the first of which, however, has (albeit limited) *political* priority over the second:

1. An ethos of peaceful coexistence, liberty, and justice, which includes

    a. the acknowledgment of a distinction between what is politically fundamental and what is morally (and religiously) highest, and the acknowledgment of the priority of the former over the latter;

b. the willingness of citizens to respect and accept, within certain limits, the outcome of the constitutional political and legal decision-making procedures, even when these outcomes do not fully correspond to or, in certain limits, contradict their own convictions, not only on what is of highest value, but also on what is politically fundamental (this is a certain priority of positive law); and

c. a fundamental engagement for equality, at least in the sense of the equality of basic liberties, which is the idea of reciprocity.

2. The conviction that politics and therefore any publicly endorsed conception of justice and public reason are in the service of *some* basic goods that are prior to politics and define its scope. These include:

a. basic liberties and rights of the individual;

b. respect for the basic and naturally given characteristics of human society—and, therefore, the naturally social character of human existence—and a thereby defined political common good, in the service of which every political organization of society and public reason is to be put; which is, as we will see, tantamount to respect for natural law, *as far as it is politically relevant.*

Now, the problem of most forms of contemporary theories of liberalism[53] and especially of John Rawls's "Political liberalism" is to be found on level (2b). Rawls's theory lacks an adequate concept of society and the human person *as a naturally social being.* His concept of "free and equal citizens" is already a result of political constructivism that makes abstraction from what persons naturally are as social beings and, therefore, also as citizens.

Already in *A Theory of Justice,* Rawls defines society as a "more or less self-sufficient association of persons" and then as a "cooperative venture for mutual advantage," of course, "of persons."[54] That society is a cooperative venture for mutual advantage over time is certainly true and intuitively acceptable; but what is certainly not true is that "society" can be described as simply a cooperative venture *of individual citizens.* Politics refers not only to "individual citizens" as "free and equal," but also to citizens as naturally social beings.[55] Politics refers moreover to what "citizens" also are: parents,

---

53. There are important exceptions, like Joseph Raz's *The Morality of Freedom* (Oxford: Oxford University Press, 1986) and in a certain way also antineutralist positions like William A. Galston's, *Liberal Purposes: Goods, Virtues, and Diversity in the Liberal State* (Cambridge: Cambridge University Press, 1991).

54. *A Theory of Justice* (Cambridge, Mass.: Harvard University Press, 1971), 4.

55. A similar defect seems to me to characterize Ronald Dworkin's fundamental emphasis on

family members, children (even unborn), property owners, neighbors, part-ners in business and other kinds of exchange and cooperation correspond-ing to the elementary fact of division of labor. Politics also refers, finally, to the social units in which this social dimension of human persons *naturally* unfolds (although they may be natural and elementary in different degrees). Thus, by defining "society" in his way, Rawls illegitimately makes abstrac-tion from the reality of society as it is—to adopt a contractarian terminology —in "the state of nature." He only considers society as political and, thus, as a result of political constructivism. This is at odds with classical liberal methodology based on contract theory, which always aimed at securing by political structures the *pre-political,* that is, natural social essentials. Al-though methodological individualism is typical for contractarianism, the interests of these individuals were always thought to be shaped by what in the "state of nature" was essential for persons as social beings.

It is true that sometimes Rawls calls a "well-ordered society" a "union of social unions,"[56] and he acknowledges "the social nature" of man, because we "need one another as partners" in our life.[57] Rawls even accepts the fam-ily as a, if not the, basic unit of society, mentioning it together with "friend-ships, and other groups" as "social unions."[58] In his later essay, "The Idea of Public Reason Revisited," he finally equates the family to all other forms of voluntary associations, "churches or universities, professional or scien-tific associations, business firms or labor unions."[59] This, however, seems to be quite unreasonable. It contradicts basic empirical facts about the repro-ductive nature of the marital union and about the family. The family is not voluntary: nobody has chosen his parents or his family, nor has he chosen to be born. And, inversely, parents do not choose their offspring. The family clearly is not a voluntary association; and marriage, though voluntary, is not associative.

The marital union, though being voluntary, is the origin of society not only causally and temporarily, but in a natural way, and it shapes what hu-man society basically is: an ordered multitude rooted in the reproductive union of male and female.[60] Thus, marital union, its extension through pro-

---

"equal respect and concern," which also only refers to individual citizens; see for example Dworkin's *Taking Rights Seriously* (London: Duckworth, 1978), 272ff.

56. For example, *Theory,* 525.   57. Ibid., 522–23.

58. Ibid., 525.

59. "The Idea of Public Reason Revisited," §5.2, in Rawls, *The Law of Peoples,* 158.

60. This cannot be said of same-sex unions: they have no relation to the natural constitution of so-

creation to becoming a family, its goals and goods, created and transmitted by it, form the naturally basic structure of society. To refer, therefore, to "society" as simply a cooperative venture of "free and equal" individual citizens is, so it seems to me, incomplete and reductive in a way that makes it misleading and perverts the very concept of the "political," which, also in Rawls thought, is shaped by reference to the "social."

In a significant section in which Rawls argues that society is "neither a community nor an association," it becomes clear that his concept of society is clearly reductive.[61] This is so not because Rawls denies that societies have "final ends and aims," as associations typically have, or that societies have a shared comprehensive conception of the good, which is typical for communities.[62] Rawls is right in emphasizing that we do not join society "at the age of reason, as we might join an association," but are "born into society where we will lead a complete life."[63] Nothing is truer than that. The problem is that when talking in this context about "society," Rawls means the "well-ordered democratic society,"[64] that is to say, he is speaking of society *already shaped by a political conception of justice:* the society of citizens or political society.

Now, when we are born we are certainly born into political society, becoming thus citizens of a determinate state. However, this is neither our first nor our entire social identity; first we are born as children of determinate parents and as members of a specific family, a social reality that logically precedes one's becoming a citizen. We also belong to determinate local communities that are all prior to political society and *naturally* exist with a proper aim and a specific nature before civil or political society is well-ordered by a political conception of justice. The latter must take into account *these* pre-political social realities. It cannot reconstruct them as parts of the basic structure of society by a political conception of justice elaborated on the idea that the only preexisting reality to such a conception is "free and equal" individual citizens. Any well-ordered political society is essentially subsidiary to, and must be respectful toward, *what naturally constitutes its citizens as social beings.*

Therefore, in my view the basic flaw of Rawls's original position is not

---

ciety, because they are not reproductive. If they naturally were reproductive, things would be different. Yet, this would also be a different world and not the one we are living in.

61. *Political Liberalism*, Lecture 1, § 7, 40–43.

62. Ibid., 41–42.   63. Ibid., 41.

64. Ibid., 40.

the "veil of ignorance." The problem is not the basic assumption that in order to shape or adopt a principle of justice the participants must abstract
from their own identity. The problem is rather that they are made out to represent exclusively individual citizens as "free and equal" and their interests.
In effect, they are allowed to represent themselves only as individuals, and
not as representatives of what, in such an original position, should be represented *as well:* the basic natural social unions to which belong above and
before all the marital union and the family. The reason for this is that the
principles of justice to be decided on in the original position refer to a real
social world—although nobody knows his own place in it—and not to a fictitious universe, or a social universe yet to be created by individual persons
and shaped by the logic of something like the original position.

This criticism is not implicitly to deny that in an ontological way we
exist only as individual persons, and that *as citizens*—on the level of politically organized society—we have to be thought of and recognized as free
and equal (this is the aim of classical contractarianism); nor do I mean to
reject, on principle, Rawls's political concept of the person.[65] Yet, a publicly endorsed political conception of justice must refer to, and politics generally is called to deal with, human beings as they are in reality; that is,
as fundamentally social beings that naturally are related to each other in
very determined forms that are part of the nature of human society. And
this means that any reasonable political conception of justice and of public reason must consider that the identity of citizens is shaped not only by
their political condition as "free and equal," but also by those facts through
which they naturally become social beings—and such, before all, is the reproductive marital union of male and female, and with it the family springing from and founded on this union. They, therefore, are presuppositions
and integral parts of any reasonable political conception of justice.[66]

What I have said has nothing to do with advocating a "comprehensive"
doctrine of the good or of moral values. What I am talking about is simply
a fundamental part of any form of reasonableness that starts with the basic

65. Ibid., 29ff. See also "Justice as Fairness: Political Not Metaphysical" (1985), in Rawls, *Collected Papers*, ed. Samuel Freeman (Cambridge, Mass.: Harvard University Press 1999), 388–414.

66. Surprisingly, in *Theory*, 137, Rawls says about the parties in the original position: "It is taken for granted, however, that they know the general facts about human society." This is an important affirma-
tion that does not, however, seem to prevent Rawls from exclusively considering as "facts about human society" what concerns citizens as free and equal *individuals*. In Rawls's theory, the pre-political values to be recognized by the parties in the original position are the "primary goods," which exclusively are goods of persons thought of as individual citizens.

facts of our existence as real human beings in the real world we are living in. To adduce against this the fact of reasonable pluralism based on the "burdens of judgment" would not make sense because it is simply unreasonable—a lack of sound judgment—to ignore that human society is originated in the reproductive union of two persons of different sex and that as citizens we all naturally have our origin in such a union. Ignorance of this kind cannot be explained by the "burdens of judgment" nor can it be explained as belonging to *reasonable* pluralism. So, some basic truths—very few, though each important—concerning the nature of society and human persons as naturally social beings cannot be excluded from a publicly endorsed political conception of justice. They certainly must be endorsed and defended by public reason. The fact that at a given moment some of these truths may be controversial does not mean that they cannot be publicly justified or should be excluded from public reason.

To illustrate my point against Rawls let me briefly go back to Bodin. In some central aspects Bodin's political thinking explicitly claims to be anti-Aristotelian. Unlike Aristotle, Bodin held that the most fundamental political good is not the perfection of moral virtue or happiness. Yet, in another most important sense, Bodin does not deviate from central suppositions of the Aristotelian conception of the *polis:* like Aristotle Bodin holds that the state and generally the domain of the public presuppose, and are in service of, social unions and realities as they exist prior to the political.

Therefore, it is significant that Bodin does not define political society as a multitude of *citizens.* The public power of the "republic," he writes, is "power of government, based on law, and sovereign, *over a multitude of families and over what is common to them.*"[67] Bodin's sovereign power is not absolute; it is limited, though not by political institutions restricting the sovereign's power, but by natural law, by the fundamental law of (in France) the *Lex salica* and, most importantly, by the social unit of the family and property, realities that are prior to, as we would say today, the "basic structure" of political society, and that shape the very nature and scope of a political conception of justice publicly endorsed.[68]

---

67. Bodin, *Six livres de la République*, 1.1.

68. It is typical that the same analytical method—to dissolve, in thought, society in its most basic components—leads Aristotle and Hobbes to a different result: Aristotle arrives at the basic unit of society as the conjugal union of male and female; for Hobbes it is the individual. Both views have their merits. The Aristotelian view is certainly closer to truth, but it is not complete either: it is excessively communitarian. Hobbes's individualism is not to be rejected as such, but because it is a one-sided

Rawls clearly departs not only from Bodin and the antiabsolutist features of his thought, but also from the liberal tradition as represented, for example, by Locke. For Locke, any social contract and the creation of community that entrusts its interests to a parliamentary government are related to a previous state of nature where the "Law of Nature" obtains and regulates human conduct. As was already mentioned before, Locke's state of nature is a state of perfect freedom, not simply of individuals, but of the reproductive unity of the family, of land owners and workers (take only chapter 5 about "Property" and chapter 6 on "Paternal Power" of the *Second Treatise*). Because—and, as it seems to me, perhaps *only* because—Rawls works with a deficient concept of society exclusively focused on the democratic and well-ordered, that is *political,* society, his entire theory not only of justice but also of political liberalism stands on one leg only and sees reality with only one eye.

Once we have acknowledged that human society is not just an association of individual persons, representing themselves, and only themselves, but that prior to the phenomenon of the political and the public there are certain natural social facts to which any reasonable conception of justice must refer and from which it also naturally receives its basic content, we will automatically find that some basic assumptions of Rawls's political liberalism—in my view correct and valuable in themselves—will yield rather different results. This applies to Rawls's "liberal principle of legitimacy," his "criterion of reciprocity," and his concept of "public reason," as well as to their mutual relation. It also is relevant for the very nature of Rawls's concept of an "overlapping consensus" and, most importantly, for the analysis of the relations between a political conception of justice and comprehensive doctrines.

Rawls's Principle of Liberal Legitimacy and the Criterion of Reciprocity

Let me, then, turn to Rawls's liberal principle of legitimacy. This principle says that "our exercise of political power is fully proper only when it is exercised in accordance with a constitution the essentials of which all citizens as free and equal may reasonably be expected to endorse in the light

---

individualism. Although it rightly declares the moral and political priority of the individual person, it wrongly excludes from its horizon that these persons are also naturally constituted as social beings (which is empirically erroneous).

of principles and ideals acceptable to their common human reason."[69] This formulation has caused discussions and provoked criticism, mainly from defenders of natural law.

John Finnis has called this principle "bafflingly ambiguous": when one says of an assertion that all citizens may be "reasonably expected to endorse it," is one "predicting the behavior of people or assessing the rational strength of the thesis?"[70] Thus, if I have correctly understood Finnis, he thinks that the ambiguity is whether constitutional essentials and corresponding contents of public reason are legitimate (1) insofar as they in effect *will be* or are at least very likely to be accepted by all reasonable citizens, or (2) insofar as they *should* be accepted by all reasonable citizens; that is, they are legitimate because those citizens who refuse to endorse them give proof of being unreasonable.

I have some difficulties in understanding these doubts because I do not see the alleged ambiguity. If the liberal principle of legitimacy is read in its wider and specific *Rawlsian* context, its meaning seems to me rather clear. In my opinion, the problem of this principle lies elsewhere. In the following I will first explain why I think that the ambiguity Finnis reproaches Rawls for does not, and cannot, exist. I then will try to make out what in Rawls's liberal principle of legitimacy such "reasonable expectation" precisely means. By this procedure we will detect where, in my view, the real crux of Rawls's liberal principle of legitimacy lies: in his (politically underdetermined) concept of "reciprocity" and its unclear relation to the concept of public reason. Notice that in some respects my criticism of Rawls comes to similar results as Finnis's, yet with significant differences regarding the evaluation of the idea of political liberalism and some practical implications of political ethics.

Let me start with the second case of what—according to Finnis—is a possible reading of the phrase "may reasonably be expected" (the meaning of "assessing the rational strength of the thesis"). Provided we assume it is this that Rawls had in mind, then the question obviously would only be postponed. To make the principle of legitimacy workable we would need additional standards of reasonableness, and so the principle of legitimacy would not settle any question. We would have to be able to distinguish rea-

<hr />

69. *Political Liberalism*, 137; see also 217.

70. John Finnis, "Abortion, Natural Law, and Public Reason," in *Natural Law and Public Reason*, ed. Robert P. George and Christopher Wolfe (Washington, D.C.: Georgetown University Press, 2000), 75–105, 79.

sonable from unreasonable substantive claims. Now, Finnis and others argue that it is most proper to natural law to provide exactly such standards of reasonableness for public reason. Therefore, so Finnis's argument runs, provided this is the meaning of Rawls's formulation, then natural-law reasons *are* public reasons.

It seems to me obvious that Rawls could never accept such a characterization of natural-law reasons as public reasons—and that the possibility of such an interpretation of the meaning of Rawls's principle must therefore be dismissed—because, according to him, it would deprive the principle of legitimacy of one of its central features, which is that the principle reflects, and works under, the condition of reasonable pluralism. "Natural law," however, with its substantial claims about the good is, so Rawls would certainly argue, itself exposed to the "burdens of judgment"; it is not, in Rawls's logic, capable of creating consensus and thus being part of public reason, but rather itself controversial and a cause of civil disagreement. Therefore, to correctly understand Rawls's liberal principle of legitimacy in the context of his "political liberalism," the second interpretation must be discarded as a possible reading of Rawls. Rawls's liberal principle of legitimacy includes a *specific* kind of reasonableness that is not dependent on any other kind of reasons except the one specifically proper to the political domain and to public reason. The point of this principle is that it purports to be part of a freestanding *moral* view of the political, as it is developed in *Political Liberalism*. This view, Rawls says, is the focus of an overlapping consensus of those endorsing it as a publicly valid political conception of justice embodied in the basic structure of society.

The first interpretation, however, that the "reasonable expectation" predicts the behavior of (reasonable) citizens and, therefore, legitimates all those political positions that in effect *will be* or are at least very likely to be accepted by all reasonable citizens seems at first sight to be a better candidate for a right understanding of Rawls's principle. Yet, if this meant to equate liberal legitimacy to the simple acceptability or foreseen acceptance of a position by a vast majority of citizens, then the liberal principle of legitimacy would simply coincide with the majority principle. But this is certainly not the way Rawls understands it. As I mentioned, Rawls's "political liberalism" is not a strategic or pragmatic conception, but purports to be a—"freestanding"—*moral* view. Although the majority principle has certainly a moral content, for Rawls foreseeing a law or a policy will be endorsed by majority is not yet sufficient to be a moral principle of public legitimation of the endorsed law or policy.

Therefore, for a moral conception of political justice to be morally legitimate, being accepted by a majority is not sufficient; according to Rawls, such a conception must be accepted additionally *for the right reasons.* These reasons must express the respect for other citizens as free and equal persons. So, the likelihood of being accepted could mean that legitimate political positions are those that in effect *will be* or are very likely to be accepted by *reasonable* people because they meet with an essential requirement of the kind of agreement and consensus that characterizes what Rawls calls the "right reasons" for endorsing a political conception of justice and statutes and laws enacted on its grounds: they are *fair,* that is, *they satisfy the criterion of reciprocity,* and this is why they may be *reasonably* expected to be accepted by virtually all *reasonable* citizens. This again means (for Rawls): if people are left to make their own choices, where there is a major disagreement such political positions do not enforce substantial values at the cost of other people's autonomy. Now, exactly this is what Rawls's concept of public reasons implies. It has been rightly criticized by natural law theorists (including Finnis), in the sense that "it almost always has the effect of making the liberal position the winner in morally charged political controversies."[71]

I would argue, however, that if this critique is true—as I think it is—it is not because of Rawls's liberal principle of legitimacy *as such,* nor because of the criterion of reciprocity *as such.* In my view, rather, the first and main problem is Rawls's already mentioned counterfactual and thus unreasonable disregard of the nature of pre-political human society and thus, of human persons not only as "free and equal" citizens but also in the dimension of what makes them naturally social beings. This is not without consequences for the specifically *political* sense of reciprocity. The second problem is how Rawls connects reciprocity with the idea of public reason (see next section).

Thus, provided we read Rawls's liberal principle of legitimacy in its proper context and as a part of his conception of political liberalism, it seems to me to have a clear and rather unambiguous meaning. The meaning of the principle of legitimacy, in fact, depends upon what Rawls understands by "reasonable." To grasp the exact Rawlsian meaning of this term

71. Robert P. George and Christopher Wolfe, eds., "Introduction," in *Natural Law and Public Reason,* 1–2.

is important for correctly—and effectively—focusing any criticism of Rawls's liberal principle of legitimacy.

With the terms "reasonable" and "reasonableness," Rawls refers to a characteristic of citizens that is specifically political and that he distinguishes from citizens' "rationality." Persons are to be called *rational* insofar as they pursue a conception of the good, seeking to employ the proper means to attain their personal goals. According to Rawls, however, one is *reasonable* when one owns a "particular form of moral sensibility that underlies the desire to engage in fair cooperation as such, and to do so on terms that others as equals might reasonably be expected to endorse."[72] This kind of reasonableness, Rawls says, is adequately expressed in the idea of reciprocity.

The idea of reciprocity for Rawls is linked to his conception of a society as a "fair system of cooperation over time, from one generation to the next."[73] People are reasonable in the sense of meeting the criterion of reciprocity "when, among equals say, they are ready to propose principles and standards as fair terms of cooperation and to abide by them willingly, given the assurance that others will likewise do."[74] So, "the reasonable is an element of the idea of society as a system of fair cooperation and that its fair terms be reasonable for all to accept is part of its idea of reciprocity."[75] The conceptions of the good, personal life plans, and so on, which persons pursue as *rational* agents, however, are comprehensive views referring to personal goals and life plans that are often mutually in conflict. It is not rationality but reasonableness that, as a political form of morality, seeks to find an overlapping consensus between them *so as to make possible society as a system of cooperation for mutual advantage over time.* A *reasonable* comprehensive view, whether it be true or not, is a view the adherents of which are disposed to peaceful political cooperation with adherents of other—with respect to their truth claims conflicting—comprehensive views.[76]

---

72. *Political Liberalism*, 51.   73. Ibid., 15.

74. Ibid., 49.   75. Ibid., 49–50.

76. In contrast to this, Rawls talks in *Political Liberalism*, 152–53, of the "rationalist believer," which, as Rawls remarks, corresponds to Joshua Cohen's "rationalist fundamentalist" as described in his "Moral Pluralism and Political Consensus," in *The Idea of Democracy*, ed. David Copp, Jean Hampton, and John E. Roemer (New York: Cambridge University Press, 1993), 270–91, 286. Such a "rationalist believer" (or "fundamentalist") is a person who wants a determined doctrine of salvation to be politically endorsed, thinks that the need of it can be rationally proven, and, thus, is not disposed to find a politically common ground of cooperation with those who do not share his religious doctrines or are nonbelievers altogether. As it seems to me, in his critique of Rawls, Robert George grossly misreads *Political Liberalism*, 152–53, thus misunderstanding the concept of "rationalist believer." Rawls applies it to the very "uncommon view" of those religious fundamentalists (or fanatics) who think that certain questions are so fundamen-

Rawls emphasizes that "being reasonable is not an epistemological idea (though it has epistemological elements). Rather it is part of a political ideal of democratic citizenship that includes the idea of public reason," because "the reasonable, in contrast with the rational, addresses the public world of others."[77] In contrast to "truth," reasonableness is essentially a political category referring to the virtue of civility, the capacity of cooperating on the basis of a shared political conception of justice despite the "practical impossibility of reaching reasonable and workable political agreement in judgment on the truth of comprehensive doctrines."[78] Constitutional essentials and the public conception of justice must be shaped in a way that allows all peacefully to cooperate for mutual advantage in society as free and equal citizens. This is also the idea of the *political* priority of the right over the good that corresponds to the idea of the *political* priority of the reasonable over the rational—without opposing them to each other—and the *political* priority of the public over the private.

It seems to me that, with this, Rawls not only expresses the modern political ethos of constitutional democracy in its quintessential form, but also formulates a principle of reasonableness that seems to be nothing other than what we all understand to be the basis of any workable and just political order. Specifically, the criterion of reciprocity must be inherent in any conception of political justice capable of creating conditions of peaceful cooperation and equal liberty. Without accepting the criterion of reciprocity and its proper reasonableness neither a peaceful public order nor constitutional democracy (*rule of law* with its procedural logic of neutrality and justice, equal basic liberties and democratic participation in government) would be possible. So, the idea underlying Rawls's liberal principle

---

tal that "the salvation of a whole people" depends on their being rightly settled; according to Rawls, the rationalist believer thinks that his comprehensive religious views about salvation "are open to and can be fully established by reason." By claiming the latter, Rawls affirms, the "rationalist believer" is mistaken because he disregards the fact of reasonable pluralism. George takes the term "rationalist believer" out of this very specific and limited context, asserting that Rawls's verdict generally applies to claims based on natural law and defended as both fundamental and open to rational and public justification. Unfortunately, large parts of George's critique of Rawls are based on this overinterpretation of the concept of a "rationalist believer." See especially Robert P. George, *In Defense of Natural Law* (Oxford: Oxford University Press, 1999), chap. 11: "Public Reason and Political Conflict: Abortion and Homosexuality," especially 202ff. (At page 202 George says: "If I understand accurately what Rawls means by 'rationalist believers', then I am something of one myself." I think George both did not accurately understand what Rawls meant and—clearly and fortunately—is far from being a "rationalist believer" himself, because as a Catholic he certainly holds that essential features of his religious convictions cannot be "fully established by reason" but can be known only by divine revelation and with the help of supernatural grace.)

77. *Political Liberalism*, 62.
78. Ibid., 63.

of legitimacy is nothing else than the expression not simply of "liberalism," but of the soul of constitutional democracy as it has developed through the last centuries of European and American history, and since then has been spreading all over the civilized world.

Yet, Rawls gives this idea a turn that is clearly hostile to "natural law" in the sense that it does not allow natural-law reasons as such—that is, on the basis of their claim of containing truth, open to everyone's understanding—to be public reasons. Before we are able to defend natural law as belonging to public reason, we therefore first have to detect those elements that in Rawls's theory create this hostility toward the public function of natural law, show them to be at odds with the liberal tradition of constitutional democracy, and so deconstruct them, without, however, jeopardizing what is the truth in Rawls's position, that is, the ethos of liberal constitutional democracy.

The real problem, therefore, is how the principles of liberal constitutional democracy, namely the idea of reciprocity, in Rawls's theory of political liberalism work. This depends on how his conception of society bears upon them. Yet, this is exactly what Rawls does not really analyze. As we have seen, he simply presupposes, in the tradition of Hobbes, a concept of society composed by free and equal individuals and by nothing but individuals. The question, then, is how in Rawlsian political liberalism the criterion or reciprocity relates to public reason. Let me now turn to this important question.

The Criterion of Reciprocity and Public Reason

The introduction to the 1996 paperback *Political Liberalism* is revealing, in that it shows Rawls's argument to be circular and, in an important aspect, self-defeating. In this new introduction, the "criterion of reciprocity" is defined as follows: "our exercise of political power is proper only when we sincerely believe that the reasons we offer for our political action may reasonably be accepted by other citizens as a justification of those actions." Rawls emphasizes that the liberal principle of legitimacy is *derived* from this understanding of reciprocity. This means that only what—on the level of the constitutional structure itself and of particular laws and statutes enacted in accordance with that structure—satisfies the criterion of reciprocity is in a liberal sense legitimately enforceable upon the totality of citizens.[79]

---

79. Ibid., xliv. Later in his above quoted paper (on page 85)—in my view too late—and in a different context Finnis mentions Rawls's criterion of reciprocity and rightly calls it "the source of the liberal principle of legitimacy."

Now the following question arises: does to "sincerely believe that the reasons we offer for our political action may reasonably be accepted by other citizens as a justification of those actions" mean that—in order to meet with the criterion of reciprocity—we must expect others to be able to *accept* our reasons in the sense of *agreeing* with them?[80] In my view this is impossible; in Rawls's own logic such an expectation would be utterly unreasonable and contradict the very fact of reasonable pluralism and the existence of burdens of judgment. Reciprocity cannot and must not demand so much. Moreover, it would simply not work because then *any* disagreement would be a cause for abstaining from *any* legal enforcement in the sphere of that controversial issue. Yet, such a minimalist practice of legal enforcement has nothing to do with liberalism but rather resembles anarchism, or at least an extreme form of libertarianism.

Consequently, the criterion of reciprocity can mean only that the reasons by which we justify the exercise of political power and coercion on others must be reasons *of the kind* that is proper to public reason and must therefore, as such reasons, be acceptable for reasonable citizens, even if they do not agree with them. (In case someone does not accept this kind of reason, this, then, would mean not that the *reasons* are unreasonable, but that this person, who does not accept them, is unreasonable.) This is exactly what Rawls says in his later "Idea of Public Reason Revisited," and it is a crucial point: Rawls tells us that public reason is "a view about *the kind of reasons* on which citizens are to rest their political cases in making their political justifications to one another when they support laws and policies that invoke the coercive powers of government concerning fundamental political questions."[81]

Now, this implies an important point about the logical status of the criterion of reciprocity: if we do not want simply to reduce "public reason" to the "criterion of reciprocity," the latter cannot be what defines the very content of public reason. Rather, the converse: what "reciprocity" means

---

80. Notice that this question is different from the questions Finnis had asked. It does not refer to the meaning of the phrase "may reasonably be *expected*" (to be accepted or endorsed by other citizens). The problem I am dealing with here is not a possible ambiguity of the term "reasonable expectation," but the problem of the (political) meaning in Rawls's theory of political liberalism of the concept of *reciprocity* (and thus the conditions of reasonable acceptability of our reasons given for determinate policies or laws). Moreover, my question is situated not at the level of the liberal principle of legitimacy (which, as such, does not seem to me to be the problem), but at the level of the "criterion of reciprocity," which is the rationale of the liberal principle of legitimacy. In my view, the real problem is the way Rawls uses—and in my opinion politically misuses—the concept of "reciprocity."

81. "The Idea of Public Reason Revisited," 165–66 (the emphasis is added).

must be derived from the logic and content of public reason; that is, in Rawls's words, it must be derived from the "view about the kind of reasons on which citizens are to rest their political cases in making their political justifications to one another when they support laws and policies that invoke the coercive powers of government." To assert that this view and this "kind of reasons" alone are the criterion of reciprocity would be ridiculous. To assert it would render public reason a politically empty formula.

Hence, what *in a political context* "reciprocity" means, and how it works, cannot be understood independently from, and prior to, what "public reason" is fundamentally about. The concept of public reason—or of public reasons generally—has a foundational function and gives to the criterion of reciprocity its specifically political meaning. Consequently, the idea of public reason and of what public reasons properly are must be defined independently from, and prior to, the criterion of reciprocity. Otherwise the content of public reason would simply be reduced to a vague and general idea of reciprocity without further qualification by a view about the *kind of reasons* that are proper to the public and political domain. Such a reduction of public reason to the simple idea of unqualified reciprocity would be politically unreasonable. It would mean to reduce public reason to something like the golden rule, and nothing more. Such a form of public reason wouldn't work because it would not allow enforcing anything if it happens to be in contrast to the preferences of some citizens.

"Reciprocity," therefore, must be politically qualified. Of course, the idea of "reciprocity" *as such* is perfectly understandable independently of the idea of public reason. But this is not yet a *political* concept of reciprocity; it would be much too broad and underdetermined. Obviously, the same obtains for the liberal principle of legitimacy and the concept of "reasonableness": as Rawls says, it is derived from the concept of reciprocity, and this is why the principle must be primarily defined in terms not of reciprocity as such, but of the idea of public reason.

So, in order to know what kind of reasons satisfy the criterion of reciprocity—and what, in a political sense, therefore is fully reasonable—we must previously determine what public reason and its basic contents are. Yet, Rawls does not do that. In some passages of his "The Idea of Public Reason Revisited" he instead does exactly the opposite: he affirms that the content of public reason simply is defined by the criterion of reciprocity.[82]

82. Ibid., 136–37, 141, 175.

In the 1996 introduction to *Political Liberalism* he affirms that his political liberalism is "a freestanding political conception having its own intrinsic (moral) political ideal expressed by the criterion of reciprocity."[83] So, in effect this criterion has in Rawls's theory the function of a kind of joker or of a *Deus ex machina*. It is used in a politically unqualified and uncontrollable way, independent from a previously determined concept of public reason. The concept of public reason does not in Rawls's theory perform its properly foundational role; it becomes instead dependent on the simple idea of reciprocity, which *as such* has no specific *political* content. Without being embedded in a concept of public reason and thus in a specifically *political* conceptual framework, it arbitrarily works as a leverage for the preferences of individuals conceived as "free and equal citizens." It tends to reduce society to an aggregate of individuals who pursue their personal preferences, and public reason to a means of furthering such preferences, often at the expense of the political common good of society.[84] (A recent and actual case for this is the claim to equate in the name of liberal nondiscrimination "same-sex marriages" to the naturally reproductive marital union of male and female, which, however, as a fundamental part of the political common good of society cannot be reasonably equated in public reason to the naturally nonreproductive private sexual preference of individual citizens.)[85]

Since "public reason" necessarily includes reference to certain elementary and politically relevant tasks that spring from the nature of human society and of persons as naturally social beings, the meaning of reciprocity must include not only considerations of the interest of individuals persons as free and equal, but also of the natural reproductive union of male and female, of the family and its educational task, as well as the interests of lo-

83. *Political Liberalism*, xlvii.

84. This is why (as already mentioned before) it has mostly the effect of "of making the liberal position the winner in morally charged political controversies" (George and Wolfe, *Natural Law and Public Reason*, 1–2). Most interestingly and somewhat paradoxically, in his *Justice as Fairness: A Restatement*, ed. Erin Kelly (Cambridge, Mass.: Harvard University Press, 2001), 90–91, Rawls defines public reason and the liberal principle of legitimacy without any reference to reciprocity! He instead says: "Citizens must be able, then, to present to one another *publicly acceptable reasons* for their political views in cases raising fundamental political questions" (emphasis added). This means, as Rawls asserts in the preceding paragraph, that political power should be exercised "in ways that all citizens can publicly endorse *in the light of their own reason*" (emphasis added). Rawls seems to have recognized that the criterion of reciprocity alone is too shallow a principle to define public reason and liberal legitimacy. He seems to have, at least intuitively, acknowledged that the definition of "public reason" is prior to the definition of (political) "reciprocity."

85. With "naturally" I mean "by its own nature," "essentially"; though heterosexual unions in some cases may not be reproductive, unlike homosexual relations they are still sexual relations of a reproductive *kind*.

cal communities—basic and quasi-natural structures of the division of labor (with which we perhaps can also count in, in some way, enterprises, but I do not want to go further into this). All this is basically relevant for shaping the meaning and content of public reason and, therefore, essentially belongs to political reasonableness.

Rawls explicitly rules out such a conception of public reason. For Rawls, public reason serves the individual citizen as "free and equal," and this is the way his original position too is designed. Political reasonableness seems to be confined to its function of securing cooperation between "free and equal" human beings under the condition of not only religious, but also deep-rooted, radical moral pluralism, that is, *overall* disagreement about what is "good" for human beings and for society. (Of course, such a description of pluralism is exaggerated; it could never realistically be defended as "reasonable" pluralism and work as a basis for juridical restrictions on public reason, although Rawls underpins his theory with exactly such an exaggerated and, at the end, morally self-defeating concept of pluralism.)

This, again, is why I think that the problem of the original position is not the "veil of ignorance." The problem of Rawls's original position is rather that the participants represent only individual "free and equal" citizens as well as their interests and preferences *as individual citizens*. In my view and to say it again, this is unreasonable. Even though a participant in the original position may not know, for example, his own sexual orientation, it would be unreasonable for him not to privilege in the framing of the principles of justice the heterosexual union. It would be unreasonable, because it is generally reasonable also for homosexual citizens to affirm that the marital union of male and female is the reproductive foundation of society and that they themselves owe their existences to such a union, and that, therefore, unlike homosexual partnerships, the marital union has a political relevance that same-sex unions are entirely lacking. Failing to acknowledge this is failing to acknowledge the social function and, thus, the political relevance of sexuality.

To assert, therefore, any violation of "reciprocity" in this context would mean to contradict basic social, and socially relevant, biological facts, which obtain in a Rawlsian original position. As with many other basic truths about the real world we are living in, they cannot be reasonably hidden by the veil of ignorance.[86] After all, participants in the original position should not be

---

86. Let me quote again what Rawls says in *Theory*, 137, about the parties in the original position: "It is taken for granted, however, that they know the general facts about human society."

ignorant to an extent that renders them *unreasonable*. The veil of ignorance should serve only to exclude personal partiality. It is of course true that nobody should be treated differently as a citizen or, say, as a member of a university simply because of his sexual orientation; but this does not mean that from a political and legal point of view heterosexual and homosexual life-unions should be treated equally, nor can it mean that a publicly endorsed political conception of justice should not express a clear and privileged interest in promoting and protecting the reproductive marital union of male and female and the family springing from it.[87]

To put it briefly: the political and legal conception of citizens as "free" and "equal" must be orientated and adjusted—and in some cases restricted —by substantial pre-political values that precede and necessarily shape any reasonable political conception of justice. Though these politically relevant pre-political values may under given circumstances be controversial, they cannot be excluded on principle from the domain of public reason, because this contradicts the very idea of public reason (provided we acknowledge the genuinely political meaning of this idea and do not make it unilaterally and exclusively dependent on an idea of reciprocity that remains politically unqualified).

Something analogous applies to the question of unborn life: all the participants in the original position know that at one time they were not-yet-born human beings. At that time they could not participate in the decision about the basic structure of society. Therefore, it would be, from the outset, fundamentally unjust, unfair, and unreasonable not to represent in the original position also the interests of the unborn (as it would be unjust not to represent the interests of children). That is to say that the status of embryos and fetuses—like the status of living human beings of the species *Homo sapiens* generally—has to be cleared *before* entering into the original position and presupposed; it cannot be a matter of deliberation in the very process of establishing principles of justice, or even afterward; this would be unfair.[88]

---

87. In *Justice as Fairness*, 87, Rawls says that to represent citizens as "free and equal" in the original position they have to be situated "symmetrically," respecting the "basic precept of formal equality" which, as he adds, corresponds to "Sidgwick's principle of equity: *those similar in all relevant respects are to be treated similarly*" (emphasis added). Nothing truer than that! This is why it is difficult to understand why in a political conception of justice heterosexual and homosexual unions should be treated equally.

88. This is not to disregard the right of women's self-determination. It only means that this right cannot be respected by simultaneously disregarding the life of the unborn, which, however, is the case in the pro-choice position. In order to value the right of self-determination of women other ways must be found. Thereby we should not forget that also getting pregnant unwillingly already is a lack of a

Although in his later writing on public reason Rawls conceded that even religious beliefs, as long as they are promoted on the grounds of public reasons, may be promoted in the public sphere, there is nevertheless a tendency in Rawls's conception of public reason toward such concessions only insofar as they satisfy the criterion of reciprocity as *he* understands it, that is, referred exclusively to individual citizens conceived as "free and equal." But this is wrong and, as we have seen, by no means genuinely *liberal*. Even if we concede that comprehensive doctrines and their components may not be legally enforced except where there are specifically public reasons for such an enforcement, these positions are not to be excluded from public reasons. They contain not only the essence of what politics is called to deal with, but the nature of the reality of human society to which political justice refers.

The criterion of reciprocity, thus, cannot possibly have the task of singling out which basic doctrines about society, the union of male and female, and the family can legitimately be a content of public reason. On the contrary, these basic empirical truths about society as a cooperative venture over time rather restrict the very criterion of reciprocity. They bestow on this criterion its properly political meaning and allow applying it properly in the political domain as a *political* criterion of legitimacy and justice for coercively imposed legal norms and public policies.[89]

The Relation between Political Conceptions and Comprehensive Doctrines: The Case of the Family

The way in which Rawls conceives the relationship between public reason and the criterion of reciprocity seems to me to be the reason why Rawls misconstrues the relation between what he calls a "political conception" and "comprehensive doctrines." At the very beginning of *Political Liberalism* Rawls asserts that a conception is not "political" but "comprehensive" "when it includes conceptions of what is of value in human life, and ideals of personal character, as well as ideals of friendship *and of familial and as-*

---

woman's self-determination. Pregnancy is not a natural event but ordinarily the outcome of a freely chosen human act, performed by self-determined and morally autonomous citizens.

89. Calling these basic truths "empirical" does not mean that they do not already include a value that is also *morally* relevant. This is so, because they are not only empirical—that is, facts about the world—but in their specific context they are also *basic*. The same is true of other basic empirical claims, such as the natural tendency to self-preservation or the need of nourishment. In their context, they formulate fundamental human goods that include, or are the basis for, moral value. Empirical claims, thus, may include moral value; it depends on their "location" and relevance. We should generally abstain from opposing "facts" to "values."

sociational relationships, and much else that is to inform our conduct, and in the limit to our life as a whole." He adds that a conception is "fully comprehensive when it comprises all recognized values and virtues within one rather articulated system" and it is only "partially comprehensive when it comprises a number of, but by no means all, *nonpolitical values and virtues* and is rather loosely articulated."[90]

This is revealing because Rawls says that a political conception must not refer to *nonpolitical* values[91] and also because he again equates the family to other associational relationships, declaring the family to be an ideal that cannot be part of a political conception. Both statements are to be rejected because political values necessarily refer to the non- or pre-political domain and corresponding values and because the reproduction of society is clearly one of the most prominent *political* values. The "political" cannot come out of nothing, and political justice, though being specifically political, does not *create* what it refers to, but is political in the *way* it refers to what is pre-political. Precisely a liberal conception of politics must refer to genuinely non-political or pre-political values such as privacy, property, individual liberty, and the like. Politics must refer to the reality of human society as it is: as composed not only of individual persons, but also of natural societal unions. The reproductive union of male and female and the family simply are the origin of society and their future; they belong to the very structure of it. This, obviously, does not apply to churches, universities, syndicates, and the like. These may all contribute to the perfection of society; but they are neither a part of its very nature nor what society is naturally rooted in.

Rawls seems to be fully aware that a theory of justice and of political liberalism must be grounded on some basic assumptions about the nature of society. Yet, Rawls gives no reason why he defines society simply as a system of cooperation of *individual citizens;* and he is not able to explain, and does not try to explain, how citizens can deliberate about a political conception of justice to be publicly endorsed in a world in which there exists no other socially and politically relevant reality except "free and equal" in-

90. *Political Liberalism,* 13 (emphasis added).
91. See also "The Idea of Public Reason Revisited," 144: "a value is properly political only when the social form is itself political: when it is realized, say, in part of the basic structure and its political and social institutions." In one sense this is obviously true, and even a truism; but it does not imply that to be politically relevant a value must not be pre-political: there are some pre-political values that become political exactly because they essentially bear upon politics. Such is, of course, the reproductive role of the family (based on the marital union between male and female).

dividuals with their personal preferences. Of course, this reveals the already mentioned problem of social-contract theories. Yet as long as contractarianism—as in the case of Locke—is not taken too seriously and is not developed in too rigorous a way, it does little harm and considerable good, making it clear that political society has to serve citizens, and not the reverse, and that in the common good there is a priority of the individual person over community. In the case of Rawls, however, contract theory is not so harmless. Here contractarianism turns out to be a device for properly constructing a conception of political justice ex nihilo—I mean, from a *social* nothing, basing the construction exclusively on the concept of "free and equal" citizens. In such an attempt of radical "Kantian constructivism," as Rawls calls it, the shortcomings of contractarianism do cause serious problems, rendering contract theory (for the reasons already given) counterintuitive and self-defeating.

I am aware that Rawls (mainly in his later writings) emphasized that the family belongs to the basic structure of society and, therefore, that it must be regulated by the publicly endorsed political conception of justice. In "The Idea of Public Reason Revisited" a whole section (§ 5) is dedicated to the family. There Rawls effectively acknowledges that the family is "the basis of the orderly production and reproduction of society and its culture from one generation to the next," and that "reproductive labor is socially necessary labor" and that "the family must ensure the nurturing and development of such citizens in appropriate numbers to maintain an enduring society."[92] Most curiously, however, in a rather strange footnote (no. 60), Rawls adds that "no particular form of family (monogamous, heterosexual, or otherwise) is required by a political conception of justice so long as the family is arranged to fulfill these tasks effectively and doesn't run afoul of other political values." Particularly "gay and lesbian rights and duties," says Rawls, may be dealt with on this principle: as long as these "are consistent with orderly family life and the education of children, they are, *ceteris paribus,* fully admissible."

The absurdity of this latter claim is so evident that one wonders whether its author is informed about the basic facts of the origin of human life (which, of course, he is). How can sexual copulation in same-sex unions take part in "reproductive labor"? Of course, Rawls is perfectly acquaint-

92. "The Idea of Public Reason Revisited," 157.

ed with the basic facts about the origin of human life, and this is why in his footnote he simply speaks of "orderly family life and the education of children," omitting precisely what is most typical and naturally character- istic of heterosexual unions: "reproductive labor" (thinking, perhaps, that same-sex unions can get children through adoption or reproductive tech- nology). Rawls seems to intentionally overlook the obvious: that, gener- ally speaking, without heterosexual reproductive acts there is nothing like "family life" and "education of children"—because there are no children and, without them, no mutual cooperation of citizens *over time*. Civil law cannot possibly disregard this fact and equate unions that are by nature of a nonreproductive kind to the naturally reproductive kind of union that we call "marriage."[93]

To deny that reproduction is a political value and, therefore, a neces- sary part of a political conception of justice, would simply be to deny that the existence of society as cooperation of citizens *over time* is politically rel- evant and a political value. This, however, would contradict the very basis of Rawls's political theory and the fundamental role his theory gives to the idea of society as a fair system of cooperation over time.

Thus, to achieve his goal of grounding his concept of public reason on reciprocity between single citizens and their "rights and duties," Rawls must manipulate or disregard the basic natural facts of society. It is true, he does not disregard the family as belonging to the basic structure of society; but he disregards it as a pre-political reality that is not created in the pro- cess of establishing the basic political structure of society and that enters in it as something that not only is regulated *by* the publicly endorsed political conception of justice, but firstly *regulates,* that is, shapes this conception and thus the content of public reason and, in consequence, the specifically political application of the criterion of reciprocity in the sense that regard- ing *reproduction,* partners in hetero- or homosexual unions are not to be

93. A possible objection to this might be that "nature" is a sufficient guarantee that most people are heterosexual and will, or can, reproduce sexually; hence, so the objections says, there is no need to deprive homosexuals of the benefits of marriage. I think this objection simply misses the point: the point is that there is simply no *political* (or public) reason to bestow on homosexuals the benefits of marriage. Marriage possesses a legally privileged status because there is a specific public reason for it that does not apply to homosexual unions: its naturally reproductive character. On the other hand, law should not prevent homosexuals from living together according to their private preferences, as ever they happen to wish (what citizens do in their bedrooms must not be a concern of the law). Likewise it should not impede other persons from living together or forming naturally nonreproductive communities of any kind (such as female or male religious communities), provided they do not interfere with public order.

considered to be equal, and thus, in order to uphold justice, they have also to be treated unequally by civil law.[94]

Constitutional Democracy, Public Reason, and the Political Recognition of Natural Law

Natural Law, Public Reason, the Domain of the Political, and the Concept of "Common Good"

What I have outlined so far was obviously a natural-law argument. Although natural law is not public reason, it shapes in a fundamental way its content. Natural law is *prior* to public reason in such a way that public reasons, though being different from natural-law reasons, include natural law. But public reason includes natural law in a restricted and limited way, that is, it includes natural law insofar as it is politically relevant. Yet, what exactly is the criterion for "political relevance"?

Natural law is politically relevant insofar as it refers to the common good of political society. Take such a simple case as murder. Natural law commands us not to commit murder because this is intrinsically unjust and contrary to human good. But this alone is not the reason why we think it reasonably repressed by criminal law. Positive law does not repress certain acts simply because they are immoral or opposed to natural law. The reason why murder—deliberate homicide—is declared to be a crime and punished by public authority is a specifically *political* one: it is necessary in order to allow citizens to live together in peace and security and, thus, to prevent society from disintegrating. Thus, already for Aquinas the reason why murder must be prohibited by positive law is its relevance for the "common good of justice and peace."[95] Aquinas, therefore, says human criminal law is re-

---

94. A similar point is made by Michael Pakaluk, "The Liberalism of John Rawls: A Brief Exposition," in *Liberalism at the Crossroads: An Introduction to Contemporary Liberal Political Theory and Its Critics*, ed. Christopher Wolfe, 2nd ed. (Lanham, Md.: Rowman and Littlefield, 2003), 1–19, 14. *Pace* Pakaluk, however, I think that to settle what counts as the basic structure of society no *comprehensive* doctrine on the family is needed, but only some basic empirical truths that, for a person normally informed about the basic facts of the origin of human life and "reproductive labor," rather seem to me to belong to common sense.

95. *Summa Theologiae* I-II, q. 96, a. 3: "Nevertheless human law does not prescribe concerning all the acts of every virtue: but only in regard to those that are ordainable to the common good—either immediately, as when certain things are done directly for the common good, or mediately, as when a lawgiver prescribes certain things pertaining to good order, whereby the citizens are directed in the upholding of the common good of justice and peace." See also I-II, q. 98, a. 1: "For the end of human law is the temporal tranquility of the state, which end law effects by directing external actions, as regards those evils which might disturb the peaceful condition of the state."

stricted to those vices "without the prohibition of which the preservation of society would not be possible—just as human law forbids murder, theft, and similar things."[96] The rest of the enforcement of natural law is left to God's judgment. According to Aquinas, therefore, "human laws leave many things unpunished, which according to the Divine judgment are sins, as, for example, simple fornication; because human law does not exact perfect virtue from man, for such virtue belongs to few and cannot be found in so great a number of people as human law has to direct."[97] But general human imperfection is not the only reason. Aquinas also asserts that human laws are *on principle* limited to matters of justice, along with, in fact, stating a kind of concept of "public reason" (which is surprisingly close to Mill's harm principle):

> Now human law is ordained for one kind of community, and the Divine law for another kind. Because human law is ordained for the civil community, implying mutual duties of man and his fellows: and men are ordained to one another by outward acts, whereby men live in communion with one another. This life in common of man with man pertains to justice, whose proper function consists in directing the human community. Wherefore human law makes precepts only about acts of justice; and if it commands acts of other virtues, this is only in so far as they assume the nature of justice, as the Philosopher explains. (Ethic. v, 1)[98]

Natural law forbids adultery, sodomy, or lying: these are as natural practical reason prescribes, intrinsically immoral acts. But this does not mean that the natural-law reasons forbidding these acts are also public reasons and that corresponding moral norms should be legally enforced or corresponding vices repressed by the criminal law. To be apt for public justification, natural-law reasons must first be converted into public reasons. They become public reasons only insofar as they can be justified in terms of referring to the common good of political society. So, for example, it is forbidden both by natural law and by public reason to lie in court or in making contracts, as generally fraud is forbidden by law. So, the whole set of public reasons contains a part of the whole set of natural-law reasons, or saying it in another way, some (but not all) natural-law reasons are, because of

96. *ST* I-II, q. 96, a. 2.

97. *ST* II-II, q. 69, a. 2 ad 1. See also q. 77, a. 1 ad 1: "human law is given to the people among whom there are many lacking virtue, and it is not given to the virtuous alone. Hence human law was unable to forbid all that is contrary to virtue; and it suffices for it to prohibit whatever is destructive of human intercourse, while it treats other matters as though they were lawful, not by approving of them, but by not punishing them."

98. *ST* I-II, q. 100, a. 2. Very helpful for this entire subject is John Finnis, *Aquinas, Moral, Political, and Legal Theory* (Oxford: Oxford University Press, 1998), chap. 7, especially 222ff.

their referring to the political common good, also valid as public reasons.

From this it follows that public reason is at least partly based on natural-law reasons. Natural-law reasons, thus, are to public reasons what conscience is to prudence: the voice of objectivity that commands, warns, admonishes, or prohibits in the name of moral truth and the truth about the human person. But this does not imply that the whole of natural law belongs to public reason or that what is a valid natural-law reason is also valid as a public reason. Even though we agree that such or such norm pertains to natural law, we can still disagree, not only for prudential reasons, but also on principle, on whether it should be implemented politically. Natural law theory, therefore, is not a sufficient theory of public reason if it is not simultaneously part of a specific political theory of public reason.

What has been said cannot only be justified in Thomistic terms, but also seems to me to belong to the central tradition of natural law (though I am aware that there also exist other interpretations of this tradition[99]). There is, however, a second aspect regarding the relation between natural law and public reason to be mentioned. It specifically concerns the ethos of modern constitutional democracy. An essential feature of natural law is that its claim of validity is identical with its claim of being both *right* reason and open to *anyone's* understanding. Natural law, in fact, makes its claim in the name of moral truth and of right reason so that, according to this logic, a person who does not accept a natural-law reason turns out to be considered as morally corrupted or at least unreasonable.

From the view that natural-law reasons rightly claim to be public reasons just *because* they are natural-law reasons—that is, because they are *right* reason[100]—it immediately follows that a public reason generally can claim to be such only once it is shown to be true and "right reason." Now, this is precisely the logic that constitutional democracy intends to overcome. Not in the sense of precluding the question of right reason or of truth from the political agenda, but in the sense of creating a public platform on which conflicting views about truth and right reason can be settled in

---

99. See, for example, Robert P. George, *Making Men Moral: Civil Liberties and Public Morality* (Oxford: Clarendon Press, 1993), chap. 1. To this I have partly responded in chapter 2 of the present work, entitled "The Liberal Image of Man and the Concept of Autonomy: Beyond the Debate between Liberals and Communitarians." This was originally published as "L'immagine dell'uomo nel liberalismo e il concetto di autonomia: al di là del dibattito fra liberali e comunitaristi," in *Immagini dell'uomo. Percorsi antropologici nella filosofia moderna*, ed. Ignacio Yarza (Rome: Armando, 1997), 95–133.

100. This, so it seems to me, is the view Robert P. George and Christopher Wolfe defend in their "Introduction" to *Natural Law and Public Reason*, 2.

what modernity has learned to be the only politically reasonable way, that is, without jeopardizing social peace, cooperation, and basic liberties. To identify "public reason" with "right reason," however, is politically conflictive and unwise, because it is to make the recognition of other citizens' reasonableness—and thus the *political legitimacy* of their views—dependent on their agreement with what others (be they a majority or not) consider "right reason." As it was clearest in the case of religious freedom, such identification of public reason with right reason subordinates reciprocity to truth claims. As we have seen, wherever in a historical context of deep ideological conflict this attitude became the *last and decisive* criterion of political legitimacy, it turned out to make civil cooperation impossible and finally cause civil war.[101]

The question is not resolved by referring, rightly, to the fact that differing in opinion in some fundamental matters "can only be rooted in ignorance or some subrational influence" and to the fact that by appealing to "natural right" we appeal to "principles and norms that are reasonable, using criteria of evidence and judgment that are accessible to all."[102] I fully agree with Finnis on that. In my view, however, this only shows that natural-law reasons are, in fact, valid candidates for public reasons and that full reasonableness of public reason is attained only when it does not contradict natural law. It does not show, however, that the claim of being a valid public reason can be *politically* legitimated by their being based on criteria of evidence and general accessibility. As a *political* and, thus, public criterion, this simply would not work.

Hence, my point is that for a reason to be legitimated as public reason it is *politically* not sufficient to be "right," "true" and based on "criteria of evidence and judgment that are accessible to all" (though these are all real criteria of full reasonableness of public reasons). The reason for this is that "ignorance," "subrational influence," and, additionally, bias caused by personal (perhaps illegitimate) interests, cultural or religious prejudices, and many other factors—true "burdens of judgment," although perhaps not exactly in the Rawlsian sense—seriously interfere with and diminish the evi-

101. In my view, it is also the reason that explains how religious truth-claims could be easily mixed with a political (social, nationalist, etc.) agenda, misusing in this way religion for political purposes, causing in consequence what are falsely called "religious wars"; in reality these wars were very political, but additionally fueled and enraged people by abusively linking a concrete political cause to religious truth-claims and thus converting religion into a political ideology.

102. Finnis, "Abortion, Natural Law, and Public Reason," 83.

dence of natural law and its rational accessibility. The only possible solution to convert "truth" and "right reason" into public standards of political and, hence, juridical legitimacy and validity would be to advocate a kind of political guardianship of the "truly virtuous" or "saint," or a kind of submission of the political to a higher authorized spiritual power, a new form of *polis*-ethic founded on a comprehensive conception of moral perfection.[103] This is what political modernity has abandoned, due to long and painful historical experience.[104]

Modern democratic societies, thus, need a concept of public reason that does not legitimate itself by being *true* or *right* reason; here I partially agree with Rawls. What is needed is in a certain sense a "freestanding"—or perhaps better, "specific"—public reasonableness in the sense that it refers to fundamental and specifically *political* values. This, to repeat, is far from meaning that the question of truth or "right reason" is removed from public reasonableness or that political values have no relation to moral truth. It only means that truth-claims are politically legitimate only insofar as they can be shown to participate in specifically *public* reasonableness (what in turn does not contradict what I have said before, namely that public reason is fully reasonable only to the extent to which it corresponds to, or does not contradict, the truth of natural law). Now, public reasons justify themselves on the grounds of being the *kind* of reasons that can be considered politically legitimate also by those citizens who do not—perhaps unreasonably and due to prejudice, passion, or even moral corruption—agree with them regarding concrete issues, and for whom those reasons are, as such a citizen would contend, not based on criteria of evidence. Nonetheless, these citizens will be compelled to recognize them as legitimate public reasons exactly because they are presented in the public sphere in the name not of

103. See for this Robert A. Dahl's valuable "critique of guardianship" in his *Democracy and Its Critics* (New Haven, Conn.: Yale University Press, 1989), 65ff.

104. Notice that the fact that natural-law reasons are mostly invoked by what Rawls calls "citizens of faith," that is by religious believers, does not convert such reasons into religious truths (and parts of some comprehensive religious doctrine). This would be the case only if such natural-law reasons would be invoked, instead of referring to public reasons, on specific religious grounds (referring as *argument*, e.g., to the simple authority of the Magisterium of the Church, of the Bible, of the Koran, or of something similar). Even if a citizen holds a natural-law reason to be true because of his religious faith, he must defend it in the public sphere with public reasons. Otherwise he could rightly be accused by his fellow citizens who do not share his faith of trying to impose on them his religious faith. What I have just said is—I think, adequately—expressed in Rawls's *proviso*; see "The Idea of Public Reason Revisited," § 4, 152ff. This does not exclude on principle that some reasons as contained in religious comprehensive doctrines are able to work as public reasons; this, however, is not because of their religious authority, but rather because of their public reasonableness.

"right reason," but of generally recognized political values (as I do in this essay in the case of marriage, the family, abortion, and euthanasia). Thus, even if they disagree and balance these values in a different way, they must acknowledge that they are the *kind* of reasons that belong to public reasonableness. I think any serious defender of natural law must be convinced that natural law, as far as it refers to the political common good, can be, and even must be, defended in terms of political reasonableness and political values.

In virtue of such recognition as valid public reasons independent from the recognition of their truth, legislation and policy based on such reasons can be legitimately (and without jeopardizing civil peace, cooperation, and fundamental liberties) enforced also on those who do not agree with them. Again: this does not hinder citizens who advocate natural law from invoking natural-law reasons because they think them to be "right reason" and to correspond to moral truth. On the contrary, it rather entitles them to do so. Since these reasons are properly and in an argumentatively transparent way invoked as *public* reasons, it additionally provides evidence that by this they neither intolerantly impose their own views on others nor endanger civil peace, cooperation, and fundamental liberties.[105]

I do not intend to propose here a full account of the relation between natural law and public reason. In this section I only want to underline three things:

1. Although natural law may always work as a criterion for recognizing specific laws as unjust, it is not a criterion sufficient for making out what is to be *imposed* by law and the coercive apparatus of the state on the totality of citizens. For this, natural law must be specified or applied to the political sphere, according to criteria that are specifically political, that is, that belong to public reason.

2. By the same token, for being recognized as public reason, natural-law reasons must be more than simply *natural-law reasons;* they must show themselves to be capable of being justified in terms of public validity, which means they must refer to the political common good of society

---

105. Generally, fundamental liberties can be legitimately restricted by public reasons. There may be, and certainly will be, disagreement also about what *kind* of reasons are public reasons. As we will see in "Postscript" below, Rawls gives us—without intending it—good help to settle this question in favor of the public relevance and legitimacy of natural law. I will come back to the political problem of disagreement about fundamentals of public reasonableness in "Pluralism, the Public Endorsement of Injustice and Political Legitimacy: Constitutional Democracy as a *Modus vivendi*" below.

and in this way be acceptable (not as such and such reason, but as *the kind of reasons* that on principle is considered politically legitimate) also to those citizens who do not agree with them in a determinate case. I in fact think that generally natural-law reasons, precisely for the reasons given by Finnis and other natural law theorists, exactly meet with this last requirement, provided they contain an argument for their *public* (or political) relevance.[106]

3. On the other hand, public reason cannot be properly defined without *some* reference to natural law, and consequently any use of the criterion of reciprocity and consequently of the liberal principle of legitimacy is to be embedded into, and in this sense limited by, the specific context of the "political" and of what "public reason" according to its very nature is.

My argument is founded on the conviction that the domain of "the political" cannot be defined except by a conception of what we traditionally call the (political) "common good." As has been argued by Gerald F. Gaus,[107] it is characteristic of Rawls that he does not succeed in defining properly what characterizes the political or a political value. Of course, there is an intuitive idea of it, but Rawls's specifications are all circular: as we have most clearly seen in the case of the family, they define the political in terms of the public conception of justice and, in turn, define *this* conception in terms of political values (that is, as "political" as opposed to comprehensive views). In fact, Rawls's problem is that to define what a political value is he would have to refer to something that could be called a "partially comprehensive" doctrine. So, he has to abstain from defining it. As I have argued, he instead simply relies on the idea of reciprocity, which refers to his con-

106. In some respects, I consider interesting also the approach by Amy Gutmann and Dennis Thompson in their publications on "Deliberative Democracy," namely, in their essay "Moral Conflict and Political Consensus," in *Liberalism and the Good,* ed. R. Bruce Douglass, Gerald M. Mara, and Henry S. Richardson (New York: Routledge, 1990), 125–47. There they develop (moral) criteria for the aptitude of concrete positions for being legitimately included in the public political agenda. The authors argue, e.g., that in the abortion debate a pro-life position that is based on the claim of the personhood and a corresponding right to life of the unborn is to be acknowledged as a position that can legitimately claim to be part of the political agenda, *which should be recognized also by those who disagree with that position.* So, also on these grounds the argument that the pro-life position is grounded in religious or otherwise "comprehensive" private beliefs and therefore should not be endorsed by public reason turns out to be invalid. The problems of the concept of "Deliberative democracy" as developed in Gutmann and Thompson's book *Democracy and Disagreement* (Cambridge, Mass.: Harvard University Press, 1996), are critically discussed in *Deliberative Politics: Essays on "Democracy and Disagreement,"* ed. Stephen Macedo (New York: Oxford University Press, 1999). The book includes a response by Gutmann and Thompson, who also reply in their subsequent *Why Deliberative Democracy?* (Princeton, N.J.: Princeton University Press, 2004).

107. *Contemporary Theories of Liberalism* (London: Sage Publications, 2003), 182–83.

cept of society as composed of free and equal citizens willing to cooperate over time, without any further specification of what a "society" is, what its nature, goals, and specific goods are. This is why I think that Rawls's concept of the political is much underdetermined, and finally even turns out to be unreasonable.

It turns out to be unreasonable because, as I have previously argued, it tacitly implies that "society" as a system of cooperation is *created* by the basic structure and the political conception of justice that regulates it and that is worked out in the original position. So, in Rawls's view the fundamental problem of social-contract theories comes to bear, namely that political society is the product of the contract to serve the interests of individuals who are thought of as pure "individuals," not yet living in a reality that is naturally shaped by the "social." Rawls's original position, his principle of reciprocity and the concepts of public reason, and the liberal principle of legitimacy derived from it, make the natural facts of society disappear or become politically "neutral" and, therefore, subordinated to the claims of citizens' individual autonomy. So, Rawls's key principles systematically disregard the politically relevant natural properties of society, which proves that in Rawls's political liberalism these principles work in an unreasonable, that is, politically arbitrary manner.

The only social-contract theorist of modernity who has maintained that man before entering into the state of society by a contract is to be thought of as of nothing but an isolated individual was Rousseau. Neither Hobbes nor Locke nor Kant conceived of a "state of nature" as being a condition of man in which the basic facts of society do not already naturally exist. Unlike Kelsen, Hobbes wisely and explicitly bases his legal positivism on the "natural right" to self-preservation and on nineteen "natural laws," knowing that otherwise his legal positivism could not be justified.[108] Hobbes's, Locke's, and Kant's conception of a "state of nature" is one in which these natural facts of society, rather than being nonexistent, lead to conflict and war and, therefore, must be ordered politically—by law—to be conducive to the human being's flourishing and progress. As I have already mentioned, Locke's basic values of life, liberty, and property, which refer not only to in-

---

108. For understanding that—paradoxically—Hobbes's political theory in fact is legal positivism founded in natural rights and natural law, I am indebted to Norberto Bobbio's fine article "Hobbes e il giusnaturalismo," *Rivista Critica di Storia della Filosofia* 17 (1962): 470–85. See for this my *La filosofia politica di Thomas Hobbes*, 229ff. For a juridical reading of Hobbes see the important book by Simone Goyard-Fabre, *Le Droit et la Loi dans la Philosophie de Thomas Hobbes* (Paris: C. Klincksieck, 1975).

dividuals but also to the marital union and the family, and are regulated by what Locke calls the law of nature even in the pre-political state of nature, shape the meaning and content of the political. Any political conception of justice publicly endorsed must respect these realities and values as the basic content of public reason.

Ironically, it is precisely about these basic facts of society and the values connected with them that there exists most consensus in our society. On these basic questions most people actually think in quite traditional ways but, being taught in most countries by the media not to impose their views on other people, they often vote "liberal." These basic social values actually are the best candidates to form the focus of an "overlapping consensus." The fact that they are typically promoted by "citizens of faith," as Rawls calls them, does not convert them into "comprehensive doctrines" to be excluded from public reason, nor does the fact that historically they have been decisively furthered by a culture permeated by Judeo-Christian and—in other parts of the world—Islamic or other religious values, remove their characteristic of belonging to public reason and of even being the basis of any public reason claiming to be not only *public* reasons, but also public *reason*. It rather could be symptomatic of the fact that concerning some basic issues, "citizens of faith" are more reasonable because they are intellectually closer to the cultural roots of constitutional democracy. I do not think that Popper was less a liberal because he remembered, as I have quoted him at the beginning of this essay, that the values of a liberal world had these precise cultural roots, which historically cannot be separated from our religious heritage.

It is important, however, to see that, unlike the reproductive basis of society and the moral facts springing from it, the determination of religious truth or the need of the endorsement of any particular religion *is not* part of the nature of society, nor does it characterize the content of a political conception of justice. This is not to say that religion, as such, is not a basic human value which may or even should be acknowledged and the exercise of which should not be facilitated. What is outside of public reason and does not belong to the political common good of society is the question of *truth* of this or that religion; this is intrinsically not a political question. Europeans, and Christian churches, had to learn this through a long process of accommodation, and to a considerable extent, though not exclusively, this learning process is what has generated the modern political ethos of constitutional democracy.

It is therefore politically reasonable to preclude questions of religious truth from the political agenda and consider arguments based on religious authority qua religious authority as alien to public reason.[109] The same, however, does not apply to questions that concern the nature of human society, even though they have certain moral implications and are essential parts of some comprehensive moral and religious doctrine. Treating them analogously to religious freedom would be politically unreasonable because, unlike establishing a particular religion, it would pervert the very meaning of politics: politics essentially refers to the reality of society and the good common to all living in it, though it does not refer to the truth of religions that transcend the meaning and reality of human society. That an assertion so empirically obvious and socially so basic as that not all forms of sexual orientations are equal is an essential part of one or many comprehensive moral or religious doctrines does not render this teaching inappropriate for being included in a reasonable and publicly endorsed political conception of justice, but rather evidences the reasonableness of the comprehensive doctrines that include such a teaching, and the unreasonableness of those that reject it

Pluralism, the Public Endorsement of Injustice and Political Legitimacy: Constitutional Democracy as a *Modus vivendi*

Although the nature and content of public reason refers to realities regulated by natural law, and although, therefore, with regard to public reason natural-law reasons are like the voice of truth, it may and actually does happen that certain public reasons or determined constitutional provisions, and/or statutes and laws enacted on their basis, do not correspond to this truth and, thus, are in a fundamental way in contradiction with the common good. It is possible that basic values of society are not sufficiently protected by public authority against threats internal or external. Sometimes public authority undermines or even attacks the common good. In given circumstances, as the case of abortion shows, consensus may vanish and in its place there arises a moral pluralism and corresponding claims about

---

109. I do not want to discuss here the question whether or to what extent citizens may offer in public political debate reasons drawn from their comprehensive moral or religious views; I am talking only about the reasons by which state organs with coercive power may licitly justify legal enactments, judicial decisions, and state policies. For the former question and for a partly alternative view to Rawls see Paul J. Weithman, *Religion and the Obligation of Citizenship* (Cambridge: Cambridge University Press, 2002). Weithman also rejects Robert Audi's view on "secular reasons" as developed, e.g., in his *Religious Commitment and Secular Reason* (Cambridge: Cambridge University Press, 2000).

rights. Such pluralism is far from being *reasonable* pluralism (though, as I will argue, it can be politically legitimate pluralism). It is a pluralism outside the limits of what is reasonable *even in a strictly political sense*, because it denies systematically something that is fundamental and basically constitutive for society and its legal order: that the right to life of a human being cannot be overruled by conflicting interests of third parties, such as self-determination, career projects, privacy, and the like. Nothing of the sort has *ever* been considered by the liberal-constitutionalist tradition as a reasonable claim of political justice.

Other examples of fundamental and, in my view, unreasonable disagreement are the legalization of medically assisted suicide as practiced even in public health institutions, and the already mentioned equating of same-sex unions to the conjugal union of man and woman. By denying a right to abortion, to assisted suicide, or the public recognition of same-sex unions, nobody's right as a "free and equal citizen" is violated, because these things simply cannot reasonably be a politically recognized right of any citizen, nor can they be constitutive of the basic structure of society.[110]

This may be less obvious in the case of euthanasia (medically assisted suicide). Yet, for the state to establish a legal right to euthanasia does not mean taking a neutral stance on this issue and respecting citizens' autonomy "in making those grave judgments for themselves, free from the imposition of any religious or philosophical orthodoxy by court or legislature," as the crème de la crème of liberal Anglo-Saxon legal philosophers have rather

---

110. To give a summary of what has been already said on that topic, the argument against "same-sex marriages" would run somewhat like this: Considered with regard to their being a homo- or a heterosexual life-partner to another person, citizens are not equals; as partners in same-sex relationships they are reproductively and therefore politically irrelevant. Consequently, if both kinds of unions are not only differently treated by the law, but homosexual unions are not even considered by it at all, no reason exists why reciprocity should be violated. By taking into account citizens' sexual orientation their rights as "free and equal" would be violated only in those regards to which sexual orientation as such makes no immediate and obvious socially or politically relevant difference, that is, for example, insofar as citizens are students, workers, employees, artists, judges, voters, etc., and even as teachers (provided they do not, mainly if they teach kids, undermine by their public behavior and their teaching the political value of marriage and the family based on it). Notice that this does not necessarily presuppose a comprehensive moral evaluation of homosexuality and sexual acts between persons of the same sex. Rather conversely, the moral evaluation of marriage is also, though not exclusively, dependent on its singular social and political value: sexuality not only refers to the good of individuals, but also and essentially to the good of the species. This aspect is completely lacking in sexual activity between persons of the same sex. On the other side, the recognition of "same sex marriages" would imply a redefinition of the institution of marriage. "Marriage" would not be any more considered in law as an essentially reproductive institution, but would be defined independently from this role. This, in my view, is a grave structural injustice and juridical incoherence with unpredictable consequences for jurisprudence and the whole legal system.

unconvincingly argued in their famous "Philosophers' Brief."[111] Quite conversely: the legal enactment of such a right turns out to be a threat to autonomy, mainly of the elderly, the lethally sick and dying, the mentally ill, and generally the weakest among us. Legal enactment as such a right would seriously and dramatically harm their prospects of being appropriately cared for by palliative means, their dignity precisely as persons who are suffering, because they would be publicly considered as a burden for society and would have to feel pressured into alleviating society from this burden by consenting to the acceleration of their own death (such an acceleration being their *right,* it seems to be unreasonable not to make use of it).[112] Legally granting a right to euthanasia, therefore, is a serious attack on the political common good of society, although in one or another extremely hard case euthanasia may have *some* plausibility as a good for a single person and as an at least understandable act of mercy. Yet, from such single cases one cannot infer the desirability of a generalized right to medically assisted suicide and the creation of corresponding structures and institutionalized practices, because such a right wrongly presents the possibility of assisted suicide as part of the common good, and assisted suicide itself as a good. At the most, in very rare and extreme cases, one could consider the concession of immunity from prosecution.

Those who disagree with such an argument must nevertheless concede that it is based on public reasons. For some reason they may not consider the concrete argument as conclusive; but they must recognize it as the *kind* of argument that is proper to public reason and cannot reject it as "imposition of a religious or philosophical orthodoxy" (though those who offer this argument do so because they are supported by the comprehensive moral or religious doctrine they adhere to). Yet, in this case it seems that *public* reasons are rather on the side of *not* granting a right to medically assisted suicide because, looking closely to the matter, such a right would confer on personal preferences of *some* citizens, and at the expense of a significant public interest, the weight of public reasons.[113] The aggressive polemic

---

111. Ronald Dworkin, Thomas Nagel, Robert Nozick, John Rawls, and Judith Jarvis Thomson, "Assisted Suicide: The Philosophers' Brief," *New York Review of Books* 44, no. 5 (March 27, 1997).

112. For this, and the real existence of a slippery slope, there is in the meantime abundant empirical evidence. See the excellent argument and well-documented survey by Iñigo Ortega, "La 'pendiente resbaladiza' en la eutanasia: ¿ilusión o realidad?" *Annales theologici* 17 (2003): 77–124 (focusing on the practice of medically assisted euthanasia in Australia, Oregon, and the Netherlands).

113. Quite another question is the right to suicide as such, and even leaving unpunished assistance to suicide generally, provided there is no self-interested motive recognizable. We are talking here exclusively of *medically assisted* suicide, which implies the support of society's healthcare system.

against the alleged "imposition of religious or philosophical orthodoxy" reveals itself to be, in fact, the political enthroning of personal preferences, bestowing on them absolute priority over public reasons. Yet, personal autonomy as such does not automatically generate a public reason. On the contrary, personal autonomy can, and sometimes must, be restricted by public reasons (which refer to the common good).[114]

Let me consider now the problem mentioned before that (1) there may not be, and in modern societies there is not, a consensus on these topics in themselves and on how to deal with them politically, and that (2) in many existing constitutional democracies these matters are in fact regulated by law in a way that in the eyes of many citizens—including me—is at odds with the nature and basic structure of human society and, hence, with natural law and the common good. These citizens will conclude that public reason is seriously flawed, if not perverted. Does the public endorsement of laws fundamentally unjust strip—in the eyes of those citizens who judge them so fundamentally unjust—a constitutional democracy, its political institutions and decision procedures that have enacted them, as well as the decisions themselves, of their legitimacy, so that a moral duty to give support to the political system that originated them evaporates?

I don't want to tackle here the general problem of unjust laws and whether and to what extent they oblige in conscience.[115] My question is a

---

114. Of course, also the personal autonomy of citizens is an essential part of the common good. Therefore, a concept of the common good that overrules the concept of personal autonomy would be a perversion of the idea of the common good. The idea of a common good always includes the good of the individuals who belong to the multitude the common good of which is at stake. Yet, this does not imply that personal autonomy is a priori trump, because it can be restricted in favor of protecting the autonomy of citizens in general. So, in a sound understanding, autonomy is restricted . . . in favor of autonomy. This is at least one decisive reason for denying citizens a right to medically assisted active euthanasia.

115. In the tradition, this question has been treated as the question to what extent laws that command certain acts or impose burdens and duties bind in conscience. The general answer was that if laws command one to do something that is contrary to the natural or the divine law, they must be opposed; if they are otherwise unjust (too burdensome, for example), they do not oblige in conscience *as such*, but accidentally, that is for sake of the common good, however, there may be sufficient reason to comply with them. All of this is not very helpful in the present case of granting abortion or euthanasia rights because such laws (or judicial decisions), as such, do not *oblige* doing anything, but they simply *permit* citizens to do certain things. Hence, the traditional argument about unjust laws, which is an argument about obligation, does not apply in this context (it applies only indirectly to the subsequent question of the refusal for conscientious reasons of health service workers to cooperate in legally permitted abortion or euthanasia; but this question can be regulated independently from the former). Technically, by granting a right to abortion or euthanasia the state abstains from regulating by law a certain domain, leaving it to the discretion of citizens. So, what we need is not so much a doctrine about how and to what extent unjust laws oblige in conscience, but to what extent and in which areas citizens as acting for the common good and, thus, political society are obliged to regulate, promote, or restrict citizens' behavior by (civil and penal) law. For this and the question of abortion I again refer to my "Fundamental Rights, Moral Law, and the Legal Defense of Life in a Constitutional Democracy: A Constitutionalist Approach to the Encyclical *Evangelium Vitae.*"

different one: can a political system and a seriously flawed or even partly perverted public reason that allows not only such divergence on basic matters, but also laws and policies that are in contradiction with basic requirements of natural law, still be *morally* justified, and legitimate, that is to say, justified as a political order that claims to embody a definite political ethic? And do citizens—supported perhaps by their religious faith and authoritative teaching of, say, the Catholic Church to which they wholeheartedly belong—who are convinced of the profound injustice and contradiction to natural law of such a legislation, still have overriding *moral* reasons that not only do cause them in fact to support the political system, but also cause them to feel morally *obliged* to do so, and therefore to support it loyally and even as wholeheartedly as they defend natural law? In other words: do requirements of specifically political morality to a certain extent override requirements rooted in natural law? This is, put in another way, one of the central questions Rawls's *Political Liberalism* deals with, and it is a question the answer to which is intrinsic to the essence of the ethos of constitutional democracy.

To spell this answer out I first of all want to repeat what I have said before: natural law *as such*—that is, insofar it is the standard for good and evil in human actions, naturally accessible to every human being's understanding—is not public reason. Even when, in a determinate political society, public reason allows certain decisions contrary to natural law, it maintains its own specifically political reasonability as *public* reason. As a socially and widely recognized form of public justification it still realizes the fundamental political values of peaceful coexistence of citizens and the equal and impartial security for their basic liberties.[116] Such contradictions to natural law, however, do not eliminate the basic political reasonableness of the system; public reason continues to be a working political principle and fulfills most of its fundamental political functions. Nobody can say, for example, that the American Constitution and its public reason did not successfully fulfill its political role while slavery was still not abolished, even though it was thereby permitting a grave injustice.

When talking in such a way, we have reached the core of the political

---

116. Of courses, this implies a politically relevant distinction between "citizens" and "human persons," to which group the unborn also belong. The distinction does not diminish the right of the unborn to live, but it makes sense in the horizon of considering the prospect of civil war as the *summum malum* to be avoided by political cooperation. The unborn (and small children) are not a possible threat for the peaceful coexistence in society.

ethos of modernity in which its institutional ethos of peace, freedom, and basic justice is situated: The acceptance of its public reason depends not on the recognition of the *truth* of its reasonability, but on the recognition of its political legitimacy (without by this excluding the question of truth from the political or public square, but only by allowing this question in a way that does not undermine the fundamental political values of peaceful coexistence, social cooperation, and equal civil liberty).

To illustrate my point consider possible reactions to such a situation by two different defenders of natural law: the first considers that under such circumstances as those just outlined the basic political structure of society is perverted to an extent that it has lost its legitimacy or, at least, that these laws are not to be regarded as legitimate products of the political and legal system. This first defender considers the situation a grave offense to civility and thus it may be opposed by illegal and uncivil means (and only for prudential reasons—that is, because of the expectation that illegal opposition to them would be most likely to be unsuccessful and even cause a civil war that cannot be possibly won—is one obliged to abstain from this form of opposition).[117]

Consider now the second defender of natural law: he judges these laws to be similarly unacceptable. He is convinced, however, that though they are unjust, contradict natural law, and gravely violate the common good, these laws are *politically legitimate* law: being enacted correctly they do not violate the standards of civility and, therefore, on principle *must not* be opposed by illegal and uncivil means. The *political* value of peaceful civil coexistence and basic liberties for all citizens, such a defender of natural law argues, has a politically freestanding and primary moral weight that is not overridden by the injustice of concrete laws and policies, even when they concern such fundamental issues as the right to life of human persons and the reproduction of society and, thus, are gravely in contradiction with the common good.[118]

Such a defender of natural law would—as I do—hold that there are forms of pluralism that, though being unreasonable, are nevertheless po-

---

117. If I have rightly understood, this is the position of John Finnis in his *Abortion, Natural Law, and Public Reason*, 89–90.

118. Of course, generally speaking such a position can be held only within certain limits. It cannot apply to cases in which the basic structure itself and the legal system as such are used in a way contrary to fundamental justice and thus intrinsically perverted. Such an *Unrechtsstaat* as was, for example, Nazi Germany cannot demand any civil loyalty from its citizens because it is essentially uncivil.

litically legitimate. Their legitimacy lies in their participation in the public reason of constitutional democracy. It is this aspect of public reason that for strictly *political* reasons (which are *moral* reasons because they belong to political morality) has its own logic. At this point, the priority of peaceful coexistence and individual freedom is to be recognized and affirmed. Reciprocity among citizens as free and equal must be considered, too, as a basic part of that civility which is part of political justice.[119]

Of course, this seems to be less the logic of overlapping consensus than of *modus vivendi*. The latter, in fact, always was and continues to be inherent in the political ethos of the democratic constitutional state. *Modus vivendi* has more moral substance than Rawls, who is eager to distinguish his "freestanding view" of political morality from a "mere" *modus vivendi*, wants to concede. A *modus vivendi* is also more capable of securing political stability over time than Rawls is ready to admit.[120]

There are several reasons for arguing also that Rawls's conception cannot be more than a *modus vivendi* or, at least, that is must contain elements typical for a *modus vivendi*. Nothing prohibits an overlapping consensus of a Rawlsian type to be called a *modus vivendi* or to contain some elements of

119. This seems to me to be the position Rawls thinks a Catholic opposed to abortion might have (see "The Idea of Public Reason Revisited," 169–70). I substantially agree with Rawls's remarks about the possibility for, say Roman Catholics (which Rawls mentions here as though they were the only Christians opposed to abortion) to accept a decision to grant a right to abortion as "legitimate law, binding on citizens by the majority principle." Rawls does not want to say that citizens who see such a right as intrinsically illegitimate must now, as democrats, change their view (being in the minority does not imply that one is wrong, as a Rousseaunian *volonté générale* would suggest). But they should, and can, accept such a decision as legitimate law in the sense that it has the legitimacy of being enacted in accordance with the institutional rules all have accepted for the sake of peaceful coexistence, liberty, and justice. Though they think that *this* law contradicts the conception of justice underlying the political system, they still may recognize that the way this law has been enacted is in accordance with the system they sustain. As long as the law does not *impose* a determinate behavior on citizens, that is, as long as it does not force citizens to abort or to cooperate in abortion, this argumentation holds. Rawls certainly does not say that in such a case Catholics may not try to oppose this law with all legal means, trying to reverse the decision, because now they have to consider the law as a just law. He only maintains that they should consider it (formally) "legitimate law," because it has been enacted in a procedurally legitimate way. The point Rawls seems to me to want to make is that in consequence of such a decision, Roman Catholics need not refrain from supporting the political system, which has made possible such a decision (in their view gravely unjust), and that they can—and should—continue to wholeheartedly support it, trying to use it in future to promote better their own agenda.

120. See Bernard P. Dauenhauer, "A Good Word for a Modus Vivendi," in *The Idea of a Political Liberalism: Essays on Rawls*, ed. Victoria Davion and Clark Wolf (Lanham, Md.: Rowman and Littlefield, 2000), 204–20. See also John Gray, *Two Faces of Liberalism* (New York: New Press, 2000). In my view, however, in his defense of liberalism as a pure *modus vivendi* Gray goes too far: his idea of liberalism as a *modus vivendi* implies a series of presuppositions about the conflicting nature of value—in the sense of Isaiah Berlin—which is partly trivial and partly exaggerated. At least liberal *constitutionalism* does not need such a relativistic concept of value. For a liberal critique of Gray's (and Berlin's) position see Gerald F. Gaus, *Contemporary Theories of Liberalism* (London: Sage Publications, 2003), chaps. 2 and 3.

it, precisely because it can work and fulfill its political task only if it draws support from those who disagree with fundamental aspects of its endorsed conception of justice, support given for the sake of securing peaceful coexistence, social cooperation, and basic liberties.[121] Historically, it seems rather obvious that constitutionalism is a specific and highly sophisticated kind of *modus vivendi*. Rawls seems not to acknowledge this fact, thus undermining his own project of "political liberalism" in favor of some comprehensive and "closed" and sometimes seemingly rather intolerant form of liberalism. He seems to hold that wherever a "liberal" position is in the minority it undercuts public reason by appealing to the rights of "free and equal" citizens and the criterion of reciprocity understood as a leverage of these rights. Here the idea of individual rights and liberties—which are meant in principle to protect individuals from the tyranny of the majority—is abused to render irrelevant the majority principle precisely in those areas in which it is most legitimately applied, the area of our understanding of fundamental features of the political common good.[122]

It is the specifically political logic of public reason that is the focus of an overlapping consensus that originates the freestanding political conception of constitutional democracy or, if you prefer, of political liberalism, which at the same time is also a *moral* conception. On this level of argument, Rawls provides some essential and, in my view, fruitful conceptual keys enabling us to better tackle this problem, although I think he exaggerates the needed amount of *overlapping* consensus. But there is still a decisive difference: while for Rawls everything that is not part of the political conception has to be counted as being a part of an excluded (or at least excludable) comprehensive doctrine, in my view natural law, *as far as it is politically relevant,* is not part of a comprehensive doctrine, but rather the basis of any sound and reasonable political conception. It is precisely the basic standard of (practical) truth of such a conception.[123]

Yet, it is equally important to emphasize that the correspondence of

---

121. Though I am very skeptical toward Larmore's discourse-ethical conception of politics and his understanding of practical reason (as intrinsically self-contradictory), I agree with his conception of the liberal state as a kind of *modus vivendi;* see Charles E. Larmore, *Patterns of Moral Complexity* (Cambridge: Cambridge University Press, 1987), 70ff.

122. This point is constantly made with great force and certainly not without reason by Michael J. Sandel, for example in his *Democracy's Discontent: America in Search of a Public Philosophy* (Cambridge, Mass.: Harvard University Press, 1996).

123. Natural law obviously gives rise to a comprehensive doctrine of the good; but this does not mean that everything that is rooted in natural law, as a political conception of justice may be, is therefore part of comprehensive doctrine and cannot be a political conception in Rawls's sense.

public reasons to natural law must itself be understood as the result of an open political process. It cannot be achieved by simply invoking natural-law reasons insofar they are such, that is, by appealing to what those who invoke them consider to be their obvious truth, because this (as is explained by Hobbes, who on this had some essential insights) would amount to in-voking private reasons against public reason and would therefore fail to set-tle the question. Invoking natural law as "true reason" would only increase disagreement and conflict. Hobbes's famous dictum *Auctoritas non veritas facit legem*[124] expresses, apart from its problematic features, also the basic truth that in politics disputes are finally settled by legitimate authoritative decision, not by truth.[125] There is no superior sovereign, no higher moral guardianship with coercive power, able to generate the correspondence of public reason with natural law. It is the democratic political process itself—on the level of both the constituent and the constituted power—which has the task of creating this correspondence between public reason and natural law. As we have seen, to be invoked as public reasons natural-law reasons must be justified as political reasons; that is to say, they must undergo a process of political justification in the course of the democratic process itself.

In a pluralistic society there will necessarily always be a tension be-tween the widely recognized content of public reason and the requirements of natural law. It is part of the political process of liberal constitutional de-mocracies to tolerate this tension, and to maintain an institutional frame-work capable of living with such tensions, or of overcoming them, or both. This is why it seems to me to be crucial to recognize that certain forms of pluralism are both unreasonable and politically legitimate: they are *unrea-sonable* from the point of view of natural law, but still *legitimate* from the point of view of public reason. It is this very tension that permits and urges natural law, and citizens who defend it, to accomplish their function of be-

---

124. In this form this famous sentence only appears once in the works of Hobbes: in the Latin ver-sion of the *Leviathan*, which was drafted after the English version. See *Thomas Hobbes Malmesburiensis Opera Philosophica quae Latine scripsit Omnia*, ed. W. Molesworth, 5 vols. (London: 1839–45; Aalen: Sci-entia, 1962–66), 3:202. In the English version the sentence does not appear. In the famous *Dialogue be-tween a Philosopher and a Student of the Common Laws of England* instead we find the sentence in a dif-ferent form: "It is not wisdom, but authority that makes a law." See *The English Works of Thomas Hobbes of Malmesbury*, ed. W. Molesworth, 11 vols. (London 1839–45; reprint, Aalen: Scientia, 1962–66), 6:5.

125. I have discussed the sense of this dictum not only in my book about Hobbes, already men-tioned, but also in chapter 4 of the present volume, which is entitled "*Autoritas non veritas facit legem:* Thomas Hobbes, Carl Schmitt and the Idea of the Constitutional State." Originally published as "*Autori-tas non veritas facit legem:* Thomas Hobbes, Carl Schmitt und die Idee des Verfassungsstaates," *Archiv für Rechts- und Sozialphilosophie* 86 (2000): 484–98; see also my *La filosofia politica di Thomas Hobbes*, 214ff.

ing in public reason the voice of conscience and truth without, however, making the legitimacy of the political system depend on its factual endorsement of this truth.

Here, of course, the influence of what Rawls calls the "background culture" is decisive: the outcome of this democratic process depends upon citizens who are rooted in solid moral, cultural, and religious traditions. Here civil society and also religious authorities, addressing the consciences of their faithful, have a constitutive role to play. They are all, in this sense, actors in this process of shaping the background culture that is mediated, in the politically decisive way, by the political institutions of the democratic constitutional state and their fundamental respect for liberty as a political value.

I disagree, therefore, with Alasdair MacIntyre's hostile assertion that "modern politics is civil war carried on by other means."[126] Modern politics in constitutional democracies is not civil war at all, but a means of overcoming and preventing civil war by political culture, a conflictive political culture, of course, but a culture that precisely endures such conflict by avoiding the *summum malum* that is civil war, and maintaining peaceful coexistence and mutually advantageous cooperation of citizens over time. This is the basis of a culture of liberty and personal freedom. Political conflict in constitutional democracy is part of a highly differentiated political ethos that does not simply appeal to the virtues of citizens—sometimes, unfortunately, it does not do so enough—but first of all is an institutional ethos, which is not only procedural but also includes substantive, although specifically political, values. As a set, these values—peaceful coexistence, individual liberty, justice as equality of liberty—formulate a common good and work as a shared moral principle of politics and public reason.[127] The

126. *After Virtue: A Study in Moral Theory,* 2nd ed. (Notre Dame: University of Notre Dame Press, 1984), 253.

127. This is why I think that MacIntyre's verdict, "the notion of the political community as a common project is alien to the modern liberal individualist world" (*After Virtue,* 156), is at least exceedingly exaggerated: it perhaps applies to certain brands of liberalism, or rather libertarianism, but cannot be called typical for the liberal tradition at all, nor for the reality of liberal constitutional democracies. This does not exclude that the behavior of citizens in modern democracies is often to an extent individualistic, which justifies MacIntyre's assertion. But this, I should say, is not a characteristic of the idea of political liberalism, but pertains to the reality of the modern world (but perhaps not only to the *modern* world), which not only, but also, by forms of perverted liberalism has become exceedingly individualistic. At any rate is it wrong, as Robert A. Dahl in his book *Democracy and Its Critics* (New Haven, Conn.: Yale University Press, 1989), 299–300, has criticized MacIntyre, to compare modern social and political *reality* with an ancient *ideal* as it appears in the views and writings of some philosophers. Aristotelian "communitarianism" must not be compared with the reality of modern society and the behavior of its citizens, but with political liberalism as it appears equally in *writings* of political philosophers and, per-

settling of the 2000 U.S. presidential election dispute by the logic of institutional procedure was an example for the entire world of the peacemaking force of the political ethos of modernity.

In a free and "open" society many aspects of natural law and *some* natural-law reasons will always be a part of political conflict, that is, they will always be focal points or the subjects of controversy.[128] To simply rely on them as being open to everyone's natural understanding and invoke them as *public* reasons is politically illusory. The point I wish to make is that their quality of being *natural-law reasons* does not yet qualify them as public reasons because modern public reason is partly defined by the task of creating consensus in a society that is divided about what is naturally good for human persons. No natural law theory can be, as such, sufficient to provide public reasons, even though it rightly presents itself as a doctrine of limited government.[129]

Moreover, as I have argued before, many precepts of natural law are not politically relevant. Others substantially bear upon the political domain, but their doing so must be justified; this cannot be the task of a theory of natural law but only of a wider political philosophy that includes natural law as one of its essential elements. In practice, it is up to citizens to convince their fellow citizens by proposing natural-law reasons and justifying them as valid public reasons, convincing the public that because of their truth they are to be publicly endorsed. But this includes arguments able to

---

haps, with the *ideas* underlying modern constitutions inspired by liberalism. The *reality* of modern society can, then, be compared with the social reality of Aristotle's time. It would be easy, I think, to make a choice which we might prefer to live in!

128. This seems to me certain also for theological reasons, because outside the order of revelation and grace there is no full intelligibility of the natural law. What I mean by this is explained in my "Is Christian Morality Reasonable? On the Difference between Secular and Christian Humanism," *Annales Theologici* 15 (2001): 529–49.

129. See John Finnis, "Is Natural Law Theory Compatible with Limited Government?" in *Natural Law, Liberalism, and Morality: Contemporary Essays,* ed. Robert P. George (Oxford: Oxford University Press, 1996), 1–26. The response to this paper by Stephen Macedo ("Against the Old Sexual Morality of the New Natural Law," in ibid., 27–48) polemically focuses on questions (of sexual morality) raised in Finnis's paper, which, as I think, in this way are not an issue of public reason. But I cannot go into this in detail here. While I agree with Finnis on substantive positions, I would also recognize as partly true what Macedo in chapter 2 of his *Liberal Virtues, Citizenship, Virtue, and Community in Liberal Constitutionalism* (Oxford: Oxford University Press, 1990), says on "Liberalism and public justification," namely that public justification follows a logic that does not simply coincide with identifying "what are simply the best reasons" (50), "best" being what mostly coincides with "right reason." Unfortunately, Macedo's public reason, though different from Rawls's version, also remains confined to the same liberal logic of an (exclusive) "broader commitment to respecting the freedom and equality of persons" (ibid.). Provided this is really an absolute priority and a "trump," then natural-law reasons will have no chance as public reasons because they often do not respect the "equality of persons": according to natural law not all persons are equal in every politically relevant respect. Yet, justice means equality for equals.

show that they are also *politically* valid; that is, that what they claim can be reasonably enforced by the coercive apparatus of the state. The liberal principle of legitimacy must not put them aside because they are commonly held by "citizens of faith," be they Roman Catholics or other believers. In his last writings, introducing the idea of the "proviso," Rawls seems to eventually acknowledge this.

It is interesting and even fascinating to see how the Magisterium of the Catholic Church increasingly offers central teachings on natural law in the form of public reasoning. This is clearly the case for abortion, euthanasia,[130] and "same-sex marriages."[131] The fact that these reasons are embedded in a wider "comprehensive" religious doctrine about the value of human life does not affect the specifically political character of other parts of this teaching. The reasons given for this teaching fully meet with the requirements of the proviso mentioned by Rawls in his "The Idea of Public Reason Revisited."[132] Perhaps it is this that renders many liberals and European "laicists" increasingly nervous: that there are good public, that is, political, reasons for defending the political requirements of natural law and that especially the Catholic Church seems to defend natural law positions in a way that has the appeal of public reasonableness. Of course, there is much in natural law and Church doctrine that is not really part of the political common good and, therefore, cannot be legitimately imposed by the coercion of civil or penal law on the whole of the citizens. The political relevance of natural law and, therefore, the legitimate legal enforcement of morality are limited—limited by *political* reasons. The political common good does not include the perfection of moral virtue, and even less religious perfection and holiness.[133]

130. For these see the encyclical *Evangelium vitae* (1985) by John Paul II. As far as abortion is concerned, I have tried to emphasize this in my "Fundamental Rights, Moral Law, and the Legal Defense of Life in a Constitutional Democracy: A Constitutionalist Approach to the Encyclical *Evangelium Vitae.*"

131. See for this the "Instruction by the Congregation of the Doctrine of the Faith" (June 3, 2003): *Considerations Regarding Proposals to Give Legal Recognition to Unions between Homosexual Persons* (especially part 3).

132. 152ff.

133. This might be misunderstood. Of course in my opinion citizens' being virtuous is of the utmost importance for society and the common good. *Making* men virtuous (or even promoting their holiness), however, is not the task of political institutions, nor is it a part of the specifically political common good (insofar as it is the aim of political praxis). Creating social *conditions* that are favorable for living the virtues may very well be the task of laws and policies (there exists no such thing as absolute "neutrality"). But also in this respect, what will be decisive are political aspects and considerations, that is, public reasons. (Much should be said on this topic that for reasons of space cannot be said here.) It is symptomatic that following the communitarian critique of liberalism and also in response to it the civil importance of "virtue" has been rediscovered. It is not surprising that Will Kymlicka has added in

Postscript: Public Reason, Natural Law and the
Final Breakdown of Rawls's Immunization Strategy

Rawls's political liberalism characteristically tries to immunize public reason from any influence by natural-law reasons. The strategy tries to sharply and neatly distinguish the domain of the political from the domain of (moral or religious) comprehensive doctrines and, correspondingly, public reason from the background culture. I think the distinction as such is valid and useful. But Rawls misuses it. While affirming that the political conception of justice as fairness and political liberalism is the focus of an overlapping consensus, he nonetheless draws a sharp line between such a political conception and the content of comprehensive views as if they were mutually exclusive. In reality, there necessarily exists a certain tension between a political conception's freestanding character and its simultaneously being the focus of an overlapping consensus. Being a result of such an *overlapping* consensus—which implies that there are precisely some contents of *comprehensive views* that overlap—it does not anymore look so freestanding.

However, I don't think that this *necessarily* is an intrinsic contradiction of Rawls's position. In order to actually avoid open contradiction, however, a defender of Rawls will be constrained to concede that there are many things belonging to comprehensive doctrines—and to the background culture—that essentially also must belong to the overlapping consensus, the corresponding political conception of justice, and, therefore, must be part of public reason. The basic political requirements of natural law, as I have emphasized them, are precisely such. And most interestingly, they are where the most overlapping consensus is to be found between Catholics, Protestants, and Muslims, say, but also between other religions and secular comprehensive doctrines. This also applies to most of the liberal tradition itself, which cannot be referred to for justifying abortion or "same sex marriages," and not even divorce as nowadays it is commonly understood and justified (in the name of personal autonomy).

It was Jürgen Habermas who attacked Rawls on these grounds and reproached him for being incoherent. Rawls's freestanding view, so Habermas objects, is not freestanding at all, because it still depends on comprehensive

---

the second edition of his *Contemporary Political Philosophy: An Introduction* (Oxford: Oxford University Press, 2002) a whole chapter on "Citizenship Theory" (284–326).

doctrines from which it draws its moral resources. It therefore fallaciously founds public discourse on nonpublic reasons instead of acknowledging a "third perspective for the reasonable," which, according to Habermas, should be totally independent from the moral substance of any comprehensive view.[134] Yet, as Rawls had previously written in his "Reply to Habermas," Habermas's alternative discourse-ethical concept falls short, in some essential ways, of the liberal-constitutionalist understanding of modern democracy. Though Habermas's observation on Rawls is correct—though not really a critique—I would defend Rawls against Habermas's attempt to institutionalize a kind of democratic-republican permanent discourse at the expense of the "dualist" constitutionalist wisdom. It is typical of the liberal constitutionalist tradition to distinguish constituent from constituted powers, and to treat the latter—the constitution and the political and legal institutions based on it—as immune from alteration or manipulation by the former in the course of the ordinary process of lawmaking, adjudication, and daily politics. The effect, the "taming of democracy,"[135] is thus to set clear juridical limits and constraints on legislation and policy (provided they are not undermined by certain kinds of judicial activism that are more political than jurisprudential).[136]

Yet, this is the reason why Rawls's immunization-strategy has not succeeded. Precisely insofar as his political conception of justice necessarily depends on some truths contained in those comprehensive doctrines that by their overlapping form this very political conception, there is much truth in Rawls's conception of political liberalism; it tends (once properly used) to give room for public reasons expressing fundamental exigencies of natu-

---

134. Jürgen Habermas, "'Vernünftig' versus 'wahr'—oder die Moral der Weltbilder," in Habermas, *Die Einbeziehung des Anderen. Studien zur politischen Theorie* (Frankfurt am Main: Suhrkamp, 1996), 95–127. This is Habermas's answer to Rawls's "Reply to Habermas"; to my knowledge it has not been published in English.

135. András Sajó, *Limiting Government: An Introduction to Constitutionalism* (Budapest: Central European University Press, 1999), chap. 2.

136. Of course, this is a terribly complex issue, and I do not feel sufficiently competent to deal with it. Yet, I think everything is a question of measure. Also moderated judicial review should have its place, even if it comes to developing constitutional law further. Constitutions are not sacred Scripture. In all countries, constitutional law and its understanding is a historical process and must be adapted to always changing challenges and requirements. Yet, a better and from a democratic point of view more logical way of doing this seems to me to be, rather than judicial review, revisions or amendments of the constitution itself by parliamentary or even plebiscitary processes. Therefore, I would agree with Russell Hittinger that natural-law reasons have their place rather in the legislative than in the adjudicative context. See his "Natural Law in the Positive Laws: A Legislative or Adjudicative Issue?" *Review of Politics* 55 (1993) 5–34; now republished as chapter 3 of Hittinger's *The First Grace: Rediscovering the Natural Law in a Post-Christian World* (Wilmington, Delaware: ISI Books, 2003).

ral law. Moreover, although Rawls has not given up his conception of public reason, he has improved on its fine-tuning, arriving at positions that clearly undermine his own immunization-strategy, thus improving his own theory of political liberalism.

Take, for example, the famous footnote on abortion from *Political Liberalism*.[137] In this note, Rawls tries to establish that the "equality of women as equal citizens" requires that a woman's right to end a pregnancy during the first trimester may not be overridden by the "due respect for human life." To deny this, Rawls argues, would be to deny that there must be a balance of political values; any comprehensive doctrine tending to exclude such a balance is to this extent unreasonable. There are several strange assertions in this note, but at the end Rawls admits that the only thing that would be opposed to the ideal of public reason is "if we voted from a comprehensive doctrine that denied this right," that is to say, only referring, say, to the Bible or the authority of some Church teaching, but without having specifically political, that is, public reasons for such a denial.

Now, in another famous footnote contained in both "The Idea of Public Reason Revisited"[138] and the "Introduction to the 1996 Paperback Edition" of *Political Liberalism*,[139] Rawls complains that his first footnote on abortion has been misunderstood as claiming a right of women to abortion in the first trimester (which certainly, so I still think, was the meaning of the footnote). In his second footnote, however, Rawls adds what he seems to have forgotten to say three years earlier and what in my view is much more consistent with his own approach, namely that it is possible that there be public, that is, specifically political, reasons able to show that to establish a woman's right to abort as overriding the value and rights of human life is to establish an *unreasonable* balance of values. What Rawls says, then, is that it is, on principle, thinkable that there actually be valid public reasons for denying that the value of human life can ever be overridden by a woman's right to end her pregnancy (that is, to kill her baby). This is exactly what a defender of natural law would claim; according to the second footnote it now seems to be consistent with Rawls's idea of public reason. On the grounds of Rawls's reformulation, on the other hand, the pro-choice position, which considers exclusively a woman's rights *but not at all the value and possible rights of unborn life,* now runs into serious trouble: the reason

137. *Political Liberalism*, 243n32.
139. lv–lvi n31.

138. 169n80.

is that by systematically excluding from consideration the value of the un-born's right to life, the pro-choice position possesses, in strictly Rawlsian terms, *no balance of values at all.* There is scarcely an effort to establish one; there is only an argument drawn from a nonpolitical comprehensive doc-trine—ideology—of "privacy" and "women's self-determination" (which po-litically and legally, however, is of quite doubtful relevance). The pro-choice argument, then, turns out to be politically not only unreasonable but also illegitimate.

If what Rawls says in this last footnote on abortion is true, then in Raw-lsian public reason natural-law reasons are not in principle excluded. The only condition is that we do not recognize only the values that refer to in-dividual citizens as free and equal—that we do not exclude altogether, from the outset, those values that express the essential preconditions of political society and politics and that, therefore, are the "natural"—pre-political—premises of a political conception of justice. In doing this, we do not have to jeopardize the liberal concern for freedom and equality of individual citizens and corresponding reciprocity, nor do we have to give up the insti-tutional ethos of constitutional democracy. We only have to recognize that before human beings are citizens they already are human and social beings, governed by natural law, and that as citizens they are not deprived of this identity of being naturally social beings and that their right to life does not depend on their political status as citizens, but on their being human beings (which is the necessary precondition for being able to become a citizen).[140]

Any conception of political liberalism accepting this—while indeed maintaining most of its Rawlsian insights—will yield much more reasonable results than it does in Rawls's own version of it. Enriched by a sound and politically reflected theory of natural law, Rawls's theory of political liberal-ism would certainly not be any more *Rawls's* theory of political liberalism, but Rawls's original theory would still serve—as it does in this essay—as a conceptual framework and reflective background for better understanding and talking about how in liberal constitutional democracy natural law must

---

140. This means that even though the unborn child is not a "constitutional person" in the sense of the fifth and the fourteenth amendments to the Constitution of the United States of America—simply because it is not yet "born" or "naturalized," that is, a citizen—it is unreasonable and contrary to politi-cal justice not to recognize its right to life because not all rights that political justice has to take into ac-count are rights of "citizens" (including aliens); some are simply natural rights of human beings. About this see also my "Fundamental Rights, Moral Law, and the Legal Defense of Life in a Constitutional Democracy," quoted above. This is exactly the crucial point Rawls—as Dworkin and many other liberal theorists—fails to acknowledge.

be thought of as part of public reason, without thereby having to give up the specifically modern political ethos of peace, liberty, and political equality, and the peculiarly modern conception of public reason dependent on that ethos, which we wish to defend not in least because of historical experience.[141]

141. This essay was originally delivered at the University of Notre Dame Law School for the 2005 Natural Law Lecture. It was then published as "The Political Ethos of Constitutional Democracy and the Place of Natural Law in Public Reason: Rawls's *'Political Liberalism'* Revisited," *American Journal of Jurisprudence* 50 (2005): 1–70.

EIGHT

Rawlsian Public Reason, Natural Law, and the Foundation of Justice

A Response to David Crawford

A "Benign Interpretation of Liberalism"

In his article "Recognizing the Roots of Society in the Family, Foundation of Justice,"[1] David Crawford has provided a very valuable account of human society as founded in the family union, which on its turn is based on the marriage between two persons of opposite sex. The marital union, Crawford argues, is the expression of human beings' bodily constitution: individual human persons are constituted as sexually differentiated as male or female. In genuinely Aristotelian tradition, he moreover affirms that human society is not formed simply by "individuals," but by "men" and "women," mutually ordered to each other to form the basic social community called "marriage," which by its nature is reproductive. As such they form the basis of society, that is, its "first and vital cell."

Crawford stresses that it is precisely in the family where the notion of justice arises and is most basically learned, and that any public endorsement of a conception of justice and the corresponding institutions must be rooted in, and in a way reflect, the anthropology implied in the structure of what he calls the "familial person." His "familial anthropology" is not only inscribed in the structure of the human body. As a theologian, Crawford also gives it a Trinitarian-Christological foundation that he under-

---

1. *Communio* 34 (Fall 2007): 379–412.

stands as a cultural proposal, which, being a theological doctrine, is not to be "juridically impose[d]" on civil institutions, but "to be judged ... according to its intrinsic merits" (403). Crawford wants to show that, because of its voluntarist and procedural concept of justice, liberalism—as he understands it—is essentially opposed to such a cultural proposal that contains a "comprehensive" view of the good, the person, and the family. Liberalism, he claims, is instead pure proceduralism; it tries to conciliate and to legally protect and promote any individual preference, endorsing therewith individualism as a publicly valid anthropology and conception of the good that is intrinsically hostile to a true conception of the family as proposed by him. With this, Crawford concludes, liberalism contradicts its own principle of being neutral and of abstaining from publicly recognizing and promoting a determinate conception of the good.

In developing his proposal, Crawford concedes a central place to the evaluation of my, as he says, "critical engagement and qualified appropriation of Rawls' notion of 'public reason,'" as contained in my 2005 Natural Law Lecture at Notre Dame Law School.[2] Crawford tries to show that, though referring to natural law, I do not succeed in avoiding the shortcomings and errors of liberal proceduralism, and that my conservative "benign interpretation" of liberalism does not surmount the central flaw of all liberal conceptions: their incapacity of rooting the public conception of justice in a sound anthropology. A sound anthropology, on the contrary, will express a substantial and comprehensive notion of the good, such as the anthropology of the nuptial character of the human body and the "familial person" with its Trinitarian-Christological foundation, as developed in Crawford's article.

After a first reading, I was somewhat embarrassed because I agree with most of what Crawford says in his article about anthropology and the family as the fundamental and vital cell of society. I not only agree with it, but thirty years ago as a young philosopher and then a layman, I wrote a book on the family, defending its origin in natural law and arguing that it was the basic cell of society and a "school of the virtues," including first of all justice.[3] The book did not become what one usually calls "an editorial suc-

2. This is published as chapter 7 of the present volume. It was originally published as "The Political Ethos of Constitutional Democracy and the Place of Natural Law in Public Reason: Rawls' 'Political Liberalism' Revisited," *American Journal of Jurisprudence* 50 (2005): 1–70.

3. See my *Familie und Selbstverwirklichung. Alternativen zur Emanzipation* (Cologne: Verlag Wissenschaft und Politik, 1979).

cess." Besides other unquestionable defects, it too sharply contrasted with the mainstream ideology of the late seventies, which was putting individual "emancipation" above the engagement in marital bonds and the good of the family life. Yet, despite of this lack of success, I have never changed my views on these issues. My current, allegedly "benign interpretation" of liberalism is certainly not due to any change of view in this regard.

As Crawford concedes (392)—and as he does himself—I "castigate[s]" in my Natural Law Lecture Rawls's "reduction of pre-political social life to voluntary associations of individuals." This is one of the main points, if not the most important point, of my critique of Rawls. It is crucial not to overlook that—in Rawls's treatment of the family—I consider it to be a major flaw that, to quote Crawford's wording, Rawls falsely "considers the family to be a voluntary association, not essentially different from any other as far as a public doctrine of justice would go" (388). In contrast, I argue that before being free and equal as citizens, human beings are naturally social beings in different contexts; one of them is the family, where they are not "free and equal," and I argue that this naturally defined social dimension of human persons cannot remain irrelevant for public reason. Yet, Crawford does not seem to notice the weight of my rejection of the basis of Rawls's concept of society and public reason, a rejection that is based on this critique and on my reference to "human nature." Instead, Crawford bases his discussion of my alleged "benign interpretation of liberalism" on my assertion that the existence of natural and pre-social unions is not a "metaphysical" but an "empirical fact." My use of the word "empirical" and "empirical facts"— instead of "metaphysical truth"—is Crawford's only substantive argument for showing that I have in fact failed to escape from liberal proceduralism that is free to reinterpret the "empirical" as it pleases.

Yet, ironically I agree with Crawford's critique of merely procedural liberalism, which claims to be neutral but in reality publicly endorses a comprehensive liberal conception of the human person. But, even more ironically, not only do I agree, but many liberals do too—including most prominently Rawls himself! When citing on page 399, note 40, some anti-liberal authors who denounced—years ago—liberal proceduralism as being deeply flawed, Crawford could have also quoted some of my writings in which I make a similar point.[4] And, as I have just mentioned, there are even

4. Most of them are not published in English, but in German, Italian, or Spanish. Some of them are forthcoming in English. See, e.g., chapter 2 of the present volume, which was originally published

liberal thinkers who have criticized the "first" Rawls (the one of *A Theory of Justice*) for committing this error of endorsing a determinate "thin" concept of the person, while pretending to hold a position of public neutrality.[5] As a consequence of this critique by liberals, such as Charles Larmore, and antiliberals—as, for example, most importantly the one by Michael Sandel[6]—Rawls has profoundly revised his original *Theory* and developed a new position that itself contains a critique of pure liberal proceduralism as it is today represented most influentially by Jürgen Habermas, and inspired by him, by Charles Larmore, or, in a different way, by Ronald Dworkin.

The "Second Rawls" of *Political Liberalism*

One of the main problems of Crawford's article, as far as it deals with Rawls and my critical discussion of his *Political Liberalism,* is that Crawford's Rawls is still and only the Rawls of *A Theory of Justice* (henceforward referred to simply as *Theory*) while I critically discuss exclusively the "second Rawls" of *Political Liberalism*[7] (and of *The Idea of Public Reason Revisited,*[8] which contains important revision of the latter). The second Rawls seems to be unknown to Crawford. This is a major problem for his argument, because *Political Liberalism* (henceforward referred to as *PL*) is significantly different from *Theory.* Not in the sense that Rawls has substantially revised his theory of justice or that he does not hold it anymore,[9] but in the

---

as "L'immagine dell'uomo nel liberalismo e il concetto di autonomia: al di là del dibattito fra liberali e comunitaristi," in Ignacio Yarza, ed., *Immagini dell'uomo. Percorsi antropologici nella filosofia moderna* (Rome: Armando, 1997): 95–133.

5. See, e.g., Charles Larmore, *Patterns of Moral Complexity* (Cambridge: Cambridge University Press, 1987).

6. In his, as Rawls says (in *Political Liberalism,* 27n29) "important work": Michael Sandel, *Liberalism and the Limits of Justice* (Cambridge: Cambridge University Press, 1982).

7. *Political Realism* (New York: Columbia University Press, 1993); I refer to the paperback edition from 1996, which contains a new and important preface as well as (as Lecture IX) the famous "Reply to Habermas," originally published in *Journal of Philosophy* 92, no. 3 (March 1995), immediately following Habermas's "Reconciliation through the Public Use of Reason: Remarks on Rawls's Political Liberalism."

8. Originally published in the *University of Chicago Law Review* 64 (Summer 1997); I quote from the republished text in John Rawls, *The Law of Peoples, with "The Idea of Public Reason Revisited"* (Cambridge, Mass.: Harvard University Press, 1999), 129–80.

9. Nor should one assume I accept Rawls's theory of justice as fairness. My own views differ from his first and especially in that I hold what I call a kind of "modified contractarianism," modified by essentially Aristotelian elements; second, my views differ from Rawls in that I never accepted his dichotomy between the "right" and the "good"; third, I hold that public reason must forward substantial values and goods rooted in a sound anthropology; fourth, I do not entirely accept Rawls's interpretation of constitutional democracy as an "overlapping consensus" between reasonable comprehensive doctrines; I rather interpret constitutional democracy as a kind of *modus vivendi* that, however, contains elements of an overlapping consensus. This means that I think the requirements of mutual and overall

sense that *PL* deals with a different problem than *Theory* did. This new and specific theme of *PL* was also the subject matter of my 2005 Natural Law Lecture that Crawford has examined in his article and whose approach he rejects. Yet, unfortunately he disregards the specific theme both of Rawls's *Political Liberalism* and of my Natural Law Lecture, grounding his evaluation of my critical engagement with the second Rawls on the older and now classic criticism directed against *Theory,* as first set out by Michael Sandel.

What is this specific difference between the first and the second Rawls? While *Theory* offers an exposition of a determinate conception of a just society, *PL* now stresses that Rawls's own conception of justice is only one among the many possible conceptions of political justice that may fit into a political framework of constitutional democracy in the liberal tradition and thus be publicly endorsed by a constitutional consensus.[10] *PL* is, thus, not a revised theory of justice or just a different theory of justice. *PL* is a theory of liberal constitutional democracy. This theory is essentially *political* in the sense that it does not seek to provide a determinate view of what a just society would have to look like in terms of justice (something that in fact *Theory* does). Instead, it only seeks to provide an account of what is required for the basic political institutions—what Rawls also calls the "constitutional essentials"—to meet the requirements of "free and equal citizens" living together and cooperating in a world in which there is no consensus on the deepest metaphysical and religious questions. Yet this world has urgent need of a stable political order based on commonly shared political values (a theme

---

acceptability of public reasons are much lower than Rawls assumes and that therefore the majority principle has a correspondingly higher, though not absolute, weight (the majority principle must always be restricted by fundamental rights of the individual person and of minorities). For some further details of my view on an adequate approach to political justice, see chapter 7 of the present volume, entitled "The Political Ethos of Constitutional Democracy and the Place of Natural Law in Public Reason: Rawls's 'Political Liberalism' Revisited," which was originally delivered at the University of Notre Dame Law School for the 2005 Natural Law Lecture. Also see chapter 3 of the present volume entitled "The Democratic Constitutional State and the Common Good." This was originally published as "Lo Stato costituzionale democratico e il bene comune," in *Ripensare lo spazio politico: quale aristocrazia?,* ed. E. Morandi and R. Panattoni (Padua: Il Poligrafo, 1998), 57–123 (Con-tratto. Rivista di filosofia tomista e contemporanea 6/1997); "Contrattualismo, individualismo e solidarietà: per rileggere la tradizione liberale," in *Per la filosofia* 16, no. 46 (1999): 30–40.

10. The term "liberal" is used in a sense that is broader than the American "liberalism"; it also includes the continental kind of Anglo-Saxon, French, German, or Italian liberalism, which is much more conservative and less left-wing than American "liberalism," which in Europe rather corresponds to "social democracy." In *PL,* Rawls uses the term "liberalism" in this broader sense of the modern secular and constitutionalist state, democratically organized and founded in the tradition of representative parliamentarianism. This is also the way I employ the term "liberalism" when I talk about "liberal democracy" or "constitutional democracy." In this sense, the American Constitution and the Founding Fathers are "liberal," as are today's American Republicans, Democrats, and Libertarians.

that was disregarded in *Theory*). So, as Rawls puts it, unlike *Theory, PL* answers the question: "how is it possible for there to exist over time a just and stable society of free and equal citizens, who remain profoundly divided by reasonable religious, philosophical, and moral doctrines?" (*PL* 4). This essential theme of *PL* must never be lost sight of. Let me extensively quote how Rawls himself—at the end of its later article *The Idea of Public Reason Revisited*—puts the difference between *Theory* and *PL*:

> I end by pointing out the fundamental difference between *A Theory of Justice* and *Political Liberalism*. The first explicitly attempts to develop from the idea of the social contract, represented by Locke, Rousseau, and Kant, a theory of justice that is no longer open to objections often thought fatal to it, and that proves superior to the long dominant tradition of utilitarianism. *A Theory of Justice* hopes to present the structural features of such a theory so as to make it the best approximation to our considered judgments of justice and hence to give the most appropriate moral basis for a democratic society. Furthermore, justice as fairness is presented there as a comprehensive liberal doctrine (although the term "comprehensive doctrine" is not used in the book) in which all the members of its well ordered society affirm that same doctrine. This kind of well ordered society contradicts the fact of reasonable pluralism and hence *Political Liberalism* regards that society as impossible.
>
> Thus, *Political Liberalism* considers a different question, namely: How is it possible for those affirming a comprehensive doctrine, religious or nonreligious, and in particular doctrines based on religious authority, such as the Church or the Bible, also to hold a reasonable political conception of justice that supports a constitutional democratic society? The political conceptions are seen as both liberal and self-standing and not as comprehensive, whereas the religious doctrines may be comprehensive but not liberal. The two books are asymmetrical, though both have an idea of public reason. In the first, public reason is given by a comprehensive liberal doctrine, while in the second, public reason is a way of reasoning about political values shared by free and equal citizens that does not trespass on citizens' comprehensive doctrines so long as those doctrines are consistent with a democratic polity. Thus, the well ordered constitutional democratic society of *Political Liberalism* is one in which the dominant and controlling citizens affirm and act from irreconcilable yet reasonable comprehensive doctrines. These doctrines in turn support reasonable political conceptions—although not necessarily the most reasonable—which specify the basic rights, liberties, and opportunities of citizens in society's basic structure.

This brief summary of the development of his position and the shift of his concerns, provided by Rawls himself, shows why Crawford in his critique of Rawlsian political liberalism and of my "benign interpretation" of it rather misses the point. In *Theory* a consideration of the problems central to *PL*—the fact of pluralism and the problem of stability—was entirely absent. As Rawls himself admits, his solution to identify his theory of justice with public reason was therefore erroneous and impracticable. Rawls frankly, and for Crawford perhaps surprisingly, acknowledges that he advances in *Theory* a "comprehensive doctrine." *Theory* simply sets forth Rawls's conception of a just society—as he says a "comprehensive liberal doctrine"—without considering that there are other, equally reasonable people who hold other conceptions of justice, even partly on the grounds of religious or otherwise comprehensive views, that may be nonliberal, but still reasonable, that is, compatible with constitutional democracy.[11] *PL* now offers a theory of the required political framework of such a constitutional democracy, elaborating the fundamental political values and goods that should govern such a well-ordered society, which may be stable over time under the real conditions of a deeply divisive social, philosophical, and religious pluralism existing in the society it intends to order.

The "second" Rawls, the one of *PL* and even more of *The Idea of Public Reason Revisited* (henceforward referred to as *IPRR*) and the posthumous *Justice as Fairness: A Restatement,*[12] does not correspond to the picture of a merely procedural liberalism, which Crawford shows as corrosive for the family and to which I allegedly have succumbed. Rawls, and especially the second Rawls, is certainly *not* an advocate of the idea of mere "liberal proceduralism." He explicitly rejects such a view, which, as mentioned above, is rather that of Habermas's "ethics of discourse," a position argued against by Rawls in the last lecture of the paperback edition of *PL* (Lecture IX: "A Reply to Habermas"). So Rawls affirms the following about his conception of justice as fairness, also adopted in *PL*:

Justice as fairness is not procedurally neutral. Clearly its principles of justice are substantive and express far more than procedural values, and so do its political conceptions of society and person.... It seeks common ground—or if one prefers, neutral ground—given the fact of pluralism. This common ground is the political conception itself as the focus of an overlapping consensus, but common ground, so defined, is not procedurally neutral ground. (*PL* 192)

Nothing so far excludes a substantial concept of the "familial person" from being part of such a common ground.

Moreover, as the above long quotation shows, Rawls does not deny that his own liberalism as expounded in *Theory* is itself a comprehensive doc-

---

11. For a more detailed explanation of the Rawlsian term "reasonable" and the "reasonableness" of comprehensive doctrines, see chapter 7 of the present volume, 239–64.

12. *Justice as Fairness: A Restatement,* ed. Erin Kelly (Cambridge, Mass.: Harvard University Press, 2001).

trine that precisely is too comprehensive to serve as such a common ground and therefore as an expression of political justice required for the basic structure of constitutional democracy under the conditions of pluralism. Therefore, inasmuch as the second Rawls and *PL* are concerned, Crawford's attempt to delegitimize Rawls's liberalism as being itself a "comprehensive doctrine" is simply off the mark. To the extent that this charge of being a comprehensive doctrine is directed against *Theory,* it proves to be irrelevant, because Rawls himself sees *Theory* as a "liberal comprehensive doctrine," and because he admits that it cannot serve as a political background theory and political common ground required for modern constitutional democracy, and because he therefore offers such a theory in *PL.*

Finally and most importantly, Rawls's conception of political liberalism *does not* claim to be neutral to any conception of the good, because it acknowledges that public reason includes *goods* and *values* (that is, *political* goods and values) and that political society itself is a good (see *PL* 201ff.). Rawls even goes so far as to recognize that, according to the principles of political liberalism, "Catholic views of the common good and solidarity when they are expressed in terms of political values" could be publicly endorsed as a political conception of justice, because they meet the requirements of reasonableness demanded by political liberalism.[13] This may sound astonishing, yet Rawls explicitly affirms it because the course of his own revisions of his theory led him, perhaps willy-nilly, to this conclusion. There is, therefore, no reason to doubt that a constitutional democracy ordered according to the constitutional principles of Rawlsian political liberalism might publicly adopt the values and express the goods such as they are substantially contained in the anthropology of the family expounded in Crawford's essay (though it will of course not publicly adopt some of its theological rationale and argumentative basis; I will come back to this). According to Rawlsian logic, a constitutional democracy will be able to adopt it precisely insofar as it represents a *political good* that can be argued for by public reasons—which, so it seems to me, is exactly what Crawford also rightly intends (because he claims that his familial anthropology provides valid public reasons and that it is affirmed not only as a private, but also as a political, good, that is a constituent part of the political common good to be aimed at by legislation and public policy).

13. See *IPPR,* 142.

Taking Rawls at His Word:
The Problem of Natural Law

What I did in my Natural Law Lecture was an attempt to take Rawls according to his own words. I am convinced that in *PL* there is much political truth concerning the way we have to tackle the problem of modern political society under conditions of real and inescapable pluralism. Tackling this problem is the price of a freedom that today no reasonable person wishes to dismiss in favor of older "pre-liberal"—in the sense of pre-constitutionalist and pre-democratic—conceptions of an authoritarian and repressive political and social order. Rawls was an honest thinker who tried to seek coherence and to respond to all sorts of critique. By doing so, he constantly readjusted his views. As I tried to show in my Natural Law Lecture, it is this combination of truth contained in *PL* and the ongoing search for coherence and consistency that has drawn Rawls to ever more concessions, which finally lead to the "breakdown" of his most typically "liberal" stances precisely on issues such as the family grounded in heterosexual marriage or abortion.[14] I cannot deny, and never denied but rather emphasized, that exactly here his initial conception of the family as voluntary association—which is neither liberal nor illiberal, but in my opinion simply false—is still present in *PL*. Yet, in *PL* it brings Rawls into trouble because *PL* obviously excludes, without justifying it, the pre-political social nature of human beings, which reveals itself mainly in the marital and family union. He "tries to immunize public reason from any influence by natural law reasons."[15] Here Rawls is victim of a prejudice and methodological shortcoming of most twentieth-century liberalism. He could never refer to, say, John Locke for such a view, because Locke, as most of the early "liberals," was still thinking in the tradition of natural law and had a very strong idea about the family as shaping the individual person, as decisive for education and as the root of human society.

The main problem—and weakness—of Rawls's *PL*, as I see it, is precisely its complete disregard for and, as it seems to me, deep aversion to the idea of natural law. Rawls wants to absolutely avoid integrating any kind of natural law into his conception of political liberalism, and so he rejects even the slightest idea that *PL* could be understood in this way. Yet, Rawls fails

---

14. See my "The Political Ethos of Constitutional Democracy," 67 ff. (III, C.: *Postscript: Public Reason, Natural Law and Final Breakdown of Rawls's Immunization Strategy*).

15. Ibid., 67.

to succeed in his attempt to ban natural law from his political philosophy because he thereby falls into methodological arbitrariness, argumentative manipulation, and blindness toward what I called basic empirical facts. That he fails to successfully ban natural law from his political liberalism is precisely the point of my "revisiting" his conception of public reason. Ironically, Crawford has not noticed—or failed to point out—that my argument is a classical natural law argument in the tradition of Aristotle and Aquinas, perhaps because he was too much focused on detecting my being infected by the virus of procedural and "neutralist" liberalism (as others unfortunately have specialized in detecting in me the virus of Kantianism).[16] Yet, even more ironically, Crawford's own argument is definitively not a natural law argument because it is essentially theological, founded in a Trinitarian-Christological doctrine, and thus based on Christian revelation! No natural law argument can be of such a kind. At least methodologically, Crawford's argument seems therefore to be at odds with Catholic natural law tradition. Founding politics on Christian revelation and theology—especially in the revealed truth and mystery of the Trinity and in Christology—is certainly not the way the Catholic tradition has founded the relevance of marriage and the family for society and politics. That does not mean that I would deny that Christian revelation gives strong support to any sound natural law conception of society and the family, helping to render fully intelligible all the goods contained in it; on the contrary, I affirm this.[17] But Christian revelation cannot serve as its first and proper argumentative basis because this would be incompatible with the very idea of natural law, which is based on human reason unassisted by revelation. Revelation and theology can even less serve to effectively confute a secular-liberal idea of the family as a free association of autonomous individuals, or provide the ground for a public endorsement and legislation regarding an alternative view.[18]

16. While Crawford charges me with relying too much on "brute" and merely "empirical" natural facts, others reproach me for having disregarded nature in favor of reason and intention (a sign perhaps that both criticisms fail to grasp some important feature of my thought). See as an example of the latter the rather bewildering attempt by Matthew Levering to attribute to me views that are precisely the ones I explicitly reject, in his "Natural Law and Natural Inclinations: Rhonheimer, Pinckaers, McAleer," *Thomist* 70 (2006): 155–201.

17. See my "Is Christian Morality Reasonable? On the Difference between Secular and Christian Humanism," *Annales Theologici* 15, no. 2 (2001): 529–49; reprinted as chapter 1 in Martin Rhonheimer, *The Perspective of the Acting Person: Essays in the Renewal of Thomistic Moral Philosophy*, ed. William F. Murphy Jr. (Washington, D.C.: The Catholic University of America Press, 2008).

18. Notice that to say that natural law does not depend on theology does not mean that what traditionally is called "natural theology" is excluded from natural law theory. According to Aquinas, natural

Unfortunately, Crawford did not read my Notre Dame Natural Law Lecture in light of the background of the real problem I was dealing with and the obvious intentions I pursued in it, but rather in the light of his own, rather theological, concerns, which, from a political point of view (i.e., concerning public argumentation and legislation), seem to me rather misplaced. In my view, this resulted also in an inappropriate reading of the way I deal with Rawls's notion of public reason.

Natural Law and "Empirical Facts"

As mentioned above, in my Natural Law Lecture I tried to set forth an immanent critique of Rawls showing that there is nothing in Rawls's conception of public reason that contradicts the existence of natural law, which, however, he excludes by sheer methodological arbitrariness. This is shown by discussing his initial contention that human society is simply composed of "free and equal citizens," a conception that I showed to be obviously false and that I emphasized was not consistent with the most fundamental "empirical" data.

Now, Crawford has stumbled over the expression "empirical," more precisely over a sentence in which I say that "*the nature of society* and, therefore, [of] what *naturally* makes human persons to be social beings" are "not genuinely 'metaphysical' but empirical questions." As Crawford reports (on page 393 of his essay), I also called the reproductive union of male and female, the family, and other expressions of the social nature of human beings "natural social facts," "basic empirical truths," "basic facts of our existence as real human beings," or "basic empirical facts about the reproductive nature of the marital union and about the family." Yet, Crawford argues, "empirical facts," are not *goods*. The real nature of the family cannot be based simply on the "empirical"; in order to be a normative ground for public reason it must be grounded in a comprehensive conception of the good. Otherwise, he continues, it will be simply subject to continuous reinterpretation by liberal proceduralism. The merely empirical "is open to an infinite number of new 'factual' situations *because what it fails to capture, and in principle can-*

---

law is the participation of the eternal law in the rational creature; this means, as I have insistently and extensively argued in my *Natural Law and Practical Reason,* that in a Thomistic interpretation, to which I adhere, there is no natural law that is not ultimately "theonomic." In fact, as I have written, natural law is "participated theonomy," which, however, constitutes a rational (cognitive) autonomy of the acting subject that I also called "participated autonomy."

not capture without leaving liberal principles behind, is a sense of the good of the person as such, that is to say of the good as perfective of the human person, In short, what Rhonheimer's argument requires is some comprehensive view of the good" (395, emphasis in the original). But such a comprehensive view of the good, Crawford adds, is incompatible with Rawlsian public reason.

I simply think that Crawford has both overdramatized my use of the term "empirical fact" and taken it out of its context. Moreover, he disregards that I have explicitly linked these empirical facts to "values," talking, for example, about "these basic facts of society and the values connected with them" or calling them simply "social values" (instead of which I also could have said "social goods") or about "natural social essentials." Moreover, I talk at length on "the case of the family," showing that its natural social features, including its heterosexual character as reproductive union, must be—contrary to what Rawls insinuates—understood as *political goods,* fully relevant for public reason and orientating its use. So, Crawford neglects to mention that my view of the family and the "familial" character of human persons is far more than the assertion of a simple "empirical fact," as he understands it; it is—in a clearly Aristotelian sense[19]—the affirmation as a political good of a naturally, and in this sense empirically, experienced essential feature of human persons, their natural sociability (that it should be even understood as a "comprehensive good," as Crawford claims, is, as I will explain later on, not only unnecessary, but even self-defeating).

The particular context of my talking about "empirical facts" was that of an internal critique of Rawls's position, which, as is usual in such cases, induced me to adopt partly his own terminology. Now, for Rawls it is important to stress that public reason cannot be founded on "metaphysically" controversial doctrines about the good. When Rawls uses the term "metaphysical," he opposes it to "political" (most famously in his essay "Justice as Fairness: Political Not Metaphysical").[20] The "metaphysical," for Rawls, belongs to

19. See Aristotle's *Politics*, book 1, 1252a 24 - 1253a 4: "The best method of investigation is to study things in the process of development from the beginning. The first coupling together of persons then to which necessity gives rise is that between those who are unable to exist without one another, namely the union of female and male for the continuance of the species." The second social union Aristotle mentions is the domestic community (which, according to him, includes also the slaves); then comes the village; and finally the perfect, self-sufficient community that is the city-state (the *polis*). "For the city-state is the end of the other partnerships, and nature is an end, since that which each thing is when its growth is completed we speak of as being the nature of each thing.... From these things therefore it is clear that the city state is a natural growth, and that man is by nature a political animal" (Aristotle, *Politics*, trans. H. Rackham, Loeb Classical Library 21).

20. Originally published in *Philosophy and Public Affairs* 14, no. 3 (1985): 223–52; reprinted as

particular truth-claiming comprehensive doctrines such as Kant's idea of autonomy or Mill's idea of individuality, or, as Rawls says, moral values or dictates called by others "natural law" and the like. The "political," instead, belongs to the domain of the practical: it is what can and should, among reasonable human beings, serve as a common ground for establishing the basic structure of political society and what can be validly considered as "public reason" because it is the sort of reason that can be, independently from controversial religious and "metaphysical" truths (in the Rawlsian sense), understood and on principle accepted by any citizen as a public reason. Of course, adherents of natural law hold that precisely natural law arguments are of this kind—even if they imply a truth-claim (I will come back to this). They are not "comprehensive" in the Rawlsian sense, but—as is emphasized also by John Finnis and Robert George, whom I partly criticized in my Natural Law Lecture[21]—are apt to be understood and accepted by adherents of different comprehensive doctrines (including religious ones), as the *kind* of arguments characteristic of public reasons (though not all persons may accept them as *valid* reasons and *agree* with them).

To understand my move against Rawls it is, moreover, important to consider that Rawls affirms that the politically just is the object of a process of reflective construction. He calls that "Kantian constructivism." Yet, what is important is that Rawls equally affirms that in his political conception of justice *not everything is constructed.* "We must have some material, as it were, from which to begin" (*PL* 104). This is why some pages later Rawls asserts: "Without conceptions of society and person, the principles of practical reason would have no point, use, or application.... The conceptions of society and person as ideas of reason are not, certainly, constructed any more than the principles of practical reason are constructed" (*PL* 108). This is why according to Rawls—and now we come nearer to the point I wish to make—it must be admitted that no constructivist, and in this sense "political," view says "that the facts that are relevant in practical reasoning and judgment are constructed, any more than they say that the conceptions of person and society are constructed" (*PL* 121). Explaining this further, Rawls tells us that there are facts which are "right-and-wrong-making character-

chapter 18 in John Rawls, *Collected Papers,* ed. Samuel Freeman (Cambridge, Mass.: Harvard University Press, 1999).

21. See Finnis's and George's contributions to the volume *Natural Law and Public Reason,* ed. Robert P. George and Christopher Wolfe (Washington, D.C.: Georgetown University Press, 2000), and my critical remarks on 32ff. (including 35n76) and 48ff.

istics"; other facts are about the "content of justice, or the nature of the virtues, or the political conception itself. They are given by the nature of the constructivist procedure" (*PL* 121 f.). Yet, the latter does not apply to the before-mentioned "right-and-wrong-making characteristics." Rawls gives an example for both cases of facts: "To illustrate the first kind of fact, to argue that slavery is unjust we appeal to the fact that it allows some persons to own others as their property and thus to control and own the product of their labor. To illustrate the second kind of fact, we may appeal straight-away to the fact that the nature of justice condemns slavery as unjust; or to the fact that the principles of justice condemn slavery as unjust" (PL 122). Rawls adds that facts, as such, are simply facts, and that they must be deter-mined by a reasonable procedure according to their weight and relevance as *reasons*. "So understood, a constructivist political conception is not at odds with our commonsense ideas of truth and matters of fact" (PL 122).

Without going further into this theory of what Rawls calls "Kantian constructivism," it should now be clearer what I mean by saying that the questions about the natural roots of society and the social nature of human beings are "not genuinely 'metaphysical' but empirical questions" and why I talk in this context about "empirical facts." First, "metaphysical" was put into quotation marks; it refers to the Rawlsian "metaphysical" as opposed to the "political." It refers to what in the sphere of the political cannot, and need not, be constructed even in a Rawlsian sense, but to "the material from which to begin." What is an empirical fact is not, like Kantian "autonomy" or Mill's "individuality," a determined comprehensive and "metaphysical" conception of the person (or as Rawls's Kantian conception of the person of his *Theory*), but belongs to what is fundamental for any sound conception of society, independently from one's comprehensive moral or religious doc-trine. It belongs to "the material from which to begin." Yet, this "material from which to begin" also for Rawls includes a dimension of truth, because it is both not "constructed" and politically valid.

Secondly, "empirical facts" in contrast to the "metaphysical" also refers to Rawls's insistence that public reasons must "appeal only to presently ac-cepted general beliefs and forms of reasoning found in common sense, and the methods and conclusions of science when these are not controversial," which means "that in discussing constitutional essentials and matters of basic justice we are not to appeal to comprehensive religious and philo-sophical doctrines" but only to "the plain truths now widely accepted, or available, to citizens generally" (*PL* 224–25). I think it is not saying too much if one asserts that the existence of human society over time depends on the reproductive community between male and female, that heterosexual unions are therefore a political good (which cannot be said about homosexual unions), and similar things. Even if some of these topics today are, for ideological reasons, controversially debated, and even if some might advocate the substitution of "natural" forms of reproduction by reproductive technologies, this does not alter the fact that these "empirical facts" about reproductive heterosexual unions do not constitute a controversial comprehensive religious or philosophical doctrine, and that they are truths "widely accepted" and "available to citizens generally."

Therefore, Rawls does not succeed in banning every idea of "truth" from his political conception of justice. Admittedly, he tries to construct a clear dichotomy between the "metaphysical" (truth claiming comprehensive philosophical and religious doctrines) and the "political" (consensual constructions by mere practical reason for the sake of finding a "basis of informed and willing political agreement between citizens viewed as free and equal persons").[22] Yet, the political must be based at least on *some* truth about the human person; otherwise, according to Rawls, nothing could be constructed. It is precisely natural law that expresses, in the realm of the political, these basic truths that are firmly rooted in empirical data—mostly delivered by the natural inclinations of the human person—which, however are in need of being interpreted by the truth-attaining human reason.[23]

Crawford has conferred on terms such as "metaphysical" or "empirical facts" a meaning that belongs to another context and that disregards the polemical and ironical use I make of them just in order to make a point against Rawls. Perhaps because of his lack of knowledge of Rawls's thought and the argumentative context, Crawford converts my statement into the assertion that these "empirical facts," that is, the social nature of human beings, as I describe it in my lecture, are not conceived as "goods." But nothing would be more mistaken than this. Crawford too easily makes this move because he thinks that Rawls does not conceive of political values as *goods*. But this again is not the case. In *PL* Rawls has in fact abandoned the sharp opposi-

---

22. Rawls, "Justice as Fairness: Political not Metaphysical," in *Collected Papers*, 394.

23. How, in my view, this is to be understood and how it might work can be gathered from my *Natural Law and Practical Reason: A Thomist View of Moral Autonomy* (New York: Fordham University Press, 2000).

tion between the "right" and the "good," so characteristic of his earlier position. He now says that "the priority of the right does not mean that ideas of the good must be avoided; that is impossible. Rather, it means that the ideas used must be political ideas" (PL 203). I think this is an important point and, in a way, even a truism: a public conception of justice and public reason must be grounded in, and be an expression of, goods that are precisely identified as politically relevant—we could also say: relevant for the political common good—they must therefore be in some broader way *political goods.* And this is my basic affirmation against Rawls: the reproductive union of male and female, the family, and so on are not only "private," but also essentially political, goods. My main argument, as exposed in my Natural Law Lecture, is: these goods are the condition for the reproduction of society and for its being a reality that persists over time. Something similar applies to the question of abortion: the right to life of the unborn is clearly a political good, which is based on generally accessible knowledge about the genetic status of embryos and fetuses, and which overrides other rights of the born, as for example the right of the woman to self-determination, or the "right to privacy."

I concede that Crawford is right in saying that it is not sufficient to talk about marriage, sexuality, and the family only in terms of "empirical facts" and the like. To prevent Crawford's misunderstanding, I perhaps should have mentioned that these empirical facts are the basis for a sound political anthropology, which no public political philosophy can do without (and that such a political anthropology includes metaphysical truths, not in a Rawlsian, but in the classical, sense). I therefore agree that a more complete account of these basic social values or goods is needed precisely to render them intelligible as anthropological goods and in this sense metaphysical truths, and not only as something merely factual that is open to manipulation and reinterpretation. Yet, this is the task of a more elaborated natural law theory (which I have presented in other places, mainly in my *Natural Law and Practical Reason*).[24] But we should still not forget that natural law has much to do with the empirical, the factual, the natural, and so on.[25] What I wanted to stress is that Rawls excludes from his concept of society not simply what is "metaphysical" and thus politically nonrelevant. It in-

---

24. See preceding note.

25. See, for example, classic treatments mainly in the German-speaking tradition, such as the one by Johannes Messner, *Das Naturrecht: Handbuch der Gesellschaftsethik, Staatsethik und Wirtschaftsethik,* 6th ed. (Innsbruck-Vienna-Munich: Tyrolia Verlag, 1966).

stead excludes what is most real and—independently from any "metaphysical" (in the Rawlsian sense) or religious comprehensive doctrine—empirically obvious and logically compelling: that without reproduction there is no society over time, and that for reproduction human sexuality, the community of male and female, and the family are necessary, and that this is the grounds for their belonging to natural law as far as it is politically relevant and, therefore, also to public reason.

Therefore, I think Crawford unjustly charges me with having a "liberal" conception of natural law. I instead try to subvert "liberal" conceptions of public reason by traditional natural law thinking. At best, Crawford could have reproached me for not succeeding in this attempt, but not for holding "liberal" views in the Rawlsian sense! On the other side, I see a problem in the fact that Crawford in reality does not seem to work with *any* conception of natural law. He overlooks, moreover, that natural law has much to do with "empirical facts." Not simply with what actually happens to be the case, but with structure and patterns that can be experienced in the reality of things, mainly in the reality we call "human nature." To reduce the nature of human beings, as Rawls does, to their being "free and equal" is empirically false. It means to disregard what simply belongs to human nature and what is fundamental for human beings as social beings; these, which I insist should not be understood as "metaphysical" doctrines in the Rawlsian sense, cannot be reasonably excluded from the range of political goods and public reason. And this means—so my argument goes—that Rawls's principle of reciprocity and his "liberal principle of legitimacy" must also be shaped by a concept of the human person and of citizens that relies not only on their political freedom and equality, but also on what, before their being citizens, naturally constitutes them as social beings.

Natural Law and Public Reason

There is another reason why Crawford thinks that my approach "effectively views natural law from the perspective of and according to the conditioning and internal logic of the core liberal principles" (396). If I have rightly understood, he thinks it because in my Natural Law Lecture I affirm that "to be apt for public justification, natural-law reasons must first be converted into public reasons" (48) and because I add to this: "They are becoming public reasons only insofar as they can be justified in terms of referring to the common good of political society" (ibid.). Crawford seems to overlook that this is rather a traditional argumentative pattern. The argument is traditional because I understand it exactly in the sense Aquinas seems to understand it, whom I have extensively quoted in this sense: civil law does not have the same range as moral law;[26] it establishes only what is politically necessary and convenient, and it punishes only what is necessary from a strictly political point of view, which Aquinas calls the "common good of justice and peace," and to which we today might like to add liberty.

In contrast, "natural law" *as such* includes the whole moral order, as far as it is naturally knowable to unassisted human reason. It is simply "the moral law" as far as it is knowable by natural human reason; it refers to all moral virtues and regulates their rational structure. It also forbids all vices. Yet, it is common teaching that not everything that the natural moral law commands or prohibits must also be commanded or prohibited and even punished by civil law. To determine, therefore, which natural-law reasons are also *public* reasons—that is, reasons that can show that something must, or should, be also publicly endorsed by legal and political means—we need in every case a *further* argument that not only refers to "natural law as such"—to its being the moral law—but also shows why such and such a norm of natural law refers to a *political* good, is therefore politically relevant and thus a candidate for also being, on the grounds of public reason, publicly endorsed (e.g., by statutes or otherwise enforced by the juridical system). I cannot see what this has in common with viewing natural law "from the perspective of and according to the conditioning and internal logic of the core liberal principles." Of course, there is a kind of liberalism, such as, for example, classic Lockean liberalism, that would be rather congruous to such a view, and something similar applies, as I noted, to the logic of Mill's harm principle. Yet this is so simply because Locke is still very much dependent on the classic natural law tradition, and because in Mill's public philosophy some clearly Aristotelian relics have survived. My own view is not, in any case, conditioned by any kind of modern liberalism because my view also precisely accepts natural law as a *standard of truth* for public reasons. There certainly is nothing specifically "liberal"—in the sense of liberal neutralism and mere procedural-

---

26. This is also recognized by the Magisterium of the Catholic Church; see, e.g., John Paul II, Encyclical *Evangelium vitae* (1995), no. 71: "The purpose of civil law is different and more limited in scope than that of the moral law." For my interpretation of this see Martin Rhonheimer, "Fundamental Rights, Moral Law, and the Legal Defense of Life in a Constitutional Democracy: A Constitutionalist Approach to the Encyclical *Evangelium Vitae*," *American Journal of Jurisprudence* 43 (1998): 135–83.

ism—in my contention that natural law is the criterion of the truth of public reason and that "public reason cannot be properly defined without *some* reference to natural law" (52), which of course in the first place means that public reason—and civil law—must never *contradict* natural law.

Moreover and especially, Crawford has overlooked the basic problem that Rawls seeks to address with his conception of political justice and that underlies my own natural law approach: the question of "which are the standards and norms that may be licitly *enforced by the coercive apparatus of the state*"? This is one of the main points I made in my lecture: "Although natural law may always work as a criterion for recognizing specific laws as unjust, it is not a criterion sufficient for making out what is to be imposed by law and the coercive apparatus of the state on the totality of citizens." This is partly a matter of principle (I think it is rather obvious to everybody that masturbation, say, should not be prohibited by law, though it is against the moral order as established by natural law, nor should civil law generally prohibit fornication, or lying, except in forensic contexts or in commercial relations, where there precisely exists a public reason for endorsing the norm of natural law also politically and legally). All of this has nothing to do with "liberalism," though a liberal might have similar ideas. That some classical liberals, such as J. S. Mill, did have an idea very close to this does not convert me into a Millean liberal or suggest that my reading of Aquinas is wrong. Neither has it anything in common with the Hobbesian principle *Autoritas non veritas facit legem,* that is, with Hobbesian legal positivism, which, once a sovereign political power is instituted, denies the existence and legitimacy of any criterion of justice beyond the positive law established by the sovereign authority. I reject such a view because I consider that objections based on natural law can be at any time raised against positive law without thereby, as Hobbes—and later the great Austrian theoretician of legal positivism Hans Kelsen—believed, undermining the legitimate sovereignty of political power and without endangering peace; I also reject Hobbesian legal positivism because I hold that the justice of positive law has a permanent measure of truth in natural law.[27]

---

27. For a critical discussion and refutation of the Hobbesian principle see chapter 4 of the present volume, entitled, "*Auctoritas non veritas facit legem:* Thomas Hobbes, Carl Schmitt, and the Idea of the Constitutional State." This was originally published as "*Autoritas non veritas facit legem:* Thomas Hobbes, Carl Schmitt und die Idee des Verfassungsstaates," in *Archiv für Rechts- und Sozialphilosophie* 86 (2000): 484–98; and more extensively my book on Thomas Hobbes: *La filosofia politica di Thomas Hobbes: coerenza e contraddizioni di un paradigma* (Roma: Armando, 1997).

On the other side, it is also a question of the problem of a pluralistic democratic society in which we have to find a common ground for public reason and legal procedures. This again is simply a fact and a necessity of the world we are living in. The only real alternative is civil war. This is why I feel somewhat uncomfortable with Alasdair MacIntyre's affirmation that "modern politics is civil war carried on by other means."[28] Modern constitutional democracy is precisely *not* this, but the overcoming of civil war by political culture, a culture of peaceful cooperation, though not necessarily harmonious and without conflict and political striving. This culture has specifically evolved on the grounds of the experience of pluralism, mainly religious; in Rawlsian terms, it has evolved through conflicting comprehensive views. This is a theme that is entirely absent from Crawford's discourse. One cannot, however, engage in a critique of Rawls's thought without having this problem present. It is the very theme of Rawls's *Political Liberalism* (remember the above-quoted sentence from *PL* 4 that contains the initial question: "how is it possible for there to exist over time a just and stable society of free and equal citizens, who remain profoundly divided by reasonable religious, philosophical, and moral doctrines?"); and this is, of course, also one of the main subject matters of my Natural Law Lecture. This is why I think Crawford has simply missed the point of the debate. He may develop his Trinitarian-Christological conception of marriage and the family—which I consider to be true and also relevant for our moral self-understanding not only as Christians, but as human beings in general. Equally I admire John Paul II's theology of the body, its deep biblical foundation and theological richness. Yet, how in a religiously and morally pluralistic society can a biblically founded Trinitarian-Christological argument become a *politically relevant and compelling one*? What I am searching for in my work of political philosophy is such arguments, not expositions of the whole truth in all its depth. Both attempts are licit and necessary in their place; but neither should be played off against the other.

Rawls's *Proviso* and Public Reason

Now, Crawford himself admits that he does not intend to offer such a political argument. And here he surprisingly comes to say, certainly without

28. Alasdair MacIntyre, *After Virtue: A Study in Moral Theory,* 2nd ed. (Notre Dame: University of Notre Dame Press, 1984), 253.

being aware of it, something very similar to what Rawls says, mainly with his famous idea of the *proviso*. Let me explain this. Crawford writes that his "vision of the person and his relationship to the family *derived in part through the light cast by* this Trinitarian-Christological foundation ought at least to be a legitimate possibility as a cultural proposal, *to be judged of course according to its intrinsic merits as such*" (403). The crucial words here are the ones I have emphasized. I assume that I am right in understanding this in the sense that Crawford agrees that a Trinitarian-Christological foundation cannot be defended publicly as a cultural proposal to be politically and legally implemented. In other words, for nonbelievers, such a theological foundation simply lacks the required intelligibility and acceptability to provide an argumentative structure for political and legal implementation. It is, or rather belongs to, a comprehensive doctrine that is, in Rawlsian terms, reasonable, but must be publicly proposed and defended by what Crawford calls "its intrinsic merits as such." What might the expression "intrinsic merits as such" mean? I suggest that in this context it can mean only "its content insofar as it is intelligible as a specifically *political* good and relevant for the political common good of society," or "its specifically political dimension," or "its merits as a public reason."

Now, even so, Crawford thinks he holds a position essentially different from any form of Rawlsian political liberalism. But this is not the case. If my understanding of what he writes is correct, he says the same thing that Rawls does. Of course, Crawford perhaps would reply that this "public reason," as he understands it (the "intrinsic merits as such" of his Trinitarian-Christological foundation), draws on a comprehensive doctrine that moreover is a religious doctrine and not a "secular" one; and that doing this is incompatible with Rawlsian political liberalism. Yet, this again would not be true. Rawls is not Robert Audi (who identifies public reasons with secular reasons);[29] for Rawls, public reasons may licitly draw from comprehensive doctrines, and these may also be *religious* comprehensive doctrines.[30] The only conditions, he says, are two: first, such comprehensive doctrines must be "reasonable," that is, able to *politically* coexist with other (reason-

---

29. See Robert Audi, *Religious Commitment and Secular Reason* (Cambridge: Cambridge University Press, 2000). Rawls says instead (in *IPRR* 143) that secular reasons and secular values "are not the same as public reasons. For I define secular reasons as reasoning in terms of comprehensive nonreligious doctrines."

30. Equally "the acceptance of the political conception is not a compromise between those holding different views, but rests on the totality of reasons specified within the comprehensive doctrine affirmed by each citizen" (*PL* 170–71).

able) comprehensive doctrines;[31] and second, they must be in due time publicly proposed by political reasons; that is, the public reasons drawn from such comprehensive doctrines must be the kind of reasons that can be acceptable as public reasons also for those who hold other comprehensive doctrines. That is, they must express specifically political values and be presented as proper political arguments open to public debate.[32]

This latter condition is what Rawls famously calls the *proviso*. An example given by Rawls is the public reason for state support to Church schools. The argument is not that these schools represent and promote the religious truth or promote values rooted in true divine revelation; the argument, rather, includes things such as the specific contribution of the religious values promoted by those schools to the common good of society, their high standards of learning efficiency, their specific contribution to culture, and similar things. Rawls also refers to how the abolitionist movement in the nineteenth century was nurtured by religious values and rooted in religious comprehensive doctrines, though it forwarded reasons against slavery that could be defended and made intelligible to everybody as public and political values. They thus were promoted in the public square in the light of their "intrinsic merits as such"—as political goods, that is, as constituents of the political common good—and not in merit of their being part of a comprehensive religious (or philosophical, "metaphysical," etc.) doctrine.

At least for the later Rawls, there is no problem that such reasons are grounded in religious comprehensive doctrines, because the public justification itself "is still given in terms of a family of reasonable political conceptions of justice. However, there are no restrictions or requirements in how religious or secular doctrines are themselves to be expressed" (*IPRR* 153). In a famous interview with Bernard G. Prusak, in the journal *Commonweal* (September 25, 1998), Rawls explains the *proviso* as follows (emphasis not in the original):

31. This is not an epistemological judgment and thus does not exclude that there might be one comprehensive doctrine that is the only true one, as it is said in *PL* 129: "There can be but one true comprehensive doctrine, though as we have seen, many reasonable ones."

32. This does not mean that they are reasons that are acceptable or even in fact accepted by everybody, but, as Rawls stresses in *IPRR*, it means they are the *kind* of reasons that can be accepted by any reasonable person as public reasons; that is, e.g., that it is not grounded in facts or revelation, which presuppose faith. See e. g. *IPRR* 165–66: "The idea of public reason is not a view about specific political institutions or policies. Rather it is a view about the kind of reasons on which citizens are to rest their political cases in making their political justifications to one another when they support laws and policies that invoke the coercive powers of government concerning fundamental political questions."

Any comprehensive doctrine, religious or secular, can be introduced into any political argument at any time, but I argue that people who do this should also present what they believe are public reasons for their argument. So their opinion is no longer just that of one particular party, but an opinion that all members of a society might reasonably agree to, not necessarily that they would agree to. What's important is that people *give the kinds of reasons that can be understood and appraised apart from their particular comprehensive doctrines*: for example, that they argue against physician-assisted suicide not just by speculating about God's wrath or the afterlife, but by talking about what they see as assisted suicide's potential injustices. So the idea of public reason isn't about the right answers to all these questions, but about the kinds of reasons that they ought to be answered by.

And against the interviewer's suggestion that some critics might consider this as a "veiled argument for secularism," Rawls continues:

I emphatically deny it. Suppose I said that it is not a veiled argument for secularism any more than it is a veiled argument for religion. Consider: there are two kinds of comprehensive doctrines, religious and secular. Those of religious faith will say I give a veiled argument for secularism, and the latter will say I give a veiled argument for religion. I deny both. Each side presumes the basic ideas of constitutional democracy, so my suggestion is that we can make our political arguments in terms of public reason. Then we stand on common ground. That's how we can understand each other and cooperate.[33]

So far, I think, this is a reasonable argument. *It certainly does not exclude offering public reasons for a politics sustaining an understanding of marriage and family grounded in a Trinitarian-Christological conception like the one exposed by Crawford, provided he is able to render it intelligible in the public sphere "according to its intrinsic merit."* This means he must render it intelligible for those who will not share his religious belief, including his Trinitarian theology and Christology.

Notice that Crawford's conception of the person and the family, as far as it can be presented as a political good—that is, as a value forming part of the political common good—is *not* what Rawls calls a "comprehensive doctrine." In my view, it is a mistake, and self-defeating, to say, as Crawford does, that a conception of the good of the person necessary for publicly sustaining a view, like the one Crawford develops, must be a *comprehensive* doctrine in the sense Rawls uses this term. I rather consider it, as far as it is politically relevant, to belong to natural law. Natural law is not a comprehensive doctrine, especially not insofar it is politically relevant, that is,

---

33. The interview has been reprinted, though with some minor, but significant omissions, as chapter 27 in Rawls, *Collected Papers*. The omissions refer mainly to some examples given in the original interview, also the one mentioned above concerning physician-assisted suicide.

a natural *legal* doctrine (in German we call it *Naturrecht,* as distinguished from the *Naturgesetz*). Yet, the point of natural law thinking generally is that, as such (abstracting from considering it in a broader theological context), it does not represent a comprehensive doctrine.[34] It instead intends to be the expression of the natural reason that is, in principle, common to all human beings, independent of their comprehensive religious or philosophical views, and that is also apt to generate what Rawls calls public reasons.

Contrary to Crawford's suggestion, moreover, nothing in Rawls's idea of public reason implies the exclusion of public reasons stemming from, or informed by, "a theological or religious background" (403). The contrary is true: Rawls explicitly distinguishes public reason from what he calls the "background culture." As Rawls stresses, the idea of public reason, including all forms of public discourse, does not apply to the background culture. It applies only to decisions, and their public justification, that imply the imposition of legal norms and policies by the coercive apparatus of the state. Such coercion, Rawls contends, may not be, and as a matter of fact in a pluralistic democratic society cannot possibly be, exercised simply on the basis of truth-claims of comprehensive doctrines (be they secular or religious), but only on the grounds of public reasons, which are political reasons and as such open to a rational debate accessible to every citizen. I would say that they are natural-law reasons, yet not just any natural-law reasons, but those that are apt to be public or political reasons: that is, those that refer to the political common good of society. And this is why I think we need, in addition to natural law theory, also a philosophy of the political common good.

To the set of public reasons grounded in natural law belong those facts and their corresponding values that distinguish human beings as naturally social. One of those, the most basic and important one, is the role of the reproductive community of male and female—marriage or matrimony—and the family springing therefrom. The knowledge of this role of marriage and the family is based in empirical or "natural" data that are interpreted and understood as basic human values or goods that are recognizable as fundamental

---

34. This touches upon the question of the rationality of Christian morality. For a discussion, see my "Is Christian Morality Reasonable? On the Difference between Secular and Christian Humanism" in my *The Perspective of the Acting Person* (quoted in note 17). In it, I argue—among other things—that "the basic moral requirements of Christian life are in principle fully intelligible and therefore accessible to reasonable argument and defense, but they simultaneously need in many cases the support of Christian faith to preserve fully their reasonableness." I further argue that Christian morality is properly understood as an integral part of a religion of salvation, within the logic of redemption through the cross of Christ.

political goods (such as reproduction, which is a fundamental political good because it guarantees the existence of society over time, as well as, e.g., the accumulation and transmission of property, which is indispensable for development and progress, and therefore is a political good, or the transmission of knowledge, technology, or other aspects of culture).

Conclusion: Defending Natural Law in a Pluralistic Society

Rawls has gone very far in his passion for finding coherence and in meeting objections to his conception of public reason. He went so far that his immunization strategy against natural law finally broke down. To show this was the aim of my Natural Law Lecture. Yet, his theory of political liberalism and his (revisited) idea of public reason is sufficiently powerful, and contains sufficient truth, to be able to be used *against* Rawls's specifically liberal idea of considering citizens exclusively as "free and equal." This idea, together with Rawls's flawed principle of reciprocity springing from it, needs to be challenged as it disregards the whole range of essential characteristics of citizens, and of the political conception of the person, that stem from their pre-political social nature grounded in what I call "empirical facts," such as the nexus between sexuality and reproduction, and the dependency of the existence of society over time on sexual reproduction and what Rawls calls "reproductive labor" (while he disregards the simple "empirical" fact that reproduction cannot be realized by same-sex unions). Whether it is a realistic expectation that this "reproductive labor" of traditional heterosexual marriage might one day be generally substituted by artificial reproduction—*in vitro* and the like—and whether this would be not only morally licit but also politically desirable, is another question. I think it is relatively easy to argue effectively against such an attempt from a political point of view. I did not do this in my Natural Law Lecture, yet it can be done at any time. This would reinforce my view that the "natural" (qualified by sound reasons, of course) would enter into the political as part of those political goods that enter into the range of public reason.

To conclude, let me just emphasize three points: First, I think that a sound and reasonable natural law approach to social and political philosophy is more important for defending a sound conception of marital love and the family in the public sphere (i.e., for political and legal purposes) than a sophisticated Trinitarian and Christological "theology of the body." Such a natural law approach does not understand itself as a "comprehensive doctrine" in the Rawlsian sense, but as part of a sort of common reasonableness, accessible to and debatable for every reasonable citizen, which can serve as foundation of public reason.

Secondly, even if the sense of justice and the virtue of justice have their origin in the experience of interpersonal relationships as first and most essentially lived in the context of the family, political society and some specifically political features of justice are specific to the public sphere and to the political. They cannot simply be transposed from the family context to political society. In this sense there is some truth in Rawls's famous distinction between two moral powers: "a capacity for a sense of justice and a capacity for a conception of the good" (e.g., PL 19), where the former is "the capacity to understand, to apply, and to act from the public conception of justice which characterizes the fair terms of social cooperation" (ibid.). Precisely "freedom" and "equality" are not, in their specifically political meaning, present in family life. Instead, family life is much more grounded in other features of justice, which sometimes instead—and justly—stress inequality, subordination, authority, obedience, community, and so on (which are not totally absent from the political sphere either, but there acquire different configurations and meanings). One of the most importance critiques of Aristotle regarding the Platonic conception of the State was that Plato confused political government with domestic government. While domestic government is government over the nonequal and unfree, Aristotle teaches that political government is over free and equal citizens whose most significant feature is the interchangeability of those who govern and the governed. Similarly, we today should not reduce political justice simply to domestic justice, even if no conception of political justice could be developed without having first learned the virtue of justice and other virtues connected with it—most importantly solidarity and generosity and, of course, charity—in the family context.

Thirdly, Christians—and more specifically Catholics—need to reflect not only upon the ultimate foundations of their values, but also upon how in a pluralistic and free society such values or goods can be effectively promoted. This needs to be done without violating the logic of a political order, which is legitimately justified as an ethos of making it possible that people who hold different and partly conflicting convictions live together and cooperate peacefully. It is unlikely that a political party will be able to realize the whole range of what they consider to be just and ultimately valuable (majorities change as do presidents and their ideology). So, we need political philosophy as *moral* philosophy that teaches not simply about ultimate truths to be realized, but about the intrinsic morality of a public conception of justice able to provide common ground for citizens who want—despite their deep division in religious and philosophical convictions and changing majorities—to peacefully cooperate for a common good. For such reflections, views such as the one developed in Rawls's *Political Liberalism* can be helpful, not because they should be endorsed as such—this would be naïve—but because they can help Christian citizens to acquire an adequate consciousness of the underlying problem, and because they provide the categories necessary to find a more adequate solution than the one presented by Rawls's "Political Liberalism." Moreover, they also help us to learn how to propose our values, or understanding of the good, in order that they have a chance of being accepted and politically promoted by those who do not necessarily share our Christian faith and the theological and spiritual wisdom springing from it. Such persons will be able to take advantage of the wisdom of our faith and tradition in the measure that we are able—precisely in a political society based on freedom—to inspire and shape social institutions and the legal framework of society by the moral substance of our most comprehensive beliefs and convictions, using, however, sound and compelling public reasons.[35]

35. This essay was originally published as "Rawlsian Public Reason, Natural Law and the Foundation of Justice: A Response to David Crawford," *Communio: International Catholic Review* 36 (Spring 2009): 138–67.

||||||||||||||||||||||||||||||||||||||||||||||||||||||||||||||||||||||||||||||||||||||||||||||||||||||||||||||||||||

NINE

Can Political Ethics Be Universalized?

Human Rights as a Global Project

Human rights are made up of all the values that concern social and political life, and are supposed to be universal. Though their origin is Western, human rights today are to be applied globally. Taken as a global political ethos, then, they form a minimum moral standard for civilized life, meaning one that is founded on full respect for human dignity. The question I would like to respond to is this: can such political ethics truly be universalized?

What Are Political Ethics?

As I understand it in what follows, political ethics are (or include) all those values that characterize a functioning society, insofar as it is politically organized. These values include not only the goals of a society's political and legal institutions, but also the behavior required of its citizens. Political ethics are thus not simply a series of norms that define honest or moral behavior in political affairs, but rather they are the moral base of the institutions in which the political life of a country takes place. Accordingly, political ethics are an expression of political culture.

The institutions in which the political life of a country develops include, first, legal institutions such as the constitution, judicial authorities and the administration of justice, penal law, and the law in general. Second, they include political institutions, such as the parliament, the electoral system, and the bill of rights. Third, they include social institutions such as social security. It is evidently impossible to distinguish definitively between these three areas, as the political and social spheres are not entirely distinct and, in fact, overlap.

Political ethics composed of these parts make up the ethos of a nation and the fabric of its society, which is in turn the product of its history. This fact does not rule out the universal applicability of such ethics, though there is inevitably a certain tension between universality and the diversity of particular social histories. This tension, and the consequent ambivalence brought about by the particulars of history, is a chief obstacle to the universal acceptance and application of political ethics.

This obstacle is apparent in the case of human rights, which are the expression of the political ethos whose universal validity we are seeking. This form of ethics is precisely the product of the history of a particular culture. Nevertheless, the universal validity of this ethic of human rights is to be sought not because they should be exported from their origin, the Christian or post-Christian West, as a neocolonial initiative, but because they have become part of a normative global heritage. Even Islamic countries, for example, and non-Christian countries in general, declare that they consider human rights as a valid standard for what they judge to be desirable norms in politics, even if, one must acknowledge, they occasionally give "human rights" interpretations that run contrary to their original meaning. There are even authors who attempt to trace the Islamic origins of human rights, a task that is not straightforward.[1]

The viewpoint from which I will reflect upon these problems is that of political philosophy. Now, it is a fundamental feature of political philosophy, also the political philosophy of human rights, to be part of *practical* philosophy. Political philosophy belongs to ethics, which is practical, for it both reflects on practical knowledge and aims at action. Therefore, it not only is normative, but must consider the concrete conditions of realization. The rationale of political institutions and action must be understood as embedded in concrete cultural and, therefore, historical contexts and as meeting with problems that only in these contexts are understandable. A normative political philosophy that would abstract from the conditions of realizability would be trying to establish norms for realizing the "idea of the

---

1. See Heiner Bielefeldt, *Philosophie der Menschenrechte. Grundlagen eines weltweiten Freiheits-ethos* (Darmstadt: Wissenschaftliche Buchgesellschaft, 1998), 134ff.

good" or of "the just" (as Plato, in fact, tried to do in his *Republic*). Such a purely metaphysical view, however, is doomed to failure. As a theory of political praxis, political philosophy must include in its reflection the concrete historical context, the historical experiences and the corresponding knowledge of the proper logic of the political.[2] Briefly: political philosophy and ethics are not metaphysics, which contemplates the necessary order of being, but practical philosophy, which deals with partly contingent matters and aims at action.

Yet, in the context of political ethics, human rights form what we might call a "political absolute" or a categorical foundation. In this function human rights are similar to natural law, though conceptually "natural law" is not identical with "human rights."

By its very nature, natural law encompasses the whole of human life and, inasmuch it is *natural* law, it therefore cannot be a criterion for what is to be counted as *politically* reasonable. Natural-law reasons do not distinguish between the moral norms a person is obliged to impose on her own actions on one side, and what she legitimately may impose on the actions of others on the other. Although natural law may always work as a criterion for recognizing specific laws as unjust, it is not a criterion sufficient for making out what belongs to the *political* common good and therefore is to be *imposed* by law and the coercive apparatus of the state on the totality of citizens. For natural-law reasons to be valid reasons in the sphere of the political and public reason they must be a political *application, restriction, or concretization* of natural law, according to the logic of the political. This logic is not contained in the concept of natural law as such, but is specifically political; that is, it is proper to reason as *public* reason.[3]

The justification of human rights typically belongs to public reason. The concept of "public reason" has been given a new actuality by the American political philosopher John Rawls.[4] More generally, I would define "public reason" as the kind of reasonableness by which the basic political institutions of political society, its legal system and, based on them, concrete law-

2. See the first chapter of this book, which is entitled "Why Is Political Philosophy Necessary? Historical Considerations and a Response." This was originally published as "Perché una filosofia politica? Elementi storici per una risposta," *Acta philosophica* 1 (1992): 233–63.

3. For this, see chapter 7 of the present volume, which is entitled "The Political Ethos of Constitutional Democracy and the Place of Natural Law in Public Reason: Rawls's 'Political Liberalism' Revisited." It was originally published under the same title in *American Journal of Jurisprudence* 50 (2005): 1–70.

4. *Political Liberalism* (New York: Columbia University Press, 1996); "The Idea of Public Reason Revisited," in Rawls, *The Law of Peoples, with "The Idea of Public Reason Revisited"* (Cambridge, Mass.: Harvard University Press, 1999).

making—legitimately imposed by coercive state power on the multitude of citizens—can be justified in a way that is able to command general consensus and that therefore will not undermine but rather will promote social cooperation and assure stability of these basic political and legal institutions. It is the reasonableness that refers to the political common good of human society.

Which Political Ethics Are Implicit in the Notion of Human Rights?

Human rights, however, do not exist in a cultural or institutional void. Moreover, they are not indifferent to particular forms of political ethics and its embodiment in a whole set of political, legal, and social institutions. Human rights, as we understand them today, are the expression of a political culture that exists in a constitutional democracy—limited government based on democratic institutions of representations or "tamed democracy"[5]—and that is characterized by the following traits: the "rule of law," that is, the submission of governing power to the law; the guarantee of fundamental freedoms, along with security, autonomy, and individual responsibility, to all citizens; the impartiality of judges and justice, such that the rules established by the law are respected (which are, above all, rules of procedure, such as the Latin adage *nulla poena sine lege,* or "no penalty without a law"); parliamentary representation decided through elections, accompanied by universal suffrage and secret balloting; majority rule, along with protection of minorities; freedom of religion and a corresponding freedom from prejudice; the right to solidarity with others, exercised through a public authority according to the principle of subsidiarity, so that the support necessary to enjoy one's rights, freedoms, and responsibility is available. (Obviously, I have here described the ethos of various normative institutions, which does not mean people's behavior will in effect correspond to this ethos.)

The political culture developed in constitutional democracies has a long and complex history, including both indirect (or distant) causes and directly constitutive causes.

Among indirect causes, I would highlight Christian anthropology, which

---

5. I take this expression from András Sajó, *Limiting Government: An Introduction to Constitutionalism* (Budapest: Central European University Press, 1999).

has delivered to Western tradition the notion of man's creation in the image of God. This tradition has fused with the legal tradition of Roman law, which in turn formed canon law, one of the main sources of the modern notion of the sovereign state. On this background, but also influenced by the feudalistic notion of correspondence of obedience and protection, has developed the medieval tradition of the right to resistance, which asserts that a political regime can be so unjust that it is morally permissible and even necessary to oppose it. The medieval right to resistance is the nucleus of the principle of subordination of power under the law. In a sense, the modern constitutional state and *rule of law* can be understood as the institutionalization and domestication of the right to resistance. Another indirect cause certainly was the idea of government by representation, namely, that a party representing the whole should make decisions on behalf of that whole, and that its decisions should be respected by each of the members of the whole; this was entirely foreign to the ancient Greeks and Romans, and was originally practiced in the ecumenical councils of the Catholic Church and within the chapters of the religious orders. To a perhaps even more important extent, modern constitutionalism is also the indirect offspring of medieval conciliarism. The idea that the authority of the pope depends on the consent of the totality of bishops united in a council—that he is elected by them and therefore responsible to them—was theologically unorthodox and finally rejected as heretical. Yet, through its transformation into a political doctrine of legitimate resistance by the French Huguenots, adopted later also by Lutherans, this originally theological and canonistic doctrine became an additional ferment in modern development of constitutionalism and representative government. Additionally we have to count among these causes the tradition, dating back to Aristotle, that considers political institutions not as gifts of nature, but as the results of human decisions that are therefore changeable, and finally, the distinction between a person and his or her function, and the legal rules of procedure based on the meaning of this distinction.

The above are only the distant historical causes. Neither Christianity alone nor the Christian civilization of the Middle Ages has created what we might call a political culture of human rights. The notion of the equal dignity of all human beings as creatures in God's image has had no clear or immediate political effect on modern human rights, precisely because individuals were never seen qua humans, but always as members of a social stratum, in a set social position, and with a corresponding function: he or she was a peasant, noble, cleric, or trader, a citizen or stranger, a Christian or Jew, which in turn defined his or her respective dignity, rights, and duties.

In order for the modern idea of human rights and its corresponding political ethos to develop, what I have called the constitutive or direct historical causes were necessary, namely (in simplified form): the development, firstly, of the sovereign territorial state, produced by what Georges de Lagarde has called "the birth of the secular mind,"[6] and secondly, the splitting of Christianity, along with the social conflict caused by cultural and ideological pluralism; together these developments brought about the sovereign modern state, whose essential function was to ensure peace and to make a shared life possible for individuals who were profoundly divided in terms of religion and ideology. The modern political ethos thus became—and this was new—an *ethos of peace.*

The peace ethos, formulated classically by Jean Bodin and the "politiques" of the sixteenth century, affirmed the primacy of peace and of the measures that secure it over the public recognition of moral and religious truth. The peace ethos followed as a reaction, in a pluralist and heterogeneous society, to public authorities' prejudice causing the worst of social evils: civil war. The peace ethos *alone,* however, is not enough. It can justify all sorts of violations of the physical and moral integrity of the individual. The peace ethos is but a necessary precursor of what follows, which is the *ethos of liberty.*

The call for freedom rose against the abuse of power in the sovereign state, which was instituted to protect the individual against his or her equals by providing the security necessary to enjoy the fruits of his or her labor, but which had been transformed into a threat to the individual. The arbitrary power of the state had superseded individual rights and converted individuals into instruments of its own functioning. It was against this Leviathan that the liberal—in the broad political sense—constitutionalist proclaimed the priority of freedom and the rights of the individual, asserting the legitimacy of his or her own rights in the face of the false pretensions of public common interests that were constricting the rights and freedoms of the individual. Later, this upheaval led to the proclamation of the superiority of a free economy over that which had been organized *by* the state and *for* the state (as had been the case in the mercantilist system of the absolute

6. Georges de Lagarde, *La naissance de l'esprit laïque au déclin du moyen age,* 5 vols. (Louvain: Nauvelaerts, 1956–1970).

state). The new claim was based on the fundamental idea that the wealth of nations consisted not in the accumulation of riches by the state, but in the work of individuals and in the free exchange of products on the market.

The modern political ethos thus became an ethos of *freedom*, the rights of the individual, and the sovereignty of law over power ("the rule of law"), a notion that was institutionalized, along with the medieval principle of the right to resistance, with the advent of the constitutional state. The ethos of freedom equally favors the autonomy of the individual as a private person in the face of public business and the various conditions imposed by a state that pretends to use its authority to foster the happiness of its citizens. Against these collective forces, liberal constitutionalism promotes individual responsibility and autonomy.

Meanwhile, liberal freedom did not mean freedom for everyone (at least, not immediately). After the industrial revolution brought with it the formation of the working class and majority rule, a third step was imminent, which would involve the restriction of the freedom and civil rights of those with property titles, and especially those enjoyed by the landed, because they had become outdated. A redistribution of liberty was needed: equality of freedom, of representation, and of rights for all as human beings: that was the third step. It led to the *ethos of justice*, which was also an *ethos of equality and of solidarity*, an equality that was nonetheless qualified and not necessarily egalitarian, that is, equality in the sense of equal rights and freedoms for all. The understanding that for such an equality to be realized, certain socioeconomic conditions had to be met has profoundly shaped the modern conception of human rights.[7]

Thus European history became, in a sense, a global history, starting with the colonization of North America, and produced as outcome of its lengthy development a specific political culture, characterized by the language of rights, in the sense of subjective rights, telling us what is owed to a human being as a person with dignity. The characteristic feature of this ethos based on human rights is that it transformed the language of rights into an institutionalized system of fundamental rights owed to each citizen, which in turn meant that one individual's right became another's duty. In

---

7. For understanding the historical development of the modern democratic constitutional state as a three-stage process (ethos of peace, liberty, and justice) I am indebted to Martin Kriele; see his *Einführung in die Staatslehre: Die geschichtlichen Legitimitätsgrundlagen des demokratischen Verfassungsstaates*, 4th ed. (Opladen: Westdeutscher Verlag, 1990).

fact, subjective rights are a profoundly social reality that has created obligations for all those from whom a right can be claimed. A society whose political organization is based on human rights thus forms a specific network, not only of rights, but also of obligations and duties.

History, then, has provided us with a precious and decisive lesson for our subject: political ethics cannot be formed independently of the historical reality of a specific political culture and of the conditions in which they have developed (a subject we will return to). This notion does not signify that political ethics and historical reality should be considered the same thing. That is, human rights, taken together, form a normative idea of all political reality. They are, in the original sense of the word, the ideology of the modern democratic constitutional state in which we live, that is, one in which power submits to law, the freedom of each individual is respected, participation in political affairs is guaranteed, and solidarity is enjoyed; we consider this model desirable for all of the world's societies. Human rights thus play the role of instantiating moral criticism of the whole political world.

It is in this sense that we wish for morals or political ethics to be universally recognized and practiced. Is this possible? My answer will be tentative and rather an exploration of the difficulties one encounters in giving a clear answer. Perhaps an exhaustive and definitive answer to this query is not possible at all. The reason is that by looking more closely at things we arrive at a certain paradox. This paradox is the simultaneity of the historically singular origin of our culture of human rights and the universality of its claim. This simultaneity of (1) genetic cultural contextuality and (2) claim of universal validity is what makes it so difficult to come to a definitive answer. In fact, everything depends on the development of cultures and of their mutual relations. We cannot predict this, and a philosopher is even less called to make any sort of prognostication about such future developments.

Can Political Ethics Be Universalized?

As I will argue in this section, universal political ethics cannot be formed simply from abstract or general principles, or from cross-cultural formulas, because they must themselves be *culture, ethos,* rooted in people's social life. Yet they must be multicultural, meaning precisely that they must respect cultural differences and must be rooted in *diverse* cultures. Insofar as they are universal political ethics, they must *be* a cultural and social reality, a part of these different cultures, which in a sense will undergo a certain homogenization.

Neither, as it was already mentioned above, can the political ethics we are seeking consist simply of universal principles of "natural rights." The teaching of natural rights is always, and has always been, replete with interpretations that originate in concrete historical and social contexts. As I have outlined in the beginning, ethics must be oriented toward action, toward behavior. To be practical, political ethics must make reference to a historical and cultural reality and must *be* an expression of a concrete cultural reality; they must contain more than abstract notions and formulas.

This necessity explains why universalizing political ethics based on human rights seems to depend, today and in the real world we live in, on the possibility of the global expansion of the political culture of the democratic constitutional state, in one of its many possible incarnations. The modern conception of human rights cannot be separated from the idea and practice of constitutional democracy.

We often complain of the manner in which human rights are ignored internationally. While these violations of human rights appear in all of the nations of the world, we may still note that systematic violations occur in the absence of the political culture of constitutional democracy. The absence of respect for human rights is not due in the first place to the lack of an international judicial system—such a system could have an important complementary function—but to the fact that on the level of the particular nation-states human rights have not yet found their institutionalization and a corresponding political culture.

Universal political ethics, then, would not overlap on a nation's other cultural and moral systems, but would become an integral part of its culture. Thus, these ethics would become universal through universal implementation, on a national level, of the determinate institutional reality of constitutional democracy, and not through the perhaps illusory creation of an ethical superstructure on a global plane. (To this end, international organizations could serve as catalysts and supporters.)

However, various cultural conflicts present problems for this idea. To answer a reproach against Western neocolonialism regarding human rights, one could point out that today human rights have become a global standard. Even though certain countries, Islamic ones above all, do not accept the universal declaration of human rights, for instance, except with certain reservations, the normative value of human rights is, at least officially, hardly contested.

The problem lies in the domain of enculturation. It seems that in countries with non-Christian traditions, the public does not recognize a political ethos that is based essentially on the idea of the equality of rights for all people, as human beings, and of the equality of freedom for everyone. Or they do not share our secular conception of citizenship, for which it is essential not to link civil rights to one's religious allegiance or other nonpolitical qualities. The Christian West has been able to get rid of some of the historical conditioning that made it impossible to accept such political ethics. In Islamic countries certain liberal thinkers are making serious efforts to interpret the *sharia* as nonlegal and nonpolitical, and rather as exclusively moral and religious (by distinguishing it from the *fiqh*, traditional Islamic jurisprudence). Generally, however, Islam is bound to its tradition of actually *not* separating the legal order and its justification from theology.

Seen in this light, the possibility of universalizing political ethics depends on finding an overlapping intercultural consensus that would be based on human rights and their implementation through the institutions of a constitutional democracy of the Western type. The advantage of such a consensus would be precisely that it would not demand any homogenization of cultures or religions, though it would not remove the problem posed by cultures and religions (or elements within particular religions) that are obstacles to institutionalizing a human rights–based political culture. Such a consensus has to be *political* and to disregard interculturally incompatible ways of public justification of human rights. Particularly, it should disregard types of justification which are nonpolitical, that is, essentially connected with divergent and mutually incompatible cultural premises (which, in practice, might be very difficult).

The Western political culture of the democratic constitutional state is not just a cultural acquisition but also an ethical value that must be defended. In its flexibility and variability, it has a universal value, a value that must be defended from the pressures of an excessive multiculturalism that endangers such conquest. A policy of "multicultural citizenship" (Will Kymlicka) and the "recognition of difference" (Charles Taylor) must therefore always be also a policy of integration, of assimilation, of socialization.[8]

8. On this, see chapter 11 in this volume, "Multicultural Citizenship in Liberal Democracy: The Proposals of C. Taylor, J. Habermas, and W. Kymlicka," which was originally published as "Cittadinanza

This applies also to the international community, though it is formed by sovereign states. This does not mean uniformity or disrespect for cultural diversity and the people who subscribe to different values. It means, however, not to give up what is politically necessary, nor to impair the achievements of the political culture of freedom and civic equality; to do so would be to impair the possibilities for peaceful cooperation, reconciliation, and consensus-building in a political culture of freedom.

Yet, this political culture—with its typical claim of being universally valid—has grown in a determinate historical context: Western Christianity, a combination of Judeo-Christian revelation, Greek scientific rationality, and Roman legal traditions. As I have tried to show, it is a historical singularity, but simultaneously it claims to be a universally and transculturally valid standard of political justice. This seems to be paradoxical, though it is not more paradoxical than the claim of the three great Abrahamic religions—Judaism, Christianity, and Islam—to be universally valid despite their historically, geographically, and culturally singularized and contingent origin. Even more paradoxical seems to be that the modern ethos of human rights has developed as a result of the emancipation of political thought from the political institutions and practices of earlier Christianity. On the other hand, one cannot deny that human rights, as they are institutionalized in the modern democratic constitutional state, appear to be a suitable expression of political humanism that is of Christian inspiration. In my view, the cause of the paradox is that human rights are a secular fruit of the message of Christian salvation, a fruit that could ripen only under the conditions of secular modern society. Today the question arises whether it does not need again the Christian leaven —of a however historically "purified" and enlightened kind—to maintain its vigor and universal dynamism.

In front of the challenges of multiculturalism—mostly in its Islamic form—which in fact tries to undermine essential features of a secular political culture of the human rights, we should defend this secularity as an offspring of Christian Europe. In my view only the acknowledgment of the ultimately *nonsecular* origin of Western secularity will help us to both respect other cultures and try to implement in them our understanding of human rights. Paradoxically, however, in some bioethical questions non-Christian cultures, precisely Islamic ones, seem to have views that are closer to those

multiculturale nella democrazia liberale: le proposte di Ch. Taylor, J. Habermas e W. Kymlicka," *Acta Philosophica* 1, no. 1 (2006): 29–52.

of the Christian tradition, although perhaps in some cases—considering their still discriminating views regarding the role of women in society—not for entirely the same reasons.

Finally, the effective implementation of human rights and the capability of defending and promoting them depend on certain givens and social conditions. Human rights alone cannot create a truly humane civilization, that is, one that is characterized by love, rather than simple justice (even if there is no love without justice). Political ethics can be a base, a framework, and are an absolutely necessary one, but they are insufficient alone. Now, the language of love, as the language of virtue generally, is typically and primarily learned within the family. The bosom of the family must produce citizens of a global culture of human rights, citizens who are aware of the irreplaceable transcendent value of each human life, and in this manner it will also be a school of respect for human rights.[9]

---

9. "Which Political Ethics Are Implicit in the Notion of Human Rights?" in this essay was reworked for inclusion in my "Christian Secularity, Political Ethics and the Culture of Human Rights," which was published in the *Josephinum Journal of Theology* 16, no. 2 (August 2009): 250–72.

TEN

Christian Secularity and the Culture of Human Rights

Religious Freedom and the Secular State: Two Traditions, European and American

It is well known that the Catholic Church has come to fully acknowledge the secularity of the state and the political principles of constitutional democracy as a cultural achievement only after a long period of mutual hostility and conflict. Yet, by doing so, the Church has reconciled itself with an essential part of its own cultural heritage marked by the genuinely Christian dualism of spiritual and temporal power and the affirmation of the intrinsic secularity of the latter. This development has been possible because already in the first centuries of its existence, Christianity had assimilated the philosophical spirit of Greek rationality and culture as well as the rational spirit of Roman legal thinking.

It is equally well known that, while European Catholicism and Protestantism were marked by long modern traditions of alliances between "throne and altar" and of the confessional state, in the United States of America the recognition of the secularity of state power and of government was a feature of the founding project of the U.S. Constitution from the very beginning. Non-established religion was part of the solution to finding a peaceful way of bringing together citizens and social groups with divergent religious and philosophical views in a common constitutional project. In consequence, religion developed into a constructive force in American public life, and the secularity of the state and religion were not necessarily perceived as incompatible values.

In Europe, however, religion was seen since the Protestant Reformation and the subsequent religious wars as a major problem. Hence, the European Enlightenment and liberal constitutionalism came to understand religious liberty as instrumental for assuring the independence and secularity of state power in order to neutralize, if not destroy, the divisive influence of religion on politics. In the current European understanding "secularity" and "laicism" frequently mean a sort of public areligious political credo that implies even the unwillingness to acknowledge the Christian tradition at least as the common *cultural* heritage containing the resources that made the modern secular state possible.

This partly anti-Christian, and even anti-Catholic and anti-Church, character of European modernity has survived in some extreme forms of "laicism" (most typically in France). This process has led to misleading alternatives: "secularity" is played off against "religious faith," "the right to religious liberty" (falsely identified with "religious indifferentism") against the "existence of religious truth," and so on. The process has also led to an unfortunate ideological and institutional equilibrium between these alternatives. The secularization of state power, its independence and autonomy, especially under conditions of democratic popular sovereignty, as well as the secularization of society in the sense of its de-clericalization, was, from a religious or even clerical vantage point, perceived as essentially directed against the very mission of the Church. Yet, with the Second Vatican Council, the Catholic Church has come to fully acknowledge the secular, religiously neutral state as a positive value and as cultural achievement, and with this also the modern idea of human rights. It seems to me significant that in his Christmas address to the Roman Curia on December 22, 2005, Benedict XVI not only positively referred to the "model of a modern state" originated by the American Revolution, but also distinguished the second—the Jacobin or "radical"—phase of the French Revolution, "that practically no longer wanted to allow the Church any room," from its first, liberal-constitutionalist phase. Yet, it was this first phase that was marked by the *Déclaration des droits de l'homme et du citoyen*," at that time, however, condemned by Pope Pius VI as national apostasy from Catholic faith. This change of attitude toward the earthly reality of the state and of politics—which was not a change in the doctrine of faith—is not only a prudential adjustment, understandable because the Catholic Church nowadays exists in a secular and pluralistic environment. As shown in the council's Declaration on Religious Freedom, *Dignitatis humanae,* it is rather a change of attitude reflecting a principled turn toward what is now judged to be more congruent to the spirit of the Gospel.

"Christian Secularity": The Seeming Paradox of "Double Identity" as Christian and as Citizen

Yet, in my view, not all problems are resolved by this acknowledgment of the secular political culture and the modern idea of human rights. A crucial question for Christians, posed by modernity, remains unanswered. This question might be formulated in the following way: "What does it mean for Christians to participate *as Christians* in a political culture and in public life defined by the modern idea of secularity?" Or in other words: "Is it possible for a Christian who believes in a determinate religious truth and cherishes objective moral values rooted in it to participate in a political culture that is defined by secular values, pluralism, and neutrality regarding this religious truth and the moral claims depending on it?"

The problem addressed with these questions is not the problem of multiculturalism. This is a quite different problem. The problem raised with these questions concerns the simple fact that the pluralism of occidental modernity is the outcome of freedom and of liberal institutions, which are characteristic for a society that recognizes human rights. Now, pluralism thus brought about is also a result of legitimate and sometimes epistemologically understandable disagreement on fundamental moral questions. On the other hand, pluralism is also the result of ignorance, the abuse of freedom, and vicious habits. Yet, it is essential for political and civil freedom that it may be misused; otherwise there would be no freedom. It is part of a political culture that fully accepts freedom, to allow, in certain limits defined by law, also this kind of pluralism. Political and civil freedom, which make it possible, do not for this reason cease to be political values.

Pluralism is defined as a kind of *internal* variety—religious, ideological, also ethnical—to a determined political culture and rooted in its common ground (part of which might be the culture of human rights). Therefore, pluralism does not jeopardize social cooperation, unity, and peace. Multiculturalism, on the other hand, is not simply pluralism, but precisely the variety of cultural common grounds, and therefore also of political and legal cultures, coexisting in one and the same society. It is a grave problem and *as such* cannot be accepted without putting into danger the constitutional order of a democratic society. In short: a multicultural society in the strict sense is not possible. By the same token, international public life and a culture of human rights presupposes a common cultural ground. The question is what kind of ground this must be.

It is precisely the challenges of multiculturalism—mostly by Islamist fundamentalism insofar as it is hostile to secular pluralism—that provides evidence that at the root of Western pluralism lies a common foundation of values, though this foundation is mostly defined in political terms of a strictly secular kind. Citizenship itself, which is a basic political and public value, must be defined on a common ground of shared cultural values; it cannot be defined in a multicultural way. The modern culture of human rights in the Western sense shapes the understanding of citizenship in a concrete and specific way that is not open to any multicultural qualification. Citizenship understood in these terms is a kind of "political absolute." This is why a "multicultural society" in the strict sense is not possible: it would cease being able to define common standards of citizenship and corresponding rights, liberties, and political values.[1]

In the European understanding, the nature of such a common ground is the idea of liberal-democratic citizenship—"liberal" in a broad sense—which is closely related to basic liberties and rights that define the status of citizens independently from their religious, cultural, or ethnic identities. "Multicultural" variety or pluralism on *this* level is impossible. There is no middle term or coexistence, for example, between the *sharia* on one side and the occidental secular understanding of the rule of law on the other. This, I think, also applies, *mutatis mutandis,* to international public life.

It also seems evident to me that wholeheartedly believing Christians, particularly Catholics, can and should share in the secular understanding of modern democratic citizenship. Equally they should share in the implementation of human rights on the international level. Yet, they will, or in my view should, do so in a different way than, for example, an atheist, agnostic, or simply nonbelieving citizen. A Christian's ideal of secular democratic citizenship might be what I wish to call "Christian secularity." "Christian secularity," as I understand it, means to develop one's Christian identity and to realize one's Christian vocation in the context of a society—and an

---

1. See chapter 11 of the present volume, entitled "Multicultural Citizenship in Liberal Democracy: The Proposals of C. Taylor, J. Habermas, and W. Kymlicka." This was originally published as "Cittadinanza multiculturale nella democrazia liberale: le proposte di Ch. Taylor, J. Habermas e W. Kymlicka," in *Acta Philosophica* 15, no. 1 (2006): 29–52.

international community—the public institutions of which are defined in secular ways, by fully accepting—informed and enlightened by historical experience—this secularity as a political value and considering this acceptance as a integral part of one's self-understanding as a Christian. To use a Rawlsian term, "Christian secularity" means for Christians to enter into an "overlapping consensus," which may be epistemologically supported and nourished by one's proper religious and moral convictions as a Christian, but is neither identical *with* them nor derived *from* them. Christian secularity, thus defined, means to be able to live a kind of "double" or "differentiated identity" as a Christian and as a citizen.

Notice that "differentiated" or "double identity" does not mean to split oneself into two existential realities, nor does it mean to live a double life, nor, as a citizen and primarily in the public sphere, to stop behaving and making decisions like a Christian. "Double identity" rather means the capacity (required by all citizens) of being able to politically cooperate under conditions of even deep disagreement on essential moral values and therewith to constructively and patiently cope with concrete configurations of pluralism that as a Christian one might consider to be alien to the true common good of human society and in need of change (for example what John Paul II has called the "culture of death"). It also signifies the capability of differentiating what on the level of political values is fundamental for a civil society and for the strictly political common good, on one side, from what is highest and according to one's religious and moral convictions most holy in the level of values, on the other. Therefore, "double identity" means the disposition to recognize the procedural legitimacy of democratic decisions even though they contradict one's fundamental convictions about the good and to therefore support political institutions *as legitimate* even though in determinate cases they generate decisions one considers to be deeply unjust and corruptive of the common good. This, finally, implies the disposition to overturn such decisions or to amend these institutions only by legal, democratic means, trying to convince other citizens of the reasonableness of one's claims, which actually strengthens the legitimacy of democratic institutions (that is, not to act so only because one considers illegal or even violent means to be unlikely to succeed).

In the past, something like "Christian secularity" has been understood as a paradox. So, it was typical for Catholics to claim a right to religious freedom only for Catholics and to concede to other faiths—at most—prudential toleration. There was no acceptance of the principle of reciprocity that is implied in the acceptance of a constitutional democracy because the Catholic tradition before the Second Vatican Council did not accept as a political value the fundamental reciprocity of political right claims independent from their being used in conformity with truth. Reciprocity is essential also for a culture of human rights on the international level. For it presupposes for members of other cultures and religions something analogous to what I have called "Christian secularity."

The above-mentioned "double identity" as a Christian and as a citizen does not mean that the world-transforming character of Christianism has to be given up or that Christians *as Christians* do not have to make a specific contribution to the social and political shaping of this world and, thus, to the content of citizenship. On the contrary: the Christian faith, based on the faith in incarnation of the Divine Word, is called to continue to be a world-transforming force, but this in a secularized world and in a secular way. A secularized world is a world without religious institutions that, for spiritual reasons, are able to effectively enforce limitations of sovereignty of political institutions or to exercise some form of politically institutionalized guardianship. By the same token, a secularized world is a world in which Christians, following their well-formed consciences, are called to cooperate side by side with all men, sharing with them their common identity as citizens and claiming no other rights than those that they share with *all* citizens.

The Political Justification of Human Rights and Their Metaphysical and Religious Roots

Secularity has consequences not only for the political cooperation of citizens in general—and on the international level, for the cooperation of nations, which can be considered citizens of an international community—but in the first place for public reason and public justificatory discourses. It bears upon the way "citizens of faith" relate to the public political culture.[2] This may best be illustrated by the example of the justification of human rights. There are different discourses on human rights: exclusively political, but also religious and metaphysical discourses. The Catholic Church in fact uses both

2. I take the expression "citizens of faith" from John Rawls, "The Idea of Public Reason Revisited," in Rawls, *The Law of Peoples, with "The Idea of Public Reason Revisited"* (Cambridge, Mass.: Harvard University Press, 1999).

of them. Sometimes it is said that human rights can be firmly founded only in the metaphysical truth about man or that their stable foundation even presupposes the acceptance of Christian anthropology, according to which man is created in the image of God. Yet, given the fact of modern pluralism and of the multicultural character of the international public square and international political life, this would provide a very weak political basis for human rights. If their effective *political* recognition and *juridical* validity needed to depend on shared metaphysical assumptions about the nature of man or on a shared acknowledgment of the theological truth of his being created in the image of God, the political standing of human rights would be rather uncertain and fragile. In reality, metaphysical and theological foundations would be far from being a common ground, being rather a matter of dispute and disagreement, as metaphysical and theological issues generally are.

The Canadian political scientist Michael Ignatieff, therefore, argues that the force of a culture based on human rights is precisely to provide for them exclusively *political* justifications that are as far as possible independent from metaphysical or religious assumptions and truth-claims and rather appeal to intuitively and commonly shared convictions about the advantageous character of such rights: though we cannot agree on *why* we have rights, we can all see what they actually *do* for us and why we need them, and such "prudential grounds for believing in human rights protection are much more secure."[3]

This may sound provocative and even cynical—mainly because Ignatieff opposes to the "politics of human rights" the "idolatry of human rights"—but it is in fact the way things in modern pluralist society tend to work. Secular modernity, which is essentially pluralistic, is in need of a minimal foundation in order to achieve a maximum consensus. As mentioned before, this is even more true for international public life in a globalized world, which is both genuinely multicultural and in need of shared standards of justice and fair cooperation. In this sense, the secular character of international organizations is an advantage. In short: the modern idea of human rights is actually a political conception based on a relatively thin justificatory foundation. The more its public justification becomes linked to metaphysical and religious premises, the less ability it has to politically assert itself and become universally implemented.

---

3. Michael Ignatieff, *Human Rights as Politics and Idolatry* (Princeton, N.J.: Princeton University Press, 2001), 55.

Yet, this is only half of the truth. It is, so to speak, the strictly political half of the truth. The other half, however, is not necessarily idolatry or, as Michael Ignatieff suggests, "moral imperialism." Politics actually does live from moral resources that it cannot create by itself. Moreover, many of these moral resources, not only historically, but also in the consciousness of citizens, spring from, or are at least linked to, their religious convictions. This is, or should be, mainly the case of Christians whose creed, besides its supernaturally revealed character, also—at least in its Catholic form—includes a tradition of natural law that in itself possesses both a political and a secular, that is, purely rational, dimension. Moreover, politics itself is a specific kind of moral behavior and must be ultimately assessed by standards of morality. Therefore, even a culture of human rights justified in the public domain by means of exclusively political values must be understood by its supporters as a *moral* value. Given the secularized and pluralistic—and on the international level even multicultural—character of modern political reality, reductive political justification is a *political* necessity. Nevertheless pluralism needs categorical foundations that themselves are not pluralistic or merely political, or at least that are able to base the latter on firm moral convictions and on the kind of rational discourse on the basis of justice that we call "natural law."[4]

Therefore: a political conception of justice justified in the context of an "overlapping consensus" between citizens of different philosophical and religious orientation and the corresponding institutions, also, cannot live without being nurtured from the moral substance of the beliefs, creeds, and convictions of those who form this consensus. On this level of argument, as Christians we are convinced that only a foundation rooted in metaphysical truth about man can provide for a culture of human rights the ultimate and stable *cognitive* basis and that, therefore, *Christian* secularity has a crucially important mission. Considering the understandable difficulties not only Catholicism but wide strands of Protestantism as well had with the growing political culture of secular modernity and the very idea of human rights and civil political equality, as Christians we have to affirm this with a certain humility. At the same time, however, as Christians we should have

4. See chapter 7 of the present volume, entitled "The Political Ethos of Constitutional Democracy and the Place of Natural Law in Public Reason: Rawls's 'Political Liberalism' Revisited." This was originally given as the 2005 Natural Law Lecture at the Notre Dame Law School, and subsequently published as "The Political Ethos of Constitutional Democracy and the Place of Natural Law in Public Reason: Rawls' 'Political Liberalism' Revisited," *American Journal of Jurisprudence* 50 (2005): 1–70.

what has been called a "complex of superiority":[5] we should know that, once accepted as the logic of the secular world and of pluralism as the result of freedom, Christian revelation and Christian faith provide the strongest *cognitive*—and thus, indirectly, also political—support for a political culture based on the legal enforcement of human rights. It is precisely on this level and in this sense that the Magisterium of John Paul II on human rights has made its most decisive contribution. Particularly in his encyclical *Centesimus annus,* we find the reconciliation of secular political modernity (constitutionalism, democracy, the priority of freedom, human rights) with a transcendental, metaphysical, and ultimately religious foundation of the moral basis of modern secularity.[6] This logic of politics is necessary and fully suited to provide a common platform for the cooperation of citizens under conditions of pluralism. But the logic of this politics is not able to uphold its moral legitimacy and uprightness without having roots in what is essentially not only "political."

Secular Pluralism and Its Defense against Destructive Forms of Multiculturalism

In what I have called "Christian secularity" there is, thus, a paradox: it is the paradox of the existing need in modern secular and pluralistic societies and in international public life of both minimalist political justification of human rights, political justice, and the like, and a metaphysical ethical anchoring of these that not only goes largely beyond such merely political justifications, but also supports them.

This paradox seems to me, first, to prove the ineluctable validity of the modern—in its original Hobbesian form one-sided—principle *Authoritas non veritas facit legem,* that is, the principle of the institutional, legal, and practical primacy of the political over the metaphysical. Of course, I am far from pleading for the Hobbesian solution of this problem, which submits truth-claims and the norms of justice entirely to the factuality of positive law.[7] But I subscribe to the maxim in the sense of the need of recognizing the demo-

---

5. This expression was frequently used by St. Josemaría Escrivá.

6. See Russell Hittinger, "The Pope and the Liberal State," *First Things* 28 (December 1992): 33–41.

7. See chapter 4 of the present volume, entitled *"Auctoritas non veritas facit legem:* Thomas Hobbes, Carl Schmitt, and the Idea of the Constitutional State." This was originally published as *"Autoritas non veritas facit legem:* Thomas Hobbes, Carl Schmitt und die Idee des Verfassungsstaates," *Archiv für Rechts- und Sozialphilosophie* 86 (2000): 484–98. See also my book *La filosofia politica di Thomas Hobbes: coerenza e contraddizioni di un paradigma* (Rome: Armando, 1997).

cratic legitimacy and thus legal validity of law even though it is considered to be, in certain limits, unjust, untruthful, and in need of being overturned by equally legal and democratic means. This is the price we have to pay for peaceful social and international cooperation, prosperity, justice—always imperfect—and, mostly, political and civil freedom. Yet, this price is rather low and certainly a reasonable one to pay. As we know from history, the alternatives are the continuous threat of civil war or, in other cases, authoritarian or even totalitarian repression in the name of some truth-claiming ideology, and on the international level, unjust domination and war.

Second, and precisely because of the ineluctable practical primacy of the political over the metaphysical, the citizens' being embedded in the truth about man is to be reinforced. Because political freedom on the national level and rights of participation in international organizations are defined and legitimized not by their relation to moral and religious truth, but to political values (such as peace, liberty, equality, economic efficiency, development, and the like), the consciousness of the relation of freedom to truth must be reinforced on the nonpolitical or pre-political level. It must be primarily cultivated in the family and, generally, in educational practice. The educational system of society cannot follow the pluralistic and merely political logic of public justification, though it must also respect fundamental values of civil liberty and equality. Education has to promote moral virtues. While politics and law predominantly speak the language of "rights" (which, of course, always generate duties of third parties), education and the moral virtues must mainly, though not exclusively, speak the language of duties and of commitment to the truly good. Finally, the relation between freedom and truth should also be respected by the mass media, without thereby curtailing their freedom—not even their freedom to exhibit stupidity—but by fostering their sense of responsibility and by *democratically* sanctioning misbehavior: manipulation and stupidity should be punished by means of the laws of the market, that is, by refusing the consumption of products that offend human dignity or are simply indecent.

"Christian secularity," thus, means to acknowledge the secularity of the political institutions and to simultaneously support them and even to permeate them with the moral substance of Christian faith and uprightness; this is done mainly on the level regulated by natural law, which as such is not "Christian," but simply human, although at present it is mostly promoted and defended by Christians. For example: to legally grant a right to abortion and support corresponding choices by the public health system is certainly a great evil and opposes the common good of human society; but it is not the fault of the democratic political culture or the secularity of the state, but rather the problem of civil society and its predominant value system that renders such laws or jurisprudence possible. It is exactly and predominantly on this level where the Christian ferment is called to come to bear, and on the international level it sometimes finds allies in other cultures.

So, the famous and flogged dictum by Ernst-Wolfgang Böckenförde that the modern secular state lives from presuppositions that it itself cannot create and guarantee may be once more invoked and even extended to international public life and its institutions of political self-organization: these presuppositions are the moral substance of its citizens and of society as a whole, and of entire nations, respectively.[8] It is also on this level that I see the role of the Church as a hierarchical and authoritative institution: to act through its teaching and pastoral care upon the consciences of citizens, but not to participate directly in politics itself. To engage in politics is the task of Christian laity, and they will do this as citizens, but as citizens of faith, using thereby their political rights freely and responsibly.[9]

In my view we have still to discover the modern Christian citizen for whom the secular character of public life and pluralism is not simply nuisance or even outrage, but who feels at home in it and acknowledges pluralism as the outcome of political freedom, a fundamental political value to be defended. Secularity, however, is not a project of secularizing the public square in the sense of an ideology of laicism that aims at the absence of any reference to religion or religious values in it. Secularity is not freedom *from* religion, but freedom *of* religion, which is possible only when the state neither enters into an alliance with any religious creed nor yields to temptations in defining or even imposing some religious truth. I admit that religious freedom also means protecting public institutions that involve the coercive power of the state *from* religion. Yet, to attain this, no public culture of "nonreligion," "antireligion," "agnosticism," or anything like this is needed. What is needed, instead, is a public awareness not only of the in-

---

8. Böckenförde, "Die Entstehung des Staates als Vorgang der Säkularisation," in Böckenförde, *Staat, Gesellschaft, Freiheit. Studien zur Staatstheorie und zum Verfassungsrecht* (Frankfurt: Suhrkamp, 1976), 60.

9. See chapter 5 of the present volume, which is entitled "The Open Society and the New Laicism: Against the Soft Totalitarianism of Certain Secularist Thinking." As discussed in the author's note in chapter 5, a shorter version of this essay was published as "Laici e cattolici: oltre le divisioni. Riflessioni sull'essenza della democrazia e della società aperta," *Fondazione Liberal* 17 (2003): 108–116.

competence of coercive state power in defining and enforcing religious truth, but also, and simultaneously, of the importance for society to be formed of citizens who hold firm moral convictions—be they rooted in some religion or not—that support and nourish the secular political culture. The ideal of the secular state and secular political culture is not endangered by such a presence of religion in national and international public life.

So, even under conditions of modern secularity and pluralism there are many possibilities of integrating religious beliefs and metaphysical truth-claims with a constitutional and liberal (in the broad sense) democratic understanding of political life. The concrete shaping of this integration, on the level of single countries, will depend upon the traditions and peculiarities of different nations. In the presence of the challenges of multiculturalism, essentially the presence of an increasing number of Muslim citizens in European countries, who do not share the common occidental and Christian heritage, Europe will have to become conscious of its Christian roots, not in order to "re-Christianize" public life in the sense of reversing the process of modern secularization and discriminating against non-Christians, but exactly on the contrary: to maintain and, if necessary, defend the peace-making and integrating force of a secular political culture based on human rights and fundamental political liberties. Perhaps it will become more and more obvious that we need to recall the Christian roots of modern secularity and political culture precisely in order to successfully defend and develop it further *in its very secularity.* On these grounds we will be able to also offer real integration as citizens to those whose cultural origin is different from ours: without urging them to enter into a Christian culture, but also without denying that this secular modern world is a mature fruit of the historic civilizing feature of Christianity, able to become a global patrimony in a multicultural world. What finally will happen on the level of international public life cannot be anything other than a reaction to the successful accommodation between religion, culture, and secular values in the life of single nations.[10]

10. This essay was originally presented at the symposium "A Growing Gap: Living and Forgotten Christian Roots in Europe and the United States," which was held in Vienna on April 26–29, 2006. It was part of section 4 of the symposium, on "Guiding Principles of International Public Life," and was later published in a more developed form under the title of "Christian Secularity, Political Ethics and the Culture of Human Rights," *Josephinum Journal of Theology* 16, no. 2 (August 2009): 320–38.

ELEVEN

Multicultural Citizenship in Liberal Democracy

The Proposals of C. Taylor, J. Habermas, and W. Kymlicka

"Multicultural Citizenship": The Basic Question

The modern political culture of the democratic constitutional state is the result of a long process of conflict, from which has arisen the awareness, typically modern, of the need to distinguish the political and juridical system (enacted by the state's coercive power) from convictions concerning the highest, ultimate values of human life. These values refer to human good in all its complexity—which is as much as to say, to happiness and, in the religious dimension, to salvation. The modern formulas for religious tolerance, derived from the emergence of a liberal constitutionalism based on the rights of freedom of the individual and of the progressive democratization of liberal constitutionalism in the course of the last two centuries, have the purpose of establishing a specifically political consensus for the peaceful, free coexistence among citizens of a society that lacks a consensus on what is ultimately valid in the realm of values, and especially with respect to religious truth.[1]

Modern constitutional and liberal democracies base themselves, therefore, on a constitutional consensus, defined by a publicly binding concep-

---

1. A brief description of the intrinsic logic of this process and a defense of its legitimacy can be found in chapter 7 of the present volume, which is entitled "The Political Ethos of Constitutional Democracy and the Place of Natural Law in Public Reason: Rawls's 'Political Liberalism' Revisited." This was originally published in *American Journal of Jurisprudence* 50 (2005): 1–70.

tion of political justice. This conception establishes, at the constitutional level, the foundational structure of the political society, that is, its fundamental political and juridical institutions. Such a constitutional consensus presupposes a certain cultural homogeneity, at least with respect to those values that form the basis of its public rationale.

The phenomenon of multiculturalism has been progressively expanding for some years in the midst of relatively homogeneous societies defined by a specific cultural tradition. This phenomenon sharpens the awareness that, despite the religious neutrality and secularity of the modern state, its political culture is not *culturally* neutral, nor is it rooted in values that are exclusively secular or "lay."[2] In the light of multiculturalism, the Canadian philosopher Charles Taylor has gone as far as to claim, somewhat provocatively—referring primarily to the challenge posed by traditionalist Islam—that it is becoming ever more clear that "Western liberalism is not so much an expression of the secular, post religious outlook that happens to be popular among liberal *intellectuals*, as a more organic outgrowth of Christianity," and that "it is not a possible meeting ground for all cultures." The reason for this, says Taylor, is that for "mainstream Islam, there is no question of separating politics and religion the way we have come to expect in Western liberal society."[3]

In fact, such a separation is part of the modern political consensus, and is its historical foundation, prefigured by the traditional Christian dualism between *regnum* and *sacerdotium*.[4] Nevertheless, modern political culture is not Christian, but secular. Even if its roots are in Christianity, the great shaper of West,[5] this culture is not exclusively and directly a product of the Christian heritage (indeed in certain respects it came about in explicit opposition to that heritage); put perhaps a bit simplistically, it derives equally

2. Translator's note: The Italian word *laico* and its cognate *laicismo* would be literally translated "lay-person" and "laicism," respectively, words that in English have an almost exclusively religious meaning. The appropriate English translation would be "secularist" and "secularism" (and "secular" for the adjective, *laicale*). The Italian (and the author) also uses *secolarismo* and *secolare* (secularism and secular, respectively); rather than the confusing "lay," I will exclusively use "secular" and its cognates in what follows.

3. Charles Taylor, "The Politics of Recognition," in Taylor et al., *Multiculturalism: Examining the Politics of Recognition*, ed. Amy Gutmann (Princeton, N.J.: Princeton University Press, 1994), 62.

4. See my considerations on this in chapter 1 of the present volume, entitled "Why Is Political Philosophy Necessary? Historical Considerations and a Response." This was originally published as "Perché una filosofia politica? Elementi storici per una risposta," *Acta Philosophica* 1 (1992): 233–63.

5. As some non-Christians also hold, as, for example, Joseph H. H. Weiler, *Un'Europa cristiana: Un saggio esplorativo* (Milan: Rizzoli, 2003). On this theme see also Marcello Pera and Joseph Ratzinger, *Senza Radici: Europa, relativismo, cristianesimo, Islam* (Milan: Mondadori, 2004).

from the Enlightenment tradition (in a broad sense). The political culture of liberal constitutional democracy possesses a specific legitimacy and modernity that is proper to it and that is not deducible from the Christian tradition, even if it is essentially rooted in that tradition. The Western Enlightenment is a son of Christianity—perhaps a "prodigal son" but nevertheless still its son—in which the parent can recognize himself and which, after the necessary correction and reconciliation (which has not entirely taken place as of yet), acquires again full rights of citizenship in the father's house. The above-mentioned dualism, unthinkable without the ferment of the Christianization of the Roman Empire,[6] made possible both the secularism of the modern state *and* the Enlightenment criticism, at times unjust and exaggerated, of the post-Constantine Christian past (a criticism unquestionably not a little intolerant in certain aspects); such a dualism is also necessary today for secular political culture to survive without falling, in its turn, into a totalizing monism hostile to religion.

For this reason, the problem of "multicultural citizenship" (the title of a well-known book by another Canadian philosopher, Will Kymlicka) arises,[7] and precisely from a liberal point of view, a point of view whose backbone as a political doctrine is the referred-to Christian dualism. The basic question is: in a political culture impregnated with specific cultural premises—such as those deriving from Christianity and liberal constitutionalism, the latter having developed in the context of the former—cultural premises that, moreover, are held to be universally valid, how is it possible to integrate cultural groups whose values in part diverge from these premises, and indeed perhaps even oppose them? One can easily see that this question is part of the general theme of pluralism, even if it does have particular nuances.

In what follows I do not intend to give an exhaustive response to this question. Perhaps a clear answer cannot be given, or must inevitably be negative: to the extent that such culturally diverse groups are in contrast with a political culture that recognizes the secularity of the state—the separation between religion and politics, between theology and the juridical order—they certainly *cannot* be integrated, at least if they do not assimilate

---

6. For this history see, in addition to the classical Catholic position of Christopher Dawson in his *The Making of Europe: An Introduction to the History of Christian Unity* (London: Sheed and Ward, 1932), the book—also already a classic—of Peter Brown, *The Rise of Western Christendom: Triumph and Diversity, A.D. 200–1000*, 2nd ed. (Oxford: Blackwell, 2003).

7. Will Kymlicka, *Multicultural Citizenship: A Liberal Theory of Minority Rights* (Oxford: Oxford University Press, 1995).

with the dominant political culture in these areas. This integration is impossible not only because of the cultural diversity, but because the concept of citizenship of these groups is incompatible with that which is innate to Western political culture (Christian, constitutional, liberal, and democratic). Consequently, the response to our question will not be simply negative, but neither will it be simply positive. It will rather be negative or positive, depending on the aspect of the question that is being examined.[8]

In the following pages I will limit myself to the presentation of some important aspects of the contemporary philosophical debate on the theme of "multicultural citizenship in liberal democracy," by means of three representative positions, those of Charles Taylor, Jürgen Habermas, and Will Kymlicka. In conclusion, I will offer an evaluation of these positions, along with a tentative response to the question I have posed, in the sense in which it has just been described.

Various Aspects of the Debate Concerning "Multiculturalism"

"Multiculturalism" is a term that has a variety of meanings, depending on the different ways in which cultural diversity is considered. Some specification of terminology will therefore be helpful. Obviously, in this setting we are speaking exclusively of the multiculturalism that occurs in the context of a single, territorially defined political culture. I will not consider here the fact of the diversity of cultures as such and their encounter at an international level, nor phenomena such as the *clash of civilizations* (in Samuel Huntington's famous expression). It is equally obvious, however, that due to the ties of cultural and ethnic groups to their home countries and because of the progressive interaction between nations of different cultures, "intranational" multiculturalism cannot always be completely separated from the phenomenon of international multiculturalism.

---

8. I do not pretend, therefore, to go as far as Samuel Huntington (see S. Huntington, *Who Are We? The Challenges to America's National Identity* [New York: Simon & Schuster, 2004]), who demands of immigrants to the United States (with good historical reasons, certainly) assimilation not only to the *political* culture of the country, but to the dominant culture *tout court*, forgetting, however, that the dominant culture is also subject to evolution, and in many aspects is enriched by the culture of immigrants. This is especially valid today for the Hispanics present in the United States, who, according to Huntington, form a body foreign to American culture, which is essentially Protestant. It does seem correct to me, however, that there must always be a dominant, "directing" (so to speak) culture—what the Moslem Lebanese-German political scientist Bassam Tibi has called *Leitkultur*—to which the immigrant must assimilate; a nation that is simply a melting pot of cultures can neither have an identity nor survive.

At the national level, the level that interests us, one must distinguish—a distinction proposed by Will Kymlicka[9]—between *national minorities* (which normally result from the integration of different national territories into a larger national unit, by federation, conquest, etc.) and *ethnic groups* (which typically result from immigration). National minorities form cultures that Kymlicka calls "societal cultures,"[10] having their own political and juridical institutions; ethnic-cultural and religious minorities, on the other hand, simply form ethnic groups with their own cultural and religious traditions in the midst of the surrounding culture. Recognition and the conferral of particular rights must be handled differently with national minorities and ethnic groups: in the case of national minorities there will be rights of self-government (autonomy); with ethnic groups, on the other hand, there will be pluri-ethnic rights (able to eliminate or prevent discrimination, and to provide public support for specific cultural practices—not so much to concede autonomy, but to facilitate integration).

The distinction between multinational states (with national minorities) and pluri-ethnic states (with groups of immigrants of other cultures) provides us with the distinction between two major types of multiculturalism, that is, (1) problems of immigration/assimilation and (2) those of the self-government and statutes of national minorities.

Another problem and area for discussion is that of racism, which in part concerns both national minorities and pluri-ethnic groups of immigrants. Still another aspect of multiculturalism is indigenous peoples, which are essentially national minorities, though in some cases not having their own territory, or perhaps even being partially integrated into the dominant culture. For these peoples, the problem arises in a particular way of their representation in the political system.

Finally, one must consider the various religious groups that are immigrants from nations of different cultures (though some such groups are not immigrant, such as the Amish and Hutterite communities in the United States). Today in Europe we are concerned above all with Moslem immigrants, and the problem of the possibility of their integration in the consensus of a political culture of the liberal-style secular state, which recognizes a clear separation between the religious and political-juridical orders.[11]

9. See *Multicultural Citizenship*, 10ff.   10. Ibid., 76.

11. For an overall view of the philosophical discussion of this theme in the Anglo-Saxon context, useful is Will Kymlicka, *Contemporary Political Philosophy: An Introduction*, 2nd ed. (Oxford: Oxford University Press, 2002), 327–76.

Charles Taylor: The Politics of Recognition

The philosophical debate on multiculturalism was in a certain sense opened in 1992 by the book of Charles Taylor, *Multiculturalism and the "Politics of Recognition,"* republished in 1994 under the title *The Politics of Recognition* (with commentary and criticism by Susan Wolf, Steven C. Rockefeller, Michael Walzer, Jürgen Habermas,[12] and K. Anthony Appiah).[13] In his book, the Canadian philosopher proposes the existence of two types of liberalism: the first (that of John Rawls and Ronald Dworkin) would be blind with respect to differences, defending the principle of a formal and procedural equality. This liberalism of the equality of rights accepts only a procedural responsibility for the public sphere, not, however, the inculcation of substantial values. Given, however, the increasingly multicultural structure of our contemporary societies, this type of liberalism and its principle of formal equality, says Taylor, ends in the imposition of the hegemonic culture of the majority. In other words, it cannot function properly as liberalism, respectful of the rights of the individual and of his legitimate autonomy, and opposed to every kind of tyranny of the majority.

For this reason another type of liberalism is needed, one proposed by Taylor, which is, so-to-speak, "hospitable" toward differences and thus more respectful of the dignity of persons, but which would also be capable of defining the society in terms of collective ends and of a substantial conception of the good. This kind of liberalism does not necessarily diminish those who do not share this definition. "According to this conception, a liberal society singles itself out as such by the way in which it treats minorities, including those who do not share public definitions of the good."[14] To this end one must distinguish between fundamental liberties, which must never be violated, and privileges and immunities, which are clearly important, but can be revoked or limited for reasons of the public interest. "A society with strong collective goals can be liberal, on this view, provided it is also capable of respecting diversity, especially when dealing with those who do not share its common goals; and provided it can offer adequate safeguards for fundamental rights."[15]

---

12. Habermas's contribution was also published in the original German version, "Kampf um Anerkennung im demokratischen Rechtsstaat," in *Die Einbeziehung des Anderen. Studien zur politischen Theorie* (Frankfurt am Main: Suhrkamp, 1996), 237–76.

13. Taylor, *Multiculturalism.*   14. Taylor, *The Politics of Recognition,* 59.

15. Ibid.

Clearly, a central concern of Taylor's argument is the demands of the French-Canadian minority of the province of Quebec, a society that, in the midst of the Anglo-Saxon Canadian society that surrounds it, seeks to define itself on the basis of some specific collective ends (regarding linguistic policies, the culture in general, and schools in particular). This is the typical case of a national minority claiming for itself a certain autonomy and structures of self-government (which might make it seem that Taylor's position is not pertinent to our theme; we will see that it is). While the position of the first, merely procedural, liberalism opts for a purely formal equality among all citizens of the country, Taylor defends the principle of a specific charter for the francophone minority of Quebec, for the purpose of the *survival* and the self-understanding of this culture. The solution would be liberal to the extent that it protects the fundamental liberties of all citizens, including those in the province (of Quebec) who are not francophone.

The essence—in a certain sense communitarian, but not antiliberal—of Taylor's position, which recognizes as central the value of autonomy and of the dignity of the individual, is that a society needs a culture that defines the collective ends and a conception of the good *proper to a society*. This becomes clear precisely thanks to the phenomenon of multiculturalism, given that in a society that maintains only a formal and procedural equality, but does not allow for the recognition of cultural differences, citizens belonging to cultures other than the majority necessarily feel marginalized. A politics respectful of the dignity of the person consequently becomes impossible, meaning the loss of a value that is essential for a genuinely liberal politics.

On the other hand—and here Taylor steps into a minefield—for a politics of difference and of the recognition of particular cultures, there are limits to the expression of these cultures, and even to their public support. Not all cultures are of equal value, says the Canadian philosopher. Certainly, we must always *presume* that the values of other cultures are in fact truly values;[16] indeed, if withholding a politics of equal respect for other cultures "is tantamount to a denial of equality, and if important consequences flow for people's identity from the absence of recognition, then a case can be made for insisting on the universalization of the presumption as a logical extension of the politics of dignity."[17] The demand, however, to judge positively every value belonging to other cultures, in Taylor's view, implies relativism and subjectivism, "which I think are shot through with confusion"; and

16. See ibid., 66ff.   17. Ibid., 68.

with respect to the value of "certain cultures … it can't make sense to demand as a matter of right that we come up with a final concluding judgment that their value is great, or equal to others."[18]

To demand a specific judgment of value as a *right* would mean to demand something that is no longer a judgment. Such a step would also be counterproductive, because with this "they miss the driving force of this kind of politics, which is precisely the search for recognition and respect"; this would mean that "the peremptory demand for favorable judgments of worth is paradoxically—perhaps one should say tragically—homogenizing. For it implies that we already have the standards to make such judgments."[19] What is needed therefore is "something midway between the inauthentic and homogenizing demand for recognition of equal worth, on the one hand, and the self-immurement within ethnocentric standards, on the other." This middle way is the "presumption of equal worth" referred to above, which might have a religious foundation and justification, or might simply be based on "a sense of our own limited part in the whole human story" and the recognition that to deny such a presumption would simply be "arrogance, or some analogous moral failing."[20]

This moralizing conclusion to Taylor's essay does not change the fact that for him not all cultures are on the same level. For this reason, as we noted at the outset, Taylor holds that the political culture of liberal democracy is not culturally neutral: "liberalism can't and shouldn't claim complete cultural neutrality"—because it is also a "fighting creed."[21] There is, however, a form of liberalism that is "inhospitable," according to Taylor's formulation, toward cultural differences—the liberalism of the first, merely procedural, type—and another, Taylor's, which would be hospitable toward cultural differences because it recognizes the need for the formulation of collective ends, not only of the society in general, but also of the societal entities formed by cultural minorities.

Jürgen Habermas: Deliberative Democracy and Constitutional Patriotism

Taylor provides us with few elements for responding to our initial question, in part because his theme is not exactly the same as ours. Our

18. Ibid., 68ff.
20. Ibid., 73.

19. Ibid., 71.
21. Ibid., 62.

theme does arise, however, in the response of Habermas to Taylor's position. Habermas objects above all to the fact that the Canadian philosopher questions "the individualistic core of the modern conception of freedom."[22] In the face of the alternative proposed by Taylor between a procedural liberalism and a liberalism that admits of the formulation of collective ends and substantial values, Habermas opts for the first, proceduralism, though not in a liberal-constitutionalistic form, but in the sense of what he calls "deliberative democracy." Based on his ethics of discourse, deliberative democracy would be a "proceduralist conception of rights according to which the democratic process has to safeguard both private and public autonomy at the same time."[23]

What does this mean? In Habermas's own words, it means that "a legal order is legitimate when it safeguards the autonomy of all citizens to an equal degree."[24] For this reason, according to Habermas, the constitutional state (the German *Rechtsstaat*) presupposes democracy, that is, the permanent realization of the sovereignty of the people by means of the democratic process. The political process itself therefore comprises part of the good life, of the moral self-understanding of the citizen. The liberal difference between private and public is thus eliminated.In this way, according to a clearly Rousseauian tradition (which the liberal Taylor rejects[25]) and not without the apparent influence of his neo-Marxist past, Habermas, as John Rawls noted in his "Response to Habermas,"[26] rejects the dualism of liberal constitutionalism, that is, the idea of removing the constitutional order and the juridical institutions founded by it—the constituted power—from the ordinary political and legislative political process. For Habermas, a constitutional state that is not at every moment the expression of the popular sovereignty, and in this way also the expression of the private autonomy of citizens, would be an oppressor, undemocratic and juridically illegitimate (it is not clear what this means from the point of view of its realization at the institutional level; but this question is unimportant in the present context).

<hr />

22. "Struggles for Recognition in the Democratic Constitutional State," in Taylor, *Multiculturalism*, 109.

23. Ibid., 116. See on this also section 5 of Habermas's book *Die Einbeziehung des Anderen*, quoted above.

24. "Struggles for Recognition," 121–22; emphasis mine.

25. See his *The Politics of Recognition*, 44–51.

26. Appeared originally in *Journal of Philosophy* 92 (1995), and then was included as *Lecture IX: Reply to Habermas* in the paperback edition, which appeared in 1996, of his book *Political Liberalism* (New York: Columbia University Press, 1993); see 405–6.

From this it follows—still according to Habermas—that any juridical order is always also the expression of a particular form of life, and that ethical-political questions are an integral part of politics. One cannot, says Habermas, reduce the political process to ethical auto-clarification, as the communitarians do; yet "the process of actualizing rights is indeed embedded in contexts that require such discourses as an important component of politics—discussions about a shared conception of the good and a desired form of life that is acknowledged to be authentic."[27] The German philosopher even speaks of the "fact that every legal community and every democratic process for actualizing basic rights is inevitably permeated by ethics."[28] In this context he mentions "the institutional guarantees enjoyed by Christian churches in countries like Germany—despite freedom of religion—or in the recently challenged constitutional guarantee of status accorded the family in distinction to other marriage-like arrangements."[29]

Habermas pays a relatively high price, however, for his acceptance of the inevitability that a particular political and juridical system be permeated by substantial ethical values: the price, as we have already mentioned, of the rejection of the "dualistic wisdom" of liberal constitutionalism, which distinguishes between the basic formal and procedural constitutional juridical structure (in which is also included formal equality with respect to rights of liberty), and ordinary political-deliberative procedures, carried out within and on the basis of the constitutional structure. Contrary to what we find in Taylor, for Habermas liberal proceduralism is not completed and relativized by the acceptance of collective ends, but reinterpreted in the sense of a discourse that must at every moment express the requirements of autonomy of the citizenry, along with the other ethical-political values they consider important. In other words: Habermas rejects the limitation of the sovereignty of the people by a constitutional state, the "rule of law" and fundamental rights, which are relatively blind with respect to substantial conceptions that are moral, religious, and so on. Popular sovereignty, always active and constitutive, becomes rather the fundamental principle of the juridical order, and the constitutional state must be its permanent expression. Instead of being, as in the liberal tradition, a principle that orders and limits popular sovereignty, for Habermas the law becomes, in a Jacobin

27. Habermas, "Struggles for Recognition," 125.
28. Ibid., 126.
29. Ibid.

fashion, the current and ever-new expression of this sovereignty that, juridically, does not admit of limits.

Habermas's position has immediate consequences for his approach to the problem of multiculturalism (which he examines, however, only with respect to immigration). Multiculturalism, he states, is not a kind of "preservation of species by administrative means." That is, the "right to equal respect ... has nothing to do with the presumed excellence of his or her culture of origin, that is, with generally valued accomplishments." Taking up an idea formulated by Susan Wolf in her critical comment on Taylor's work,[30] what we have here is simply the recognition of the fact that for a particular individual, a culture and its corresponding practices and traditions possess a particular worth. The recognition, that is, not of the worth of cultures, but of the individuals who belong to them.[31] "For in the last analysis," concludes Habermas, "the protection of forms of life and traditions in which identities are formed is supposed to serve the recognition of their members."[32] Thus Habermas rejects Taylor's opinion that the recognition of different cultural traditions also presupposes a value judgment with respect to these cultures, and that such a recognition has as its object not only individuals, but also the collective ends and values implicit in the respective cultural traditions, that is, the survival of the cultures themselves.

One sees, moreover, how Habermas would apply the principle of the unity between private autonomy and public autonomy to the problem of multiculturalism, and how, according to him, the democratic process must simultaneously ensure private and public autonomy with respect to the questions of multiculturalism and of the recognition of ethnic differences and particularities.

For Habermas, immigrants who come from other cultures must have the freedom to choose between various possibilities, which would be: (a) preserve the culture from which they have come and be socialized within it, (b) renounce and abandon that culture, or (c) live a fragmented identity. In all three cases "the ethical integration of groups and subcultures with their own collective identities must be uncoupled from the abstract political inte-

---

30. See Susan Wolf, Comment, in Taylor, *Multiculturalism*, 79.

31. In her comment, Susan Wolf (ibid., 81) says: "The insult here is an insult fundamentally to individuals and not to cultures. It consists either in ignoring the presence of these individuals in our community or in neglecting or belittling the importance of their cultural identities. Failing to respect the existence or importance of their distinctive histories, arts, and traditions, we fail to respect them as equals, whose interests and values have equal standing in our community."

32. Habermas, "Struggles for Recognition," 129.

gration that includes all citizens equally."[33] Thus integration becomes possible: a "constitutional patriotism" is formed that organizes the intentions of
all citizens and establishes "an association of individuals who are free and
equal." In this way, "the political integration of citizens ensures loyalty to the
common political culture."[34] But the common adherence to the constitution,
that is, "the *ethical substance of a* constitutional patriotism cannot detract
from the legal system's neutrality vis-à-vis communities that are ethically integrated at a sub-political level." The difference between these two levels is
thus essential for Habermas. As such, "the universalism of legal principles
is reflected in a procedural consensus which must be embedded in the context of a historically specific political culture through a kind of *constitutional
patriotism.*"[35]

This solution seems to be balanced and, its problematic theoretical presuppositions notwithstanding, in fact does not present major problems.
The crucial problem surfaces, however, only toward the end of Habermas's
essay, reopening the question of his previous solution: the question of
"whether the desire for immigration runs up against limits in the right of a
political community to maintain its political-cultural form of life intact."[36]
The same also applies to the question of "legitimate conditions of entry."
Habermas resolves the problem by distinguishing between (a) assimilation
as assent to the principles of the constitution and (b) assimilation as a further level of willingness to become acculturated, that is, not only to conform
externally but to become habituated to the way of life, the practices, and
customs of the local culture. The democratic constitutional state, asserts
Habermas, must clearly distinguish these two levels of integration and ask
of immigrants only a political association of type (a), that is, the loyal approval of constitutional principles.[37]

The solution is therefore one of conforming to the political culture of
the new country without having to renounce the form of cultural life of
one's origins. Excluded, according to Habermas, are "fundamentalistic"
cultures, a term that is very unclear in this context and not later specified.
One can easily understand the problem: in some cases, these two levels of
integration are not clearly separable; this refers especially to those cases, as
with traditionalist Islam, in which the juridical-political system is not dis-

---

33. Ibid., 133ff.
35. Ibid., 134ff.
37. See ibid., 138ff.

34. Ibid., 134.
36. Ibid., 137.

tinguished from the religious system, in which theology and jurisprudence form a unity and, moreover, no justification exists for the state outside of its function that is also religious. The basis for an integration of type (a) is lacking, therefore, that is, a political integration with the formation of a corresponding constitutional patriotism and loyalty. Indeed, even the capacity to distinguish between the two levels of integration is lacking. Unfortunately, Habermas does not reflect at all on this question; he limits himself, rather, to what seems to be mere political correctness.

We can nevertheless at this point make a preliminary, tentative evaluation. Even if the positions of Taylor and Habermas are different and even opposed, they possess two points in common, both interesting and extremely important:

1. both authors recognize that the political culture of a nation is more than a structure of formal rights and procedural rules with no ethical content or substantial values;

2. both claim that the democratic constitutional state of the liberal tradition (or in the case of Habermas: the democratic "state under the rule of law," in German *Rechtsstaat*) is not compatible with every cultural tradition, but only with those that accept the constitutional consensus that—precisely—includes the differentiation between the political-juridical system (secular, "lay," allowing pluralism) and the religious-theological system. Habermas defends the idea that the ethical-political aspects must be integrated into the democratic system by means of a new type of proceduralism, democratic deliberation. Taylor, on the other hand, thinks in terms of defining collective ends at the constitutional level, at the same time guaranteeing fundamental rights to all citizens, including those who find themselves in dissent with respect to those ends.

Will Kymlicka and the Liberal Theory of Minority Rights

The positions of Taylor and Habermas are formulated at an equal critical distance with respect to liberalism properly so-called. Especially the first point—the insufficiency of a purely formal proceduralism with no content of substantial ethical values—would in fact seem unacceptable to many liberals. A liberal could argue that, for liberalism, the problem of multiculturalism is not a problem at all, given that it is already resolved: a liberal democracy grants equal rights to all, is blind with respect to cultural differences, and treats all in an equal manner. Precisely this would be the advantage of liberal proceduralism (which would be identical to the "liberalism 1" criticized by Taylor).

Not all liberals, however, think in this somewhat simplistic fashion. Another Canadian philosopher, the above-mentioned Will Kymlicka—also the proponent of a strictly liberal position—has claimed that liberals also must recognize the necessity of seeing multiculturalism as a problem and as a political challenge, and, moreover, a *liberal* theory of rights for ethnic minorities must be elaborated. Kymlicka accepts the two principles mentioned above (common to Taylor and Habermas), that is, the insufficiency of a merely formal proceduralism and the fact that the political culture of a particular nation, even a democracy with a liberal, constitutionalistic tradition, includes in it a political-ethical content that is not neutral with respect to all cultures, values, and religious traditions.

Kymlicka, therefore, tries to offer a way toward a solution within a liberalism of the first type, that is, that liberalism which, according to Taylor, would be incapable of doing justice to the phenomena of multiculturalism, being "inhospitable" with respect to the recognition of cultural differences.[38]

In his book cited above, *Multicultural Citizenship,*[39] published in 1995, Kymlicka maintains that a state cannot renounce having its own cultural identity, that is, a culture of the majority rooted in history. In this regard the possibility of neutrality does not exist, as it does, for example, in the area of religion. Separation between church and state is possible, but not that between state and culture or ethnic identity. The state can renounce having a state religion, but not having a majority culture. The state, therefore, necessarily supports the majority culture in a privileged way. The question is whether it does so in a way that is just and fair with respect to minority cultures.[40]

---

38. Michael Walzer, in his commentary on Taylor (in Taylor, *Multiculturalism,* 99ff.), also offers a solution in the context of the first form of liberalism, though a solution that seems somewhat less than straightforward and even somewhat cynical: he says that he first would choose "liberalism 2," and then within it he would implement "liberalism 1"—i.e., a pure proceduralism—as a collective end and good.

39. See also by Kymlicka his collection of other writings on this theme: *Politics in the Vernacular: Nationalism, Multiculturalism, and Citizenship* (Oxford: Oxford University Press, 2001). For a discussion of Kymlicka's theses see Matteo L. Bellati, *Quale multiculturalismo? I termini del dibattito e la prospettiva di Will Kymlicka* (Milan: Vita e Pensiero, 2005).

40. See Kymlicka, *Multicultural Citizenship,* 115.

Kymlicka shows how the exclusive application of the rules of formal rights and procedural logic easily leads to discrimination (which is also Taylor's thesis). Specific rights for minority groups therefore become necessary. Kymlicka does not address the problem of national minorities in a multinational state, focusing instead only on ethnic groups and cultures that result from immigration (i.e., multiculturalism in pluri-ethnic states); he nevertheless introduces some helpful distinctions.

According to Kymlicka, collective rights (of which Taylor speaks) claimed by ethnic groups and cultural minorities are of two different types. The first are rights that limit some fundamental rights that the surrounding, majority society confers on all of its citizens, in the name of the solidarity of the ethnic group and the survival of its cultural identity (e.g., the right to change religions or, for women, to attend certain schools or to marry a person of another religion). Collective rights that restrict, for the members of a particular group and in the name of a particular cultural tradition, some civil rights generally valid for the surrounding society, Kymlicka calls *internal restrictions.*

Collective rights of the second type are aimed at limiting the influence, political power, economic power, and so on, of the surrounding, majority society over a minority ethnic and cultural group, for the purpose of protecting the latter's institutions, traditions, and identity—which is to say, to protect them from the tyranny of the majority (as, for example, the right to have special schools, subsidies for specific cultural practices, or norms for preferred access to pedagogical institutions, such as affirmative action). Kymlicka calls these collective rights *external protections.*[41]

While internal restrictions are normally incompatible with the political culture of human rights, and thereby with a liberal-type constitutional democracy, external protections can be compatible with such a culture and at times even required by it, in that they help to promote equality between minority and majority groups, or more precisely, the equality of rights between the members of minority groups and those of the dominant culture. A liberal political culture must therefore promote some external protections, if these serve to establish equality between citizens. The general principle would be that "liberals should seek to ensure that there is equality *between* groups, and freedom and equality *within* groups."[42]

41. Ibid., 35ff.
42. Ibid., 194.

As an example of a multiculturalism *incompatible* with liberal principles, Kymlicka mentions the system of the *Millet* in the Ottoman Empire.[43] In this instance of a certain religious pluralism and a tolerant regime, Moslems, Christians, and Jews could live according to their respective religious traditions and impose the rules of their religions on their members with coercive power: a Moslem, for example, but not a Christian, could be condemned to death for apostasy. Religious freedom was thus not conceived of as a right of individuals, but as a collective right of the group. According to the modern Western conception of constitutional liberalism, however, the right to religious freedom has the fundamental characteristic of being an individual right, guaranteed by the coercive power of the state, and there can be no other coercive power that can limit that right (thus apostasy could never be a crime with civil implications). In this sense, for example, a Catholic who teaches at a Catholic university, and who publicly abandons the faith and the Church, can be deposed from his position at the university and lose the rights of a member of the Catholic Church, but he cannot be deprived of any civil right; moreover, he cannot be constrained by the coercive power of the state (which possesses a monopoly of coercive power) to remain in the Church. To confer on an ethnic, cultural, or religious group such a power over its members would thus be an "internal restriction" incompatible with the principles of a liberal state.

With this one also sees—as Kymlicka observes[44]—that the question of conferring collective rights on ethnic, cultural, or religious minorities is not an issue of the difference between "individualism" and "communitarianism." For Kymlicka, this opposition is mistaken, given that even in the case of the conferral of collective rights, the goal is always one of promoting juridical equality and equality of opportunity among *individuals*. Collective rights, as well, are at the service of the individual person, and only in this sense can they be justified. Here it seems that Kymlicka's position surpasses those of both Taylor and Habermas.[45]

Kymlicka therefore formulates the following principle: "Liberals can

43. Ibid., 156ff.

44. See ibid., 46–47.

45. For the thesis that communitarianism and liberalism are not comprehensive alternatives, and that they in a certain sense complement one another, see chapter 2 of the present volume, entitled "The Liberal Image of Man and the Concept of Autonomy: Beyond the Debate between Liberals and Communitarians." This was originally published as "L'immagine dell'uomo nel liberalismo e il concetto di autonomia: al di là del dibattito fra liberali e comunitaristi," in *Immagini dell'uomo. Percorsi antropologici nella filosofia moderna*, ed. Ignacio Yarza (Rome: Armando, 1997), 95–133.

only endorse minority rights insofar as they are consistent with respect for the freedom or autonomy of individuals."[46] Nevertheless, Kymlicka does not want to say that such rights have as their purpose *only* the promotion of the autonomy of the individual. The principle expressed is only a condition for the conferral of such rights, not the reason for which they are conferred (though in some cases it could be the reason, as well). The real reason for conferring such rights is based on the idea that justice often requires that the members of different groups also have different rights.[47]

Why? Not only because, as we have mentioned, specific rights for specific groups may be required to establish equality between minority and majority, but because the exercise of individual freedom is also linked to belonging to a group and to its culture—which is to say: the exercise of freedom requires a cultural identity and a specific social context. Otherwise it is not possible to make meaningful choices, nor is there support for one's personal identity.[48] With his "culturalist" liberal position, therefore, Kymlicka in a certain sense makes his own the "social thesis" of the communitarians, while avoiding the ambivalence and problems of communitarianism.[49]

From what has been said one can see how important it is that individuals have access to their own culture. But why is this important? Wouldn't it be better to simply wait for these cultural minorities to dissolve, and their members to mix in with the dominant culture? The reason, according to Kymlicka, is that what is at stake *is the identity of the person*, which is based on belonging and not on accomplishments (this is also a thesis of Taylor). As we have said, only through belonging to a culturally specified social context is it possible to make meaningful choices.[50]

According to Kymlicka, however, this is not the same as a communitarian conception.[51] In the first place, because it doesn't imply a communitarian conception of the self: according to the liberal conception the person always possesses the ability to change his identity and to distance himself from a prior identity, and thus also to cease belonging to a group. Neither

46. Kymlicka, *Multicultural Citizenship*, 75.

47. Ibid., 47.

48. Ibid., 105: "Liberals should recognize the importance of people's membership in their own societal culture, because of the role it plays in enabling meaningful individual choice and in supporting self-identity."

49. See ibid., 84–93; see also Kymlicka, *Contemporary Political Philosophy*, 244–68, 338ff., as well as his first work on the theme: *Liberalism, Community, and Culture* (Oxford: Oxford University Press, 1989).

50. See *Multicultural Citizenship*, 89. Kymlicka makes reference to Avishai Margalit and Joseph Raz, "National Self-Determination," *Journal of Philosophy* 87, no. 9 (1990): 439–61.

51. Kymlicka, *Multicultural Citizenship*, 91ff.

the group, nor the surrounding society, should prevent him from doing so. Second, because the politics of communitarianism aims at a common good that is not realizable at the national level—that is, at the level of the whole political society—but only at the sub-national, more local level. This, however, could lead to repressive structures that the individual would be unable to leave. At the "national" level, communitarianism in effect offers no solutions and is not practicable. The liberal solution, on the other hand, assures freedom and autonomy at the subnational level (and therefore the possibility of changing groups, changing identity, distancing oneself from certain values, etc.); at the national level, liberalism creates a community of free and equal individuals that has as its ideal precisely to make possible a life in freedom and equality. *This*, in fact, is a truly communitarian culture.

This kind of liberal cultural identity, Kymlicka says, does not presuppose any common values, even if it does form an "ethical community":[52] with the proponents of a "liberal nationalism,"[53] Kymlicka maintains the possibility and the importance of a national identity. This identity is formed by a common history, a common cultural heritage, and a common language, but also by common social and political institutions and the like. According to the liberal conception, however, such a national identity must be "thin." It must not be centered on a specific conception of the good life, thereby becoming antipluralist and exclusive, but only on those values that help citizens to fulfill their obligations of justice toward their fellow citizens. This national identity would therefore be formed by the values of coexistence and solidarity between free and equal citizens.[54]

Although one could legitimately raise the question as to whether there could be any national identity, however "weak" it may be, that is not linked to a certain conception of the good life—this perhaps also "weak"—one sees in Kymlicka (and in authors such as Yael Tamir and Joseph Raz[55]) a clear awareness of the cultural conditions necessary for a civic identity centered on freedom and equality. For this reason, the question arises of tolerance toward ethnic groups whose self-understanding is based on the rejection of liberal principles. It would seem logical that groups or individuals who

52. See *Contemporary Political Philosophy*, 266.

53. As for example Yael Tamir, *Liberal Nationalism* (Princeton, N.J.: Princeton University Press, 1993).

54. Kymlicka, *Contemporary Political Philosophy*, 265ff.

55. See notes 50 and 53 above. See, in addition to Raz's well-known work *The Morality of Freedom* (Oxford: Oxford University Press, 1996), the essay "Multiculturalism: A Liberal Perspective" in Raz, *Ethics in the Public Domain: Essays in the Morality of Law and Politics*, rev. ed. (Oxford: Oxford University Press, 1994; reprint, 2001), 170–91.

are opposed to these principles or values—and this in a politically relevant way, that is, attempting to create a subculture that competes with the political and legal system of the surrounding society—cannot be tolerated; nor can those be tolerated who attempt to, so to speak, "export" their antiliberal ideas, trying to impose them on the entire society. The question also remains of tolerance toward groups that organize themselves *internally* according to principles opposed to those of liberalism (for example, preventing girls from attending school, or members from undergoing blood transfusions, even in cases of life and death), without, however, wanting to export their principles. For Kymlicka, these are cases requiring prudential judgment; the response would depend on the specific case.[56]

According to Kymlicka, the error of proponents of "political liberalism," and particularly of John Rawls, is to think that such groups not only could be tolerated, but also could form part of an *overlapping consensus;* Kymlicka criticizes the idea that groups that do not recognize the value of autonomy internally could support a public conception of justice, proceeding from an "overlapping consensus," in which political autonomy is a central value.[57] In Kymlicka's view, it is not possible to support a conception of autonomy at the political level without also adhering to this value in private life, personal life, and so on. For this reason Kymlicka thinks that, generally speaking, groups that do not accept the idea of autonomy in the liberal sense (e.g., that of John Stuart Mill) in their private life cannot accept autonomy as a political value either.

I think that Kymlicka is only partially correct in his criticism of Rawls. He is correct in the sense that one who accepts a political consensus that includes autonomy as a central political value (in the sense of *legal* freedoms, as for example the freedom to profess and practice one's chosen religion, to express one's opinion publicly, to marry whom one pleases or to choose one's professional formation) must also accept certain "liberal" principles of this type for his private life as well, or for the internal life of his religious or cultural group, and so on. But he must first of all accept *the distinction itself* between the religious-theological sphere and the juridical and political sphere. On this basis it would then be possible to adhere to certain values precisely as *political and juridical* values. One who accepts the political val-

---

56. Kymlicka, *Multicultural Citizenship*, 163–72.

57. Ibid., 158–63. Kymlicka refers primarily to Rawls's 1985 essay "Justice as Fairness: Political Not Metaphysical," *Philosophy and Public Affairs* 14, no. 3 (1985): 223–51, as well as to the book *Political Liberalism*.

ue of autonomy can—and must—also accept the corresponding conception of citizenship and, consequently, renounce principles that are incompatible with such a conception.

For example, clearly *incompatible* with a political conception of autonomy (in the sense of the political liberalism of Rawls) is the idea that the juridical system of a society must be established according to the *sharia,* or that a purely secular definition and legitimacy of the state does not exist, that is, outside of the religious context (which is of course central to the Christian and Western tradition). To offer another example: one can certainly be convinced, at the personal and private level, that a person who abandons the Christian faith commits a serious, culpable act of infidelity, while at the same time being convinced, at the level of the rights of citizens, of the right of every person to freely choose and change religions. Moreover, one could be convinced that there is only one religion and one true church—one's own—and at the same time defend the civil right to adhere to and practice that religion which one in conscience believes to be true—or the right to not adhere to any religion—without any intervention by the state with its coercive power, or by the legal system backed by this power. It seems obvious to me that the political value of autonomy, even if distinguished *in the same subject* from his conception of moral autonomy in a broader sense (i.e., one valid for his personal life), also includes a moral substance, of precisely a *political* morality. It is moreover the expression of an ideal of social life, of coexistence, and of cooperation among citizens, and even, especially in the case of religious freedom, of a specific conception of the human being and of the relation of his freedom to truth. This shows, though, that even the "liberal community" includes a specific, even if "thin," conception of the good life.[58]

Obviously, adherents of "political liberalism" would also agree with a vision of the problem articulated in this way.[59] And yet this is in no way

58. This thesis is explicitly affirmed by "antineutralist" liberals such as William Galston and Stephen Macedo, or liberal neo-Aristotelians such as Martha Nussbaum, and in another way also by the liberal "perfectionism" of Raz. Thus, William Galston, in his book *Liberal Purposes: Goods, Virtues and Diversity in the Liberal State* (Cambridge: Cambridge University Press, 1991), 79, has written: "No form of political life can be justified without some view of what is good for individuals." See also Martha Nussbaum, "Aristotelian Social Democracy," in *Liberalism and the Good,* ed. R. Bruce Douglass, G. M. Mara, and H. S. Richardson (New York: Routledge, 1990), 203–52; Stephen Macedo, *Liberal Virtues: Citizenship, Virtue, and Community in Liberal Constitutionalism* (Oxford: Clarendon Press, 1990); for Raz, see his *The Morality of Freedom.* Critical reflections concerning some of these authors can be found in Christopher Wolfe, ed., *Liberalism at the Crossroads: An Introduction to Contemporary Liberal Political Theory and Its Critics,* 2nd ed. (Lanham, Md.: Rowman and Littlefield, 2003).

59. See, for example, the essay of Charles E. Larmore, "Political Liberalism" (1990), reprinted in Larmore, *The Morals of Modernity* (Cambridge: Cambridge University Press, 1996), 140; also Rawls, *Political Liberalism,* 138; see also 152ff.

that type of non-liberal doctrine that Rawls thinks could be part of an *over-lapping consensus* in support of a political conception of autonomy. Moreover, Rawls does not hold, as Kymlicka suggests, that our private opinions concerning political and legal values can be completely independent of the publicly reigning political conception; he rather holds that what we pursue as good in our personal life can be defined in terms different than those in which the public conception of political justice is defined. If such a personal conception of the good has political and legal implications that conflict with the public conception of justice, such a comprehensive doctrine of the good would be, according to Rawls, "unreasonable," and therefore could not form part of an overlapping consensus, nor even support such a consensus and contribute to the stabilization of society. Thus it seems to me that Kymlicka's criticism misses the mark.[60]

In fact, to be a good and loyal citizen of a state in which a public conception of political justice in the sense of political liberalism reigns, one does not need, as Kymlicka suggests, to make his own the conception of John Stuart Mill about autonomy, which I have called a "strong conception of autonomy," because according to this conception the principal value of autonomy consists *in the very possibility of choosing,* and not so much in choosing what is truly valuable or good.[61] This "strong" concept of autonomy is precisely not a concept of *political* autonomy, but rather an idea expressing a specific self-understanding of the moral subject. "Political liberalism" attempts precisely to distinguish these two levels on which one speaks of autonomy.

The Impossibility of a Properly Multicultural Citizenship

We thus arrive at the moment for making an evaluation, in which I would like to briefly propose the thesis mentioned at the beginning, that is, that a "multicultural citizenship" in a proper, "strong" sense is impossible.

60. For my critical evaluation of the political liberalism of Rawls, see chapter 7 of the present volume (see note 1 above). A rather different interpretation, more hostile with respect to Rawls and in my opinion to some degree unfortunate (as I attempt to show in the essay just mentioned), can be found in the contributions of Robert P. George, Christopher Wolfe, and John Finnis in George and Wolfe, eds., *Natural Law and Public Reason* (Washington, D.C.: Georgetown University Press, 2000); and Robert P. George, "Pluralismo morale, ragione pubblica e legge naturale," in *Etica e politica nella società del duemila,* ed. R. A. Gahl (Rome: Armando, 1998), 79–91. An identical argumentation can be found in chapter 11 of George, *In Defense of Natural Law* (Oxford: Oxford University Press, 1999), 196ff.

61. See chapter 2 of this volume, 46–67; and Rhonheimer, *L'immagine dell'uomo nel liberalismo e il concetto di autonomia,* 105ff.

Between authors as diverse as Taylor, Habermas, and Kymlicka, there nevertheless seems to be a consensus on an essential point: a political culture of freedom and equality, like that of the democratic state with a liberal and constitutional tradition, lives by specific cultural presuppositions and forms a "community of values," an "ethical community." One could cite, once again, the famous phrase of Ernst-Wolfgang Böckenförde that "the liberal, secularized state lives by presuppositions that it cannot guarantee by itself,"[62] that is, it lives "by the moral substance of individual persons and the homogeneity of the society."[63] Traditionally, liberalism has paid little attention to this aspect, because it developed under the banner of freedom, fighting against political systems that—in the name of specific communities of value, of truth (including religious), and of a social homogeneity defined in these terms—did not recognize the autonomy of the person as a citizen. The liberal political culture of modernity developed—always in opposition to that prior heritage, though not without ebb and flow—in the name of tolerance, freedom, individual rights, confessional neutrality, and the acceptance of pluralism.[64] As has already been mentioned, classical liberalism was capable of winning this battle (with such success that today, properly "liberal" parties seem like a relic of the past) only because it acted within the context of a culture that made possible the resolution of the serious conflict between power and freedom—a culture that was in this sense *secular*—and always within a community of values that had been provided by the Western tradition, thus permeated by Judeo-Christian values, Greek thought, and Roman law.[65]

In the face of the challenge of multiculturalism—and above all, as I have

62. "Der freiheitliche, säkularisierte Staat lebt von Voraussetzungen, die er selbst nicht garantieren kann." Böckenförde, "Die Entstehung des Staates als Vorgang der Säkularisation," in Böckenförde, *Staat, Gesellschaft, Freiheit. Studien zur Staatstheorie und zum Verfassungsrecht* (Frankfurt: Suhrkamp), 60.

63. Ibid.: "Aus der moralischen Substanz des einzelnen und der Homogenität der Gesellschaft."

64. See among others the 1925 classic of de Ruggiero, *Storia del liberalismo europeo* (Rome-Bari: Laterza, 2003) and Nicola Matteucci, *Organizzazione del potere e libertà: Storia del costituzionalismo moderno* (Turin: UTET, 1988) (especially chap. 8, "Costituzionalismo e liberalismo").

65. One can also appeal in this regard to a testimony that is beyond suspicion, that of Karl Popper, who wrote: "When I call our social world 'the best,' ... I have in mind the standards and values which have come down to us through Christianity from Greece and the Holy Land; from Socrates, and from the Old and New Testament" (Popper, *Conjectures and Refutations: The Growth of Scientific Knowledge*, 3rd ed. [London: Routledge and Kegan Paul, 1969], 369). Nevertheless, I am not entirely opposed to the idea of Michael Ignatieff in *Human Rights as Politics and Idolatry*, ed. Amy Gutmann (Princeton, N.J.: Princeton University Press, 2001), who claims that in order that civil liberties and rights can be universally and more effectively guaranteed, what is needed is a more *political* understanding of human rights, instead of one linked to metaphysical and religious truths, etc., which are always controversial. This may be true, but it does not mean that such rights can coexist with all cultural presuppositions, or that they could have arisen, as "secular" values, outside of the above-mentioned context.

said, of traditionalist Islam—we are again made aware of the cultural presuppositions of a political culture of freedom. The Islamic discussion, for
example, even if modernizing and tending—in authors such as Mohamed
Charfi and Mohamed Talbi,[66] both eminent Tunisian intellectuals—toward
a conciliation between the Koran and the secular state and between Islam
and liberal democracy, is still infected by the Islamic "dogma," defended
by even its most liberal and secularist representatives, that a separation between the *Islamic* religion and the state is not possible, because the state is
the necessary guarantor and overseer of the religion and cult of Islam. For
its practical realization, in fact, Islam has much more need of the state than
Christianity does. Consequently, it seems entirely uncertain to what extent
the Western model of separation between church and state would be applicable in the Islamic community,[67] even if it must be acknowledged that
in certain practical aspects the Islamic position in this area is ultimately not
that different from the Christian position of the past, whether in its Catholic
form[68] (e.g., in Gallicanism) or its Protestant form (much more inclined, at
least in Lutheranism, to leave ecclesiastical organization in the hands of the
state). It seems, however, that in the case of Islam, an evolution analogous
to that which took place among the various Christian confessions—for the
Catholic Church, definitively with Vatican II—would be possible only with
difficulty, because Islam includes an element that is absent in the Western-
Christian tradition: the idea that the state has a function that is essentially
also religious. In other words, the Islamic tradition does not acknowledge a
purely secular legitimacy and justification of the state—something that has
always been part, even if in various ways, of the Christian tradition. For this
reason it seems almost impossible that Islam could evolve in a way analogous to Christianity in this area, that is, toward a recognition of the genuine
and essential secularity of the state, even if the last word of history in this
area, it seems to me, has not yet been spoken.[69]

66. See their respective contributions in the volume of Johannes Schwartländer, ed., *Freiheit der
Religion: Christentum und Islam unter dem Anspruch der Menschenrechte* (Mainz: Matthias-Grünewald-
Verlag, 1993), 53ff., 93ff., 384ff., 387ff.

67. See for this problem the works of Arnd Uhle, *Staat—Kirche—Kultur* (Berlin: Duncker & Humblot,
2004); *Freiheitlicher Verfassungsstaat und kulturelle Identität* (Tübingen: Mohr, Siebeck, 2005).

68. See, for example, the Catholic position as it was presented at the beginning of the nineteenth
century, by some illustrious Catholic theologians, in various opinions in the course of the "process"
against the liberal Catholic Abbé Lammenais (his original name was Félicité-Robert de La Mennais),
who, among other things, asked for a separation between Church and state and the recognition of civil
liberties in the liberal sense; see the French edition of the acts of Marie-Joseph Le Guillou and Louis Le
Guillou, *La condamnation de Lamennais, Dossier présenté da* (Paris: Editions Beauchesne, 1982).

69. For a discussion of the prospects for an "Islamic liberalism"—a presupposition for a recon-

Faced with the challenges of multiculturalism, we also become aware of the secularity of the state and of the political power as *cultural conquests,* ethical values that in turn presuppose a conception of the good—of the common good, precisely at the political level. True, therefore, is the statement of Gian Enrico Rusconi, that the secularity of the state cannot be reduced to a simple multiculturalism, because the

principle of secularity ... does not limit itself to neutralizing the claims of the various cultures and religions to occupy the public space in an improper or monopolistic way; it does not limit itself to affirming the principle of a benevolent tolerance, but positively demands a reciprocal bond on which to construct a political community which is solidaristic in that it faithfully defines itself by principles, rules and institutions which prescind from particular cultural roots that are not generalizable.[70]

Nevertheless, even the *generalizable* particular cultural roots that shape the self-understanding of the Western-style secular democratic constitutional state and its sense of secularity are still *cultural* roots that, even if generalizable and perhaps even universally valid, live precisely by those cultural presuppositions in which they are rooted, and that are made present in social and political realities through the consciences of citizens.[71]

From this it can be concluded that, at the political and juridical levels, multiculturalism in the true and proper sense is not possible. It is impossible in the sense of a "multicultural citizenship," according to which *differing conceptions of citizenship,* culturally differentiated, could coexist in a single political community, that is, in a state or a nation. At least it is impossible according to the self-understanding of constitutional democracy in the liberal tradition, which defines itself precisely on the basis of a common conception of citizenship (political, secular, and egalitarian), on the for-

---

ciliation between Islamic culture and Western political liberalism—see the important book of Leonard Binder, *Islamic Liberalism: A Critique of Development Ideologies* (Chicago: University of Chicago Press, 1988). Regarding the contemporary problems of the religious integration of Muslims in the case of three European states, see J. S. Fetzer and J. C. Soper, *Muslims and the State in Britain, France, and Germany* (Cambridge: Cambridge University Press, 2005). Regarding the mentioned evolution of the Catholic position, I refer the reader to my work "Il rapporto tra verità e politica nella società Cristiana: Riflessioni storico-teologiche per la valutazione dell'amore della libertà nella predicazione di Josemaría Escrivá," in *Figli di Dio nella Chiesa. Riflessioni sul messaggio di San Josemaría Escrivá. Aspetti culturali ed ecclesiastici,* ed. Fernando de Andrés, (*La grandezza della vita quotidiana.* Atti del Congresso Internazionale, January 8–11, 2002, vol. 5/2) (Rome: Pontifical University of the Holy Cross, 2004), 153–78. A more developed version of this was published as chapter 4 of my *Changing the World: The Timeliness of Opus Dei* (New York: Scepter Press, 2009).

70. Gian Enrico Rusconi, *Possiamo fare a meno di una religione civile?* (Rome-Bari: Laterza, 1999), 74.

71. A criticism of the "secular" conception proposed by Rusconi in his later essay *Come se Dio non ci fosse: I laici, i cattolici e la democrazia* (Turin: Einaudi, 2000), can be found in chapter 5 of this book, originally published in a shorter form in my brief essay "Laici e cattolici: oltre le divisioni. Riflessioni sull'essenza della democrazia e della società aperta," *Fondazione Liberal* 17 (2003): 108–16.

mation, that is, of a "community of citizenship" in which what is common are precisely civil rights (which imply duties in the sense that every right possessed by a citizen generates a duty to one's fellow citizens to respect that right, as well as duties toward the community of citizens). Kymlicka is therefore correct in this regard, and the distinctions made by Taylor seem to have little relevance, at least for the problem of multicultural immigration and the pluri-ethnic states formed by it (which is what we have been examining).

The conception of Habermas, on the other hand, is not lacking in utopianism. Unfortunately, the German philosopher avoids facing the real problem, that is, that of the limits of multiculturalism. Habermas seems to have a quasi-mystical faith in the power of dialogue, in a deliberative democracy in which the autonomy of citizens as moral subjects is actualized through popular sovereignty. The aspects of his approach that are more plausible and worthy of acceptance seem to be those that are essentially parasitic with respect to the liberal-constitutionalist tradition, aspects that, however, are contaminated in Habermas's thought by his Rousseauian and "identificatory" conception of democracy, that is, by the old dream of an identity of rulers and the ruled.[72] Habermas seems to have offered a recipe that would reveal its utopian face if put into practice institutionally, and would perhaps even be pernicious in its practical realization.

Taylor, nevertheless, teaches us a valuable lesson that should not be forgotten: no society can define itself without also including, in the collective definition, some substantial understanding of the good. Kymlicka also ultimately admits this. A strong, typically liberal prejudice prevails in the latter, however, above all against the notion of a "common good" that, in his view, would be entirely linked to the communitarian ideal. The communitarian concept of the common good, however, is not the only one possible, even if in many respects it can be understood as a valid corrective to an excessive *rights talk*.[73] In my opinion, we must recover a specifically *political* notion of the common good, comprised precisely of the political values of autonomy, freedom, pluralism, tolerance, the culture of the secularity of the state, and the differentiation between politics and religion.[74] The Western

72. For a criticism of this conception of Habermas as it was presented thirty years ago, see Rhonheimer, *Politisierung und Legitimitätsentzug. Totalitäre Kritik der parlamentarischen Demokratie in Deutschland*, Praktische Philosophie Band 8 (Freiburg/Munich: Karl Alber Verlag, 1979), 169–91.

73. See Mary Ann Glendon, *Rights Talk: The Impoverishment of Political Discourse* (New York: Free Press, 1991); A. Etzioni, *The Common Good* (Cambridge: Polity Press, 2004).

74. Certainly, many aspects of the reflections of Jacques Maritain move in this direction. Chapter 3

political culture of the democratic constitutional state is not only a cultural conquest, but also an ethical value that must be defended. In its elasticity and variability it has universal value, a value that must be defended in the face of pressure from an exaggerated multiculturalism that threatens this conquest.

A politics of "multicultural citizenship" and of the "recognition of difference" must, therefore, always also be a politics of integration, of assimilation, and of socialization. This does not mean homogeneity or a lack of respect for cultural diversity, or for persons who adhere to a different set of values. It does, however, mean not yielding in what is politically necessary so as to not weaken the accomplishments of the political culture of freedom and civic equality, and with that the possibility of peaceful cooperation, and of reconciling pluralism and the necessary consensus in a political culture of freedom.[75]

---

of the present volume, which is entitled "The Democratic Constitutional State and the Common Good," is meant as a contribution toward a reevaluation of the notion of "common good" in the present context. It was originally published as my "Lo Stato costituzionale democratico e il bene comune," in *Ripensare lo spazio politico: quale aristocrazia?* ed. E. Morandi and R. Panattoni (Padua: Il Poligrafo, 1998), 57–123 (*Con-tratto. Rivista di filosofia tomista e contemporanea* 6/1997). In a more synthetic form see also "Contrattualismo, individualismo e solidarietà: per rileggere la tradizione liberale," *Per la filosofia* 16, no. 46 (1999): 30–40. See also Francesco Botturi, "Per una teoria liberale del bene comune," *Vita e Pensiero* 79, no. 2 (1996): 82–94; Sergio Belardinelli, *La comunità liberale: La libertà, il bene comune e la religione nelle società complesse* (Rome: Edizioni Studium, 1999); Michael Novak, *Free Persons and the Common Good* (Lanham, Md.: Madison Books, 1989).

75. This essay is a slightly amplified version of a paper given by the author as part of the "Course for the Updating of Philosophy Professors," *Aspects of the Contemporary Ethical Debate,* organized by the philosophy faculty of the Pontifical University of the Holy Cross, September 8–9, 2005. The Italian original was published as "Cittadinanza multiculturale nella democrazia liberale: le proposte di Ch. Taylor, J. Habermas e W. Kymlicka," *Acta Philosophica* 15, no. 1 (2006): 29–52. Translation by Joseph T. Papa.

TWELVE

Christianity and Secularity

Past and Present of a Complex Relationship

It is therefore the task of all believers, particularly believers in Christ, to help formulate a concept of secularity which, on the one hand, acknowledges the place that is due to God and his moral law, to Christ and to his Church human life, both individual and social; and on the other, affirms and respects the rightful autonomy of earthly affairs.

—Benedict XVI to Italian jurists, December 9, 2006

The thesis that I will propose in this essay is the following: Christianity introduced a clear separation between politics and religion into Western history, in an absolutely new way and indeed for the first time. At the same time, however, it affirms the supremacy of the spiritual with respect to the temporal, and the consequent relativization of the political power, that is, its subordination to superior and independent criteria of moral truth, natural law, justice, and criteria of an eschatological nature. For these reasons, Christianity has been the condition of possibility of the development of a secular political culture, and as we shall see—though it may seem paradoxical —is still one of its guarantors today. This secular culture was in fact nourished by a Greco-Roman civilization inspired and profoundly transformed by Christianity. The values, but also the institutions (juridical, educative, economic, etc.), that derive, even if not exclusively, from Christianity are the soul and the condition of vitality of a Western-style civilization (which tends to universalize itself in important aspects, such as those regarding human rights, or the liberal constitutional form of democracy). At the same time, Christianity and the Church are in a continual critical tension vis-à-vis secular political culture, in that the former understand themselves as witnesses to a superior, transcendent truth. That truth, of which the Church is the depositary as a supreme spiritual authority, demands the ability to judge *temporalia*, and for this reason even today considers itself authorized to illuminate political processes and developments with its moral teaching.[1]

History has seen the development, in ever-new forms, of a dialectic between the separation and mutual interpenetration of the two spheres, spiritual and temporal—a dialectic between the secularity and sacredness of the temporal power, between political-religious dualism and monism. The Middle Ages, my theory claims, were nevertheless incapable of finding an enduring solution to this problem, one consistent with the fundamental charism of Christianity. Through the centuries, especially in the wake of some very specific conditioning factors and historical contingencies, the Catholic Church implemented forms of pastoral action that were in stark contrast with what it today recognizes as a "healthy secularity of the State." In modern times the Church has sought to recover its ancient roots, which affirm a clear separation between politics and religion, just as it has sought to reconcile the recognition, originally Christian, of a political-religious dualism with its perennial and indispensable task of being the testimony of a superior, transcendent, and ultimate truth, capable of judging the exercise of political power from a privileged moral perspective.

On the basis of this historical analysis, in the second part I will propose a distinction between two conceptions of secularity: a merely political

1. I want to explain briefly why I do not, generally, distinguish in what follows between "Christianity" and "the Catholic Church." First, because from the beginning Christianity has, as a historical subject, existed as *Church*; one cannot speak about "Christianity" without speaking of the Church (even if one can and must distinguish between them in various contexts). Also, when speaking on the historical level of the "Church," one speaks not only of the ecclesiastical hierarchy, but also of theologians and theology, of Christians in general, of the Christian mentality, etc. Second, because this Church has been, from the beginning of its history, the *Catholic* Church. The Catholic Church is not the product of the rupture of the unity of the Church that resulted from the schism with the Orthodox churches, or later from the Protestant Reformation; what we today call "the Catholic Church" is the same, identical historical subject that existed at the beginning of the history of Christianity. The various divisions have not created the "Catholic Church" or "Catholicism" as one of the various Christian confessions, but have *weakened the union* of the Orthodox churches *with the Catholic Church,* and *distanced from the Catholic Church* those Christians who now belong to the various Protestant ecclesial communities. The Catholic Church, on the other hand, even if always in need of reform, has never been separated or distanced from anyone; it has existed in interrupted continuity, and is in the full sense the Church founded by Jesus Christ, gathered on the day of Pentecost in Jerusalem around Peter and the other apostles. (It must not be forgotten that those churches that are today called Orthodox churches were part of the Catholic Church in Christian antiquity and still at the beginning of the Middle Ages, and in essence are still part of it today, though imperfectly).

conception of secularity, consistent with the self-understanding of Christianity and of the Catholic Church since Vatican II; and another that I will call an "integral" conception of secularity (which I will further refer to as "integralist secularism" or "secular integralism"), integral in the sense of of John Rawls's "comprehensive," and as such a comprehensive political-philosophical doctrine essentially areligious and antireligious. It is precisely this latter form of secularity, which in continental language is referred to as "laicism," that cannot be accepted by the Church, because it sees religion—and every influence of religious claims in public life—as a danger to freedom and subversive of democracy.

Even if the secular State does not make distinctions between the various religions—assuming, of course, that they do not oppose themselves to the public order and to the minimum requirements of public morality—not every religion has an identical relationship with a given political culture. I am convinced, and I will seek to demonstrate, that in the case of the political culture of the democratic constitutional State (i.e., secular, liberal, and Western-style democracy), a genetic relationship exists with Christianity that is both determinative and constitutive. Conversely, there exists a relationship of incompatibility with other religions. This claim does not imply that one must make—even if indirectly—a "profession of faith" in the truth of Christianity, but simply indicates a fact that is of significant importance in today's world.

In particular, faced with the challenge of Islamic culture—which is, essentially, integralist—in my opinion we must defend the properly Christian roots of the secular political culture of the liberal and democratic constitutional State. In the face of Islamic integralism—considering the fact that Islam is not only a religion in the Western sense, but essentially an integral conception of the legal and political social order that is incompatible not only with modern political culture, but with the entire Christian tradition— we must today defend a political secularity of the State and of the legal order that is capable of accepting and valuing a religion like Christianity, and religious claims like those of the Catholic Church, which, *precisely as a religion and as religious claims,* confer full legitimacy on the secular character of the State and of the democratic process. By this I do not mean to say that Islam could not also exist in a secular State as a religion whose adherents enjoy full *religious freedom,* according to our Western understanding and within the limits required by public order. The problem to which I am referring consists in the fact that Islam is much more than a religion. It is, in fact, a complete religious, social, juridical, and political system, characterized by its opposition to the essence of Western political culture as such, and not only in its secular form. Though it does not intend to impose Islamic *religious belief,* and much less so upon Jews and Christians, it nevertheless proposes to extend the *juridical and social order* of the *sharia* throughout the entire world.

Throughout history Christianity, and especially the Catholic Church, has likewise known the temptation to develop in the direction of a political-religious system. But it has always had to learn to recover its original charism, that of a religion that does not intend to impose by force a social and juridical order it has formulated, even if it does claim to be the source of inspiration and the spiritual soul, so to speak, of the social order. The Church today not only understands the (relative) primacy of politics (in the sense we will specify below), its autonomy, and the sovereignty of political institutions—and thus the secularity of politics and of democratic institutions as they are proposed by a non-integralist (i.e., merely political) conception of secularity—but goes so far as to call the "secular State" "a value that has been attained and [that has been] recognized by the Catholic Church" that "belongs to the inheritance of contemporary civilization."[2] With this recognition, the Church, after a long period of hostility toward political modernity, has not only recovered its originary charism, but has become the strongest ally and supporter of a correctly understood secular political culture, without for this abandoning its task of being the representative of a higher truth, in the light of which the exercise of political power can and must be judged. For Islam, and from the point of view of the *sharia,* this type of recognition of the secular State is intrinsically impossible, since, even if Islam could "provisionally" accept secularity for pragmatic and "tactical" reasons, secularity nevertheless radically conflicts with its deepest religious identity, with its original self-understanding, and with its authoritative legal texts.[3]

2. Congregation for the Doctrine of the Faith, *Doctrinal Note on Some Questions Regarding the Participation of Catholics in Political Life,* November 24, 2002, n. 6; cit. according to *http://www.vatican.va.*

3. For an understanding of this, it would be worthwhile to study one of the manuals of the *sharia* produced by one of the great Sunni juridical schools and approved by the authoritative al-Azhar University of Cairo, as for example that of Ahmad ibn Naquib al-Misri, which is available in an Arab-English bilingual edition, *Reliance of the Traveller: A Classic Manual of Islamic Sacred Law,* trans. ed. Nuh Ha Mim Keller (Beltsville, Md.: Amana Publications, 1991 and 1994). The translation is also approved by al-Azhar University.

Part 1. The History: Christian Faith, the Catholic Church, and Political Power: Historical Evolution and the Political-Theological Structure of Christian Dualism

Two Visions of History

To explicate and justify the thesis I have just presented, a brief historical survey is necessary. History is indispensable for understanding the present; nonetheless, it can be read in many different ways. My reading will be both philosophical and theological, based on data that have been made available by broad historical research on this theme.

In this area, there are two fundamentally different visions:

1. The first vision is typical of an anticlerical secularism, but also of a certain kind of Catholic traditionalism. It sees the essence of secular modern political culture in the *negation of the Christian tradition*. According to this way of seeing things, modern political culture, and particularly the secular State, would represent the definitive overcoming of the Christian tradition or, in the traditionalist reading, the fruit of a deplorable collective apostasy.

2. The second approach, on the other hand, is characteristic of an attitude that tends to reconcile the Christian tradition and modernity, and even looks to appropriate, in a "Christian" way, some of the most characteristic aspects of contemporary political culture (the rights of man, democracy, religious freedom, etc.). That which is specifically modern, positive, and worthy of assent—and in a particular way human rights—is to be considered the genuine fruit, even if slow in coming, of Christianity. The Church's conflict with nineteenth-century liberalism and secularity was therefore merely the fruit of a misunderstanding. According to this vision, modernity would then be the most mature expression of Christianity.

In my opinion, both positions are partially true and partially incorrect. The first is characterized by a notable historical myopia, which tends to deny not only the Christian roots of Western European civilization, but also Christianity as a principal and decisive factor in progress and civilization. The second seems somewhat naive and even a bit insincere, in that it denies a certain intrinsic conflictuality between Christianity and the secular character of modernity. Nevertheless, both visions contain elements of truth, though in my view the second is nearer the truth than the first.

It seems to me certain that between the modern idea of secularity (which implies the separation between religion and political power, between religion and civil law, religious freedom, etc.) and the essence of Christianity there exists not only a communality of origin and of spirit, but also a basic divergence and tension that, in my view, will never be entirely overcome. In fact, these are divergencies and tensions that are necessary, creative, and fruitful, in that they do not weaken, but rather confirm and reinvigorate, the secularity of the State. The basic divergence is caused by the essence itself of Christianity, by what I would like to call (for lack of a better term) the "Christian paradox."

This "Christian paradox" consists in the fact that Christianity affirms the intrinsic goodness, rationality, and autonomy of earthly realities; it consequently does not subordinate them to the religious sphere from the gnoseological, metaphysical, or practical points of view. At the same time, however, it sees these same earthly realities as in need of being illuminated by a higher truth, and of redemption. This combination of the *recognition of autonomy* (in the perspective of creation, of the being of things) and the *affirmation of dependency* (in the perspective of redemption) is the principal cause of all the complexities, ambivalencies, and conflicts, not only at the theoretical level, but also at the historical, in the relationship between what has traditionally been called the temporal power and the spiritual power.

We will first focus our attention on this recognition, typical of Christianity, of the intrinsic goodness, rationality, and autonomy of earthly realities.

Origins: The Christian Dualism between Politics and Religion

Christianity introduced an absolute novelty into history of which we—the heirs of a culture impregnated with the Christian spirit—are at times no longer aware: the independence of religion from the political power and, conversely, the independence of the political power, and even more so of the legal order, from religion. "Independence," however, understood in a specific sense: on the one hand, with Christianity, the political power is no longer the representative of higher powers or divinities; on the other hand, the Christian religion does not serve as a means to more effectively exercise political power, or to assure or sustain the order of society and of the State.

It is true that Christianity, after Constantine, entered in various ways into a close symbiosis with the political power of the Roman Empire and that this symbiosis—and comingling—between the political and religious orders was also the root of the medieval system with its theocratic tendencies. But this historical process and its ultimate result, political modernity, can be adequately understood only against the background of the almost revolutionary novelty that Christianity itself introduced into history. According to nineteenth-century French scholar Fustel de Coulanges, "Christianity was the first religion that did not want to make the law depend on religion."[4] We can say more generally: for the first time in history, Christianity recognized that temporal things—politics and the juridical institutions of the earthly city—respond to an intrinsic logic that is autonomous and independent of religion. Christianity, though understanding itself as a unique and ultimate truth, does not understand this truth to be a substitute for other earthly truths and logic in the juridical, political, and philosophical fields, but as their fulfillment and their salvation. Christianity did not come to create a new temporal order, but to save the goodness of creation and thus to make it possible that the intrinsic rationality and autonomy of the realities of this world would be free from the degeneration of sin.

Precisely in this Christianity is distinguished from all other ancient civilizations, even if in Greek philosophy and in Roman law prior to the Principate the tendency to such an autonomy already existed. This explains why philosophy and Greco-Roman law could easily be integrated into Christian civilization—indeed redeemed—but also transformed and handed on to posterity.[5] In this, Christianity is radically distinguished from Islam, which arose later and which introduces exactly the opposite principle: Islam in fact defines politics and the law on the basis of religion, claiming that they have a single source, and discrediting any other, natural, source of truth, even if the unity that this implies has almost never been realized historically. Islam does not have a concept of natural truth that is prior, independent, and propaedeutic with respect to Islamic religious and revealed truth. For Islam, human beings are born Moslem; it is the parents who lead them to belong to other religions. Thus every position other than Islam is not only an error, but also a perversion of the natural condition of man, and a kind of apostasy.[6] Anti-dualism and political-religious integralism are written into the very essence of Islam (even if not always in the history of its realization).[7]

4. Fustel de Coulanges, *La cité antique* (1864), book V, ch. 3 (Paris: Flammarion, 1984), 463.

5. See Vittorio Mathieu, "Il fondamento romano e cristiano della laicità," in *L'identità in conflitto dell'Europa: Cristianesimo, laicità, laicismo*, ed. Laura Paoletti (Bologna: Il Mulino, 2005), 157–69.

6. Rémi Brague, *La Loi di Dieu. Histoire philosophique d'une alliance* (Paris: Gallimard, 2005), 199.

7. For this reason it is not surprising that Islamic culture has never shown interest in Aristotle's

It would be difficult, therefore, to overvalue this novelty of Christianity, which derives not from a prior, contingent, historical factor, but directly from the heart of the Christian religion itself. The time of the first Christians, commonly known as the time of persecutions, gives vivid testimony to the fact that, even then, it was possible to arrive at a full Christian identity and at a full practice of the Christian religion in a world and a society ruled by principles and values that did not derive from the religion, and were in fact even in part discordant with it. A social, political, and juridical system deriving from faith was not considered necessary in order to be a Christian in the full sense, or to fully live one's faith.

This is not to say, however, that the Christian faith does not have the capacity and the mission to influence the ordering of the earthly city, its social and legal institutions, and the like. Christianity, though, *is not defined* on the basis of this task, that is, that of establishing a social order. That, to repeat, *is* the case with Islam, as with certain "modern" understandings, somewhat heterodox, of Christianity, which would transform it into a program of socio-economic and political reform and liberation. Christianity—and the Church as an institution in this world and as a historical subject—*does not understand its function* to be to establish and make the existing social and political order prosper, as was the case with the "official" pagan religion of the Roman Empire. This, moreover, explains why the latter's conflict with Christianity had at times fatal consequences for the Christian faithful.

The independence and relative indifference of the Christian religion with respect to the ordering of the earthly city does not imply an indifference of the *Christian faithful* toward the progress of this city. Their position reflects the essence of the famous saying of Jesus, to render unto Caesar what belongs to Caesar and to God what belongs to God (Mt 22:21). The founder of the Christian religion refers his questioner, who had asked for a political orientation, to the latter's responsibility as a citizen, declaring himself incompetent in the area. Christ is not a political leader, and his kingdom is not of this world. This is also the substance of what St. Paul says at the beginning of chapter 13 of the letter to the Romans: "No authority exists that does not come from God, and those which exist have been es-

---

Politics, the only work of Aristotle that had no influence on Moslem culture, which has rather, on political themes, shown much more interest in the writings and ideas of Plato. See also J. H. Burns, ed., *The Cambridge History of Medieval Political Thought c. 350–c. 1450* (Cambridge: Cambridge University Press, 1988), 330.

tablished by God ... and not in vain does it carry the sword ... therefore it is necessary to be subject, not only out of fear of punishment, but also for the sake of conscience" (Rom 13:1–5). By these words is expressed the Christian idea of the directly divine origin of the political power and its juridical function—though not, however, of a religious or *ecclesiastical* origin. The divine origin of the political power indicates that it belongs to the order of creation, which possesses its own natural legitimacy and which, consequently, possesses autonomy and independence, which in juridical terms means sovereignty.

The testimonies of Tertullian and Lactantius were known among the early Christians, which shows how far Christians in the first two centuries were from seeing the temporal power as a tool for promoting, or even institutionalizing, a religious agenda. The only thing that the first Christians asked of the political power was *freedom* and their full *equality* as citizens. They desired "tranquility," and the freedom to be able to live according to their faith, to practice the Christian cult without impediment and discrimination, and to attract to their faith all those who desired it. Neither the Christian faith, nor the apostolic impulse of the Christian life, was in opposition to the non-Christian Roman power; the desire to bring the Christian truth to all did not have immediate political implications. Thus St. Paul admonishes the young bishop, Timothy: "I ask, therefore, first of all, that requests, supplications, prayers and thanksgiving be offered for all, for rulers and for all those who are in power, so that we can live a calm and tranquil life with all piety and dignity. This is good and pleasing before God, our Savior, who wants all to be saved and to come to a knowledge of the truth" (1 Tim 2:1–4). What Christianity needs in order to realize itself and to be lived out is freedom. Consequently, this is what Christianity demands of the powers of this world. The first Christians came in conflict with the power of the State, due not to a lack of civic loyalty or to the non-recognition of the legitimacy of the pagan government (an unbelieving prince, *infidelis,* as he will be called in the Middle Ages), but because by their monotheism they denied the legitimacy of the pagan cults, including the cult of the emperor.

In this sense Christianity, in theory, should have logically developed in the direction of a political culture in which the temporal and spiritual powers would have coexisted without reciprocal interference. That is, it could and should have generated a "secular" State (secular in the sense of a worldly reality—certainly not in a modern sense). For various reasons, in

part intrinsic to the essence of Christianity itself and in part due to historical contingencies, things developed differently.

The Indeterminacy of Fundamental Principles

The intrinsic reason to which the evolution that followed early Christianity can be attributed is the indeterminate character—in a certain sense
ambivalent and even paradoxical—of the genuinely Christian idea of the independence and autonomy of earthly realities with respect to religion. This
indeterminacy became obvious at the moment when the Church appeared
as an actor on the public scene in the Roman Empire. In the Church's battle
for its freedom from interference by the Christian emperors—who, in continuity with the typically Roman idea of the political function of religion, and
considering themselves to be invested with episcopal power, interfered in
properly ecclesiastical tasks in an increasingly dangerous way—over time
the Church articulated a structure of principles suitable for defining the relationship between the ecclesiastical power and the temporal power. These
principles themselves, though belonging to the essence of the Church's self-
understanding, were not (and still are not) without a significant degree of
indeterminacy, and therefore remain susceptible of being applied in very
different ways, depending on the circumstances. Without changing in their
doctrinal and dogmatic essence, throughout history these principles have
been interpreted and applied in extremely contrasting ways and, if we consider the Second Vatican Council, even in ways that are mutually contradictory.[8]

In the present context, we are dealing essentially with two principles:
first, *the primacy of spiritual realities over temporal realities* and, second,
the ordination of what is earthly and temporal to what is heavenly and eter-

---

8. In my opinion, the Second Vatican Council must be read simultaneously as a continuity (at the
level of principles, i.e., of Catholic doctrine properly speaking) and a discontinuity (regarding certain
applications and concretizations, especially with respect to politics and social doctrine). Benedict XVI
emphasized this in his important discourse of December 22, 2005, *The Second Vatican Council, 40 Years
Later,* in which he emphasizes that Vatican II was not a simple continuity, or a discontinuity, but a *reform*: "It is clear that in all these sectors, which all together form a single problem, some kind of discontinuity might emerge. Indeed, a discontinuity had been revealed but [one] in which, after the various
distinctions between concrete historical situations and their requirements had been made, the continuity of principles proved not to have been abandoned. It is easy to miss this fact at a first glance. It is precisely in this combination of continuity and discontinuity at different levels that the very nature of true
reform consists" (cit. according to http://www.vatican.va). As an example, Benedict XVI used precisely
the Church's doctrine on religious freedom.

nal. These are two principles that, for the Catholic Church, are fundamental claims that are theologically and doctrinally indispensable, because it sees its essential task as one of leading human beings to eternal salvation, though recognizing the goodness of earthly realities as created by God, and their just autonomy. In a certain sense, these principles are a consequence of the separation itself, genuinely and originally Christian, of politics and religion, that is, of the conviction that religion is not a "department" of politics, that it does not follow the logic of reasons of state and that neither should it replace politics or the temporal power, absorbing them into its own logic.

At the same time, however, Christianity presents itself as *truth*—and in this it distinguishes itself from all previous religions, which were national cults of specific peoples or societies, the highest expression, in the case of the Roman religion, of the *mos maiorum.* Christianity presents itself not only as truth, but as a *unique, complete, and universal* truth. In this sense, precisely because of its independence from every political order, the Christian faith claims to be the measure and judge of every such order, because it sees them in the light of the dignity of human beings as created in the image of God and, therefore, having an eternal destiny.

The indeterminate and paradoxical character of these principles, with their ambivalent consequences on the properly political level, very quickly became apparent on the occasion of their first application, in the battle for the defense of the *libertas ecclesiae.* The paradox consists in the twofold historical fact whereby, on the one hand, in the course of this struggle for freedom spiritual truth was declared to be independent of the political power and superior to it, and therefore exempt from every interference on the part of the political and temporal power. On the other hand, however, the Church simultaneously asked the political power to promote the true religion, Catholicism, to the point where the Church itself came to accept, and even to demand, the support of the temporal political power against heresies. These latter, according to the law, came to be equated with superstitions and were declared to be illicit religions.[9]

Put otherwise, the paradox is that before the political power, the primacy and freedom of conscience is defended in the name of truth; and in the name of the same truth, and indeed with the help of the political power,

9. See the intelligent and sensible introductions to the documents edited by Hugo Rahner, *Kirche und Staat im frühen Christentum* (Munich: Kösel-Verlag, 1961), especially the introduction to part 2.

there is at the same time a tendency to impose uniformity on consciences, considering every attempt to contest the integrity of the Christian faith as illegal. In my view, this should be considered not a direct and necessary consequence of Christianity, but rather the fruit of the Roman, "imperial" mentality generally diffused in the culture of late antiquity—including among Christians—together with other specific historical circumstances. In addition, the enormous success and rapidity of the Christianization of ancient society and culture inevitably (and I would say fatally) created a pressure toward social conformity, which intellectuals and the ruling classes of society in particular could not easily avoid, if they did not want to end up "socially dead" and discriminated against in their social and professional prospects. This could also explain a widespread loss of the Christian fervor of the early centuries, due to a Christianization that was often perfunctory and superficial.[10]

Augustinian Dualism: The Collapse of the Empire and a New Role for the Church

As we have already pointed out, the first position-takings by Church leaders, especially by some popes and bishops in union with them (in particular Ambrose of Milan and Athanasius), were provoked by the battles for the Church's freedom against the caesaropapist interference of the emperors. The Church very readily, even enthusiastically, saw in the political power, and especially in the power of the emperor, the guarantee not only of its freedom, but also of the maintenance of religious orthodoxy. In the parts of the empire dominated by Arianism, this tendency was even stronger. In places where Arianism was opposed, on the other hand, the tendency to entrust the maintenance of orthodoxy to the imperial authority was, again, in a certain aspect paradoxical. Against Arianism, faith in the divinity of Christ provided the Catholic Church with a strong antidote against the temptation to attribute to the emperor, and to the temporal power in general, a quasi-priestly or quasi-episcopal function over the Church itself, allowing their intrusion into the Church's sanctuary. Appealing for the help of State authority to suppress the Arian heresy thus meant rejecting the sacralization

---

10. As is asserted by Henri-Irénée Marrou, *Décadence romaine ou antiquité tardive? IIIe–VIe siècle* (Paris: Éditions du Seuil, 1977), 153. For the theme of the social mechanisms that favored conversions, see also Bruno Dumézil, *Les racines chrétiennes de l'Europe: Conversion et liberté dans les royaumes barbares Ve–VIIIe siècle* (Paris: Fayard, 2005).

or clericalization of the imperial power, thereby preserving the "secular" conception of the temporal power. The political essence of the fight against Arianism was, in fact, the fight against caesaropapism, that is, the fact of conceiving the imperial power as an ecclesial-episcopal power, which, as we shall see, had some very specific reasons, though always contingent, for existing for a brief period in the Western Middle Ages. It is characteristic of Catholic Christianity to have overcome this historical phase and restored the separation of the spiritual and temporal powers, not with *political* reasons and arguments, but precisely *theological* ones. Moreover, beginning in the eleventh century, this restoration was the work not of politicians, but of the popes themselves, through what is today called the "Papal Revolution" (to be dealt with below).

At the same time, the Catholic fight against the Arians and thus against caesaropapism in the first centuries of Christianity, though we are still far from the medieval system, does not change the fact that even then the Church considered it correct that the Catholic religion be raised, as religious truth, to the rank of the official religion of the State. This fact, which many consider the "original sin" of the post-Constantine era—and I tend to agree with this perspective—later developed in the direction of a *respublica christiana,* in which, juridically, the Catholic religion would become the supreme law, and the pontifical power the first authentically sovereign power in the history of the post-ancient West.

To understand this post-Constantinian evolution, one should bear in mind that the Catholic bishops, and Christians generally, were Romans and acted with a Roman mentality. This mentality, rooted in the imperial tradition, continued to include the idea of political-religious unity, and especially the idea of the need to venerate the true God for the health and prosperity of the earthly city. The idea was prevalent, among both statesmen and churchmen, that the cult of the true God brought with it the well-being of the empire. Constantine's *in hoc signo vinces* before the decisive battle at the Milvian Bridge was in fact an essentially political aspiration: the hope that the God of the Christians would be the one who could give security, stability, and prosperity to the empire. When the shock of Alaric's invasion happened in 410, this was not only a political blow, but also, and perhaps above all, a religious one, causing the foundations of the imperial Roman theology, by this time based on Christianity, to shake. It was St. Augustine who then defended the Christian religion against the attacks of the last remaining pagans, who reproached Christians for having abandoned the tradition of the Roman religion, claiming that the disaster of the fall of Rome was the consequence and sign of this abandonment.[11]

Saint Augustine responded with his epocal work *De civitate Dei,* in which he takes a crucial step: he dissolves, again—but this time on the level of a more mature theological reflection, by now informed by the history of an entire century—the perilous link between empire and Church, between political prosperity and religious truth. At the theoretical level, *De civitate Dei* signified the abandonment of Roman imperial logic. Although St. Augustine's political thought is often not linear, given that it is immersed in a variety of always polemical situations, and under certain aspects is even contradictory, it could nevertheless have perhaps served as a new point of departure for a clear separation between religion and politics, and in this sense could have contributed to the emergence of a merely secular understanding of the temporal power.[12]

Again, however, things did not develop in this direction. So-called political Augustinianism, the later application of St. Augustine's thought from the beginning of the Middle Ages, gave birth to an interpretation that legitimated an evolution in precisely the opposite direction, that is, along the lines of the theology of the empire and its tendency to a fusion between religion and politics. This interpretation was also greatly facilitated by a historical fact that was no less decisive for being contingent, and was in other aspects also providential: the collapse of the Roman Empire, and with it the beginning of a new role for the Church, that of becoming the guarantor of the public order and of the maintenance of juridical institutions in vast areas occupied by new barbarous and warrior peoples, where the empire no longer existed. The Church, alongside the pursuit of its missionary task and supported by the nascent monasticism, began to acquire an ever-increasing educational role, not only regarding the faith, but also regarding how to live a more dignified life in this world. It is impossible to exaggerate the importance that the Catholic Church, assuming this role, had on the development

---

11. See Pierre Chuvin, *Chronique des derniers païens. La disparition du paganisme dans l'Empire romain du règne de Constantin a celui de Justinien,* 2nd ed. (Paris: Les Belles Lettres/Fayard, 1991), 86ff.

12. St. Augustine's appeal to the imperial power to discipline the Donatists was not so much motivated by religious reasons, i.e., the repression of a heresy (to that end the bishop of Hippo preferred the way of dialogue and persuasion), but because, as the Donatists were extremely violent, they represented an obvious disturbance to civil peace, and a danger to the legitimate freedom of the Catholic faithful. Expressed in modern terms, the Donatists egregiously transgressed the limits of religious freedom, endangering the public order and the fundamental rights of their fellow citizens.

of European civilization, even if—here we would have to draw up a sort of *List der Vernunft?*—the price to be paid in terms of the "clericalization" of society and of the State was high. Finally, we must mention another contingent factor, not properly religious, but of a more pragmatic and political nature: the decisive fact of the alliance of the papacy with the Frankish kings—the latter as protectors and guarantors of the independence of the Apostolic See of Rome—and the new Christian empire that arose from this alliance.

One must never forget that the missionary task of the Church was not conceived of solely as a "religious" and spiritual task. It was, rather, in the self-understanding of Christians of that time and of the Church, an integral proposition of inculturation and civilization, a true and authentic offer of liberation to those peoples who lived in the darkness of ignorance, in the fear of demons, and at a very primitive level of civilization. Christianity brought not only the promise of freedom from sin through baptism and an end to the fear of demons but also—with Roman law—a new juridical order, a legal system, bureaucratic administration based on law, and the doing away with merely customary, "tribal" law. It also introduced letters, progress in agricultural techniques, and other similar things and, not to be forgotten, a decisive improvement in the situation of women who, with the matrimonial law imposed by the Church, were for the first time treated as equals with respect to their husbands.[13]

As Harold J. Berman has shown in his important research on the formation of the Western juridical tradition, Christianity put an end to the "fiction of the immutability of the [Germanic] folklaw." The idea of the fundamental equality among human beings improved the position of women and slaves, and protected the poor and those incapable of defending themselves.[14] Later, beginning with Gratian, the ecclesiastical cultivation of natural law emerged, which allowed the definitive overcoming of a certain "positivism" of customary law, through a critical enhancement according to rules of moral rationality.[15] Gratian "started by interposing the concept of natural law between the concepts of divine law and human law,"[16] a fact of singular importance and an essential presupposition for modernity, be-

---

13. For this entire process I refer the reader to Peter Brown, *The Rise of Western Christendom: Triumph and Diversity A. D. 200–1000*, 2nd ed. (Oxford: Blackwell, 2003); Dumézil, *Les racines chrétiennes de l'Europe;* Marrou, *Decadence romaine ou antiquité tardive?*

14. Harold J. Berman. *Law and Revolution. The Formation of the Western Legal Tradition* (Cambridge, Mass.: Harvard University Press, 1983), 65–66.

15. Ibid., 144ff.

16. Ibid., 145.

cause "the theory of Gratian and his fellow canonists provided a basis for weeding out those customs that did not conform to reason and conscience," which "meant that custom lost its sanctity; a custom might be binding or it might not."[17] In this way the fundamental distinction between natural law and positive law, already present in Greek philosophy and Roman jurisprudence, again entered the Western juridical tradition[18]—a distinction, moreover, that came to be applied even to the law of the Church! "The laws of the church itself were to be tested by their conformity to natural law."[19] Thus, medieval natural law became the cradle of a development that terminates in the modern concept of human rights as subjective rights.[20]

In all of these developments, the Church did not forget the primacy of its spiritual mission, even if, obviously, the consciousness of this mission was obscured in not a few aspects. Indeed, with the system of the Ottonian and Salian emperors, there was an astonishing intermingling of the Church and the political power, with the "worldliness" of the Church that accompanied this. Certainly, the principles mentioned above were not forgotten, that is, the primacy of spiritual things *(spiritualia)* over temporal *(temporalia)*, and the ordination of these latter to eternal things. Nevertheless, with the subsequent combination of canon law and feudalism, these principles, indispensable for the Church, more and more acquired a political configuration, or, to be more precise, political-ecclesiastical. They culminated, with the theory of the *plenitudo potestatis* of the pope, in a genuine and authentic theory of sovereignty. The road that led to this point was complex, and this evolution again shows the ambivalence of the principles that caused it.

From the Gelasian Formula to the Triumph of "Political Augustinianism"

When Pope Gelasius, at the end of the fifth century, formulated the famous principle "There are two powers on this earth: the sacred authority [*auctoritas sacrata*] of the popes and the royal power [*potestas regalis*],"[21]

17. Ibid.   18. Ibid., 146.

19. Ibid., 146–47.

20. See Brian Tierney, *The Idea of Natural Rights: Studies on Natural Rights, Natural Law, and Church Law 1150–1625* (Grand Rapids, Mich.: William B. Eerdmans, 1997). For the important impact, in part negative and in part positive, of Protestantism on the development of juridical thought until the modern conception of the rights of man and of the great law codifications, see also Harold J. Berman, *Law and Revolution II: The Impact of the Protestant Reformations on the Western Legal Tradition* (Cambridge, Mass.: Harvard University Press, 2003).

21. Rahner, *Kirche und Staat im frühen Christentum*, 256.

he could not have foreseen the later evolution that the interpretation of this lapidary phrase would have.[22] Even the Gelasian formulation itself is an expression of the original indeterminacy of the two principles we have mentioned (to repeat, the primacy of spiritual realities over temporal, and the ordination of what is earthly and temporal to what is heavenly and eternal). According to the Gelasian formula, the rulers of this world possess the *potestas*, whereas the Church possesses the *auctoritas*. The first is a coercive, earthly power, which concerns the things of this world; the second, on the other hand, is a sacred power of a dogmatic, pastoral, and moral nature, which is exercised in the name of a truth that is, also, the measure of goodness of the exercise of every temporal power.

The question is, how to apply such a distinction in practice and, especially, what would its juridical and institutional consequences be?

Considering the Gelasian formula in itself, it does not speak of a simple dualism of two equal and *juxtaposed* claims. It speaks rather of a clear superiority of one over the other: the *auctoritas sacrata,* given that it represents truth—indeed a divinely revealed truth—is necessarily superior to any human *potestas*. The *auctoritas sacrata,* however, is not a governing-coercive power, though it is still superior to every coercive power of this world, in that it is a power responsible for the world before God and is called to judge the exercise of temporal power in this world. For this reason Gelasius added, "the priestly office involves more responsibility, in that priests *must render account before the divine tribunal for kings themselves.*" Consequently, the formula does not primarily express the relationships between *institutions* in the modern sense, but between *persons,* or, better said, between the pastoral authority of the Church and the persons invested with royal power (emperors, kings, princes) and who, as Christians and sons of the Church, are subject to the pastoral responsibility of the *sacerdotium*; the latter, says Gelasius, is also responsible for the salvation of temporal rulers, and must ensure that these rulers respect the pastoral supremacy of the Church.

One can see how the Gelasian formula is in fact in continuity with the other, earlier, formulation of St. Ambrose: *Imperator intra ecclesiam, non supra ecclesiam* ("the emperor is in the Church, not above the Church").[23] In

---

22. See Burns, *The Cambridge History of Medieval Political Thought c. 350–c. 1450,* 88ff.

23. St. Ambrose of Milan, "Speech against Auxentius" (Migne, Patrologia Latina 16, 1007–1018), cited by Rahner, *Kirche und Staat im frühen Christentum* (Document 13b), 184. The importance of this sentence for juridical history is emphasized by Hans Hattenhauer, *Europäische Rechtsgeschichte* (Heidelberg: C. F. Müller Juristischer Verlag, 1992), 120ff.

this sense, Gelasius had previously formulated, as secretary to Pope Felix II, the statement that the emperor is not a bishop of the Church, but a son of the Church. The Church, therefore, claims to judge—always on the basis of spiritual criteria—the exercise of temporal power, and this judgment is essentially a judgment on the actions of the *person* who represents this power. For this reason—and this seems to me important—at least at the theoretical level a Gelasian-type subordination does not yet put in doubt the "secular" character of the temporal power as an *institution*.[24] It is clear that this subordination remains within a strictly pastoral logic—the subordination of the person who exercises temporal power to the discipline of the Church in the areas of faith and morals—and it makes use of exclusively spiritual means. It is not "politics," given that it does not make use, as it will later on, of juridical means apt for joining priestly authority and the ruling power (with regard to power and coercion), thus constituting, at least in theory, a properly *governing* hierarchy that is also coercive.

With the Gelasian formula, Christianity expressed a truly epochal principle, the spirit of which is still legitimately present and alive today, even in the "postconciliar" Church. In evaluating it we must not allow ourselves to be guided by the later applications of this principle, whether medieval or modern (e.g., in the denominational principle of "union between throne and altar"), which were certainly problematic. These applications, favoring the aspect of hierarchical subordination, tended toward a political-religious unity that was in essence foreign to a genuine Gelasian dualism. It is worthwhile, prior to and independent of the various later evolutions, to grasp the fundamental theological and moral sense of Pope Gelasius's principle: it says that, independently of the political powers of this world and of that which these powers prescribe, *there exist a moral rationality, an axiological truth, and an authority capable of rendering a judgment, in terms of justice, on the exercise of this power.* To say it again, this was the great novelty introduced into history by Christianity.

The Gelasian formula is an expression of this novelty, and at the same time includes what I have called "the Christian paradox": the simultaneous recognition of the autonomy of the powers of this world and affirmation that these are in need of redemption and salvation. This implies that the worldly

---

24. Nevertheless, assuming that the person of the emperor and of any other earthly ruler is identified with the governing institution, this requirement of submission to the Church implicitly refers to the emperor not only as a private Catholic, but also in the exercise of his duties.

powers depend on the spiritual power, in the sense that they can and must be judged according to objective criteria of value and truth by authorities that possess such truth. The Gelasian principle establishes that the worldly power does not contain within itself the ultimate criteria of its rectitude, morality, and justification; its exercise is subject to, and can at all times be evaluated on the basis of, independent criteria of truth and moral objectivity, which are by nature superior to the worldly power itself. This separation, therefore, also implies subordination, and this also bears with it the danger of destroying the just autonomy of the political and civic sphere, even though—again, paradoxically—the subordination *presupposes* separation and mutual autonomy. We are thus dealing with a fluid relationship that is always open to imbalance—which is also true for the principle that attempts to define this relationship in terms of "two powers." In any case, the Gelasian principle expresses a fundamental principle that has shaped Western civilization until our day, and without which the forces that shaped the modern secular State would never have been able to develop. Without the essence of this principle—the autonomy of the political power and the simultaneous dependency on external criteria of truth and morality—a secular political culture risks turning into some form of political totalitarianism.

Nevertheless—and with this we touch on a central point—moral subordination is not necessarily equivalent to *juridical* and *political* subordination, in the sense of the assertion of the legal supremacy of the spiritual power as an institution, and, consequently, its effective sovereignty with respect to every other worldly power. It was precisely in this direction, however, that the subsequent medieval application of the Gelasian principle headed.

The application of these principles, which in essence are not only Christian but, to put it anachronistically, also antitotalitarian, was increasingly realized according to the logic of so-called political Augustinianism.[25] The logic of this unilateral and, in my opinion, erroneous interpretation[26] of the great Father of the Church was summed up in the famous expression of Pope Gregory the Great that "who governs has received his power over all men from above, so that the earthly city be in service of the heavenly."[27] At

---

25. A term created by H. X. Arquillière, *L'augustinisme politique. Essai sur la formation des théories politiques du Moyen-Age*, 2nd ed. (Paris: J. Vrin, 1955). For a synthetic exposition of political Augustinianism, see also Jean-Jacques Chevalier, *Storia del pensiero politico*, vol. 1, 2nd ed. (Bologna: Il Mulino, 1989), 256–80.

26. Also the opinion of Arquillière himself: see *L'augustinisme politique*, 52ff.

27. *Epist.* III, 65.

a time of intense missionary activity by the Church among the new pagan peoples, and a time when the Church—through strong bishops and missionaries—presented itself as the only institution capable of investing the temporal power with a sense of legality and morality, this already represented a basically "political" interpretation of the principle of the primacy of spiritual things and the ordering of what is temporal to what is eternal, to the heavenly city. In fact, for Gregory the Great, the two tasks of the temporal power are the *dilatatio* of the cult of the true God and the *defensio* of the Church. At the same time, Gregory justified war for the expansion of the *respublica* that practices the cult of the true God.[28] The interpretation thus gradually evolved in the direction of the assertion that the temporal power is at the service of the spiritual power of the Church, being its secular arm. This is the idea that St. Isidore of Seville expressed succinctly in the seventh century: the power of princes, he wrote, is needed so as to impose "by the fear of punishment what the clergy is unable to bring about by words alone."[29] This is simply the necessary prelude to what, at first sight, could seem a new direction, but in fact is a logical consequence: the sacralization of the temporal power, beginning in the ninth century. With a work dedicated to Pipin of Aquitaine, the *De institutione regia* of Jonah of Orléans (bishop of Orléans, d. ca. 843), it became obvious that, according to a position that understood the royal power and politics in general as sacred functions, "Christian law" ultimately absorbed natural law, and the royal ministry became an ecclesiastical function. The first duty of the king, wrote Jonah of Orléans, is to defend the Church, to watch over and support priests in the exercise of their ministry, and to protect, with the force of arms, the Church of God.[30]

Thus, with the consolidation of the new empire at the time of the Carolingians, the Ottonians, and the Salians, political Augustinianism triumphed. The earthly city became a means for serving the heavenly kingdom, the latter increasingly indentified with the visible Church on earth. The *regalis potestas,* and to a much greater extent the power of the emperor, became an instrument for reaching the highest goal of the Church itself, and increasingly acquired an ecclesial and sacred character. Already at

28. Burns, *The Cambridge History of Medieval Political Thought*, 293–94.
29. *Sententiae,* book III, ch. 51 (P.L. 83, 723–724); the Latin text of this passage can be found in Arquillière, *L'augustinisme politique,* 142.
30. See Arquillère, *L'augustinisme politique,* 149.

the time of Charlemagne, royal consecration was considered a sacrament, and the emperor took the title, used in antiquity by the bishops, of *vicarius Christi*.[31] Moreover, political Augustinianism was characterized by a successive absorption of natural law into divine law, and of civil law into the law of the Church (the specific characteristic, according to Arquillière, of political Augustinianism). While Pope Gelasius had spoken of two powers *on earth (in terra)*—subordinate, not juxtaposed—in the periods that followed, until the end of the Middle Ages, two powers *in the Church* will be spoken of—subordinate, that is, because they in essence belong to the same ecclesiastical sphere.[32]

The "Papal Revolution" and Medieval Dualism

Until the high Middle Ages, the temporal power was in fact conceived of as an originally ecclesiastical power. Empire and Church were identified, initially in the person of the emperor, and later, at least in the understanding of the Papal Curia, in the person of the pope. In the first phase, that is, prior to the fight over investitures, it was the emperor who fulfilled a sacred and ecclesiastical function. His first task was the protection of the Church and the expansion of the Christian faith. The Church became part of the empire, with the bishops, their functionaries, and the local churches being under the guidance of the princes, and to a large extent their property.

This system eventually became a prison for the Church, from which it had to free itself through what we call "the fight over investitures," so as to recover its freedom in the exercise of its essentially pastoral mission. In this process of liberation, however, the theological premises did not change at all; indeed, they were confirmed, reinforced, and, through Roman law (which had become canon law) and in the logic of the feudal system, transformed into a unified juridical system. Now it was the Church, in the person of the Roman pontiff, who claimed the right to represent the continuity of imperial power, not in a properly political sense—given that the empire, according to medieval understanding, was above all a spiritual entity—but in the sense that the supreme power of the pope, who for the first time assumed the title of "vicar of Christ," also claimed the *plenitudo potestatis*. It was no longer only an *auctoritas sacrata* over the ruling power, but also the

---

31. For some aspects of this theme, see Ernst H. Kantorowicz, *The King's Two Bodies: A Study in Medieval Political Theology*, 3rd ed. (Princeton, N.J.: Princeton University Press, 1973).

32. Burns, *The Cambridge History of Medieval Political Thought*, 298ff.

fullness of that governing power which also decided concerning the right use of coercive power, though this was left in the hands of temporal rulers with regard to its actual exercise (according to the doctrine of the indirect power—*potestas indirecta*—of the pope over temporal affairs). This power of the popes was justified by the claim that it derived directly from their quality of being the successors of the apostle Peter who, it was said, received it directly from Christ.[33]

The pope was thus the only one who originally possessed the fullness of power that came from Christ,[34] to which every other power was juridically subordinate. According to this understanding, expressed in the famous theory of the two swords that summed up the doctrine of the *potestas indirecta*,[35] the pope could depose princes and dissolve feudal bonds of fidelity according to his judgment. This judgment, clearly expressed by Innocent III (called by his contemporaries *arbiter mundi*) and reaffirmed by Boniface VIII, was not effected according to "political" criteria in the strict sense, but, in the classical formulation, exclusively *ratione peccati,* that is, for reasons that were strictly of the moral and spiritual order, and always within the logic of the (pastoral) subordination of the *person* and of relations between persons (the pope as feudatory, kings as vassals).[36] The medieval doctrine of the *plenitudo potestatis* of the pope, though being a true and proper theory of sovereignty due to its juridical nature (and therefore, in the medieval context, also political), because it remained on the level of indirect power, did not intend to appropriate the temporal power to itself.

---

33. On this I refer the reader to Walter Ullmann, *Principles of Government and Politics in the Middle Ages* (London: Methuen, 1961), part 1.

34. This despite the fact that Jesus Christ never claimed any governing power over this world, and in fact he explicitly rejected it. I think one could argue, theologically, that Christ, *as man*, did not possess the *plenitudo potestatis* in the sense in which the medieval popes claimed it based on the doctrine of the two swords. If this is true, the fact of having received their power directly from Christ, as the successor of Peter, does not include this type of *plenitudo potestatis*, but only the ecclesial and pastoral power that canon law still today attributes to the pope (see CIC of 1983, can. 331–33).

35. A well-documented summary of this theory can be found in Burns, *The Cambridge History of Medieval Political Thought,* 300–305.

36. Innocent III, the decretal *Novit ille* of 1204: "non enim intendimus iudicare de feudo ... sed decernere de peccato ... nullus, qui sit sanae mentis, ignorat, quin ad officium nostrum spectet de quocunque mortali peccato corripere quemlibet Christianum, et, si correctionem contempserit, ipsum per districtionem ecclesiasticam coercere.... Licet autem hoc modo procedere valeamus super quolibet criminali peccato, ut peccatorem revocemus a vitio ad virtutem, ab errore ad veritatem, praecipue tamen quum contra pacem peccatur, quae est vinculum caritatis"; cit. according to Emil Friedberg, *Corpus Iuris Canonici,* vol. 2, reprinted by the Editio Lipsiensis secunda (Graz: Akademische Druck- u. Verlagsanstalt, 1955), cols. 242–44; for Boniface VIII, see the texts cited in Jean Rivière, *Le problème de l'Eglise et de l'Etat au temps de Philippe le Bel* (Louvain: Spicilegium Sacrum Lovaniense, 1926), 77–78: "Dicimus quod in nullo volumus usurpare iurisdictionem regis.... Non potest negare rex, seu quicumque alter fidelis, quin sit nobis subiectus *ratione peccati.*"

It was thus not meant to be—as some of the theologians of the Curia understood it—properly a *potestas directa*, which is to say a hierocracy,[37] but was simply the concise and clear statement, in terms of "powers," of the superiority of the spiritual over the temporal. This superiority, however, was ensured through a law that converted the temporal power into the secular arm of the spiritual, conferring on the pope the right to institute and depose kings. Within the logic of the superiority of the spiritual, therefore, it conferred sovereignty on the pope.[38]

Without entering into the specifics of this medieval order—which from the beginning was doomed to failure, in that it paradoxically nurtured the forces that in the end would overturn it—I would like to point out what, in my opinion, was its decisive and key element, though perhaps also its most irksome and contingent element, and one that in our day has been rightly overcome. This element does not consist in the two fundamental principles we have cited, which are genuinely Christian and indispensable (the primacy or superiority of the spiritual power over the temporal, and the ordering of earthly realities to the heavenly city and eternal life, with the consequent possibility of judging the temporal power). The specific, decisive element consists in the fact that in the high Middle Ages, these fundamental principles—and thus also the Church's fight for its legitimate freedom with respect to the temporal power—took on an openly *juridical* structure. Consequently, according to the logic of things, this structure was also inevitably politically coercive. Thus the Church, which in the system of the Ottonians and Salians had already become part of the governmental and legal system, now, after its "liberation," found itself in the position of being the *dominate and supreme* part. The spiritual power was politicized and invested with elements of coercion and, by means of the secular arm, of violent repression. The Roman pontiff was in reality the only true sovereign: the "vicar

---

37. As, for example, Egidio Romano and Giacomo of Viterbo; see on these "curialists" Alois Dempf, *Sacrum Imperium: Geschichts- und Staatsphilosophie des Mittelalters und der politischen Renaissance,* 3rd ed. (Darmstadt: Wissenschaftliche Buchgesellschaft, 1962), 441ff.; Beonio Fumagalli and Maria Teresa Brocchieri, *Il pensiero politico medievale* (Bari: Manuali Laterza, 2004), 115ff.; Martin Grabmann, "Studien über den Einfluss der aristotelischen Philosophie auf die mittelalterlichen Theorien über das Verhältnis von Kirche und Staat," in *Sitzungaberichte der Bayerischen Akademie der Wissenschaften, Phil-hist,* vol. 2 (Munich: Verlag der Bayer, 1934), 41–60. See also Iring Fetscher and Herfried Münkler, eds., *Pipers Handbuch der politischen Ideen,* Band 2 (Munich: Piper, 1993), 371ff. Opposed to the curialists was, principally, Giovanni Quidort of Paris, who in 1302 developed an anti-hieratic, strictly dualist concept in his *Tractatus de potestate regia et papali* (see ibid., 379ff., and the entry *Giovanni di Parigi (detto Quidort ...)* by S. Simonetta, in *Enciclopedia Filosofica,* vol. 5 (Milan: Bompiani, 2006), 4793ff.

38. Ullmann, *Principles of Government and Politics in the Middle Ages,* 72–86.

of Christ" was at the same time the holder of an imperial power that, as we have seen, from the time of Charlemagne had been understood as an essentially sacred and ecclesiastical reality. After what Harold Berman called the "Papal Revolution,"[39] which took place during the fight over investitures, and the consequent desacralization of the figure of the emperor (and of the temporal power generally), who was returned to a simple lay state, the hierarchy was simply overturned: now it was the pope who understood himself as the possessor of the ultimate sacred ecclesiastical power that had characterized the Carolingian and post-Carolingian imperial ideal.

I repeat, this was not the fruit of a will on the part of the popes to seek a fusion of the temporal and spiritual powers, or to arrogate to themselves the task of governing the world.[40] Such a notion would have been foreign to the essence of Christianity, and to the consciousness that the popes had of their mission (magnificently expressed in the *De considerazione* of St. Bernard, which affirmed that the pope is the successor not of Constantine, but of Peter).[41] The process was rather the consequence of the self-understanding of the Church—from a correct and undeniable ecclesiastical perspective—of knowing itself to be possessor of the supreme, revealed truth necessary for eternal salvation. It was also the result of a desire to understand the pastoral care of souls in a global sense, at the level of a *respublica christiana* as a political-spiritual community, and of the idea that for this reason the spiritual power, by nature superior to the temporal, had to be independent and free from any interference by worldly powers, so as to be able to judge the exercise of that power. The medieval political and juridical order is the expression of a unilaterally religious conception of the world and of society, and of a unitary and universal pastoral project. Though problematic, and in many respects linked to its time, this conception did not originate from the pretense of the Church to replace the temporal power and to dominate the world politically. In this sense, the recognition remained implicit of the secular nature of the temporal and political power; indeed, it was precisely the Papal Revolution that reaffirmed this, perhaps contrary to the original and principal intentions of that juridical and pastoral revolution.

In the logic of things, however, and in order to be able to defend its free-

39. See Berman, *Law and Revolution,* 85–119 and passim.
40. As some authors seem to suggest, as for example Johannes-Jürgen Meister, "Sacerdotium ac imperium," in *Respublica Christiana: Politisches Denken des orthodoxen Christentums im Mittelalter,* ed. Peter von Sivers (Munich: List Verlag, 1969), 19–46.
41. St. Bernard of Clairvaux, *De consideratione ad Eugenium Papam,* book IV, III, 6.

dom and exercise its task as ultimate spiritual and moral authority, and in
the logic of the historical situation, this spiritual power became the source
and judge of every law. This law was first and foremost Roman civil law,
restored, studied anew, adapted to the pastoral and organizational needs of
the Church and thereby becoming also "canon law," the law of the Church.[42]
The fact was that the world was ruled by the Church's law, which found its
direct application, its fulfillment, and its range of jurisdiction not only in
the strictly ecclesiastical sphere, but also in the temporal. No other law or
legal provision could prevail if it contradicted that of the Church.

Paradoxical Effects and Merits of the Gregorian System

The Effects: The "Secularization" of the Political Power and the Dynamization of Its Autonomy

The effect of the Gregorian system was paradoxical. The doctrine of
the great popes of this period, from Gregory VII and Innocent III through
Boniface VIII, reduced temporal Princes, including the Emperor himself, to
simple laymen. They radically desacralized the temporal power, thus creating the conditions for the formation of a new secular spirit in civil and
political life. Paradoxically, it was precisely the medieval canonical juridical doctrine of the *plenitudo potestatis* of the Pope that reconfirmed the
radical secularity of the temporal power, even if in an initial phase this was
only in the sense of a secularity at the service of the spiritual power. At the
same time, in the confrontations with the Emperor that were necessary to
impose this doctrine, the Popes promoted the power of the Princes subject
to the Emperor, who gradually consolidated their governmental and administrative power over their territories, thus preparing the birth of the modern territorial State. With the famous decree *Per venerabilem*, Innocent III established the principle that a king *in temporalibus* has no superior,[43] a principle which was later crystallized in the phrase *rex est imperator in regno
suo*, thus equating the royal power, in the territory of a kingdom, with that
of the emperor. This phrase would soon become the formula of sovereignty
for territorial states, later claimed against the *plenitudo potestatis* of the

---

42. This process is amply described in Berman, *Law and Revolution*.
43. The complete text is in Friedberg, *Corpus Iuris Canonici*, cols. 714–76.

pope.[44] In an analogous way, papal policy promoted the power of the com-munes in Italy, so as to weaken the imperial power in favor of the *plenitudo potestatis* of the Pope.[45] The strong development of urban civilization and the space provided for corporative self-organization in the new universi-ties,[46] for the most part founded by the Church itself, created other condi-tions for resistance to the medieval system. The first literary expression of this resistance was the *Defensor pacis* (1324) of Marsilius of Padua, rector of the University of Paris from 1313. This amounted to a frontal attack on the doctrine of the pontifical *plenitudo potestatis,* in the name of the autonomy of the temporal power (for denying, incorrectly, *any* right of jurisdiction of the Church, Marsilius was condemned for heresy in 1327). Ultimately canon law itself, which had also assumed in itself the essence of Roman public law, became the source for the law of the new territorial states that chal-lenged the legislative sovereignty of the Popes. Thus canon law, elaborated as a means for the supremacy of the spiritual power over the temporal, in its secularized form became the means by which this supremacy was chal-lenged and finally abolished.

The "Papal Revolution," set in motion by Gregory VII in the eleventh century, thus paradoxically became the point of departure for the modern emancipation from the medieval system, and the presupposition of the sec-ularity of the modern State.[47] In the present context, these historical facts interest us precisely to the extent to which they show us, in general and somewhat abstract terms, in what consists the essence of an order *opposed* to a secular state: an order in which the State is subjected to the supremacy, not moral but *juridical,* of a religious claim, and is therefore not fully sover-eign. Or, it may be subjected to institutions which claim to be depositaries of religious truth, and for this reason to possess an authentic legislative, judicial and, consequently, also coercive sovereignty (even if, according to

44. See Sergio Mochi Onory, *Fonti canonistiche dell'idea moderna dello stato* (Milan: Vita e pen-siero, 1951), 271ff.

45. For the implications of this process for juridical and political thought see the first chapter of Quentin Skinner, *The Foundations of Modern Political Thought,* vol. 1, *The Renaissance* (Cambridge: Cambridge University Press, 1978).

46. See on this important theme, which shows once again the decisive importance—and the supe-riority—of Christianity for the development of modern Western culture: Toby E. Huff, The *Rise of Early Modern Science: Islam, China and the West,* 2nd ed. (Cambridge: Cambridge University Press, 2003).

47. Berman's study, *Law and Revolution,* shows not only this, but also how much the modern ju-ridical tradition owes to canon law and to the acceptance and subsequent evolution of Roman law on the part of the Church. Under this aspect, also, the Church became the great teacher of the West, and indirectly of the entire world. See also Huff, *The Rise of Early Modern Science,* 118ff.

the idea of *potestas indirecta*, it renounces the direct exercise of this power, leaving it in the hands of the "secular arm").[48]

I personally think that the idea of a temporal sword (as an original and legitimate possession of the Church, even if not used by it, and left to worldly rulers) was a theological and juridical fiction which expressed, on the one hand, the Church's clear awareness that "governing" this world was not its task, and on the other, that it nonetheless had a direct pastoral responsibility toward this world and the persons living in it. Thus, a responsibility for the just exercise of temporal power, and a responsibility for the good of the Church and of souls, as well as for peaceful coexistence among people. In its mature, high medieval form, the theory of the two swords had the hybrid, incoherent character of a strategy of retreat which, in that historical context, ultimately meant only to affirm the supremacy of spiritual and moral values over the practical activities of power, that is, the primacy of the eternal destiny of man with respect to all considerations of the temporal order. To do this, the Church made use of the means at its disposal: ecclesiastical law and sanctions. It did not, however, have any real power (except, obviously, in the Papal States). The only power it possessed was based, in fact, on the force and penetration of the Christian faith in medieval society, and the indisputable spiritual authority of the ecclesial hierarchy. The medieval person, including the politician, was a believer, and this was the basis of the Church's power.

The fact that the Catholic Church did not intend to rule the world, or to seek dominion in this world in a "political" sense, reveals an essential characteristic of Christianity, one which radically distinguishes it from Islam, which from its beginning was conceived of *simultaneously* as a religion, as a force for social order, and as a political and military power. Although unity between religion and politics was inscribed from the beginning in the idea of Islam, this Islamic integralism has almost never been fully realized in the course of history (especially due to the political weakness of the Baghdad caliphate of the Abassids).[49] Whereas for Islam the separation of politics

48. This "leaving" also oscillates between various senses: that of a mere *delegation* of a temporal power and jurisdiction that would nevertheless be originally, essentially, and by right in the hands of the Roman pontiff; or that according to which the "leaving" means that the temporal power and jurisdiction *in temporalibus* belong, not in a delegated way, but *originarily, properly, and essentially* to the temporal power, but that its exercise must be realized within the limits and under the direction of the spiritual power. A classical exposition of the traditional doctrine of indirect power can be found in Charles Journet, *La Juridiction de l'Église sur la cité* (Paris: Desclée, 1931).

49. On this strange dichotomy between "theory and practice" in Islam, I refer the reader again to Brague, *La Loi de Dieu*, 189 and 309.

and religion is contrary to its original self-understanding (as represented by Mohammad himself, a political and military genius) and to its theology (as is found in the Koran and in Islamic *sharia* law), for Christianity, exactly the opposite is true. The essence of Christianity is dualistic, separating religion and politics, though historical contingencies provoked a commixture of the two terms in ever-new forms—which, in my view, significantly distanced themselves in not a few respects from the founding charism and from the essence itself of Christianity. Though it may seem paradoxical, this fact is confirmed by history: a civilization permeated by the Christian spirit favors a secular understanding of politics, while a society formed by Islam, whose concept of law depends on religion, always has a tendency to unite in some way the religious and political powers.

The Merits: The Relativization of Political Power and the Creation of a Public Juridical Culture

It would undoubtedly be a mistake to judge the medieval system by modern, "liberal," or even democratic categories. The times offered no other alternatives. But the essence of the medieval system, which today for many reasons we consider to be a failed system (and rightly so, precisely because it was Christian), internally contradictory and in various aspects morally unacceptable, nevertheless possesses its own greatness, truth and, in my view, perennial validity. These are found precisely in its "antitotalitarian" character, that is, in the *principle of the subordination of the political power to external, independent, and superior moral criteria,* and especially to criteria of justice; criteria, that is, which are not at the free disposition of those who exercise political power. While according to modern theories, that is, the absolutist theories (of the seventeenth and eighteenth centuries) of the "divine right of kings," absolute power precludes a judgment concerning the exercise of temporal power, the Middle Ages asserted the opposite: the princes of this world, including the emperor, can be judged by the spiritual power, which is ultimate and full, though not political, and which itself can be judged by no one. In other words, in the Middle Ages, the Church recognized no absolute political power. To do this, however, it had to declare itself to be a *nonpolitical* absolute power. That this was the intention is beyond question; equally certain is the assertion that such an "a-politicalness" of an absolute, and in truth *sovereign,* spiritual power was an illusion. Such a spiritual power could never avoid being politicized, especially once the modern territorial State was born and in an epoch no longer characterized by the unity of the faith. It was the modern period that taught us that the political power must be controlled not by a spiritual-religious power, but by another *political* power. This would become the essence of constitutionalism, of parliamentarianism, and of modern constitutional, representative, and parliamentary democracy. Nevertheless, as we shall discuss below, this does not render superfluous an independent spiritual power such as that of the Church.

The medieval Church, however, did not merely have good intentions. It offered accomplishments and contributions that were essential to the formation of the world in which we live today. Having affirmed the primacy of the moral over the political and, from this perspective, subjected the powers of this world to criteria of justice that are ultimately indispensable—criteria, however, *that in their essence were always considered to be secular and independent of faith (i.e., natural law)*—the Church, in fact, acted as the great educator of the West and, indirectly, of humanity. In this way, it unquestionably prepared the spiritual ground for the modern idea of human rights.[50]

Considering the essence of what animated the Church's action, the medieval system also contained in itself the realization of authentic Christian principles, though in a way that was contingent and distorted by historical factors. Despite its tendency to hierocracy (the mixture of religion and politics), *this system did not deny the genuine separation between religion and politics* so typical of the Christianity of the times of persecution. Indeed, it confirmed this separation and organized it according to pastoral criteria, making use not only of Roman law—developed according to the new needs and unified, enacted in the last instance by the Church—but also of the secular arm, the coercive force of the temporal power.

This last aspect, which is the problematical one and, in the eyes of a modern spectator, even scandalous, was nevertheless in a certain sense a "fruitful" error, given that canon law—on the basis of which the Church erected itself as a kind of sovereign entity—derived in large part from secular Roman law, especially public law (and above all the so-called *lex regia* of the times of the Roman Principate). As has been shown in many studies on the topic, in this way the medieval Church and the culture created by it, including urban and university culture, became the origin of the mod-

---

50. It should not be forgotten that the idea of the papal *plenitudo potestatis* had to be, at least in the conception of the great theologians such as St. Bernard, joined to the task of protecting the rights—including judicial—of the weak and the poorest against the powerful; see *De consideratione*, Lib. IV, VII, 23, and all of book III.

ern State and of the principal juridical institutions of the modern world.[51] A scholar of the history of European law has written that

in the history of medieval Europe, the Church, with all her experience in law, became the master of the secular law. Whatever new developments were needed in that area, had already been thought out and tried in the ecclesiastical legal framework. When the Church claimed priority for her law over secular law, up to the end of the Middle Ages such a position could be justified not only in theological and canonical terms; it was also justified politically—through the undeniable reality that every secular government had to "go to school" with the Church before it could learn how to stand on its own legs.[52]

Nevertheless, the price that the Church paid for its civilizing mission and the consequent involvement in temporal affairs and responsibilities was high. The application of the great Christian principles mentioned at the outset (the primacy of the spiritual and the idea that this life is a passage to a definitive and eternal life) slowly became a global vision of the political and juridical organization of society. As a consequence, the application of the two principles was, so to speak, politically tainted. The elevation of the Catholic faith—that is, of a religious orthodoxy—to a condition of citizenship and to the foundation and supreme law of an entire society and civilization created intolerable and scandalous discrimination. Above all, it turned religious heresy into a crime, since it saw it as something politically relevant and even dangerous—an attack on the "constitutional" foundations of the public order and of the peace, ultimately a crime of *lèse-majesté*, punishable by death. The logical consequence was the Inquisition, itself an instrument of Roman law, which was begun with the idea of halting unjust accusations, often anonymous, of heresy and the lynching of persons who

---

51. In addition to the already cited works of Harold J. Berman and Toby E. Huff, see: Sergio Mochi Onory, *Fonti cononistiche dell'idea moderna dello stato*; Helmut Quaritsch, *Souveränität: Entstehung und Entwicklung des Begriffs in Frankreich und Deutschland vom 13. Jh. bis 1806* (Berlin: Athenäum, 1986); Dieter Wyduckel, *Princeps legibus solutus: Eine Untersuchung zur frühmodernen Rechts- und Staatslehre* (Berlin: Duncker & Humblot, 1979); Helmut G. Walther, *Imperiales Königtum, Konziliarismus und Volkssouveränität: Studien zu den Grenzen des mittelalterlichen Souveränitätsgedankens* (Munich: Fink, 1976).

52. Hattenhauer, *Europäische Rechtsgeschichte*, 126: "In der Geschichte des europäischen Mittelalters wurde die Kirche mit dieser Rechtserfahrung zur Lehrmeisterin des weltlichen Rechts. Was immer sich dort an Neuem ausbilden sollte, war in der Rechtsgestalt der Kirche vorgedacht und erprobt worden. Wenn die Kirche für ihr Recht den Vorrang vor dem weltlichen beanspruchte, so war dieses bis zum Ende des Mittealters nicht nur theologisch-kirchenrechtlich zu begründen. Es war politisch gerechtfertigt durch die unübersehbare Tatsache, dass alle weltliche Regierung bei der Kirche in die Lehre gehen musste, ehe sie auf eigenen Beinen zu stehen lernte." Similarly, also see Wolfgang Reinhard, *Geschichte der Staatsgewalt: Eine vergleichende Verfassungsgeschichte Europas von den Anfängen bis zur Gegenwart* (Munich: C. H. Beck, 1999), 285ff. The same can be said of the juridical roots of the modern sovereign state; see the study of Paolo Prodi, *Il Sovrano Pontefice: Un corpo e due anime: la monarchia papale nella prima età moderna* (Bologna: Il Mulino, 1982).

were unjustly suspected, but later became an instrument of terror and the grave violation of human rights. Though it was originally, through the introduction of the Roman instrument of the *inquisitio,* an attempt at humanization according to the rules of procedural fairness, the Inquisition was contrary to the Christian tradition as represented by the Fathers of the Church. Thus when the medieval system collapsed—which occurred precisely at the high point of its development—the Church found itself faced with an enormous failure and loss of prestige which, through the centuries, negatively conditioned its action in the world, and the consequences of which are still evident today.

The Modern Ethos of the Primacy of the Political, and Its Specific Legitimacy

The Paradigmatic Case of Marsilius of Padua

Even before the breakup of Christian unity that followed on the various Protestant reforms, the medieval system had been called into question by jurists, theologians, and philosophers, on both the practical and theoretical levels. On the practical level, some territorial princes, such as Philip the Fair of France, began with the help of their lawyers and courts to use essential elements of canon law, apt for limiting the power of the emperor in favor of papal power, to legitimize their own sovereignty. On the theoretical level, the challenge came prominently from Marsilius of Padua, who, in his *Defensor pacis,* rejected the subordination of the temporal power to the supremacy of the pope. To the vision of the *plenitudo potestatis*—a doctrine that he considered the cause of disunity and of all political conflict—Marsilius opposed a purely Aristotelian, monist ethic of the *polis.* The Church and the clergy, wrote Marsilius, must not exercise any kind of power, but limit themselves to preaching the Gospel and administering the sacraments. The crucial point of this argument is the denial—later condemned as heretical—of the Church's right to exercise *any* form of jurisdiction, even ecclesiastical and pastoral, and the assertion that the Church does not even have the right to determine, in a juridically binding way, if a doctrine is heretical and to condemn it. This, says Marsilius, is the task of the temporal power, after hearing the opinion of the clergy. Not that the temporal power should become a spiritual power, but it alone possesses the *plenitudo potestatis*: it has the competence for the competence (what in German is simply

Kompetenz-Kompetenz), possesses sovereignty, and the last word belongs solely to it.

Marsilius had no intention of resacralizing the temporal power, nor did he intend to establish State control over the Church. His approach is more modern, in that he pursues a purely political logic, which is in fact expressed in the title of his work: *Defensor pacis*. Like Thomas Hobbes two centuries later, Marsilius is interested in a political value: peace, and as was later the case with Machiavelli, unity among the Italians. His anticlericalism is thus the expression of a political, secular goal. For the resolution of a political problem, he defends the *plenitudo potestatis* of the State, that is, the full political and juridical sovereignty of the temporal power. We have here, for the first time, something like the modern idea of public reason, which in its sphere is autonomous, sovereign, and not subject to the judgment of any superior claim. According to Marsilius, a State should be governed only by civil laws: the authority and power of the government are entirely derived from the will of the people.[53]

Marsilius thus becomes one of the medieval authors who pass on what we can call Aristotelian constitutionalism, but he is also a testimony to the presence of that Aristotelian "political naturalism" that was widely cultivated in the scholasticism of the high Middle Ages. The greatest "political naturalist" in this sense—that is, in the sense of considering political life, society, and government not as realities existing only in a fallen world, but as realities of creation, pertaining to human nature and having their own, autonomous justification—is St. Thomas Aquinas, who nevertheless did not reach the "anticlerical"—and on some points heretical—conclusions of Marsilius.[54] The specific novelty of Marsilius—who will become the teacher not only of Machiavelli, but of all modernity—is certainly the unambiguous assertion of the primacy and autonomy of the political sphere. His solution, however, is ambiguous: despite his Aristotelian constitutionalism and the assertion of the supremacy of the law based on popular sovereignty, in affirming the primacy of the political he subordinates the spiritual authority and priestly power of the Church to that of the State, elevating the political power to the final arbiter of truth and justice. In this he also reveals, pre-

---

53. *Defensor pacis*, part 1, ch. 12; see Horst Kusch, ed., *Marsilius von Padua, Verteidiger des Friedens (Defensor Pacis)*, Latin text and German translation (Berlin: Rütten & Loening, 1958), 117ff.

54. See on "political naturalism" Georges de Lagarde, *La naissance de l'esprit laïque au déclin du moyen age*, vol. 2: *Secteur social de la scolastique* (Louvain: Nauvelaerts, 1958), 51ff.

maturely, one of the ambivalences of the "secular State": the possibility of yielding to the temptation to understand itself as the exclusive interpreter of every norm, criterion of justice, and even of morality. Marsilius, therefore, shows us not only an essential property of modern statehood, but also the politically problematic, and even dangerous, face of what will become modern laicism.

The Loss of Christian Unity and the Birth of the Modern Political Ethos

The affirmation of the primacy of politics and of its corresponding autonomy would come to exercise its influence in a new context, that of the rupture of Christian unity. The clear consciousness of the supremacy of politics over religion is the consequence of a long history of conflicts, bloody wars, and the inability to coexist peacefully under conditions of religious disagreement and pluralism. This set of circumstances is linked to the birth of the modern territorial State: aspirations for unification, pacification, and the consolidation of the power of the princes were joined, above all in Protestant areas, to the problem of resolving religious conflict, thus perpetuating the division among the various Christian confessions.

The fracture of religious unity in the West led to an urgent need for specifically *political* solutions, like what occurred in an exemplary way in France, where the party of the so-called politicians sought a solution capable of putting the question of religious *truth* in parentheses, in favor of peaceful coexistence. Thus, in the well-known formulation of Michel de l'Hôpital, chancellor to the king of France: "It is not important which is the true religion, but how the people can live together in peace."[55]

The great theorist of the primacy of the political was also the first great modern theoretician of State sovereignty: Jean Bodin, also a member of the party of the *politiques*. In his monumental work *Six Livres sur la République* (1576), he proposes the idea of a State focused on what is essential from a strictly political point of view. He distinguishes public goods from private, a distinction that serves to formulate the political conditions for civic co-

---

55. The party of the *politiques* in the civil war of the sixteenth century was influenced above all by jurists: see on the theme Roman Schnur, *Die französischen Juristen im konfessionellen Bürgerkrieg des 16. Jahrhunderts. Ein Beitrag zur Entstehungsgeschichte des modernen Staates* (Berlin: Duncker & Humblot, 1962). Also see Nicola Matteucci, *Organizzazione del potere e libertà: Storia del costituzionalismo moderno* (Turin: UTET, 1988), 37ff.; and Joseph Lecler, *Histoire de la tolérance au siècle de la Réforme* (1955) (Paris: Albin Michel, 1994), 479ff.

existence in a world characterized by conflicts resulting from differing religious, as well as philosophical, truth-claims. Bodin's idea of a *modus vivendi* (which nevertheless still respects natural law and the *lois fondamentaux*, the *lex salica*, the constitutional law of the French monarchy, and is therefore not a positivism or a pure absolutism) is based on the distinction between, on the one hand, those values that are highest and most important in a religious, moral, and existential sense, and on the other hand values of lesser dignity, but *politically more fundamental and urgent*. This *modus vivendi* includes a political ethic that is an ethic of responsibility, based on the willingness to renounce the political implementation of particular values, even if—as, for example, with eternal salvation—they are considered to be the highest values, in favor of assuring those fundamental political values that are necessary for peaceful coexistence: something like the motto *primum vivere, deinde philosophari*.[56]

This *ethos of peace* presupposes, says Bodin, the sovereignty of the State: a State, that is, that distinguishes between what is public and what is private, that is capable of imposing what is politically fundamental, and that knows how to preserve peace, having no other power alongside it that could prevent it from doing so. In a similar spirit, Thomas Hobbes constructed his "Leviathan," a type of pacifying political mechanism, created by man through a contract authorizing a sovereign power. Ignoring for now all the problematic and dangerous characteristics of the Hobbesian solution,[57] it is worth pointing out the underlying objective: to find a political way out of a state of civil war, which is always latent when people turn the answer to questions of truth (whether religious, or concerning questions of natural law, justice, etc.) into a condition of peace. According to Hobbes, these questions must be excluded from the public discourse and left to the decision of the sovereign, not allowing another authority—such as the Church—to question these decisions.

Obviously, this solution is both unilateral and myopic precisely from a *political* point of view. It ignores the question of freedom before a State that is sovereign, oppressive, and without institutional controls. The sovereignty of the political power, seen initially as a solution to the problem of the paci-

---

56. For an understanding of this implicit political ethic in Bodin's thought, an indispensable resource is Martin Kriele, *Einführung in die Staatslehre: Die geschichtlichen Legitimitätsgrundlagen des demokratischen Verfassungsstaates*, 6th ed. (Stuttgart: Kohlhammer, 2003).

57. See Martin Rhonheimer, *La filosofia politica di Thomas Hobbes: coerenza e contraddizioni di un paradigma* (Rome: Armando, 1997).

fication of society, becomes a cause no longer of civil war, but of resistance in the name of freedom.

Against the early-modern State—powerful, monarchic, and absolute— arose the liberal-style constitutional movement. Modern constitutionalism opposed a State in which the power considered itself to be the owner of its "subjects," and was not subject to any real institutional control—nor to the control of a spiritual authority, like the Church in the Middle Ages.[58] The ethos of peace of the modern State had to be completed by an *ethos of freedom,* which found its expression in contractualism, especially that of John Locke, which became the most influential. Despite its obvious argumentative deficiencies, modern contractualism had the merit of expressing the primacy of the individual, as a citizen, over the State, the idea of mutual advantage and equality, and with this the idea that every government must serve its citizens (and not the other way around, i.e., that subjects must serve the interests of the State and be simply subject to it), and even the idea that it would be possible to overthrow an unjust government.[59] Thus, with modern contractualism rooted in the idea of natural law, a secular form of moral and juridical control of power had its beginning. The great merit of liberal contractualism was that of being able, over time, to submit the modern State to legal limitations and controls: of subordinating power to law, according to the ancient Anglo-Saxon idea of the rule of law. This latter derived from an older, medieval tradition, and ultimately became the foundation of our modern democracies, with the modern idea of fundamental rights, civil rights, and the rights of man.[60]

58. Contrary to the medieval order, according to the political theology—"drawn from Sacred Scripture," but even more from Hobbes—of Bossuet, bishop of Meaux, tutor of the dauphin Louis XIV and theoretician of French absolutism, the king was the incarnation of a supreme reason, which had to give account of itself only to God. "The King cannot commit an injustice"—in his actions as king—and can be judged by no one. On this theme see Bertrand de Jouvenel, *De la souveraineté. A la recherche du bien Politique* (Paris: Éditions M.-Th. Génin, 1955). British representatives of the *Divine Right of Kings* argued analogously, as, for example, James I of England in his work *Basilikon doron.*

59. See chapter 2 of this volume, "The Liberal Image of Man and the Concept of Autonomy: Beyond the Debate between Liberals and Communitarians," which was originally published as "Contrattualismo, individualismo e solidarietà: per rileggere la tradizione liberale," in *Per la filosofia* 16, no. 46 (1999): 30–40.

60. That modern liberal constitutionalism had its roots, in its various aspects, in the Christian Middle Ages is not questioned today, and is a widely studied theme. This is shown by the Anglo-Saxon tradition of the rule of law; the medieval tradition of the right of resistance, but also of popular sovereignty; the tradition of the doctrine of the *regimen mixtum,* the ideas of representation and parliamentarianism, and the conciliarist conception (which, though theologically erroneous, had great political impact). Some of these themes are treated in Brian Tierney, *The Idea of Natural Rights: Studies on Natural Rights, Natural Law, and Church Law 1150–1625* (Grand Rapids, Mich.: William B. Eerdmans, 1997); see also

The Complex Nature of Modern Democracy:
The "Democratic Constitutional State"

Modern democracies, in fact, are not simply "democratic" in the ancient sense. They have nothing to do with Athenian democracy, in which all of the people (male and non-slaves) gathered in an assembly, which, under the guidance of the demagogues, decided on matters of life and death, war and peace. Democratic representative government was unknown to antiquity. Modern democracies, on the other hand, are essentially based on the idea of representation; they are a mixture of various elements, some of which come down from the Middle Ages. They presuppose the institution of the rule of law, of representative bodies (parliaments), the separation of powers—especially the independence of the judiciary—and thus the fragmentation, indeed almost the abolition, of the (internal) sovereignty of the State (meaning the distribution of the functions of sovereignty among various state bodies, which are separate among themselves and in a relationship of mutual control). Modern, liberal-type democracy is in reality a "democratic constitutional State"; it is the product of the democratization of Anglo-Saxon-style constitutional parliamentarianism, based on universal suffrage and on the principle of majority. These are elements that, in isolation, could lead to another kind of system: the plebiscitary and even totalitarian democracy[61] in the Rousseauian tradition, which opposed precisely the idea of representation. The democratic principle, which was historically the last to be realized, means the democratization of a constitutional, parliamentary State, based on the rule of law and the division of powers. The presumed foundation of democracy on a pure "sovereignty of the people," and on this alone, is an ideological formula that has been abandoned, and that corresponds to neither historical reality nor the political reality of our day.[62] The

---

Quentin Skinner, *The Foundations of Modern Political Thought*, vol. 2: *The Age of Reformation* (Cambridge: Cambridge University Press, 1978); and the great classic: Carl J. Friedrich, *Constitutional Government and Democracy* (New York: Blaisdell, 1950); in German, *Der Verfassungsstaat der Neuzeit* (Berlin/Göttingen/Heidelberg: Springer, 1953). See also by the same author *L'uomo, la comunità politica, l'ordine politico* (Bologna: Il Mulino, 2002), 149: "The authoritarian aspects of Catholicism must not close our eyes to the fact that during the entire Middle Ages the Church was the bastion of efficacious limitations, and therefore of constitutionalism." For a detailed historical study on medieval constitutionalism, especially on the level of jurisprudence, see Kenneth Pennington, *The Prince and the Law 1200–1600: Sovereignty and Rights in the Western Legal Tradition* (Berkeley: University of California Press, 1993).

61. According to the famous expression of Jacob L. Talmon, *The Origins of Totalitarian Democracy* (1952) (London: Sphere Books, 1970).

62. Peter Graf Kielmannsegg, *Volkssouveränität: Eine Untersuchung der Bedingungen demokratischer Legitimität* (Stuttgart: Klett, 1977).

"democratic constitutional State," therefore, simultaneously bears within it a threefold ethos, developed through the course of history: the ethos of peace (which created the modern *State*), the ethos of freedom (which created the *constitutional* State), and the ethos of the equality of freedom and justice (which created the *democratic* constitutional State).[63] Here we have the essence of the modern secular State, the result of a long, intricate process of successive secularization and awareness of the primacy of the political values of peace, freedom, equality, participative justice, and so on, over those values that are properly religious.

The solution of the sixteenth century French *politiques* of excluding religious questions from the public sphere did not mean the establishment of a nonconfessional State, but the guarantee of a wide tolerance, to the point of rendering subjects' religion politically indifferent. This effort had success in the Edict of Nantes (1598), which, however, did not last long; the edict was later revoked by Louis XIV. What triumphed everywhere was in fact an intolerant confessional State, characterized no longer as a religious-spiritual project, as in the Middle Ages, but as a project of unification, stabilization, political utility, and above all, after the experience of the wars of religion, pacification (though not always easily distinguishable from the simple will of sovereigns to increase their power). Thus, in the religious peace of Augsburg and confirmed after the Thirty Years' War, the insidious principle of *Cuius regio, eius religio* was established as a formula of pacification but also of territorial sovereignty. Consequently, as the Middle Ages were characterized by the primacy of the spiritual, modernity came to be characterized by the primacy of the political. In its first phase, this primacy of the political—justified on the basis of historical experience—was realized monistically: religion itself was treated as an element of the political order. In the modern confessional State, both Catholic and Protestant, religion was considered to be a constituent factor of the public order, also defining the identity of the political organization of a society and its juridical institutions. In a certain sense, modernity prior to the French Revolution and the restoration regressed to a "Roman" mentality, of seeing in religion the guarantee of the stability of the social order and of political prosperity. This mentality was especially present in the States that arose from the Protestant Reformation, in which Christianity was established as the State religion and

---

63. For this threefold formation of the democratic constitutional State, see Kriele, *Einführung in die Staatslehre.*

the prince was invested with ultimate authority, including episcopal. But it is also found in French Gallicanism, and in other equally Catholic forms of the fusion of nationalism and religion.

A very important historical fact, at times forgotten, is that the secular-liberal movement developed, no longer in opposition to the medieval system—which by that time had completely disappeared and was no longer understood—but against the modern system of the union between "throne and altar." Similarly, one must bear in mind that the system defended by the Church in its fight with modernity after the French Revolution was not in fact the medieval system, but that of the modern confessional absolute State. Consequently, the conflicts between laicists and Christian faithful (or, in the present context, Catholics), and the alternatives that arose as a result, were a typical fruit of the modern situation. The theological and Christian essence of the medieval system—that which arose from the Papal Revolution—was increasingly less well-understood, and even forgotten. In particular its dualistic and "antitotalitarian" character was no longer understood (perhaps it is better understood today), its merit of submitting the temporal power to objective values and moral criteria. As a consequence, the secular battle against the modern confessional State, especially in its Catholic form, at times assumed forms that tended to forget the submission of the political power to higher criteria. Instances of State arrogance in the name of secularity and liberal progress reached such a point as to lead a noted Italian liberal, in 1925, to say that "one who reflects on the harshly authoritarian character of contemporary democratic civilization cannot deny that, in reality, the Church represents a bulwark and a defense of freedom against State 'tyranny,' even if the intimate motivation of the latter is anything but liberal."[64]

It seems to me certain that the world would have been spared the great tragedies of the twentieth century—totalitarian regimes, genocides, and wars—if European politics had remained not only impregnated with, but also "checked" and mollified by, Christian values and behavior, and especially if, in many areas, the voice of the Catholic Church had been listened to and followed. Such an observation, however, is rather futile, in that due to its profound incomprehension of the positive aspects of political modernity, the Church was incapable of fulfilling this function; already by the

---

64. Guido De Ruggiero, *Storia del liberalismo europeo* (1925), 3rd ed. (Bari: Laterza, 1984), 429. An English translation was published as *The History of European Liberalism* (Boston: Beacon Press, 1966).

nineteenth century, it had become irrelevant to the discussion. In particular, it had lost the working class (papal social teaching began at least half a century too late, with the 1891 encyclical *Rerum novarum*, and was in fact a reaction to an already accomplished fact: the conquest of the working classes by socialism and the union movement, more or less influenced by Marxism). Moreover, it had also frustrated the efforts, at times premature perhaps, of those intellectuals and liberal Catholic politicians who had a vision not only of the past, but of the future.

The Doctrinal Evolution within the Catholic Church
From the Clash with Political Modernity to the Recognition of Modern Political Culture

From the time of the French Revolution, the Catholic Church, in its conflict with liberal-constitutional and democratic modern political culture—and in its self-consciousness rooted not only in principles from the medieval past but also from the modern territorial, monarchical, and confessional State—made an effort, understandably, to distinguish between what was historically contingent in its position and what was indispensable from the perspective of the deposit of faith. The same, however, was true for nineteenth-century secularism, which identified the political position in favor of the secular State and freedom with a religiously antidogmatic, subjectivist, and relativist position that tended to base the necessary public and political neutrality regarding claims of religious truth on the denial of the existence itself of such truth. This claim was made even to the point of denying the link between conscience and truth, which is to say to the point of denying that the dignity of individual conscience is based not only on the fact that the conscience is "mine," but also that conscience is capable of being a voice of truth—even if it does not lose this dignity when in error—and enables the person to freely seek the truth.[65]

The negative disposition of the Church toward the liberal and democrat-

---

65. Even today there are those, as for example one of the great teachers of the twentieth century, Norberto Bobbio, who succumb to the old myth that the right to religious freedom presupposes the nonexistence, and indeed the impossibility, of truth in religious matters; see his "Sul fondamento dei diritti dell'uomo," in Bobbio, *L'età dei diritti* (Turin: Einaudi, 1990), 10. The paradox is: if a knowable religious truth were to exist, would the right to religious freedom no longer exist? Ironically, a secularist who thinks on this as Bobbio does thinks in the same way that Catholic theologians and popes of the eighteenth century thought: the right to religious freedom implies that there is no religious truth, i.e., "indifferentism"!

ic movement of the nineteenth century was nevertheless due not only to the latter's aggressive and baldly anticlerical character, but also to the fact that the Church focused one-sidedly on particular versions of this movement, specifically those in Catholic countries of Latin tradition such as France and Italy. Both the teaching of the Magisterium and the theology of the time were particularly focused on the theory of the sovereignty of the people and of plebiscitary democracy, as proposed by the disciples of Rousseau.[66] These latter preached an *absolute* popular sovereignty, in no way limited by prior, natural law considerations of a moral and juridical character; they also preached the right of the people to overthrow any type of government at any time. The Magisterium and the theology of the Church of the nineteenth century ignored that other tradition which would become the origin of contemporary political culture, that is, the Anglo-Saxon tradition of the constitutional State, the rule of law and the corresponding conception of a parliamentary, representative democracy that is subject to law and to constitutional restrictions, based on the separation of powers, and sensitive to the protection of minorities. In particular, they failed to appreciate the liberal theory, classically set forth by Emmanuel-Joseph Sieyès (the "Abbé Sieyès"), of the differentiation between "constituting power" (the people and the constitutive assemblies with full legislative freedom and, from the legal perspective, unlimited sovereignty) and "constituted power," which, once in place, subjects the sovereignty of the people to the limitations and the institutional and legal controls provided in the constitution (and thus effectively abolishes and renders inoperative the absolute sovereignty of the people, subjecting it to the rules of the law). Liberal constitutionalism, in its first elitist and antiegalitarian phase, but also in its later democratic phase, was in fact more in line with the ancient and medieval tradition (as expressed in the theory of the *regimen mixtum*) than with the vision of the Christian State (always monarchic, with a Christian monarch who was more or less absolute) promoted by the Church of the nineteenth century (and not without nostalgia toward the times prior to the French Revolution, in which the State was a reliable support for the Church and its pastoral task).[67]

66. This was noted some time ago by Hans Maier, "Kirche und Demokratie," in Maier, *Kirche und Gesellschaft* (Munich: Kösel Verlag, 1972), 82–107.

67. See Josef Isensee, "Die katholische Kritik an den Menschrechten. Der liberale Freiheitsentwurf in der Sicht der Päpste des 19. Jahrhunderts," in *Menschrechte und Menschenwürde. Historische Voraussetzungen—säkulare Gestalt—christliches Verständnis*, ed. Ernst-Wolfgang Böckenförde and Robert Spaemann (Stuttgart: Klett-Cotta, 1987), 138–74; Manfred Brocker and Tine Stein, eds., *Christentum*

Other kinds of factors, no less important, should also be mentioned. On the one hand was the fact that "modern freedoms," and the associated political demands, were incompatible with the existence of the temporal power of the pope in the Papal States, in which the Roman pontiff was the temporal sovereign, canon law had civil validity, and the Holy Office controlled the press and other publications via censorship and reserved important governmental and administrative positions to members of the clergy, except during the brief period at the beginning of the pontificate of Pius IX. Even if liberal Catholics in France such as the Count Charles de Montalembert (about whom we will speak more below), or in Italy, the adherents of neo-Guelphism, wholeheartedly defended—perhaps ingenuously—the temporal power of the pope in the Papal States, the popes themselves did not nourish illusions on this point: liberal and constitutionalist demands were incompatible with the existing clerical regime. On the other hand, it must not be forgotten that the French episcopate in the nineteenth century, strongly allied to the old monarchic, antirevolutionary regime, was comprised exclusively of members of the aristocracy. Both the French Revolution and liberal constitutionalism were in fact more anti-aristocratic than anti-monarchical: the Revolution did not intend to abolish the monarchy, but the privileges of the aristocracy (it was Louis XVI who refused to cooperate with the revolution, and not vice versa). Thus, the first polemical and revolutionary writing to have a great impact was not the *Social Contract* of Rousseau (which was little known and little read before the Revolution), but the pamphlet "Against Privileges" by the Abbé Sieyès. Both sociologically and by mentality, therefore, neither the pope nor the high levels of the episcopate could have been much inclined toward a recognition of "modern freedoms." Rather, both the bishops and the pope (then Leo XIII) defended the "legitimism" of the restoration; they could not recognize a regime that was the result of a revolutionary process, that is, they could not legitimize *juridical discontinuity.*

The evolution during the last two centuries within the Catholic Church is characterized by a slow, yet continuous and progressive, awareness of these historical factors, and by a growing freedom with respect to them. The

---

und Demokratie (Darmstadt: Wissenschaftliche Buchgesellschaft, 2006), especially the contributions of Uertz and Ballestrem; for Germany: Rudolf Uertz, *Vom Gottesrecht zum Menschenrecht: Das katholische Staatsdenken in Deutschland von der Französischen Revolution bis zum II. Vatikanischen Konzil (1789–1965)* (Paderborn: Schöningh, 2005).

process, which will culminate in the fifth chapter of John Paul II's encyclical *Centesimus annus,* began with Leo XIII and his attempt to create a *ralliment* in France—the acceptance of the secular republic by Catholics and their cooperation with it, with the aim of impregnating it with a Christian spirit. Above all, however, it was affirmed by the doctrine of the autonomy and supremacy, each in its own sphere, of both the temporal power and the spiritual power *(utraque potestas est in genere suo maxima).*[68] With this affirmation of a sovereign autonomy of the State, Leo XIII signaled the definitive abandonment of the vision created by Gregory VII, and an openness to new solutions. After the final vision of a Catholic State pursued during the pontificate of Pius XI by means of the mobilization of the laity as the *longa manus* of the hierarchy, the evolution passes through the hesitant and conditional, but in the end irreversible, acceptance of the idea of democracy by Pius XII,[69] and the positions taken by John XXIII regarding the rights of man in his encyclical *Pacem in terris.* Finally, Vatican Council II and the postconciliar social Magisterium, which culminates, as mentioned, in the encyclical *Centesimus annus* of John Paul II and the second part of Benedict XVI's *Deus caritas est,* indicate a decisive turn.

The Problem in the Nineteenth Century: The Weight of a Centuries-Old Canonical and Theological Tradition

The reactions of the Church to modern liberal claims were characterized, from the time of the French Revolution, by lack of understanding, fear, and defensive reactions, originating not only from the at times aggressively anticlerical way in which these claims were put forth, but—as noted above—

68. "The Almighty, therefore, has given the charge of the human race to two powers, the ecclesiastical and the civil, the one being set over divine, and the other over human, things. *Each in its kind is supreme,* each has fixed limits within which it is contained, limits which are defined by the nature and special object of the province of each, so that there is, we may say, an orbit traced out within which the action of each is brought into play by its own native right" (Leo XIII, Encyclical *Immortale dei,* 1885; cit. according to http://www.vatican.va). For the Latin text (which, strangely, is not available at this site) see *Enchiridion delle encicliche 3* (Bologna: Edizioni Dehoniane, 1999), 342.

69. Christmas message *Benignitas* of December 24, 1944. The problem appears in statements such as the following: "A healthy democracy founded on the immutable principles of the natural law and of revealed truths, will be resolutely opposed to that corruption which attributes to the legislation of the State a power without controls or limits, and which also makes of the democratic regime, despite vain appearances to the contrary, a pure and simple system of absolutism" (trans. from the text cit. according to www.totustuus.biz/users/magistero/p12benig.htm). One sees the clear and correct intention along the lines of a subjection of power to law and morality, but also a profound incomprehension of the institutional reality and the intrinsic political rationality of modern democracy in a pluralistic society, which of its nature cannot offer such guarantees.

also from a fundamental incomprehension on the part of the Church of the liberal, constitutionalist, and secular project.[70] Besides the aspects already mentioned, this incomprehension was rooted in the survival in theology and canon law, practically unaltered, of frames of thought originating in the Middle Ages and in the tradition of political Augustinianism, and the corresponding interpretation of the principles of the primacy of the *spiritualia* over the *temporalia* (the interpretation, i.e., that the *potestas* of temporal princes must be at the service of the *auctoritas* of the spiritual power). Even more problematic was the fact that these mental schemes were present in their typically modern form of the "confessional State," which was ideally Catholic. On this basis, the Church could not accept any political proposal that meant the dissolution of the juridical—and therefore also political—bond between religious truth, temporal power, and citizens' rights, as in fact liberalism and secular constitutionalism intended to do. The Church could not accept a State—a political power—indifferent toward religious truth. Also unacceptable was a conception of freedom and of civil rights recognized as independent with respect to religious truth, regardless of whether their use was "true" or "erroneous" (given that it was held that "only the truth has rights, not error").

In the condemnation by Pius IX's encyclical *Quanta cura* of Catholic liberalism and "modern freedoms," particularly the religious freedom that Charles de Montalembert demanded (in 1863 at the Congress of Malines) to be recognized by the Church, the traditional principle was still operative according to which the Church claimed its right to be able to use the coercion of the secular arm, certainly not to impose the Christian faith on nonbelievers (something that the Church has always held to be illicit), but to prevent the Catholic faithful from abandoning the faith, that is, to discipline them in cases where they fall into heresy.[71] The principle according to which coercion would be necessary and licit to prevent apostasy and heresy, and the medieval interpretation of the principle according to which the temporal power is at the service of the supernatural end of the Church, went together with the idea that error in religious matters must be censured and repressed, even by the State authority (a principle that was of course

70. I refer the reader again to Isensee, *Die katholische Kritik an den Menschrechten*.
71. See the well-documented and thoroughly useful work (even if I do not share the traditionalist theological orientation and its rejection of the doctrine of Vatican II on religious freedom) of Bernard Lucien, *Grégoire XVI, Pie IX et Vatican II: Études sur la Liberté religieuse dans la doctrine catholique* (Tours: Éditions Forts dans la foi, 1990). On the congress of Malines and Montalembert's addresses see 163ff.

practiced in an immediate way by the organs of the Holy See in the Papal States, and was vital for the maintenance of the temporal power of the pope in these territories).

Based on such premises, "modern freedoms" appeared as doctrinal and dogmatic impossibilities, given that, logically, the freedom of the moderns would have led to the undifferentiated equality of all religious beliefs.[72] Still valid, therefore, was the classical principle expressed by St. Thomas according to which, while no one could be constrained to embrace the Christian faith (because *accipere fidem est voluntatis*), nevertheless a Christian must be constrained to not abandon it (because *tenere iam acceptam est necessitatis*).[73] This principle, stated by St. Thomas to justify coercive measures against heretics, later became a general political principle, causing "modern freedoms" to be seen as a direct attack on the faith and making necessary the protection of the faith by the State.[74]

The above-mentioned *logical* impossibility—based on traditional premises—of the acceptance of what we call "modern freedoms," is obvious: in the view of the nineteenth-century Church, such freedoms, which put the rights of persons above the "rights of truth," presupposed religious indifferentism, the denial of the truth of the Christian religion. For traditionally Catholic nations, to concede these rights of freedom—and especially the civil right of religious freedom, conscience, and worship—was, from such a view, the equivalent of a collective and public apostasy. This, in fact, was precisely the argument with which Pius VI in 1791 condemned the French Declaration of the Rights of Man and of the Citizen.[75]

72. Various reports of expert theologians in the trial of Lammenais were along these lines, material that has been fully published in French; see *La condamnation de Lammenais,* Dossier présenté par M. J. Le Guillou et Louis Le Guillou (Paris: Beauchesne, 1982).

73. *Summa theologica* II-II, 10, 8, ad 3: "Acceptance of the faith is a matter of the will, whereas keeping the faith, when once one has received it, is a matter of obligation. Wherefore heretics should be compelled to keep the faith."

74. Thus the argumentation of Luigi Bilio, charged with drawing up *Quanta cura*: see Lucien, *Grégoire XVI, Pie IX et Vatican II,* 180–90. Bilio in fact defended, as essentially traditional and Catholic, the licitness of recourse to the "material force" of the state in favor of the true religion. He considered as heretical, for example, the principle of liberal Catholics that "l'Église n'a pas de droit de réprimer les violateurs de ses lois par des peines temporelles" (ibid., 185). For Bilio and the entire process of the redaction of *Quanta cura* see also Giacomo Martina, S.J., *Pio IX (1851–1866)* (Rome: Editrice Pontificia Università Gregoriana, 1986), 315–48.

75. Pius VI, *Quod aliquantum* (March 10, 1791): the Holy Father emphasizes the difference "quod intercedit inter homines qui extra gremium Ecclesiae semper fuerunt, quales sunt infideles et Judaei, atque inter illos, qui se Ecclesiae ipsi per susceptum baptismi sacramentum sujecerunt. *Primi etenim constringi ad catholicam obedientiam profitendam non debent; contra vero alteri sunt cogendi.*" In Basile Valuet, *La Liberté religieuse et la tradition catholique* (Le Barroux: Abbaye Sainte-Madeleine du Barroux, 1998), tome 2, fasc. A, 1035.

The great problem to be resolved was therefore to reconcile the modern claim of the primacy of the political—and of the consequent autonomy and secularity of the political power, as well as the ideas of popular sovereignty, democracy and the principle of majority—with the Christian claim of the primacy of the spiritual with respect to the temporal, and with the self-understanding of the Church as the voice of a truth that would be the ultimate measure not only regarding the human person's eternal destiny, but also regarding human affairs, that is, regarding the common good of the earthly city. In other words, the question was: how to reconcile the just autonomy and secularity of the political sphere—especially if organized democratically—and the freedom of conscience of citizens and their right to be immune from State oppression in religious matters, with the Church's responsibility to be the voice of a truth that includes moral criteria for judging the exercise of political power and the ordering of human society?

The first solution, proposed in the nineteenth century by the Jesuit theologians charged by Pius IX with defending Catholic principles in print through the magazine *La Civiltà Cattolica*,[76] was the distinction between "thesis" and "hypothesis."[77] By "thesis" was understood universal, Catholic, traditional, and integral doctrine—in this case, the defense of the Catholic State and of the principle that only truth has the right to exist, and consequently the denial of a right to religious freedom for those who do not profess the true religion. By "hypothesis," on the other hand, was meant the acceptance, to the end of arriving at a *modus vivendi* with modern culture, of modern claims and modes of action, so as to use these in the most advantageous way possible for the Church's own purposes, especially where the Church and Catholics were a minority. This was a kind of *reservatio mentalis,* an acceptance of what was inevitable, and a flexibility so as to be able to get along in the modern world, while reserving, at the doctrinal level, the principles—the "thesis"—of the Catholic tradition. Gregory XVI had already acted according to this logic, intransigently condemning all of the "modern freedoms" and the most passionate Catholic defender of these, Félicité de Lammenais, even if not by name. At the same time, however, he resisted the suggestion of his advisors to condemn the new Belgian constitution of 1831, created by liberal Catholics under the inspiration and with the direct collaboration of Lammenais himself. In the later, quasi-official version pro-

---

76. For the history of the magazine see Giuseppe de Rosa, S.J., *La Civiltà Cattolica. 150 anni al servizio della Chiesa 1850–1999*, (Rome: La Civiltà Cattolica, 1999).

77. See also Martina, *Pio IX (1851–1866)*, 349.

posed by the Jesuits of *La Civiltà Cattolica*, the distinction between "thesis" and "hypothesis" was joined to the idea that modern freedoms, accepted hypothetically, could ultimately be used to the advantage of the Catholic religion in many situations, even if, at level of the "thesis," they could not be granted to non-Catholics.[78]

This was a pragmatic solution, proposing a consideration of the theme that was somewhat schizophrenic and ultimately less than transparent, to say the least. It was also a violation of the principle of reciprocity (a right was claimed that was not granted to others), which today is clearly recognized as a moral obligation of a culture based on democratic and human rights. (In a certain way, the principle of reciprocity can even be called the soul of secular democracy.)[79] The distinction between thesis and hypothesis remained in effect until Vatican II.[80] Catholic theologians continued to maintain the idea that a right to religious freedom was incompatible with the dogma and truth of the Catholic religion.[81] This view, and with it the distinction between thesis and hypothesis, was definitively abandoned with the Vatican II declaration *Dignitatis humanae* on religious freedom, which no longer focuses on the "right of the truth," but on the right of the *person* to follow his own conscience in matters of religious practice, freely and without interference or coercion by the State, even if, from the point of view of religious truth, it is erroneous.

The declaration of Vatican II on religious freedom in fact dissolves, on the doctrinal level, the link between truth and the right to religious free-

---

78. This was the argumentation of Carlo Maria Curci, S.J., in *La Civiltà Cattolica* of October 2 1863 (Series V, vol VIII, fasc. 326): 129–49 in a famous article entitled "Il congresso cattolico di Malines e le libertà moderne" [The Catholic Congress of Malines and modern freedoms]. The article was an unofficial response to Montalembert and the liberal Catholics, as they were going to be condemned a year later in the encyclical *Quanta cura* of Pius IX. P. Curci concludes: "Those freedoms considered as a thesis, i.e. as universal principles regarding human nature in itself and the divine order, are absolutely worthy of condemnation and have been repeatedly condemned by the Roman Pontiffs.... But considered as a hypothesis, i.e. as provisions appropriate to the special conditions of this or that people, they can be legitimate; and Catholics can love and defend them, doing beautiful and useful work, when they use them, as effectively as they can, in the service of religion and of justice"(149). As Giacomo Martina says, "the hypothesis in reality triumphed over the thesis" (354); from the doctrinal point of view, however, it was a very unsatisfying situation for many.

79. John Rawls also theorized in this way in his work *Political Liberalism* of 1993. However, in my opinion the use that Rawls makes of this principle is vitiated and incorrect; see chapter 7 of this book, which was originally published as "The Political Ethos of Constitutional Democracy and the Place of Natural Law in Public Reason: Rawls' 'Political Liberalism' Revisited," *American Journal of Jurisprudence* 50 (2005): 1–70.

80. Even in Catholic political theory, as for example in the important book of the Belgian jurist Jean Dabin, *L'État ou le Politique. Essai de Définition* (Paris: Jurisprudence Générale Dalloz, 1957), 2.1, §5.

81. Still in 1952, for example, *La Civiltà Cattolica* uses the same argumentation; see Antonio Messineo, S.J., "Laicismo politico e dottrina cattolica," *La Civiltà Cattolica* 103 / Vol. II (1952): 18–28.

dom. This means that today, the Church no longer asks for *its* right to religious freedom, for the individual Catholic faithful and for the Church as an institution, based on the assertion that the Christian religion is the *true* one, while conceding at most tolerance to the adherents of other religions or confessions "to avoid greater evils." According to the doctrine of Vatican II, this right is today claimed based on the common obligation of all people to seek religious truth, and to freely adhere to it. To this is added that the temporal power is incompetent in religious matters, and therefore does not have the task of, and indeed must abstain from, giving a judgment on the truth of any religion and making it a public norm.[82] It is also important to emphasize that *Dignitatis humanae* does not make the right to religious freedom depend on the truth of the religion that one confesses; indeed, it attributes this right also to those who do not seek the truth at all. As a civil right, therefore, the right to religious freedom has a formal, procedural, and negative character, which is to say *against the State*, as the protection of a personal space of freedom into which the public power must not enter. The limits of this right are formulated based not on religious criteria, but solely on *political* criteria, in reference to that aspect of the common good that is called the "public order" (which includes public morality).[83]

The Problem of the Acceptance of the Ethos of Secular Democracy: From Pius XII to the Encyclical *Centesimus Annus*

The historical path leading to an authentic recognition, including at the doctrinal level, of political (and economic) modernity—even if in a suitably critical way and with appropriate reservations—is completed only with the encyclical *Centesimus annus* of John Paul II. The Church's social doctrine, as well, enters a new phase with this encyclical.[84] This change is particu-

---

82. With this the classical vision is abandoned, which was expressed by Messineo in 1952 ("Laicismo politico e dottrina cattolica," 24–25): "The juridical equality of all cults, above all, cannot be sustained, if one does not want to ignore the transcendence of the Christian religion and its divine origin ... to be applicable, all religions would have to have the same value.... That is, the consequence of the juridical equality of the cults could not come about again except by the failure to recognize that the Catholic religion is the only true religion and that the Catholic Church is the only true Church."

83. With the concept of "public morality," one touches on a difficult theme, since, as with violations of the public order in general, violations of public morality must also be defined by law. For this reason, what is juridically valid as public morality cannot be defined at a pre-political and general level, but is the result of the legislative process and has, therefore, a politically consensual character. In other words: even the concept of public morality does not escape the logic of democracy. Consequently, the standards of public morality always depend on the society and on the culture (which shows the responsibility of Christians in this regard).

84. This thesis is further justified in my essay, "La realtà politica ed economica del mondo mod-

larly evidenced with respect to the Church's doctrine on democracy and the recognition of its specific ethos.

This ethos, within the limits formulated by the constitution (and therefore within the limits of fundamental rights, both human and of citizens), is formal and procedural. The democratic decision-making process, even if linked to rules and constitutional limitations of sovereignty, is a continually open process. As Böckenförde has written, good electoral law is more important for modern democracy than good scholastic law. Moreover, democracy cannot coercively guarantee particular requirements of natural law; it can only be open to them, that is, make their realization possible by means of the democratic process. More important, therefore, than the realization of specific postulates of justice, even if these remain indispensable at the level of the constitutional foundation, is the goal of realizing the peaceful coexistence of free persons in a pluralistic society, who seek a common good that is nonetheless not pre-defined.[85]

This idea is in conflict with the tradition of the social doctrine of the Church, in that the Church in the past made the acceptance of a political system dependent on the fact that it would offer guarantees assuring a minimum of requirements at the level of natural law (according to the Catholic interpretation) and of substantial values. In this spirit, the Church typically declared its "indifference" toward all political systems, *assuming* they respect these fundamental truths and demands. Based on this traditional "doctrine of indifference," the acceptance of democracy posed a problem, given that democracy, by its nature, cannot offer such guarantees. Thus, when Pius XII expressed a hope for the acceptance of modern democracy on the part of the Church toward the end of World War II, he still understood the legitimacy of any democratic system to be dependent on these doctrinal presuppositions. In his famous Christmas radio message in 1944 on "healthy democracy," he linked his acceptance to a series of substantial demands having to do not with constitutional limitations along the lines of fundamental freedoms and the rights of citizens, but with limits of a moral and doctrinal type. Pius XII did not understand democracy as a *procedure*

---

erno e i suoi presupposti etici e culturali. L'enciclica Centesimus annus," in *Giovanni Paolo teologo—Nel segno delle encicliche*, ed. Graziano Borgonovo and Arturo Cattaneo, preface by Camillo Card. Ruini (Rome: Edizioni Arnoldo Mondadori, 2003), 83–94.

85. Ernst-Wolfgang Böckenförde, "Das Ethos der modernen Demokratie und die Kirche," in Böckenförde, *Der deutsche Katholizismus im Jahre 1933. Kirche und demokratisches Ethos*, Schriften zu Staat—Gesellschaft—Kirche, Band 1 (Freiburg: Herder, 1988), 21–38; the cited passages: 29 and 33.

capable of reconciling divergent interests in a pluralistic society and of creating compromise, a political order continually open to solutions that could be, though *democratically legitimate*, nonetheless erroneous from a moral and religious point of view, and in opposition to what the Church holds to be required by natural law. Even if Pius XII made a decisive step with his acceptance of the idea of democracy, this radio message can be interpreted as a final attempt by the Church's spiritual authority to lay conditions on the political autonomy of the modern State, even if only at the doctrinal level, by stipulating *moral conditions of its legitimacy*—though still without adequately understanding its properly political nature in the modern sense.

It would be unfair, however, to evaluate Pius XII's intervention in favor of democracy only from this perspective. Under the impression left by the totalitarianisms of the twentieth century and the wars they provoked, and also considering the traditional antidemocratic attitude of not a few pastors of the Church—which certainly weakened their ability to resist the attraction especially of authoritarian and fascist movements, and to recognize their at times even totalitarian character[86]—the intervention of Pius XII represented a real change. From today's perspective, however, one cannot avoid also seeing the limitations and insufficiencies of this step in 1944.

One can better understand the still limited and unsatisfactory character of this early recognition of democracy if the doctrine on democracy of Pius XII is compared with that of John Paul II in the encyclical *Centesimus annus* (which itself goes well beyond the doctrine of Vatican II, expressed in the pastoral constitution *Gaudium et spes*). A superficial reading of John Paul II's encyclical could lead one to think that such a difference doesn't exist. The following frequently cited passage from the fifth chapter (n. 46) might especially suggest this:

Nowadays there is a tendency to claim that agnosticism and skeptical relativism are the philosophy and the basic attitude which correspond to democratic forms of political life. Those who are convinced that they know the truth and firmly adhere to it are considered unreliable from a democratic point of view, since they do not accept

---

86. A famous case was that of the German bishops who—as, for example, Cardinal Faulhaber of Munich, who despised the democratic system—had a certain sympathy with the authoritarian traits of the National Socialist state; they condemned its extreme racist ideology, without, however, losing hope of arriving at an understanding with the forces that were considered to be less extreme (among whom some, such as Faulhaber, counted even Hitler). It was an enormous error of judgment that, in part, explains a certain propensity, in 1933, to come to an agreement with the new regime, and the subsequent line of action of the German bishops. See also on this the famous essay of 1961, which, though controversial, is certainly worthy of consideration, of Ernst-Wolfgang Böckenförde, "Der deutsche Katholizismus im Jahre 1933," in the volume by the same title cited in the previous note, 39–71.

that truth is determined by the majority, or that it is subject to variation according to different political trends. It must be observed in this regard that if there is no ultimate truth to guide and direct political activity, then ideas and convictions can easily be manipulated for reasons of power. As history demonstrates, a democracy without values easily turns into open or thinly disguised totalitarianism.

The decisive difference from Pius XII, however, consists in the fact that John Paul II speaks here not of the *conditions of legitimacy* of democracy, but of the *conditions of its maintenance*. The cited text, that is, speaks of the possible degeneration of a democracy toward a totalitarian system, but it does not teach the prerequisites to be fulfilled so that a democratic system may be accepted and *legitimate*. With this, John Paul II recognizes an essential characteristic of modern democracy: its openness to abuse, without the system for this fact losing its procedural and *political* legitimacy. This, therefore, is the minimum requirement for the recognition of the autonomy of politics, of the State and of the democratic system: it is not necessary that every democratic decision be recognized as *morally valid;* it is enough to recognize such decisions, even if considered morally invalid, as *politically legitimate*. And even if they are politically legitimate, they can always be criticized from a moral perspective, without for this violating the autonomy of the political.

It is significant in this context that *Centesimus annus* no longer mentions the traditional "doctrine of indifference"; or rather, it mentions it in a radically new way, stating that the Church "respects the *legitimate autonomy of the democratic order* and is not entitled to express preferences for this or that institutional or constitutional solution" (n. 47). And even if it is not said explicitly, according to *Centesimus annus* the "legitimate political order" seems to be equivalent to "democratic political order." Whereas traditionally (and prior to the rise of the totalitarian states) the Church in essence was indifferent toward all political systems *except democracy*, which was rejected, now it declares itself indifferent toward all political systems *assuming they are democratic* (in the sense defined by the encyclical). The condition of the recognition of a democratic system is, as expressed in no. 47, its guarantee of human rights. Democracy must be integrated in a constitutional order that guarantees these fundamental rights.[87]

87. Given that in no. 47, the encyclical mentions in a privileged way among these rights the right to life, which includes "to develop in the mother's womb from the moment of conception," one could argue that a democracy that permits abortion would lose its *legitimacy* (and we are back again to where we were with Pius XII). This does not seem, however, to be the intention of John Paul II, who a few

This "preferential option" for modern democracy is now based on a more realistic and adequate conception of it, as is expressed at the beginning of the fifth chapter (n. 44): modern democracy is seen as integrated into a system characterized by "legislation capable of protecting the freedom of all. To that end, it is preferable that each power be balanced by other powers and by other spheres of responsibility which keep it within proper bounds. This is the principle of 'the rule of law,' in which the law is sovereign, and not the arbitrary will of individuals." It is precisely on this basis— the Anglo-Saxon tradition of the constitutional State and the rule of law— that the Church today accepts and respects the democratic system. (This is the decisive element still lacking in the doctrine of the conciliar constitution *Gaudium et spes,* which emphasizes almost exclusively the participative aspect of democracy, an inadequate concept of it.)

When *Centesimus annus* says finally in no. 46 that "freedom attains its full development only by accepting the truth" and that "in a world without truth, freedom loses its foundation and man is exposed to the violence of passion and to manipulation, both open and hidden," it does not fall back into an anachronistic position that would make the legitimacy of political freedom depend on its link with religious truth. These words are an appeal not to the "State" or to State authority and its coercive governmental apparatus, but to the responsibility of Christian citizens who are involved in various ways in political life. Thus it continues: "The Christian upholds freedom and serves it, constantly offering to others the truth which he has known (cf. Jn 8:31–32), in accordance with the missionary nature of his vocation. While paying heed to every fragment of truth which he encounters in the life experience and in the culture of individuals and of nations, he will not fail to affirm in dialogue with others all that his faith and the correct use of reason have enabled him to understand." The hermeneutical key for reading this passage was already provided in the preceding paragraph, which speaks of "the danger of fanaticism or fundamentalism among those who, in the name of an ideology which purports to be scientific or religious, claim

---

lines below mentions the "scandal of abortion" as one of the aspects "of a crisis within democracies themselves, which seem at times to have lost the ability to make decisions aimed at the common good." Even if the right to life is obviously a fundamental human right, without the recognition of which a democratic system would lose its *legitimacy,* the "scandal of abortion" does not mean that our democracies have arrived at this point of illegitimacy, but rather that the *understanding* of the right to life, which is clearly recognized by all secular democracies, is in crisis (since they exclude from this right and thus discriminate against the unborn, with the argument, e.g., that they are not persons).

the right to impose on others their own concept of what is true and good."
The Church intends to abandon this way of "imposition," since *Christian
truth* is not of this kind. Since it is not an ideology, the Christian faith does
not presume to imprison changing socio-political realities in a rigid sche-
ma, and it recognizes that human life is realized in history in conditions
that are diverse and imperfect." Christianity is not an ideology or a political program that tends to a perfect realization. On the contrary, "constantly
reaffirming the transcendent dignity of the person, the Church's method is
always that of respect for freedom."

Present-Day Church Doctrine on Democracy and the Secular State

In my opinion, despite this most recent doctrinal clarification, not all
problems have been resolved. A final step is still lacking—a step that the
Church could obviously never take. This would be the step of the Church
putting itself, so to speak, at the level of the democratic system and the secular State, of understanding itself as part of these, and with this proclaiming a secular, democratic political doctrine, fully adapted to the nature of
modern democracy, as a doctrine of the Church. Because the Church cannot
do this, there will always be a certain inevitable and necessary ambivalence
in its social teaching and in its actions in the public forum, regarding its
recognition of the autonomy of the State and of politics.

Given that the Church could never understand itself as part of the secular State and the democratic system, it does not need to integrate the self-
understanding of these into its own Magisterium. Which is to say that it
does not need to become a teacher of politics, secularity, and democracy—
the idea would be ridiculous! The doctrine of the Church could never be a
properly *political* doctrine, that is, a doctrine on the essence of the democratic and secular constitutional State, because this is a question for philosophy, for political science, for sociology, and so on. The Church can give
a judgment concerning political realities only from its specific doctrinal and
pastoral perspective, a perspective that defends the transcendent dignity of
the human person and the temporal conditions that respect that dignity. Ultimately, therefore, the Church gives its evaluation of secular democracy in
the light of the two great principles that have been present from the beginning of its history: the primacy of the spiritual over the temporal, and the

ordering of what is earthly and temporal to what is heavenly and eternal.

More than providing a doctrine on the nature, legitimacy, and functioning of modern democracy, the Church, in fulfillment of its pastoral task, offers —and is fully justified in doing so—its own conceptual *ideal* of democracy, full of substantial values that can be realized democratically, along with a conception of the common good. This does not mean that the Church wants to make the *legitimacy* of democracy depend on the effective realization of these values, or on a particular conception of the common good; this would be contrary to the nature of democracy as a political order, which is by its nature open to a plurality of conceptions of the common good that differ among themselves. While not being formulated as a condition of legitimacy, however, the Church's conception can and must be defended *within* the democratic process. In a democratically organized society, the Church's position would be only one *political* position among others—though proposed with the weight of its spiritual authority, which, depending on circumstances, is more or less recognized—partially or wholly adopted by individual citizens involved in politics and by particular political parties, without making the legitimacy of the democratic process itself depend on the effective realization of the substantial conception of the common good the Church holds to be true. The Church's social teaching, and the public positions it takes up, are not to be understood as a new form of the exercise of a *potestas indirecta,* given that such a *potestas* simply doesn't exist based on the premises of the secular State and modern democracy.

In its social doctrine, therefore, the Church proposes only a doctrine regarding *its ideal conception* of democracy, the State, the economy, and the like. For this reason its concept of the secularity of the State and of democracy, while being reasonable and true, is perhaps a concept that cannot be generalized democratically. In democracy's public forum, what the Church proposes as a doctrine of the secularity of the State can be only *its* conception of the secularity of the State, of democracy, of the economic order, and of the natural law. To avoid misunderstandings, it is important that this point be grasped correctly: the voice of the Church proposes a truth, but not an institutional or a procedural alternative to democracy. It means to admonish, not to delegitimize; and even if it condemns certain legislative solutions or political moves, it does not invite disloyalty toward democratic institutions, but their different use within the rules of the constitution.

I am convinced that the conception of democracy and the common good that the Church proposes is a conception that is not only valid, but also entirely reasonable and in accordance with the truth of man and his genuine dignity. This, however, does not in any way change the fact that—precisely because of the secularity of the State and its corresponding political-functional autonomy—this conception must present itself in the democratic process as only one of the various competing conceptions, which attempt to prevail through the existing constitutional procedures and the corresponding political process. It would be incompatible with the acceptance of modern democracy for the Church to turn the effective realization of its substantial conception of the good society and of the common good into a *condition of legitimacy* of democracy (which would also imply inciting Catholic citizens loyal to the Church to rebel against the constitutional order or, at least, to behave according to the logic of the historical *non expedit* of Pius IX, i.e., in disloyalty toward this order).

Even if it is true that ethical relativism is a real danger for democracy, democracy itself is based on a certain "relativism" of a political nature: a specifically political relativism, politically justified, which makes a plurality of political conceptions and conceptions of justice possible without a priori determining which is better or more just—that is, it does this institutionally. As a political order, the democratic constitutional State intends to formulate the rules according to which decisions can be made on conceptions of politics and of justice; it does not presuppose these conceptions. In this precise sense, every true democracy is both politically and functionally relativist —which is to say open.

This functional and political relativism must be distinguished from what I would call the *categorical foundation of values* of a democratic order (human rights and the fundamental rights of citizens). It is this foundation that is directly corrupted by what the Church denounces as ethical relativism. Even if here the Church's voice as the voice of truth is considered to be particularly important—as the Church itself in fact claims—this voice, to say it again, can *be made effective* only by means of the democratic process itself. This, in essence, is acceptance of the secular State and of secular democracy: the Church accepts being able to realize its conception of the truth only through a process that, by its nature, is also open to other conceptions, that is, through a political process precisely of a secular character. Even the authoritative and legally binding interpretation of basic human and civil rights is part of the political process. Only one who accepts this fact as a characteristic and requirement that is both inexorable and *just* also accepts the secularity of the State. At the same time, however, it must be asserted: one who is a member of a democratic society has the right to participate in this public process of the interpretation of the fundamental and human rights of the citizen. The interpretation of these rights proposed by the Catholic Church today is certainly an interpretation compatible with democracy and with the secularity of the State; indeed, it can strengthen them.

Part 2. The Present: Modern Democracy, the Secular State, and the Spiritual Mission of the Church: Ideas for a "Healthy" Political Conception of Secularity

Two Forms of Secularity: Political and Integralist Conceptions of Secularity

Religious Freedom and Secularity

As we have seen, the declaration of the Second Vatican Council on religious freedom, *Dignitatis humanae,* dissolves the link between the right to religious freedom (freedom of conscience and worship) and truth. This is a separation at the juridical and political level, which does not imply the nonexistence of religious truth or that all religions are equal. It is a position of *political* indifference—of the State—not of a *theological* indifference or "indifferentism." With its doctrine on the right to religious freedom, therefore, the Church after Vatican II recognizes the secularity of the State as the institutional separation between religion and politics.

Nevertheless, in the Church's view, this political indifference of the State and of public persons with respect to religious truth (not necessarily, however, of statesmen, i.e., of politicians as citizens who are co-responsible for the common good) does not mean that the State may not, and even must not—always respecting the culture of the country in question—help religious communities and their faithful create the conditions that will allow them to live according to their religious beliefs (especially with respect to worship and education). Religious freedom and the corresponding neutrality of the State do not mean a-religiosity or public "atheism." A public atheism would not be religious neutrality, but a creed, albeit negative, of an antireligious character. Antinomy and the *denial* of something—in this case of religion and every theist belief—are never "neutral" positions! Atheism and agnosticism are *not* neutral positions regarding religion! Rather, they are extreme and very partial positions given that, depending on the case, they are the denial of the truth, value, and existential relevance of *every* religion—at times even asserting their harmfulness! The neutral position is rather one that abstains from any evaluation regarding the truth of either position. The kind of behavior to which impartiality would lead from case to case remains an open question that depends on the concrete cultural circumstances of each country.[88] Clearly, an attitude of political neutrality cannot close its eyes to the presence of a religion that is a traditional and majority cultural reality in a given country.

Moreover, religious freedom and the corresponding neutrality of the State are compatible with a public recognition, even if nonconfessional, of the existence of a divine transcendence, and with the facilitation of the religious practice of the various believers, according to their own self-understanding. This is shown by the practice of a great number of countries, and the constitutional texts of many European and non-European countries, which, fully respecting the secularity of the State and the religious freedom of their citizens, do not reduce religion to a purely private matter.[89] Nonetheless, in the logic of the secularity of the State and in a constitutionally pluralistic political society, any recognition of religious practices is based not on a judgment concerning the truth of a specific religion, but, as we shall see, on criteria of political justice.

There is, however, an understanding of secularity that goes beyond the requirements of the neutrality and autonomy of the temporal power with respect to claims of truth. It holds that religion—every religion—is a type of belief and practice that must be relegated entirely to the sphere of the private life of citizens, because in itself it would be a competition and even a contradiction with a secular political culture. In this view, religious freedom means not so much the right of the citizen to exercise his religion according to the dictates of his conscience, limited only by the requirements of public order and morality, but the freedom (or liberation) of the State and the public sphere *from* religion and its influence. In what follows, I will call this form of secularity the "integralist conception of secularity" or "secular

---

88. The theme is studied from a historical, philosophical, and juridical perspective by Arnd Uhle, *Staat—Kirche—Kultur* (Berlin: Duncker & Humblot, 2004).

89. This has been well-emphasized by the Jewish jurist Joseph H. H. Weiler, *Ein christliches Europa: Erkundungsgänge* (Salzburg: Anton Pustet, 2004).

integralism," which I will distinguish from a merely "political" understanding of secularity, articulated and limited as such.

Before describing these two forms of secularity, however, I would like to justify this terminological choice. Both "secularity" and "laicism" are flexible terms, and in the course of history they have not always been used univocally.[90] According to their origin in France at the end of the nineteenth century, *laïcité* and *laïcisme* mean (1) complete separation between Church and State and (2) maximum possible reduction of the influence of the Church on public life. In this context, "laicism" is the antithesis of "clericalism," the latter in the sense of a certain domination, including institutional and coercive, of the ecclesial hierarchy (i.e., the clergy) in society and public life. Thus the French politician Gambetta ended his famous speech of May 4, 1877, with the cry: "Clericalism? It is the enemy."[91] In the twentieth century, however, various forms of secularism or laicism developed that were not so anticlerical or anti-Catholic and, in fact, not too far from what the Church today accepts as a "healthy secularity of the State."[92]

The fact is that in most languages, the term "laicism" means an understanding of secularity in a politically antireligious sense. Even the contemporary Magisterium of the Church continues to use the term "laicism" exclusively in this negative sense. Initially, I thought of proposing the distinction between two types of laicism: one unhealthy, and the other corresponding to the conception of a "healthy secularity of the State." It does not seem wise, however, to go against the already established terminology. Even if I respect, therefore, the negative connotation of the term "laicism," it nevertheless seems opportune to observe that certain essential aspects of the traditional "laicism" that were once opposed by the Church are today recognized as positive, or as aspects of what the Church itself now calls a "healthy secularity" of the State; indeed, some of these aspects were explicitly condemned by the earlier Magisterium, such as that of Pius VI, Gregory XVI, and especially Pius IX, especially those aspects regarding the separation of Church and State.

90. Useful are the entries *Laicismo,* by T. Goffi and G. Dalla Torre, and *Laico-Laicità,* by G. Dalla Torre, in the *Enciclopedia Filosofica* (Fondazione Centro di Studi Filosofici di Gallarate) (Milan: Bompiani, 2006), 6:6169ff.

91. See Jean Marie Mayeur, *La question laïque. XIXe et XXe siècle* (Paris: Fayard, 1997), 41. (This seems to be a paraphrase of the anti-Semitic cry "the Jew is the enemy," which was very popular at that time, including in certain circles of the French clergy, especially in the Catholic newspaper *La Croix*).

92. For a documented history of anticlericalism in France see René Rémond, *L'anticléricalisme en France de 1815 à nos jours,* new rev. and expanded ed. (Paris: Fayard, 1999).

This must be kept firmly in mind when reading texts such as the classic statement of Pius XI in the encyclical *Quas primas* of 1925:

> We refer to the plague of anti-clericalism [the original says: "so-called laicism"], its errors and impious activities. This evil spirit, as you are well aware, Venerable Brethren, has not come into being in one day; it has long lurked beneath the surface. The empire of Christ over all nations was rejected. The right which the Church has from Christ himself, to teach mankind, to make laws, to govern peoples in all that pertains to their eternal salvation, that right was denied. Then gradually the religion of Christ came to be likened to false religions and to be placed ignominiously on the same level with them. It was then put under the power of the State and tolerated more or less at the whim of princes and rulers. Some men went even further, and wished to set up in the place of God's religion a natural religion consisting in some instinctive affection of the heart. There were even some nations who thought they could dispense with God, and that their religion should consist in impiety and the neglect of God.[93]

To conceive of "laicism" (or "anticlericalism") as the "rejection of the empire of Christ over all nations" and the denial of the Church's "right … to teach mankind, to make laws, to govern peoples in all that pertains to their eternal salvation," although this could be understood in an exclusively spiritual and pastoral way, in the context in which it was formulated—a lament over the loss of the "Christian" or "Catholic State"—represented also a condemnation of that "healthy secularity" of the State that is today accepted by the Church, lamenting as well the loss of the indirect power of the Church over temporal affairs (a power that was justified precisely "for the good of souls," i.e., for "their eternal salvation"). The vision of Pius XI took up again that of Pius VI, when the latter condemned the right to religious freedom of the French Revolution as the apostasy of an entire nation from the Catholic faith. From this same perspective, though in a different context, Pius XI called laicism an "apostasy of contemporary society which wants to distance itself from God and thus from the Church."[94]

Before such a conception of "laicism," it seems to me useful to identify, using the "political concept of secularity," that ingredient of "secularity" that is acceptable and justifiable, is recognized today by the Church, *and was already present*—together with other completely unacceptable elements—in the traditional forms of laicism that were rejected by the Magisterium of the above-mentioned popes.

93. Cit. according to *Welcome to the Catholic Church on CD-ROM* (Brooks, Ore.: Harmony Media, 2006).

94. Pius XI, *Dilectissima Nobis*, June 3, 1933; trans. from *Enchiridion delle Encicliche, 5: Pio XI* (Bologna: Edizioni Dehoniane, 1995), 943 (the document is addressed to the Church in Spain).

The Political Concept of Secularity

The essence of what I call the "political concept of secularity"[95] can be defined as the exclusion from the public political and juridical sphere of every normativity that would make reference to a religious *truth*—precisely as truth—and with that, neutrality and public indifference with respect to any claim of truth in religious matters. In addition, even though a secular State does not adopt criteria of truth in religious matters, it would deal with the various religions, applying criteria of political justice, which include impartiality and neutrality. This is compatible with the recognition, including on the educational level, of the importance of the religious dimension as a source of culture and moral orientation for citizens and as a stimulus to social commitment.[96]

This does not mean that the State is "believing," but rather that the public life of a country is not closed a priori to the presence of the religious dimension of human existence. This religious dimension is never an abstract or ahistorical fact, but is always shaped according to the real history of a people, a nation, or an entire civilization. The religious dimension of human existence can thus be present in the life of a country only in the form of a concrete religion and in the institutional form pertaining to it. (In a society that is highly pluralistic religiously, as for example the United States of America, such a public presence of religion would also necessarily reflect that pluralism.) A secularism that would deny the public relevance of religion, or would want to remove every religious reference from consideration in the public sphere, would be a political position that is ahistorical, rigidly doctrinaire, and abstract.[97] Such an "integralist" concept of secularity might even acquire the form of a true "cultural revolution," promoted by the ruling class of a country, as was the case for example in the French republicanism of the Third Republic in the final decades of the nineteenth

95. I propose this term in a certain analogy with the concept of "political liberalism" as it has been elaborated by John Rawls, even if I differ from him in important aspects. See the above-cited chapter 7 of this volume, "The Political Ethos of Constitutional Democracy and the Place of Natural Law in Public Reason: Rawls's 'Political Liberalism' Revisited."

96. Conversely, when the State ceases to be secular, and recognizes and pays homage to a particular religious truth, it also subjects itself to the supreme interpretive competence of the respective religious and spiritual authority and its consequent supremacy in defining the public and civil implications of that truth.

97. Even if, it must be admitted, a phenomenon like French *laïcité* is understood precisely historically, i.e., as a defense of the Republic against legitimist and monarchic clericalism; after more than a century, however, maybe it is time to look more to the future than to the past.

century.[98] In any case, this type of secularity would in no way be "neutral" in the proper sense of the word.[99]

The secular State—"secular" in a merely political sense, "nonintegralist" —in place of a religious or confessional identity of political and civic life, substitutes a secular, political identity, an ideal of citizenship and of the common good. It entirely separates the rights of citizens and their exercise from religious belonging or confession. It understands the ethos of peace, freedom, and equality inherent in the idea of the democratic constitutional State as an authentically political value with its own intrinsic legitimacy, in itself independent of any religious creed and capable of forming and animating a political society and an ethic of citizenship common to all, whatever their religious creed may be. The secular State is not, therefore, a multicultural State, at least not in the political and civic sense: "the secularity of the State" cannot mean systemic multiculturalism. "Multiculturalism" in a strict sense means a lack of cultural unity; "political" and systemic multiculturalism is rather the lack of a unified and unifying political culture. The secular ethos of the democratic constitutional State is a true political *culture* with its own ethos, and a unifying force for social and public life, defining itself through a common project rather than in multicultural or culturally particularistic terms.[100] Or, as Gian Enrico Rusconi, with whom I agree on this point, wrote: "The secular principle ... does not limit itself to affirming the principle of a benevolent tolerance, but positively demands a mutual bond on which to construct a political community characterized by solidarity, in that it loyally recognizes, in principle, rules and institutions which prescind from particular cultural roots that cannot be generalized."[101]

The political conception of secularity admits a foundation of values, beyond properly political institutions, and accepts authorities that promote

98. See Claude Nicolet, *L'Idée républicaine en France (1794–1924): Essai d'histoire critique* (Paris: Gallimard, 1982); idem, *République et laïcité*, in Nicolet, *La république en France. État des lieux* (Paris: Éditions du Seuil, 1992), 100–121; Mayeur, *La question laïque*.

99. Even if, as in the above-mentioned case of France, it also possesses some understandable aspects, such as that of promoting secular public schools in a society in which Catholics, including the clergy, generally adhered to the monarchic tradition of the *ancien régime* and were openly anti-republican; this was an effort to form republican citizens, loyal to the institutions of the republic, and to break what was considered an illegitimate *political* power of the Catholic Church and the clergy.

100. See also chapter 11 of this volume, "Multicultural Citizenship in Liberal Democracy: The Proposals of C. Taylor, J. Habermas, and W. Kymlicka," originally published as "Cittadinanza multiculturale nella democrazia liberale: le proposte di Ch. Taylor, J. Habermas e W. Kymlicka," *Acta Philosophica* 15, no. 1 (2006): 29–52. The perspective of Will Kymlicka seems to me to be particularly pertinent, in his book *Multicultural Citizenship: A Liberal Theory of Minority Rights* (Oxford: Oxford University Press, 1995).

101. Rusconi, *Possiamo fare a meno di una religione civile?* (Rome-Bari: Laterza, 1999), 74.

them, even critically, with respect to the political power. It also allows for the presence in the public discourse of values derived from religious beliefs, when they are appropriately adapted to the political discourse in such a way that they can be understood and accepted by all citizens, and generalized.[102] The secularity of the State as promoted by a *political* conception of that secularity is not so much a "secular project" as it is a political morality of peaceful coexistence, respect, and guarantees of the freedom of citizens. *It leaves the society free, however, to formulate its own project of values,* without imposing a project of "secularization" *of* the society through the coercive force of the public power—even if democratically legitimate—as does secular integralism. For this reason merely political secularity has need of a political morality of citizenship, of that mutual bond that defines what the German political theorist Dolf Sternberger has called *Verfassungspatriotismus* ("constitutional patriotism"), a civic attitude of loyalty to the political institutions of the democratic constitutional State and to its "rules of the game," even if many times this means renouncing the realization of values that one considers of higher worth, or an integral project regarding one's own conception of the good society.

The "Comprehensive" Concept of Secularity (or "Secular Integralism")

The "comprehensive" (in the sense of Rawls) or *integralist concept of secularity* (or "secular integralism") goes beyond the mentioned "reciprocal bond" based on culturally generalizable elements. The "comprehensive" or "integralist" conception of secularity is not only a more radical variation—with respect to a merely political conception—of separation between Church and State, between politics and religion, but is something essentially different. It is a form of the exclusion of religion, and of everything that, with respect to ethics, could derive from a truth and from a teaching rooted in religious truths. I also call it "comprehensive," following the terminology of John Rawls, who calls *comprehensive doctrines* those philosophical and

---

102. In the wake of the proposals of John Rawls, there is a broad discussion on this theme with widely divergent positions, especially in the Anglo-Saxon world; for example: Robert Audi, *Religious Commitment and Secular Reason* (Cambridge: Cambridge University Press, 2000); Paul J. Weithman, *Religion and the Obligation of Citizenship* (Cambridge: Cambridge University Press, 2002); Michael J. Perry, *Religion in Politics: Constitutional and Moral Perspectives* (Oxford: Oxford University Press, 1997); and by the same author: *Under God? Religious Faith and Liberal Democracy* (Cambridge: Cambridge University Press, 2003). Recently Jürgen Habermas joined the debate, as well; see "Religion in der Öffentlichkeit. Kognitive Voraussetzungen für den 'öffentlichen Vernunftgebrauch' religiöser und säkularer Bürger," in Habermas, *Zwischen Naturalismus und Religion. Philosophische Aufsätze* (Frankfurt am Main: Suhrkamp, 2005), 119–54.

religious doctrines that deny a differentiation between political sphere and reasoning on the one hand and an integral interpretation of the world on the other. There is a secularism that is "comprehensive," "integral," or total-izing in this sense, and not only politically, because it interprets the logic of politics from a vision of the world that is, precisely, comprehensive. As with an integralist doctrine in a religious context, such a comprehensive and "secular" conception of secularity is also a form (negative, so to speak) of integralism.

This type of secularity tends to eliminate, by its nature and in principle, the distinction between power and morality. That is, it tends to exclude, at least implicitly, the fact that there are objective criteria of value, indepen-dent of the practical exercise of political power, on the basis of which the exercise of that power can be judged. Secularity of this second type not only opposes religion, but is a kind of "political exclusivism" in the sense that, in the public discourse, it accepts as criteria of morality and justice only those secular claims that are subject to the control of the political process, and as they comprise part of it (a process that obviously would ideally be demo-cratic, and therefore regulated by the principle of majority). This leads to the submission of criteria of morality and justice—unfortunately in an ever-increasing measure—to the results of surveys that show a presumed "major-ity" and "democratic" opinion (forgetting that, in parliamentary and rep-resentative democracy, the opinion of the majority must no longer express itself via plebiscite or through polls, but through election to representative institutions as provided by the constitution).[103]

Such a "secular integralism" implies a sovereignty of politics that is not only functional, but sovereign also in a moral sense, that is, the *moral* sovereignty of political facts (decisions, laws). Even if this were democrati-cally legitimated, such a moral sovereignty would be problematic, since it would cause solely the "normative force of what in fact exists" to prevail (the *normative Kraft des Faktischen,* according to the expression of the

103. "Demoscopic democracy," at least past a certain point, is in truth a grave violation of the ethos of modern parliamentary democracy, which is based on the principle of representation. Representation means competence for the whole on the part of some, appropriately deputed for the task, without them having a "political mandate," i.e., without their being elected with a mandate other than to promote the electoral platform of their party. As deputies, they do not simply represent their electors, still less the concrete, immediate preferences of the latter. Rather, as representatives, deputies must decide accord-ing to conscience and on their own responsibility—with due adherence to the discipline of their party—what they consider to be advantageous to the common good. A democracy based on polls destroys this freedom and responsibility proper to representatives, and introduces an irrational and dysfunctional plebiscitary element into the democratic process.

nineteenth-century German jurist Georg Jellinek). To the extent that such a political normativity is recognized also as a moral normativity beyond appeal, the difference between legality and legitimacy disappears, and what is legally and procedurally justified becomes what is morally legitimate. Thus the integralist conception of secularity is, in the purest sense, a type of juridical-political positivism,[104] which attempts to found a kind of new spiritual power.[105] This integralist understanding of secularity coincides in part with the old proto-totalitarian myth of the *volonté générale*, created by Rousseau, according to which the majority is always right and the minority position is mistaken and morally illegitimate. Not that the principles of legality and procedural correctness are not also moral values, but they must not be considered to be absolute values. They can always be surpassed by higher moral considerations, even those of a minority (for example, considerations of natural law, even if by this the question is not resolved of how, in a democracy, such considerations could become politically and juridically relevant;[106] what is important, for the moment, is to affirm that in a non-totalitarian or "open" political system, such considerations *can* exist and *must be able* to exist).

For all these reasons, integralist secularity sees a competitor in the religious phenomenon, an enemy to the secular character of the State. Even more importantly, it sees in it an enemy of the "secular" autonomy of the consciences of citizens. Integralist secularity is a kind of paternalism that wants to protect citizens from every religious influence—and from institutions such as the Catholic Church—an influence that it considers to be irrational and corrosive of freedom. This occurs precisely because, according to such a conception of secularity, religion speaks not in the name of a democratic procedural legitimacy or a majority principle, but in the name of a *truth*. Secular integralism, such as that at the beginning of the Third French Republic, can behave peacefully toward religion, convinced that it will die of itself as science and modern society progress,[107] but it can also become aggressively antireligious and anticlerical, as also in France from the begin-

---

104. This is also shown by the republican secularism of the Third French Republic, which was intimately linked to the positivism of Auguste Comte, who was considered the true teacher of secularism; see Nicolet, *L'idée républicaine en France*, 187–248, and passim.

105. Ibid., 268: "il s'agissait de fonder un nouveau pouvoir spirituel."

106. I have amply treated this in chapter 7 of this volume.

107. For an understanding of the ideology of the secular republic, I again refer the reader to the cited work of Claude Nicolet, *L'Idée républicaine en France*; idem, *République et laïcité*; Mayer, *La question laïque. XIIe et XXe siècle.*

ning of the twentieth century, or in the liberal Piedmont of Cavour in Italy (or perhaps better of Umberto Rattazzi, who was the one responsible for the violently anticlerical—"laicist"—radicalism of Cavour's government).[108]

Consequently, such a hostility toward religion does not seem to be due to the properly *religious* character of religion, which, as a collection of pious and cultic practices, could also ultimately be accepted by a secular State, and even helped to survive as a cultural and folkloristic fact. Rather, it must be attributed to the claim of religion to represent a truth of a higher order and a structure of objective values, capable of subjecting the exercise of political power and of civil freedom to a moral evaluation according to criteria that claim to be *true,* and able to actually exercise an influence through its public presence, for example in the education system. A secularity that understands the political process itself, when it is democratic or procedurally legitimate, as the exclusive criteria of rectitude and justice, would in any case be incapable of accepting such an axiological relativization, or the effective influence of a spiritual power such as the Catholic Church on the conscience of its citizens. It would end, therefore, by discrediting and declaring illegitimate every voice that opposes itself to its claims of being the only power. Legality and procedural justice are one thing (political, democratic legitimacy), and they are certainly moral values, but of a *political* morality (and therefore partial, limited, sectional, and relative); moral legitimacy is another thing in an exhaustive, comprehensive, or absolute sense.

What the integralist conception of secularity really opposes is any interference in the political process of a criterion of value, independent of a "secular" point of view, which understands itself to be higher and objective. "Laicists" discredit such criteria as a dogmatism that is destructive of freedom. Moreover, the "secular" points of view that are traceable to this secular integralism are not necessarily defined by a specific and proper rationality. With respect to their content, they can even coincide with "Catholic" positions (for example in the demand for the abolition of the death penalty). The "secular point of view," in fact, is simply that of those who, at a particular time, define it as "secular" because it is put forward by "laicists" (nonbelievers, non-Catholics, etc.), and that for this reason can be, according to them, legitimately imposed on the entire society through the

---

108. A concise summary can be found in Roger Aubert, *Il Pontificato di Pio IX (1846–1878),* vol. 21, pt. 1: *Storia della Chiesa,* ed. Augustine Fliche and Victor Martin, Edizioni Paoline (Milan: Cinisello Balsamo, 1990), 119–33.

democratic process. Democratically speaking, this is certainly valid, but it shows that the alarmist defense of such a "secular integralism" against the presumed intrusions of the Church (or of Catholics) is in fact a game of propaganda and political power. The reason for this is that "Catholics," as well—and even the Church itself—propose policies and legislation that, considered essentially, are fully justifiable in terms of *secular* public reasoning, but are considered by "laicists" to be "nonsecular"—and therefore not generalizable or apt to being imposed through the democratic process—merely because they are proposed by "Catholics" (or other Christians); or, as happens at times, they are officially defended by the Church, and therefore acquire the stigma of being "religious" positions. Thus, in various instances, the defense of the secular character of the State is nothing other than the refusal to enter into a true public debate on the *arguments* put forward by "non-laicist" citizens and by the Church.

Here we are faced with a political game, played by those who fear losing a majority. In these cases, the political game fails to respect one of the normative characteristics most typical of the "open society": the acceptance of any kind of opposition, assuming it respects the rules of democracy and uses generally understandable arguments and constitutionally legitimate proposals.[109]

The Autonomy of Politics and the Distinction between Political Facts and Criteria of Value

Integralist secularism, therefore, understands the autonomy of political institutions not only as political, institutional, and juridical autonomy, but—in a comprehensive sense—also as moral autonomy and therefore as the ultimate and supreme moral criteria in the effective exercise of such autonomy. This form of secularity therefore denies—at least implicitly—criteria of value that transcend mere facts and their normative force, and tends to turn the facts themselves—actual majorities, legislative measures, and so on—into supreme political values beyond moral appeal. This can be easily seen to be an authentic secular "integralism," just as it is easy to observe that, in

---

109. For more arguments, see chapter 5 of this volume, "The Open Society and the New Laicism: Against the Soft Totalitarianism of Certain Secularist Thinking," which was originally published as "Laici e cattolici: oltre le divisioni. Riflessioni sull'essenza della democrazia e della società aperta," *Fondazione Liberal* 17 (2003): 108–16 (which is a response to Gian Enrico Rusconi's book, *Come se Dio non ci fosse. I laici, i cattolici e la democrazia* [Turin: Einaudi, 2000]).

the opposition between such secular powers and the Catholic Church, the medieval structure of conflict between temporal and spiritual powers is in a certain sense repeated today.

This, in fact, is the scandal of the Christian religion—as it was in the time of pagan Rome—that is, the fact that it means to represent a truth that, without taking away the intrinsic and justly autonomous value of earthly realities, nevertheless relativizes them and subjects them to its judgment. It does not admit of an absolute created by man. It is precisely for this reason that religion is essentially hostile to every form of idolatry. There exist today, in fact, the idolatry of politics and of the State, secularized forms of the idolatry of the emperor of Roman times and of the sacralization of the political power in the Middle Ages. The scandal today is not in the fact that Christianity or the Church denies the political legitimacy and autonomy of democracy—which they don't—but in their claim to be a source and an ultimate guarantee of value, including for the democratic political community. The State is not obligated to, nor is it even able to, recognize such a claim as true. But neither can it consider the public presence of such a claim and its influence on the society and on the political life of a country as an attack on its secularity.

That not all "secularists" and adherents of liberalism deny the principle of the dichotomy between political power and values is shown by the case of Karl Popper, who is entirely above suspicion in this regard.[110] According to him, the "open society," secular and democratic, rests on the "dualism between facts and criteria": the facts (e.g., concrete laws, the legal system, institutions) might be formulated in such a way as to fail to conform—according to Popper—to "just, valid and true moral criteria." The dualism between facts and criteria implies therefore that any political or social fact—including the results of democratic processes—can be measured on the basis of moral criteria that are external to, and superior to, those processes. To deny such a dualism is the same for Popper as asserting the identification of power with the law.[111]

In his work *Conjectures and Refutations* (1963), the theoretician of the

110. See on what follows chapter 5 of this volume, and also my article *Laici e cattolici: oltre le divisioni*.

111. Popper shows this in his "Facts, Standards, and Truths: A Further Critique of Relativism," in Popper, *The Open Society and Its Enemies*, 5th ed. (Princeton, N.J.: Princeton University Press, 1971), 2:369–93. See especially section 12, "Dualism of Facts and Standards," and section 16, "The Dualism of Facts and Standards and the Idea of Liberalism."

open society articulates the reasons why, in his opinion, our present society is to be considered the best that has ever existed. Moreover, claims Popper, if this is true, it is certainly not due to its technical achievements, but because of "the standards and the values which, through Christianity, have come down to us from Greece and from the Holy Land, from Socrates and from the Old and New Testaments."[112] For Popper these values mean, above all, respect for the individual and for his inalienable dignity. He therefore clearly thinks that even an open society must rest on a stable system of values *that it is incapable of producing on its own,* and that constitutes the criteria on the basis of which its results and accomplishments must be measured; the values themselves in fact originate in a specific religious tradition.[113]

A "healthy" conception of secularity—that is, nonintegralist and noncomprehensive, but purely political—will respect the principle of the existence of objective criteria of law, justice, and political morality, independent and superior with respect to the effective exercise of every human power, and thus principles on the basis of which this exercise can be judged. A healthy secularity must not only accept, but also hope, that there would be authorities outside the political process that, in the name of a proposal of a higher truth, would step forward to oppose themselves to mere "facts" created by the political process or by an actual democratic majority (always assuming that none of these claims to truth can impose themselves on the State with coercive power, replacing the constutional order and the democratic process).

From a political point of view, it makes no difference whether these authorities are religious, scientific, or come from other groups within civil society. The only important thing—and here we touch on the central point— is that these authorities respect *the political and juridical autonomy* of the State and the procedural legitimacy of democratic processes, as provided by the constitution. In other words: what a secular point of view requires

---

112. Karl. R. Popper, *Conjectures and Refutations: The Growth of Scientific Knowledge* (London: Routledge and Kegan Paul, 1963), 69.

113. Others have said the same thing regarding the secular State, such as Ernst-Wolfgang Böckenförde in his saying, often cited and by now a classic formulation, that "the liberal, secularized State lives by presuppositions that it can no longer guarantee by itself," and because of this it must be based on something that comes from without, i.e., on the "moral substance" of its citizens and on a certain homogeneity of the society; see "Die Entstehung des Staates als Vorgang der Säkularisation," in Böckenförde, *Staat, Gesellschaft, Freiheit. Studien zur Staatstheorie und zum Verfassungsrecht* (Frankfurt: Suhrkamp, 1976), 42–61, at 60.

is not the silencing of the Church and its voice, which speaks in the name of a higher truth that many citizens in fact embrace, but the submission of the Church's actions on the public political scene to the common political and civil rules that are valid for every actor in the public sphere, leaving it, however, the full freedom to express itself and to attempt to have its reasoning prevail in the public debate (even if, with this, it exercises a real *power* in the sense of a spiritual authority that is more or less socially recognized and followed in the various situations). It is only the political authority of the State, however, that should impose laws and sanctions of any kind with coercive force and civil effects (as Marsilius of Padua had in fact asked in his day).

An "unhealthy," and even dangerous, conception of secularity, on the other hand, is one that—in the name of the autonomy of temporal things, and particularly of the secular State—rejects any kind of external judge concerning the political process itself, and tries to "protect" its citizens from every influence of religious and ethical teaching coming from a religious authority. Such a secularity—antireligious, "integral," almost fundamentalist— is, it seems to me, one of the expressions of what Cardinal Ratzinger, in his memorable speech immediately prior to being elected Pope Benedict XVI, called the "dictatorship of relativism." Such a secularity would be a form of relativism of *values,* a new "weak" metaphysics—Giovanni Vattimo's *pensiero debole* ("weak thought") and thus, as is said, essentially "secular"—hostile to any affirmation of truth, and simultaneously an absolutization of the political power with respect to any other claim of goodness, truth, and value. In truth, it is only values that can be absolute; the political process and its results, on the other hand, are always something relative, debatable, reformable, subject to error, provisional, and capable of being judged.

The Secular State and Religion: From Criteria of Truth to Criteria of Political Justice

An attitude of "secular integralism" could be motivated, it is true, by a fear of falling back into an overbearing ecclesiality or a re-clericalization of society. A merely political secularity, however, is sufficient for avoiding this outcome. Such a conception of secularity is sufficient for avoiding any kind of commixture—of either the medieval or modern variety—between religion and politics, Church and State, spiritual and temporal power. To go beyond this, as a comprehensive and integralist concept of secularity intends to do, means not only to define the rules of the political game circumventing all religious belief and every claim of truth, that is, "as if God didn't exist,"[114] but it would also mean the assertion that God *does not exist* and that every religion is a pernicious illusion—at least for the public sphere—and consequently, politically speaking, an evil to be repressed (and tolerable only if relegated to the completely private sphere). Such a "secularism," essentially antireligious, today attempts to impose with the force of State power the truth of the nonexistence and nonrelevance of God, and of the consequent irrelevance—even the harmfulness—of religion. This type of secularity— "laicism"—is not neutral, just as atheism is not a religiously neutral doctrine. Jürgen Habermas has gone as far as to say that that the "neutrality of the state authority on questions of world views" is "incompatible with a political universalization of a secular world view."[115]

A certain historical myopia unfortunately hides behind the position that confuses the secularity of the State with public agnosticism or atheism, that is, a considerable ignorance regarding the decisive and constructive role of the Christian religion and the Church in the formation of Western civilization and indeed precisely of the secular character of the State (as has been shown in the first part of this essay). A myopia, as well, regarding the fact that Christian values are the foundation of our Western society, to the point where our most important juridical and social institutions are crystallizations of the Christian spirit, and without this spirit are condemned to degeneration in the long term.

The public presence of religion, and with it the consciousness of the existence of God and of a transcendence, is not without importance even for the secular State. I am not speaking properly of a "civil religion," but of the "civil function of religion,"[116] that is, that function that in fact exists as a cultural presence in a given country. The religion or religions that actually exist in a society can fulfill an important role if they are compatible with the secular political culture of the democratic constitutional State, without for

---

114. This is the title of the book by Gian Enrico Rusconi mentioned above, *Come se Dio non ci fosse*.

115. Jürgen Habermas, "Pre-political Foundations of the Democratic Constitutional State," in Habermas and Joseph Ratzinger, *The Dialectics of Secularization: On Reason and Religion* (San Francisco: Ignatius Press, 2007), 51.

116. See Sergio Belardinelli, "A che serve parlare di Dio? Sulla funzione civile della religione," in *L'identità in conflitto dell'Europa*, ed. Laura Paoletti (Bologna: Il Mulino, 2005), 141–55; and by the same author: *La comunità liberale: La libertà, il bene comune e la religione nelle società complesse* (Rome: Edizioni Studium, 1999).

this imposing a religious creed or claims of truth on the entire population of citizens.

A secular State that conceives of itself as "publicly atheist" is a State that does not recognize the transcendence of values with respect to politics; it declares publicly that the human will and human decisions are the ultimate criteria of value and justice. On the other hand, a State that in some way, including publicly, cultivates a consciousness of the existence of a God, and with this of a transcendence, knows itself to be subject to "objective" criteria of value and of justice, in the sense that it opens the possibility of the dualism between "facts" and "values," as explained above. Such a civil religion, assuming that it is not confessional and would therefore not impair the principle of religious freedom, does not contradict the secularity of the State. The imposition of a public atheism or agnosticism, on the other hand, violates one of the essential requirements of this secularity: its neutrality. Ultimately, a complete neutrality is impossible, and one must choose what is more reasonable, even politically: an atheist/agnostic secularity or one that recognizes transcendence. As I have explained, what seems more reasonable, even for the modern political culture of the secular State, is the public presence of the consciousness that man is not the supreme being in the universe and, therefore, any political decision can and even must be evaluated according to criteria of value whose origin is independent of the human will and superior to it (in the terminology of the Magisterium of the Catholic Church: "objective"). It is for this reason that the *Grundgesetz,* the German constitution, after the experience of a totalitarian regime that put man in the place of God, begins with the words: "In the consciousness of its responsibility before God and before men ... the German people has decided ..."

The neutrality of the secular State requires, however, that the religion or religions practiced by the citizens of a particular society be treated *according to rules of political justice.* The rules of political justice are based on criteria of freedom, equality, and procedural fairness. From this political perspective, religion is accepted as part of the reality and the cultural heritage of a society or of a nation, and thus, logically, religious practice and its facilitation come to be part of the common good. A secularity that represses and excludes religion would be legitimate only for political reasons, which is to say, because a religion endangers the constitutional order or the public order and does not respect the minimum requirements of public morality (prescribing, for example, sexual acts with minors or human sacrifice as cultic acts).

It is understandable why, based on the above-mentioned premise of an integralist conception of secularity that represses and eliminates religion, an authority such as that of the Catholic Church and the other Christian churches, capable of directly influencing the consciences of citizens, could be perceived as a danger for the secularity of the State. I think that such an attitude would be justified only in cases where the Church, or any other religious community, attempted with the force of its authority to combine its moral judgment on behaviors, decisions, laws, and public measures with a judgment on the legitimacy of the political institutions themselves, and asked, in the name of a supreme authority, the relativization of the juridical and political sovereignty of these institutions, or even the overthrow of the constitutional order. Which is to say, the fears of the adherents of an integralist conception of secularity would be justified if the Church claimed for itself the "competence for the competence," which is the final cogent judgment on who can make legitimate and politically binding decisions.

"Free Church in a Free State"?

The acceptance of the secularity of the State does not mean complete harmony between Church and State, but rather "constructive conflict," in the mutual recognition of freedom and autonomy. The relationship between Christianity, which makes present a universal proposal of truth and an equally universal project of redemption, and democratic, secular, and pluralistic modern political culture will always be a relationship full of problems and tensions. Throughout the whole history of the Church's presence in the world, it has always been this way: it belongs to the nature of the relationship between Christian truth and the Church on the one hand, and the world on the other, given that this relationship is precisely one between the offer of redemption and a world fallen as a result of original sin.

Consequently, both Christianity in general and the Church as its institutional expression and as a historical subject and public actor (which is true for all the Christian confessions) can never understand themselves to be a simple portion of society, as a mere social group, as simply one associative phenomenon among others, or, at the institutional level, as a kind of nongovernmental organization (NGO) that attempts to promote its agenda in competition with other similar institutions, being nothing other than one more actor on the worldwide public scene.

Recall the formulation of Pope Gelasius, *"There are two powers on this earth ... "*: the Church, as the *auctoritas sacrata* that represents a divine, redemptive truth, claims for itself to be a *power* that stands in opposition to political-temporal powers, and to all the powers of this world. The big question is: is this self-understanding compatible with modern, secular, democratic political culture, and with the pluralism that is in part its cause and in part its effect?

With the declaration on religious freedom, the Church has clearly indicated the manner in which it intends to respond to this question. It now chooses a path that it considers, as the declaration itself affirms, to be more in line with the Gospel and with the actions of the apostles.[117] It asks for freedom, not on the basis of a presumed duty of the State—of the powers of this world—to recognize its characteristic as the one true religion, but on the basis of a right to religious freedom that belongs to *all* believers of every type, in virtue of their dignity as rational and free beings.[118]

With this the Church does not renounce its self-understanding as a "power" in the Gelasian sense: as a power that is precisely not political, but *auctoritas sacrata*. Sacred authority, because it makes the redemptive action of Christ present in this world through the ministry of the word and the administration of the sacraments, and thus also a moral authority that influences the consciences of believers and of every person able to be enlightened by its doctrine; and finally, a prophetic power, which claims to be capable of issuing moral judgments, criticisms, and evaluations concerning the exercise of temporal power, in the light of the integral vocation and the eternal destiny of every human being. For this reason it also asks for the freedom and independence, including organizational, that make it possible to exercise without impediment or political concerns—*opportune, importune* ("in season and out")—all that it is convinced of being obligated to carry out "by divine mandate": "Go into the whole world and preach the gospel to every creature";[119] a message, therefore, as the Church believes, entrusted to it not by men, by society, or by the nation, but by God.

This is why the Church had difficulties, in its day, with Cavour's formula "a free Church in a free State," a formula inspired by the liberal Catholic politician Charles de Montalembert.[120] Even if this formula in its origi-

---

117. See *Dignitatis humanae*, no. 11.   118. Ibid., no. 13.
119. Ibid.
120. For Montalembert, see his speech at Malines in *Le libéralisme catholique*, ed. Marcel Prélot

nal version referred to the Roman question (i.e., the idea of "freeing" the Church of its temporal power so as to leave it free to fulfill its pastoral mission, in an Italy equally free from ecclesiastic oversight), the formula was little by little used to characterize the relationship between the secular State and a Church reduced to a simple associative phenomenon within society, regulated by civil laws (and thus "freed" from its patrimony and, consequently, from its organizational and pastoral independence). The truth of the formulation, together with its deeply problematic character in its concrete application, comes out clearly in some statements of one its most jealous adherents, the liberal Catholic politician Marco Minghetti, a close collaborator of Cavour, head of the government and follower of so-called jurisdictionalism.[121]

On the one hand, it is striking the exactness with which the Florentine politician grasps, in an exemplary—and thus in the present context highly illustrative—way, the essence of the modern secular State. According to Minghetti, with modern liberalism the idea of the "two powers" has been definitively overcome. The Church could no longer be considered a "power" that enters into contact with the State. "For us, true power, in the legislative and coercive sense, i.e. the faculty of sanctioning laws with force—*imperium*—is not, nor can it be, other than unitary; and this belongs to the State."[122] The Church is not a "power," because it does not have "the faculty to make laws accompanied by coercive power, that is, to obligate citizens to observe them, including with force." To say that there are two powers "would imply admitting two States coexisting in the same time and space, and therefore in mutual conflict." The Church is of another nature: "The commandments of the Church must not be imposed with force, its ministry is wholly of persuasion, directed at the souls of believers, it is an authority which must win spontaneous obedience." On the other hand, it is worth noting "the incompetence of the State in dogmatic and religious matters."[123]

---

and F. Gallouédec Genuys (Paris: Armand Colin, 1969), 227ff. (excerpts); for the relevant passages of Cavour's speeches see Camillo Benso conte di Cavour, *Libera Chiesa in libero State*, commentary by Fancesco Ruffini and preface by Mario Pirani (Genova: Il Melangolo, 2001). Montalembert reproved Cavour for having "stolen" the formula, and "distorting" it: Francesco Ruffini, *Relazioni tra State e Chiesa*, ed. F. Margotta Broglio (Bologna: Il Mulino, 1974), 156.

121. On Marco Minghetti see Carlo Jemolo, *Chiesa e State in Italia: Dalla unificazione ai giorni nostri* (1955) (Turin: Einaudi, 1965), 29ff.

122. "Discorso del 8 maggio 1873," in Marco Minghetti, *Discorsi Parlamentari, raccolti e pubblicati per deliberazione della Camera dei deputati* (Rome: Tipografia della Camera dei deputati, 1890), 5:302.

123. Marco Minghetti, *State e Chiesa*, 2nd ed. (Naples: Ulrich Hoepli, 1878), 77–80.

With these premises, Minghetti thinks he has resolved the problem (as Marsilius of Padua had thought earlier, something impossible not to recall in this context).

After having brilliantly laid out what truly characterizes the modern secular State—that is, the issue of sovereignty and the consequent political, legislative, and procedural autonomy—now comes the problematic point. For Minghetti, from the two premises just enunciated, "it follows that the Church cannot be, in contrast with the State, other than a complete or partial association of citizens, directed toward a specific religious end, that offends neither the rights of others nor the security of the State itself."[124] This means that the Church is reduced to an associative phenomenon of civil society, regulated by the State and by the directives of civil law. The formula "a free Church in a free State" thus comes to mean that the Church is an entity within the State that enjoys no proper corporate autonomy, and that must be organized according to the directives of civil law (something that becomes relevant especially with respect to all that regards the Church's patrimony, the administration of its goods, etc.).[125] A "free" Church, but free according to the rules formulated by the liberal and secular State.

Such an understanding of the charter of a religious institution like the Catholic Church certainly does not correspond to the idea that the Church has of itself; nor does it correspond to the essence itself of Christianity, which cannot be regulated in this way by temporal powers. Certainly, the Church today wants to leave sovereign autonomy to the State—in this respect the positions of both Marsilius of Padua and Marco Minghetti are confirmed; it no longer claims juridical and coercive power over the temporal power (even if it continues to excommunicate politicians, though this without civil consequences). The Church nevertheless continues to conceive of itself as a "power" opposite the State: an independent spiritual power, representing a higher truth that is definitive, salvific, and enlightening, even concerning the things of this world. And so as to be able to exercise this task of a specific moral authority, not only with respect to its own faithful but also toward the whole culture of a country (and today even at the international level), the Church claims the appropriate freedom and independence.

124. Ibid., 81.
125. See now the exhaustive study of Martin Grichting, *Das Verfügungsrecht über das Kirchenvermögen auf den Ebenen von Diözese und Pfarrei*, Münchner Theologische Studien 3, Kanonistische Abteilung 62 (Ottilien: EOS Verlag, 2007), 224ff.

The freedom of the Church in a "free (i.e., secular) State" means for it to have a charter such as to assure complete independence of internal organization and pastoral action, at both the local and universal levels. I am convinced, moreover, that this has always been the intimate motivation of the Church's action. And in this sense, in today's Church we can still recognize the same Catholic Church of centuries past, continuing to defend its freedom and independence.

I cannot enter in this setting into this complex question in greater detail. I will limit myself to simply noting that, despite the impossibility of a "jurisdictionalism" as proposed by the followers of Cavour at the end of the nineteenth century, an important part of the formula "free Church in a free State" remains valid: that concerning the understanding of the "freedom of the State," that is, precisely its secularity, its full political-juridical autonomy, meaning its sovereignty with respect to the ecclesiastical power (and to the spiritual power of any other religious authority or community). Equally valid is the request that in a "free," that is, secular, State, the Church observe the laws of the State, with clerics being citizens just like any others, without privileges on the political and jurisdictional level. Remaining inconsistent with the Church's self-understanding, however, is the idea that it must be considered as a simple association, social group or—at the international level—a kind of NGO. According to its perennial and indispensable self-understanding, the Church is not of this world, and represents a truth and a salvific praxis of transcendent origin, with a transcendent purpose. What causes difficulties is this twofold characteristic of the Church, that is, that of existing and acting in this world—in our day, in the modern world of secular democracy—and simultaneously not being of this world, being established rather as a power that is above it. The Church today does not mean to constrain anyone, not even the State, to recognize *the truth* of such a self-understanding. But it will always oppose any political or legal measure that attempts to hinder it from organizing itself and acting according to this self-understanding. Consequently, even today it asks for the *libertas Ecclesiae,* no longer threatened, as in the Middle Ages, by emperors and princes wanting to integrate it into their political system, but now by a secular integralism that wants to distance it from public life and, in essence, submit the Church to its own control so as to render it socially and politically irrelevant.

The Church does not expect to live in complete harmony with the secular State, or to insert itself into public life as one peaceful interlocutor among others, adapting itself to the political and juridical logic of the State. Rather than *inserting itself* into the democratic and secular constitutional State, submitting itself to the logic of the latter's political and juridical organization, the Church wants to *coexist* with this State, while preserving its own identity, its organizational freedom, and its independence (through measures, for example, such as concordats, which presuppose recognition as a subject of international law, or, at the national level, by seeking a charter of public law in the area of state-church law). This "coexistence" with the secular State and independent public presence cannot mean, however, a type of interference with State institutions, or even opposition to their legitimacy. Rather, as acting in public life and exercising, according to its self-understanding, the task of teacher of humanity and of morality, the Church must do so respecting the rules of the secular State that—as we have seen—the Church itself recognizes as a "value that has been attained" that "belongs to the inheritance of contemporary civilization."

This does not mean that the Church would realize its evangelizing and apostolic task in a so to speak "corporate" way, that is, in the sense of an institution that forms a power group within society, under the guidance of the clergy and employing the body of the lay faithful as its *longa manus,* a new type of secular arm. I think rather that the Church should commit itself today to the path of helping the lay faithful to act as Christians in the midst of society as responsible citizens, providing them with the necessary formation and indicating the requirements and the nonnegotiable limits of their civic and political action, without, however, considering them merely as a "passive body" or "secular arm." The presence of the Church in public life will be effected primarily through the presence of responsible Catholic citizens, capable of exercising their civil rights in a way consonant with their faith. Moreover, the public presence of the Church does not mean that it must comment on, evaluate, and judge all of the political events of a country, or be continually present with proposals, judgments, and directives for its faithful. So as to avoid any "magisterial hypertrophy," the Church must always remind itself of its specific mission and its supernatural end, and limit itself to intervening in what for it is truly "nonnegotiable" from the perspective of the dignity of man and his eternal destiny.

"Interference" of the Church in Public Life
in Defense of Natural Law

I believe that the above-mentioned insuperable tension between transcendent origin and contemporaneous immersion in the immanence of history and human society is the element that has always caused the problems between *sacerdotium* and *regnum* (as was once said), between the spiritual and the temporal power. This tension is still present today in certain reservations the Church has with respect to the secular State, and regarding those formulations that refer to "secularity" and "secularism." The tension also surfaces when the Church proposes a doctrine of natural law that in its view is entirely reasonable and capable of being understood by everyone independent of faith, but that, precisely as taught by the Church, is necessarily perceived by non-Catholics as a "Catholic" natural law doctrine because it has been interpreted by the Church—and thus a teaching linked to a religious claim that speaks in the name of a higher competency and truth.

To confer a public legitimacy and acceptability on the natural law taught by the Church it is therefore not enough to emphasize its "secular" character. Precisely *in that it is a teaching of the Church,* it cannot fulfill the typically "secular" function of natural law: the function of a common, universal rationality that is independent of religion. It can do so only to the degree that the Church—together with Christian theologians and philosophers—is able, in the public discourse, to convince citizens of the justice and intrinsic truth of its conception of natural law. Which is to say to the degree that the Church does not propose natural law in virtue of a magisterial competence to which the entire political society would be subordinate, but rather acts as an actor on the stage of modern democracy, according to its rules.[126] In this sense it has been justly said that "the natural law has remained—especially in the Catholic Church—the key issue in dialogues with the secular society and with other communities of faith in order to appeal to the reason we share in common and to seek the basis for a consensus about the ethical principles of law in a secular, pluralistic society."[127]

126. To avoid a possible misunderstanding: this applies only to the relationship between Magisterium and State/political society/political and democratic processes; it obviously does not apply to the relationship between the Magisterium and the Catholic faithful. For these latter, the authority of the Magisterium does not depend on the force of the arguments, but on the fact that, and on the way in which, a particular doctrine (including those of natural law) is proposed as Catholic doctrine, to which a response of faith is due even when it is not understood.

127. Joseph Ratzinger, "That Which Holds the World Together: The Pre-political Moral Foundations of a Free State," in Habermas and Ratzinger, *The Dialectics of Secularization*, 69.

In my opinion, the Catholic Church today has understood this challenge, and therefore its teaching in this field offers arguments that are ever more adapted to democratic public discourse (even if, at times, those with whom the Church would desire to enter into dialogue seem not very open or interested in doing so: rather than interesting themselves in the "secular" arguments put forward by Catholics, they unfortunately busy themselves highlighting the "Catholic," and thus "religious," as they say, origin of the arguments, so as to denounce them as mere clerical "impositions"). The Congregation for the Doctrine of the Faith's *Doctrinal Note on Some Questions Regarding the Participation of Catholics in Political Life* of November 24, 2002, cited above, in fact makes a significant distinction: it affirms that the Church recognizes secularity "as the autonomy of the civil and political sphere from the religious and ecclesiastical—*but not from the moral.*" The mere fact, moreover, that some moral truths "may also be taught by the Church does not lessen the political legitimacy or the rightful 'autonomy' of the contribution of those citizens who are committed to them" (no. 6). With this the Church affirms and defends the freedom of those citizens who, precisely in the exercise of their freedom and civic responsibility and following their conscience, give ear to what the Church teaches on a given politically relevant issue.

The fact persists, however, that this teaching is interpreted by many as an illegitimate interference by the Church in the political process, an interference that could destroy the secularity of the State. Indeed, it is logical that the positions taken by the Church, to the point of publicly declaring particular political positions or support for this or that project of law as incompatible with Christian morality, would be interpreted by some as undue interference. In a certain sense those who raise these criticisms are correct, because these are in fact "interferences." What we have here is a conflict of two authentic powers, even if that of the Church limits itself (today) to using exclusively noncoercive, and in this sense nonpolitical, means. For this reason, citing the above-mentioned *Doctrinal Note* of 2002, the "Compendium of the Social Doctrine of the Church" defends the legitimacy and compatibility of the Church's way of acting in regard to the secular State:

When the Church's Magisterium intervenes in issues concerning social and political life, it does not fail to observe the requirements of a correctly understood autonomy, for "the Church's Magisterium does not wish to exercise political power or eliminate the freedom of opinion of Catholics regarding contingent questions. Instead, it intends—as is its proper function—to instruct and illuminate the consciences of the faithful, particularly those involved in political life, so that their actions may always serve the integral promotion of the human person and the common good. The social doctrine of the Church is not an intrusion into the government of individual countries. It is a question of the lay Catholic's duty to be morally coherent, found within one's conscience, which is one and indivisible.[128]

This passage shows all the complexity and, in a certain sense, the paradox of the situation. It seems obvious that the Church wants to influence the consciences of citizens, and especially of those involved in political and legislative decisions! It cannot be denied that a spiritual power is exercised here. How, then, can it be claimed that this in no way constitutes an intrusion or an illegitimate practice, however indirect, incompatible with the secularity of the State?

The response seems obvious and confirms the essence of the secularity of the State: the Church says that this is not an "intrusion *into the government* of individual countries." In fact, the Church's action does not interfere at all with the autonomy and sovereignty of the secular State, or with the democratic process: no legal or political appropriation takes place with regard to the functioning of political or civil institutions. Even an ecclesiastical penalty, as for example the excommunication of a politician, can have no civil effect; the effects will be only ecclesiastical (even if they can have—and are intended to have—repercussions in the electoral behavior of citizens; this practice, however, falls within the sphere of that legitimate political freedom and civil autonomy that the State must never coerce, "direct," protect, or control).[129] On the other hand, the nonacceptance of the Church's teachings, even by members of the Church itself, does not involve any *civil effect*. And nor can their acceptance be coerced by any political means. Precisely this demonstrates that such "interventions" are not illegitimate from the perspective of the secularity of the State.

I think this is precisely what Benedict XVI wanted to express on December 9, 2006, in his speech to the participants in the National Study Congress organized by the Union of Italian Catholic Jurists, when he said that "Any direct intervention from the Church [in the political field] would be undue

128. *Compendium of the Social Doctrine of the Church*, no. 571; cit. according to http://www.vatican.va.

129. Even for a political philosopher like Charles Larmore, this is fully compatible with a liberal society. Likewise the fact that the Church is not, internally, "liberal": "The Catholic Church, for example, is a legal institution in our society, but it does not manage its ecclesiastical affairs on the basis of tolerance. It cannot burn heretics at the stake, because this violates their rights as citizens, but it can still excommunicate them" (Charles Larmore, "Liberalismo politico," in *Comunitarismo e Liberalismo*, ed. Alessandro Ferrara [Rome: Editori Riuniti, 1992], 184).

interference. Moreover, 'healthy secularism' implies that the State does not consider religion merely as an individual sentiment that may be confined to the private sphere alone. On the contrary, since religion is also organized in visible structures, as is the case with the Church, it should be recognized as a form of public community presence." This, continues Benedict XVI, has a variety of consequences; for our purposes we wish to emphasize those contained in the following statement:

> To refuse the Christian community and its legitimate representatives the right to speak on the moral problems that challenge all human consciences today, and especially those of legislators and jurists, is not a sign of a healthy secularity. *Thus, it is not a question of undue meddling by the Church in legislative activity that is proper and exclusive to the State* but, rather, of the affirmation and defence of the important values that give meaning to the person's life and safeguard his or her dignity. These values are human before being Christian, such that they cannot leave the Church silent and indifferent. It is her duty to firmly proclaim the truth about man and his destiny. (Emphasis added)[130]

The power that the Church exercises through its influence on the consciences of its faithful who are involved in political decisions is, therefore, not a *political* power in the strict sense (i.e., that according to which the secularity of the State is defined)—it is not "undue interference by the Church in the proper and exclusive legislative activity of the State." Rather it is, shall we say, a cultural power, a real influence on the culture of a country, on the opinion of citizens and on their way of thinking—if they allow themselves to be influenced by it—and on the conception of public morality. The Church acts in society and influences society, things that cannot obviously be without political relevance—especially in a democratic culture! The indignation of a certain kind of integralist secularity over this type of spiritual power and cultural influence of the Church consequently shows itself to be inconsistent with the very idea of a free, pluralist, "open," and, indeed, secular society. It shows itself purely as a political game, essentially intolerant and doctrinaire, of political authorities and institutions that, with the help of the mass media, arrogate to themselves the right to set themselves up as in fact a new spiritual power, while at the same time having in their hands all the coercive apparatus of political sovereignty.

It would be difficult, moreover, to argue that Catholic positions in the field of marriage, family, and bioethical policy could be considered incom-

130. Cited according to http://www.vatican.va.

patible with a "secular" point of view. It would be difficult for no other reason than the fact that many contemporary "Catholic" positions in these areas were, a few decades ago, generally also shared by "secularists" (and in
part still are today). The privileged status of heterosexual unions ordered
to the reproduction of society, called "marriage," and the nonconcession of
such a status to unions of persons of the same sex, was the norm in secular States of the past—and not because they were victims of ecclesiastical
pressure, but because it was considered *politically just* that this be so. Even
secularists of the past saw in abortion, for example, a practice that, in principle, must be considered a crime in the juridical order (the protection of
the unborn arose out of the great legal codifications of the Enlightenment
and the development of embryology at the end of the eighteenth century).[131]
At one time, the equation of homosexual unions with marriage between a
man and a woman was unacceptable for purely "secular" reasons. In natural law questions it is thus *not possible* to identify positions that, with respect to content, would in themselves be "secular" or "Catholic"—that is,
confessional positions that are therefore incompatible with the secularity
of the State! Even if the acceptance of a right of homosexual couples to form
"marriages" recognized by the State, for example, or of a "right to abortion," are more *modern*—and thus believed by many to be more consonant
with human rights—such positions are not for this reason more *secular,* or
conversely their denial a confessional position incompatible with the secularity of the State. An incompatibility or illicit confessionality could only exist in the *way* in which the Church and Catholics attempted to make their
positions prevail and impose them, that is, through coercive interventions in
the legislative process of the State. But such an interference in and violation
of the sovereignty of the State does not occur, is not possible, and is not even
desired by the Church. The incompatibility, therefore, simply does not exist.

With the Church's teaching in the area of natural law, despite the fact that
in a pluralistic society it is perceived as "Catholic" natural law, the Church
remains faithful to the centuries-old, perennial tradition of Christianity.[132] We

---

131. See John Keown, *Abortion, Doctors, and the Law: Some Aspects of the Legal Regulation of Abortion in England from 1803 to 1982* (New York: Cambridge University Press, 1988). See also chapters 6 and
7 of my book *Ethics of Procreation and the Defense of Human Life: Contraception, Artificial Fertilization,
Abortion,* ed. William F. Murphy Jr. (Washington, D.C.: The Catholic University of America Press, 2010).

132. The situation of the Orthodox churches is of course completely different; the reason for this is,
on the one hand, their insertion into the political structure of a country and, on the other, their mutual
independence and therefore their national character. The Orthodox churches understand themselves as
an essential part of the political system of their respective countries, in the sense of being the guarantee

have already shown above how important was the cultivation of natural law by medieval jurists, and the emancipating and egalitarian function that was carried out in the face of a customary law and practices that were degrading to human nature. If we look at things from a broad historical perspective and with a vision of the future, we become aware of the fact that still today the Church must fulfill a civilizing and educational function, in the face of those who want to subject man to the tyranny of custom and to habits that, for different reasons than in the past, are incongruent with human dignity. To appeal here to the "secularity of the State" would only be to want to replace political debate with casting aspersions on the interlocutor.[133]

The task of the Church in a pluralistic society politically organized according to secular principles does not mean, as we have already mentioned, that the Church, as an ecclesiastical institution and as Magisterium, would "engage in politics," being constantly present in the public forum to provide criteria and solutions for current political questions. It does this only in questions that are directly connected to positions that are vital for the Christian faith, and specifically regarding what concerns Catholic dogma and morality. Today, the Church wants to be present in this world primarily through its faithful, citizens who are immersed in social realities and who, in various ways and degrees, are also engaged in politics, at least as voters. According to the most recent Magisterium, it belongs to these, with the responsibility and freedom they possess as citizens of a democratic constitutional State, to create a society ever more worthy of the dignity of the human person. But they would do so with a conscience inspired by and formed according to their Catholic faith, to which the ecclesial Magisterium provides an indispensable orientation.

Conclusions: Coexistence and Inevitable Tension between Secular State and Christianity

Modern political secularity retrieves authentically Christian values, but it also inevitably enters into conflict with the essence of the Christian proj-

---

of value and orientation, including and especially with respect to the education system. At the same time, they are dependent on the state and do not enjoy that freedom and independence that the Catholic Church has always sought and defended (even if in various countries and historical periods it has at times betrayed these).

133. No one reproaches the Church for its commitment to social justice or, to cite a concrete example, its opposition to racial discrimination. In fact, for having publicly fought against the latter in

ect, and with the Church as an institution whose task it is, according to its self-understanding, to make present in a fallen world the voice of divine truth and the efficacy of redemption through Jesus Christ, who, according to the Christian faith, is the one mediator between human beings and God.

In such a situation, the voices of the Church and of Christian preaching in general—but also the action of authentic Christians—are necessarily voices that contrast and potentially conflict with a secular State that understands itself as the agent of a pluralistic society—and it is good that this is so. This conflict is a sign of the just autonomy of the civil and political sphere, of a healthy secularity that is also fully acceptable from a Christian point of view. At the same time, this conflict is the expression of what in the Church is held to be a theological truth, that is, of the fallen condition of this world and the mission of the Christian religion (or rather of the Church) to be a witness of the truth, a light for consciences and a remedy for sin. That this is a service to society is beyond question for the believer, who will consequently seek to act with a conscience enlightened by the truth that issues from his faith. He will do so, however, as a citizen of the earthly city, respecting democratic procedural rules and the pluralistic logic of this city.

Today, the real "power" of Christianity and of the Church resides in the action of Christian faithful who, with consciences formed as Christians, act in every environment in society as "salt of the earth" and "light of the world." A new evangelization consequently must not abolish the foundations of the modern secularity of the State. Not only are the ethos of peace, freedom, and equality of the modern constitutional State and its secularity cultural accomplishments that should maintain their value in a newly "Christianized" society, but it might be even more important that such a society not yield to the temptation to again unite religion with the coercive force of the temporal power and to overthrow citizens' rights of freedom and the legitimate pluralism of the society.

In my opinion, therefore, a *Christian secularity* is not only thinkable but *necessary*, not in a confessional and anti-pluralistic sense, but from the point of view of the values that are present and dominant in society.[134]

---

the United States, the Church was highly praised by the liberal and secular press in the 1950s. There are many examples that show that often secularists call "secular" simply that position which at a particular historical moment is considered *desirable* by secularists.

134. Some reflections and concretizations can be found in my contribution "Il rapporto tra verità e politica nella società cristiana. Riflessioni storico-teologiche per la valutazione dell'amore della libertà nella predicazione di Josemaría Escrivá," in *Figli di Dio nella Chiesa. Riflessioni sul messaggio di San Jo-*

Precisely through the action of Christians in the midst of society, the "axiological coefficient" of pluralism and of the consequent democratic process can vary and shift. A society impregnated with Christian values can still be a pluralistic, secular, democratic society, assuming that the change in this "coefficient," that is, the "Christianization" of the society, would not be the result of a legal and political subordination to the spiritual power of the Church, with the abolition of effective freedoms—especially of religious freedom—and the autonomy of the democratic process. It must rather be the fruit of the Christian consciousness of citizens who, precisely *democratically*, construct a legal and social order more consonant with what from a Christian point of view defines human dignity and the common good at the level of natural law. Such a State would not be confessional or Catholic, but simply a State that has a different conception of what is politically required and indispensable in view of the common good and in the area of natural law. It stands to reason that adherents of an integralist conception of secularity would view such a process with uneasiness—indeed as a kind of nightmare—and attempt to prevent it. Those, however, with a merely political concept of secularity need not be concerned; they can consider such a development to be the fruit of an authentically secular and, in the best sense of the word, democratic political culture.

The conflict that is always present between Christianity and secular political culture is inevitable and necessary. Moreover, the desire to find a clean and perfect institutional solution to resolve it, or make it go away, seems to me an illusion. This conflict is a consequence of the specific mission of the Church as the light of revealed truth in a world in need of redemption. But it is also a consequence of the nature of earthly realities, which legitimately require their own autonomy and with that—as regards the political power—secularity, that is, institutional and juridical independence from every imposition in the name of truth on the part of the Church or any other religious authority The Church today wants to respect this secularity with all the imperfections and fallibility it implies, and accepts the resulting pluralism. In this it sees not merely a strategic position, but a moral and evangelical doctrinal requirement—without ceasing to simultaneously

---

semaría Escrivá. *Aspetti culturali ed ecclesiastici* (*La grandezza della vita quotidiana*. Atti del Congresso Internazionale, January 8–11, 2002, vol. 5/2), ed. Fernando de Andrés (Rome: Pontificia Università della Santa Croce, 2004), 153–78; reprinted as chapter 4 in Martin Rhonheimer, *Changing the World. The Timeliness of Opus Dei* (New York: Scepter Press, 2009).

exercise its mission of proclaiming the truth and clarifying consciences. Its victory, however, is not in imposition through coercive mechanisms, but in convincing, in conversion of hearts, in persecution—and in the Cross. The Church wants to continue to awaken consciences, proclaiming the superiority of what is spiritual and of what pertains to eternal life over merely temporal realities. It also wants to provide criteria of justice proper to its vision of man and of his dignity as a person called to communion with the eternal God, the Creator of this world.

To the extent to which natural law, too, is part of the "public reason"—which is to say to the extent that natural law is part of the argumentative rationality generally recognized in the public forum and considered legitimate for political and legal decisions involving the coercive power of the State—it would also be a task of the Church to continually emphasize its requirements and demands. Even if in doing so the Church exercises a true and proper influence on consciences and, through these, on the political process and democratic choices, this would be entirely legitimate, including from the perspective of a purely political secularity, provided that it respects the institutional and juridical autonomy of political processes. In this sense, and only in this sense, I would subscribe to the validity of the principle "free Church in a free State." The State—the political process—must be free from institutional constraints on the part of the Church, which must recognize a political freedom that is not linked to forms of coercion dictated by the spiritual power of the Church or of any other religious authority.

In a reciprocal way, the Church must enjoy the freedom to say to holders of political power and to citizens (who also hold power in modern democracies) what it considers opportune to be said. In this way, with the authority proper to it, it exercises an influence on the conscience of citizens. In a modern democracy this could admittedly constitute a genuine power, though not of a coercive type, but moral and cultural. Such a power could be denied to the Church only by a State that wants to erect itself as the ultimate source of value, uprightness, and justice—which is to say a State that erects the relativity and political negotiability of all values into an absolute value, not tolerating alongside it any voice apt to relativize this claim.

The Church therefore asks to have a voice in public life, legitimately exercising its influence on the consciences of its faithful, who, as citizens, especially in a democratic society, are directly involved both in the way that political power is exercised and in legislative choices. At the same time, however, the ecclesiastical hierarchy must, in my view, refrain from considering the lay faithful as a simple *longa manus* or tool for influencing society. The Church does not engage in politics in this sense. It wants faithful Catholics to act with freedom and on their own responsibility, even if regarding potential conflicts (i.e., between loyalty and obedience to the legitimate pastors of the Church, on the one hand, and the freedom and responsibility of the Catholic citizen and politician, with the demands of loyalty to the political party or organization in which he is legitimately engaged, on the other), perhaps not every problem has been so far clarified in a satisfactory manner.

A secularity, on the other hand, that, beyond requiring the juridical and institutional autonomy of the mechanisms by which political power is exercised, would also limit the public presence of the voice of the Church and its cultural influence, and would render difficult—or even fail to facilitate—religious freedom and the related exercise of religion according to impartial rules of justice, would be a secular State in an "unhealthy," "integralist" sense: it would turn secularity into an a-religious, even antireligious, fundamentalist creed. Rather than respecting the religious fact as an essential dimension of human life, including in its social and public dimensions, it would neutralize it with the coercive force of the power of the State.

In this sense, faced with the arrogance of the State, Christianity would still have the task today, as always in the past, of defending the freedom of citizens and the submission of political power to moral values, to truths of law and justice that are "natural"—and in this sense also universally valid—and to guarantees of the true dignity of the human person. The true enemy of the secular State is not Christianity, or the Catholic Church, but a culture, like that of Islam, which understands itself as a unitary political-religious project that makes legal and political institutions depend on a theology based on a sacred, revealed text, and on a body of law that is religiously defined and administered by jurist-theologians with no democratic legitimization. The Catholic Church has never promoted such a project, which would be completely foreign to it, contradicting its very essence. The natural ally of the secular State, in fact, is Christianity, and—it would not seem an exaggeration to say so if one considers the whole of history impartially—above all the Catholic Church, which has existed since the time of the apostles under the guidance of their successors, the members of the episcopal college, whose head and guarantee of unity is the bishop of Rome, the successor of the apostle Peter. The task today, therefore, is to defend the historically Christian foundations of the secularity of the modern State, of its juridical system, and of the political institutions of the democratic constitutional State.[135]

135. The original Italian version of this essay has been published as "Cristianesimo e laicità: storia ed attualità di un rapporto complesso," in *Laicità: la ricerca dell'universale nelle differenze*, ed. Pierpaolo Donati (Bologna: Il Mulino, 2008), 27–138. This translation by Joseph T. Papa. A much more extended version of this essay is available as a book: Martin Rhonheimer, *Christentum und säkularer Staat. Geschichte —Gegenwart—Zukunft. Mit einem Vorwort von Ernst-Wolfgang Böckenförde* (Freiburg i. Br.: Herder, 2012).

THIRTEEN

Benedict XVI's "Hermeneutic of Reform" and Religious Freedom

Continuity or Rupture: How Did Vatican II Understand the Church's Relation with the Modern World?

In a notable Christmas message given before the Roman Curia on December 22, 2005, Pope Benedict XVI cautioned against a widespread interpretation of the Second Vatican Council that would posit that the Church after the council is different from the "preconciliar" Church.[1] Benedict called this erroneous interpretation of the council a "hermeneutic of discontinuity and rupture."

The warning was enthusiastically taken up by Catholics plainly faithful to the Magisterium of the Church, with the opinion spreading that in his speech Benedict had opposed the "hermeneutic of discontinuity" with a "hermeneutic of continuity." Robert Spaemann also seems to have understood it this way, as the idea seems to him consistent with current efforts at harmonization in the area of religious freedom, efforts that defend the existence of an uninterrupted continuity between pre- and postconciliar doctrine.[2]

---

1. See "Address of His Holiness Pope Benedict XVI to the Roman Curia Offering Them His Christmas Greetings (Thursday, 22 December 2005)," available at www.vatican.va/holy_father/benedict_xvi/speeches/2005.

2. See *Die Tagespost* 49 (April 25, 2009): 5. Some months later Robert Spaemann further specified his position in an article appearing in the *Frankfurter Allgemeine Zeitung*. See R. Spaemann, "Legitimer Wandel der Lehre," in *Frankfurter Allgemeine Zeitung* 228 (October 1, 2009), 7. Spaemann also speaks of a "change of magisterium," specifically in analogy with the change of the Church's doctrine on usury and the interdiction of the corresponding practice of lending for interest. The actual relevance of that analogy, however, seems doubtful to me.

This understanding, however, is unfounded. In the pope's address, there is no such opposition between a "hermeneutic of discontinuity" and a "hermeneutic of continuity." Rather, as he explained: "In contrast with the hermeneutic of discontinuity is a hermeneutic of reform." And in what lies the "nature of true reform"? According to the Holy Father, true reform is found "in the interplay, on different levels, between continuity and discontinuity."

The Relationship with the State

"Continuity," therefore, is not the only hermeneutical category for understanding the Second Vatican Council. The category of "reform" is also necessary, a category that includes elements of both continuity and discontinuity. But as Benedict emphasized, the continuity and discontinuity are "on different levels." It is important, therefore, to identify and distinguish these levels correctly.

On this point the pope first asserted: "The council had to define anew the relation between the Church and modernity"—and in two regards. First, regarding the modern natural sciences. "Secondly, the relation between the Church and the modern state had to be newly defined: a state which gave space to citizens of different religions and ideologies, acting with neutrality toward those religions, and which assumed responsibility only for guaranteeing the orderly and tolerant cohabitation of citizens, and the freedom to practice their own religion." It is clear, Benedict continued, that regarding the Council's teaching, "in all of these areas, which as a whole represent a single problem, there could seem to be a certain discontinuity; and in a certain sense, there was discontinuity." At the same time, it can be said that, "in principle, nothing of continuity was given up." Thus: "Precisely in this interplay on different levels between continuity and discontinuity lies the nature of true reform."

Benedict XVI then gave as an example of the "hermeneutic of reform" the understanding of the conciliar teaching on religious freedom, as though in anticipation of the current debate. In doing so, he made precisely that separation of the "different levels" that the preconciliar Magisterium, for very specific theological and historical reasons, had been unable to accomplish. Gregory XVI and Pius IX—to mention just these two popes—considered that the modern fundamental right to freedom of religion, conscience, and worship was necessarily joined to the denial of the existence of a true religion. They thought this because they could not conceive that, since there was religious truth and there was a true Church, these should not also receive the support of the state-political order and the civil legal order. It is also true that many of their liberal opponents used precisely the opposite argument to defend religious freedom: such a freedom must exist, because there is no true religion.

The liberal view held that the state had neither the competence nor the obligation to assure the prevalence in society of the true religion, which contrasted with the traditional idea of not conceding to other religions the right to exist, but at most only tolerating them within certain limits. Similarly, the liberal view held that the state must not, in service of the true religion, place limits on freedom of press and expression through state censorship, which to the nineteenth-century Church was tantamount to a denial of the unique truth of the Christian religion, and to both "indifferentism" and "agnosticism." In the preconciliar Magisterium, therefore, the doctrine on the unique truth of the Christian religion was linked to a doctrine on the function of the state and its duty to assure the prevalence of the true religion and to protect society from the spread of religious error. This implied the ideal of a "Catholic state," in which, ideally, the Catholic religion is the only state religion and the legal order must always serve to protect the true religion.

Precisely here lies Vatican II's discontinuity with the doctrine of the nineteenth-century popes—a discontinuity, however, that brings into view a deeper and more essential continuity. As Pope Benedict explained in his address: "With the Decree on religious freedom, the Second Vatican Council both recognized and assumed a fundamental principle of the modern state, while at the same time re-connecting itself with a deeply rooted inheritance of the Church." This fundamental principle of the modern state that is simultaneously a deeply rooted inheritance reassumed by the Church is, for Benedict, the rejection of a state religion. "The martyrs of the early Church died for their faith in the God revealed to them in Jesus Christ, and as such they also died for freedom of conscience and for the freedom to confess their faith."

In the modern conception, after all, "freedom of conscience" meant above all freedom of worship, that is, the right, in the contexts of public order and morality, of individuals and the various religious communities to live their faith and to profess it—publicly and communitarily—without impediment by the state. This is exactly what the first Christians asked during the age of persecutions. They did not demand that the state support religious truth, but asked only for the freedom to profess their faith without state interference. Vatican II now teaches that this is a fundamental civil right of the person—that is, a right of all people, regardless of their religious faith. This right implies the abrogation of the earlier claim of the so-called rights of truth to political and legal guarantees, and the renunciation of state repression of religious error. However one views the question, the conclusion is unavoidable: precisely this teaching of the Second Vatican Council is what Pius IX condemned in his encyclical *Quanta Cura*.

Pope Benedict concluded his exemplification of the "hermeneutic of reform" with the doctrine of religious freedom with a concise statement: "The Second Vatican Council, with its new definition of the relations between the Church's faith and certain basic elements of modern thought, reelaborated or corrected some decisions made in the past." This correction does not imply a discontinuity at the level of Catholic doctrine on faith and morals—the competency of the authentic Magisterium and possessed of infallibility, even as ordinary Magisterium. The pope thus spoke here only of an "apparent discontinuity," since, in rejecting an outdated teaching on the state, the Church "has recovered and deepened its true nature and identity. The Church was and is, both before and after the council, the same Church: one, holy, Catholic and apostolic, making its pilgrim way through time."

In short: the teaching of Vatican II on religious freedom does not imply a new dogmatic orientation, but it does take on a new orientation for the Church's social doctrine—specifically, a correction of its teaching on the mission and function of the state. The council gave the same immutable principles a new application in a new historical setting. There is no timeless dogmatic Catholic doctrine on the state—nor can there be—with the exception of those principles that are rooted in the apostolic Tradition and in sacred Scripture. The idea of a "Catholic state" as the secular arm of the Church falls outside these principles, which in fact suggest a separation between the political and religious spheres.

The partial dissolution of the genuinely Christian dualism between civil and spiritual power, and their historical intermingling, was a later development, the result of specific contingent historical circumstances: first, as a consequence of the elevation of Christianity to the state religion of the Roman Empire and the conflict with Arianism (which once again claimed a divinization of the state); then, during the early Middle Ages, due to the integration of the Church with imperial governmental structures; and finally, as a reaction against this integration in the medieval political-canonical doctrine of the *plenitudo potestatis* of the popes, out of which grew the modern idea of the confessional Catholic monarchial state—the view that was still held by Pius IX, with of course its corresponding Protestant version.

We find a clear break here in the teaching of Vatican II, which once and for all abandoned a historical burden. The council's doctrine on religious freedom is essentially a doctrine on the functions and limits of the state, as well as on a fundamental civil right—a right of persons, not of truth—involving a limitation in the sovereignty and competence of the state in religious matters. It is also a doctrine on the Church's freedom, based on the corporate right to religious freedom, to exercise its salvific mission without hindrance, even in a secular state—a right that also belongs to every other religion. Finally, it is a doctrine on the state's responsibility to encourage, in a neutral and impartial way, the creation of the necessary conditions in the public and moral order within which religious freedom can flourish and citizens can fulfill their religious duties.

Unsuccessful Attempts at Harmonization

It is precisely this new political-legal doctrine, which asserts that the state is no longer the secular arm of the Church or the representative of religious truth, that traditionalists reject. In fact, Fr. Matthias Gaudron of the German branch of the Society of St. Pius X, responsible for dialogue with Catholic institutions, identified the essential point in a letter published in *Die Tagespost* (June 6, 2009). Whereas some harmonizing positions, such as that of H. Klueting (*Tagespost* 64 [May 30, 2009]: 18), reduce Vatican II's doctrine on religious freedom to "freedom from forced conversion"—thus falsely suggesting an unbroken continuity—Fr. Gaudron put his finger on the key point: the dissent is not over the question of the rejection of forced conversions, about which there is unanimity, but regards "whether and to what degree the public exercise and propagation of a false faith may be limited." He thus correctly identifies a break in continuity or, in the words of Benedict XVI, discontinuity.

This is stated even more clearly in the memorandum sent by Fr. Franz Schmidberger, superior in Germany of the Society of St. Pius X, to the German bishops, entitled "The Time Bombs of Vatican II." According to Fr. Schmidberger, the council's teaching implies "the secularization of states and of society" and "state agnosticism"; it denies the right and duty of states "to prevent adherents of false religions from promoting their religious convictions in the public sphere through public gatherings, missionary activities and the erection of buildings for their false cult." In short, with its teaching on religious neutrality—read, secularity—the council abandoned the traditional teaching on the Catholic state and the social kingdom of Jesus Christ. In fact, says Schmidberger, here simply following Archbishop Lefebvre, "Jesus Christ [is] the only God, and his Cross the only source of salvation"; consequently "this claim of universal representation must be made efficacious in society to the greatest extent possible, through the prudent policies of state leaders."

Here we have neither communion nor continuity with the doctrine of Vatican II. I think that attempts at harmonization such as those of Basil Valuet[3] (to whom Spaemann refers) and Bertrand de Margerie[4]—despite their laudable efforts to reconcile traditionally minded thinkers with the teaching of Vatican II—are fraught with objective difficulties and doomed from the start. Ultimately they sow confusion, since such attempts obscure not only the real problem, but also the originality of the teaching of Vatican II. The arguments used are false, inasmuch as these efforts at harmonization fail to consider the political-legal context or the distinction of levels called for by Benedict XVI.

Thus it cannot be claimed—with de Margerie—that neither for Gregory XVI nor for Vatican II is freedom of press "unlimited" and that there is therefore continuity between Gregory's condemnation of freedom of press and Vatican II's doctrine. Gregory asked for ecclesiastically controlled state censorship of the press in the service of the true religion, whereas Vatican II—as did nineteenth-century liberals—situated the limits of freedom of opinion and the press in the rights of citizens, legally defined and juridically enforceable, and in the requirements of public order and morality. These limits correspond fully with the logic of the secular, liberal, constitutional, and democratic state, which is neutral with respect to religious truth claims, and have nothing—repeat, *nothing*—to do with the "defense of religious truth" or the protection of citizens from the "scourge of religious error," and thus also nothing to do with state censorship in the service of and according to the dictates of the Church (a censorship that, in the nineteenth-century Papal States, where canon law functioned as civil law, was enforced by the Holy Office—predecessor of today's Congregation for the Doctrine of the Faith).

3. Basile Valuet, *La liberté religieuse et la tradition catholique*, 3 vols. (Le Barroux: Abbaye Sainte-Madeleine du Barroux, 1998).
4. Bernard de Margerie, *Liberté religieuse et règne du Christ* (Paris: Editions du Cerf, 1988).

Similarly, neither can the tolerance taught by Pius XII in his address "Ci riesce" of December 6, 1953—a tolerance that could be exercised in religious matters "under certain circumstances" and according to the discretionary judgment "of Catholic statesmen"—be considered a form of religious freedom, precisely because this fundamental civil right of the person limits the competence of the state power in religious questions. According to this right, a place for the discretionary judgment of "Catholic statesmen" would no longer be possible, and would even be illegal. A supposed "right of tolerance," therefore, which Basil Valuet attributes to Pius XII and says corresponds to the doctrine of Vatican II, would be a contradiction and cannot exist.

For all these reasons, we are faced here not with, in Robert Spaemann's words, a "battle over principles devoid of consequences," but with a basic question of the relation of the Church with the modern world, and especially with the free democratic constitutional state. Even more, it is a question of the Church's self-understanding and its response to the question of coercion in religious matters. Although the Church has always rejected the idea of forced conversions, it has not generally rejected coercion in religious matters. On the contrary. Pius XI's encyclical *Quanta cura* was not directed against liberals who denied God, but against the influential group of liberal Catholics gathered around the French politician Charles de Montalembert. These were orthodox Catholics, who even defended the existence of the Papal States (it was Montalembert who coined the slogan "A free Church in a free State," later taken up by Cavour in a different sense), and who at the Congress of Malines in August 1863 demanded that the Church recognize freedom of assembly, press, and worship.

This demand, however, collided with the "traditional" position—a legacy of the high Middle Ages—that the Church had the right to use coercion to protect Catholics from apostasy, with the help of legal-punitive state measures. "The acceptance of the faith is a matter of freedom," according to St. Thomas Aquinas; "but one is obligated to preserve the faith once it has been embraced" (*Summa theologiae* II-II, q. 10, a. 8, ad 3). The theologians who prepared *Quanta cura* appealed to this principle, understanding it to be the task of the state, as the Church's secular arm, to protect the faithful from influences threatening to the faith and apostasy, by means of state censorship and civil penal law.

On this basis Pius VI, in his Brief "Quod aliquantum" (1791), had earlier condemned the French Revolution's General Declaration of the Rights of Man and of Citizens as the public apostasy of an entire nation. Religious freedom could be demanded by Catholics in an unbelieving or Jewish state, but France was a Christian nation, and the French were baptized Christians, and thus a generalized civil freedom could not be granted regarding adherence to any religion other than the true one—the Catholic faith. Pius VI said it well: the unbaptized "cannot be compelled to obey the Catholic faith; the rest, however, must be compelled [*sunt cogendi*]."

In his 2005 discourse Benedict XVI defended precisely the first, "liberal" phase of the French Revolution, distinguishing it from the second, Jacobin, plebiscitary, and radical-democratic phase that brought with it the Reign of Terror. He thus rehabilitated the 1789 Declaration of the Rights of Man and of Citizens, which had been born of a spirit of representative parliamentarianism and American constitutional thought.

The Perspective of Vatican II

It is thanks to Vatican II that the identification of religious freedom with "indifferentism" and "agnosticism," typical of preconciliar doctrine, has been overcome. This is an epochal transition for the Church's Magisterium, one that can be understood only according to the "hermeneutic of reform" proposed by Benedict XVI. This transition should be embraced, not watered down by the search for a false continuity that would ultimately distort a genuine continuity and, with it, the nature of the one, holy, Catholic, and apostolic Church.

And what of the "traditional Catholic teaching on the moral duty of individuals and societies toward the true religion and the one Church of Christ," which according to the conciliar declaration, remains "intact"? This statement, in fact, has often been called up to suggest an uninterrupted "continuity" in the Church's teaching on religious freedom as well. The council's teaching here seems to be ambivalent. The statement, however, is not as ambivalent as it might appear. These duties—as is stated immediately prior to the cited phrase—presuppose a "freedom from coercion in civil society." It seems that, when the declaration speaks of the duty "of individuals and societies towards the true religion and the one Church of Christ," the old doctrine on the functions of states as the secular arm of the Church has already been set aside.

What these duties consist in is specified in what can be considered an authentic interpretation of the debated passage. The passage is quoted in the *Catechism of the Catholic Church,* no. 2105, which explains that it refers to the duty of individuals and of society of "offering God genuine worship." This is realized when, "constantly evangelizing men, the Church works toward enabling them 'to infuse the Christian spirit into the mentality and mores, laws and structures of the communities in which [they] live.'" In their personal involvements and activities in family and professional life, Christians are required "to make known the worship of the one true religion which subsists in the Catholic and apostolic Church." This, concludes the present section of the *Catechism,* is how the Church "shows forth the kingship of Christ over all creation and in particular over human societies."

That is, the perspective of Vatican II calls for the proclamation of the Gospel by the Church and for the apostolate of the Christian faithful so that these penetrate the structures of society with the spirit of Christ—not a word on the state as the secular arm of the Church, which by state coercion must protect the "rights of truth," and in this way impose the kingdom of Christ in human society. The discontinuity is obvious. And even more obvious is the continuity, where it is truly essential, and therefore necessary.

Appendix: Does the Existence of Discontinuity Call into Question the Infallibility of the Magisterium?

The reactions of some theologians to the reflections above have emphasized that my interpretation would bring into doubt the infallibility of the Church's Magisterium, and that it is thus not acceptable because my observations would suggest a real rupture in the continuity of the universal ordinary Magisterium. According to their opposing view, in declaring religious freedom a natural right, Vatican II's doctrine on religious freedom did introduce a genuine novelty, though without for this reason coming into conflict with earlier magisterial declarations that had not yet contemplated such a natural right. We should therefore, according to their view, not speak of discontinuity, but of a broadening of perspective. In fact, the condemnations of religious freedom by the popes of the nineteenth century would have a disciplinary and not a doctrinal value.

Although it is not the task of moral or political philosophy to address questions such as these—which properly belong to fundamental theology—it is nonetheless necessary in this case to fill out my argument, so as to avoid any misunderstanding. For my part, I consider the question to have been

settled by what I have already said. In fact, from my interpretation of the relations between the historical dimension and the purely theological dimension, it has already been clearly shown that neither the infallibility of the
Church's solemn Magisterium nor that of its universal ordinary Magisterium
is in any way called into question. This was shown by the distinction between two levels: on the one hand, the level of the principles of the doctrine
of the Catholic faith; on the other hand, that of their concrete historical application, as was also advocated in Benedict XVI's discourse. Of course, one
who cannot agree to this distinction will certainly have difficulty in accepting my argumentation.

In order to show, then, why I consider the criticism expounded above to
be erroneous and the related fears unfounded, I will attempt here to explain
this distinction at more length, refuting the above-mentioned objections. In
doing so, I will proceed in five steps.

The Question of Infallibility

The infallibility of the Magisterium—the *Compendium of the Catechism
of the Catholic Church* affirms in number 185—"is exercised when the Roman
pontiff, in virtue of his office as the supreme pastor of the Church, or the
college of bishops, in union with the pope especially when joined together
in an ecumenical council, proclaim by a definitive act a doctrine pertaining
to faith or morals." In the same way, the infallibility of the universal Magisterium of the college of bishops is exercised "when the pope and bishops
in their ordinary magisterium are in agreement in proposing a doctrine as
definitive." This infallibility regards not only dogma in the strict sense, but
the totality of the teaching on faith and morals, including the interpretation of the natural moral law and any other proclamation that might have
an intrinsic historical or logical relationship with the faith, without which
dogma could not be correctly understood or preserved.

The first case—definition "ex cathedra" or ecumenical council—clearly
does not obtain with the question of freedom of religion. In effect, the first
and so far the only council to have expressed itself on this subject has been
Vatican II. It was precisely this council that recognized religious freedom. In
the same way, not even the universal ordinary Magisterium seems to be affected here, because never before had the pope and the bishops condemned
religious freedom and proclaimed this condemnation as a definitive doctrine of the Church. This was rather the case of a few isolated popes, over a

span of about a hundred years, and never of an explicit assertion of wanting to present a definitive doctrine in a matter of faith or morals (even if this was the implicit understanding of the nineteenth-century popes).

Prima facie, therefore, it seems at the least very improbable that the discontinuity highlighted above in the Church's doctrine on the freedom of religion could in some way bring into question the infallibility of the Magisterium, including the universal ordinary Magisterium. This initial claim should be confirmed by what follows.

The Doctrinal Substance of the Condemnation of Religious Freedom by Pius IX

If this is considered under the aspect of his condemnation of both indifferentism and relativism in religion—according to which there is no exclusive religious truth, all the religions are in principle equal, and the Church of Christ is not the only way of salvation—it is undeniable that the condemnation of religious freedom issued by Pius IX in effect touched on a central aspect of Catholic dogma. Upholding the truth of the Catholic Church against this challenge of indifferentism and religious relativism seemed, in any case, what was at stake at the time. If I say "seemed," it is because—as Vatican II demonstrated—the doctrine of the exclusive truth of the Christian religion and of the unicity of the Church of Jesus Christ as the way of eternal salvation is in reality not in the least harmed by the acceptance of freedom of religion and worship.

As Vatican II teaches, the right to freedom of religion and worship does not in any way imply that all religions are equivalent. This right is in effect a right of persons; it does not concern the question of knowing to what extent that which persons believe might contradict the truth. In other words, recognizing that the faithful of all religions enjoy the same civil right to freedom of worship does not mean that, because it is a right of all, all religions must be "equally true."

As shown above, the conviction of the popes and the dominant theology of the nineteenth century was that a civil right to freedom of religion (or freedom of worship) implied precisely such indifferentism. For them, this also meant abandoning the principle according to which the government of a Catholic country has the task and duty of protecting and favoring the Catholic truth, and of denying the right of any deviant religious confession to exist. At the most, such religious error could be *tolerated* within certain limits and to the extent reasonable (in order to avoid greater evil). To concede, however, a (civil) *right* to profess and cultivate a religion that was not the true one was considered to imply *ipso facto* the admission not only that there is not one true religion and Church, but that all religions are equivalent. Now, it goes without saying that at the time the Church could not accept such a view of things, nor, moreover, can it do so today. Nonetheless, today the Church has modified its conception of the function of the state and of its duties toward the true religion, a conception that in reality is not at all of a purely theological nature; nor has it to do with the nature of the Church and its faith, but it concerns the nature of the state and its relationship with the Church. So at the most, this is a question concerning an aspect of the social doctrine of the Church.

So when Benedict XVI says that Vatican Council II "recognized and made its own an essential principle of the modern state with the decree on religious freedom," he is clearly manifesting a conception of the nature and duties of the state very different from and opposed to Pius IX's conception of the state; he also departs from the traditional view of the subjection of temporal power to spiritual power. Such a discontinuity does not signify rupture with the dogmatic doctrinal Tradition of the Church, nor a deviation from the *depositum fidei* and thus from the canon of Vincent of Lérins: "quod ubique, quod semper, quod ab omnibus creditum est" (from what has been believed everywhere, always, and by all). As a result, there can be no contradiction here, not even with the infallibility of the universal ordinary Magisterium of the Church, since such a contradiction is in itself not possible.

Admittedly, the doctrine on temporal power that was developed on the basis of apostolic Tradition, and especially of sacred Scripture (including the letters of St. Paul), also contains elements of natural law that are also the object of the infallible Magisterium of the Church. This applies in particular to the doctrine that teaches that all power comes from God, that civil governors and authorities are part of the order of creation, and that in conscience, and thus for moral reasons, everyone owes obedience to the civil authority and must also acknowledge its right to adopt punitive measures. Yet it would be excessive to affirm that these principles of Scripture and Tradition also contain guidelines on the relationship between the Church and the state, on the duties of the state toward the true religion, or on the right of the Church to assert its claims by the secular arm of the state, as an instrument of both temporal penalties and civil consequences. It was only in the course of time and under the influence of different situations and histor-ical needs that such positions or doctrines were constituted, principally in relation to the Church's battle for the *libertas ecclesiae,* the freedom of the Church from civil and political control and oversight. This was an extremely complex process (the stages of which I have discussed in another essay in this volume).[5]

In this regard, it must also be emphasized that the discontinuity pointed out by Benedict XVI at the level of the application of principles does not im-ply any rupture in the continuity of the understanding of the mystery of the Church. On the contrary, Benedict XVI notes that "the Church, both before and after the Council, was and is the same Church, one, holy, catholic and apostolic, journeying on through time." One grasps here, it seems to me, Benedict XVI's real concern for a "hermeneutic of discontinuity and rup-ture" that sees in the Church of Vatican II another Church, a new Church. According to the pope, the supporters of a "hermeneutic of discontinuity and rupture" have considered the council "as a sort of constituent that elim-inates an old constitution and creates a new one." In reality, Benedict XVI explains, the council fathers had not received such a mandate. Speaking of continuity and of discontinuity at different levels—on the one hand that of dogma, of the understanding of the mystery of the Church, and, on the other, the level of the always concrete and contingent ways of applying it—"the hermeneutic of reform" defended by Benedict XVI does not establish any rupture in the understanding of the Church. The Church is instead un-derstood there as "a subject that increases in time and develops, yet always remaining the same, the one subject of the journeying people of God."

Natural Right or Civil Right? The Heart of the Doctrine of Vatican II on Religious Freedom

As argued in another objection in the criticism cited at the beginning of this appendix, Vatican II proclaims in its declaration *Dignitatis humanae,* at number 2, that "the right to religious freedom has its foundation in the very dignity of the human person as this dignity is known through the re-

---

5. See chapter 12 of this volume, entitled "Christianity and Secularity: Past and Present of a Com-plex Relationship." It was previously published in Italian as "Cristianesimo e laicità: storia ed attualità di un rapporto complesso," in *Laicità: la ricerca dell'universale nella differenza,* ed. Pierpaolo Donati (Bologna: Il Mulino, 2008), 27–138; in Spanish, see *Cristianismo y laicidad: Historia y actualidad de una relación compleja* (Madrid: Rialp, 2009). A much-expanded German version has been published as *Christentum und säkularer Staat. Geschichte—Gegenwart—Zukunft* (Freiburg i. Br.: Herder, 2012).

vealed word of God and by reason itself." Now, this means that for Vatican II, religious freedom is a natural right. In declaring this, the infallible Magisterium of the Church extends the interpretation of the natural moral law and of natural rights. As a result, the objection concludes, there can be no discontinuity or contradiction here, and so it would be false to affirm that Vatican II explicitly taught that which Pius IX condemned, that is, the right to freedom of religion and of worship.

In effect, the *Catechism of the Catholic Church,* at number 2106, states the grounds of this right clearly: "This right is based on the very nature of the human person." It is therefore certainly correct to say that the Second Vatican Council considers religious freedom as part of natural law. But it is equally true to say that *Dignitatis humanae* at number 2 asserts: "This right of the human person to religious freedom is to be recognized in the constitutional law whereby society is governed and thus it is to become a civil right." The perspective of Vatican II is therefore not simply and solely that of natural law, but is always also that of religious freedom "as a civil right," meaning, in the final analysis, as the right to freedom of worship. In fact, this was also the perspective of Pius IX, because the freedom of religion that he was condemning was nothing other than the civil right to freedom of worship asserted by, among others, the Catholic liberals. It is therefore correct to say that the assertion by Vatican II of religious freedom as a demand proper to natural law, meaning the civil right to freedom of worship, is nothing other than what had been condemned in the encyclical *Quanta cura* of Pius IX and in its supplement, the "Syllabus" of errors.

Natural law as such is therefore not at all affected by the discontinuity that is in question here. The contradiction arises only at the level of the assertion of the civil right, and is therefore only of the political order. The doctrine of Vatican II and the teaching of *Quanta cura* with its "Syllabus errorum" are therefore in contradiction not at the level of the natural law, but at the level of natural law's legal-political application in situations and in the face of concrete problems. Besides, the innovation introduced by Vatican II rests not only on its teaching of religious freedom as a natural right but also on the need for this to be recognized as a civil right, as freedom of worship. In other words, from the well-attested conception of religious freedom as a natural right, Vatican II was able to draw a new consequence concerning the positive legal order of the state. And yet, Pius IX had not drawn this same consequence; he considered it, on the contrary, harmful and false because—in his view—it necessarily implied religious indifferent-ism and relativism, both from the doctrinal point of view and in its practi-cal consequences. Vice versa, if the Second Vatican Council was able to do so, that is because it started from a different conception of the state and of its relationship to the Church, which allowed the Council to move the em-phasis from the "right to the truth" to the right of the person, of the citizen considered as an individual and of his religious conscience.

So once again, what is at stake here is not the infallibility of the ordi-nary Magisterium in its interpretation of the natural law, because saying "application" is not the same thing as saying "interpretation." In effect, in-terpretation essentially rests on that which concerns the natural moral law and the corresponding moral norm, but it says nothing about the manner in which the natural law or natural rights must be applied, nor is it con-cerned with the consequences that must be drawn from a given historical situation. That the Magisterium should sometimes express itself on such an application is inevitable, and can also be helpful. That having been said, it still cannot be affirmed that these are cases of magisterial *interpretations* of natural rights or of the natural moral law, capable of being the object of infallibility. They are concrete realizations and applications, which, at the time in which they are made, can be binding for the Catholic faithful and demand their obedience. But this is not in any way a matter of teachings that could not be recused by subsequent magisterial decisions.[6]

Discontinuity in Doctrine or Only in Relationship with the Political-Practical (Disciplinary) Orientation?

In order to escape from the supposed threat of a doctrinal contradiction, one could nonetheless take refuge in the argument that the condemnations of Pius IX were not doctrinal condemnations, but only disciplinary. In that case, there would not be any doctrinal discontinuity.

Now, in the first place, the pope's speech of 2005 does not oppose doc-trinal affirmations on the one hand to simple "decisions" (of a practical and disciplinary nature) on the other. In reality, Benedict XVI goes further, in distinguishing between "principles" and "the ways of their application." In the second place, I consider this objection to be mistaken from the histori-

---

6. Montalembert, too, submitted to the pontifical verdict, certainly in the more moderate interpre-tation, approved by Pius IX, of Bishop Félix Dupanloup of Orléans.

cal point of view as well, because in the nineteenth century this question was clearly of a doctrinal nature. In effect, Pius IX understood his condemnation of religious freedom as a necessity of the dogmatic order, and not solely as a disciplinary measure. As we have already said, the assertion of religious freedom or the affirmation that the Church does not have the right to impose upon the faithful, with the help of the "secular arm," punishments or coercive temporal measures was perceived at the time as a heresy, or at least as a way leading to heresy.[7] So it seems to me historically as well as objectively mistaken to interpret the condemnation of religious freedom on the part of the authorities of the time as a simple measure of practical-disciplinary order.

For Pius IX, what was in danger was the very safeguarding of the essence of the Church, of its claim to be the sole bearer of the fullness of truth and source of salvation. So for him, recognizing the freedom of religion meant denying these truths; it equally meant religious indifferentism

---

7. It is true that the main editor for the preparatory work of the encyclical *Quanta cura*, consultor to the Holy Office Fr. Luigi Bilio, qualified as *heretical* the statement defended by Montalembert that "L'Église n'a pas le droit de réprimer les violateurs de ses lois par des peines temporelles" (The Church does not have the right to suppress violators of its laws by means of temporal punishments). See on the theme the remarkably well-documented study of Bernard Lucien, *Grégoire XVI, Pie IX et Vatican II: Études sur la Liberté religieuse dans la doctrine catholique* (Tours: Éditions Forts dans la foi, 1990), 184–85. (Incidentally, Lucien is himself opposed to Vatican II's doctrine of religious liberty.) See also Giacomo Martina, S.J., *Pio IX (1851–1866)* (Rome: Editrice Pontificia Università Gregoriana, 1986), 336–48. It is important to emphasize that the above position, censured as heretical, does not simply refer to the right of the Church to impose, in the case of the baptized, ecclesiastical penalties that might also include "temporal" aspects—as, for example, the withdrawal of an ecclesiastical office or of a church benefice. The context of the present case makes it clear that with "temporal" the consulters of the Holy Office referred to *state authority* as being in the service of enforcing Church laws on the baptized. (The consulters explicitly stated that Montalembert's condemnable proposition referred to the "freedom of worship and press and to material coercion for religious reasons," and so in this context "temporal" precisely did not refer to ecclesiastical power and penalties, but to the coercive power of the state in the service of the true religion.) It is important to emphasize this, because the problem raised by the Catholic liberals around Montalembert was not whether the Church had the right to use coercion by imposing ecclesiastical penalties (spiritual, as for example, excommunication, and temporal, as the examples mentioned above); the question rather was whether the Church had the right to recur to the support of the temporal power of the state to impose its jurisdiction over the baptized, and whether the state, or Catholic state officials, had the duty to serve the Church in that respect. This is why Thomas Pink (a professor of philosophy at King's College, London) is mistaken in blaming me for having falsely asserted that with Vatican II the Church has renounced to its right to impose temporal penalties to enforce its jurisdiction over the baptized; he is also wrong in writing that, according to me, this was the idea that in 1864 was considered heretical by Bilio and the other consulters of the Holy Office (see Thomas Pink, "Rhonheimer on Religious Liberty: On the 'Hermeneutic of Reform' and Religious Liberty in *Nova et Vetera*," *RorateCaeli blogspot*, August 5, 2011, at http://rorate-caeli.blogspot.com/2011/08/on-religious-liberty-and-hermeneutic-of.html). My point was precisely that Bilio and the other theologians consulting the Holy Office referred "temporal" to the state as the secular arm of the Church for the enforcement of ecclesiastical jurisdiction over the baptized and to corresponding "material coercion for religious reasons," as they expressed it.

and relativism. The greatness of this pope resides precisely in this: that on the basis of the theological positions of his time (the historical character of which he was unable to discern), he unquestionably acted in a spirit of heroic fidelity to the faith and stood firm as a rock in the midst of a tempest of unbridled relativism. The time was evidently not yet ripe for the Church to join this defensive battle in a new and more differentiated way.[8]

It is in the rejection of religious indifferentism and relativism that the still-valid heart of this nineteenth-century condemnation is found. Nonetheless, this battle against religious indifferentism and relativism has become a battle against the civil right to freedom of religion and worship because of the conception that the state is the guarantor of religious truth and the Church possesses the right to make use of the state as its secular arm to ensure its pastoral responsibilities. Now, such a conception of the state did not rest in the slightest on the principles of Catholic doctrine on faith and morality, but rather on the traditions and practices of ecclesiastical law of medieval origin, as also on their theological justifications.

To this it must be added that magisterial discontinuity as such is not at stake here. For Benedict XVI, this is primarily a matter not of the continuity of the Magisterium, but of continuity of the Church, and of the understanding of the Church. He is opposed to the idea of a rupture between the "preconciliar" and "postconciliar" Church, as it is presented by the supporters of a "hermeneutic of discontinuity and rupture." In the magisterial declarations—in particular in those touching on political, economic, and social issues—many elements are found that depend upon historical circumstances. The Magisterium of the Church in the field of social teaching also contains, together with immutable principles founded on the doctrine of the faith, a mass of implementations that are often, in hindsight, rather dubious. What is involved here is not a type of "teaching" similar to Catholic teaching in matters of faith and morals, where the Church interprets the natural law in an obligatory manner—as in the cases of questions concerning contracep-

---

8. For this reason, Pius IX also later approved the distinction between "thesis" and "hypothesis," which was elaborated by the journal *Civiltà Cattolica* (founded by the Jesuits on Pius IX's request). According to this distinction, one must, from a practical-political perspective, accept and even demand modern freedoms as a "hypothesis" for the sake of Catholic causes, but one must never affirm them as a "thesis," that is, as being genuinely true and just. See the statement made, in this decisive context, by Fr. Carlo Maria Curci, S.J., "Il congresso cattolico di Malines e le libertà moderne," *La Civiltà Cattolica*, ser. 5, vol. 8, fasc. 326 (October 2, 1863): 129–49. With some important exceptions (for example, Jacques Maritain, Yves Congar, and John Courtney Murray), Catholic theology would maintain this distinction between "thesis" and "hypothesis" until Vatican II.

tion, abortion, euthanasia, and other moral norms in the field of bioethics. In these last cases, it is a matter not of simple applications of the natural law and concrete situations, but of determinations of that which belongs precisely to the natural law and to the corresponding moral norm. In this field, the universal ordinary Magisterium is also infallible.

The conceptions dominant in the nineteenth century with regard to the role and duties of the temporal power toward the true religion—conceptions that were founded on models of the Middle Ages and of late Christian antiquity, but that acquired their definitive form only within the modern confessional state—can claim for themselves only with great difficulty the privilege of resting on the apostolic Tradition or of being a constitutive element of the *depositum fidei*. In the same way, it seems very improbable that these conceptions belong to the truths that possess a historical or necessary logical relationship with the truths of the faith or of dogma, truths that would be necessary to maintain for the purpose of preserving and interpreting correctly the *depositum fidei,* as it is explained in several documents of the Magisterium.[9]

On the contrary, it would seem that at its origin Christianity even adopted a rather different position. It was born and developed in a pagan environment; it was conceived, on the basis of the Gospel and the example of Jesus Christ, as founded essentially on the separation between religion and politics, and it demanded from the Roman Empire only the freedom to develop without obstacles. In recognizing and making its own through its decree on religious freedom an "essential principle of the modern state," Benedict XVI affirms in his speech, the Second Vatican Council "has recovered the deepest patrimony of the Church. By so doing she can be conscious of being in full harmony with the teaching of Jesus himself (cf. Mt 22:21), as well as with the Church of the martyrs of all time."[10]

9. See Congregation for the Doctrine of the Faith, *Doctrinal Note on the "Professio fidei,"* and especially John Paul II, apostolic letter issued *motu proprio Ad tuendam fidem* of May 18, 1998. In the latter document one reads regarding the second paragraph of the *Professio fidei*: "This second paragraph of the *Profession of faith* is of utmost importance since it refers to truths that are necessarily connected to divine revelation. These truths, in the investigation of Catholic doctrine, illustrate the Divine Spirit's particular inspiration for the Church's deeper understanding of a truth concerning faith and morals, with which they are connected either for historical reasons or by a logical relationship." It seems difficult to prove that such as relation exists in the case in question.

10. In his article "Rhonheimer on Religious Liberty," Professor Pink wrongly asserts that *Dignitatis humanae* did not pronounce a teaching on the relations between Church and state; Pink arrives at this conclusion because he interprets *DH* no. 3, the last paragraph (that is, the teaching that the state has no competence in directing or prohibiting religious acts because this contradicts the very nature of the state, which is ordered only to the temporal common good) as referring only to the fact that, by its very

Nonetheless, the reference to the Gospel and to the first Christians is a theme mentioned not solely by Benedict XVI. Even earlier it constituted the heart of the argumentation of *Dignitatis humanae*, which dedicates two paragraphs, 11 and 12, to a reflection on the origins of the Church. The council explains laconically: "In faithfulness therefore to the truth of the Gospel, the Church is following the way of Christ and the apostles when she recognizes and gives support to the principle of religious freedom as befitting the dignity of man and as being in accord with divine revelation." It is precisely the reference to the Gospel, to the apostolic Tradition, and to the testimony of the first Christians, who, as Benedict XVI emphasizes, "clearly rejected the religion of the state," that truly characterizes the doctrine on religious freedom of Vatican II. Thus the conception of the tasks and duties of the state toward the true religion, which had been taken as authoritative by Pius IX, was tacitly shelved by the act of solemn Magisterium of an ecumenical council.[11]

---

nature ("under natural law," as Pink says), the state has no such competence, but that it has "a duty of reason under natural law" to profess and promote the true religious faith and that baptized state officials have the corresponding moral obligations toward the Church; it is precisely the *Church* that has the right to demand this on the basis of its jurisdiction over the baptized. Vatican II, Pink argues, has not abandoned this doctrine but simply sidestepped it for prudential (or pastoral) reasons—for example, the impossibility of enforcing this teaching under modern conditions—thus leaving the traditional teaching intact. Now, this quite sophisticated interpretation actually is nothing other than a new version of the above-mentioned distinction between "thesis" and "hypothesis," elaborated by the nineteenth-century Jesuits. Many passages of *Dignitatis humanae* make it clear, however, that the council intended precisely much more: to abandon the centuries-old, but certainly not apostolic, tradition of conceiving the temporal power as being in the service of the spiritual power and to return to the message of the Gospel, the teaching of the apostles, and the practice of the early Christians (see *DH* nos. 10–12). Unfortunately, Thomas Pink disregards those texts of the Magisterium that contradict his interpretation—most importantly, Benedict XVI's 2005 Christmas message to the Roman Curia, which is never mentioned and in which, as I have repeatedly quoted, the pope speaks about the Church's having "made its own an essential principle of the modern state." This signifies that Vatican II not only omits mentioning—for prudential reasons—the traditional doctrine, but that it actually proffers a new teaching. The novelty of that teaching does not rest in an innovation in Catholic dogma or morals; it rather consists in a different, soundly *secularist* conception of the state, which logically and necessarily also implies a different understanding of the relation between Church and state. (Another key text of the postconciliar Magisterium, disregarded by Professor Pink, is the *Doctrinal Note on Some Questions Regarding the Participation of Catholics in Political Life* by the Congregation for the Doctrine of the Faith of November 24, 2002.)

11. It seems clear to me that a confessional state, in the traditional sense of the term, would be essentially incompatible with the doctrine of Vatican II and in general with the civil right to freedom of religion, since, necessarily, civil discrimination would be inevitable in a confessional state, especially in the public sphere. The statement of Vatican II in number 6 of *Dignitatis humanae* ("If, in view of peculiar circumstances obtaining among peoples, special civil recognition is given to one religious community in the constitutional order of society, it is at the same time imperative that the right of all citizens and religious communities to religious freedom should be recognized and made effective in practice") should not be understood in the sense that the council maintained here a compatibility between the confessional state and religious freedom, but in the sense that the council proffered here an admonition to do away with all religious discrimination, addressed to those states in which historical vestiges of privileges accorded to a particular religion still survived.

Fidelity to the Faith, Tradition, and "traditions," and Political Modernity

The Second Vatican Council freed the Church from a centuries-old historical burden, the origins of which date back not to the apostolic Tradition and to the *depositum fidei* but rather to concrete decisions of the post-Constantinian era of Christianity. These decisions ultimately crystallized in canonical traditions and in their respective theological interpretations, with which the Church tried to defend its freedom, the *libertas ecclesiae*, from the incessant attacks of the temporal powers: one might think in particular of the medieval doctrine of the two swords, which, at the time, sought to justify theologically and biblically the understanding of the pope's *plenitudo potestatis*. Nonetheless, over the course of the centuries, these canonical traditions and their theological formulations have changed their function and tone. Afterward, and in the tradition of the confessional modern sovereign states, these became a justification of the ideal Catholic state, in which "the throne and the altar" existed in close symbiosis, and Catholic statesmen zealously upheld the cause of the "rights of the Church" instead of the civil right to religious freedom. This symbiosis and this unilateral vision that led to clericalism (in the sense of the unsound meddling of clerics in political and generally worldly affairs) and to a clerical society did not fail to obscure the authentic face of the Church.

The Second Vatican Council dared to take a step here that defined an era. Nonetheless, this did not change the Church's understanding of itself, or the Catholic doctrine on faith and morals. There was only a redefinition of the manner in which the Church conceives of its relationship with the world, and in particular with the temporal power of the state, a redefinition that in fact hearkens back to the origins, to the founding Christian charism, so to speak, and in particular to the very words of Jesus, who invites us to give to Caesar what is Caesar's and to God what is God's. Neither the infallibility of the pope nor that of the universal ordinary Magisterium of the college of bishops was harmed or diminished by such a step. On the contrary, through the doctrine of Vatican II on religious freedom there is a much clearer manifestation of the identity of the Church of Jesus Christ and of the extent to which the Magisterium of the Church in matters of faith and morals possesses continuity, in spite of all the historical discontinuities; this continuity in matters of faith and morals, moreover, constitutes the foundation and the most convincing argument for the possibility of its infallibility. For this reason, it seems to me that any interpretation that would seek to smooth over, by means of complicated expedient arguments, any sort of discontinuity in this picture of completeness is of no support in the defense of the Magisterium of the Church. Although motivated by pastoral reasons that are in themselves comprehensible and valid (but are shown to be mistaken in the light of the facts), such an interpretation complicates things unnecessarily. Through the evidence of the concrete intentions regarding ecclesiastical politics of those who promote such an interpretation, smoothing over any discontinuity can even have a counterproductive effect and so damage the credibility of the Magisterium.

Against those who, instead, like the traditionalists gathered around the Society of St. Pius X of Archbishop Lefebvre, are no longer able to see in the Church of Vatican II "the one, holy, catholic, and apostolic Church" of Tradition, and who speak of a disastrous rupture with the past, one can reply that in effect there is an irreconcilable dispute here over the conception of the Church, and also of the state and its duties. It is for this reason that these traditionalists, for whom "tradition as such" and "the ecclesial traditions" are clearly more important than the apostolic Tradition[12]—the only one that is ultimately normative—will find it difficult to accept the attempts at mediation mentioned above, because these skirt the heart of the problem, which is none other than the discontinuity that really does exist.

In a response, published online, to Robert Spaemann and to my statements on the theme of religious freedom, Fr. Matthias Gaudron cites a statement of mine: "There is no timeless dogmatic Catholic doctrine on the state—nor can there be," commenting on it as follows: "If this is true then the new Magisterium of Vatican II is no longer dogmatic, but is itself subject to change. By this same fact, then, no one can reproach the Society of St. Pius X for criticizing this Magisterium."[13] Indeed, the teaching of Vatican II on religious freedom as a civil right is certainly not *dogmatic* in nature. It is, however, the Magisterium of an ecumenical council and, as such, must be accepted by the faithful with religious obedience (not less, but indeed much more so, than the condemnations of Pius IX in their time). In any case, this does not justify a division in the Church.

12. See, in the opposite sense, the *Catechism of the Catholic Church* 83, and the Second Vatican Council, Dogmatic Constitution *Dei Verbum* on divine revelation.

13. *Sie haben ihn entthront! Eine Antwort von Pater Matthias Gaudron zur Diskussion um die Religionsfreiheit* (November 26, 2009), to be found at http://www.piusbruderschaft.de.

The position of the traditionalists, moreover, does not confine itself to saying that one *may criticize* this teaching; it instead goes so far as to say that this teaching means apostasy from the Church of Christ and is—at least implicitly—*heretical,* and it claims that the Church of Vatican II is no longer the true Church of Jesus Christ. This is why Fr. Gaudron's argumentation also skirts the real issue when he writes: "It should therefore be permitted, in the very bosom of the Church, to criticize a teaching that contradicts the body of the Church's earlier declarations, as well as to raise important objections from a juridical and political perspective. It is a matter here of a right to a different opinion." I consider this statement rather to conceal the facts, because the issue is not that members of the priestly Society of St. Pius X "criticize" the conciliar teaching, but that they claim that the traditional conception of the state and of the relations between the state and the Church—in particular the vision in which the state has the duty to promote the Catholic religion and to the extent possible to hinder the spread of other religions, through coercive means such as the condemnation of a civil right to freedom of religion and worship—would be *a constitutive element of the doctrine of the Catholic faith,* so that in the rejection of such a conception, Christ is "dethroned" and the Church betrayed. Before such a conception, the liberal principle of religious freedom seems an apostasy, the Church of Vatican II is no longer the true Catholic Church, and the schismatic episcopal ordinations of 1988 would ultimately be justified.[14]

In a later response to my affirmation above that the members of the Society of St. Pius X consider the doctrine of Vatican II about religious freedom *heretical,* Fr. Gaudron has replied that this is not true, that what I described above is not the position of the Society of St. Pius X, but that of the so-called *sedevacantists.*[15] According to Fr. Gaudron, the doctrine of the Second Vatican Council on religious freedom, in its opposition to Pius IX's understanding of the duties of the state toward the true religion, does not oppose a dogma of Catholic faith (and thus it is not heretical), but only a theological *sententia certa.*[16] Admittedly, this would be a significant precision, and I

14. See also Archbishop Marcel Lefebvre, *Ils l'ont découronné. Du libéralisme à l'apostasie. La tragédie conciliaire* (Escurolles: Éditions Fideliter, 1987); Lucien, *Grégoire XVI, Pie IX et Vatican II.*

15. See Gaudron's article "Religionsfreiheit und Unfehlbarkeit der Kirche," May 18, 2011, at www.piusbruderschaft.de.

16. According to the article "Qualifikationen, theol.," in *Lexikon für Theologie und Kirche,* 2d ed., ed. Michael Buchberger, Josef Höfer, and Karl Rahner. 10 vols. (Freiburg: Herder, 1963), 8:918, a sentence that is "theologically certain" *(theologice certum)* is a theological affirmation about whose relationship to revelation the Magisterium has not yet decided definitively, the denial of which, however, would be

would like to accept it if there were not considerable doubts about whether Fr. Gaudron is really putting all of his cards on the table. For, like Archbishop Lefebvre, he also quotes Pius VII's apostolic letter *Post tam diurnitas* (1814),[17] which says that the right to freedom of worship signifies the equivalence of all religions (that is, religious indifferentism), and that this is "implicitly the disastrous and ever deplorable heresy which St. Augustine mentions with the following words: 'They assert that all the heretics are on the good way and tell the truth.'"

Now Pius IX later condemned, in the encyclical *Quanta cura,* the following opinion of the Catholic liberals (Montalembert): "that is the best condition of civil society, in which no duty is recognized, as attached to the civil power, of restraining by enacted penalties, offenders against the Catholic religion, except so far as public peace may require" (this is the wording of *Quanta cura*). Pius IX adds that this opinion is "against the doctrine of Scripture, of the Church, and of the Holy Fathers"; he therefore suggests what Pius VII, in *Post tam diurnitas,* mentioned above, had already indicated to be the core point, namely to "put on the same level the Church, outside of which there is no salvation, with the heretic sects and even with the Jewish faithlessness." This is the decisive point that Fr. Gaudron seems to fail to address and even obscures: the traditional coupling of religious freedom and indifferentism, which necessarily meant that the defense of religious freedom would imply the equivalence of all religions, something that clearly is "against the doctrine of Scripture, of the Church, and of the Holy Fathers" and, thus, a heretical position. Exactly this equating of religious freedom with indifferentism, however, was undone with the Second Vatican Council. With it, what the popes of the nineteenth century rejected as heretical still is heresy: religious indifferentism. But religious freedom as a civil right is no longer affected by this verdict.

On the grounds of their understanding of Church and state, however,

---

tantamount to a denial of a doctrine of faith or at least indirectly threaten it. According to the article "Theological Censures," in the *Catholic Encyclopedia,* vol. 3 (New York: Robert Appleton, 1908), online edition at http://www.newadvent.org/cathen/03532a.htm, "[a] proposition is branded heretical when it goes directly and immediately against a revealed or defined dogma, or dogma de fide; erroneous when it contradicts only a certain (certa) theological conclusion or truth clearly deduced from two premises, one an article of faith, the other naturally certain. Even though a statement be not obviously a heresy or an error it may yet come near to either. It is styled next, proximate to heresy when its opposition to a revealed and defined dogma is not certain, or chiefly when the truth it contradicts, though commonly accepted as revealed, has yet never been the object of a definition (proxima fidei)."

17. See Matthias Gaudron, "Die Religionsfreiheit, Das wahre Verhältnis von Kirche und Staat," *Civitas. Zeitschrift für das christliche Gemeinwesen* 10 (2010): 1–19, at 7.

the followers of Archbishop Lefebvre reject exactly this uncoupling of the equation of religious freedom and indifferentism. To the extent that they hold to this position, the doctrine of Vatican II must seem to them heretical, at least regarding its implications. Consider also the following sentence by Montalembert (which was qualified as heretical by Fr. Luigi Bilio, consultor of the Holy Office and main drafter of *Quanta cura*): "The Church does not have the right to suppress violators of its laws by means of temporal punishments."[18] Yet, this position of Montalembert was exactly the one targeted by Pius IX in *Quanta cura*. The core of the "traditional" and "preconciliar" doctrine included the affirmation that—in religious matters and for the salvation of souls—the Church, by its very essence, had the right to use the temporal power. In modern language, it had the right to rely on the means of state coercion, a right whose defense, as Archbishop Lefebvre has stressed emphatically, was the core of the papal condemnation of religious freedom.[19]

This is why we have to ask how Fr. Gaudron, and with him the Society of St. Pius X, can possibly avoid the consequence of asserting that the Second Vatican Council's doctrine on religious freedom at least implicitly is opposed to the Catholic doctrine of faith and thus is implicated in heresy. He must, moreover, recognize the legitimacy of being asked how he can possibly justify the schismatic act of the 1988 episcopal ordinations on the grounds of the incongruence of the teaching of Vatican II on religious freedom with a mere theological *sententia certa* (which incongruence he claims the doctrine on religious freedom reflects). Together with Archbishop Lefebvre, the founder of the Society of St. Pius X, he should rather hold that this teaching implies the "heresy of liberalism" and a general apostasy of the Church and the entire human society from Jesus Christ, and that it therefore puts the whole of Catholic faith at stake.[20] Provided, however, Fr. Gaudron only intended to defend—against the idea of the religiously neutral, secular state—the integralist idea of a state, which has the task and the right to use

18. See note 7 above.

19. See Lefebvre, *Ils l'ont décourorné*, 76: "Ce qui est commun à tous les libéralismes, c'est la revendication du droit à ne pas être inquiété par le pouvoir civil dans l'exercice public de la religion de son choix; leur dénominateur commun (comme le dit le cardinal Billot) c'est la libération de toute contrainte en matière religieuse. Et cela, les papes l'ont condamné." This shows again why Thomas Pink, in "Rhonheimer on Religious Liberty," is wrong: the question is not about ecclesiastical power as such and its right to impose, besides strictly spiritual penalties such as excommunication, also so-called temporal penalties such as, for example, withdrawing a Church office or benefice, but the question of the relation between the ecclesiastical power and the power of *worldly* authorities, that is, the temporal power of the state (see also note 7 above).

20. Ibid.

coercion for the salvation of souls, this would only be a *political* position (though a theologically grounded one), which I would not consider to be heretical, but anachronistic and regrettable.

Vatican Council II effectively places us before a choice: the choice between, on the one hand, a Church that seeks to affirm and impose its truths and its pastoral duties by means of civil power, and on the other hand, a Church that recognizes—as *Dignitatis humanae* maintains in number 1—that "the truth cannot impose itself except by virtue of its own truth, as it makes its entrance into the mind at once quietly and with power." It is not a matter here of two Churches that are distinct in the dogmatic or constitutive sense, but of two Churches that have different ways of understanding their relationships with the world and with the temporal order. Vatican II does not speak out either for a strictly "laicist" state in the sense of traditional French *laïcité* or for the relegation of religion to the private sphere, but for a Church that no longer presumes to impose the kingship of Christ by means of temporal power, and that for this very reason acknowledges the political secularity of the modern secular—not militantly laicist—state.

This is precisely the perspective of Vatican II. It has been confirmed by the Congregation for the Doctrine of the Faith's *Doctrinal Note on Some Questions Regarding the Participation of Catholics in Political Life* of November 24, 2002. In number 6 of this note we read that "*laïcité,* understood as autonomy of the political or civil sphere from that of religion and the Church" represents for Catholic moral doctrine "a value that has been attained and recognized by the Catholic Church and belongs to [the] inheritance of contemporary civilization."[21] Though not autonomous *morally*—it must satisfy basic, objective moral criteria—the state is at the same time not obliged to recognize one religious truth or one true Church over other confessions or religious communities. As state and as coercive civil power,

21. I have slightly changed the wording of the official English translation, because it does not correctly reproduce the Italian original, which speaks of *laicità* (the Italian equivalent to the French *laïcité*) and of "autonomy" *without any further qualification* (and not, as the English translation does, of "rightful autonomy," which is out of place, because the autonomy of the state regarding the religious and the ecclesiastical spheres is autonomy *tout court*, without any further qualification). The Italian original thus says: "Per la dottrina morale cattolica la laicità intesa come autonomia della sfera civile e politica da quella religiosa ed ecclesiastica—*ma non da quella morale*—è un valore acquisito e riconosciuto dalla Chiesa e appartiene al patrimonio di civiltà che è stato raggiunto." Of course, this does not mean that the state must be indifferent regarding the religious life of its citizens or that religion must be absent from public life, as it is in the case of French *laïcité* (see the passage of *Dignitatis humanae* quoted in continuation). The point is the institutional independence and sovereignty of the political sphere with respect to religious authorities such as the Church, that is, the absence of any form of establishment of a determinate religion.

it declares itself incompetent to judge on religious questions of truth or on any associated privileges. The duties and aims of the state are of a different nature, even when it shows concern for the religious life of its citizens or when it recognizes a particular religion, deeply anchored in a nation's tradition, as a reality belonging to its culture and its public life. The state's activity is ultimately oriented toward the *political* principles of justice and of the equality of all confessions, and toward the recognition of the same rights of all persons. "Government therefore ought indeed to take account of the religious life of the citizenry and show it favor, since the function of government is to make provision for the common welfare. However, it would clearly transgress the limits set to its power, were it to presume to command or inhibit religious acts."[22]

The mission of preaching the Gospel, on the part of the Church and by the apostolate of the lay faithful who found themselves upon that Gospel, consists in penetrating the structures of society with the spirit of Christ, and by this means favoring the manifestation of the kingship of Christ.[23] The kingdom of Christ does not begin with the public confession of the true religion; it begins with the proclamation of the Gospel by the Church, which is received in the hearts of men and women, and it continues to grow through the apostolic action of the ordinary faithful, who establish it in all of human society, in all the structures and realities of life.[24]

22. *Dignitatis humanae,* no. 3.

23. See my reflections on this subject in my book *Changing the World: The Timeliness of Opus Dei* (New York: Scepter Press, 2009).

24. The present article first appeared in German in *Die Tagespost* 115 (September 26, 2009): 14, and online at KATH.NET, September 28, 2009 (www.kath.net/detail.php?id=24068). A Spanish translation of the article appeared in Appendix I of Martin Rhonheimer, *Cristianismo y laicidad. Historia y actualidad de una relación compleja, Ediciones* (Madrid: Rialp, 2009), 167–79. The version presented here includes the text of that article in its entirety, expanded and provided with an appendix, which deals with specific questions concerning the continuity and infallibility of the ordinary universal Magisterium, questions inherent to the problem discussed here. This expanded version was first published in French as "L' 'herméneutique de la réforme' et la liberté de religion," *Nova et Vetera* 85 (2010): 341–63 (online at www.novaetvetera.ch/Art%20Rhonheimer.htm) and in a slightly abridged version in *Die Neue Ordnung* 65, no. 4 (August 2011): 244–61. Parts of these texts were previously published online also in English: http://chiesa.espresso.repubblica.it/articolo/1347670. Compared with the version of the French edition of *Nova et Vetera,* this complete English version is slightly updated, including at the end a further response to a critic from the ranks of the Society of St. Pius X.

I thank Joseph T. Papa, Matthew Sherry, and William F. Murphy, all of whom have contributed to this English translation.

||||||||||||||||||||||||||||||||||||||||||||||||||||||||||||||||||||||||||||||||||||||||||||||||||||||||||||||

FOURTEEN

Capitalism, Free Market Economy, and the Common Good

The Role of the State in the Economy

Author's note: The following is a piece of moral and political philosophy—or political ethics—rather than of economics or political science. It tries to provide, however, a philosophical treatment of the topic embedded in, and—as I hope—enlightened by, basically sound economic thinking, as far as this can be successfully achieved by a noneconomist. At any rate, I am convinced that it is not possible to say something reasonable specifically from a moral point of view, which is also the viewpoint of political philosophy, about a topic like "Capitalism, Free Market Economy, and the Common Good" without respecting the logic proper to economic thinking. When speaking about so-called social justice, both moral philosophers and theologians should be always aware of this logic and the respect which it is owed. Economists reading this chapter, on the other hand, may forgive me for any misapprehension of economic issues, lack of clarity, or undue simplifications they will possibly find.

The Traditional Criticism of Capitalism and *Laissez-Faire* and the Call for State Intervention

In his famous and brilliantly written pamphlet *The End of Laissez-faire*, the great British economist John Maynard Keynes calls the essential characteristic of capitalism the "intense appeal to the money-making and money-loving instincts of individuals."[1] In this same line, he somewhat contemp-

---

1. John Maynard Keynes, *The End of Laissez-Faire* (1926), republished in Keynes, *The End of Laissez-Faire: The Economic Consequences of the Peace* (New York: Prometheus Books, 2004), 43.

tuously depicts an image of businessmen and entrepreneurs, governed by such capitalist instincts, whose evil economic consequences must be overcome by new forms of public business regulations. In his 1926 text, Keynes, somewhat surprisingly, contends that "progress lies in the growth and the recognition of semi-autonomous bodies within the state—bodies whose criterion of action within their own field is solely the public good as they understand it, and from whose deliberations motives of private advantage are excluded," returning thereby "towards medieval conceptions of separate autonomies." These bodies, Keynes continues, should be "subject in the last resort to the sovereignty of the democracy expressed through Parliament."[2] Such a solution, therefore, "would involve Society in exercising directive intelligence through some appropriate organ of action over many of the inner intricacies of private business, yet it would leave private initiative and enterprise unhindered."[3]

This, in my view, somewhat utopian proposal appropriately describes a spirit of interventionism—although it pretends to "leave private initiative and enterprise unhindered"[4]—a position that was generally advocated after the First World War, albeit in different ways, in both democratic and nondemocratic societies (it is known that Keynes's ideas not only inspired left-wing politics of government planning and regulation, but also fascist corporatism). Government curbing of entrepreneurial initiative and bureaucratic state regulation of business activity was considered to be the remedy for the principal failures of capitalism. Due to its monopolistic structure and increasing state interventions (which, rather than aiming at breaking the power of monopolies, tended to bureaucratically control and direct business activity), the former economic system was considerably degenerated at that time. After the 1929 New York Stock Exchange crash, caused by a speculative financial bubble, and the succeeding slump, such policies were increasingly recognized as beneficial and necessary.[5] However, as historians have

---

2. Ibid., 37.   3. Ibid., 41.

4. Notice, however, the formulation on page 41: "These measures would involve Society in *exercising directive intelligence through some appropriate organ of action over many of the inner intricacies of private business,* yet it would leave private initiative and enterprise unhindered" (emphasis added). This sounds somewhat contradictory; I suppose, however, that what Keynes had in mind was something widely practiced some years later by one of the last German pre-Nazi governments, presided over (1930–32) by chancellor Heinrich Brüning, and afterward systematized by the Nazi regime. This involved leaving business as such—the means of production and enterprise generally—as private property while the government regulated and directed concrete business decisions. This policy turned out to be fatally unsound; however, it provided the natural presupposition for Hitler's later war economy.

5. A still useful summary and analysis of the international situation during these years is provided

argued on the basis of Milton Friedman's and Anna Schwartz's study of the financial history of the United States, these politics led to a mistaken, restrictive monetary policy by the Federal Reserve Board, suffocating the recovery of private business activity.[6] Others, however, most prominently Murray N. Rothbard, have argued against this idea on the grounds of the "Austrian" understanding of the business cycle as elaborated by Ludwig von Mises. They insist that the real cause of the depression was not restrictive money policy after the slump but rather continuous inflationary state intervention during the "roaring twenties (which because of permanent price stability remained unnoticed)" and the attempt by the Hoover administration to impede readjustment of the economy after the 1929 crash.[7] Rothbard further argues that far from having followed a politics of laissez-faire, as a persistent myth continues to tell, the Republican administrations of the twenties, together with the Federal Reserve Board—in close, quasi-conspiratorial coordination with the Bank of England and the British government[8]—was in reality highly interventionist, causing continuous inflationary credit expansion. This policy necessarily brought about a depression and the final explosion of the malinvestment bubble in October (the consequence, not the cause, of the beginning of the depression, initiated already in July 1929). Moreover, the unfortunate protectionist measures taken by the Hoover administration (e.g., the Smoot-Hawley tariff in 1930), disintegrated the world economy and dramatically increased unemployment everywhere. Finally, under the successor to this administration, Franklin D. Roosevelt, these politics took the unprecedented form of "big government," famously called by its inventors the "New Deal" (although, in fact, it only continued the politics of the Hoover administration, pushing them to the extreme).[9]

Inspired by a Keynesian spirit—a line of thought much less original than is commonly believed as it primarily rationalized what at that time was

---

by the W. Arthur Lewis's classic book, *Economic Survey 1919–1939* (London: Allan and Unwin, 1949; 9th impression 1970); reprinted in the Routledge Reprint ed. (London: Routledge Chapman & Hall, 2003).

6. Milton Friedman and Anna J. Schwartz, *A Monetary History of the United States, 1867–1960* (Princeton, N.J.: Princeton University Press, 1963), 299–419.

7. See Murray N. Rothbard, *America's Great Depression* (1963), 5th ed. (Auburn, Ala.: Mises Institute, 2000). Rothbard's and Friedman's views, I think, do not strictly contradict each other since they perceive, although in different ways, the cause of the problem in the state's monetary policy and its grave distortion of economic equilibrium

8. See ibid., 131–45.

9. For the details of the truly interventionist politics of the Hoover administration (e.g., its fight against the readjustment of price-cost relations by impeding the fall of wages, thereby causing heavy and persistent unemployment), see ibid., 167–295.

widely in vogue[10]—Roosevelt's politics of the New Deal tried to overcome the economic depression not only by extensive public deficit spending and huge government programs such as the Tennessee Valley Authority (TVA), but also by interventions into the price system, by meticulous bureaucratic regulations of entrepreneurial activity—with the justification of protecting society from greedy predators—and by imposing increasingly higher tax rates on the business profits of the wealthy (causing them to hoard rather than to invest their riches in business). As the economic historian Amity Shlaes has recently argued in her book *The Forgotten Man: A New History of the Great Depression,* in reality Roosevelt's politics, though not *causing* the depression, "helped to make the Depression Great"[11] (although, provided the Austrians are right, this honor should already be attributed to President Hoover). With their bias for central planning and state regulation of productive activity through several government-run agencies, their public projects like the TVA, their interventions into the price system, and the imposition of high taxes on the profits of the wealthy, the New Dealers, united in Roosevelt's "brain trust,"[12] were convinced that they were not only stimulating the economy, but fighting against what they regarded as the cause of all evils: the capitalist's, and even ordinary businessman's, greed for money and profit. This was also the message Roosevelt effectively transmitted to the public through his regularly broadcast "Fireside Chats," which additionally contributed to deteriorating the image of private business and those engaged in it. Roosevelt's policy, as Amity Shlaes points out, "made government into a competitor that the private sector could not match."[13] Although not all the measures taken by the Roosevelt administration were harmful—some actually were beneficial—most of them caused much damage. Their immediate effect was to strangle entrepreneurial initiative and the readiness of businessmen and the rich to take risks, not only thereby withholding new prosperity from the economy, but also making simple recovery more difficult by interfering with the only forces that could have reestablished economical dynamics and innovation: entrepreneurial risk behavior in view of the reward of profit—that is, the alleged "evil" of

10. See for this argument Henry Hazlitt, *The Failure of the "New Economics": An Analysis of the Keynesian Fallacies* (1959) (Auburn, Ala.: Mises Institute, 2007).

11. Amity Shlaes, *The Forgotten Man: A New History of the Great Depression* (New York: HarperCollins, 2007), 9.

12. This term was created and first applied to Roosevelt's board of consulters at this very time.

13. Shlaes, *The Forgotten Man,* 11, 262–68.

capitalism—and a corresponding expansion of productive activity.[14] Contrary to encouraging this force of renewal, its interventionist character and strong belief in the superiority of state planning and regulation as well as its continuously experimental and volatile character caused arbitrariness and unpredictability. In this manner, the politics of the New Dealers made entrepreneurial risk calculation and long-term foresight impossible and thus greatly discouraged investment.[15] At the same time, Roosevelt, cherishing the myth of a society of classes—actually partially existing as a product of the failures of the first period of the New Deal—increasingly served interest groups. Basing his politics on constituencies, he was rewarded with votes and reelected twice. Hence, as Amity Shlaes concludes, "the New Dealer's economic failures were working to their own political advantage."[16]

This continues to be a well-known pattern: successful electoral politics united to generally harmful economic policies that, however, are held to be salutary by a majority of voters. This error is due to the strong influence of organized interest groups, who will gain from these policies, upon public opinion. This was first practiced systematically by the Roosevelt administration and greatly contributed to the following myth that the state—comprising public deficit spending and job creation by government-run enterprises —is not only the necessary and single remedy against slumps and similar economic crises, but the ordinary means to regulate economic cycles and to achieve social justice.[17]

14. "The story of the mid-1930s is the story of a heroic economic struggling to recuperate but failing to do so because of perverse federal policy. The worst factor was Roosevelt's war on business.... The private sector, desperate, was incredibly productive—those who did have a job worked hard, just as our grandparents told us. But the government was taking all the air in the room. Utilities are a prime example. In the 1920s electricity was a miracle industry. There was every expectation even in the 1930s that growth in utilities might pull the country through hard times in the future. And the industry might have indeed done that, if the government had not supplanted it. Roosevelt believed in public utilities, not private companies" (ibid., "Afterword" to the paperback edition, 2008, 392–94).

15. Some observers think that at present the Obama administration commits the same mistake: due to the unpredictability of government policy and the subsequent creation of a lack of confidence, private business and investment is discouraged so that the economy is not recovering as it should to decrease unemployment.

16. Shlaes, *The Forgotten Man*, 267.

17. One of the clearest European critics of the New Deal (and of Keynes), Wilhelm Röpke—after the Second World War he was among those greatly inspired by "neoliberalism" and the German *Soziale Marktwirtschaft*—remarked that if Keynes had only taught that as an incentive the state should contribute by some deficit spending to reanimate a depressed economy, he would have said something very reasonable and generally accepted. However, with this position, he certainly would not have gained the reputation he received by teaching that the medicine for an ailing patient should also be the ordinary nourishment for ordinary and more healthy times; see Wilhelm Röpke, "Was lehrt Keynes? Die Revolution der Nationalökonomie," in *Universitas*, December 1952, 1285–95, reprinted in Röpke, *Gegen die Brandung*, ed. Albert Hunold, 2nd ed. (Erlenbach-Zürich: Eugen Rentsch Verlag, 1959), 256–69. See also

The effective economic failures of the politics of the New Deal were never fully realized, thanks to the outbreak of the Second World War and the transition to a war economy, strongly based on state regulation.[18] On the other hand, the New Deal has left to posterity what today is generally accepted as its most beneficial outcome: the social security system. This must not cause us to forget that the basis for the legitimization of the New Deal was a pro-socialist ideology of anti-laissez-faire, advocated by those members of Roosevelt's brain trust very much influenced by socialist ideas—at that time the Soviet Union still seemed to many of them to be an interesting experiment from which something could be learned. Moreover, joined to this socialist bias was the idea, openly supported by the president himself, that the government needed to bring morality into the immoral and selfish world of capitalist business by means of state regulation.

An Alternative View: Walter Eucken's Ordoliberalism

In the opening pages of his seminal work *Grundsätze der Wirtschaftspolitik* (Principles of economic policy), first published in 1952, the influential "ordoliberal" (or, as they were called at that time, "neoliberal") economist Walter Eucken extensively criticizes the nineteenth-century idea of laissez-faire. In a short footnote,[19] Eucken remarks that Keynes, though having been quite right in criticizing pure laissez-faire, had not, however, understood the very essence of capitalism and, thus, the other side of the coin, that is, the positive and beneficial features of the idea of laissez-faire. These features were principally to be elaborated as the entrepreneurial freedom to make, on the basis of the information delivered by the price system in a free market shaped by the division of labor, decisions regarding the choice of what to produce, of which factors of production to employ, and of output

---

Röpke's devastating 1934 judgment about the first period of the New Deal, still worthwhile reading: "Die Nationalökonomie des 'New Deal,'" first published in *Zeitschrift für Nationalökonomie* 5 (1934): 577–95, reprinted in Röpke, *Gegen die Brandung*, 60–84.

18. Notice that in September 1931, unemployment amounted to 17.4 percent; in July 1935, in the fifth year of the New Deal, it had risen to 21.3 percent, to come down in August 1937 to 13.5 percent, yet rising again to the initial amount of 17.4 percent in January 1938. In January 1940, when Roosevelt won reelection to his third term, it was still 14.6 percent. In the meantime, the Dow Jones Industrial Average was 140 (in 1931), 119 (1935), 187 (1937), 121 (1938), 151 (1940). Before the 1929 crash, it registered at 168 (1927) and 343 (October 1929, immediately before the crash). So, after eight years of the Roosevelt administration, the New Deal generated only little recovery, and certainly no new prosperity. Moreover, as far as unemployment was concerned, its results were rather poor.

19. Walter Eucken, *Grundsätze der Wirtschaftspolitik*, 4th ed. (Tübingen: J. C. B. Mohr [Paul Siebeck], 1968), 27n1.

numbers, as well as the unfettered freedom to invest privately owned monetary assets at one's own risk, motivated by the expectation of future profit.[20]

Contrary to what Keynes wrote, *as such* this entrepreneurial behavior of the real businessman has nothing to do with "money-loving." Even if in most cases love of money, personal enrichment, and what this actually involves are the innermost motive of a capitalist's undertakings—which, however, is by no means necessarily the case, but admittedly very natural and always most probable, it is simply flawed logic to assert that the *motive* or *intention* with which people do what they are doing is equal to, and the essence of, *what* they are doing. Now, the essence of capitalism is to be seen in *what* a capitalist is actually doing, and not in *why* he does it or what *motivates* him to do it.[21]

Eucken dedicates many pages of his seminal book to criticizing nineteenth-century laissez-faire. However, he elegantly demonstrates that there are both sound and unsound elements in the idea of laissez-faire. The traditional laissez-faire political economy is completely correct in insisting on the freedom of entrepreneurial activity, personal responsibility, and the freedom to make the typical business decisions. Eucken further shows that

20. With this description, which I admit is a simplification, it is not ignored that in modern, mainly big business companies, the capital owners—mostly shareholders—and those who take the concrete and current entrepreneurial decisions, the top managers, are not the same persons. Yet, this does not change the basic idea of capitalism; it only affects the way, the idea is practically carried out. In fact, already in his above-quoted 1926 anti-*laissez-faire* pamphlet, Keynes had noticed that in big companies "the owners of the capital, *i.e.* the shareholders, are almost entirely dissociated from the management, with the result that the direct personal interest of the latter in the making of great profit becomes quite secondary" (*The End of Laissez-faire*, 38). Keynes applauds this, thinking it to be a first step of big companies toward "socializing themselves," which, as he notes, is one of "the advantages of State Socialism" (ibid., 39; for other reasons, however, Keynes did not advocate what he called State Socialism). Today, we have come to understand the disadvantages of this kind of "self-socializing" of big companies, that is, of top managers being paid independently from the business success and profit of the companies they direct.

21. A further differentiation should be made between the "real economy" market and financial markets; yet, as I understand the difference should not be stressed too much, because the nature and aim of financial markets is not just making money, as many people think, but in fact serving and making work precisely the "real economy" (through financing, credit, insurance, etc.). Therefore, financial markets and also speculative activity are, in principle, useful and necessary, and engaging in them is an absolutely honorable profession. In my view, the problem starts when finance transactions and speculation become totally uncoupled from any real economic substratum, that is, when they have no connection anymore to the world of the "real economy" that leads to the creation of economic value. Such a kind of financial speculation is far away from the real entrepreneurial spirit that is characteristic of capitalism; rather than being a long-term project for value creation, as it is typical for capitalism, its only "economical" function rather is to serve short-term personal enrichment. It has been proven to be very dangerous and detrimental to the international finance system to let it, without any further security measures, fall prey to these kinds of financial sharks, who are lacking any real entrepreneurial spirit or are perverting this spirit from inside great firms (such as banks, insurance companies, etc.), and thus are also tending to "moral hazard and to taking exaggerated and irrational risks, which an authentic "capitalist" and classic entrepreneur would never take.

this sound element of capitalistic laissez-faire is linked to the idea of free competition—which precisely contradicts a monopolistic structure of the market—and finally depends upon an unfettered price system as the *sole and unique* regulatory principle of decisions concerning production and consumption (according to the laws of supply and demand). Government intervention aimed at curbing, controlling, or fettering this entrepreneurial liberty, at partially annulling the regulatory role of the price system, or even at competing, through government-run companies, with private business, Eucken argues, is both economically and socially harmful. Hence, it is also essentially opposed to the common good.

On the other side, Eucken contends, the error of nineteenth-century laissez-faire was the conviction—based rather on philosophical, moral, or even theological assumptions (often also on popularized forms of Darwinism, or better, "Spencerism"), than on economic thinking—*that this entrepreneurial freedom alone* could positively establish a complete harmony between private interests and the common good. Therefore, even egoistic motivations were socially beneficial.[22] During the second half of the nineteenth century, united to the Industrial Revolution, capitalism undoubtedly led to unprecedented economic innovation and growth as well as to a constant rise in real wages and the affluence of all social classes.[23] Yet, several factors, some intrinsic to the logic of the market—and the financial system— and others due to extrinsic causes, primarily harmful state interventions, led to fatal imbalances and distortions of the capitalist economy.

The free coordination of individual interests by market forces, without any ordering and correcting activity by the state, Eucken forcibly argues, does not necessarily and automatically lead to the common good. The free market needs a political framework developed by the state *(Ordnungspolitik)*. Despite this, in Eucken's eyes the essential truth of laissez-faire and the insights of the classical theoreticians of economic liberalism remain valid: by undermining and even, although only partially, annulling the spontaneous market forces through government intervention in the economic process itself, the common good is undermined and positively counteracted.

---

22. This was expressed in its purest form by the great French economist Frédéric Bastiat; see, e.g., his *Harmonies économiques* (Paris: Guillaumin, 1851). Notice that also Keynes, in his aforementioned pamphlet, interprets capitalism in terms of the Darwinist—that is, "Spencerist"—"survival of the fittest."

23. See, e.g., Peter Mathias, *The First Industrial Nation: An Economic History of Britain 1700–1914,* 2nd ed. (London: Routledge, 1983); Fernand Braudel and Ernest Labrousse, *Histoire économique et sociale de la France,* vol. 3: *1789–années 1880* (Paris: Presses Universitaires de France, 1976).

Thus, Eucken emphasizes, laissez-faire in the sense of entrepreneurial freedom and self-responsibility concerning production decisions, based on the information delivered by the price system, undistorted by state regulations, is a *necessary* condition for obtaining the common good. Laissez-faire, however, is not a *sufficient* condition, and therefore, if other conditions are not met, it cannot be in the public interest and may even be harmful.[24]

In other words: Adam Smith's "invisible hand" in fact does work. The invisible hand was actually Adam Smith's landmark discovery. Essentially, it is an argument against the mercantilist economic and trade policy of an absolutistic state, based on the idea that the *visible* hand of the state has to organize the whole economy, thus creating the wealth and power of a nation.[25] For Adam Smith, instead, the pursuit of self-interest—which, as I will argue below more in detail, does not necessarily mean egoism—and the division of labor do create a spontaneous order of coordinated activities of supply and demand, regulated by the price system, and an optimal allocation of resources. Therefore, they also most forcefully promote the public interest and the common good. A "visible hand" of politicians and bureaucrats neither exists nor is needed. There is no system of central planning or any super-intelligent human mind that could possibly fulfill this task of coordination, because such coordination *can* be achieved only as the outcome of the whole *system* of, on the level of individual intentionality, uncoordinated and thus "spontaneous" economic transactions.

Now, the point of all this is that in a free market economy, as conceived by Adam Smith, *there is actually no such thing as an invisible hand at all.* The metaphor of the invisible hand only indicates what really and truly *happens* in a market economy. To those who do not understand the mechanism of markets, the division of labor, and free competition, an "invisible hand" *seems* to be there (they seek a "hand" that explains the otherwise seemingly miraculous outcome, according to the logic of conspiracy theories, which always look for the "invisible hand": one single cause explaining complex

24. Ibid., 360.
25. Notice that Mandeville's famous *Fable of the Bees* (with its moral "private vices are public benefits"), which is commonly held to be an authentic expression of the *laissez-faire* ideology and of Adam Smith's invisible hand, actually is based on a mercantilist outlook. This is clarified at the end, where the author remarks that such private vices are certainly beneficial for the public good provided "that Private Vices by the dextrous Management of a skilful Politician may be turn'd into Publick Benefits." Now, such "dextrous Management of a skilful Politician" is exactly the opposite of Smith's invisible hand! See Bernard Mandeville, *The Fable of the Bees: Or Private Vices, Publick Benefits,* ed. with an introduction by Philip Harth (London: Penguin Books, 2010), 371.

patterns). Yet, in the free market economy, there is no "one hand" that explains the result. In reality, the invisible hand is the feedback system of the "many hands," that is, of the market that, through the price system, spontaneously coordinates private interests in such a way as to concur with an optimal allocation of resources. The hand, thus, is "invisible" because this indicates the market as a kind of black box: we know the result, but, despite knowing the basic mechanism, we are unable to comprehend all the steps having brought it about, precisely *because in none of these steps did somebody actually intend to bring it about.*

Adam Smith was not an extremist; but he knew that an individual engaged in business does not, and cannot, intend to promote the public interest. Yet, when Smith writes, "By pursuing his own interest he frequently promotes that of the society more effectually than when he really intends to promote it,"[26] he not only simply describes what obviously happens, but also moderately and wisely says that this is the case only "frequently." In fact, nothing in the idea of the invisible hand denies that laissez-faire is only a necessary *but not a sufficient condition* for coordinating private interests, attaining thereby the common good. Further, there is not any denial that there are many circumstances and cases in which the invisible hand would not work because some condition for its proper functioning fails.[27]

Unfortunately, there persists a confusing and detrimental attitude of those who, beginning from the insight into the insufficiency of laissez-faire and its unsatisfactory outcome if the market is left to itself, conclude that a free market is *intrinsically* harmful. Thus, entrepreneurial decisions and the regulatory force of the price system should *on principle* be checked by government intervention or even by directly converting the state into a competitor of private business to overcome its alleged egoism and greed of profit—of course by unjustly subsidizing economic state activity with taxpayers' contributions (also with those of citizens engaged in private business who thus are unjustly constrained to subsidize their often even less efficient state-run competitors). Such people think that capitalist laissez-faire, instead of be-

26. Adam Smith, *An Inquiry into the Nature and Causes of the Wealth of Nations,* IV, 2, ed. R. H. Campbell and A. S. Skinner; textual ed. W. B. Todd (Oxford: Oxford University Press, 1979), 456.

27. When I say *optimal* allocation this precisely does not mean *perfect* allocation. "Optimal" is always relative to concrete circumstances and their constraints. The outcome may also be *suboptimal,* due to market-distorting lacks of equilibrium. It seems to me reasonable to assert, however, that even the suboptimal allocation of resources is usually the best we can achieve in this real world, so that the difference between "optimal" and "suboptimal" becomes rather theoretical. On the other hand, to demand perfection, and to criticize the market economy on these grounds, is unrealistic and intellectually unsound.

ing as it actually is, though very imperfectly, a cause of prosperity, is in reality a problem and a cause of misery. This is the great confusion to which Keynes, among economists—Marx, after all, was only a philosopher—has contributed certainly in the most influential way. This is not to deny that the capitalist or free market economy avoids causing problems or undesirable side effects. Yet, these should be resolved not by abolishing or fettering capitalism and the dynamics proper to it, but by making it work better and more efficiently, according to truly just rules, so that it can develop its true potential.

The Free Market: An Order Both Natural to Man and Created, Which Should Be Supervised by the State

The popularity of the anti-capitalist bias, which is actually an anti-free-market-economy bias, has survived right up to the present day. People who have no education in basic economics and, therefore, have difficulties in understanding economic logic commonly believe, generally and as a matter of principle, that *the market is a problem* and that the state, however, is the solution. As Bryan Caplan has shown in his *The Myth of the Rational Voter,*[28] citizens of modern democracies apply economic thinking very well in their daily lives, but are much less able to understand it on the level of the public and democratic choice of government policies. Consequently, in crucial issues they vote for bad politics, which is opposed to their own interests. By challenging the myth of the rational voter, Brian also attacks the whole school of rational choice economics, based on its vision of a *homo oeconomicus* who is always and exclusively driven by pure economic rationality, even in his publicly relevant choices.

Bryan Caplan's argument is based on statistical evidence from the United States (I suppose, however, that some of the biases mentioned by him may even be stronger in quite a few European countries because generally U.S. citizens are much more pro–free market than Europeans, who have a much stronger tradition of "state-devoutness" and, thus, of expecting solutions for public needs and social problems to come from the government). Now, regarding U.S. citizens, Caplan identifies four widespread biased beliefs concerning economics. First, he makes out an *anti-market bias,*

28. Bryan Caplan, *The Myth of the Rational Voter: Why Democracies Choose Bad Politics* (Princeton, N.J.: Princeton University Press, 2007).

which is a "tendency to underestimate the economic benefits of the market mechanism" (an expression of the most common error concerning the basic features of markets, trade, and the logic of entrepreneurial activity). Secondly, Caplan states an *anti-foreigner bias,* "which underestimates the economic benefits of interaction with foreigners," benefits that exist even if foreign countries are much poorer, and which leads to being sympathetic toward protectionist policies. Thirdly, Caplan speaks of a *make-work bias,* which leads voters "to underestimate the economical benefits of conserving labor," ignoring that normally the destruction of jobs by bankruptcy of inefficient industries or by downsizing firms in order to increase efficiency and thus secure their survival, rather than being a loss, means economic growth (this bias favors state intervention in favor of maintaining, and subsidizing with the taxpayers' money, inefficient enterprises). Finally, he sketches out a *pessimistic bias,* which is "a tendency to overestimate the severity of economic problems and underestimate the (recent) past, present, and future performance of the economy"—a bias readily used by politicians to enhance the agenda of government intervention, instead of spreading optimism in the creative and innovative forces of freedom.[29]

Because of the—at least at first glance—counterintuitive character of many basic economic truths, the idea that the market is the problem and the state the solution "is a deeply rooted pattern of human thinking that has frustrated economists for generations."[30] With most, perhaps not all, economists—from F. A. Hayek to Milton Friedman, Amartya Sen to Paul Krugman and even Joseph E. Stiglitz, independently of their belonging to the political right or left—I am convinced that, generally speaking and as a matter of principle, exactly the opposite is true: *normally* and *as a matter of principle,* the solution is the market. The problems, however, are created by state and government policies aimed at checking and "correcting" the market mechanism, trying at least to partially replace it by bureaucratic regulations, or even by the state's seeking to directly participate in the game.[31]

29. Ibid., chap. 2 (30–49).
30. Ibid., 31.
31. Pointing out the failures of financial markets in recent times and taking advantage of the financial crisis, Joseph Stiglitz seems to me to somewhat demagogically overstate the defects and insufficiency of the free market. Also Stiglitz knows well that the state can never do what markets alone are able to do: to assure the optimal allocation of resources. State intervention can help markets to better attain this goal, or correct certain outcomes for political or moral reasons. So, despite of his Keynesian viewpoint (pleading for the state having, as a primary economic goal, the task of assuring full employment), Stiglitz, as an economist, in fact is much more an advocate of the free market than he seems to admit. To call

Now, market failures are an obvious fact, but state failures are much more frequent and more harmful. State failures have a tendency to become institutionalized and thus an enduring solution for resolving the problems created by the very government interventions that claimed to remedy alleged market failures. Normally, state failures are less obvious and less perceived—as, for example, the huge failures of promoting and subsidizing real estate property by the U.S. government through the huge mortgage associations of Fannie Mae and Freddie Mac, most probably one of the main causes, if not the condition *sine qua non,* of the recent subprime bubble and the following financial crisis. Hence, according to many who have commented on the crisis, the "underpricing of risk," which by providing biased information and nourishing the urges of greedy hunters of short-term gain distorted the financial markets, was greatly caused by previous state intervention (thus, provided this is a correct assessment of what happened, greed was not the *cause,* but already a consequence of, and a reaction to, a government policy creating the conditions to fuel such greed). As far as state failure is concerned, something analogous, although in a different order, seems to apply to the 1929 stock market crash and the following slump. What really caused the Depression and made it Great was not simply the greedy predators on the financial markets—they also had their part in causing the bubble and the 1929 stock exchange crash—but, as mentioned above, previous inflationary credit expansion during the "roaring twenties," causing a cluster of malinvestment and the subsequent state failure in reacting to the slump following the stock exchange crash. According to the Friedman-Schwartz analysis, these latter failures, attributed to the actions of the Federal Reserve Board (contracting instead of expanding credit),[32] the

(in his *Making Globalization Work* [New York: Norton, 2006], xvi) "pollution" or "too little basic research" market failures is not really to the point, because even the most liberal advocates of the free market admit that the market, by itself and without any state regulation, is not able to internalize external effects such as pollution, or to provide sufficient resources for research and education. See also Stiglitz, *Freefall: America, Free Markets, and the Sinking of the World Economy* (New York: Norton, 2010), where it becomes rather evident that Stiglitz has no real alternative to offer to the market economy; his proposals are rather moral appeals than concrete proposals for institutional alternatives to the market economy.

32. Cf. a short account in Niall Ferguson, *The Ascent of Money: A Financial History of the World* (London: Penguin, 2008), 158–65. Ferguson also refers to Milton Friedman and Anna J. Schwartz, *A Monetary History of the United States, 1867–1960* (an explanation, however, not accepted by the adherents to the Austrian theory of business cycles). As Niall Ferguson argues, there were similar stock exchange crashes also after the Second World War, but they never caused a depression as the reaction of the government was quite different; the lesson of the period following 1929 had been well learned. But this also signifies that the catastrophic effect of the 1929 crash was not so much due to a failure of capitalism, but rather to state failures regarding government reaction to a speculative bubble, which periodically and

fatal protectionist measures that converted the U.S. depression into a world-wide economic crisis, the interventionist measures taken by the Hoover administration impeding the readjustment of price-cost relations (including wage rates), and eventually the aforementioned state activities and regulations of the New Deal, were the real causes of the disaster (though regarding this last point, perhaps also for obvious ideological reasons, there seems to be less consensus among historians). Contrarily, having at least partially learned from history, at present we are amazed about how rapidly and relatively spontaneously—at least outside the United States, in countries that have reacted with much less state stimulation of the economy—the market forces have succeeded in overcoming not only the 2008 financial crisis, but also the worldwide recession and the contraction of international trade it caused (though it should be noted that it is not clear whether this recovery will be sustainable, considering not only the huge state-indebtedness of most European countries in the Eurozone, but also that of the United Kingdom, and the structural imbalances among them, which are still a menace for the success of this monetary community, their economies, and the survival of their social security systems).

Now, to say that the market is the solution, admittedly, is not true for all economic and much less for all social problems. And it is certainly not to say that the state is *always* the problem while the market is *never* a problem. As liberals from Adam Smith to F. A. Hayek have noted, the logic of capitalism and the market mechanism certainly do not suffice for providing those public goods that are necessary but cannot be provided by private initiative "because the profit could never repay the expense to any individual or small number of individuals, though it might frequently do much more than repay it to a great society."[33] Therefore, no private businessman will reasonably engage in them. Something similar applies to external costs, which can be internalized and thus managed only by legal measures and regulations imposed by the state.

Yet, there is more to say than what Adam Smith said—not in opposition to his basic insight into the nature of the free market as a system of *spon-*

---

perhaps inevitably occurs in societies in which the government together with central banks has control over the money supply, being able to inflate it for political reasons. This monetary system, as such, has nothing to do with capitalism or the market economy; both developed without it. It is rather a perhaps inevitable, but very dangerous, political decision.

33. Smith, *The Wealth of Nations*, IV, 9, 688; F. A. Hayek, *The Road to Serfdom* (1944), in *The Collected Works of F. A. Hayek*, vol. 2, ed. Bruce Caldwell (Chicago: University Press of Chicago, 2007), 87; see also Milton Friedman, *Capitalism and Freedom* (1962) (Chicago: University of Chicago Press, 1982), 22–36.

taneous coordination of private interests in benefit of the public interest or common good, an outcome that, however, is *not intended by individual actors*. But Adam Smith—still living in a pre-industrialized world dominated by agriculture, manufacture, and traditional trade and ignoring the effects of the Industrial Revolution and the antagonism of interests between employers and wage earners typical for the era of industrialized capitalism—still believed that by the market mechanism "the obvious and simple system of natural liberty establishes itself of its own accord."[34] Better informed by historical experience and the intrinsic shortcomings, failures, and imperfections of the market mechanism under conditions of industrialized capitalism, we have to add: the assertion that the market is the solution and the state is the problem is correct if, and only if, *there exists a real and functioning market*, that is: an order of competition not perverted by monopolistic structures (including the labor market!) and a price system providing reliable information not only for the allocation of resources and entrepreneurial decision making, but also for the choices to be made by consumers. The most important insight of Walter Eucken's "Ordoliberalism" (which in many aspects is close to Friedrich A. Hayek's "Catallactics,"[35] or even Milton Friedman's vision of capitalism as an order of freedom,[36] and certainly very close to what in Germany after the second World War successfully developed as *Soziale Marktwirtschaft*) is the following: *a market can be a system of coordinating individual choices to the benefit of the common good only if there exists a legal and economic order imposed and enforced by the state that creates and guarantees by legal and political measures an order of free competition.*

This is achieved not only by providing a legal framework—enforceable rules of the game—and the basis of a sound monetary and fiscal system with the corresponding institutions and policies, such as central banks that ensure the stability of the monetary system, even though this is the most important part. It also requires an active government politics of guaranteeing the functioning of the price system and the existence of a functioning order of competition freed from the distortions caused by monopolistic concentration, cartels, and trusts. As Adam Smith already had remarked, it is intrinsic to business activity to try to overrule and even to eliminate competitors by

34. Smith, *The Wealth of Nations*, IV, 9, 687.
35. See his *Law, Legislation and Liberty: A New Statement of the Liberal Principles of Justice and Political Economy* (London: Routledge and Kegan, 1982).
36. See his *Capitalism and Freedom*, quoted above.

collusion and creation of cartels (this is most effectively and unjustly done by government itself, when it becomes a competitor of private business). According to Eucken, the market therefore possesses an intrinsic tendency to destroy itself. It does not naturally and necessarily tend to harmony between private and public interest, even though *the market mechanism* as such is precisely the means for bringing private and public interest into a certain correspondence—provided, to say it again, the market mechanism really works.

Eucken's main point is that in our real world and because of its inherent logic the market itself cannot guarantee the upholding of the functioning of its mechanism without support from public authorities. This is not properly a defect of the market mechanism, but a limitation due to a defect of the world in which this mechanism has to work and which it cannot remedy by itself. It is a consequence of the human condition. Freedom tries to use this mechanism against its proper logic of fair exchange, that is, unfairly or taking advantages of imperfect information or positions of power. Human beings tend to use—or abuse—good things in a way that renders them harmful for others and the community. Notice that this economic vision is embedded in wider anthropological presuppositions. Interestingly enough, it opens the way to seeing how human virtues and ethical behavior in general might and should be the necessary and salutary corrective of the factual forces of the market mechanism.[37]

Because of his deeply anthropological outlook, Eucken is very close to the perhaps most important twentieth-century representative of the Austrian school of economics, Ludwig von Mises, whose economic theory is a widely anthropological theory as well as a theory of human action.[38] This is a truly humanistic approach to economics. Though being perhaps flawed, and in some respects one-sided,[39] nevertheless it provides an impressive corrective to rational choice–economists who, like Gary Becker—and unlike Adam Smith[40]—perceive human beings only as *homo oeconomicus*.[41]

37. This is the basic idea of Peter Koslowski's excellently argued and in my view highly recommendable *Prinzipien der Ethischen Ökonomie* (Tübingen: J. C. B. Mohr—Paul Siebeck, 1988); English edition: *Principles of Ethical Economy* (Dordrecht: Springer Netherlands, 2000). Koslowski, a disciple of Robert Spaemann, holds degrees both in economy and in philosophy.

38. See his *Human Action: A Treatise on Economics*, (London: William Hodge, 1949).

39. See a good critique of these insufficiencies in Koslowski, *Prinzipien der Ethischen Ökonomie*, 205–7 and passim.

40. Amartya Sen argues very well against the view that Adam Smith favored the idea of *homo oeconomicus*; see Sen's recent book *The Idea of Justice* (Cambridge, Mass.: Harvard University Press, 2009), 184ff.

41. An interesting comparison between the different liberal systems of Ludwig von Mises and Gary

The conclusion is thus: the goal of state politics ought to be to render the market an efficient tool by securing the correct functioning of the market mechanism.[42] This is not equal to creating "social justice," but to efficiently coordinating individual interests and the allocation of resources (the outcome of market processes is to be called neither "just" nor "unjust," as only the *rules* of the game can be just or unjust; the outcome, however, can be called "desirable" or "undesirable," also for moral reasons. Thus these outcomes can reasonably call for correction). Consequently, a functioning free market order is not a solution for problems of "social justice." Rather, it is a necessary and indispensable, or at least the best, presupposition for being able to achieve, with additional *political* measures, the maximum possible approximation of what we usually, but sometimes misleadingly, call the requirements of "social justice" and which should better be called demands of *solidarity*. Nobody is really able to clearly define the content of "social justice," because it is a matter that—in a world of limited and even scarce resources—is by its very nature highly controversial and about whose requirements reasonable people can certainly hold different views. Moreover, it seems to me difficult to reasonably hold that less well-off people and those in real need have properly a *right* to corrections of the outcome of market processes by redistributive measures—that is, that they properly have a *right* to get a share of the property of other people—and that such redistribution thus is a demand of *justice* properly spoken. I rather think that the correction of market outcomes by redistribution is to be grounded on an *obligation*—a *moral* obligation—of solidarity of the better-off toward the needy, an obligation citizens justly and reasonably delegate to democratically controlled public authorities to be carried out on their behalf by redistributive measures (whose amount and limitations are to be measured precisely by the criterion of the moral obligation of solidarity of those better-off toward the worse-off, not by the criterion of some pattern or program of an egalitarian "just society").[43]

Becker can be found in Javier Aranzadi, *Liberalism against Liberalism: Theoretical Analysis of the Works of Ludwig von Mises and Gary Becker* (London: Routledge, 2006).

42. I do not, as I should, differentiate between the "real economy" markets and financial markets. The latter are a special case, and, as far as I can judge, to the extent that regulation and protection could be justified, it would be of a different kind.

43. See more about this in my "Lo Stato costituzionale democratico e il bene comune," in Ripensare lo spazio politico: quale aristocrazia?, ed. E. Morandi and R. Panattoni (Padua: Il Poligrafo, 1998), 57–123 (Con-tratto. Rivista di filosofia tomista e contemporanea 6/1997); an English version of this essay appears as chapter 3 in this volume.

As has been already mentioned, such a vision is based on essential anthropological assumptions that, among other things, also involve the principle of subsidiarity. The market economy is *natural* to human beings (in the sense of *secundum naturam*), but the market itself is not something "natural" in the sense of being "naturally given" *(a natura)*. It must be organized, arranged, ordered, controlled, and protected by the governing part of society, that is, the public authority of the state and its legal system. The market, though being based on the natural tendency of human beings to enter into relations of exchange and barter and thereby an attempt at a coordination of interests, is more than something spontaneously created by human natural inclinations: it is also and always *an institution* created by the legal system, by the obtaining culture, and by the ordering political framework activity of the state.[44]

In order to settle this point with conceptual clarity, Walter Eucken helpfully distinguishes between two fundamentally different kinds of economic action aiming also at pursuing two different goals: first, "the shaping of the *forms of order* of an economy" *(Gestaltung der Ordnungsformen der Wirtschaft)*, and secondly, "the direction of the economic process" *(die Lenkung des Wirtschaftsprozesses)*. The former task, that is, shaping the forms of economic order (like creating a legally ordered market and an order of free competition and guaranteeing this order with a policy aiming at maintaining such an order, not at *replacing* or *directing* its inner mechanism by state interventions and bureaucratic regulations), is properly the task of government, backed by the legal system and its coercive power. The latter, that is, directing the economic process itself, is the task of the market, the price system, and the incentives it provides for the producer's and consumer's decisions, with the following allocation of resources according to the real needs of those who participate in the market.

This means that not the state and state activity or even state intervention *as such,* or its amount and intensity, is a problem, but the *quality*, the meaning, and the aim of such intervention.[45] The state transgresses the lim-

---

44. Some of these features of the market are happily, though in my opinion also somewhat haphazardly, expressed in chapter 3 of Benedict XVI's encyclical *Caritas in veritate,* to which I will briefly return below.

45. This was already expressed by Ludwig von Mises, in his *Kritik des Interventionismus: Untersuchungen zur Wirtschaftspolitik und Wirtschaftsideologie der Gegenwart* (Stuttgart: Gustav Fischer Verlag, 1929); Von Mises clearly distinguishes, e.g., between the nationalization of some means of production or a railway company (which is not an "intervention" in his sense) and a state-induced change of the economic factors, that is, a state command that forces the private owners of means of production to

its of its proper tasks when instead of organizing, ordering, and—mainly by the suppression of monopolistic structures, collusion, and cartels, as far as this is possible—protecting the market as a system of free coordination of the interests of free citizens and economic actors, it tries to take over part or the whole of the function of the market. The state does so by participating in the economic process itself, regulating entrepreneurial decisions or intervening in the price system and thereby depriving it of its function of providing reliable information for producers and consumers; such a state, Eucken's Ordoliberalism contends, certainly acts in detriment to the common good. As far as I can judge, this position seems to me to be basically sound.

The Systemic Conflict between Economic and Political Logic

Now, what has been outlined so far is not the whole story. One problem of Walter Eucken's vision of ordoliberalism is certainly that in the real world it will never be possible to have perfect competition: a market free from any monopolistic or oligopolistic structures. The idea that producers normally are bound to *take* the price for which they sell *from* the market, does not correspond to reality, or at least, it does not usually correspond to all sectors of a market economy. It is, therefore, important not to have a too idealistic picture of a real market economy. In many cases, producers who have a factually monopolistic position can *give* or *dictate,* or at least *influence,* the price for which they sell their products. Thus, the market is not, and can never be, the perfect mechanism it should be. This in no way diminishes its real merits, however. Moreover, there is no reasonable alternative to the free market economy. As Milton Friedman noticed, even though monopolies are bad, they are sometime inevitable, and so we have to choose between three evils: private monopoly, public monopoly, or public regulation. While Walter Eucken opted for public regulation, Friedman thinks that "private monopoly may be the least of the evils."[46]

Yet, I wish to leave such questions to economists; this also applies to the burdensome question to what extent it is possible to neatly distinguish between acts of "shaping the forms of order" and acts of "directing the eco-

---

employ them in a way that is different from the one they would have chosen if no such command existed (see ibid., 5–6).

46. Friedman, *Capitalism and Freedom,* 28.

nomic process" (much depends on whether one believes, as Keynes and his Keynesian followers did, in the possibility and efficiency of the macroeconomic steering of the concrete process of the economy). There is a second problem, however, that needs to be mentioned here and that I wish to briefly tackle. It is the *problem of democracy,* related to economics. Like markets, democracy is a very imperfect political system, though without a real alternative. Winston Churchill famously said: "Many forms of Government have been tried and will be tried in this world of sin and woe. No one pretends that democracy is perfect or all-wise. Indeed, it has been said that democracy is the worst form of government except all those other forms that have been tried from time to time."[47] This may be criticized as a commonplace complaint or a truism, justifying scandalous inequalities and the lack of social justice. Be that as it may, one of democracy's imperfections is that there is *a gap between the logic of economy and the logic of democratic politics.* Roughly speaking—and perhaps at a first glance this may sound odd—real and cold economic logic essentially and on principle aims at serving the common good, that is, the *long-term* outcome and interests of the *whole* of society, while the logic of politics is rather focused on *short-term* outcome and *group* interests.

Let us not fool ourselves by appearances: apart from *Ordnungspolitik* in Walter Eucken's understanding (the politics of shaping and securing the form of the economic order) and except for providing evidently necessary public goods, there is no such thing as an *economic* politics capable of directly aiming at and realizing the common good (I said *economic* politics, not excluding there being *other kinds* of politics, e.g., social, or redistributionist, actually aiming at the common good). As seems to be now largely accepted by most economists, the Keynesian idea widely practiced in the decades after the Second World War, the macroeconomic steering of the economy, has been proven to be doomed to failure. As far as the allocation of material resources and the satisfaction of material needs is concerned—which up to a certain point is the supposition for satisfying higher human needs—only the economic logic of the market, that is, the logic of the coordination of individual plans pursuing individual interests regulated by the price system, can do the job.

For politics, however, it is typical to serve rather short-term goals, the in-

47. Winston Churchill, Speech in the House of Commons, November 11, 1947, in *The Official Report, House of Commons* (5th Series), November 11, 1947, vol. 444, 206–7.

terests and needs of determinate groups whose claims are perceived, some-times by means of public persuasion, as being identical with the common good. This is not only a problem of modern democracies, but it also was the case during eighteenth-century absolutism and its mercantilist politics. As Adam Smith forcefully criticized in his *Inquiry into the Nature and Causes of the Wealth of Nations,* the mercantilist system unilaterally served the interests of the state and the established groups of producers, manufacturers, trades-men, and such. It did not, however, favor the interests of consumers, which were the needs of the broad population. Yet, as it seems to me, *the goal of the economy* is neither public enrichment, nor production, nor the satisfy-ing of producers' interests; it is not even the creation of jobs and the provi-sion of labor opportunities. The goal of the economy is *consumption,* that is, the satisfying of the needs of *all* the persons living in a determinate territory. Production, jobs, and the supply of produced commodities and services are supposed to serve concrete needs and the corresponding demand. Therefore, it seems to me to be unsound to conversely think of the economy as a sys-tem of demand or purchase power *with the goal of creating production, sup-ply, and jobs.* This would be doing things back to front. For this reason, full employment cannot be a reasonable *goal* of the economy. About whether it is a reasonable means, *auctores disputant,* I would tend to rather adhere to the arguments of those who assert that it is not—not only for economic but also for moral reasons.

One may of course consider jobs and employment—opportunities to work—as a basic need of human persons, corresponding to their dignity, and even a moral right, and thus think of a policy of full employment as satisfying such a need and basic right of the human person. Yet, this would not be an *economic* policy, but one that is part of social politics, guided by moral principles. Even if it is believed to be politically or socially just, it can still be economically unsound. Consider, however, that also from a political, "social," or moral viewpoint, only the provision of *useful* and *economically efficient* jobs makes sense and thus corresponds to human dignity. Perform-ing, even with the help of public funding, a useless job, *is not dignifying.* Now, the politics of full employment are mostly based on the creation of jobs by inflating bureaucracies or work opportunities created by govern-ment programs, whose usefulness is at least very doubtful, or by supporting inefficient and ailing industries. This is both economically harmful and—precisely from the viewpoint of "social justice"—morally problematic, because it is tantamount to subsidizing with public funds inefficient and use-less jobs *at the expense of other, useful, and efficiently working sectors of the economy.* Rather than subsidizing ailing industries or companies, it would be much more just, and thus morally upright, in such cases to let inefficient firms go bankrupt, and instead use public funds to help those who thereby lose their jobs to find new and useful employment, even by subsidizing pro-grams of retraining. This is why it seems to me possible to reasonably and in a morally justified way hold that a certain amount of unemployment is both economically healthy and socially just (to say it again, provided the unem-ployed are not simply forgotten, but rather supported in obtaining new jobs or in being retrained).

The problem is that this kind of economically sound logic aims at long-term and overall effects. Fighting for them is politically not very reward-ing. Another example of politically unrewarding economic logic is the ar-gument that *in the long run* free trade is always better than protectionism *for everybody.*[48] This is why Princeton's emeritus professor in international political economy, Robert Gilpin, has written that "economists of every persuasion are convinced that free trade is superior to trade protection,"[49] and why according to the rather left-wing liberal economist Alan Blinder, from Princeton as well, "enthusiasm for free trade is axiomatic to econo-mists."[50] Yet, in a short-term perspective, without considering all sectors of the economy, but only a determinate group, protectionism actually may be advantageous—for the time being. Politics, mainly democratic politics, aims at serving determinate groups of producers, industries, and their em-ployees. Such policies normally fail to serve the interests of consumers, and they certainly hurt other industries, which are not protected or aided by these measures. These protected interests are normally articulated in short-term perspectives and, in such a restricted perspective, may seem plausible and thus become popular.[51] But in the long run, policies of protectionism

48. The main arguments against protectionism and in defense of free trade can be found (apart from standard textbooks of international economics such as, e.g., Paul R. Krugman and Maurice Obst-feld, *International Economics: Theory and Policy,* 8th ed. [Boston: Pearson—Addison Wesley, 2009]), in Douglas A. Irwin, *Free Trade under Fire* (Princeton, N.J.: Princeton University Press, 2002) and Jagdish Bhagwati, *Free Trade Today* (Princeton, N.J.: Princeton University Press, 2002).

49. Robert Gilpin, *Global Political Economy: Understanding the International Economic Order* (Princeton, N.J.: Princeton University Press, 2001), 196.

50. Alan S. Blinder, *Hard Heads, Soft Hearts: Tough-Minded Economics for a Just Society* (Cam-bridge, Mass.: Perseus Books, 1987), 111.

51. In his 1926 pamphlet (33), Keynes also actually rejected protectionism—together with Marxist socialism ("a doctrine so illogical and so dull")—as a "poor quality" opponent proposal to *laissez-faire.*

or the public subsidizing of ailing industries to conserve jobs also harm the interests of those they first pretended to serve. So, from the outset and on principle, as well as in regard to the *common* good, they are certainly harmful.[52] This is why political logic in so many cases does not promote the common good—even though politicians emphatically invoke the common good for advancing their agenda and denounce economic thinking as egoistic, serving only the interests of the rich. Again, according to Alan Blinder, the problem of politicians—and voters—choosing bad economic policies is not just "bad luck, bad judgment" or due to "human errors," but is "rather systemic": "Economic policy is made by politicians, not by economists—which is just as it should be in a democracy. But politicians do not accept and reject economists' advice at random. They choose solutions that they perceive to be politically correct. Unfortunately, there seems to be a systematic tendency for good economics to make bad politics."[53]

This is not the whole story, however. Sometimes and in some ways, political decisions that run against economic logic may perhaps be justified or inevitable. The clearest case is wartime: a war economy is in itself an economic absurdity and economically harmful, yet it may be to a certain extent necessary as a short-term or emergency policy in order to win a war. Unfortunately, governments and the bureaucracies created by them like state-controlled war economy, so they tend to conserve its structures also during peacetime (this first happened, mainly in Germany, after the First World War; and in many countries, especially in the United States, it was repeated after the Second World War as well). Moreover, if they are big and important enough, the subsidizing or saving of ailing companies by the government with the taxpayers' funds is—more in Europe, however, than in the United States—very popular, though certainly opposed to the common good in terms of long-term and overall economic benefits (because, as said above, helping a determinate industry or saving a determinate company inevitably hurts other sectors of the economy and other companies, who by this are

52. So Alan Blinder—not a right-wing economist, nor a conservative, but a liberal (in the American sense)—says about protectionism: "Protectionism's allure stems not from the economics of the national interest, but from the politics of special interests. Politics turns trade policies that are economic turkeys into political peacocks. But to understand why, we must look beyond the abstract arguments for and against free trade to the specific lists of winners and losers from protection. Then we will see that trade protection secures concentrated and highly visible gains for a small minority by imposing diffuse and almost invisible costs on a vast and unknowing majority. That makes protectionism at once economically graceless and politically fetching" (*Hard Heads, Soft Hearts*, 112).

53. Ibid., 3.

penalized for being more efficient). For example, maybe it would have been more advantageous for the world economy, for poorer countries, and for future generations if the U.S. government had let General Motors go bankrupt and disappear. For obvious reasons, however, this would have been at the moment *politically* a very risky option because of the social problems it would have immediately caused. But there are good reasons to think that, regarding the *common good,* it would have been both economically more efficient and socially more just. In this special case, it would have possibly been even more popular, not in the Detroit region, but everywhere else in the United States, because U.S. citizens are not happy about the government spending their money to save an inefficient and poorly managed industry (and are now—in August 2010, when this was written—expecting the government to sell the factually nationalized GM at a decent price on the stock market by its forthcoming IPO).[54]

As Henry Hazlitt noticed in his classic *Economics in One Lesson*—first published in 1946—it was a mistake of classical economists not to perceive the deep divergence between the economic and the political logic. This led them to overlook the endemic political inefficiency of economic arguments and, thus, to neglect trying to make economic thinking more accessible and more popular. "The art of economics"—Hazlitt explains—"consists in looking not merely at the immediate but at the longer effects of any act or policy; it consists in tracing the consequences of that policy not merely for one group, but for all groups."[55] All economic fallacies, Hazlitt argues, "stem from one of two central fallacies, or both: that of looking only at the immediate consequences of an act or proposal, and that of looking at the consequences only for a particular group to the neglect of other groups." Hazlitt superbly illustrates this fallacy in all of its different variations, pointing out the counterproductive and sometimes even absurd consequences of widely accepted and practiced yet fallacious economic policies (such as price fixing, the subsidizing of ailing industries, protectionism, etc.). Hazlitt, however, does not close his eyes to the political viewpoint and its merits. In fact, he remarks: "It is true, of course, that the opposite error is possible. In considering a policy, we ought not to concentrate *only* in its long-run results to the community as a whole. This is the error often made by the classical economists. It resulted in a certain callousness toward the fate of groups

54. "Initial Public Offering" (at the stock exchange).
55. Henry Hazlitt, *Economics in One Lesson* (1946), new ed. (New York: Three Rivers Press, 1979), 17.

that were immediately hurt by policies or developments which proved to be beneficial on net balance and in the long run."[56]

There actually exists a conflict, often ignored by free market economists, between the logic of economics and politics. Economics is grounded on a specific technical rationality, aimed at optimizing overall benefits. As said above, and perhaps somewhat ironically, an economics that is aimed at optimizing the *overall* and *long-term* effects of the economy *in its totality*, and not only regarding the interests of determinate groups, is in the highest degree focused precisely on the *common good*. Simultaneously, however, economic thinking seems callous and coldly contemptuous, as Hazlitt wrote, "toward the fate of groups that were immediately hurt by policies or developments which proved to be beneficial on net balance and in the long run." Politics, on the other hand, both democratic and autocratically plebiscitarian politics, aim at satisfying the needs of the moment and of those groups who are able to most convincingly persuade a majority that their interest is a common or public interest. This is why politicians rather focus on short-term effects and effects regarding determinate social groups and their actual problems (mainly the groups that hold out the prospect of the best election returns). *Long-term* common good and the interests of *all parts* of society, as well as the interests of *future generations*, tend to be taken into account only insofar as this is politically profitable—according to Keynes's well-known, somewhat cynical comment that, after all, "in the long run we are all dead."[57]

Economic and political logic, then, are often in mutual conflict. The political logic is in most cases *economically* unsound; but it is popular and promises to promote social justice. Unfortunately, though, it normally produces undesired long-term effects that run directly afoul of the original intentions of those who supported the corresponding policies and turn out to be neither social nor just. On the other side, economic logic is often rather counterintuitive and seemingly hard-hearted and "socially cold." The long-term advantages, even for the particular industries or sectors of trade that economic logic will hurt in short-term, are not generally understood, so that usually to advocate and promote the corresponding policies turns out to be politically suicidal.[58]

56. Ibid.
57. The above-quoted dictum "in the long run we are all dead" is to be called cynical because future generations are not even born yet, but will have to pay for what we are doing now.
58. To have systematically studied these interconnections between the economy and democratic

This is a real dilemma, which, however, is not to be understood as an argument against democracy. Nondemocratic regimes usually behave even worse in this respect, or at least *not sustainably* well (because dictators or otherwise authoritarian regimes systematically tend to undermine, or to neglect to build, the institutions warranting long-term sustainability of reasonable policies). After all, democracies are able to change majorities, and thus lead to a certain learning effect. At the very least, democratic politics tend to correct one error with its contrary, which is not the best of politics either, yet perhaps in many cases brings about acceptable results in the form of only limited harm. Moreover, liberal democracy, based on political freedom, participation, and majority rule, is still the best, if not the only appropriate, environment for a good and successful market economy. The market economy is an exercise in freedom, and thus supposes institutions securing freedom.

We should never forget: neither liberal constitutional democracy nor the free, capitalistic market economy simply aims at maximizing "technical" efficiency. They first of all are based on, and aim at, securing freedom—individual freedom—convinced that only in a society in which this freedom is trump, social justice can finally be realized as much as possible in this broken and imperfect world.[59]

Capitalist Economy, Social Justice, and Catholic Social Doctrine: Traditional Misunderstandings and the Genesis of a New Vision of the Role of the State

The historical record seems to be clear: during the last two centuries, capitalist free market economy and free trade without tariff barriers have continuously improved the conditions of life of *all social levels, always* and *everywhere.* Conversely, all kinds of state interventionism, bureaucratic planning

---

politics is the merit of the work of Bruno S. Frey and his school; see, e.g., his *Theorie demokratischer Wirtschaftspolitik* (München: Vahlen, 1981; 2nd ed., together with coauthor Gebhard Kirchgässner, 2001); English ed., *Democratic Economic Policy* (New York: Palgrave Macmillan, 1983).

59. See for this the classical liberal "monument," F. A. Hayek's *The Constitution of Liberty* (Chicago: University of Chicago Press, 2001). Even if there may be considerable shortcomings and flaws from an anthropological viewpoint, and considering that Hayek is little sensitive to Hazlitt's above-mentioned caveat concerning "the error often made by the classical economists," that is, "a certain callousness toward the fate of groups that were immediately hurt by policies or developments which proved to be beneficial on net balance and in the long run," the merits of this book remain beyond discussion. In order to be able to criticize Hayek for such shortcomings, one has first to well understand the merits of his approach and to reach his level of learning and argument.

of the economy, and socialism (or semi-socialism) have deteriorated conditions of life and welfare of *all social levels, always* and *everywhere*. Paradoxically, however, people generally think the opposite is true: that capitalism is good only for the rich, and that, if not checked and contained, it causes progressive pauperization of the masses. It was Karl Marx who most effectively promoted this distorted view, based on a profoundly mistaken analysis of the capitalist economy—and not a few Christians as well as Catholics, both "left-wing" and conservative, have been influenced by this view.

Yet, all the Marxist predictions about pauperization of the working class as well as the *eherne Lohngesetz* (the Iron Law of Wages) formulated by the German socialist Ferdinand Lasalle (1825–64) have been refuted by history. However, this prejudice still exists, working in the heads of a great number of people, although historians know perfectly well that it is not true. The same applies to the merits of free trade as it has been theoretically grounded by the English economist David Ricardo and his law of "comparative advantage" (a principle already known and expressed by Adam Smith). In practice, this principle was successfully promoted by the "Manchester school," another name for Richard Cobden's Anti-Corn Law League, which was later to be much defamed and condemned as "Manchester liberalism." During the second half of the nineteenth century, thus, free trade became a spectacular motor of economic progress, with a continuous rise of real wages at *all* social levels and a general increase in welfare. Where it created mutual bonds and interdependence between trading countries, it also secured peace in a way unknown in earlier periods. The renowned historian Eric Hobsbawm, himself a Marxist, writes that the spectacular expansion of world trade in the second half of the nineteenth century really benefitted all countries, "even if it benefitted the British disproportionately." It was the first and definitive step to globalization, "the creation of a single expanded world." At its root was "the liberation of private enterprise, the engine which, by common agreement, powered the progress of industry."[60] This was the presupposition to overcoming the living conditions of pre-industrialized society that, we should not forget, sometimes and in some places were much more miserable than the sometimes miserable conditions during the process of industrialization (though the first period of English industrialization—the period of so-called pauperism—cannot be compared

60. Eric Hobsbawm, *The Age of Capital 1848–1875* (1975) (London: Abacus, 1997), 47–54.

with the second half of the nineteenth century, precisely the *liberal* "age of capital").[61]

So, as history teaches, a capitalist economy based on a free market, entrepreneurial creativity, and free trade without tariff barriers is more realistic and in the long run more beneficial for everybody. State interventionism, socialism, and protection of job opportunities by tariffs and strict regulations of the labor market (as exaggerated protection against wrongful dismissal), though they may look charitable, socially just, and benevolent, focus exclusively on a just and equal distribution of the cake. However, they are not concerned with the effective production and enlargement of this common cake. In reality, they rather tend to be harmful in the long run, especially for the less advantaged, and thus to undermine the common good—even if normally this becomes evident only to the next generations (or at least when the next election round approaches). This is not to say that in the past, socialist pressure, or pressure by the syndicates, creating legal protection of the workers and the improvement of working conditions, has not been necessary and beneficial precisely for relieving the often callous economic logic of capitalism toward determinate groups and their short-term needs. Yet, we have also to add that true and unfettered capitalism and free international trade have existed only during a very short period in history: between 1850 and 1870. We do not know how nineteenth-century laissez-faire capitalism would have developed without the First World War, which was the beginning of intense and lasting state interventionism in the economy of all countries, and of the modern welfare state (which in Germany started already with Bismarck's social laws, which, though being beneficial for workers, were in the first place meant to be a political tools for stopping the socialists).

One problem with economic progress is that it creates inequality. By sound economic transactions, the rich become even richer, even though the poor profit as well. If I, having 100, start trading with you, who have only 10, and both of us thereby increase our wealth by, say, 10 percent, I will afterward have 110, and you 11. So, the gap between us has increased. Yet, the bargain may be beneficial for both: having now 11 instead of 10 increases your potential for sustainable growth and for doing business with others.

61. As to living conditions in pre-industrialized England, which were rather diverse according to the time and place, see Peter Laslett's classic *The World We Have Lost: Further Explored* (1965) (London: Routledge, 2000); especially chap. 6 (122–52): "Did the peasants really starve? Famine and pestilence amongst English people in the pre-industrial past."

Generally speaking, it is thus a question of promoting sound political and economic incentives and environments favorable for investment in order that the wealth of the rich may become the motor of progress for the poor. Yet, there is an egalitarian logic of envy that, against any economic logic, prefers to rather expropriate from the rich by exaggerated measures of redistribution in order to create "social justice," instead of encouraging them to enlarge the cake by investment and entrepreneurial activity. This, again, is the fruit of the great confusion of thinking that capitalism as such is a *problem* that must be resolved by government intervention, checking the profit greed of capitalists. Again, this is not to deny that capitalism and the market economy do cause problems that have to be solved by government policies and, in the sense of basic solidarity, even redistributive measures.[62] The problem is not material inequality; it is first *inequality in rights and opportunities* that makes it impossible for individual persons or whole social groups to participate in the market; it is second the way in which economic inequality is managed so that, rather than harmful, it becomes beneficial also for the less well-off.

For several decades, anti-capitalist and anti-market biases were rather typical for Catholic social doctrine. In 1931, in his encyclical *Quadragesimo anno,* Pope Pius XI rejected the idea that "in the market, i.e., in the free struggle of competitors" the economy has "a principle of self direction which governs it much more perfectly than would the intervention of any created intellect." The encyclical acknowledges that free competition is "justified and certainly useful provided it is kept within certain limits"; it, however, bluntly declares that free competition "clearly cannot direct economic life" and that therefore other principles of regulation of the economy must be sought. These are, as the encyclical teaches, "social justice" and "social love," which are "loftier and nobler principles" and which "public authority ought to be ever ready effectively to protect and defend."[63]

Now the idea that it is not the market forces based on free competition and the price system, but government—by implementing programs of social justice and love—that is to be the regulatory or directive principle of the economic process itself seems to be economically unsound. We can, of course, read *Quadragesimo anno* in terms of Ordoliberalism—the formulations used by the encyclical actually admit of a broad interpretation—but this is not

---

62. See my "Lo Stato costituzionale democratico e il bene comune."
63. Pius XI., Enyclical *Quadragesimo anno,* no. 88.

what the text really says, and it is not how it was immediately understood.[64] Its critique of the monopolistic and "dictatorial" structure of capitalism at this time was certainly to a large extent justified. However, the encyclical did not distinguish between "free competition" and such a system. The system Pius XI criticized was not exactly a system of free competition, but one of domination by monopolies and a high degree of political control by large firms. Now, the role of the state cannot be to *replace* competition and the price system by another regulatory principle such as "social justice" and "social love" promoted by public authority; it is rather to destroy the monopolistic structure of the economy and to reestablish, as far as this is possible, a real order of competition. Afterward, and complementary to this, social justice and social love may come in and perhaps *correct* the outcome of market processes, or else *compensate* for their undesired side effects. They are unable, however, to replace free competition and the price system—and with them the laws of supply and demand—as the directing and regulatory principle of the economy without gravely damaging the common good.

As the 1931 encyclical *Quadragesimo anno* at least implicitly delegitimized the directive and regulatory role of competition and the price system on the free market of a national economy, so the 1967 encyclical *Populorum progressio* by Pope Paul VI delegitimized it on the international level of free trade. Again, this is how the encyclical *was understood* when it appeared (something I remember perfectly: it was commonly praised by pro-socialists as a left-wing encyclical). Like *Quadragesimo anno, Populorum progressio* was right in rejecting a kind of economic liberalism that believed in the automatically harmonious self-regulation of markets. The evil, however, was again located in the wrong place, that is, in free competition and capitalist profit-making.[65] Here again it must be emphasized that free competition is good and beneficial. The problem is not *competition,* but the lack of an order provided by a legal framework and of just rules—in this case, international treaties or a legal framework as provided by the WTO; by capital flows, caused by political instability, into more secure countries; by public indebtedness; by distorted market structures, typically caused by the anticompetitive behavior of global monopolies;[66] and—most importantly—by

64. See, e.g., the commentary of the encyclical by its main drafter, Oswald von Nell-Breuning, *Die soziale Enzyklika. Erläuterungen zum Weltrundschreiben Papst Pius' XI über die gesellschaftliche Ordnung* (Köln: Katholische Tat-Verlag, 1932), 166–73.

65. See Paul VI, *Populorum progressio,* no. 26.

66. See Stiglitz, *Making Globalization Work,* 200 (a nice example of how even a left-wing and Keynesian liberal cannot help emphasizing the importance of the competitive structures of a free mar-

the protectionism of the rich countries that closes their markets to the products of agriculture and manufacture of poorer countries (not always openly with tariffs, though, but sometimes by imposing so-called fair trade or antidumping laws, or by enforcing, even through WTO rules, environmental or labor standards and corresponding restrictions for imported products).[67] Profit as the "motor" of entrepreneurial activity is not the problem. Rather, it is state regulations and other factors that impede or discourage capital owners from taking the risk of investing in such economies. *Populorum progressio* unfortunately promoted the idea that free trade is not really beneficial for poor countries.[68] It is true that not *only* the establishment of free trade is sufficient to secure the progress of poor countries. Free market and free trade *alone* do not do the job. The approach must be more complex and multifaceted.[69] But this does not negate the fact that free trade is always beneficial for everybody and a *necessary,* though not a sufficient, condition precisely for poor countries to develop economically and socially.[70]

Admittedly, Catholic social thinking contains an admirable outlook on solidarity and the fulfillment of the human person in all its dimensions. Moreover, the social doctrine of the Church rightly stresses the importance of the common good. These features, however strangely, combine with a long-lasting opposition against the soundness of the economic logic and the logic of business. Among other things, this bias was certainly based on the confusion, in a way connatural for theologians but not confined to them alone (see the case of Keynes), between self-interest and egoism.[71]

We have to remember that for Adam Smith, self-interest was not the only motivation of human behavior. He clearly did not hold the idea of *homo oeconomicus.* Self-interest dominates, according to him, only in actions of

---

ket and even referring to Adam Smith, who has clearly seen the problem): "The problem of anti-competitive behavior has been evident since the birth of economics: as Adam Smith put it, 'People of the same trade seldom meet together, even for merriment and diversion, but the conversation ends in a conspiracy against the public, or in some contrivances to raise prices.' When there is a lack of competition, the potential for abuses of multinationals grows much worth."

67. See for this rather complicated matter Irwin, *Free Trade under Fire,* chaps. 4 and 6.

68. *Populorum progressio,* no. 58.

69. See, e.g., the many good arguments provided for this by Amartya Sen, *Development as Freedom* (New York: Anchor Books/Random House, 2000), 126–27.

70. I again refer to Irwin, *Free Trade under Fire,* and Bhagwati, *Free Trade Today.*

71. See for this Michael Novak, *Catholic Social Thought and Liberal Institutions* (previously published as *Freedom with Justice*), Second Edition (New Brunswick: Transaction Publishers, 1989), 8ff.; see also by the same author *The Catholic Ethic and the Spirit of Capitalism* (New York: Free Press, 1993). Concerning the anti-capitalist bias primarily in Catholic countries such as Spain and France see from a historical viewpoint Rodney Stark, *The Victory of Reason: How Christianity Led to Freedom, Capitalism, and Western Success* (New York: Random House, 2006).

exchange. But he also speaks of many other motivations underlying people's acts, such as sympathy, humanity, justice, generosity, and public spirit.[72] Yet, as I will argue below, even self-interest is not necessarily selfishness or egoism, but rather the typically economic way most of us think in everyday life.

But before addressing this topic, let me try to make the following point: it seems to me essential to notice that already the very idea underlying "capitalism" is something *structurally* non-egoistic and rather social and beneficial for others (even if the concrete *motivations* of the capitalist may be egoistic and "money-loving" greed): capitalism is the achievement of people who, instead of consuming and using their property and riches for themselves, postpone or partly renounce consumption in order to invest *at their own risk* their riches in productive or otherwise entrepreneurial activity, therewith creating jobs, paying wages, generating purchase power and demand. This in turn stimulates investment by more people, leading to the accumulation of capital that, through the public tax system, creates the possibility for state authorities to provide public goods such as basic infrastructure, education, basic health care, and the like. Again, this does not mean that capitalists are "good" or altruistic persons, or even that "renouncing consumption" means that they lead a modest and sober life (though there were and certainly still are many examples, mainly in the Puritan tradition, for which this was beyond doubt the case). Yet, by its very dynamics, capitalism and its competitive nature based on the division of labor has proven to promote innovation and to continuously increase productivity—the capacity of producing more and better things with less labor—and with this, welfare and opportunities for entire populations.

During this process some people, families, and countries will become richer than others, some of them very and even incredibly rich. Despite normally being beneficial—since it encourages investment—inequality sometimes also presents a political problem of uncontrolled and disadvantageous social and political power that needs to be solved, or at least mitigated, by adequate political and legal means. Much more harmfully, however, inequality creates quite another type of problem, a *psychological* problem: the tendency to equate "inequality" as such with "injustice." The origin of this error lies in considering economy and business as a zero-sum game, that is,

---

72. Adam Smith, *A Theory of Moral Sentiments*, ed. D. D. Raphael and A. L. Macfie (Oxford: Oxford University Press, 1976; reprint: Indianapolis: Liberty Fund, 1984), 190–91. For a discussion of this topic I refer again to Sen, *The Idea of Justice*, 184ff. See also the classical critique of the idea that economics is the characterization of *homo oeconomicus* by the founder of the liberal Austrian School of economics, Ludwig von Mises, in his *Human Action*, 62ff.

as if that great wealth was based on the rich having taken something away from those who remain worse off, or even poor. Yet, such an idea is wrong and harmful. A capitalist economy is not a zero-sum game, in which one can gain only when others lose, but essentially a process in which *new wealth is created*. It is a common misunderstanding that wealth, also the "wealth of nations," consists in the possession of economic assets in the form of money, gold, silver, diamonds, or other things of value (whose amount at a given time is always limited and, therefore, can be possessed only in the degree to which others do not possess them). The belief that this possession, in opposition to a non-possession, was what made a nation rich and powerful—that is, to have, while others have not—was the main error of the economics of mercantilism, typical for the absolutist, and for this reason essentially imperialist, state. It was the error that Adam Smith set out to refute by his *The Wealth of Nations*. If anything, wealth consists in *capital*, that is, a productive asset, and therefore, apart from machines or technological knowhow, it consists in the creativity and innovative potential of a social system of the division of labor, of productive labor, and of mutually beneficial exchange. I am rich only provided I am able to *sell* what I have or produce—for this, however, others must have purchasing power; thus they cannot be poor. Equally, I am rich only provided I am able to *buy* with my money something that is useful and necessary for me—and this again supposes others having something to sell. Money alone, in an environment where others are poor, is of no use. Thus, I am rich only to the extent that there are others who are rich as well.

If capitalism works (and throughout history it *has* indeed worked), this wealth, or its results, is distributed to all social levels, even though some gain disproportionally—and, of course in single cases, because of fraud or ruthlessness also unjustly—more than others. Others will not gain at all, but rather lose (be it by their own fault, or by misfortune, discrimination, natural disadvantage, or handicap). Yet, the very existence of inequality tends to provoke irrational politics of exaggerated egalitarian redistribution, tantamount to the expropriation of the rich. As many examples show, in the long run this is mostly to the detriment of those who are not as well off, because it hurts the dynamics of the economy by fettering the forces of creativity and innovation, even though it may be rewarding for those who are politically taking advantage of the forces of envy.[73]

73. Once again, it provides a rather distorted view of free market economy to say, as does Joseph E. Stiglitz, that its advocates assume "that markets, by themselves, without government intervention, are efficient, and that the best way to help the poor is simply to let the economy grow—and, somehow, the

Now, as mentioned above, self-interest, the motor of the capitalist market economy, is not equal to egoism or selfishness. Of course, there are many cases of the sheer love of money and greed. Morally speaking, this is detrimental in the first place to the capitalist himself, not materially perhaps, but for his spiritual well-being; it can be, and in the past very often was, harmful to workers. Yet, it can still be also economically advantageous. Many great and beneficial discoveries, inventions, and entrepreneurial achievements have had their immediate cause in some form of profit-seeking or greed.

More important, however, is that one can, and most people actually do, pursue *altruistic* self-interests, *because their self-interest is precisely to also promote the good of others.* This is not a paradox. Notice that those who care for their family will still act in their self-interest, that is, "economically": trying to obtain more or better things with less money or work. Businessmen will seek to produce more and better, more competitive products with less labor and for lesser costs; and consumers will always be interested in buying more and better things for a better price. Both in the first place care for making a living for themselves and those persons for whom they care. This is the sort of economic, truly self-interested thinking we all apply in our everyday calculations. It is "self-interested" not because it is selfish, but because it pursues the interest of the actor, and not some general or public interest for which the actor sacrifices what interests *him*. As the housekeeper tries to make a good buy when shopping, without thinking thereby of the good of neighbors, of the national textile industry, or of the agriculture of poor countries, so the entrepreneur will produce with an eye not on developing some other countries, but on advancing the good of the company in order to assure the income, jobs, and other goals he pursues—which are all a part of the entrepreneur's self-interest, that is, economic calculation. Admittedly, and as already emphasized above, contrary to what rational choice economists contend, self-interest is not the only motivation of human beings. The *homo oeconomicus* is a limited, one-sided, and unrealistic model.

---

benefits will trickle down to the poor" (*Making Globalization Work,* xvi). Growth of the economy is truly a precondition of helping the poor; but those who defend this basic insight do not deny therewith that for various reasons also government policies, or other public-minded organizations and institutions, should enable the poor to participate in the benefits of a growing economy (by providing opportunities for education, health care etc., which are not produced by the mechanism of the free market, without at least some intervention of the state). But again: the fact that the market alone is not able to achieve this has nothing to do with a *market failure,* as Stiglitz seems to suggest; it simply shows the limits, but not failures, of the market (market *failures* are possible only in those sectors for which the market is supposed to be the solution, not in those which by its very nature—which is an exchange between equivalents—it cannot possibly be a solution).

As such, self-interest and the behavior of the *homo oeconomicus* have nothing to do with egoism, and sometimes they have quite much to do with altruism and caring for others. To take Adam Smith's example:[74] the butcher who delivers his meat, not driven by benevolence, but rather by self-interest (Adam Smith says "self-love"), perhaps is the loving and caring head of a family who thinks of the well-being of his wife and the upbringing and education of his children. If he delivered to his clients the commodity he produces *by mere benevolence,* and not for making a profit, he most probably would violate both justice and charity toward his own family. Additionally—and this was Smith's main argument—this type of behavior is more advantageous for the client, because he knows that he will get his meat not only today, sometimes, or once, depending on the benevolence and humanity of the butcher—who actually perhaps has no reason at all to be benevolent toward him—but that he will get it also tomorrow and in a continuous and *reliable* way (which enables him to enter into business too, because he can, within certain limits, foresee and calculate the future).

To be precise: Adam Smith does not say that *the butcher acts* not by benevolence, but by self-love; what he says is that *we do not expect* our dinner from his benevolence and humanity, but from his self-love! So, Smith talks not about the *intentions of the butcher,* but about the *reasonable expectations of the client.* If we really knew that we could reasonably and reliably expect our daily dinner on the grounds of the butcher's humanity and benevolence, this would certainly be a much better, but also a very different, world from the one in which we actually live. It would be a world of saints. In the real world, however, such an expectation is simply unreasonable. This does not exclude that a world and an economy in which butchers, though acting by economic logic and in their well-understood self-interest, do this *additionally* by benevolence toward their client—or are even saints—is a much better world and a much better economy as well (because it will generally improve the butcher's service and prevent him from fraudulently seeking profit). Yet, even if we should tend to improve our world exactly in this direction, this is not the point with which Smith was concerned.

The condemnation of self-interest and profit is at the basis of most confusion concerning capitalism and the free market economy. As I have argued, Church social doctrine in the past was not unaffected by this attitude. Moreover, it had a certain bias for state interventionism and regula-

---

74. From his *The Wealth of Nations,* I, 2, 27.

tions even though this was not in accordance with its own basic principles, for example, subsidiarity and property rights. It entirely overlooked the fact that the very idea of capitalism already included in a way, that is, *structurally*, a social commitment of private property since the capitalist is an owner not simply of property and riches, but of *capital*, that is, of means of production: he puts his riches at society's disposal. The profit of the capitalist is the reward he or the shareholders of a company are justly entitled to expect and to receive for taking their own risk. Even though reality is not always in accord with this idea, it has been proven to be successful, leading to a real advantage for society as a whole. Therefore, even if a capitalist's profit is much more than he may seem to merit by standards of justice, his *expectation* of profit and the motivation following from it are highly useful for the entire society and, thus, serve the common good.

The overlooking of such logic can perhaps be explained by the fact that, as part of theology and made by theologians, the social teaching of the Church tends to be "charitable." It must show that it takes the side of the poor, the disadvantaged. Moreover, the Church's social Magisterium has its starting point (with Leo XIII's encyclical *Rerum novarum*, 1891) in a time in which Catholicism was generally opposed to the modern world, namely to the modern spirit of business and capitalism, which by leading theologians and those in the Catholic press was commonly identified with an essentially un-Christian, even "Jewish," spirit. Therefore, the widespread Catholic, socially motivated anti-Semitism was also intrinsically anti-capitalist.[75] The fact is that not only among left-wing and pro-socialist Christians, but also in more conservative ecclesiastical circles, sound economic thinking, which is truly very advantageous for the poor, is still today often disregarded or even condemned as heartless, egoistic, and serving only the rich.

In this respect, however, and for many people very surprisingly, John Paul II's encyclical *Centesimus annus*, published in 1991, opened a new area. This encyclical contains a clear-cut argument in favor of "capitalism" insofar as it is conceived as "an economic system which recognizes the fundamental and positive role of business, the market, private property and the resulting responsibility for the means of production, as well as free human creativity in the economic sector."[76] It equally advocates the free market economy

75. From the second part of the nineteenth century until the eve of the Second World War, this message was spread over and over again by the Vatican-authorized journal *La Civiltà Cattolica*, run by the Jesuit Fathers, which had also a great influence on the entire Catholic press of the time.

76. See John Paul II, Encyclical *Centesimus annus*, no. 42.

that "on the level of individual nations and of international relations, ... is the most efficient instrument for utilizing resources and effectively responding to needs."[77] Moreover, the encyclical also adopts a vision of the rule of law, a separation of powers, democracy, and the role of the state regarding the economy in the best tradition of liberal constitutionalism and Ordoliberalism.[78] With this promulgation, John Paul II actually abandoned the idea that the Church's social doctrine is "a 'third way' between liberal capitalism and Marxist collectivism"—as was already announced in his 1987 encyclical *Sollicitudo rei socialis*—"nor even a possible alternative to other solutions less radically opposed to one another: rather, it constitutes a category of its own."[79] Since *Centesimus annus*, thus, the social doctrine of the Church espouses the idea of a capitalist free market economy, rightly understood, including the "legitimate role of profit as an indication that a business is functioning well" and "that productive factors have been properly employed and corresponding human needs have been duly satisfied;[80] it also understands the merits of free trade and opts for the rather limited role of the state.[81]

In *Centesimus annus*, John Paul II actually depicts a clear-cut conception of the role of the state in the economic sector. So, according to *Centesimus annus*, the state has first to guarantee "individual freedom and private property, as well as a stable currency and efficient public services." Secondly, the state has the role of "overseeing and directing the exercise of human rights in the economic sector," which, however, does not mean to "directly ensure the right to work for all its citizens," because this the state could do only if it "controlled every aspect of economic life and restricted the free initiative of individuals," which, however, would be harmful. Therefore, in the sense of subsidiarity, the state has rather "a duty to sustain business activities by creating conditions which will ensure job opportunities, by stimulating those activities where they are lacking or by supporting them in moments of crisis." Thirdly, the state must "intervene when particular monopolies create delays or obstacles to development." Furthermore, and "in

---

77. Ibid., no. 34.

78. Ibid., nos. 44–48.

79. John Paul II, Encyclical *Sollicitudo rei socialis*, no. 41.

80. *Centesimus annus*, no. 35 (wisely adding, however, that "profitability is not the only indicator of a firm's condition").

81. For a synopsis of the main themes of this encyclical and an appreciation of its innovative character, see my "La realtà politica ed economica del mondo moderno e i suoi presupposti etici e culturali. L'enciclica *Centesimus annus*," in: *Giovanni Paolo teologo—Nel segno delle encicliche*, ed. Graziano Borgonovo and Arturo Cattaneo (Roma: Edizioni Arnoldo Mondadori, 2003), 83–94. An English version appears as chapter 6 in this volume.

exceptional circumstances the state can also exercise a substitute function, when social sectors or business systems are too weak or are just getting under way, and are not equal to the task at hand." Yet, "such supplementary interventions, which are justified by urgent reasons touching the common good, must be as brief as possible, so as to avoid removing permanently from society and business systems the functions which are properly theirs, so as to avoid enlarging excessively the sphere of state intervention to the detriment of both economic and civil freedom."[82]

It is obvious that this program is very close to, if not in a large part identical with, the best tradition of Ordoliberalism (once called "neoliberal," a label that for some years has become a swear word, being identified with something totally alien to original neoliberalism: a not only economic, but also social, order of the purest and most extreme socially insensible laissez-faire, linked not with the names of the great economists of the postwar neoliberal tradition, but rather to names such as Margaret Thatcher and Ronald Reagan. These protagonists, though having unquestionable merits, were certainly not the champions of neoliberal economical *thinking*, but only of certain politics called Thatcherism or Reagonomics—while the Laffer-curve, after all, has nothing to do with "neoliberalism" either, but simply seems to be bad economics).[83] According to the ordoliberal outlook of *Centesimus annus*, the state must create and secure the order of a real free market economy in which the forces of capitalism and free competition can develop and cooperate for the common good. So, the role of the state, rather than being an actor by bureaucratically intervening in the economic process and interfering with business decisions, is to be responsible for ordering the framework and regulating the parameters of the process as a whole, while leaving its intrinsic forces to develop their proper potential. Hence, what *Centesimus annus* presents is actually a program of capitalist laissez-faire, but of laissez-faire—according to Eucken's differentiation—in the positive sense as economic liberty, spontaneity, and creativity embedded in an order of competition created, guaranteed, and actively overseen by the state and

---

82. *Centesimus annus*, no. 48.

83. A telling example of how "neoliberalism" is seen by a left-wing, Marxist historian is provided by David Harvey's *A Brief History of Neoliberalism* (Oxford: Oxford University Press, 2005), where one can find assertions such as (on page 7) the "assumption that individual freedoms are guaranteed by freedom of the market and of trade is a cardinal feature of neoliberal thinking." No "neoliberal" economist or social theorist would maintain such nonsense (that "individual freedoms are *guaranteed* by freedom of the market"); they would rather say that freedom of the market and of trade *is an essential part* of individual freedom, which, however has to be *ordered and guaranteed by the State and its legal system.*

the rule of law. Most importantly, in *Centesimus annus* there is also a guiding principle for the role of the state in the economic sector: it is "economic and civil freedom." More than any previous document of the social Magisterium of the Church, *Centesimus annus* has definitively enriched Catholic social doctrine with the idea that the common good contains, and needs to be achieved by, both economic and civil freedom.

The Role of the State Regarding the Economy as Part of an Ethics of Institutions

In order to properly describe the role of the public authority of the state, it is necessary to emphasize the *importance of institutions*. The encyclical *Centesimus annus* presents a clear-cut doctrine about the state, democracy, and the capitalist market economy, based on the insight that the first and principal task of state authorities is establishing and upholding institutions that are able to guarantee those freedoms of citizens. These citizens, in turn, cooperate for the common good—including the competitive order of a free market economy. The state is not viewed by *Centesimus annus* as a superior agency, equipped with a higher and privileged insight and wisdom into the concrete material requirements of this common good. Rather, the first and basic requirement of the common good is precisely held to be *the establishment and functioning of the basic political, legal, economical, and social institutions*.

At first glance, however, the last social encyclical of the Catholic Church, Benedict XVI's *Caritas in veritate,* seems to be less clear-cut. It focuses on so many topics that it is difficult to identify its main argument. Now, despite its title, which gives the impression that the encyclical intends to focus on charity, *Caritas in veritate* actually stresses not so much "charity" but the ideas of *justice* and the *common good*. As the pope argues, they are precisely what render charity *true* charity, and not only a sentimental taking the part of the poor and disadvantaged.[84]

By focusing on justice and the idea of the common good—with the aim of making out what real charity demands—like *Centesimus annus, Caritas in veritate* also opens the way to integrating sound economic thinking into the *whole* of Catholic social doctrine, which is concerned with the human person

---

84. Benedict XVI, Encyclical *Caritas in veritate*, no. 6.

in his integrity and the fullness of his earthly and eternal destiny. Now, what do "justice" and "common good" mean? In *Caritas in veritate,* there is actually a passage that seems to me to be crucial, and also quite innovative, in this respect. It is the affirmation that "to take a stand for the common good is on the one hand to be solicitous for, and on the other hand to avail oneself of, that complex of institutions that give structure to the life of society, juridically, civilly, politically and culturally, making it the *pólis,* or 'city.'"[85] The common good is not so much seen as a determined outcome, a social pattern, or a pattern of distribution of wealth and opportunities, but as the *institutional framework,* which then generates, as a *result* of free cooperation of citizens, an outcome that is to be considered just and coherent with the common good. It is so because it has come about in a just and ordered manner.

Such perspectives might be the starting point for a missing piece of Catholic social doctrine: an *ethics of institutions* that focuses not on moral norms for personal conduct, but on *moral norms concerning the creation and securing of political, juridical, economical, and social institutions,* and this precisely as *moral* requirements. In this context, they would be requirements of justice and charity. That this is not entirely opposed to the meaning of the passage of *Caritas in veritate* quoted earlier is shown by the astonishingly bold assertion that immediately follows: "*This is the institutional path—we might also call it the political path—of charity,* no less excellent and effective than the kind of charity which encounters the neighbor directly, outside the institutional mediation of the *pólis*" (emphasis added).[86]

Admittedly, it might sound somewhat odd to talk in this context about "charity," mediated by the institutions of the *polis.* Yet, I think one of the profound inspirations of *Caritas in veritate,* expressed in its profoundly theological introduction, was precisely to bring Christian charity down to the conditions of its concrete application to the real world in which we are living. This includes indicating that Christian charity is not only what is commonly called "charitable" actions, but that this charity must be concretized as justice and social and political *institutions* able to bring about what personal, private, and privately organized "charity" is not able to achieve.

Some commentators, such as George Weigel, have seen in this encyclical a clear left-wing or "red" antithesis to the rather right-wing-liberal or "golden" *Centesimus annus.*[87] This is perhaps correct regarding some formulations that

---

85. Ibid., no. 7.   86. Ibid.
87. See George Weigel, "*Caritas in Veritate* in Gold and Red: The Revenge of Justice and Peace (or

might seem to be a kind of retraction from *Centesimus annus*'s advocation of the free market economy. Yet, *Caritas in veritate* need not necessarily be understood in this way. Perhaps Weigel had in mind some propositions contained in the encyclical aiming at correcting or complementing the logic of exchange of equivalents ("giving in order to acquire") typical for the market economy, by a "market of gratuitousness." As the encyclical says, this market is characterized by solidarity and communion[88] as well as by "the *principle of gratuitousness* and the logic of gift as an expression of fraternity" that "in *commercial relationships* can and must *find their place within normal economic activity*" and is even "demanded by economic logic."[89] I am not sure how exactly this is to be understood. There seems to be a clear allusion to the late medieval and Renaissance tradition of civic humanism as it has recently been retrieved by some Italian economists.[90] In any case, when *Caritas in veritate* speaks of the "continuing hegemony of the binary model of market-plus-State" that "has accustomed us to think only in terms of the private business leader of a capitalistic bent on the one hand, and the State director on the other,"[91] it should be remarked that this "binary model of market-plus-State" does not necessarily belong to the best of liberal tradition. The best of liberal tradition has always claimed that the binominal of market and state must be complemented by other forms of relationships and forms of solidarity, rooted in civil society. Twentieth-century liberals have stressed the importance of recognizing that a free market economy must be embedded in a system of values that the market itself cannot create but presupposes. Thus, in his last book, *Jenseits von Angebot und Nachfrage* (Beyond offer and demand), one of the leading neoliberal German economists and social philosophers, Wilhelm Röpke, emphasized that in order for it to work properly and in a human and freedom-enhancing way, the market mechanism, based on the laws of supply and demand, actually depends on what is *beyond* supply and demand.[92] Liberals have usually also stressed the importance of the *corps intermédiaires;* these are public-spirited charities and other organizations, yet neither state-

---

So They May Think)," *National Review Online,* July 7, 2009, http://article.nationalreview.com/399362/icaritas-in-veritatei-in-gold-and-red/george-weigel.

88. *Caritas in veritate,* no. 39.   89. Ibid., no. 36

90. See, e.g., Luigino Bruni and Stefano Zamagni, *Economica civile: Efficienza, equità, felicità pubblica* (Bologna: Il Mulino, 2004); as is well known, Stefano Zamagni, as consultor for the "Pontifical Commission for Justice and Peace"—charged by Benedict XVI with drafting this encyclical—was one of the main contributors to this work and one of those who officially presented the new document to the press.

91. *Caritas in veritate,* no. 41.

92. Wilhelm Röpke, *Jenseits von Angebot und Nachfrage,* 4th ed. (Erlenbach-Zürich: Eugen Rentsch Verlag, 1966); English ed.: *A Humane Economy* (Chicago: Henry Regnery, 1960).

run nor economically spirited or profit-seeking institutions; they arise from and are located in civil society, and many of them are also run by the Church and different religious communities. They have even pleaded for many publicly relevant services, for example, in the field of education, research, or health care, to be privately organized and funded (as are most of the best universities in the United States). It also seems that in societies with a rather more developed market economy and less developed state-run welfare institutions, the civil society is more creative and there is an especially high intensity of volunteering (which is the case in the United States, while people in countries such as Italy, Spain, or Germany rely much more on state-run aid).[93]

However, as far as the state and its relation to the economy is concerned, it is important to thoroughly understand the role of the state as precisely both *fundamental* and *limited*. It is equally important to recognize the establishment and the upholding of the institutions that are fundamental as part of the political ethics involved in the economic order of the free market. In my judgment, with the idea of an ethics of institutions—political, juridical, economic, and social institutions as basic *moral* requirements of justice and Christian charity—*Caritas in veritate* has complemented the fundamental vision of *Centesimus annus*, concerning the role of the state in the economic sector, in an important and promising way.

Conclusion: The Trade-Off between Economic Efficiency and Equity and the Necessarily Limited Role of the State

As was said above, the outcome of the capitalist economy and the market is neither morally good nor evil, neither just nor unjust; it can, however, still

93. See, e.g., the detailed report *Volunteering in America: State Trends and Rankings 2002–2005*, ed. Corporation for National and Community Service, Office of Research and Policy Development, Washington, D.C., June 2006, www.nationalservice.gov. A 2010 fact sheet indicates as the most recent key findings: "Approximately 1.6 million more volunteers served in 2009 than in 2008, making this the largest single-year increase in the number of volunteers since 2003 (annual data collection for volunteering statistics started in 2002). A total of 63.4 million volunteers contributed 8.1 billion hours of service in 2009, equaling an estimated dollar value of approximately 169 billion for their services. The volunteering rate increased in 2009 to 26.8 percent, up from 26.4 percent in 2008" (www.nationalservice.gov/pdf/10_0614_via_2010_fact_sheet_6_10_10.pdf).

See data for European countries on the website of the the European Volunteer Centre (CEV) in Brussels: www.cev.be/66-cev_facts_e_figures_reports_-EN.html . According to the information provided by the CEV, Italy had in 2003 a total number of 825,995 persons engaged in volunteering (USA: 65 million in 2005), which, taking into account the difference in population size (Italy about 58 million, USA 307 million)—and provided the figures are correct and comparable—signifies that the percentage of persons engaged in volunteering in the United States (22%) is about fifteen times higher than in Italy (1.45%).

be considered more or less *desirable,* and thus demands correction precisely for moral reasons. Provided the market mechanism really works, the market is certainly the most efficient way of coordinating human energies, resources, and their allocation. As Peter Koslowski in his *Ethics of Capitalism*[94] has convincingly argued, capitalism, which he strongly defends as an economic order, cannot, however, also be a *social order* because the market itself is unable to decide between preferences of goals and values. In other words, the totality of the social order cannot be understood solely as a market, and the market cannot be conceived of as the whole of society.[95] The idea of the market and free competition (F. A. Hayek's "Catallactics") forms an ideal of coordination, but they are not yet a complete theory of society. Moreover, not all human needs are "marketable," that is, possible objects of exchange transactions of equivalents. There are people who first must be helped in order to become players in market relations; there are others who never will be able to participate. No one of the often defamed important "neoliberal"—or ordoliberal—economists has ever denied this. Moreover, the goal to attain and the values to realize are certainly not the market itself. The market is an optimal, if not the only working, mechanism for allocating resources in the most efficient way and therefore specifically regards the common good of the most beneficial *economic* order. But the efficiency of allocation, although a *condition* for social justice, does not yet select the goals that human beings living together and cooperating in a determinate society desire to attain. Economic efficiency and legally correct procedures are not yet sufficient criteria for just distribution.[96] In the same way, the goal of freedom and self-choice cannot be mere freedom. "Self-choice as an ideal makes sense only because some *issues* are more significant than others.... Which issues are significant, *I* do not determine. If I did, no issue would be significant.... So the ideal of self-choice supposes that there are *other* issues of significance beyond self-choice."[97] The common good cannot simply be an ideal of freedom and self-choice; it must also contain the conditions that render possible the realization of one's freedom in view of *valuable* goods.[98] Social or redistribu-

---

94. I refer to the original German edition: Peter Koslowski, *Ethik des Kapitalismus. Mit einem Kommentar von James M. Buchanan,* 6th ed. (Tübingen: Mohr Siebeck, 1998). The English edition is part of Koslowski, *Ethics of Capitalism and Critique of Sociobiology: Two Essays with a Comment by James M. Buchanan* (Berlin: Springer, 1996).

95. See for the following Koslowski, *Ethik des Kapitalismus,* 55–72.

96. Ibid., 55–56.

97. See Charles Taylor, *The Ethics of Authenticity* (Cambridge, Mass.: Harvard University Press, 1992), 39 (first published in 1991 as *The Malaise of Modernity* by the Canadian Broadcasting Corporation).

98. See Joseph Raz, *The Morality of Freedom* (Oxford: Clarendon Press, 1986), 400ff.

tive justice is thus sometimes required to realize the goals and the "common good" we aim at, to a certain and prudent measure, even at the expense of long-term and overall economic efficiency.

It must be clear, however, that there is a trade-off between the freedom of the market and social justice, between economic efficiency and equity, though, as Alan Blinder thinks, it is not necessarily inevitable.[99] What seems to be certain, however, is that social justice will never be attained by *systematically* contravening economic efficiency. Social justice at the expense of freedom and self-responsibility, as is the case in the paternalistic welfare state or the "Social Assistance State," deplored and criticized also by *Centesimus annus*,[100] is not a desirable ideal either. It leads to a society with less solidarity, because when citizens know that the state taxes away a great amount of the fruits of their labor, returning it in form of social security, public health care, and the like, they will be less motivated to show personal solidarity or engage in volunteering. Rather, they will try to use for themselves the best of what the state does not tax away. "By intervening directly and depriving society of its responsibility"—John Paul II wrote rather prophetically in *Centesimus annus*— "the Social Assistance State leads to a loss of human energies and an inordinate increase of public agencies, which are dominated more by bureaucratic ways of thinking than by concern for serving their clients, and which are accompanied by an enormous increase in spending. In fact, it would appear that needs are best understood and satisfied by people who are closest to them and who act as neighbors to those in need."[101] Extreme welfare state plus capitalism is not an ideal combination at all. Besides systematically violating the principle of subsidiarity, it also provides a justification for employers, entrepreneurs—if they still exist—businessmen, and citizens in general to act more egoistically. Today, as we know, the welfare state is not any more affordable: it has turned out to be too expensive, causing an ever-increasing state indebtedness. Understandably, however, politicians are reluctant to call these problems by their real name.

Anti-capitalism is as unsound as thinking that capitalist economic efficiency alone does the job. Therefore, even if government intervention may be required to sometimes protect weaker social groups from the immediately damaging effects of sound economic policy, it should not be concerned *too much* or *primarily* with this kind of social justice; otherwise, it will tend

---

99. See Blinder, *Hard Heads, Soft Hearts*, especially the remarks on 30–31.
100. No. 48.
101. Ibid.

to advocate structural economic inefficiency, which in turn will undermine all the efforts to achieve precisely the social justice one intends to attain.

Unfortunately, there are and will always be politicians who take advantage of the economic inefficiencies of the market economy; this legitimizes their advocation for more government interventionism, thus creating even more market failures. This was, as mentioned above, the sort of self-fulfilling-prophecy policy first practiced in the United States during the thirties by the Roosevelt administration. Hopefully, however, responsible politicians and responsible citizens with a better education in basic economics will in the future better see through such political calculations and correspondingly penalize such politicians by refusing to cast their vote for them.

But notice again that defending economic liberalism means defending not only, or in the first place, *economic efficiency*. Liberalism is not a political and economic doctrine aiming at money making, maximum productivity, and profit. It is part of a vision of society that is based on freedom and that sees in freedom an essential part of the common good. Liberals believe, more than in economic efficiency, in freedom. This is a strength, but also an obvious weakness of liberalism. Traditional liberalism is somewhat reductionist, one-sided, and in some respect flawed in its anthropology. As a purely secular mode of thinking, it most importantly lacks the knowledge of what is basic for any Christian approach to human and social problems: not only the awareness of the real condition of mankind as a consequence of sin, but also its real and eternal destiny. Such knowledge, of course, is not immediately relevant for economics and politics. It does, however, help to see things in another perspective. I think it is mainly here, and not in trying to find better economic models, that the social teaching of the Church can contribute to economics—not by being anti-capitalist, but by complementing the idea of a capitalist and free market economy with a vision of the common good that is not simply economic, but much more integral.

I am convinced that Catholic social thinking can also learn much from the liberal tradition, namely the insight that for those who are pursuing the common good, freedom—and not only justice and peace—is both an essential basis and a goal. On the other hand, the perennial and most valuable insights and achievements of the liberal tradition will certainly be supported and even enhanced by being integrated into a wider anthropology and vision of society, characteristic of the tradition of Catholic social doctrine.[102]

102. This essay was originally published in *Free Markets and the Culture of Common Good*, ed. M. Schlag and J. A. Mercado (New York: Springer, 2012).

Bibliography

Ackermann, Bruce. *Social Justice in the Liberal State*. New Haven, Conn.: Yale University Press, 1980.

Alting von Geusau, Frans A. M. "Die liberale Gesellschaft und der Rechtsstaat." In *Die liberale Gesellschaft: Castelgandolfo-Gespräche, 1992*, edited by Krzysztof Michalski. Stuttgart: Klett-Cotta, 1993.

Aranzadi, Javier. *Liberalism against Liberalism: Theoretical Analysis of the Works of Ludwig von Mises and Gary Becker*. London: Routledge, 2006.

Arblaster, Anthony. *The Rise and Decline of Western Liberalism*. Oxford: Blackwell, 1984.

Arendt, Hannah. *The Human Condition*. Chicago: University of Chicago Press, 1958.

Aristotle. *Politics*. Translated by H. Rackham. Loeb Classical Library 264. Cambridge, Mass.: Harvard University Press, 1932.

Arquillière, Henri-Xavier. *L'Augustinisme politique. Essai sur la formation des théories politiques du Moyen Age*. 2nd ed. Paris: J. Vrin, 1955.

Aubert, Roger. *Il Pontificato di Pio IX (1846–1878)*. Vol. 21, pt. 1: *Storia della Chiesa*, edited by Augustine Fliche and Victor Martin. Edizioni Paoline. Milan: Cinisello Balsamo, 1990.

Audi, Robert. *Religious Commitment and Secular Reason*. Cambridge: Cambridge University Press, 2000.

Bagehot, Walter. *The English Constitution (1867)*. Oxford: Oxford University Press, 2009.

Bastiat, Frédéric. *Harmonies économiques*. Paris: Guillaumin, 1851.

Bastit, Michel. *Naissance de la loi moderne: La pensée de la loi de saint Thomas à Suarez*. Paris: Presses Universitaires de France, 1990.

Beauté, Jean. *Un grand juriste Anglais: Sir Edward Coke 1552–1634: Ses idées politiques et constitutionelles, ou aux origines de la démocratie occidentale moderne*. Paris: Presses Universitaires de France, 1975.

Belardinelli, Sergio. "A che serve parlare di Dio? Sulla funzione civile della religione." In *L'identità in conflitto dell'Europa: Cristianesimo, laicità, laicismo*, edited by Laura Paoletti. Bologna: Il Mulino, 2005.

———. *La comunità liberale: La libertà, il bene comune e la religione nelle società complesse*. Rome: Edizioni Studium, 1999.

Bellamy, Richard. *Liberalism and Modern Society: An Historical Argument*. Cambridge: Polity Press, 1992.

Bellati, M. L. *Quale multiculturalismo? I termini del dibattito e la prospettiva di Will Kymlicka*. Milan: Vita e Pensiero, 2005.

Benedict XVI. "Address of His Holiness Pope Benedict XVI to the Roman Curia Offering Them His Christmas Greetings." December 22, 2005. (www.vatican.va/holy_father/ benedict_xvi/speeches/2005)

———. *Caritas in veritate*. June 29, 2009.

Benestad, J. Brian. *Church, State, and Society: An Introduction to Catholic Social Doctrine*. Catholic Moral Thought Series. Washington, D.C.: The Catholic University of America Press, 2011.

Berlin, Isaiah. "Two Concepts of Liberty." In *Four Essays on Liberty*. Oxford: Oxford University Press, 1969.

Berman, Harold J. *Law and Revolution: The Formation of the Western Legal Tradition*. Cambridge, Mass.: Harvard University Press, 1983.

———. *Law and Revolution II: The Impact of the Protestant Reformations on the Western Legal Tradition*. Cambridge, Mass.: Harvard University Press, 2003.

———. *Recht und Revolution. Die Bildung der westlichen Rechtstradition*. Frankfurt am Main: Suhrkamp Verlag, 1991.

Berti, Enrico. *Le vie della ragione*. Bologna: Il Mulino, 1987.

Bhagwati, Jagdish. *Free Trade Today*. Princeton, N.J.: Princeton University Press, 2002.

Bielefeldt, Heiner. *Philosophie der Menschenrechte. Grundlagen eines weltweiten Freiheitsethos*. Darmstadt: Wissenschaftliche Buchgesellschaft, 1998.

Binder, Leonard. *Islamic Liberalism: A Critique of Development Ideologies*. Chicago: University of Chicago Press, 1988.

Blackstone, Sir William. *Commentaries on the Laws of England*. 4 vols. (1765, 1766, 1768, and 1769), edited by William G. Hammond. San Francisco: Bancroft-Whitney, 1890.

Blinder, Alan S. *Hard Heads, Soft Hearts: Tough-Minded Economics for a Just Society*. Cambridge, Mass.: Perseus Books, 1987.

Bobbio, Norberto. "Hobbes e il giusnaturalismo." *Rivista Critica di Storia della Filosofia* 17 (1962): 470–85.

———. *L'età dei diritti*. Torino: Einaudi, 1990.

Böckenförde, Ernst-Wolfgang. *Der deutsche Katholizismus im Jahre 1933: Kirche und demokratisches Ethos (Schriften zu Staat—Gesellschaft—Kirche, I)*. Freiburg: Herder, 1988.

———. *Kirchlicher Auftrag und politisches Handeln. Analyse und Orientierungen*. Schriften zu Staat—Gesellschaft—Kirche, Band 2. Freiburg-Basel-Vienna: Herder, 1989.

———. *Religionsfreiheit. Die Kirche in der modernen Welt (Schriften zu Staat— Gesellschaft—Kirche, III)*. Freiburg-Basdel-Vienna: Herder, 1990.

———. *Staat, Gesellschaft, Freiheit. Studien zur Staatstheorie und zum Verfassungsrecht*. Frankfurt: Suhrkamp, 1976. In English: *State, Society and Liberty*. New York: Berg, 1991.

Bodin, Jean. *Les Six Livres de la République*. Paris: Chez Iaques Du Puys, 1576.

Borgonovo, Graziano, and Arturo Cattaneo, eds. *Giovanni Paolo Teologo. Nel segno delle encicliche*. Rome: Edizioni Arnoldo Mondatori, 2003.

Botturi, Francesco. "Per una teoria liberale del bene comune." *Vita e Pensiero* 79, no. 2 (1996): 82–94.

Boutmy, Émile. "La déclaration des droits de l'homme et M. Jellinek." *Annales des sciences politiques* 17 (1902): 415–43. Reprinted in Émile Boutmy. *Études Politiques.* Paris: Armand Colin, 1907.

Brague, Rémi. *La Loi de Dieu. Histoire philosophique d'une alliance.* Paris: Gallimard, 2005.

Braudel, Fernand, and Ernest Labrousse. *Histoire économique et sociale de la France.* Vol. 3: *1789–années 1880.* Paris: Presses Universitaires de France, 1976.

Brocker, Manfred, and Tine Stein, eds. *Christentum und Demokratie.* Darmstadt: Wissenschaftliche Buchgesellschaft, 2006.

Brown, Peter. *The Rise of Western Christendom: Triumph and Diversity, A.D. 200–1000.* 2nd ed. Oxford: Blackwell, 2003.

Bruni, Luigino, and Stefano Zamagni. *Economica civile: Efficienza, equità, felicità pubblica.* Bologna: Il Mulino, 2004.

Burke, Edmund. *On Government, Politics and Society.* Edited by B. W. Hill. Glasgow: Fontana/Harvester Press, 1975.

Burns, James Henderson, ed. *The Cambridge History of Medieval Political Thought c.350–c.1450.* Cambridge: Cambridge University Press, 1988.

Calvez, Jean-Yves. *Les silences de la doctrine sociale catholique.* Paris: Les Éditions de l'Atelier e Éditions Ouvrières, 1999.

Caplan, Bryan. *The Myth of the Rational Voter: Why Democracies Choose Bad Politics.* Princeton, N.J.: Princeton University Press, 2007.

Carlyle, Robert Warrant, and Alexander James Carlyle. *A History of Mediaeval Political Theory in the West.* 6 vols. Edinburgh/London: William Blackwood, 1903–36. Last printing in 1970.

Catholic Church. Second Vatican Council. Dogmatic Constitution *Dei verbum.* November 18, 1965.

———. Pastoral Constitution *Gaudium et spes.* December 7, 1965.

———. Declaration *Dignitatis humanae.* December 7, 1965.

———. Congregation for Catholic Education. *Guidelines for the Study and Teaching of the Social Doctrine of the Church in Priestly Formation.* December 30, 1988.

———. *Catechism of the Catholic Church.* 2nd ed. Citta del Vaticano: Libreria Editrice Vaticana, 1997.

———. Congregation for the Doctrine of the Faith, *Doctrinal Commentary on the Concluding Formula of the "Professio fidei."* June 29, 1998.

———. Congregation for the Doctrine of the Faith. *Doctrinal Note on Some Questions Regarding the Participation of Catholics in Political Life.* November 24, 2002.

———. Congregation of the Doctrine of the Faith. *Considerations Regarding Proposals to Give Legal Recognition to Unions between Homosexual Persons.* June 3, 2003.

———. Congregation for the Doctrine of the Faith. *Note on the Banalization of Sexuality Regarding Certain Interpretations of "Light of the World".* December 22, 2010.

———. Pontifical Council for Justice and Peace. *Compendium of the Social Doctrine of the Church.* Washington D.C.: USCCB Publishing, 2005.

Catholic Encyclopedia. New York: Robert Appleton, 1908.

Cavour, Camillo Benso conte di. *Libera Chiesa in libero State.* Genoa: Il Melangolo, 2001.

Chandler, Ralph R., Richard A. Enslen, and Peter G. Renstrom. *The Constitutional Law Dictionary.* Vol. 1: *Individual Rights.* Santa Barbara: Clio Press, 1985.

Chevalier, Jean-Jacques. *Storia del pensiero politico.* Vol. 1. 2nd ed. Bologna: Il Mulino, 1989.

Chuvin, Pierre. *Chronique des derniers païens. La disparition du paganisme dans l'Empire romain du règne de Constantin a celui de Justinien.* 2nd ed. Paris: Les Belles Lettres/Fayard, 1991.

Cohen, Joshua. "Moral Pluralism and Political Consensus." In *The Idea of Democracy,* edited by David Copp, Jean Hampton, and John E. Roemer, 270–91. New York: Cambridge University Press, 1993.

Constant, Benjamin. *Political Writings.* Translated and edited by Biancamaria Fontana. Cambridge: Cambridge University Press, 1988.

Corporation for National and Community Service, Office of Research and Policy Development. *Volunteering in America: State Trends and Rankings 2002–2005.* Washington, D.C., 2006.

Coulanges, Fustel de. *La cité antique.* Paris: Flammarion, 1984. (First published 1864.)

Crawford, David. "Recognizing the Roots of Society in the Family, Foundation of Justice." *Communio* 34 (Fall 2007): 379–412.

Curci, Carlo Maria. "Il congresso cattolico di Malines e le libertà moderne." *La Civiltà Cattolica,* series 5, vol. 8, fasc. 326 (October 2, 1863): 129–49.

D'Agostino, Francesco. *Il diritto come problema teologico.* Recta Ratio 17. Turin: G. Giapichelli, 1992.

Dabin, Jean. *L'État ou le Politique. Essai de Définition.* Paris: Jurisprudence Générale Dalloz, 1957.

Dahl, Robert Alan. *Democracy and Its Critics.* New Haven, Conn.: Yale University Press, 1989.

Dalle Fratte, Gino, ed. *Concezioni del bene e teoria della giustizia: Il dibattito tra liberali e comunitari in prospettiva pedagogica.* Rome: Armando, 1995.

Dauenhauer, Bernard P. "A Good Word for a Modus Vivendi." In *The Idea of a Political Liberalism: Essays on Rawls,* edited by Victoria Davion and Clark Wolf. Lanham, Md.: Rowman and Littlefield, 2000.

Dawson, Christopher. *The Making of Europe: An Introduction to the History of Christian Unity.* London: Sheed and Ward, 1932.

Dempf, Alois. *Sacrum Imperium: Geschichts- und Staatsphilosophie des Mittelalters und der politischen Renaissance.* 3rd ed. Darmstadt: Wissenschaftliche Buchgesellschaft, 1962.

Detjen, Joachim. *Neopluralismus und Naturrecht: Zur politischen Philosophie der Pluralismustheorie.* Politik- und Kommunikationswissenschaftliche Veröffentlichungen der Görres-Gesellschaft 1. Paderborn: Schöningh, 1988.

Devlin, Patrick. *The Enforcement of Morals.* Oxford: Oxford University Press, 1965.

Donati, Pierpaolo, ed. *Laicità. la ricerca dell'universale nelle differenze.* Bologna: Il Mulino, 2008.

————. *Teoria relazionale della società*. Milan: Franco Angeli, 1991.

Douglass, R. Bruce, and David Hollenbach, eds. *Catholicism and Liberalism: Contributions to American Public Policy*. Cambridge Studies in Religion and American Public Life. Cambridge: Cambridge University Press, 1994.

Dumézil, Bruno. *Les racines chrétiennes de l'Europe: Conversion et liberté dans les royaumes barbares Ve-VIIIe siècle*. Paris: Fayard, 2005.

Dunn, John. *The Political Thought of John Locke: An Historical Account of the Argument of the "Two Treatises of Government."* Cambridge: Cambridge University Press, 1969.

Dworkin, Ronald. "Freiheit, Gleichheit und Gemeinschaft." In *Die liberale Gesellschaft. Castelgandolfo-Gespräche 1992*, edited by Krzysztof Michalski. Stuttgart: Klett-Cotta, 1993.

————. "Liberal Community." *California Law Review* 77 (1989): 479–504.

————. "Liberalism." In *Public and Private Morality*, edited by Stuart Hampshire. Cambridge: Cambridge University Press, 1978.

————. *Taking Rights Seriously*. London: Duckworth, 1977; 1978.

Dworkin, Ronald, Thomas Nagel, Robert Nozick, John Rawls, T. M. Scanlon, and Judith Jarvis Thomson. "Assisted Suicide: The Philosophers' Brief." *New York Review of Books* 44, no. 5 (March 27, 1997): 41–45.

Engberg-Pedersen, Troels. *Aristotle's Theory of Moral Insight*. Oxford: Oxford University Press, 1983.

Ensslin, Wilhelm. "Auctoritas und Potestas. Zur Zweigewaltenlehre des Papstes Gelasius I." *Historisches Jahrbuch* 75 (1955): 661–68.

Escrivá, Josemaría. *L'avventura della libertà*. Milan: Edizioni Ares, 1972.

Etzioni, Amitai. *The Common Good*. Cambridge: Polity Press, 2004.

————. *New Communitarian Thinking: Persons, Virtues, Institutions, and Communities*. Charlottesville: University of Virginia Press, 1995.

————. *The Spirit of Community: Rights, Responsibilities and the Communitarian Agenda*. London: Fontana Press, 1995.

Euchner, Walter. "Auctoritas non veritas facit legem: Zur Abgrenzung von Politik und Nicht-Politik bei Thomas Hobbes." In *Furcht und Freiheit. Leviathan-Diskussion 300 Jahre nach Thomas Hobbes*, edited by U. Bermbach and K.-M. Kodalle. Opladen: Westdeutscher Verlag, 1982.

Eucken, Walter. *Grundsätze der Wirtschaftspolitik*. 4th ed. Tübingen: J. C. B. Mohr–Paul Siebeck, 1968.

Ferguson, Niall. *The Ascent of Money: A Financial History of the World*. London: Penguin, 2008.

Ferrara, Alessandro. *Comunitarismo e Liberalismo*. Rome: Editori Riuniti, 1992.

Fetscher, Iring. *Rousseaus politische Philosophie: Zur Geschichte des demokratischen Freiheitsbegriffs*. 3rd ed. Frankfurt am Main: Suhrkamp, 1975.

Fetscher, Iring, and Herfried Münkler, eds. *Pipers Handbuch der politischen Ideen*. 5 vols. Munich: Piper, 1987; 1993.

Fetzer, J. S., and J. C. Soper. *Muslims and the State in Britain, France, and Germany*. Cambridge: Cambridge University Press, 2005.

Fijalkowski, Jürgen. *Die Wendung zum Führerstaat: Ideologische Komponenten in der Philosophie Carl Schmitts.* Cologne: Westdeutscher Verlag, 1958.

Finnis, John. "Abortion, Natural Law, and Public Reason." In *Natural Law and Public Reason,* edited by Robert P. George and Christopher Wolfe. Washington, D.C.: Georgetown University Press, 2000.

———. *Aquinas, Moral, Political, and Legal Theory.* Oxford: Oxford University Press, 1998.

———. "Is Natural Law Theory Compatible with Limited Government?" In *Natural Law, Liberalism, and Morality: Contemporary Essays,* edited by Robert P. George. Oxford: Oxford University Press, 1996.

———. "Public Reason, Abortion, and Cloning." *Valparaiso University Law Review* 32, no. 2 (1998): 361–82.

Fraenkel, Ernst. *Deutschland und die westlichen Demokratien.* Edited by Alexander von Brünneck. 8th ed. Frankfurt am Main: Suhrkamp, 1991.

Franz, Günther, ed. *Staatsverfassungen: Eine Sammlung wichtiger Verfassungen der Vergangenheit und Gegenwart in Urtext und Übersetzung.* Munich: R. Oldenbourg, 1975.

Frey, Bruno S. *Democratic Economic Policy.* New York: Palgrave Macmillan, 1983.

———. *Theorie demokratischer Wirtschaftspolitik.* München: Vahlen, 1981.

Frey, Bruno S., and Gebhard Kirchgässner. *Theorie demokratischer Wirtschaftspolitik.* München: Vahlen, 2001.

Friedberg, Emil. *Corpus Iuris Canonici.* 2 vols. Reprinted by the Editio Lipsiensis secunda. Graz: Akademische Druck- u. Verlagsanstalt, 1955.

Friedman, Milton. *Capitalism and Freedom.* 1962. Chicago: University of Chicago Press, 1982.

Friedman, Milton, and Anna J. Schwartz. *A Monetary History of the United States, 1867–1960.* Princeton, N.J.: Princeton University Press, 1963.

Friedrich, Carl J. *Constitutional Government and Democracy.* New York: Blaisdell, 1950; 3rd ed., Boston: Ginn, 1951. In German: *Der Verfassungsstaat der Neuzeit.* Berlin/ Göttingen/Heidelberg: Springer, 1953.

———. *L'uomo, la comunità politica, l'ordine politico.* Bologna: Il Mulino, 2002.

Fuenmayor, Amadeo de. *La libertad religiosa.* Pamplona: EUNSA, 1974.

Fumagalli, Beonio, and Maria Teresa Brocchieri. *Il pensiero politico medievale.* Bari: Manuali Laterza, 2004.

Galston, William A. *Liberal Purposes: Goods, Virtues, and Diversity in the Liberal State.* Cambridge: Cambridge University Press, 1991.

Gaudron, Matthias. "Die Religionsfreiheit, Das wahre Verhältnis von Kirche und Staat." *Civitas. Zeitschrift für das christliche Gemeinwesen* 10 (2010): 1–19.

Gaus, Gerald. *Contemporary Theories of Liberalism: Public Reason as a Post-Enlightenment Project.* London: Sage Publications, 2003.

Gelasius I. *Tractatus 4.* In *Sources chrétiennes,* edited by H. de Lubac and J. Daniélou. Vol. 65. Paris: Cerf, 1960.

George, Robert P. *In Defense of Natural Law.* Oxford: Oxford University Press, 1999.

———. *Making Men Moral: Civil Liberties and Public Morality.* Oxford: Clarendon Press, 1993.

————. "Pluralismo morale, ragione pubblica e legge naturale." In *Etica e politica nella società del duemila*, edited by R. A. Gahl. Rome: Armando, 1998.

George, Robert P., and Christopher Wolfe, eds. *Natural Law and Public Reason.* Washington, D.C.: Georgetown University Press, 2000.

Gierke, Otto von. *Das deutsche Genossenschaftsrecht.* Vol. 1: *Rechtsgeschichte der deutschen Genossenschaft.* Berlin: Weidermann, 1868; reprint, Darmstadt: Wissenschaftliche Buchgesellschaft, 1954.

————. *Johannes Althusius und die Entwicklung der naturrechtlichen Staatstheorie: Zugleich ein Beitrag zur Geschichte der Rechtssystematik.* 2nd ed. Breslau: Verlag Marcus, 1902.

Gilpin, Robert. *Global Political Economy: Understanding the International Economic Order.* Princeton, N.J.: Princeton University Press, 2001.

Glendon, Mary Ann. *Rights Talk: The Impoverishment of Political Discourse.* New York: Free Press, 1991.

Gough, John Weidhofft. *The Social Contract: A Critical Study of Its Developments.* London: Oxford University Press, 1936; 2nd ed. 1957/1963/1976; reprint, Westport, Conn.: Greenwood Press, 1978. In Italian: *Il contratto sociale. Storia critica di una teoria.* Bologna: Il Mulino, 1986.

Goyard-Fabre, Simone. *Le Droit et la Loi dans la Philosophie de Thomas Hobbes.* Paris: C. Klincksieck, 1975.

Grabmann, Martin. "Studien über den Einfluss der aristotelischen Philosophie auf die mittelalterlichen Theorien über das Verhältnis von Kirche und Staat." In *Sitzungsberichte der Bayerischen Akademie der Wissenschaften, Philos.-hist. Abt.* Vol. 2. Munich: Verlag der Bayerischen Akademie der Wissenschaften, 1934.

Grasso, Kenneth L., and Robert P. Hunt, eds. *Catholicism and Religious Freedom: Contemporary Reflections on Vatican II's Declaration on Religious Liberty.* Lanham, Md.: Rowman and Littlefield, 2006.

Gray, John. *Two Faces of Liberalism.* New York: New Press, 2000.

Grichting, Martin. *Das Verfügungsrecht über das Kirchenvermögen auf den Ebenen von Diözese und Pfarrei.* Münchner Theologische Studien 3, Kanonistische Abteilung 62. Ottilien: EOS Verlag, 2007.

Gutmann, Amy. "Communitarian Critics of Liberalism." *Philosophy and Public Affairs* 14 (1985): 308–22.

Gutmann, Amy, and Dennis Thompson. *Democracy and Disagreement.* Cambridge, Mass.: Harvard University Press, 1996.

————. "Moral Conflict and Political Consensus." In *Liberalism and the Good*, edited by R. Bruce Douglass, Gerald M. Mara, and Henry S. Richardson. New York: Routledge, 1990.

————. *Why Deliberative Democracy?* Princeton, N.J.: Princeton University Press, 2004.

Häberle, Peter. *Le libertà fondamentali nello Stato costituzionale.* Edited by P. Ridola. Rome: Nuova Italia Scientifica, 1993.

Habermas, Jürgen. *Die Einbeziehung des Anderen. Studien zur politischen Theorie.* Frankfurt am Main: Suhrkamp, 1996.

————. *Faktizität und Geltung. Beiträge zur Diskurstheorie des Rechts und des demokratischen Rechtsstaats.* Frankfurt am Main: Suhrkamp, 1992.

————. "Religion in der Öffentlichkeit: Kognitive Voraussetzungen für den 'öffentlichen Vernunftgebrauch' religiöser und säkularer Bürger." In Habermas, *Zwischen Naturalismus und Religion: Philosophische Aufsätze.* Frankfurt am Main: Suhrkamp, 2005.

Habermas, Jürgen, and Joseph Ratzinger. *The Dialectics of Secularization: On Reason and Religion.* San Francisco: Ignatius Press, 2007.

Hale, Matthew. "Reflections by the Lord Chief Justice Hale on Mr. Hobbes His Dialogue of the Lawe" (manuscript). In *History of English Law,* edited by W. S. Holdsworth, vol. 5, app. 3, 500–513. 13 vols. 7th ed. London: Sweet & Maxwell, 1956–64.

Hart, H. L. A. *Law, Liberty and Morality.* Oxford: Oxford University Press, 1963.

Harvey, David. *A Brief History of Neoliberalism.* Oxford: Oxford University Press, 2005.

Hattenhauer, Hans. *Europäische Rechtsgeschichte.* Heidelberg: C. F. Müller Juristischer Verlag, 1992.

Hayek, Friedrich A. *The Constitution of Liberty.* Chicago: University of Chicago Press, 1960.

————. *Law, Legislation and Liberty: A New Statement of the Liberal Principles of Justice and Political Economy.* London: Routledge and Kegan, 1982.

————. *The Road to Serfdom.* 1944. Reprinted in *The Collected Works of F. A. Hayek,* vol. 2, edited by Bruce Caldwell. Chicago: University Press of Chicago, 2007.

Hazlitt, Henry. *Economics in One Lesson.* 1946. New ed. New York: Three Rivers Press, 1979.

Heller, Ágnes. *Beyond Justice.* Oxford: Basil Blackwell, 1987.

Hittinger, Russell. "Natural Law in the Positive Laws: A Legislative or Adjudicative Issue?" *Review of Politics* 55 (1993): 5–34. Reprinted in Hittinger, *The First Grace: Rediscovering the Natural Law in a Post-Christian World.* Wilmington, Del.: ISI Books, 2003.

————. "The Pope and the Liberal State." *First Things* 28 (December 1992): 33–41.

Hobbes, Thomas. *The English Works of Thomas Hobbes of Malmesbury.* Edited by W. Molesworth. 11 vols. London, 1839–45; reprint, Aalen: Scientia, 1962.

————. *Leviathan.* Edited by C. B. Macpherson. Harmondsworth: Penguin, 1986.

————. *Man and Citizen: "De Homine" and "De Cive".* Edited by B. Gert. Indianapolis: Hackett 1991.

————. *Thomas Hobbes Malmesburiensis Opera Philosophica quae Latine scripsit Omnia in Unum Corpus Nunc Primum Collectae studio et labore Gulielmi Molesworth.* Edited by W. Molesworth. 5 vols. London, 1839–45; reprint, Aalen: Scientia, 1962–66.

Hobsbawm, Eric. *The Age of Capital 1848–1875.* 1975. London: Abacus, 1997.

Höffe, Otfried. *Politische Gerechtigkeit: Grundlegung einer kritischen Philosophie von Recht und Staat.* Frankfurt am Main: Suhrkamp, 1989.

————. "Ragione pubblica o ragione politica? A proposito di Rawls II." In *Concezioni del bene e teoria della giustizia,* edited by Gino Dalle Fratte. Rome: Armando, 1995.

Hoffmann, Rupert. "Die Zumutungen des Grundgesetzes. Zur verfassungsstaatlichen Entwicklung der Bundesrepublik Deutschland am Ende der siebziger Jahre." *Zeitschrift für Politik* 27 (1980): 129–54.

Hofmann, Hasso. *Legitimität gegen Legalität.* Neuwied: Luchterhand, 1964; 4th ed., Berlin: Duncker & Humblot, 2002.

Holdsworth, William Searle. *History of English Law.* 13 vols. 7th ed. London: Methuen, 1956–64.

Holmes, Stephen. *The Anatomy of Antiliberalism.* Cambridge, Mass.: Harvard University Press, 1993.

———. *Passions and Constraint: On the Theory of Liberal Democracy.* Chicago: University of Chicago Press, 1995.

Honneth, Axel. "Grenzen des Liberalismus. Zur politisch-ethischen Diskussion um den Kommunitarismus." *Philosophische Rundschau* 38 (1991): 83–102.

Huff, Toby E. *The Rise of Early Modern Science: Islam, China and the West.* 2nd ed. Cambridge: Cambridge University Press, 2003.

Humboldt, Wilhelm von. *Ideen über Staatsverfassung, durch die neue Französische Constitution veranlasst* (1791). In *Wilhelm Von Humboldt's Gesammelte Werke*, vol. 1. Charleston, S.C.: BiblioBazaar, 2008.

———. *The Limits of State Action.* Translated by J. W. Burrow. Cambridge: Cambridge University Press, 1969.

Huntington, Samuel. *Who Are We? The Challenges to America's National Identity.* New York: Simon and Schuster, 2004.

Ignatieff, Michael. *Human Rights as Politics and Idolatry.* Edited with an introduction by Amy Gutmann. Princeton, N.J.: Princeton University Press, 2001.

Irwin, Douglas A. *Free Trade under Fire.* Princeton, N.J.: Princeton University Press, 2002.

Isensee, Josef. *Das Grundrecht auf Sicherheit: Zu den Schutzpflichten des freiheitlichen Verfassungsstaates.* Berlin: Walter de Gruyter, 1983.

———. "Die katholische Kritik an den Menschrechten. Der liberale Freiheitsentwurf in der Sicht der Päpste des 19. Jahrhunderts." In *Menschrechte und Menschenwürde. Historische Voraussetzungen—säkulare Gestalt—christliches Verständnis*, edited by Ernst-Wolfgang Böckenförde and Robert Spaemann. Stuttgart: Klett-Cotta, 1987.

Jänicke, Martin. "Die 'abgründige Wissenschaft' vom Leviathan—Zur Hobbes-Deutung Carl Schmitts im Dritten Reich." *Zeitschrift für Politik* 16 (1969): 401–15.

Jellinek, Georg. *Die Erklärung der Menschen- und Bürgerrechte.* 3rd ed. Munich: Duncker & Humblot, 1919. Reprint of the 4th ed. (identical to the 3rd) in *Zur Geschichte der Erklärung der Menschenrechte*, edited by R. Schnur. Darmstadt: Wissenschaftliche Buchgesellschaft, 1964.

Jemolo, Carlo. *Chiesa e Stato in Italia: Dalla unificazione ai giorni nostri.* Turin: Einaudi, 1965.

Joblin, Joseph, and Réal Tremblay, eds. *I cattolici e la società pluralista. Il caso delle "leggi imperfette."* Bologna: ESD, 1996.

John Paul II. *Ad tuendam fidem.* May 18, 1998.

———. *Centesimus annus.* May 1, 1991.

———. *Sollicitudo rei socialis.* December 30, 1987.

Journet, Charles. *La Juridiction de l'Église sur la cité.* Paris: Desclée, 1931.

Jouvenel, Bertrand de. *De la souveraineté. A la recherche du bien Politique.* Paris: Éditions M.-Th. Génin, 1955.

Kant, Immanuel. *Political Writings.* Cambridge: Cambridge University Press, 1991.

Kantorowicz, Ernst. *The King's Two Bodies: A Study in Medieval Political Theology.* 3rd ed. Princeton, N.J.: Princeton University Press, 1973.

Kaufmann, Francis-Xavier, ed. *The Public Sector: Challenge for Coordination and Learning.* Berlin: De Gruyter, 1991.

Kavka, Gregory S. *Hobbesian Moral and Political Theory.* Princeton, N.J.: Princeton University Press, 1986.

Keown, John. *Abortion, Doctors, and the Law: Some Aspects of the Legal Regulation of Abortion in England from 1803 to 1982.* New York: Cambridge University Press, 1988.

Kern, Fritz. *Gottesgnadentum und Widerstandsrecht im früheren Mittelalter. Zur Entwicklungsgeschichte der Monarchie.* 7th ed. Reprint of the 2nd edition of 1954, edited by Rudolf Buchner. Darmstadt: Wissenschaftliche Buchgesellschaft, 1980.

Kersting, Wolfgang. *Die politische Philosophie des Gesellschaftsvertrags.* Darmstadt: Wissenschaftliche Buchgesellschaft, 1994.

Keynes, John Maynard. *The End of Laissez-Faire.* 1926. Reprinted in Keynes, John Maynard, *The End of Laissez-Faire: The Economic Consequences of the Peace.* New York: Prometheus Books, 2004.

Kielmannsegg, Peter Graf. *Volkssouveränität: Eine Untersuchung der Bedingungen demokratischer Legitimität.* Stuttgart: Klett, 1977.

Kluxen, Wolfgang. *Ethik des Ethos.* Freiburg: Alber, 1974.

Koslowski, Peter. *Ethics of Capitalism and Critique of Sociobiology: Two Essays with a Comment by James M. Buchanan.* Berlin: Springer, 1996.

———. *Ethik des Kapitalismus. Mit einem Kommentar von James M. Buchanan.* 6th ed. Tübingen: J. C. B. Mohr–Paul Siebeck, 1998.

———. *Gesellschaft und Staat. Ein unvermeidlicher Dualismus.* With a foreword by Robert Spaemann. Stuttgart: Klett-Cotta, 1982.

———. *Gesellschaftliche Koordination. Eine ontologische und kulturwissenschaftliche Theorie der Marktwirtschaft.* Tübingen: J. C. B. Mohr, 1991.

———. *Principles of Ethical Economy.* Dordrecht: Springer Netherlands, 2000; Berlin: Kluwer Academic Publisher/Springer, 2002.

———. *Prinzipien der Ethischen Ökonomie.* Tübingen: J. C. B. Mohr–Paul Siebeck, 1988.

Kriele, Martin. *Die Herausforderung des Verfassungsstaates: Hobbes und die englischen Juristen.* Neuwied: Luchterhand, 1970.

———. *Einführung in die Staatslehre: Die geschichtlichen Legitimitätsgrundlagen des demokratischen Verfassungsstaates.* 4th ed. Opladen: Westdeutscher Verlag, 1990.

———. *Einführung in die Staatslehre: Die geschichtlichen Legitimitätsgrundlagen des demokratischen Verfassungsstaates.* 6th ed. Stuttgart: Kohlhammer, 2003.

Krugman, Paul, and Maurice Obstfeld. *International Economics: Theory and Policy.* 8th ed. Boston: Pearson–Addison Wesley, 2009.

Kukathas, Chandran. "Liberty." In *A Companion to Contemporary Political Philosophy,* edited by Robert E. Goodin and Philip Pettit. Oxford: Blackwell, 1993.

Kurz, Hanns. *Volkssouveränität und Volksrepräsentation.* Cologne: Carl Heymanns, 1965.

Kusch, Horst, ed. *Marsilius von Padua, Verteidiger des Friedens (Defensor Pacis)*. Latin text and German translation. Berlin: Rütten & Loening, 1958.

Kymlicka, Will. *Contemporary Political Philosophy: An Introduction*. Oxford: Oxford University Press, 1990; 2nd ed. Oxford: Oxford University Press, 2002.

———. *Multicultural Citizenship: A Liberal Theory of Minority Rights*. Oxford: Oxford University Press, 1995.

Lacey, Nicola. *State Punishment: Political Principles and Community Values*. London: Routledge, 1988.

Lagarde, Georges de. *La naissance de l'esprit laïque au déclin du moyen age*. 5 vols. Louvain: Nauvelaerts, 1956–70.

Larmore, Charles E. "Liberalismo politico." In *Comunitarismo e Liberalismo*, edited by Alessandro Ferrara. Rome: Editori Riuniti, 1992.

———. *Patterns of Moral Complexity*. Cambridge: Cambridge University Press, 1987.

———. "Political Liberalism." *Political Theory* 3 (1990): 339–60. Reprinted in Larmore, *The Morals of Modernity*. Cambridge: Cambridge University Press, 1996.

Laski, Harold. *Authority in the Modern State*. New Haven, Conn.: Yale University Press, 1919.

———. *Studies in the Problem of Sovereignty*. New Haven, Conn.: Yale University Press, 1917.

Laslett, Peter. *The World We Have Lost: Further Explored*. London: Routledge, 2000.

Le Guillou, Marie-Joseph and Louis Le Guillou. *La condamnation de Lamennais*. Textes Dossiers Documents 5. Paris: Éditions Beauchesne, 1982.

Lecler, Joseph. *Histoire de la tolérance au siècle de la Réforme*. In 2 vols. Paris: Aubier, 1955; reprinted in 1 vol. Paris: Albin Michel, 1994.

Lefebvre, Marcel. *Ils l'ont découronné. Du libéralisme à l'apostasie. La tragédie conciliaire*. Escurolles: Éditions Fideliter, 1987.

Leo XIII. Encyclical *Immortale Dei*. Latin text in *Enchiridion delle encicliche 3*. Bologna: Edizioni Dehoniane, 1999.

Levering, Matthew. "Natural Law and Natural Inclinations: Rhonheimer, Pinckaers, McAleer." *Thomist* 70 (2006): 155–201.

Lewis, W. Arthur. *Economic Survey 1919–1939*. London: Allan and Unwin, 1949. Reprinted in the Routledge Reprint edition. London: Routledge Chapman and Hall, 2003.

Lewis, V. Bradley. "The Common Good against the Modern State? On MacIntyre's Political Philosophy." *Josephinum Journal of Theology* 16, no. 2 (Summer/Fall 2009): 357–78.

Lexikon für Theologie und Kirche. 2nd ed. Edited by Michael Buchberger, Josef Höfer, and Karl Rahner. 10 vols. Freiburg: Herder, 1963.

Locke, John. *Second Treatise of Government*. Edited with an introduction by C. B. Macpherson. Indianapolis: Hackett, 1980.

Loewenstein, Karl. *Volk und Parlament nach der Staatstheorie der französischen Nationalversammlung von 1789*. Munich: Drei Masken Verlag, 1922; reprint, Aalen: Scientia, 1964 and 1990.

Lübbe, Hermann. "Dezisionismus—eine kompromettierte politische Theorie." In Lübbe, *Praxis der Philosophie, praktische Philosophie, Geschichtstheorie*. Stuttgart: Reclam, 1978.

Lucien, Bernard. *Grégoire XVI, Pie IX et Vatican II: Études sur la Liberté religieuse dans la doctrine catholique*. Tours: Éditions Forts dans la Foi, 1990.

Macedo, Stephen, ed. *Deliberative Politics: Essays on "Democracy and Disagreement."* New York: Oxford University Press, 1999.

———. *Liberal Virtues: Citizenship, Virtue, and Community in Liberal Constitutionalism.* Oxford: Clarendon Press, 1990.

MacIntyre, Alasdair. *After Virtue: A Study in Moral Theory*. Notre Dame: University of Notre Dame Press, 1981; 2nd ed., Notre Dame: University of Notre Dame Press, 1984.

———. *Dependent Rational Animals: Why Human Beings Need the Virtues*. Chicago: Open Court, 1999.

———. "Politics, Philosophy and the Common Good." In *The MacIntyre Reader*, edited by Kelvin Knight. Notre Dame: University of Notre Dame Press, 1998.

———. *Three Rival Versions of Moral Enquiry: Encyclopedia, Genealogy, and Tradition.* Notre Dame: University of Notre Dame Press, 1990.

———. *Whose Justice? Which Rationality?* Notre Dame: University of Notre Dame Press, 1988.

Maier, Hans. *Kirche und Gesellschaft*. Munich: Kösel Verlag, 1972.

Mandeville, Bernard. *The Fable of the Bees: Or Private Vices, Publick Benefits*. Edited with an introduction by Philip Harth. London: Penguin Books, 2010.

Margalit, Avishai, and Joseph Raz. "National Self-Determination." *Journal of Philosophy* 87, no. 9 (1990): 439–61.

Margerie, Bertrand de. *Liberté religieuse et règne du Christ*. Paris: Editions du Cerf, 1988.

Maritain, Jacques. *Man and the State*. Chicago: University of Chicago Press, 1951.

Maritain, Jacques, and Raïssa Maritain. *Oeuvres complètes*. 16 vols. Paris, Fribourg-Paris: Éditions Universitaires Fribourg-Suisse/Éditions Saint-Paul, 1988.

Marrou, Henri-Irénée. *Décadence romaine ou antiquité tardive? IIIe–VIe siècle*. Paris: Éditions du Seuil, 1977.

Martina, Giacomo. *Pio IX (1851–1866)*. Rome: Editrice Pontificia Università Gregoriana, 1986.

Mathias, Peter. *The First Industrial Nation: An Economic History of Britain 1700–1914.* 2nd ed. London: Routledge, 1983.

Mathieu, Vittorio. "Il fondamento romano e cristiano della laicità." In *L'identità in conflitto dell'Europa: Cristianesimo, laicità, laicismo*, edited by Laura Paoletti. Bologna: Il Mulino, 2005.

Matteucci, Nicola. *Organizzazione del potere e libertà: Storia del costituzionalismo moderno*. Turin: UTET, 1988.

Mayer-Tasch, Peter C. *Thomas Hobbes und das Widerstandsrecht*. Tübingen: J. C. B. Mohr–Paul Siebeck, 1965.

Mayeur, Jean Marie. *La question laïque: XIXe et XXe siècle*. Paris: Fayard, 1997.

Meister, Johannes-Jürgen. "Sacerdotium ac imperium." In *Republica Christiana: Politisches Denken des orthodoxen Christentums im Mittelalter*, edited by Peter von Sivers. Munich: List Verlag, 1969.

Mendus, Susan. *Toleration and the Limits of Liberalism.* London: Macmillan, 1989.

Mesnard, P. *L'essor de la philosophie politique au XVIe siècle.* Paris: J. Vrin, 1951.

Messineo, A. "Laicismo politico e dottrina cattolica." *La Civiltà Cattolica* 2, no. 103 (1952): 18–28.

Messner, Johannes. *Das Naturrecht: Handbuch der Gesellschaftsethik, Staatsethik und Wirtschaftsethik.* 6th ed. Innsbruck-Vienna-Munich: Tyrolia Verlag, 1966.

Michalski, Krzysztof, ed. *Die liberale Gesellschaft: Castelgandolfo-Gespräche 1992.* Stuttgart: Klett-Cotta, 1993.

Mill, John Stuart. *Principles of Political Economy.* In *Collected Works of John Stuart Mill.* 33 vols. Edited by J. M. Robson. Toronto: University of Toronto Press; London: Routledge and Kegan Paul, 1963–91.

———. *Utilitarianism, On Liberty, and Considerations on Representative Government.* Edited by H. B. Acton. London: J. M. Dent, 1972.

Minghetti, Marco. *Discorsi Parlamentari, raccolti e pubblicati per deliberazione della Camera dei deputati.* Vol. 5. Rome: Tipografia della Camera dei deputati, 1890.

———. *State e Chiesa.* 2nd ed. Naples: Ulrich Hoepli, 1878.

Mises, Ludwig von. *Human Action: A Treatise on Economics.* London: William Hodge, 1949.

———. *Kritik des Interventionismus: Untersuchungen zur Wirtschaftspolitik und Wirtschaftsideologie der Gegenwart.* Stuttgart: Gustav Fischer Verlag, 1929.

Misri, Ahmad ibn Naquib al-. *Reliance of the Traveler: A Classic Manual of Islamic Sacred Law.* Translated and edited by Nuh Ha Mim Keller. Beltsville, Md.: Amana Publications, 1991 and 1994.

Mochi Onory, Sergio. *Fonti canonistiche dell'idea moderna dello stato.* Milan: Vita e pensiero, 1951.

Montesquieu. *De l'esprit des lois.* Edited by R. Derathé. Paris: Garnier, 1973.

Mulhall, Stephen, and Adam Swift. *Liberals and Communitarians.* Oxford: Blackwell, 1992.

Murphy, William F., Jr. "Craniotomy and Treatments for Tubal Pregnancy: Progress toward Consensus on Extreme Vital Conflicts?" *Angelicum* 87 (2010): 871–910.

———. "Revisiting Contraception: An Integrated Approach in Light of the Renewal of Thomistic Virtue Ethics." *Theological Studies* 72, no. 4 (December 2011): 812–47.

Nell-Breuning, Oswald von. *Die soziale Enzyklika: Erläuterungen zum Weltrundschreiben Papst Pius' XI über die gesellschaftliche Ordnung.* Köln: Katholische Tat-Verlag, 1932.

Nicolet, Claude. *L'Idée républicaine en France (1794–1924): Essai d'histoire critique.* Paris: Gallimard, 1982.

———. "République et laïcité." In Nicolet, *La république en France: État des lieux.* Paris: Éditions du Seuil, 1992.

Nino, Carlos Santiago. *The Ethics of Human Rights.* Oxford: Oxford University Press, 1991.

———. *Etica y derechos humanos.* Buenos Aires: Paidós, 1984; 2nd ed., Buenos Aires: Astrea, 1989.

Novak, Michael. *The Catholic Ethic and the Spirit of Capitalism.* New York: Free Press, 1993.

———. *Catholic Social Thought and Liberal Institutions: Freedom with Justice.* New Brunswick: Transaction Publishers, 1989.

———. *Free Persons and the Common Good.* Lanham, Md.: Madison Books, 1989.

Nozick, Robert. *Anarchy, State, and Utopia.* New York: Basic Books, 1974.

Nussbaum, Martha. "Aristotelian Social Democracy." In *Liberalism and the Good,* edited by R. Bruce Douglass, G. M. Mara, and H. S. Richardson. New York: Routledge, 1990.

Oakeshott, Michael. *Hobbes on Civil Association.* Oxford: Oxford University Press, 1975.

Ortega, Iñigo. "La 'pendiente resbaladiza' en la eutanasia: ¿ilusión o realidad?" *Annales theologici* 17 (2003): 77–124.

Pakaluk, Michael. "The Liberalism of John Rawls: A Brief Exposition." In *Liberalism at the Crossroads: An Introduction to Contemporary Liberal Political Theory and Its Critics.* 2nd ed. Edited by Christopher Wolfe. Lanham, Md.: Rowman and Littlefield, 2003.

Palmer, Robert Roswell. *The Age of Democratic Revolution.* Vol. 1: *The Challenge.* Princeton, N.J.: Princeton University Press, 1959.

Paul VI. *Humanae vitae.* July 25, 1968.

———. *Populorum progressio.* March 26, 1967.

Pennington, Kenneth. *The Prince and the Law 1200–1600: Sovereignty and Rights in the Western Legal Tradition.* Berkeley: University of California Press, 1993.

Pera, Marcello, and Joseph Ratzinger. *Senza Radici: Europa, relativismo, cristianesimo, Islam.* Milan: Mondadori, 2004.

Perry, Michael J. *Morality, Politics, and Law.* Oxford: Oxford University Press, 1988.

———. *Religion in Politics: Constitutional and Moral Perspectives.* Oxford: Oxford University Press, 1997.

———. *Under God? Religious Faith and Liberal Democracy.* Cambridge: Cambridge University Press, 2003.

Pink, Thomas. "Rhonheimer on Religious Liberty: On the 'Hermeneutic of Reform' and Religious Liberty in *Nova et Vetera.*" RorateCaeli blogspot, August 5, 2011. (http://rorate-caeli.blogspot.com/2011/08/on-religious-liberty-and-hermeneutic-of.html)

Pius XI. *Dilectissima nobis.* June 3, 1933. In *Enchiridion delle Encicliche, 5: Pio XI.* Bologna: Edizioni Dehoniane, 1995.

———. *Quadragesimo anno.* May 15, 1931. In *Enchiridion delle Encicliche, 5: Pio XI.* Bologna: Edizioni Dehoniane, 1995.

Popper, Karl R. *Conjectures and Refutations: The Growth of Scientific Knowledge.* London: Routledge and Kegan Paul, 1963; 3rd ed., Routledge and Kegan Paul, 1969; London: Routledge Classics, 2002.

———. *The Open Society and Its Enemies.* 5th ed. Princeton, N.J.: Princeton University Press, 1971.

Possenti, Vittorio. *Le società liberali al bivio: Lineamenti di filosofia della società.* Perugia: Marietti, 1991.

———. *Una filosofia per la transizione: Metafisica, persona e politica in J. Maritain.* Milan: Massimo, 1984.

Prélot, Marcel, and F. Gallouédec Genuys, eds. *Le libéralisme catholique*. Paris: Armand Colin, 1969.

Prodi, Paolo. *Il Sovrano Pontefice. Un corpo e due anime: la monarchia papale nella prima età moderna*. Bologna: Il Mulino, 1982.

Quaritsch, Helmut. *Souveränität: Entstehung und Entwicklung des Begriff in Frankreich und Deutschland vom 13. Jh. bis 1806*. Berlin: Athenäum, 1986.

Rahner, Hugo. *Kirche und Staat im frühen Christentum*. Munich: Kösel-Verlag, 1961.

Ratzinger, Joseph. *Wendezeit für Europa? Diagnosen und Prognosen zur Lage von Kirche und Welt*. Einsiedeln-Freiburg: Johannes Verlag, 1991.

Ratzinger, Joseph, and Jürgen Habermas. *The Dialectics of Secularization: On Reason and Religion*. San Francisco: Ignatius Press, 2007.

Rawls, John. *Collected Papers*. Edited by Samuel Freeman. Cambridge, Mass.: Harvard University Press, 1999.

———. "Domain of the Political and Overlapping Consensus." *New York University Law Review* 64 (1989): 233–55.

———. "The Idea of an Overlapping Consensus." *Oxford Journal of Legal Studies* 7 (1987): 1–26.

———. *Justice as Fairness: A Restatement*. Edited by Erin Kelly. Cambridge, Mass.: Harvard University Press, 2001.

———. "Justice as Fairness: Political not Metaphysical." *Philosophy and Public Affairs* 14, no. 3 (1985): 223–51.

———. "Kantian Constructivism in Moral Theory: The Dewey Lectures." *Journal of Philosophy* 77 (1980): 515–72.

———. *The Law of Peoples, with "The Idea of Public Reason Revisited."* Cambridge, Mass.: Harvard University Press, 1999.

———. *Political Liberalism*. New York: Columbia University Press, 1993; 1996.

———. "Political Liberalism: Reply to Habermas." *Journal of Philosophy* 92 no. 3 (March 1995): 132–80. Also published as "Lecture IX: Reply to Habermas." In *Political Liberalism*. New York: Columbia University Press, 1996.

———. "The Priority of Right and Ideas of the Good." *Philosophy and Public Affairs* 17 (1988): 251–76.

———. *A Theory of Justice*. Cambridge, Mass.: Harvard University Press, 1971; Oxford: Oxford University Press, 1972.

Raz, Joseph. *Ethics in the Public Domain: Essays in the Morality of Law and Politics*. Rev. ed. Oxford: Oxford University Press, 1994; reprint, 2001.

———. *The Morality of Freedom*. Oxford: Oxford University Press, 1986; 1996.

Reibstein, Ernst. *Volkssouveränität und Freiheitsrechte: Texte und Studien zur politischen Theorie des 14. bis 18. Jahrhunderts*. 2 vols. Freiburg-Munich: Alber, 1972.

Reina, Victor de. "Los términos de la polémica Sacerdocio-Reino." *Ius Canonicum* 6 (1966): 153–99.

Reinhard, Wolfgang. *Geschichte der Staatsgewalt: Eine vergleichende Verfassungsgeschichte Europas von den Anfängen bis zur Gegenwart*. Munich: C. H. Beck, 1999.

Rémond, René. *L'anticléricalisme en France de 1815 à nos jours*. Rev. ed. Paris: Fayard, 1999.

Rhonheimer, Martin. "*Autoritas non veritas facit legem:* Thomas Hobbes, Carl Schmitt und die Idee des Verfassungsstaates." *Archiv für Rechts- und Sozialphilosophie* 86 (2000): 484–98.

———. "Benedict XVI's 'Hermeneutic of Reform' and Religious Freedom." *Nova et Vetera* (English edition) 9, no. 4 (Fall 2011): 1029–54. This is a minor expansion of the English version previously published online, which was updated to include a further response to a critic.

———. "Can Political Ethics Be Universalized? Human Rights as a Global Project." In *Ethics and Health in the Global Village: Bioethics, Globalization and Human Rights,* edited by Emilio Mordini, preface by Franco Frattini. Rome: CIC Edizioni Internazionali, 2009.

———. "Capitalism, Free Market Economy, and the Common Good: The Role of the State in the Economy." In *Free Markets and the Culture of Common Good,* edited by M. Schlag and J. A. Mercado. New York: Springer, 2012.

———. *Changing the World: The Timeliness of Opus Dei.* New York: Scepter Press, 2009.

———. *Christentum und säkularer Staat. Geschichte—Gegenwart—Zukunft.* With a preface by Ernst-Wolfgang Böckenförde. Freiburg im Breisgau: Herder, 2012.

———. "Christianity and Secularity: Past and Present of a Complex Relationship." In *The Common Good of Constitutional Democracy.* Washington: The Catholic University of America Press, 2012.

———. "Christian Secularity, Political Ethics and the Culture of Human Rights." *Josephinum Journal of Theology* 16, no. 2 (August 2009): 320–38.

———. "Cittadinanza multiculturale nella democrazia liberale: le proposte di Ch. Taylor, J. Habermas e W. Kymlicka." *Acta Philosophica* 15, no. 1 (2006): 29–52.

———. "Contrattualismo, individualismo e solidarietà: per rileggere la tradizione liberale." *Per la filosofia* 16, no. 46 (1999): 30–40.

———. "Cristianesimo e laicità: storia ed attualità di un rapporto complesso." In *Laicità: la ricerca dell'universale nella differenza,* edited by Pierpaolo Donati. Bologna: Il Mulino, 2008.

———. *Cristianismo y laicidad. Historia y actualidad de una relación compleja.* Madrid: Rialp, 2009.

———. "Die 'Hermeneutik der Reform' und die Religionsfreiheit." *Die Tagespost* 115 (September 26, 2009): 14; online at KATH.NET, September 28, 2009 (www.kath.net/detail.php?id=24068). This was the original publication in German.

———. *Ethics of Procreation and the Defense of Human Life: Contraception, Artificial Fertilization, Abortion.* Edited by William F. Murphy Jr. Washington, D.C.: The Catholic University of America Press, 2010.

———. *Familie und Selbstverwirklichung. Alternativen zur Emanzipation.* Cologne: Verlag Wissenschaft und Politik, 1979.

———. "Fundamental Rights, Moral Law, and the Legal Defense of Life in a Constitutional Democracy: A Constitutionalist Approach to the Encyclical *Evangelium Vitae.*" *American Journal of Jurisprudence* 43 (1998): 135–83.

———. "'Hermeneutic of Reform' and Religious Freedom." (http://chiesa.espresso.repubblica.it/articolo/1347670?eng=y) This corresponds to the version published in the French edition of *Nova et Vetera.*

———. "'Hermeneutica de la reforma' y libertad religiosa." *Palabra* 553 (October 3, 2009): 62–67. Also appeared in M. Rhonheimer, *Cristianismo y laicidad. Historia y actualidad de una relación compleja*, Apéndice I, 167–79. Madrid: Rialp, 2009. (http://chiesa.espresso.repubblica.it/articolo/1347670?sp=y) This was a translation of the German original.

———. "Il rapporto tra verità e politica nella società Cristiana: Riflessioni storico-teologiche per la valutazione dell'amore della libertà nella predicazione di Jose-maría Escrivá." In *La Grandezza della vita quotidiana* (Atti del Congresso Internazionale, January 8–11, 2002). Vol. 5, part 2: *Figli di Dio nella Chiesa: Riflessioni sul messaggio di San Josemaría Escrivá: Aspetti culturali ed ecclesiastici*, edited by Fernando de Andrés. Rome: Pontifical University of the Holy Cross, 2004.

———. "Is Christian Morality Reasonable? On the Difference between Secular and Christian Humanism." *Annales Theologici* 15, no. 2 (2001): 529–49.

———. *La filosofia politica di Thomas Hobbes: coerenza e contraddizioni di un paradigma*. Rome: Armando, 1997.

———. "L' 'herméneutique de la réforme' et la liberté de religion." *Nova et Vetera* (French edition) 85 (2010): 341–63. (www.novaetvetera.ch/Art%20Rhonheimer.htm and http://chiesa.espresso.repubblica.it/articolo/1347670?fr=y) This was an expanded translation of the German original, enhanced with an appendix that deals with specific questions concerning the continuity and infallibility of the ordinary universal Magisterium.

———. "Laici e cattolici: oltre le divisioni. Riflessioni sull'essenza della democrazia e della società aperta." *Liberal* (Fondazione Liberal), no. 17 (2003): 108–16.

———. *La prospettiva della morale: Fondamenti dell'etica filosofica*. Rome: Armando, 1994.

———. "La realtà politica ed economica del mondo moderno e i suoi presupposti etici e culturali. L'enciclica *Centesimus annus*." In *Giovanni Paolo Teologo—Nel segno delle encicliche*, edited by Graziano Borgonovo and Arturo Cattaneo. Preface by His Eminence Camillo Cardinal Ruini. Rome: Edizioni Arnoldo Mondatori, 2003.

———. "L'immagine dell'uomo nel liberalismo e il concetto di autonomia: al di là del dibattito fra liberali e comunitaristi." In *Immagini dell'uomo. Percorsi antropologici nella filosofia moderna*, edited by Ignacio Yarza. Rome: Armando, 1997.

———. "Lo Stato costituzionale democratico e il bene comune." In *Ripensare lo spazio politico: quale aristocrazia?* edited by E. Morandi and R. Panattoni. Padua: Il Poligrafo, 1998. (*Con-tratto—Rivista di filosofia tomista e contemporanea* 6/1997).

———. "Natural Law and Moral Reasoning: At the Roots of Aquinas's Moral Epistemology." *Josephinum Journal of Theology* 17, no. 2 (Summer/Fall 2010): 341–81.

———. *Natural Law and Practical Reason: A Thomist View of Moral Autonomy*. Translated by Gerald Malsbary. New York: Fordham University Press, 2000.

———. "Perché una filosofia politica? Elementi storici per una risposta." *Acta Philosophica* 1, no. 2 (1992): 233–63.

———. *The Perspective of Morality: Philosophical Bases of Thomistic Virtue Ethics*. Washington, D.C.: The Catholic University of America Press, 2011.

———. *The Perspective of the Acting Person: Essays in the Renewal of Thomistic Moral*

Philosophy. Edited with an introduction by William F. Murphy Jr. Washington, D.C.: The Catholic University of America Press, 2008.

―――. "The Political Ethos of Constitutional Democracy and the Place of Natural Law in Public Reason: Rawls's 'Political Liberalism' Revisited." *American Journal of Jurisprudence* 50 (2005): 1–70.

―――. *Politisierung und Legitimitätsentzug. Totalitäre Kritik der parlamentarischen Demokratie in Deutschland.* Reihe Praktische Philosophie 8. Freiburg: Karl Alber Verlag, 1979.

―――. *Praktische Vernunft und Vernünftigkeit der Praxis: Handlungstheorie bei Thomas von Aquin in ihrer Entstehung aus dem Problemkontext der aristotelischen Ethik.* Berlin: Akademie Verlag, 1994.

―――. "Rawlsian Public Reason, Natural Law and the Foundation of Justice: A Response to David Crawford." *Communio: International Catholic Review* 36 (Spring 2009): 138–67.

―――. "Religionsfreiheit—Bruch mit der Tradition?" *Die Neue Ordnung* 65, no. 4 (August 2011): 244–61. This was a slightly abridged version of the original "Die 'Hermeneutik der Reform' und die Religionsfreiheit."

―――. "Vital Conflicts, Direct Killing, and Justice: A Response to Rev. Benedict Guevin and Other Critics." *National Catholic Bioethics Quarterly* 11, no. 3 (Summer 2011): 519–40.

―――. *Vital Conflicts in Medical Ethics: A Virtue Approach to Craniotomy and Tubal Pregnancies.* Edited by William F. Murphy Jr. Washington, D.C.: The Catholic University of America Press, 2009.

Rhonheimer, Martin, G. B. Sadler, and Michael Zuckert. "Forum: Hobbes on Laws of Nature and Moral Norms." *Acta Philosophica* 16, no. 1 (2007): 125–31 and 139–41.

Rivière, Jean. *Le problème de l'Eglise et de l'Etat au temps de Philippe le Bel.* Louvain: Spicilegium Sacrum Lovaniense and Champion, 1926.

Rodríguez Luño, A. *"Cittadini degni del vangelo" (Fil 1, 27): Saggi di etica politica.* Rome: Edizioni Università della Santa Croce, 2005.

―――. "Le ragioni del liberalismo." In *I cattolici e la società pluralista. Il caso delle "leggi imperfette,"* edited by J. Joblin and R. Tremblay. Bologna: Edizioni Studio Domenicano, 1996.

Röpke, Wilhelm. *Gegen die Brandung.* 2nd ed. Edited by Albert Hunold. Erlenbach-Zürich: Eugen Rentsch Verlag, 1959.

―――. *Jenseits von Angebot und Nachfrage.* 4th ed. Erlenbach-Zürich: Eugen Rentsch Verlag, 1966. In English: *A Humane Economy.* Chicago: Henry Regnery, 1960.

Rorty, Richard. *Contingency, Irony and Solidarity.* Cambridge: Cambridge University Press, 1989.

―――. "The Priority of Democracy to Philosophy." In *Philosophical Papers,* vol. 1. Cambridge: Cambridge University Press, 1991.

Rosa, Giuseppe de. *La Civiltà Cattolica. 150 anni al servizio della Chiesa 1850–1999.* Rome: La Civiltà Cattolica, 1999.

Rothbard, Murray N. *America's Great Depression* (1963). 5th ed. Auburn, Ala.: Mises Institute, 2000.

Rousseau, Jean-Jacques. *Oeuvres complètes*. Edited by Bernard Gagnebin and Marcel Raymond. 4 vols. Bibliothèque de la Pléiade. Paris: Gallimard, 1959–69.

Ruffini, Francesco. *La libertà religiosa: Storia dell'idea*. New ed. Edited by Carlo Jemolo. Milan: Feltrinelli, 1991.

———. *Relazioni tra State e Chiesa*. Bologna: Il Mulino, 1974.

Ruggiero, Guido de. *Storia del liberalismo europeo*. Bari: Laterza, 1984. First published in 1925; republished in 2003. In English: *The History of European Liberalism*, translated by R. G. Collingwood. Boston: Beacon Press, 1959.

Rumpf, Helmut. *Carl Schmitt und Thomas Hobbes*. Berlin: Duncker & Humblot, 1972.

Rusconi, Gian Enrico. *Come se Dio non ci fosse: I laici, i cattolici e la democrazia*. Turin: Einaudi, 2000.

———. *Possiamo fare a meno di una religione civile?* Rome: Laterza, 1999.

Sabine, George H. *A History of Political Thought*. 4th ed. Revised by Thomas Landon Thorson. Hinsdale: Dryden Press, 1973.

Sajó, András. *Limiting Government: An Introduction to Constitutionalism*. Budapest: Central European University Press, 1999.

Sandel, Michael J. *Democracy's Discontent: America in Search of a Public Philosophy*. Cambridge, Mass.: Harvard University Press, 1996.

———. *Liberalism and the Limits of Justice*. Cambridge: Cambridge University Press, 1982.

———. *Liberalismus und Republikanismus: Von der Notwendigkeit der Bürgertugend*. Vienna: Passagen Verlag, 1995.

———. "Moral Argument and Liberal Toleration: Abortion and Homosexuality." *California Law Review* 77 (1989): 521–38. Reprinted in *New Communitarian Thinking: Persons, Virtues, Institutions, and Communities*, edited by Amitai Etzioni. Charlottesville: University Press of Virginia, 1995.

———. "Political Liberalism." *Harvard Law Review* 107 (1994): 1765–94.

———. "The Procedural Republic and the Unencumbered Self." *Political Theory* 1 (1984): 81–96.

Sartori, Giovanni. *The Theory of Democracy Revisited*. Chatham, N.J.: Chatham House, 1987.

Schall, James. *Roman Catholic Political Philosophy*. Lanham, Md.: Lexington, 2004.

Schiller, Friedrich. "Über die aesthetische Erziehung des Menschen in einer Reihe von Briefen." In Schiller, *Sämtliche Werke*, vol. 5. Munich: Carl Hanser Verlag, 1962.

Schmitt, Carl. *Der Begriff des Politischen*. Berlin: Duncker & Humblot, 1932, 1963.

———. *Der Leviathan in der Staatslehre des Thomas Hobbes: Sinn und Fehlschlag eines politischen Symbols*. Edited by G. Maschke. Cologne: Hohenheim, 1982.

———. *Die Diktatur: Von den Anfängen des modernen Souveränitätsgedankens bis zum proletarischen Klassenkampf*. Munich: Duncker & Humblot, 1921.

———. *Politische Theologie: Vier Kapitel zur Lehre von der Souveränität*. 2nd ed. Munich: Dunker and Humblot, 1934.

———. *Über die drei Arten des rechtswissenschaftlichen Denkens (Schriften der Akademie für Deutsches Recht)*. Hamburg: Hanseatische Verlagsanstalt, 1934.

———. *Verfassungslehre*. Munich: Duncker & Humblot, 1928.

————. "Weiterentwicklung des totalen Staats in Deutschland." In Schmitt, *Verfassungsrechtliche Aufsätze aus den Jahren 1924–1954: Materialien zu einer Verfassungslehre.* Berlin: Duncker & Humblot, 1958.

Schmitz, Mathias. *Die Freund-Feind Theorie Carl Schmitts: Entwurf und Entfaltung.* Cologne-Opladen: Westdeutscher Verlag, 1965.

Schneider, Peter. *Ausnahmezustand und Norm: Eine Studie zur Rechtslehre von Carl Schmitt.* Stuttgart: DVA, 1957.

Schnur, Roman. *Die französischen Juristen im konfessionellen Bürgerkrieg des 16. Jahrhunderts: Ein Beitrag zur Entstehungsgeschichte des modernen Staates.* Berlin: Duncker & Humblot, 1962.

Schwartländer, Johannes, ed. *Freiheit der Religion: Christentum und Islam unter dem Anspruch der Menschenrechte.* Mainz: Matthias-Grünewald-Verlag, 1993.

Scoppola, Pietro. *La repubblica dei partiti: Profilo storico della democrazia in Italia (1945–1990).* Bologna: Il Mulino, 1991.

Sen, Amartya. *Development as Freedom.* New York: Anchor Books/Random House, 2000.

————. *The Idea of Justice.* Cambridge, Mass.: Harvard University Press, 2009.

Shlaes, Amity. *The Forgotten Man: A New History of the Great Depression.* New York: HarperCollins, 2007.

Siéyès, Emmanuel-Joseph. *Politische Schriften 1788–1790.* Translated and edited by Eberhard Schmitt and Rolf Reichardt. Neuwied: Luchterhand, 1975.

Skinner, Quentin. *The Foundations of Modern Political Thought.* Vol. 1: *The Renaissance.* Cambridge: Cambridge University Press, 1978.

————. *The Foundations of Modern Political Thought.* Vol. 2: *The Age of Reformation.* Cambridge: Cambridge University Press, 1978.

Smith, Adam. *An Inquiry into the Nature and Causes of the Wealth of Nations.* Edited by R. H. Campbell and A. S. Skinner; textual editor W. B. Todd. Oxford: Oxford University Press, 1979.

————. *A Theory of Moral Sentiments.* Edited by D. D. Raphael and A. L. Macfie. Oxford: Oxford University Press, 1976; reprint, Indianapolis: Liberty Fund, 1984.

————. *The Wealth of Nations.* New York: Great Mind Series, Prometheus Books, 1991.

Sorabji, Richard. "Aristotle and the Role of Intellect in Virtue." *Proceedings of the Aristotelian Society,* new series, 74 (1973–74): 107–29.

Spaemann, Robert. *Der Ursprung der Soziologie aus dem Geist der Restauration: Studien über L. G. A. de Bonald.* Munich: Kösel, 1959.

————. "Legitimer Wandel der Lehre." *Frankfurter Allgemeine Zeitung* 228 (October 10, 2009): 7.

Spragens, Thomas A., Jr. "Communitarian Liberalism." In *New Communitarian Thinking: Persons, Virtues, Institutions, and Communities,* edited by Amitai Etzioni. Charlottesville: University Press of Virginia, 1995.

————. *The Irony of Liberal Reason.* Chicago: University of Chicago Press, 1981.

Stark, Rodney. *The Victory of Reason: How Christianity Led to Freedom, Capitalism, and Western Success.* New York: Random House, 2006.

Stiglitz, Joseph. *Freefall: America, Free Markets, and the Sinking of the World Economy.* New York: Norton 2010.

———. *Making Globalization Work*. New York: Norton, 2006.

Storing, Herbert J. "William Blackstone." In *History of Political Philosophy*, edited by Leo Strauss and Joseph Cropsey. 3rd ed. Chicago: University of Chicago Press, 1987.

Sullivan, William M. *Reconstructing Public Philosophy*. Berkeley: University of California Press, 1986.

Sutor, Bernhard. *Politische Ethik: Gesamtdarstellung auf der Basis der Christlichen Gesellschaftslehre*. Paderborn: Schöningh, 1991.

Talmon, Jacob L. *The Origins of Totalitarian Democracy*. London: Sphere Books, 1970.

Tamir, Yael. *Liberal Nationalism*. Princeton, N.J.: Princeton University Press, 1993.

Taylor, Charles. "Cross Purposes: The Liberal-Communitarian Debate." In *Liberalism and the Moral Life*, edited by Nancy L. Rosenblum. Cambridge, Mass.: Harvard University Press, 1991.

———. *The Ethics of Authenticity*. Cambridge, Mass.: Harvard University Press, 1992. First published 1991 as *The Malaise of Modernity* by the Canadian Broadcasting Corporation.

———. *Philosophy and the Human Sciences*. Philosophical Papers 2. Cambridge: Cambridge University Press, 1985.

———. *Sources of the Self: The Making of the Modern Identity*. Cambridge: Cambridge University Press, 1989.

Taylor, Charles, et al. *Multiculturalism: Examining the Politics of Recognition*. Edited and introduced by Amy Gutmann. Princeton, N.J.: Princeton University Press, 1994.

Tierney, Brian. *The Idea of Natural Rights: Studies on Natural Rights, Natural Law, and Church Law 1150–1625*. Grand Rapids, Mich.: William B. Eerdmans, 1997.

Tocqueville, Alexis de. *De la Démocratie en Amérique*. 2 vols. Paris: Charles Gosselin, 1835–40.

Uertz, Rudolf. *Vom Gottesrecht zum Menschenrecht: Das katholische Staatsdenken in Deutschland von der Französischen Revolution bis zum II. Vatikanischen Konzil (1789–1965)*. Paderborn: Schöningh, 2005.

Uhle, Arnd. *Freiheitlicher Verfassungsstaat und kulturelle Identität*. Tübingen: Mohr, Siebeck, 2005.

———. *Staat—Kirche—Kultur*. Berlin: Duncker & Humblot, 2004.

Ullmann, Walter. *Medieval Papalism: The Political Theories of the Medieval Canonists*. London: Methuen, 1949.

———. *Principles of Government and Politics in the Middle Ages*. London: Methuen, 2nd ed., 1966; 3rd ed., 1973.

Valuet, Basile. *La Liberté religieuse et la tradition catholique*. Le Barroux: Abbaye Sainte-Madeleine du Barroux, 1998.

Vialatoux, Joseph. *La Cité de Hobbes: Théorie de l' état totalitaire*. Paris: Lecoffre, 1935. Reprinted under the title *La Cité totalitaire de Hobbes*. Lyon: Chronique sociale de la France, 1952.

Villey, Michel. *La formation de la pensée juridique moderne: Cours d'histoire de la philosophie du Droit*. New rev. ed. Paris: Éditions Montchrétien, 1975.

Vittorio. Possenti. *Le società liberali al bivio: Lineamenti di filosofia della società*. Turin: Marietti, 1991.

Vossler, Otto. "Studien zur Erklärung der Menschrechte." *Historische Zeitschrift* 142, no. 3 (1930): 516–45. Reprinted in Roman Schnur. *Zur Geschichte der Erklarung der Menschenrechte.* Darmstadt: Wissenschaftliche Buchgesellschaft, 1964.

Walther, Helmut G. *Imperiales Königtum, Konziliarismus und Volkssouveränität: Studien zu den Grenzen des mittelalterlichen Souveränitätsgedankens.* Munich: Fink, 1976.

Walzer, Michael. "The Communitarian Critique of Liberalism." *Political Theory* 18 (1990): 6–23.

———. *Politics in the Vernacular: Nationalism, Multiculturalism, and Citizenship.* Oxford: Oxford University Press, 2001.

Wasser, Hartmut. *Parlamentarismuskritik vom Kaiserreich zur Bundesrepublik: Analyse und Dokumentation.* Stuttgart-Bad Cannstatt: Frommann-Holzboog, 1974.

Weiler, Joseph H. H. *Ein christliches Europa: Erkundungsgänge.* Salzburg: Anton Pustet, 2004.

———. *Un'Europa cristiana: Un saggio esplorativo.* Milan: Rizzoli, 2003.

Weiss, Ulrich. *Das philosophische System von Thomas Hobbes.* Stuttgart-Bad Canstatt: Fromman-Holzboog, 1980.

Weithman, Paul J. *Religion and the Obligation of Citizenship.* Cambridge: Cambridge University Press, 2002.

Willms, Bernard. *Die Antwort des Leviathan: Thomas Hobbes' Politische Theorie.* Neuwied u. Berlin: Luchterhand, 1970.

Wolfe, Christopher, ed. *Liberalism at the Crossroads: An Introduction to Contemporary Liberal Political Theory and Its Critics.* 2nd ed. Lanham, Md.: Rowman and Littlefield, 2003.

———. *Natural Law Liberalism.* Cambridge: Cambridge University Press, 2006.

Wolterstorff, Nicholas. *Justice: Rights and Wrongs.* Princeton, N.J.: Princeton University Press, 2008.

Wyduckel, Dieter. *Princeps Legibus Solutus: Eine Untersuchung zur frühmodernen Rechts- und Staatslehre.* Berlin: Duncker & Humblot, 1979.

Yale, D. E. C. "Hobbes and Hale on Law, Legislation and the Sovereign." *Cambridge Law Journal* 31, no. 1 (1972): 121–56.

Index

The Common Good of Constitutional Democracy: Essays in Political Philosophy and on Catholic Social Teaching was designed in Meta Serif with Meta display type by Kachergis Book Design of Pittsboro, North Carolina. It was printed on 50-pound Natures Recycled and bound by Sheridan Books of Ann Arbor, Michigan.